PLANNED SOCIAL INTERVENTION

Chandler Publications in Anthropology *and* Sociology
Leonard Broom, *General Editor*

Sociology
Charles M. Bonjean, *Editor*

PLANNED SOCIAL INTERVENTION

INTERVENTION

AN INTERDISCIPLINARY ANTHOLOGY

Edited by

LOUIS A. ZURCHER, Jr.
CHARLES M. BONJEAN

The University of Texas at Austin

Expanded from the *Social Science Quarterly*, December, 1969

CHANDLER PUBLISHING COMPANY
An Intext Publisher • Scranton / London / Toronto

CONTENTS

VI. Methodological Issues in
Intervention Research   395

PREFACE

The notion that social policy *should* be based on valid social and economic information—if not, in fact, on principles of human behavior—is as old as the social sciences. Yet few would deny that relatively little social science (with economics a possible exception) has actually *been* the basis for programs designed to ameliorate social problems.

Encouragingly, events during the past few years have suggested some degree of rapprochement between social scientists and those who make and administer public policy. At the very least, we have noticed that our colleagues seem to be more interested in policy-related research than they were only a few years ago. Much of this research, in turn, has been stimulated by grants from relevant policy organizations, most of them a part of the federal government.

To sample social scientists' current points of view and research activities relevant to planned social intervention, the *Social Science Quarterly* put out its first call for papers on the topic in September 1968. The response was immediate and overwhelming. Between that date and September 1969, more than 200 intervention-related manuscripts by scholars representing eight social-science disciplines were submitted for publication. The 30 surviving a rather rigorous review process were published in the December 1969 issue of the *Quarterly*. Those articles are reprinted here with another 12 selected to round out or provide background for the six topical areas explored.

All 42 contributions are intervention-oriented, although they run the gamut from think pieces to research reports, from the role of social science to the roles of the individuals studied, and from traditional to "new" orientations. Variety among selections was assured from the outset, since the co-editors were not and are not in agreement in regard to such basic matters covered in this volume as, for example, the role of the social scientist vis-à-vis the implementation of social policy. Thus, one suggested a contribution by Mills to introduce the reader to the topic, while the other immediately countered with an article by Hauser, who represents a different stance. Both have been included, and we hope that other, similar compromises will ultimately be in the interest of the reader.

In preparing this anthology, we tried to keep in mind the interests and levels of the advanced undergraduate student and the graduate student. We hope it will aid them in defining the role of social science in social policy, identifying the problems associated with the use of social-science research in the development of policy, locating the types of research most suitable for guiding policy, and sampling the nature of social criticism based on social science. These topics are likely to be central to courses in social planning, social policy, and social welfare. Beyond this, the reader may find the collection of readings useful as a supplement to courses in, for example, social problems, social control, urban sociology, community development, poverty, community mental health, and methods of applied social research.

We are indebted to more individuals than there is space to acknowledge. In addition to the contributors, our *Quarterly* staff members and graduate assistants—Cynthia Gardner, Jean P. Baker, Ann C. Hardy, Paula Miller, Angelica Martinez, Arthur Frakes, and Marilyn Bidnick—were of special help. Associate and advisory editors who provided helpful suggestions to the authors for revision included Harold Osborne, Robert Cushing, Dan D. Nimmo, Coldwell Daniel, William Breit, E. Dale Odom, Jim B. Pearson, Oleh Fedyshyn, James Chase, J. Allen Williams, Joe Colwell, Robert L. Lineberry, Frederick Whitam, Harry Scoble, Walter Firey, James Anderson, Russell Curtis, George Ragland, C. Norman Alexander, David Gottlieb, and Norval D. Glenn. Also assisting us in the review of manuscripts were Edward Taborsky, Thomas Curtis, Ivan Belknap, Louis Gould, W. Lee Hansen, Richard J. Hill, Richard Henshel, Harley Browning, Wallace Mendelson, Howard Bahr, Willis Sutton, Arthur Shostak, Richard Cramer, Rex Enoch, Lawrence Saha, Reece McGee, Joseph Lopreato, Gideon Sjoberg, Cora Martin, Louis Schneider, Herbert Hirsch, Harry Martin, Nancy Kutner, John Stephenson, Charles Mulford, Robert Evans, John Lane, Hiram Friedsam, Eleanor Wolf, and Frank Bean.

Financial support for the extra-length issue of the *Social Science Quarterly* was made possible by its cosponsoring organizations, the Southwestern Social Science Association and the University of Texas at Austin, and by a grant from the Hogg Foundation for Mental Health, Austin, Texas.

Austin, Texas   Louis A. Zurcher
March 25, 1970   Charles M. Bonjean

CONTRIBUTORS

FREDERICK L. AHEARN, JR., is assistant professor of community organization and social planning at Boston College.

VICTOR G. ALICEA is staff associate with the Institute of Urban Environment at Columbia University.

ROBERT L. BEE is assistant professor of anthropology at the University of Connecticut.

WILLIAM C. BERLEMAN is assistant professor in the school of social work at the University of Washington.

HYMAN BERMAN is associate professor of history and director of social-science programs at the University of Minnesota.

CHARLES M. BONJEAN is professor of sociology at the University of Texas at Austin.

FRANCIS G. CARO is assistant professor of sociology at the University of Colorado and assistant director for evaluation research at the Institute of Behavioral Science at the University of Colorado.

RICHARD X. CHASE is assistant professor of economics at the University of Vermont.

JOSEPH M. CONFORTI is assistant professor of sociology at Rutgers University (Newark).

HERBERT COSTNER is professor of sociology at the University of Washington.

WAYMAN J. CROW is director of the Western Behavioral Sciences Institute at La Jolla, California.

J. RONNIE DAVIS is assistant professor of economics at Iowa State University.

AMITAI ETZIONI is professor of sociology at Columbia University.

JOHN W. EVANS is chief of the evaluation division of the OEO Office of Research, Plans, Programs, and Evaluations.

ROBERT EVANS, JR., is associate professor of economics at Brandeis University.

WILLIAM FREITHALER FORD is associate professor of economics as Texas Tech University.

ELI GINZBERG is Hepburn professor of economics in the graduate school of business at Columbia University.

DAVID GOTTLIEB is professor of human development at Pennsylvania State University.

WALTER GOVE is assistant professor of sociology at Vanderbilt University.

PHILIP M. HAUSER is professor of sociology and director of the Population Research Center at the University of Chicago.

RALPH K. HUITT is professor of political science at the University of Wisconsin.

BYRD L.JONES is associate professor of education at the University of Massachusetts.

MICHAEL KATZ is associate professor of law at the University of North Carolina.

ELLIOTT A. KRAUSE is assistant professor of sociology at Northeastern University.

GENE LABER is assistant professor of economics at the University of Vermont.

ROBERT L. LINEBERRY is assistant professor of government at the University of Texas at Austin.

FREMONT JAMES LYDEN is associate professor in the graduate school of public affairs at the University of Washington.

LEON MAYHEW is associate professor of sociology at the University of Michigan.

PATRICK H. MCNAMARA is assistant professor of sociology at the University of Texas at El Paso.

C. WRIGHT MILLS was a leading critic of American society and was professor of sociology at Columbia University.

DANIEL P. MOYNIHAN is Assistant to the President for Urban Affairs.

JOHN H. NOBLE, JR., is project director at the Medical Foundation, Inc. (Boston).

NEIL A. PALOMBA is assistant professor of economics at Iowa State University.

GASTON V. RIMLINGER is professor and chairman of the department of economics at Rice University.

PETER H. ROSSI is chairman of the department of social relations at Johns Hopkins University.

HAROLD L. SHEPPARD is a staff social scientist at the W. E. Upjohn Institute for Employment Research.

JOSEPH J. SPENGLER is professor of economics at Duke University.

HANS B. C. SPIEGEL is professor of urban affairs at Hunter College of the City University of New York.

THOMAS W. STEINBURN is data-analysis consultant for the Institute for Sociological Research at the University of Washington.

BRUCE C. STRAITS is assistant professor of sociology at the University of California at Santa Barbara.

WILLIS A. SUTTON, JR., is professor of sociology at the University of Kentucky.

JERRY V. THOMAS is a graduate student in the department of political science at the University of Washington.

ROBERT TOLLISON is assistant professor of economics and finance at Cornell University.

WALTER I. TRATTNER is associate professor of history and social welfare at the University of Wisconsin.

JAMES J. VANECKO is senior study director at the National Opinion Research Center and assistant professor at the University of Illinois at Chicago Circle.

J. ALLEN WILLIAMS, JR., is associate professor of sociology at the University of Texas at Austin.

ELEANOR P. WOLF is professor of sociology at Wayne State University.

WILLIAM L. YANCEY is assistant professor of sociology at Vanderbilt University.

MAYER N. ZALD is professor of sociology at Vanderbilt University.

LOUIS A. ZURCHER, J., is associate professor of sociology at the University of Texas at Austin.

Part I

THE SOCIAL SCIENTIST'S ROLE
IN SOCIAL INTERVENTION

There can be no doubt that the role of the academic in stimulating and guiding social change is one of the major issues in the several social sciences today. Within these disciplines, relationships among scholarship, social policy, and social intervention are being debated anew. The debate has been heated and visible at recent national meetings of professional societies such as the American Sociological Association, the American Political Science Association, the American Historical Association, the American Psychological Association, and the American Philosophical Association. That the issues are major and their implications possibly profound seems documented by the observation that even the mass media give them more than routine attention. *Newsweek* magazine, for example, saw fit to note the changing tenor of professional meetings:

> In the past, annual meetings of U.S. scholarly organizations were little more than occasions for reading professional papers in musty hotel public rooms and for "slave markets" where bright graduate students seeking jobs tried to impress department heads. But these days the brightest students—and the most promising young instructors—are also the most politically aware. And last week, their collective academic weight was felt across the country as scholars found themselves locked in vigorous debate over the war in Vietnam, government "repression"

and, most important, their own responsibilities as academics in taking stands on the political and moral issues of the day.[1]

While one may be tempted to suspect that the mass-media attention given such events was more a matter of registering some surprise at finding a sign of life in the ivory tower than an attempt to record academic change, scholars who have attended national meetings over a period of years (or, for that matter, who are sensitive to changing orientations in their classrooms) would be among the first (along with the "brightest students" and the "most promising young instructors") to be likely to exclaim that in this instance a news medium was "telling it like it is."

In most cases such activities have not been spontaneous, but have reflected the strategies of "radical" and "concerned" groups of social scientists and graduate students who have been urging more "relevance" and less sterile "objectivity" in social research. Prior to and during the 1969 meetings of the American Sociological Association, many members received copies of *The Insurgent Sociologist,* a newsletter calling for a "counterconvention" and suggesting that "truth squads" attend regular sessions of the meetings. At meetings themselves, the "truth squads" were in evidence, as were other strategies of the Sociology Liberation Movement. That these interventionists were "successful" in achieving their goals could be debated; that they had some impact on the convention and the discipline cannot. Similar, more or less organized groups of students and faculty members have articulated their concerns and orientations at meetings of other professional societies. In most instances the majority view has been the traditional view—a desire to keep academic social science free of politics and thus, at least implicitly, out of the policy process.

Most members of the vocal minority perceive their position as "new." Thus, interventionist-oriented political scientists call themselves "The Caucus for a New Political Science." *Time* magazine recently labeled the "type of scholar who respects no scientific boundaries, least of all his own, and who rejects the traditionalist's antiseptic analyses of how society works in favor of passionate prescriptions for its betterment" as "The New Sociology."[2] Certainly, if such an orientation becomes dominant in any discipline, it would be "new" in terms of the recent history of social science, but concern on the part of social scientists with the relevance and usefulness of their findings for society is as old as the social sciences themselves. At times such men have been few and at other times many, just as the orientation itself has sometimes been fashionable, sometimes not. Occasionally, a social scientist has emerged who so competently, convincingly, and vociferously called his colleagues' attention to the role of social science in confronting social problems that he, at least temporarily, captured his audience—Pitirim Sorokin, Kurt Lewin, Thorstein Veblen, Karl Mannheim, Wesley Mitchell, John Maynard Keynes, Ralph

[1] "Politics in Academe," *Newsweek* (January 12, 1970).
[2] "The New Sociology," *Time* (January 5, 1970), p. 38.

Bunche, and Woodrow Wilson, to name a few. Occasionally, a national crisis has become so sweeping and urgent that the social-science enterprise was expected to mobilize research and expertise, as in the cases of World Wars I and II and the Great Depression.

Even during noncrisis periods, the action approach in social science has been sufficiently pervasive to be recognized. Organizations such as sociology's Society for the Study of Social Problems and psychology's Society for the Psychological Study of Social Issues have been around for more than a decade and distinguish themselves from other professional social-science associations by their applied or interventionist orientation.

More often than not, however, the application and relevance of research to contemporary social problems has been left to "practitioners." Most universities, professional organizations, and other systems important to the social scientist have supported (and continue to support) that stance and provide rewards accordingly to those engaged in "pure" research. There are social scientists who at this moment are conducting research that bears directly on social problems or are providing data which will be useful in the formulation of social policy and intervention. Social scientists are serving in government positions, as consultants to policy makers, and on ad-hoc commissions and task forces. But their number is small and, as will be discussed in chapters of this book, their impact is problematical.

While the traditional-interventionist or—to shift the focus to ideology— the establishment-radical dichotomies have been apparent in the several social sciences for some time, only recently have the issues emerged as sufficiently important to result in some polarization within disciplines, with recognized leaders and significant numbers of followers in both camps. Thus, to political scientists, Christian Bay and Robert Dahl represent respectively the political and the science aspects of the discipline. In sociology C. Wright Mills has been a hero of the radicals, while Philip M. Hauser, a former president of the American Sociological Association, has perhaps best articulated the views of the establishment. Mills and Hauser have points of agreement as well as disagreement. Both men manifest concern for human suffering. But while Hauser feels that value judgments concerning human problems and suffering are incompatible with the role of social scientist, Mills argues that no social scientist can or should operate without them. Whereas Mills sees the social scientist at once being and acting as citizen, scholar, researcher, and actionist, Hauser sees those roles as separate, and self-defeating if simultaneously enacted. Mills urges social scientists to take positions on social, economic, and political issues, to create "publics" for rational discourse, and directly to influence the wielders of power and the makers of policy. Hauser contends that it is not the role of the social scientist or his professional organization to take such positions unless they are concerned with threats to the effective functioning of the discipline. These views are elaborated in the two contributions which follow.

Contribution 1 is from *The Sociological Imagination*, one of the most stimulating volumes completed by Mills before his recent and untimely death. Three types of roles which the social scientist may take are outlined by Mills—philosopher-king, advisor to the king, or simply social scientist directing his work at kings and to publics. When he wrote the essay, the distance between academia and the polity was greater than it had been before or has been since. But one of Mills' basic questions— "Where is the intelligentsia that is carrying on the big discourse of the Western world *and* whose work as intellectuals is influential among parties and publics and relevant to the great decisions of our time?"—is as pertinent today as it was in the late 1950's.[3] Some pundits are convinced that another, even more drastic schism between academics and politicians is upon us. However, others (including Spengler in contribution 5) argue that the paths taken by social scientists and government officials are likely to cross more frequently in the future.

Hauser, in contribution 2, also delimits three types of roles—social thinker, social scientist, and social actionist. He notes that at different times different roles have been dominant, and he presents arguments lending support to the traditional viewpoint that the major orientation in sociology today should be professional and scientific rather than political. At the same time, he makes it clear that within this framework the sociologist "can still relate to the solution of the evils of the day even if he is not in an actionist posture in respect of them."[4]

The Mills and Hauser contributions not only will enable the reader to assess his own posture in regard to the social scientist's role in social intervention, but will serve as a relevant point of departure for assessing the other contributions to this volume. The contributions, in turn, may be used to assess the orientations set forth by Mills and Hauser.

Parts II through VI of this anthology are concerned with differing but related aspects of the social scientist's role in social intervention. Each part contains contributions by some scholars one would associate with the Mills interventionist orientation and by some more closely aligned with the traditional orientation discussed by Hauser.

In Part II an economist, a political scientist, and three sociologists— all widely experienced interventionists, but with differing orientations— react to Daniel P. Moynihan's critique of the role of social science in the war on poverty as presented in his *Maximum Feasible Misunderstanding*. Beyond this, they discuss current and potential relationships between social science and social policy.

Part III presents some historical examples of the involvement of social scientists in the formulation of national social policy. Some of the contributions also demonstrate that the historian, by making available analyses of the dynamics and impact of past decisions, can himself contribute greatly to the interventionist perspective.

The social scientist as intelligencer, reflecting upon the nature of

[3] C. Wright Mills, *The Sociological Imagination* (New York: Oxford University Press, 1959), p. 183.

[4] Philip M. Hauser, "On Actionism in the Craft of Sociology," *Sociological Inquiry* 39 (Spring, 1969), p. 147.

social problems and conducting a public critique of the social phenomena which perpetuate them, is exemplified throughout the contributions in Part IV. The topics discussed range from the military draft to population policy, from guiding a society to controlling a local school system. In the role of intelligencer, the social scientist can stimulate or express the opinions of publics and can call the attention of policy makers to the several facets of an issue.

Some social scientists are funded by intervention agencies themselves and are expected to provide usable evaluations of ongoing social programs. The contributions in Part V report examples of such work and include evaluations of health-care facilities, urban renewal, and assorted poverty programs. The orientations vary from microscopic to macroscopic, and the methods are as diverse as participant observation and large-scale surveys.

Part VI is concerned with intervention research as such. The contributions discuss or illustrate methodological problems and techniques in the evaluation of intervention programs and are concerned with the validity of the evaluations for social policy.

Throughout the volume, the approach is interdisciplinary. Just as political scientists and economists, for example, are likely to find the Mills-Hauser perspectives applicable to their disciplines, sociologists are likely to find that later contributions by other social scientists not only are relevant to sociological perspectives on social problems, but also contain insights they might otherwise miss.

·1·
ON POLITICS

C. WRIGHT MILLS

THERE IS NO NECESSITY FOR WORKING SOCIAL SCIENTISTS TO ALLOW the political meaning of their work to be shaped by the 'accidents' of its setting, or its use to be determined by the purposes of other men. It is quite within their powers to discuss its meanings and decide upon its uses as matters of their own policy. To a considerable, and largely untested, extent, they can influence or even determine these policies. Such determination requires that they make explicit judgments, as well as decisions upon theory, method, and fact. As matters of policy, these judgments are the proper concern of the individual scholar as well as of the fraternity. Yet is it not evident that implicit moral and political judgments have much more influence than explicit discussions of personal and professional policy? Only by making these influences matters of debated policy can men become fully aware of them, and so try to control their effects upon the work of social science and upon its political meaning.

There is no way in which any social scientist can avoid assuming choices of value and implying them in his work as a whole. Problems, like issues and troubles, concern threats to expected values, and cannot be clearly formulated without acknowledgment of those values. Increasingly, research is used, and social scientists are used, for bureaucratic and ideological purposes. This being so, as individuals and as professionals, students of man and society face such questions as: whether they are aware of the uses and values of their work, whether these may be subject to their own control, whether they want to seek to control them. How they answer these questions, or fail to answer them, and how they use or fail to use the answers in their work and in their professional lives determine their answer to the final question: whether in their work as social scientists they are (a) morally autonomous, (b) subject to the morality of other men, or (c) morally adrift. The catchwords with which these problems have been carried along—often, I am certain, with good intentions—are no longer good enough. Social scientists must now really confront these quite fateful questions. In this chapter I am going to suggest some of the things it seems necessary to consider in any answer to them, and also to set forth the kind of answer I have come, in the last few years, to believe reasonable.

1

The social scientist at work is not suddenly confronted with the need to choose values. He is already working on the basis of certain values. The values that these disciplines now embody have been selected from the values created in Western society; elsewhere social science is an import. Of course some do talk as if the values they have selected 'transcend' Western or any other society; others speak of their standards as if they were 'immanent' within some existing society, as a sort of unrealized potential. But surely it will now be widely agreed that the values inherent in the traditions of social science are neither transcendent nor immanent. They are simply values proclaimed by many and within limits practiced in small circles. What a man calls moral judgment is merely his desire to generalize, and so make available for others, those values he has come to choose.

Three overriding political ideas seem to me inherent in the traditions of social science, and certainly involved in its intellectual promise. The first of these is simply the value of truth, of fact. The very enterprise of social science, as it determines fact, takes on political meaning. In a world of widely communicated nonsense, any statement of fact is of political and moral significance. All social scientists, by the fact of their existence, are involved in the struggle between enlightenment and obscurantism. In such a world as ours, to practice social science is, first of all, to practice the politics of truth.

But the politics of truth is not an adequate statement of the values that guide our enterprise. The truth of our findings, the accuracy of our investigations—when they are seen in their social setting—may or may not be relevant to human affairs. Whether they are, and how they are, is in itself the second value, which in brief, is the value of the role of reason in human affairs. Along with that goes a third value —human freedom, in all the ambiguity of its meaning. Both freedom and reason, I have already argued, are central to the civilization of the Western world; both are readily proclaimed as ideals. But in any given application, as criteria and as goals, they lead to much disagreement. That is why it is one of our intellectual tasks, as social scientists, to clarify the ideal of freedom and the ideal of reason.

If human reason is to play a larger and more explicit role in the making of history, social scientists must surely be among its major carriers For in their work they represent the use of reason in the understanding of human affairs; that is what they are about. If they wish to work and thus to act in a consciously chosen way, they must first locate themselves within the intellectual life and the social-historical structure of their times. Within the social domains of intelligence, they must locate themselves; and they must relate these domains, in turn, to the structure of historical society. This is not the place to do such work. Here I want only briefly to distinguish three political roles in terms of which the social scientist as a man of reason may conceive of himself.

Much social science, perhaps especially sociology, contains the theme of the philosopher-king. From Auguste Comte to Karl Mannheim, one finds the plea for and the attempted justification of greater power for 'the man of knowledge.' In a more specific statement the enthronement of reason means, of course, the enthronement of 'the man of reason.' This one idea of the role of reason in human affairs has done much to cause social scientists to keep very general indeed their acceptance of reason as a social value. They have wished to avoid the foolishness of such an idea when it is considered alongside the facts of power. The idea also goes against the grain of many versions of democracy, for it involves an aristocracy, even if an aristocracy of talent rather than of birth or wealth. But the rather foolish idea that he should become a philosopher-king is only one idea of the public role that the social scientist may attempt to enact.

The quality of politics depends very much upon the intellectual qualities of those who are engaged in it. Were the 'philosopher' king, I should be tempted to leave his kingdom; but when kings are without any 'philosophy,' are they not incapable of responsible rule?

The second, and now the most usual role is to become an advisor to the king. The bureaucratic uses which I have described are a current embodiment of this. The individual social scientist tends to become involved in those many trends of modern society that make the individual a part of a functionally rational bureaucracy, and to sink into his specialized slot in such a way as not to be explicitly concerned with the structure of post-modern society. In this role, we have seen, social science itself often tends to become a functionally rational machine; the individual social scientist tends to lose his moral autonomy and his substantive rationality, and the role of reason in human affairs tends to become merely a refinement of techniques for administrative and manipulative uses.

But that is the role of advisor to kings in one of its worst forms; this role need not, I believe, assume the shape and meaning of the bureaucratic style. It is a difficult role to fulfill in such a way as to retain moral and intellectual integrity, and hence, freedom to work on the tasks of social science. It is easy for consultants to imagine themselves philosophers and their clients enlightened rulers. But even should they be philosophers, those they serve may not be enlightenable. That is one reason I am so impressed by the loyalty of some consultants to the unenlightened despots they serve. It is a loyalty that seems strained neither by despotic incompetence nor by dogmatic silliness.

I do not assert that the role of advisor cannot be performed well; in fact, I know that it can, and that there are men who are doing it. Were there more such men the political and intellectual tasks of those social scientists who elect the third role would become much less burdensome, for it overlaps this one.

The third way in which the social scientist may attempt to realize the value of reason and its role in human affairs is also well known, and sometimes even practiced. It is to remain independent, to do one's own work, to select one's own problems, but to direct this work *at* kings as well as *to* 'publics.' Such a conception prompts us to imagine social science as a sort of public intelligence apparatus, concerned with public issues and private troubles and with the structural trends of our time underlying them both—and to imagine individual social scientists as rational members of a self-controlled association, which we call the social sciences.

In taking up such a role, which I shall explain more fully in a moment, we are trying to *act* upon the value of reason; in assuming that we may not be altogether ineffective, we are assuming a theory of history-making: we are assuming that 'man' is free and that by his rational endeavors he can influence the course of history. I am not now concerned to debate the *values* of freedom and reason, but only to discuss under what theory of history they may be realizable.

2

Men are free to make history, but some men are much freer than others. Such freedom requires access to the means of decisions and of power by which history may now be made. It is not always so made; in the following, I am speaking only of the contemporary period in which the means of history-making power have become so enlarged and so centralized. It is with reference to this period that I am contending that if men do not make history, they tend increasingly to become the utensils of history-makers and also the mere objects of history-making.

How large a role any explicit decisions do play in the making of history is itself an historical problem. It depends very much upon the means of power that are available at any given time in any given society. In some societies, the innumerable actions of innumerable men modify their milieux, and so gradually modify the structure itself. These modifications are the course of history; history is drift, although in total 'men make it.' Thus, innumerable entrepreneurs and innumerable consumers, by ten thousand decisions per minute, may shape and re-shape the free-market economy. Perhaps this was the chief kind of limitation Marx had in mind when he wrote, in *The 18th Brumaire:* 'Men make their own history, but they do not make it just as they please; they do not make it under circumstances chosen by themselves. . . ."

Fate, or 'inevitability,' has to do with events in history that are beyond the control of any circle or group of men having three characteristics: (1) compact enough to be identifiable, (2) powerful enough to decide with consequence, and (3) in a position to foresee these consequences and so to be held accountable for them. Events, according to this conception, are the summary and unintended results of innumerable decisions of innumerable men. Each of their decisions is minute in consequence and subject to cancellation or reinforcement by other such decisions. There is no link between any one man's intention and the summary result of the innumerable decisions. Events are beyond human decisions: History is made behind men's backs.

So conceived, fate is not a universal fact; it is not inherent in the nature of history or in the nature of man. Fate is a feature of an historically specific kind of social structure. In a society in which the ultimate weapon is the rifle; in which the typical economic unit is the family-farm and the small shop; in which the national-state does not yet exist or is merely a distant framework; in which communication is by word-of-mouth, handbill, pulpit—in *such* a society, history is indeed fate.

But consider now, the major clue to our condition: Is it not, in a word, the enormous enlargement and the decisive centralization of all the means of power and decision, which is to say—all the means of history-making? In modern industrial society, the facilities of economic production are developed and centralized—as peasants and artisans are replaced by private corporations and government industries. In the modern nation-state, the means of violence and of political administration undergo similar developments—as kings control nobles, and self-equipped knights are replaced by standing armies and now by fearful military machines. The *post-modern* climax of all three developments—in economics, in politics, and in violence—is now occurring most dramatically in the United States and the USSR. In our time, international as well as national means of history-making are being centralized. Is it not thus clear that the scope and the chance for conscious human agency in history-making is just now uniquely available? Elites of power in charge of these means do now make history—to be sure, 'under circumstances not of their own choosing'—but compared to other men and other epochs, these circumstances themselves certainly do not appear to be overwhelming.

Surely this is the paradox of our immediate situation: The facts about the newer means of history-making are a signal that men are not necessarily in the grip of fate, that men *can* now make history. But this fact is made ironic by the further fact that just now those ideologies which offer men the hope of making history have declined and are collapsing in the Western societies. That collapse is also the collapse of the expectations of The Enlightenment, that reason and freedom would come to prevail as paramount forces in human history. And behind it there is also the intellectual and political default of the intellectual community.

Where is the intelligentsia that is carrying on the big discourse of the Western world *and* whose work as intellectuals is influential among parties and publics and relevant to the great decisions of our time? Where are the mass media open to such men? Who among those who are in charge of the two-party state and its ferocious military machines are alert to what goes on in the world of knowledge and reason and sensibility? Why is the free intellect so divorced from decisions of power? Why does there now prevail among men of power such a higher and irresponsible ignorance?

In the United States today, intellectuals, artists, ministers, scholars, and scientists are fighting a cold war in which they echo and elaborate the confusions of officialdoms. They neither raise demands on the powerful for alternative policies, nor set forth such alternatives before publics. They do not try to put responsible content into the politics of the United States; they help to empty politics and to keep it empty. What must be called the Christian default of the clergy is as much a part of this sorry moral condition as is the capture of scientists by nationalist Science-Machines. The journalistic lie, become routine, is part of it too; and so is much of the pretentious triviality that passes for social science.

3

I do not expect (nor does my present argument as a whole require) that this view be accepted by all social scientists. What I want most to say here is that, having accepted the values of reason and freedom, it is a prime task of any social scientist to determine the limits of freedom and the limits of the role of reason in history.

In assuming the third role, the social scientist does not see himself as some autonomous being standing 'outside society.' In common with most other people, he *does* feel that he stands outside the major history-making decisions of this period; at the same time he knows that he is among those who take many of the consequences of these decisions. That is one major reason why to the extent that he is aware of what he is doing, he becomes an explicitly political man. No one is 'outside society'; the question is where each stands within it.

The social scientist usually lives in circumstances of middling class and status and power. By his activities in these milieux, he is often in no better position than the ordinary individual to solve structural problems, for their solution can never be merely intellectual or merely private. Their proper statement cannot be confined to the milieux open to the will of social scientists; neither can their solutions, which means, of course, that they are problems of social and political and economic power. But the social scientist is not only an 'ordinary man.' It is his very task intellectually to transcend the milieux in which he happens to live, and this he does when he considers the economic order of nineteenth-century England or the status hierarchy of twentieth-century America, the military institutions of Imperial Rome, or the political structure of the Soviet Union.

In so far as the values of freedom and reason concern him, one of his themes for study has to do with the objective chances available for given types of men within given types of social structure to become free and rational as individuals. Another of his themes has to do with what chances, if any, men of differing positions in differing types of society have, first, by their reason and experience, to transcend their everyday milieux, and second, by virtue of their power, to act with consequence for the structure of their society and their periods. These are the problems of the role of reason in history.

In considering them, it is easy to see that in modern societies, some men have the power to act with much structural relevance and are quite aware of the consequences of their actions; others have such power but are not aware of its effective scope; and there are many who cannot transcend their everyday milieux by their awareness of structure or effect structural change by any means of action available to them.

Then, as social scientists, we locate ourselves. By the nature of our work, we are aware of social structure and somewhat aware of the historical mechanics of its movement. But clearly we do not have access to the major means of power which now exist and with which these mechanics can now be influenced. We do, however, have one often fragile 'means of power,' and it is this which provides a clue to our political role and to the political meaning of our work.

It is, I think, the political task of the social scientist who accepts the ideals of freedom and reason, to address his work to each of the other three types of men I have classified in terms of power and knowledge.

To those with power and with awareness of it, he imputes varying measures of responsibility for such structural consequences as he finds by his work to be decisively influenced by their decisions and their lack of decisions.

To those whose actions have such consequences, but who do not seem to be aware of them, he directs whatever he has found out about those consequences. He attempts to educate and then, again, he imputes responsibility.

To those who are regularly without such power and whose awareness is confined to their everyday milieux, he reveals by his work the meaning of structural trends and decisions for these milieux, the ways in which personal troubles are connected with public issues; in the course of these efforts, he states what he has found out concerning the actions of the more powerful. These are his major educational tasks, and they are his major public tasks when he speaks to any larger audience. Let us now examine some of the problems and tasks set by this third role.

4

Regardless of the scope of his awareness, the social scientist is usually a professor, and this occupational fact very much determines what he is able to do. As a professor, he addresses students, and on occasion, by speeches and by writings, publics of larger scale and more strategic position. In discussing what his public role may be, let us stick close to these simple facts of power, or if you like, to the facts of his powerlessness.

In so far as he is concerned with liberal, that is to say liberating, education, his public role has two goals: What he ought to do for the individual is to turn personal troubles and concerns into social issues and problems open to reason—his aim is to help the individual become a self-educating man, who only then would be reasonable and free. What he ought to do for the society is to combat all those forces which are destroying genuine publics and creating a mass society—or put as a positive goal, his aim is to help build and to strengthen self-cultivating publics. Only then might society be reasonable and free.

These are very large goals, and I must explain them in a slightly indirect way. We are concerned with skills and with values. Among 'skills,' however, some are more and some are less relevant to the tasks of liberation. I do not believe that skills and values can be so easily separated as in our search for 'neutral skills' we often assume. It is a matter of degree, with skills at one extreme and values at the other. But in the middle ranges of this scale, there are what I shall call sensibilities, and it is these which should interest us most. To train someone to operate a lathe or to read and write is in large part a training of skill; to help someone decide what he really wants out of his life, or to debate with him Stoic, Christian, and Humanist ways of living, is a cultivation or an education of values.

Alongside skill and value, we ought to put sensibility, which includes them both, and more besides: it includes a sort of therapy in the ancient sense of clarifying one's knowledge of self. It includes the cultivation of all those skills of controversy with oneself that we call thinking, and which, when engaged in with others, we call debate. An educator must begin with what interests the individual most deeply, even if it seems altogether trivial and cheap. He must proceed in such a way and with such materials as to enable the student to gain increasingly rational insight into these concerns, and into others he will acquire in the process of his education. And the educator must try to develop men and women who can and who will by themselves continue what he has begun: the end product of any liberating education is simply the self-educating, self-cultivating man and woman; in short, the free and rational individual.

A society in which such individuals are ascendant is, by one major meaning of the word, democratic. Such a society may also be defined as one in which genuine publics rather than masses prevail. By this, I mean the following:

Whether or not they are aware of them, men in a mass society are gripped by personal troubles which they are not able to turn into social issues. They do not understand the interplay of these personal troubles of their milieux with problems of social structure. The knowledgeable man in a genuine public, on the other hand, is able to do just that. He understands that what he thinks and feels to be personal troubles are very often also problems shared by others, and more importantly, not capable of solution by any one individual but only by modifications of the structure of the groups in which he lives and sometimes the structure of the entire society. Men in masses have troubles, but they are not usually aware of their true meaning and source; men in publics confront issues, and they usually come to be aware of their public terms.

It is the political task of the social scientist—as of any liberal educator —continually to translate personal troubles into public issues, and public issues into the terms of their human meaning for a variety of individuals. It is his task to display in his work—and, as an educator, in his life as well—this kind of sociological imagination. And it is his purpose to cultivate such habits of mind among the men and women who are publicly exposed to him. To secure these ends is to secure reason and individuality, and to make these the predominant values of a democratic society.

You may now be saying to yourself, 'Well, here it comes. He is going to set up an ideal so high that in terms of it everything must seem low.' That I might be thought to be doing so testifies to the lack of seriousness with which the word democracy is now taken, and to the indifference of many observers to the drift away from any plain meaning of the word. Democracy is, of course, a complicated idea about which there is much legitimate disagreement. But surely it is not so complicated or ambiguous that it may no longer be used by people who wish to reason together.

What I mean by democracy as an ideal I have already tried to indicate. In essence, democracy implies that those vitally affected by any decision men make have an effective voice in that decision. This, in turn, means that all power to make such decisions be publicly legitimated and that the makers of such decisions be held publicly accountable. None of these three points can prevail, it seems to me, unless there are dominant within a society the kinds of publics and the kinds of individuals I have described. Certain further conditions will presently become evident.

The social structure of the United States is not an altogether democratic one. Let us take that as a point of minimum agreement. I do not know of any society which is altogether democratic—that remains an ideal. The United States today I should say is generally democratic mainly in form and in the rhetoric of expectation. In substance and in practice it is very often nondemocratic, and in many institutional areas it is quite clearly so. The corporate economy is run neither as a set of town meetings nor as a set of powers responsible to those whom their activities affect very seriously. The military machines and increasingly the political state are in the same condition. I do not wish to give the impression that I am optimistic about the chances that many social scientists can or will perform a democratic public role, or—even if many of them do so—about the chances that this would necessarily result in a rehabilitation of publics. I am merely outlining one role that seems to me to be open and is, in fact, practiced by some social scientists. It happens also to be a role that is in line with both liberal and socialist views of the role of reason in human affairs.[1]

My point is that the political role of social science—what that role may be, how it is enacted, and how effectively—this is relevant to the extent to which democracy prevails.

If we take up the third role of reason, the autonomous role, we are trying to act in a democratic manner in a society that is not altogether democratic. But we are acting as if we were in a fully democratic society, and by doing so, we are attempting to remove the 'as if.' We are trying to make the society more democratic. Such a role, I contend, is the only role by which we may as social scientists attempt to do this. At least I do

[1] In passing, I should like to remind the reader that, quite apart from its present bureaucratic context and use, the style of abstracted empiricism (and the methodological inhibition it sustains) is not well suited for the democratic political role I am describing. Those who practice this style as their sole activity, who conceive of it as the 'real work of social science,' and who live in its ethos, cannot perform a liberating educational role. This role requires that individuals and publics be given confidence in their own capacities to reason, and by individual criticism, study, and practice, to enlarge its scope and improve its quality. It requires that they be encouraged, in George Orwell's phrase, to 'get outside the whale,' or in the wonderful American phrase, 'to become their own men.' To tell them that they can 'really' know social reality only by depending upon a necessarily bureaucratic kind of research is to place a taboo, in the name of Science, upon their efforts to become independent men and substantive thinkers. It is to undermine the confidence of the individual craftsman in his own ability to know reality. It is, in effect, to encourage men to fix their social beliefs by reference to the authority of an alien apparatus, and it is, of course, in line with, and is reinforced by, the whole bureaucratization of reason in our time. The industrialization of academic life and the fragmentation of the problems of social science cannot result in a liberating educational role for social scientists. For what these schools of thought take apart they tend to keep apart, in very tiny pieces about which they claim to be very certain. But all they could thus be certain of are abstracted fragments, and it is precisely the job of liberal education, *and* the political role of social science, *and* its intellectual promise, to enable men to transcend such fragmented and abstracted milieux: to become aware of historical structures and of their own place within them.

not know of any other way by which we might try to help build a democratic polity. And because of this, the problem of the social sciences as a
prime carrier of reason in human affairs is in fact a major problem of
democracy today.

5

What are the chances of success? Given the political structure within
which we must now act, I do not believe it is very likely that social
scientists will become effective carriers of reason. For men of knowledge
to enact this strategic role, certain conditions must be present. Men make
their own history, Marx said, but they do not make it under conditions of
their own choice. Well then, what are the conditions *we* require to play
this role effectively? What are required are parties and movements and
publics having two characteristics: (1) within them ideas and alternatives
of social life are truly debated, and (2) they have a chance really to
influence decisions of structural consequence. Only if such organizations existed, could we become realistic and hopeful about the role of
reason in human affairs which I have been trying to outline. Such a
situation, by the way, I should consider one major requirement for any
fully democratic society.

In such a polity social scientists in their political roles would probably
'speak for' and 'against' a variety of movements and strata and interests,
rather than merely address an often vague, and—I fear—dwindling,
public. Their ideas, in short, would compete, and this competition (as a
process as well as in its result at any given time) would be politically
relevant. If we take the idea of democracy seriously, if we take the
democratic role of reason in human affairs seriously, our engagement in
such a competition will in no way distress us. Surely we cannot suppose
that all definitions of social reality, much less all statements of political
ways and means, much less all suggestions of goals, would result in some
undebatable, unified doctrine.[2]

In the absence of such parties and movements and publics, we live in
a society that is democratic mainly in its legal forms and its formal expectations. We ought not to minimize the enormous value and the considerable opportunity these circumstances make available. We should
learn their value from the fact of their absence in the Soviet world, and
from the kind of struggle the intellectuals of that world are up against.
We should also learn that whereas there many intellectuals are physically
crushed, here many morally crush themselves. That democracy in the
United States is so largely formal does not mean that we can dodge the
conclusion that if reason is to play any free part in a democratic making
of history, one of its chief carriers must surely be the social sciences. The
absence of democratic parties and movements and publics does not mean

---

[2] The idea of such a monopoly in the sphere of social ideas is one of the authoritarian notions which lie under the view of 'The Method' of the science-makers as
administrators of reason, and which is so thinly disguised in the 'sacred values' of
grand theorists. . . .

that social scientists as educators ought not to try to make their educational institutions a framework within which such a liberating public of individuals might exist, at least in its beginnings, and one in which their discussions might be encouraged and sustained. Nor does it mean that they should not try to cultivate such publics in their less academic roles.

To do so of course, is to risk 'trouble'; or what is more serious, to face a quite deadly indifference. It requires that we deliberately present controversial theories and facts, and actively encourage controversy. In the absence of political debate that is wide and open and informed, people can get into touch neither with the effective realities of their world nor with the realities of themselves. Nowadays especially, it seems to me, the role I have been describing requires no less than the presentation of conflicting definitions of reality itself. What is usually termed 'propaganda,' especially of a nationalist sort, consists not only of opinions on a variety of topics and issues. It is the promulgation, as Paul Kecskemeti once noted, of official definitions of reality.

Our public life now often rests upon such official definitions, as well as upon myths and lies and crackbrained notions. When many policies—debated and undebated—are based on inadequate and misleading definitions of reality, then those who are out to define reality more adequately are bound to be upsetting influences. That is why publics of the sort I have described, as well as men of individuality, are, by their very existence in such a society, radical. Yet such is the role of mind, of study, of intellect, of reason, of ideas: to define reality adequately and in a publicly relevant way. The educational and the political role of social science in a democracy is to help cultivate and sustain publics and individuals that are able to develop, to live with, and to act upon adequate definitions of personal and social realities.

The role of reason I have been outlining neither means nor requires that one hit the pavement, take the next plane to the scene of the current crisis, run for Congress, buy a newspaper plant, go among the poor, set up a soap box. Such actions are often admirable, and I can readily imagine occasions when I should personally find it impossible not to want to do them myself. But for the social scientist to take them to be his normal activities is merely to abdicate his role, and to display by his action a disbelief in the promise of social science and in the role of reason in human affairs. This role requires only that the social scientist get on with the work of social science and that he avoid furthering the bureaucratization of reason and of discourse.

Not every social scientist accepts all the views I happen to hold on these issues, and it is not my wish that he should. My point is that one of his tasks is to determine his own views of the nature of historical change and the place, if any, of free and reasonable men within it. Only then can he come to know his own intellectual and political role within the societies he is studying, and in doing so find out just what he does think of the values of freedom and of reason which are so deeply a part of the tradition and the promise of social science.

If individual men and small groups of men are not free to act with historical consequence, and at the same time are not reasonable enough to
see those consequences; if the structure of modern societies, or of any
one of them, is now such that history is indeed blind drift and cannot be
made otherwise with the means at hand and the knowledge that may be
acquired—then the only autonomous role of social science is to chronicle
and to understand; the idea of the responsibility of the powerful is foolish;
and the values of freedom and of reason are realizable only in the excep-
tional milieux of certain favored private lives.

But that is a lot of 'ifs.' And although there is ample room for disagreement over degrees of freedom and scales of consequence, I do not believe
that there is sufficient evidence to necessitate abandoning the values
of freedom and reason as they might now orient the work of social science.

Attempts to avoid such troublesome issues as I have been discussing are
nowadays widely defended by the slogan that social science is 'not out to
save the world.' Sometimes this is the disclaimer of a modest scholar;
sometimes it is the cynical contempt of a specialist for all issues of larger
concern; sometimes it is the disillusionment of youthful expectations; often
it is the pose of men who seek to borrow the prestige of The Scientist,
imagined as a pure and disembodied intellect. But sometimes it is based
upon a considered judgment of the facts of power.

Because of such facts, I do not believe that social science will 'save
the world' although I see nothing at all wrong with 'trying to save the
world'—a phrase which I take here to mean the avoidance of war and
the re-arrangement of human affairs in accordance with the ideals of
human freedom and reason. Such knowledge as I have leads me to embrace rather pessimistic estimates of the chances. But even if that is
where we now stand, still we must ask: If there *are* any ways out of the
crisis of our period by means of intellect, is it not up to the social scientist
to state them? What we represent—although this is not always apparent
—is man become aware of mankind. It is on the level of human awareness
that virtually all solutions to the great problems must now lie.

To *appeal* to the powerful, on the basis of any knowledge we now have,
is utopian in the foolish sense of that term. Our relations with them are
more likely to be only such relations as they find useful, which is to say
that we become technicians accepting their problems and aims, or ideolo-
gists promoting their prestige and authority. To be more than that, so
far as our political role is concerned, we must first of all re-consider the
nature of our collective endeavor as social scientists. It is not at all utopian
for one social scientist to appeal to his colleagues to undertake such a
re-consideration. Any social scientist who is aware of what he is about
must confront the major moral dilemma I have implied in this chapter—
the difference between what men are interested in and what is to men's
interest.

If we take the simple democratic view that *what men are interested in*
is all that concerns us, then we are accepting the values that have been
inculcated, often accidentally and often deliberately by vested interests.

These values are often the only ones men have had any chance to develop. They are unconsciously acquired habits rather than choices.

If we take the dogmatic view that *what is to men's interests*, whether they are interested in it or not, is all that need concern us morally, then we run the risk of violating democratic values. We may become manipulators or coercers, or both, rather than persuaders within a society in which men are trying to reason together and in which the value of reason is held in high esteem.

What I am suggesting is that by addressing ourselves to issues and to troubles, and formulating them as problems of social science, we stand the best chance, I believe the only chance, to make reason democratically relevant to human affairs in a free society, and so realize the classic values that underlie the promise of our studies.

·2·
ON ACTIONISM IN THE
CRAFT OF SOCIOLOGY

PHILIP M. HAUSER
University of Chicago

S OCIOLOGY HAD ITS ORIGINS IN THE CONVERGENCE OF THREE DEVELOP-
ments—the development of social thought, the desire to improve the
lot of man, and the application of the method of science to social
phenomena. In its brief history as a science, which by rigorous criteria
does not begin until perhaps the second quarter of this century, these
three strains have remained distinguishable in the literature and in the
activities of sociologists. In fact, contemporary sociologists may be classified into three broad categories on the bases of their time-budgets and
their works—as predominantly social thinkers or social scientists or social
actionists. These categories are, of course, not mutually exclusive and most
sociologists to some extent straddle all three. But prototypes exist of
sociologists who fall predominantly into one of these categories. Although
readers will undoubtedly be able to make their own identifications, to
avoid distractive dissension I shall refrain from naming prototypes active
or inactive (deceased or retired).

The development of sociology during the course of this century has
effected significant changes in the balance of the sociological life-style.
Although no rigorous empirical investigation is available on the point, it
is probably correct to say that in the first two or three decades of the
century sociologists were predominantly social thinkers and secondarily
social actionists. In the second three decades of the century sociologists
can be characterized as primarily social scientists and secondarily social
thinkers. With the acceptance of the natural science model of science the
proportion of the sociological life-space devoted to social action diminished. Certainly up to very recently the proportion of persons recruited
to sociology who were primarily motivated by the desire to "do good," as
represented, for example, by those with religion or social work oriented
backgrounds diminished.

In the evolving of sociology there has emerged a large literature on the
role of social thought or "theorizing," empirical research, and social action
as distinct activities within the craft as well as on their interrelationships.
There is certainly less disagreement about theorizing and empirical
research being essential ingredients of sociology than about the place of
social actionism in the craft. There has been and there is now increasing
disagreement on the Weberian model of science as the model most applicable to sociology or to the social sciences in general. But this model
has certainly become the dominant one, and still is, for most practitioners
of sociology. Sociologists do not regard social action as a major concern of
the craft.

♦ Originally published in Vol. 39, No. 2 of *Sociological Inquiry*. Reprinted by
permission.

There has, of course, never been any dispute about the prerogative of the sociologist, as a citizen or social engineer, to engage in social action. Moreover, by reason of his more than average awareness of social problems, sociologists as citizens or as social engineers have probably been well above average in their participation in action programs designed to remedy existent social evils.

With the emergence of the "new politics," and especially the "new left," however, the craft of sociology has been infiltrated by an actionist ideology which constitutes the greatest threat to the Weberian conception of social science that has yet emerged. In the vanguard of the actionists are the new left graduate students and younger members of sociology faculties who accuse sociology and sociologists of being elements of "the establishment" which must be overthrown. They conceive it to be the obligation and function of sociology to dissociate itself from the established order and to work for its overthrow. They accept as techniques for the achievement of this objective, among others, disruption and violence. They reserve the right to determine who shall and who shall not be heard. They have adopted the language as well as the tactics of Chairman Mao without, to a large extent, his or any other positive program. Their closest approach to the statement of a positive objective consists of their vague references to effect a "redistribution of power." Sociologists who attended the Sixty-Third Annual Meeting of the Association in Boston in 1968 had the opportunity to observe at first hand the persons and the tactics, to read the literature and to hear the remarks of these self-appointed "liberators" of sociology—the members of the "Sociology Liberation Movement."

It is relevant to observe that most of the personnel involved in this movement are at best marginal sociologists in that they are still graduate students or nontenured members of faculties who have yet to demonstrate that they can win their places as professional journeymen sociologists. They are still very young, very inexperienced, and still presumably engaged in learning the craft of sociology. They appear to be, in the main, excellent students who are very much disillusioned about their elders, sociologists as well as others; and they are convinced that our society is a sick society that must be destroyed. They are especially sensitive to the horrors of Vietnam and of war in general, to the iniquities of racism, to the blight of poverty, to the deficiencies of systems of governance, and to the evils of machine politics and its attendant limited options in the selection of political leaders. They are certainly extraordinarily conscientious citizens with a deep sense of obligation to correct the evils they perceive and with a major commitment to bring this about. They are perhaps the closest manifestation in contemporary life to a religious sectarian movement characterized by a sense of moral fervor and absolute righteousness.

This description of the new left sociologists is not intended to be pejorative. One cannot lightly dismiss or condemn as undesirable a movement that addresses itself to the elimination of the acute and chronic evils with which society is admittedly afflicted. On the contrary, one must extoll the perception, the concern, the dedication, the commitment, and even the fervor of those who would solve the sore problems which beset us. One can question the righteousness and absolutism which characterizes the movement and evaluate in various ways its present and potential effectiveness. But these are not the purposes of this essay. It is rather the purpose of this discussion to consider the place of this actionist ideology and behavior in the craft of sociology.

To do so, it is desirable, first of all, to indicate the premises underlying the discussion. These are: First, that science has as its major goals the achievement of predictability and explanation of a specifically delineated set of phenomena—physical, biological, or social.

Second, that science by its nature can produce existential and instrumental judgments but not value judgments. Value judgments, which underlie all action, may draw upon the fund of knowledge produced by science but are not the product of any scientific process or procedure, as such, and are necessarily dependent on an arbitrarily selected set of norms used as criteria in reaching the judgment.

Third, that sociology is one of the social sciences.

Fourth, that actionist ideology and behavior, necessarily based on value judgments, are incompatible with the role of sociologists as scientists.

Fifth, that it is possible for the individual sociologist to play many roles in addition to his role as scientist—that of husband, father, musician, religious believer and, also, that of citizen or social engineer.

Sixth, that actionist behavior and ideology are a prerogative of sociologists but not as scientists, any more than their roles as husband or musician, etc., are roles as scientists.

These premises lead to the conclusion that the value judgments of scientists, including those of sociologists, all other things being equal, have no more validity than the value judgments of anyone else. For example, the judgment by the new left and others that the Vietnam War is a horrible, nightmarish, devastating, bestial, imperialist enterprise on the part of the United States, whether held by sociologists or non-sociologists, is not based on sociology or any other science. It, as other value judgments, derives from the norms used as criteria in reaching the judgment, norms that do not have their origin in science but, rather, in the cultures that mankind has evolved. The conception of science adopted here is, of course, not the only conception extant, but it is certainly the predominant one and, for sociologists, is that of the Weberian model.

If my premises are accepted, then it is clear that actionist ideology and behavior have no place in sociology except, of course, on those matters that pertain to the craft itself. That is, sociologists cannot ignore developments that constitute a threat to the effective functioning of the discipline of sociology. Examples of such threats include any constraints on freedom of research, teaching, recruitment of personnel or, in general, violations of academic freedom. In respect of such matters sociologists must be prepared to defend the sociological establishment, and, indeed, the entire academic establishment; and, appropriately, should be prepared to mobilize and take action against any efforts designed to impinge upon these freedoms. In becoming actionists in such situations sociologists would be acting in their capacities as members of a profession rather than as scientists. Such actionist behavior would be in defense of their roles and functions as scientists.

Resolutions by the American Sociological Association, in accordance with its constitution, aimed at defense of freedom of research and teaching and related matters, are then consistent with the premises set forth above. But what about resolutions of the type proposed by the Sociology Liberation Movement and others relating to the Vietnam War or any other social, economic or political evil? Certainly, each sociologist is free to have a position on such matters and to take such action as seems indicated in his role as a citizen or in his role as a social engineer if he is engaged in action programs. "Such action as seems indicated" is a matter for individual determination and conceivably could include civil disobedience if the person feels this is justified and is prepared to risk the penalties likely to be imposed. The essential point is that in such a circumstance the sociologist is acting as a citizen or as a social engineer and not as a member of the craft of sociology. He acts as an individual and must assume individual responsibility for his behavior. He certainly cannot contend that he is acting as a sociologist, as a member of a scientific profession, in the sense that the science of sociology justifies his course. For neither sociology nor any other science can produce the value judgment that underlies the individual's behavior.

Should the American Sociological Association take a stand on social, economic and political issues beyond those directly affecting the craft of sociology as an academic discipline? It is my contention, based on the premises above, that the answer must be decisively in the negative. For to pursue such a course is to confuse the roles of the scientist and the citizen or social engineer. It necessitates a value judgment that the science of sociology cannot produce, on which sociologists may and do disagree, and which perverts the role of sociologists as scientists. The American Sociological Association as a professional association of scientists has no special ability beyond that of any other organization to make a value judgment; and any actionist behavior which the Association as such may take transcends its competence as a scientific organization. It may be argued that just as the doctrine of "guilt by association" is to be deplored, so, also, is the doctrine of "validity by association." The fact that the American Sociological Association or any other organization of scientists makes a value judgment does not give that judgment any greater validity than a value judgment made by a nonscientific association. Yet, sociologists, in the heat of emotional reaction and anger, in confusion of their roles as scientists and citizens or social engineers, may act with a righteousness that makes even them believe their value judgments have a superior validity. In fact, what they may demonstrate is that sociologists, even if good scientists, can be as frail, as emotional, as irrational, and as downright silly as anybody else.

I am arguing that in taking positions on social, economic, or political issues sociologists would compromise their position as social scientists in revealing their weaknesses rather than their strengths. Sociologists, as citizens or as social engineers, can express their value judgments through many other channels without destroying the image of the craft of sociology, dragging sociology as a profession into the heat of the political arena, and impairing sociology's ability to perform its basic tasks in investigation and education. For the sociologist may be a good scientist even if he is a naive citizen or an incompetent social engineer. To confuse his roles is to gain nothing while risking his potential to be an effective scientist. It is the task of the sociologist as a scientist to illuminate rather than to exhort, to analyze rather than to prescribe, to delineate problem areas rather than to confront them.

The Boston Annual Meeting provided a good example of the fact that sociologists, in the heat of emotional reaction, can be as irrational as anybody else. The resolutions of the business meeting not to meet in Chicago for the next three meetings scheduled in that city extending to 1976, is a case in point. To meet in Chicago is certainly not to condone either Mayor Daley's or his police department's shortcomings, any more than to meet in San Francisco in 1969 in lieu of Chicago constitutes condoning of the events at San Francisco State College. To decide not to meet in Chicago until after 1976 is to demonstrate that sociologists as human beings can be as emotional and irrational as any group of non-scientists; that they can act without benefit of knowledge of the facts, that is, in advance of the several investigations launched to determine what actually happened; and in a fit of anger presumably intended to punish the city even beyond the term of its incumbent mayor. Moreover, the same emotional binge during the business meeting resulted in the passing of a resolution to establish a Committee on Social Policy which conceivably could initiate an era of pronouncements by the Association on social, economic and political issues—pronouncements, I repeat, incompatible with its role as an association of scientists.

Fortunately, the membership of the Association, in less emotional moments and in keeping with its knowledge of human behavior, including the behavior of sociologists, adopted a constitution which prevents the members who happen to attend a business meeting from passing resolutions in the name of the American Sociological Association. This power is reserved to the Council which receives the actions of the business meeting as recommendations and which, in more sober deliberation, acts in the name of the Association. Even this provision does not guarantee rational behavior for the Council, meeting in Boston with the emotional surcharge provided by the business meeting, also voted not to meet in Chicago until after 1976. But it is possible that this action will be reversed for meetings subsequent to 1969. If the Association were to adopt the position that it would not meet in any city in which undesirable situations or events were to be found it is clear no more annual meetings could be held—except perhaps, for the time being, on the moon.

Assuming that the American Sociological Association is prepared to conduct itself as a professional and scientific organization rather than as a political grouping, what should be its attitude toward efforts to drag it into the political arena and, more specifically, what should be its attitude toward the Sociology Liberation Movement?

The answer to the first part of the question is already given. To summarize, the Association, and the craft of sociology, in general, is well advised to concentrate on the professional and scientific matters which it was formed to consider. The answer to the second part of the question is likewise clear. The Association should refuse to be liberated by our self-appointed liberators. The Association and the craft, in general, should do its utmost to help to complete the sociological education of our would-be liberators for, on the whole, they undoubtedly include many persons with first-rate capacities who potentially could make fine scientists. We should continue, by the same token, to provide them with ample opportunity to be heard through all the channels of communication open to members of the Association, including the annual meeting.

In the Boston meeting this policy was scrupulously pursued. Rooms were provided for their meetings despite the fact that their requests came much later than normal arrangements would make possible. They were given ample opportunity to distribute their literature and to participate in programs. They were invited to have a discussant at the plenary session at which their chief target, Secretary of Health, Education and Welfare, Wilbur Cohen, spoke. In brief, they were given every opportunity to present their case to the members of the Association.

Just as the Association must be zealous in its efforts to protect the right to be heard of the Sociology Liberation Movement or other dissident groups, so, also, it must be zealous in its insistence on its right to conduct its meetings without disruption. It must not permit the Sociology Liberation Movement or any dissident group to determine who can and who cannot be heard. This is not just a rhetorical argument, for the Sociology Liberation Movement threatened disruption of the plenary session at which Secretary Cohen spoke and, also, of other sessions. In its righteousness, the group reserves unto itself the decision to employ tactics of disruption and violence, as its literature makes explicitly clear. While the Association should be quite tolerant of those militants who make up the Movement, it must not allow itself to be cowed by the threat of disruption or refuse to muster such force as may be necessary to prevent this small minority group from interfering with Association activities. It is in order to report that, as President of the Association, I forewarned the leaders of the Sociology Liberation Movement that superior force would be employed if necessary to assure the right of all speakers to be heard; and it was ironic to be called "Fascist" by those who were prepared to use storm trooper tactics to prevent speakers with whom they disagreed from being heard.

The Association should not rule out as members sociologists or potential sociologists who are primarily actionists any more than it should rule out those who are primarily social thinkers or empirical researchers. Sociologists who are primarily social engineers and, therefore, actionists appropriately are eligible for membership in the Association. But actionists who aim at "liberating" sociology by behavior that is disruptive of Association activities and which violates the rights of others to freedom of speech and association should lose their eligibility for Association membership. The Association should tolerate in its members any and all postures in respect of what constitutes science, what constitutes the mission of sociology, what constitutes appropriate balance among social thinkers, empirical researchers, and social actionists. But it must adamantly be intolerant of those who exercise tactics of disruption to prevent normal means of communication and dialogue among all members of the sociological fraternity. In this respect, it must be made clear that those who utilize disruption and violence demonstrate their incapacity to be members of a scientific community whose very existence is posited on freedom of research, freedom of teaching and freedom of communication. There is nothing compulsory about being a sociologist any more than there is anything compulsory about being enrolled at a university. To be a member of a professional and scientific association or of an academic community requires complete adherence to the principle of freedom of communication. One not prepared to live by this rule should not be considered eligible for membership in an intellectual community; and this posture should be emphatically communicated by the Association and, I might add, by universities and colleges as well.

The November issue of *The American Sociologist* arrived as this essay was being written. A considerable proportion of its contents is devoted to actionism in sociology.[1] Amitai Etzioni, in his piece "On Public Affairs Statements of Professional Associations," on the whole is in agreement with the stand I have taken on the general role of sociologists and of the Association in respect of public policy pronouncements. He inquires "are there any circumstances under which the general rule against such statements may be suspended?" He agrees the Association should take a public stand "when public events adversely affect the members' professional work" (p. 279). But he holds that the general rule should also be suspended when a "unique" case calls for it (p. 280). The unique case arises when "the macroscopic effects of an issue are of such magnitude that a *crisis* is reached in the sense that basic needs or values *of the society* are undermined . . ." (p. 280).

Within the framework I have developed above I would disagree with Etzioni's position if it requires the Association to issue a policy pronouncement in the name of the profession of sociology. The basic premises I have set forth would be violated and such an act would, therefore, be incompatible with the behavior of sociologists as scientists. Yet, I would see no objection to a polling of sociologists as one group whose opinions as

---

[1] I would particularly commend to the reader William A. Gamson's piece on "Sociology's Children of Affluence," containing hypotheses for explaining the changing attitudes of sociologists toward actionism, as are also the "Letters" which are concerned with various effects of actionism in the field. I also regard Stuart A. Rice's "Why I wanted to become a Sociologist" as must reading for all, and especially younger sociologists concerned with this issue of actionism. In response to being awarded the first "Certificate of Merit" of the District of Columbia Sociological Society, Rice traces his sociological career and has words of wisdom consistent with the position I have outlined above. . . .

citizens are sounded. The recent vote of the members of the Association on the Vietnam resolution is a case in point and supports the stand I am advocating. That is, the Association membership voted almost two to one against the Association, as such, taking any position on the proposed resolution, even as a majority in one way or another voted as citizens against the Vietnam War. The distinction was much more than a superficial one, for such actions carefully recognized the difference between the role of the sociologist as a scientist and as a citizen.

ACTIONISM IN A SOCIOLOGICAL CAREER

By reason of the emphasis placed by the editors on the personal experience and judgment of the contributors to this issue I shall present a brief biographical account of how one sociologist—namely myself—has managed to achieve a satisfying balance of sociology and actionism in a sociological career.

To begin with, my training in sociology at the University of Chicago during the late twenties and early thirties led me to accept the Weberian model of sociology. That sociology was a science, not a vehicle for social action, was a tenet of faith on the part of the faculty and the predominant proportion of graduate students at Chicago including those who had been recruited from action-oriented backgrounds.

Yet, interestingly enough, it was clear that many members of the faculty, permanent and visiting, were making major contributions to action programs. Examples included Park, in race relations; Burgess, in treatment of delinquent and criminal behavior; Ogburn, in the development of facilities for psychoanalysis; Wirth, in urban problems; Sutherland, in penology; and Rice, in the development of statistical organization in government. I reconciled the apparent contradictions in my own mind, then and since, by accepting the proposition that the sociologist could play multiple roles—that of scientist as his major profession but, simultaneously, also, that of social engineer or citizen. The important thing it seemed to me then, as now, is that the roles not be confused because such confusion would compromise excellence in performance in both.

The development of career lines rarely follow plan. They are more likely to be the result of opportunities—unanticipated as well as promoted. With major training in theory and general sociology the course of events led me to concentrate my activities, research and actionist, in social statistics, demography and urban sociology. After a three-year leave of absence from my post as Instructor in Sociology at the University of Chicago to participate, as a social statistician, in the FERA and WPA programs in Washington during the depression (1934–1937), a disagreement with a university administrator and the opportunity to participate in a decennial census (that in 1940) led me to spend about a decade as an official of the U.S. Bureau of the Census.

This assignment provided an admixture of opportunities for thought, for research, and for action in the development of decennial census and current statistical programs. Moreover, the development of statistical programs provided an opportunity to illuminate many of the more serious problems which confronted the nation—urban, racial, educational, economic, and housing as well as demographic. My Washington activities were a most satisfying experience from almost every standpoint and certainly provided ample opportunity for the exercise of technical and scientific skills even while providing the fulfillment which comes with direct participation in action programs. For, in addition to playing a role in the expansion and improvement of social statistics, I was drawn into activities which led directly to significant innovations such as the establishment of the Social Security System, the Atomic Energy Commission, the National Science Foundation, the public housing and urban renewal programs, the Employment Act of 1946, and the Marshall Plan. Even after my return to the University of Chicago in 1947 it remained possible, while pursuing the academic life, to participate in such developments as federal aid to education, the anti-poverty programs, the welfare programs and the population programs of the Federal Government. Moreover, participation in various projects on the state and local levels was also possible including activities relating to the Illinois Centennial of the Emancipation Proclamation and the Illinois mental health program; and on the city level, work on projects relating to public school education, city planning, urban renewal, public housing and public health.

Finally, I should mention that participation in action programs was also possible on the international level throughout Asia, Latin America, and Africa in activities including the development of census and statistical systems, of policies and programs in respect of urban and regional planning, of programs in population training, research and action, and work with the United Nations and UNESCO on the formation of social development policy.

I recite these activities to indicate that the sociological life need not be one divorced from the reality of world, national, state or local affairs. Opportunities for the sociologist to engage in social engineering activities in addition to research and teaching activities will undoubtedly increase, not decrease, in the coming years. The sociologist who becomes restive if confined to research and educational activities can find many ways to become actionist in the social engineering sense. With the proliferation of economic and social planning and the increase in welfare functions of government, the need for sociologists has increased both for the performance of scientific and social engineering tasks.

In fact, there are few, if any, fields of sociology which do not have social action implications. To those who feel they must be involved in action programs there is almost always a way, in the role of social engineer or citizen, in which involvement is possible. In the short run the sociologist can function as a scientist even though, in addition, he participates in action roles as a social engineer. In the longer run a division of labor between the roles of the scientist and the social engineer will be both desirable and inevitable. It will be desirable because of the diverse orientations and skills which are required to perform these different functions and because maximum proficiency will result from specialization in one or the other. Even now, actionist roles by sociologists can be performed only at the expense of scientific activity. Keeping up with the literature in one's own field of specialization is virtually a full-time job. In the longer run, it is safe to predict that the increasing fund of sociological knowledge, the more complex character of research techniques, and the demands upon social engineers to be familiar with a much broader spectrum of sociological and social science knowledge than the specialist sociologist scientist can possibly acquire will force a greater division of labor between social science and social engineering activities. Moreover, the number of social engineering professions will undoubtedly proliferate and require specialized engineering training and experience.

En route to the long run, what does the sociologist and especially the younger sociologist do? He is well advised, first of all, to decide on a relatively narrow spectrum of activities on which to concentrate both as scientist and engineer. It is very tempting to respond to the many and growing opportunities to engage both in ongoing research and social engineering projects. This is a mandate much easier to transmit than to exemplify. My major criticism of my own activities, especially now that I near the end of my formal academic career, is that my energies are much too diffused and much more controlled by the pressures and demands generated by the course of events and by others to permit the orderly and efficient completion of priority tasks. It is becoming imperative for the advancement of sociology as a science for sociologists to learn to say "no"—both in response to invitations to attend the round of endless meetings and conferences and to the invitations to social action which impair research productivity. One of my teachers, Professor William F. Ogburn, advised me and others many years ago to avoid becoming "a committee bum." But I am afraid I have not heeded his advice and in addition to two badly overdue research monographs, at the moment, I can think of a relatively long list of undone researches which I had hoped to do over the years.

With the hindsight that comes with nearing retirement age, I suggest that all sociologists under 45 hold to a minimum their committee, conference, consulting, and social action assignments—perhaps restrict their non-university committee assignments to only one, that most clearly related to their fields of research. The predominant inputs of sociologists under 45 should be in research—while they have the combination of maturity, energy, and skills to be at their prime.

After age 45 for some, and perhaps older ages for others, an increasing admixture of social engineering activities may be desirable and even called for. The more senior sociologists may find it increasingly difficult to compete with younger sociologists in the conduct of significant research in a world in which the half-life of an engineer's education is estimated at about seven years and that of a sociologist is probably not too much greater. The older sociologist may have wisdom rather than research competence to contribute towards the advancement of sociology, a wisdom that may well serve social engineering projects as well, at least for the time being in the absence of a well-staffed cadre of social engineers. Moreover, it is probably the wisdom of the older sociologists, more than the impatience, energy and righteousness of the young, that can best contribute to amelioration of society's ills. This proposition is likely to stand up even if it is the revolutionary actionist who opens the way to some types of change.

CONCLUDING OBSERVATIONS

By eschewing political action as a professional and scientific body the Association would by no means be failing to contribute to the resolution of the acute and chronic problems which afflict this nation and the entire world. This would no more be the case than the refusal of the biochemist engaged in cancer research to treat a cancer patient. Biochemical research may contribute more to the elimination of cancer in the longer run than will the biomedical engineer, the physician, who treats the cancerous patient. Similarly, the fund of knowledge produced by sociological research may contribute infinitely more to the solution of social problems than the disruptive and violent tactics of the new left actionists including the Sociology Liberation Movement.

Yet sociologists as scientists do have options in respect of the relevance of their research to social problems and, therefore, can to a considerable extent relate to current social problems. That is, sociologists do have freedom in determining the subjects of their investigations and, therefore, they can opt to conduct their studies on problems which they regard as the most significant from a social problematic as well as a disciplinary point of view. Moreover, although the organizations with funds for research in some ways exercise undue influence in the direction research may take they, on the whole, and certainly the private foundations, tend to focus on society's most severe problems. For example, there is little difficulty, at this time, in obtaining funds for study of many aspects of minority group problems; housing problems; urban problems in general; population problems, especially if related to high fertility and family planning; education problems; problems relating to mental health; problems relating to child development and the process of socialization, in general; problems of aging; and a host of other problems which are of concern either to private or public sources which fund research.

The sociologist even as scientist, then, can still relate to the solution of the evils of the day even if he is not in an actionist posture in respect of them. Of course, if he is very deeply emotionally involved in the problem it is possible that he may not be in a position to conduct objective research. On the other hand, his emotional involvement if controlled, and good training should make control possible, may provide desirable motivation and increase input into the research enterprise.

As I indicated in my Presidential Address to the American Sociological Association (*American Sociological Review*, February, 1969), there is a great gap between the knowledge which the social sciences, including sociology, have produced and society's employment of that knowledge in social policies and programs. This gap is itself an important area for investigation. But despite this fact the knowledge of the social sciences in general, and of sociology in particular, is still quite limited and there is need for continued and increased research output. The sociologist as scientist need not, in any sense, feel apologetic for his role as a scientist nor need he feel any sense of detachment from reality by concentrating on his scientific and professional functions. Indeed, the sociologist who cannot restrict himself to such activities and whose citizenship activities do not provide fulfillment has the choice of becoming a part-time or full-time social engineer. There are increasing numbers of such opportunities, including the role of policy advisor to officials in the public or private sector.

In conclusion, it is the mission of the sociologist *qua* scientist to add to sociological knowledge. He should not yield to the temptation to turn activist at the expense of his functions as a scientist. If he prefers action he has the alternative of becoming a social engineer—a practitioner employed in the application of sociological and other bodies of knowledge. If out of impatience or other characteristics he must become an actionist employing the tactics of disruption and violence, he is acting as a revolutionary, certainly not as a scientist. There may be need for revolutionaries and for tactics of disruption—but the revolutionary and the employment of violence should not be confused with, nor permitted to, contaminate the craft of sociology. Moreover, sociology as a craft would do well to avoid direct participation of any kind in the general political arena in the interest of maximizing its contribution to the funding of knowledge and, thus, indirectly—but more powerfully and more appropriately—to the elimination of the evils which beset man and society.

Part II

SOCIAL SCIENCE AND SOCIAL POLICY

In January, 1968, political scientist Daniel P. Moynihan, Assistant to the President for Urban Affairs, published *Maximum Feasible Misunderstanding*—an account of the evolution of the Economic Opportunity Act of 1964 (the war on poverty) and its subsequent amendments. Moynihan's narrative focuses upon the social-science underpinnings of the act's mandate for "maximum feasible participation" of the poor in the conduct and development of poverty programs. The emergence of that mandate from social-science theory is reported to have been fraught with avoidable naiveté, blunders, and distortions, and at least to the present time to have resulted in a rather resounding failure. Moynihan concludes from his and others' experiences in the war on poverty that *"The role of social science lies not in the formulation of social policy, but in the measurement of its results"* (emphasis in the original; see p. 41 in this volume). In drawing that conclusion, he agrees with Hauser (contribution 2): social scientists trip over their own feet when they attempt simultaneously to walk the paths of researcher *and* reformer. Moynihan's discussion concerning the role of social science in social policy (the concluding section from *Maximum Feasible Misunderstanding*) is presented as contribution 3 below.

Sociologist David Gottlieb, himself a former Washington antipoverty warrior and a "new sociologist" according to *Time*, introduces a symposium of scholars, by no means "ivory tower" types, who in part react to Moynihan and in part speculate about current and future relations between social scientists and public policy. In most cases, their essays permit them to be classified unambiguously in either the Hauser or the Mills camp.

Gottlieb, in contribution 4, is at once pessimistic and sanguine. He does not see social scientists in the near future actively proposing strategies of social intervention. If they were to do so, he says, they probably would not be taken seriously by policy makers anyway. Gottlieb agrees with Moynihan that most social scientists lack implementation awareness, and thus generally are unable to bridge their research findings with practical applications. Perhaps, both concur, the style and methodology of social science will change enough one day to facilitate such bridging.

While recognizing the utility of conceptually and statistically sophisticated research reports *for* the social sciences, there is little doubt that most reports today have considerably less utility for those who might seek to apply their findings. Any perusal of the major social-science journals will document this assertion. That an implementation awareness has been a recent development in the social sciences having some appeal to nonsocial scientists seems demonstrated by the recent establishment and subsequent success of such publications as *Trans-action* and the *Journal of Applied Behavioral Science*. Special issues dealing with intervention topics have recently characterized other journals such as the *American Behavioral Scientist*, the *Journal of Social Issues*, and the *Social Science Quarterly*. Yet implementation awareness is not an attribute characteristic of most social scientists.

Economist Joseph J. Spengler, in contribution 5, is not surprised by the setbacks in the war on poverty. He assesses contemporary social science in general to be short on theory, long on clichés, overdependent upon misleading survey data, and too quick to generalize from meager data. With social science in this state of immaturity, he continues, its practitioners are apt to be sloppy and their applications plagued with implicit value judgments or ideological biases. That social-science practitioners would let "maximum feasible participation" become a Frankenstein's monster should have been anticipated and perhaps could have been avoided. Nonetheless, Spengler advises that social science is more ready to meet the challenge of planned social intervention than social scientists themselves are. Agreeing substantially with Hauser, Spengler suggests that social scientists should devote themselves to basic research, and then conduct only such research as they can accomplish with validity and reliability, without value judgment and ideological influence. To promise more than can be delivered, even if such promises are rewarded with increasingly precious funding, is to invite failure and to be guilty of a disservice.

Sociologist Peter H. Rossi writes, in contribution 6, that it may be too early to accept Moynihan's declaration that "maximum feasible participation" was a failure. Rossi points to the fact that participation of the poor continues to be a mandate in the Model Cities Program of the Department of Housing and Urban Development and similarly can be seen to influence the current decentralization of some school systems. He argues further that there were actually only a few bona-fide social scientists involved in the planning and implementation of the Economic Opportunity Act, so that the selective use of tenuous theoretical perspectives cannot fairly be blamed on social scientists. Rossi thinks that Moynihan assigns social scientists an unnecessarily conservative role when he suggests that they should only *evaluate* planned social intervention. In Rossi's view, the evaluation of a program can indicate only that the program was better or worse than no program at all; it does not allow for the systematic assessment of alternative interventions. Social scientists are competent to design and to test such alternatives, and can provide data valuable to large-scale intervention planning—*if* they have the funds and the freedom to do so. Rossi cites the example of the experimental income-maintenance programs being studied by the University of Wisconsin's Institute for Research on Poverty.

Rossi's consideration of the disadvantages of restricting social scientists to evaluation tasks is well taken—especially since social scientists are usually hired to begin evaluation research after programs have already begun. Ideally, social scientists should be present when program goals and strategies are decided, so that they can isolate the independent and dependent variables central to evaluation. Research should be funded at such a time as to allow investigators the opportunity to prepare their tools and gather sufficient baseline data *before* assessing program impact. Perhaps such timing is politically or systemically difficult. Perhaps, given the present state of their measures or the complexity of the program dynamics, social scientists would have trouble doing a complete job of evaluation no matter how much preparation time and funding were made available (as Moynihan points out, it took four and a half years just to prepare the proposal for the Mobilization for Youth program; yet horrendous measurement problems were encountered). The point is that even if social scientists are limited to evaluation research, the whole system of funding, timing, and feedback of findings needs to be examined and subsequently streamlined.

Rossi closes his contribution in harmony with Mills. He sees social scientists actively engaged in the roles of advisor to policy makers and social critic, and he questions the practicality, efficacy, and sagacity of a value-free social science.

Political scientist Ralph K. Huitt, former Assistant Secretary for Legislation for the Department of Health, Education, and Welfare, describes in detail, in contribution 7, the ponderous but time-honored policy process of the federal government. He concludes by agreeing with Moynihan that program evaluation, not policy formulation, is the appropriate bailiwick for social scientists. There is little they can actually do directly to influence the policy process, except perhaps to *demonstrate* priorities for program goals. Huitt argues, as does Rossi, that social scientists should press for the design and evaluation of experimental intervention programs *before* the programs are escalated by billions of dollars and hundreds of staff members to national scope.

Sociologist Harold L. Sheppard, in contribution 8, concurs with Rossi that the problem with the OEO Community Action Program was not too much but *too little* social science. He suggests that the OEO policy formulators failed to conceive of poverty as a multivariate problem, as existing in a network of macrolevel phenomena such as the tax structure, economic development and manpower training programs, employment levels—conceptions of which and data for which social scientists had readily available. Sheppard illustrates that the social scientist can contribute immensely to assessments of planned social intervention, providing baseline data on the characteristics of target populations and taking readings of postintervention changes in those characteristics. If epidemiology is crucial for the assessment of public-health intervention programs, then demography similarly can be crucial for the assessment of social intervention programs. Essentially, he speaks to the importance of providing "social indicators," as stressed by Moynihan and Rossi. However, Sheppard urges that having the data is not enough. Social scientists should take steps toward better communication with and greater influence of policy makers. His summary of the functions of social scientists in planned social intervention is an admixture of Mills and Hauser—demanding experimental, evaluative, and advisory expertise.

Are enough social scientists ready and willing to accomplish these tasks? Are social-science graduate programs prepared to train such men? If we accept that implementation awareness is to be an important attribute of at least some social scientists, how can it be encouraged? Where is it first learned, if not in the graduate schools? If Hauser's interpretations of the role of social scientists (contribution 2) are to be followed, then graduate schools need not modify their curricula for academic and research-oriented students. But since implementation awareness would be important for "social engineers," then perhaps separate or parallel training programs should be established for them, that they might acquire the knowledge and skill which would allow them to bridge the basic and applied aspects of their disciplines. The so-called professional-degree programs being started in a few universities might be viable approaches to that division of labor (that is, academics and basic researchers are awarded the doctor of philosophy degree; "applied" professionals are awarded doctorates of sociology, psychology, economics, political science, and so on). Interdisciplinary Ph.D. programs, such as the University of Michigan's Sociology and Social Work graduate sequence could be another approach.

If, on the other hand, Mills' interpretation of the role of social scientists is preferred (contribution 1), then students must simultaneously be trained both in the basic discipline and in the applications of the discipline. Thus, consideration should be given to augmenting traditional programs which speak to those applications and facilitate the bridging role.

Rossi writes that policy makers often have a naive view of social science, while Moynihan attributes political naiveté to most social scientists. If both these views are correct and it is important to rectify the situation, then social scientists are faced with several challenges. They must acquaint themselves with political realities and at the same time educate policy makers about the scope and methods, potentials and limitations, of social science. Either policy-relevant research reports must be written or reports must include summaries which are written in such a manner that decision makers, interveners, and implementers will read and understand them. Further, it can be argued that more social scientists should be willing to serve in or support closely policy-formulating roles. Can social-science professional organizations do more to advance the mutual education process of social scientists and social administrators? Would it be appropriate for them to establish postdoctoral fellowships or internships (patterned after the Russell Sage Foundation Internships or the White House Fellowship Program) by which young social scientists could become less politically naive and perhaps, at the same time, share the complexity of their disciplines with policy makers?

·3·
THE ROLE OF SOCIAL SCIENCE
IN SOCIAL POLICY

DANIEL P. MOYNIHAN
Assistant to the President for Urban Affairs

W HAT THEN IS TO BE SAID OF THE ROLE OF SOCIAL SCIENCE IN SOCIAL policy? Not, that is, of social scientists: a teeming and irrepressible group, they will be on hand proferring proposals for universal improvement doubtless for all time to come. And no bad thing. But this they do in their capacity as citizens, as interested, sentient beings. But is there something called social science, a body of knowledge, a methodology that men of quite disparate politics and temperaments will nonetheless agree upon, that can contribute to the formulation of public policy? I will propose that the answer is a limited but emphatic Yes.

I have sought to argue, by illustration, that social science is at its weakest, at its worst, when it offers theories of individual or collective behavior which raise the possibility, by controlling certain inputs, of bringing about mass behavioral change. No such knowledge now exists. Evidence is fragmented, contradictory, incomplete. Enough snake oil has been sold in this Republic to warrant the expectation that public officials will begin reading labels. This precaution, if growing, is nonetheless far from universal. In the late 1960's the circles in New York that a decade earlier had conceived community action as a cure for delinquency, came forward with the notion that a slightly different form would cure educational retardation on the part of minority group public school children. Community control *might* improve the school performance of slum children. It might *not*. No one knows. It might have other effects that are quite desirable, *or* undesirable. It is a perfectly reasonable proposal to try out. But at this point in time it is almost unforgivable that it should be put forth as a "proven" remedy for anything. About the only forecast that could have been made with any confidence would have been that the effort to impose community control would lead to a high level of community conflict, which in New York City it has been doing, and which will presumably be the case elsewhere.

This does suggest one area of social science usefulness. For while the reforming spirit is very much abroad in such circles, so also is the critical spirit, often creatively present in the same individual. Government, especially liberal government, that would attempt many things very much needs the discipline of skeptical and complex intelligence repeatedly inquiring "What do you mean?" and "How do you know?" The expectations of such government needs to be controlled by insights such as Nisbet's on the unlikelihood of final social peace:[1]

---

[1] [Robert A.] Nisbet [*The Quest for Community* (New York: Oxford University Press, 1953)], p. 73.

The quest for community will not be denied, for it springs from some of the powerful needs of human nature—needs for a clear sense of cultural purpose, membership, status, and continuity. Without these, no amount of mere material welfare will serve to arrest the developing sense of alienation in our society and the mounting preoccupation with the imperatives of community. To appeal to technological progress is futile. For what we discover is that rising standards of living, together with increases in leisure, actually intensify the disquietude and frustration that arise when cherished and proffered goals are without available means of fulfillment. "Secular improvement that is taken for granted," wrote Joseph Schumpeter, "and coupled with individual insecurity that is acutely resented is of course the best recipe for breeding social unrest."

This will seem to some a formula for immobilism, but it is nothing of the sort. The two national political figures of the 1960's closest to the style and content of this tradition in social science thought have been John F. Kennedy and Eugene McCarthy. Both exceptionally creative innovators in politics. But both men whose minds were touched by a certain sadness at having perceived the complexity and difficulty of it all: both men for whom the achievement of limited goals lacked nothing in glory, as they knew all too well how problematic even that would be. Arthur M. Schlesinger, Jr., captured this quality with respect to Kennedy's seeming caution and seeming reluctance to move when all about him hot young blood demanded frontal assaults in all directions:[2]

> I believe today that its basic source may have been an acute and anguished sense of the fragility of the membranes of civilization, stretched so thin over a nation so disparate in its composition, so tense in its interior relationships, so cunningly enmeshed in underground fears and antagonisms, so entrapped by history in the ethos of violence. . . . His hope was that it might be possible to keep the country and the world moving fast enough to prevent unreason from rending the skin of civility. But he had peered into the abyss and knew the potentiality of chaos.

The great failing of the Johnson administration was that an immense opportunity to institute more or less permanent social changes—a fixed full employment program, a measure of income maintenance—was lost while energies were expended in ways that very probably hastened the end of the brief period when such options were open, that is to say the three years from the assassination of Kennedy to the election of the Ninety-first Congress. In a sense, the repeated message of contemporary social science is that of the scarcity of social opportunity, rather as in earlier ages the scarcity of resources preoccupied the thoughts of economists. The consequence of such a sensibility is not so much great *caution*, as great *care*. Those who govern will do well to provide access for persons with such sensibilities: their views will commonly prove highly convergent with and congenial to the pragmatic liberal political mind that continues to provide much that is most to be valued in the American polity.

But this is a matter, primarily, of advice and counsel. What institu-

[2] Arthur M. Schlesinger, Jr., *A Thousand Days* (Boston: Houghton Mifflin Company).

tional role may the social sciences expect to play in public affairs? The answer seems clear enough. *The role of social science lies not in the formulation of social policy, but in the measurement of its results.*

The great questions of government have to do not with what *will* work, but what *does* work. The best of behavioral sciences would in truth be of no very great utility in a genuine political democracy, where one opinion is as good as another, and where public policies emerging for legislative-executive collaboration will constantly move in one direction, then another, following such whim, fashion, or pressure that seems uppermost at the moment. What government and the public most need to know in the aftermath of this process is whether there was anything to show for the effort, and if so, what. Causal insights of the kind that can lead to the prediction of events are interesting, absorbing, but they are hardly necessary to the management of a large, open political system. All that is needed is a rough, but hopefully constantly refined, set of understandings as to what is associated with what. A good deal of medicine is no more than this, yet people are healthier as a result, and so might be the consequence for the body politic.

Perhaps the foremost example of this function to appear in the 1960's was the report on *Equality of Educational Opportunity*, known for its principal author James S. Coleman, which was issued by the U.S. Office of Education in 1966. Commissioned by Section 402 of the Civil Rights Act of 1964, the study began with a clear and untroubled understanding as to what the world was like. The U.S. Commissioner of Education was instructed within two years to report to the President and Congress "concerning the *lack* of availability of educational opportunities for individuals by reason of race, color, religion, or national origin in public educational institutions." (My italics.) Two years later the second largest social science research project in history was released, almost furtively, by the Office of Education. The things "everybody knew" about education appeared from the massive collection of data—not to be so! School facilities were not especially unequal as between the races, and where differences did exist they were not necessarily in the presumed direction. In any event it did not appear that school facilities had any great influence on educational achievement, which seemed mostly to derive from the family background of the child and the social class of his schoolmates. The whole rationale of American public education came very near to crashing down, and would have done so had there not been a seemingly general agreement to act as if the report had not occurred. But it had, and public education will not now be the same. The relations between resource input and educational output, which all school systems, all legislatures, all executives have accepted as given, appear not to be given at all. At very least what has heretofore been taken for granted must henceforth be proved. Without in any way purporting to tell mothers, school teachers, school board superintendents what *will* change educational outcomes, social science has raised profoundly important questions as to what does not.

This hardly precludes experimentation. On the contrary, as techniques of evaluation evolve, outright laboratory-type investigations of social issues are likely to become more frequent, and certainly more useful. In 1967, for example, the Office of Economic Opportunity entered a $4 million contract with the Institute for Research on Poverty of the University of Wisconsin to carry out an experimental study of the effects of a negative income tax on one thousand low-income, intact, urban families in New Jersey, to extend over a period of fifty months. A generation ago such an undertaking would have seemed strange, if not outrageous. But the OEO announcement was accepted without apparent comment, perhaps owing to the professional reputations of the social scientists who would be engaged on the project. Quietly a new style in social innovation is emerging. The negative income tax project can be thought of in ways as a second generation of the PCJD "experiments." Much more money is available, more time, more expertise, or at all events more economists. In the judgment of Norton E. Long, who has looked into the matter, there would not appear to be much else to show for the delinquency programs. "The conduct of valid social science in hot policy areas," he writes, "is probably one of our society's prime needs." It did not come out of the PCJD, but OEO, that followed and continued the effort, and in terms that Norton would approve:[3]

> The recommendation that would seem to follow from analysis of the materials is the necessity of separating research from the political action of innovation. The demonstration needs to be recognized as an attempt to influence which cannot be studied by those engaged in it, whose needs must be threatened by objective evaluation.

The circumstance of a University of Wisconsin team working in New Jersey would at least in part meet these terms. Similarly, OEO has engaged professional research organizations to evaluate some of its work, and these results have been of value. Thus a study of nine CAP's conducted in the winter of 1966–67 by Daniel Yankelovich, Inc., showed quite positive results for those individuals actually reached by the programs:[4]

> The large majority of the poor reached by CAA programs report significant changes in their own and their children's lives as a result of their participation. For their children, they report improvements both in school and at home. For themselves, they report a mix of tangible and intangible benefits including new jobs, special training, more earnings, education, stretching available dollars further, improvement of neighborhoods, and increased hope, self-respect and confidence in the future (mixed with an intense impatience especially on the part of the Negro families to share in the affluence they see in the rest of the society).

A measure of reality testing would seem in order here: were the "reported" improvements, for example, observable to others besides those

[3] Robert K. Merton, *Social Theory and Social Structure*, rev. ed. (New York: The Free Press, 1957), p. 3.

[4] "Detailed Findings of Study to Determine Effects of CAP Programs on Selected Communities and Their Low Income Residents," prepared for Office of Economic Opportunity, Daniel Yankelovich, Inc., March 1967, pp. 8–9.

who reported them? Even so, the Yankelovich survey would suggest that community action agencies can produce results even if such do not always add up to social revolution. A similar set of enquiries might well be directed to the consequences of the abrupt discontinuation of efforts so hopefully begun. Was it the case, for example, that much of the discontent evident in Negro communities in the summer of 1967 was stirred by community action workers who either had been or were threatened with being *declassed* by cutbacks in the program?

Corresponding to the development of experimental technique in social innovation is the far more significant, if directly related, emergence of "social measurement," to use the term of John R. Meyer, as an area of special interest to social scientists, and in particular economists. On assuming direction of the National Bureau of Economic Research in 1968 Meyer reported the wide interest of his associates that "the Bureau in the 1970's should do for social statistics what it did for economic statistics in the 1930's."[5] With a sustained annual growth rate of 4 to 5 per cent in real national product seemingly increasingly feasible—that itself a tribute to the work of the Bureau—he asked whether it was not now time to turn the powerful methodology of modern economics to the analysis of social problems. "For example, have we come to a time when it makes sense to systematically document the status and changes in the status of the American Negro?"

Very much as the national government began compiling economic statistics that were to make economic planning feasible years before such planning became politically acceptable, the Federal establishment has for some time been expanding the collection of the raw social data to which Meyer proposes the new methodologies he directed. The Bureau of the Census, one of the truly noble institutions of the Federal government, has quietly been transforming its decennial survey into a continuous measurement process. Much room remains for improvement. (In 1960, some 10 per cent of the nonwhite population was missed, with proportions twice that and more among young adult males.) But there are not many mysteries left as to *how* to conduct an adequate census, and with more support the Bureau will be able to do just that. The truth of John Kenneth Galbraith's observation remains: statisticians are key actors in the process of social change, for it is often only when it becomes possible to measure a problem that it also becomes possible to arouse any political interest in solving it. For all its attenuated mandate, the provision of the Employment Act of 1946 committing the American national government "to promote maximum employment, production, and purchasing power" brought about the years of analysis that in turn led to the singularly successful political economy of the 1960's. With more foresight, might not a commitment to "maximum feasible participation" lead to a similar process of measurement and feedback? Something very like this has been proposed by Bertram M. Gross who was associated with

[5] John R. Meyer, "The National Bureau: Continuity, Change and Some Future Perspective," Toward Improved Social and Economic Measurement, Forty-eighth Annual Report, National Bureau of Economic Research, Inc., 1968, p. 1.

the establishment of the Council of Economic Advisors, as was provided by the Employment Act. Responding to these initiatives, Senator Walter Mondale of Minnesota in 1967 introduced legislation, the Full Opportunity and Social Accounting Act of 1967, providing for the establishment of a Council of Social Advisors who would perform for the President, and the nation generally, the counterpart of the economists' role. Others have proposed that a social scientist be substituted for one of the three economists on the present council. The concept of a social report of the President, to parallel the economic report, has been widely discussed, and a group under the leadership of Daniel Bell began work on a prototype. In 1966 Raymond A. Bauer and a group at the American Academy of Arts and Sciences published a group of papers under the heading *Social Indicators* which marked the beginning of systemic inquiry into the issue.

The potential of these proposals is easily underestimated, as are the dangers implicit in some of the present trends in social measurement. The demands of rational resource allocation, so compelling on so many grounds, have already led to an extensive development of "social measurement" techniques in the executive branches of American government, especially the Federal government. This very largely is what the renowned, if somewhat over-touted Program Planning Budgeting System (PPBS) represents, a system largely developed in the Defense establishment and under Johnson colonized throughout the Federal establishment. Should this trend continue, and it will, the result will be a considerable exacerbation of a situation already to be observed, namely, a pronounced and growing imbalance between the "knowledge" as to what works and what does not, what is needed and what is not, available to the executive branch of government, as against the legislature. In hearings before the Subcommittee on Executive Reorganization of the U.S. Senate Committee on Government Operations in December 1966, I had occasion to comment on this development in terms that seem relevant here:

> There is nothing sinister about this state of affairs. Serious evaluation research is only just approaching the state of a developed, as against an experimental, technique. Inevitably it has been sponsored in the first instance by executive departments. However, precisely because the findings of such research are not neutral, it would be dangerous to permit this imbalance to persist. Too often, the executive is exposed to the temptation to release only those findings that suit its purposes; there is no one to keep them honest. Similarly, universities and other private groups which often undertake such research on contract are in some measure subject to constant, if subtle, pressure to produce "positive" findings. The simple fact is that a new source of knowledge is coming into being; while it is as yet an imperfect technique, it is likely to improve; and if it comes to be accepted as a standard element in public discourse it is likely to raise considerably the level of that discourse. This source of knowledge should not remain an executive monopoly.
>
> What is to be done? I would offer a simple analogy. In the time this nation was founded, the principal form in which knowledge was recorded and preserved was in printed books, and accordingly in 1800

Congress established the Library of Congress as a source of information. Over the next century, techniques of accounting and budgeting developed very rapidly, and in 1921 Congress established the General Accounting Office to keep track of federal expenditures. I would like to suggest that Congress should now establish an Office of Legislative Evaluation in the GAO which would have the task of systematically reviewing the program evaluations and "PPBS" judgments made by executive departments. This office would be staffed by professional social scientists. On occasion they would undertake on their own to assess a Federal program, just as on occasion the GAO does an audit of its own; but in general their task would be to "evaluate the evaluators" and in this way both maintain and improve the quality of the regular ongoing work of the executive departments in this field, and also routinely make these findings available to the Congress. It should not be expected that their findings will be dramatic or that they will put an end to argument—just the contrary is likely to occur. But the long-run effect could be immensely useful, if only because Congress would have some clearer idea than it now has as to what it is doing.

Some will feel that the very existence and distribution of knowledge of this kind is a threat to continued experiment and innovation. I disagree. I would argue, for example, that the General Accounting Office has in its 45 years of activity raised the level of financial honesty in the programs of the Federal government to the point that it is no longer even a remote obstacle to federal legislation. Federal money may get wasted, but it rarely gets stolen. The American people know this, and I am persuaded that it profoundly affects their willingness to pay taxes for the support of federal programs. I believe further that if we began to be as careful and as open about assessing the results of social programs as we are in ensuring the personal honesty of those involved with running them, we might begin to see a more enduring willingness to keep trying— as well, perhaps, as a welcome reluctance by cabinet officers to "oversell" their program to begin with.

We have set ourselves goals that are, in some ways, unique in history: not only to abolish poverty and ignorance, but also to become the first genuinely multi-racial and, we hope, in the end non-racial democracy the world has seen. I believe that in moving toward these goals, and in seeking to change the present reality, an unflinching insistence on fact will be a major asset.[6]

And there is an issue beyond objectivity. The "movement of the social system into self-consciousness" has been accompanied by increasingly sophisticated efforts to shape and direct that system. Increasingly social scientists are recruited for such attempts; increasingly they themselves initiate them. There arises then a range of questions of ethical behavior that correspond to the canons of professional practice with respect to individual clients. Social workers have developed, and in some cases borrowed from other professions, a quite extensive set of rules governing and protecting professional conduct. They can, for example, purchase

[6] Daniel P. Moynihan, "A Crisis of Confidence?" The Public Interest, Spring 1967, pp. 9–10, adapted from Testimony given before Subcommittee on Executive Reorganization, Committee on Government Operations, Federal Role in Urban Affairs, December 13, 1966.

insurance for suits against malpractice. *But what is malpractice with respect to a community?* At what point are risks taken that are not justified? In what way is it to be determined whether advice was incompetent or treatment negligent? Difficult, perhaps unavailing questions. But questions withal. A generation ago Reinhold Niebuhr forewarned us that the major difficulty of our time would be that of imposing ethical standards on the behavior of large organizations, an effort suddenly imposed on society after three millenia of slowly developing standards of personal conduct. Rather the same challenge faces those who would "engineer" social change. The problem goes beyond individual measures of professional competence to the question of the very possibility of such competence. Looking back it is clear, for example, that the community action programs of the war on poverty lent themselves to a rise in internal domestic tensions only in part because of their intrinsic qualities, and far more because of a rise of upper middle class white disaffection with the direction of American society occurring in conjunction with an even more powerful surge of the civil rights movement associated with an inevitable, and in ways much overdue rise of militant black assertiveness. Had these developments been foreseen it may well be that wisdom in government would have dictated another course for the antipoverty program, there having developed on its own an altogether sufficient potential for community activism. Prescriptions for arousing the "silent" students and inert mass as of the Eisenhower era, may only have exacerbated the tendencies of the period of the Students for a Democratic Society and the Black Panthers. But who was to know this would be the case? Exactly. It was not possible to know: it *is* not possible. Wisdom surely bespeaks moderation in projections of the future, and restraint in its promises for it.

This is, of course, first of all a challenge for those who practice the most demanding calling of all, that of government itself. For them, Edmund Burke's conception of successive generations as possessing their society's laws and customs of governance in the form of an entailed estate, given them for lifetime use, with the condition that it be passed on at least not diminished and hopefully enhanced, seems especially relevant now in the United States. The 1960's, which began with such splendid promise of a new and higher unity for the nation, are ending in an atmosphere of disunity and distrust of the most ominous quality. For it is not the old and weak and excluded who have been ill used, or think themselves such. Rather it is the vibrant, established, *coming* young people of the nation who in large numbers have learned to distrust their government, and in many ways to loathe their society. They are not yet in power. *They will be.* When that day comes, however moderated their views may have become, their understanding of their country will have been shaped by the traumas of the 1960's. Not least of these shocks has been the debacle of the community action programs of the war on poverty: the soaring rhetoric, the minimum performance; the feigned constancy, the private betrayal; in the end, to their understanding, the sell-out. All this will be part of a past that has already shaped the future. It will then be asked, by some at least, how well the men who held office in that near to heartbreaking decade exercised their brief authority.

·4·

SOCIAL SCIENCE AND SOCIAL POLICY:
AN INTRODUCTION TO A SYMPOSIUM

DAVID GOTTLIEB

The Pennsylvania State University

E ARLY IN 1961 PRESIDENT KENNEDY CALLED FOR A MAJOR EFFORT IN SPACE exploration. The ultimate goal was to land an American on the moon by the year 1970.

In 1966 Sargent Shriver, then Director of the Office of Economic Opportunity, noted that this nation could commemorate its two-hundredth year of independence by a successful completion of the war on poverty. The magic year was to be 1976.

The Kennedy prophecy was fulfilled. The Shriver goal, taken seriously by few in 1966, was abandoned by Congress in 1967.

Numerous explanations can be offered to account for the contrasts between these two national efforts. Generally, however, it would seem safe to say that success in one and failure in the other reflect two essential societal characteristics. First, as a nation we have always invested most heavily in technological as opposed to social change; hardware as opposed to software; physical as opposed to human resources. Even in long-range planning, while the Department of Defense is able to make projections as to our "military needs" to the year 2000 and beyond, the Department of Health, Education, and Welfare is unable to note with any degree of accuracy or certainty our needs for education and welfare even over the course of the next few years. Second (and it is difficult to determine which is the dependent and which is the independent variable), our social sciences (and perhaps our social scientists) are not as clean, precise, predictive, or dependable as are our natural and physical sciences.

As a result social scientists (with the possible exception of economists —although they too have slipped from the pinnacle of influence they enjoyed during the Kennedy administration) rarely hold positions of power in the federal government; rarely are able to guide the development and implementation of social policy; rarely are able to determine the type and scope of research and evaluation which should be an integral part of social policy and social programming; and rarely come close to getting more than a few per cent of the total federal investment in research and science building.

Looking to the future, Joseph J. Spengler, an economist and contributor to this symposium, predicts that money for science is destined to decline and hence there will be an increase in competition between the sciences. Spengler goes on to point out that the need for the social sciences (not necessarily social scientists) will be great and continue to grow. Social problems will be with us and social science will be expected to provide some solutions.

Not unlike other social scientists, Professor Spengler expresses some concern other whether or not the forms of social intervention proposed by

♦ First published in *Social Science Quarterly* 50, No. 3 (December, 1969).

social scientists "merely worsen the 'evils' they are intended to alleviate." Further, he feels that the competition for dollars may lead social scientists to promise more than they can possibly deliver.

I for one doubt that Professor Spengler has anything really to worry about. Based on the past performance of federal government agencies and social scientists I do not believe that social scientists will seek to propose strategies of social intervention nor do I think that what they do propose will be taken seriously by those in a position to implement social policy and social change. Although social scientists talk and write much about social problems, they rarely are willing to promise very much. Obviously we will not feel very secure in proposing solutions to problems at the "macro" level if we are unable to deal with problems at the "micro" level. Even with all of our research on youth socialization we are either unable or unwilling to propose strategies of intervention in dealing with student alienation on our own campuses. Although we know something about the characteristics of drug abusers and the reasons for dependency on drugs we have failed to come up with workable solutions to that problem. No matter whose theory of juvenile delinquency we endorse, none is so clear that we are able to translate their content into programs which will in fact minimize delinquency. Finally, despite years of research involvement in matters of race and race relations we did not come close to predicting the emergence of a black revolution nor are we even now able to agree upon whether there is "empirical evidence" available to support either the claims of the black separatists or the black integrationists.

Whatever the real value of our knowledge and sophistication of our science, I think we would be hard pressed to identify any social policy or social program which was brought about primarily as the result of social science input. Certainly the testimony of some prominent social scientists might help the case being made by a particular congressman or agency head. References to social science research findings are frequently included by those engaged in arguing for or against particular social legislation. At the same time it is not the research findings or the social scientists' observations which have the most influence on whether or not a particular social policy or program is accepted or rejected. Social science and social scientists had little to do with the Supreme Court decision on school desegregation (Alsop to the contrary); desegregation of the military; organization of the Peace Corps, the Neighborhood Youth Corps, or the Job Corps; emergence of a black power ideology and organization; SDS; the Office of Economic Opportunity generally; or the Community Action Program more specifically.

It is for this reason that I for one was somewhat surprised at the degree of interest which Moynihan's *Maximum Feasible Misunderstanding* appears to have generated among social scientists. Perhaps it was Moynihan's placing social scientists in a role they seldom play—national policy brokers—which helps account for why this Moynihan report has aroused social scientists. No doubt the fact that the author also holds a position of power with the current administration adds to interest in his observations.

Peter H. Rossi in his contribution to the symposium identifies the three primary areas with which Moynihan deals in his book: the role of social scientists and social science theory in the development of the maximum feasible involvement concept; the failure of this concept when put into pracice in many American communities; and the role that social scientists should play in the business of social policy and social intervention.

Rossi notes that few if any of the people named by Moynihan as being involved in the initial stages of CAP were in fact bona fide social scientists. From my own experience with OEO (three full years from task force days to the days of OEO dismemberment) I would agree with Rossi and then some. Few real social scientists were present at the start, the middle, or the end of the war on poverty. There were, of course, some who were employed full time in the non-programmatic shop entitled Research, Planning, Program and Evaluation. There were a few others with acceptable social science credentials in the Job Corps, Neighborhood Youth Corps, VISTA, and Head Start. With the possible exception of RPP&E, however, it was virtually impossible for social scientists in the OEO to be straight and at the same time meet the day-to-day demands of the job. This is not meant to be an apology or a cop-out. Any of the social scientists involved who felt they were being asked to compromise their professional self-concept, could, if they chose to do so, make a public statement claiming they were deceived, that the program was a hoax and a fraud, and then return to the campus. (One can only wonder why Moynihan, admittedly a licensed social scientist and early designer of the CAP strategy, waited all these months to blow his whistle.)

In CAP particularly there may have been an abundance of social reformers and social workers but there were few social scientists. And even if there had been more social scientists in CAP or in other OEO programs I really doubt if the outcomes would have been different.

As pointed out by Ralph Huitt in his contribution to this symposium, the legislative process is such that what is enacted as social policy is not so much that which is best, that which is based on empirical research, or that which comes from days, months, or years of study by some blue ribbon committee. Rather, as Huitt notes: "The commission's report may be helpful to the President, *if it recommends what he wants to do.*" The point could be carried a step further by noting that what the President does in fact recommend will be dependent on a variety of other constraints over which the commission has little or no control.

Obviously at the lower level all government agencies are faced with similar constraints. In many instances the strategy is to push for what has a chance of being accepted, that which will alienate the fewest legislators, that which will keep the wolves from your door for just a little while longer.

I believe this was particularly true of OEO, which many of us recognized was doomed from the start. From the arrival of the first youth in Job Corps, factors other than what was best for poor adolescents took control of program and policy implementation. Political processes must be involved in the establishment of equitable social policy. When, however, the political process is responsive only to select special interest groups, social science input, no matter how worthwhile, becomes a less than salient factor.

Given this obvious professional and personal value conflict, how and why does one remain with the operation? It would be presumptuous to speak for others and hence I can only share some of my own reasons. Among my considerations was a belief that I might be able to make a difference; that if I were not on the scene the situation would be worse; and that so far no social scientist had come through the door with a strategy or solution that we had not tried and found wanting when applied to the real life world of a Job Corps center.

I would agree with both Professors Rossi and Sheppard that there should have been more social science research and certainly more in the way of evaluation. At the same time I would insist that it is misleading to create the impression that social scientists were not encouraged to do their thing or that there were not some in OEO (social scientists as well as others) who did not make every attempt to come up with fairly acceptable evaluative methodology and procedures.

Weeks before the arrival of the first Job Corps enrollee in the first Job Corps center we did have a fairly extensive research and evaluation plan. The materials and tests included in the evaluation plan were in fact put together by a number of different social scientists (outside consultants) and had, I believe, the social science seal of approval. What the social scientists and others did not realize were the very real logistical problems that come with any type of massive research or evaluation. The Job Corps plan called for a pre-test upon arrival at the center, a second look once the enrollee had been at the center for a period of six to eight weeks, and a final testing and evaluation prior to departure from the center. The testing and evaluation materials were printed up and placed neatly into a single package. Select center personnel were trained in proper procedures and given a "test-giver's handbook." Arrangements were made for data processing and report writing. Unfortunately the entire plan broke down with the arrival of the first enrollees in the first center. We had naturally made some assumptions about how long enrollees would stay at the center. In the first group there were several who took one look at the center and headed for the hills. What was the ordering of priority to be? Hold the youngster for testing purposes or take steps that might ease entrance into this new life for those remaining? We made assumptions about what we would find. We assumed that the youth coming to Job Corps would be able to handle the paper and pencil materials, and we were wrong. There is a great difference between captive audiences (i.e., students in a classroom, adults in a living room, and soldiers in their barracks) and massive populations who can come and go without permission from researchers. Rossi might recall that one reason there was no adequate evaluation information in Job Corps was not because Job Corps was not interested, but because NORC had a terrible time finding and holding onto a control group. In fact, I recall a representative of NORC noting that one difficulty stemmed from the fact that after talking with a poor adolescent, NORC interviewers could not resist helping the respondent get into one poverty program or another (thereby adding to the shortage of subjects in the control group).

The point here is that it is one thing to design and plan research and evaluation and another to understand and control the logistical factors that do in fact intervene and determine research and evaluation outcomes.

I would also want to take exception with the observation that there was an avoidance of research on the part of social scientists in OEO. In fact I am somewhat surprised that none of the contributors to this symposium has much to say about the Institute for Research on Poverty funded by OEO and housed at the University of Wisconsin. Whether the research reports produced by the Institute could have improved OEO programs and operations is difficult to say. Some of us in OEO who were responsible for day-to-day program decisions were somewhat reluctant to take these reports seriously since each report had stamped across the cover *Discussion Papers*. Many of us felt that a social science which concentrated almost exclusively on the study of social problems as opposed to the study of solutions to social problems was of little use to those engaged in programs of social intervention.

The Job Corps did allocate funds for research and evaluation. While the end products may have benefited the individual scholar or perhaps his discipline, I would suggest that they were of little practical value. I recall, particularly, a study funded by OEO which was to deal with proposed strategies for minimizing conflict between black and white Job Corps enrollees. The investigators were reputable scholars and their methodology was appropriate. They conducted numerous personal interviews, they circulated paper and pencil questionnaires, they observed, they submitted their final report. Briefly, they concluded that there were two alternatives available to us: either we could control the input of enrollees into Job Corps centers by establishing racial quotas (a clear violation of the law) or we could concentrate on changing attitudes. The how of changing attitudes with this particular population was never really dealt with by the investigators.

It is this lack of implementation awareness, I believe, that minimizes the potential value of social science in matters of social policy and social programming. Social scientists can identify variables. They can say something about how a change in certain independent variables will alter certain dependent variables. What they are unable to demonstrate is how one goes about the business of manipulating these same variables in an ongoing social process. I feel that it is in bridging the gap between research and demonstration that social scientists are least competent. At the same time it would be unjust to blame them for a lack of experience or ability in application. Generally this has not been part of the social science bag. Our approach has usually been to do research, point out and then leave it to social engineers (whoever they might be) to translate our research papers into social policy and programmatic guidelines.

Perhaps in the years to come, social science style and methodology will allow for basic research leading to demonstration and experimentation, with an ongoing evaluation of processes and change, and with a final feedback into research. I would think that such a model would contribute to the building of social science theory, the improvement of our methodology, and place us in a better position to assist in the development of social policy and in the solving of social problems which confront our world.

Finally, I can only support and applaud Rossi's closing statement:

> I think we have reached the stage of maturity where we can turn again to these problems, for a completely value-free social science is a social science of little value.

·5·

IS SOCIAL SCIENCE READY?

JOSEPH J. SPENGLER
Duke University

> The story of the impact of the social sciences will not be written for five-hundred years. . . . The full impact . . . may not be felt for a hundred years.[1]

MAN'S HISTORY CONSISTS IN PART IN THE REPLACEMENT OF OLD BY NEW superstitions. Today's overriding superstition is the belief that scientists can intervene in human affairs in such wise as to make men far happier than ever before. Our multiplying futurists are anticipating a Golden Age, albeit one that a stubborn minority finds inferior to that situated in the past or at some transcendent destination.[2] Even smaller is the minority which recalls J. B. Say's advice that "time is a necessary element in all great revolutions," or Turgot's warning (in *Fondation*), "how easy it is to do harm in wishing to do good."

In this Age of Intervention, the Future is viewed as the product of Science of the Present, of social science as well as of organic and inorganic science. Science costs money and the *relative* amount available for its support is destined to decline. One may therefore anticipate conflict among the three branches of science competing for funds, probably accompanied by excessive pretensions to capacity to deliver the goods. Having reviewed this conflict, I touch upon past and prospective interventionist performance of social scientists and their suitedness to assume (as some would) the role of oracle and high priest, or capacity to deliver what a prospective Delphian market is likely to call for.

THE FUTURE DEMAND FOR SOCIAL SCIENCE

It may be taken for granted that the need for social science will be great and growing. Doubts may, however, be inspired by Utopian spokesmen for the coming Cybernetic Revolution who foresee the disappearance of most if not all problems, certainly of those which troubled Marx. Glenn T. Seaborg writes:

> The time may someday come when the computer will enable the production of enough consumer products and the performance of enough individual services so quickly and efficiently that it may require little if any sacrifice to perform the additional work necessary to achieve most of our desired social goals. Cybernation will, of course, also be effective in this area, and enhance its productivity as well.
>
> Eventually, in the era of abundance we are seeking, many new economic and social phenomena will take place. No one will be deprived of the means to an adequate income and, above this, there will be many

[1] K. E. Boulding, *The Impact of the Social Sciences* (New Brunswick: Rutgers University Press, 1960), pp. 19–20.

[2] For example, see D. N. Michael, *The Unprepared Society* (New York: Basic Books, 1968).

* First published in *Social Science Quarterly* 50, No. 3 (December, 1969).

incentives for creativity and productivity on numerous scales. Probably the highest status and rewards will not come from money or material possessions. Their value will some day become almost meaningless. In this regard, it is interesting to recall what the great economist, John Maynard Keynes, wrote in his 1932 *Essays on Persuasion*. Keynes said this: "When the accumulation of wealth is no longer of high social importance there will be great changes in the code of morals. We shall be able to rid ourselves of many of the pseudo-moral principles which have hagridden us for two hundred years, by which we have exalted some of the most distasteful of human qualities into the position of highest values."[3]

Social scientists would be ill advised, however, to hasten to Lloyds for insurance against this utopian eventuality. Just as new diseases and ailments replace old, so do new problems replace old ones, and so do new scarcities replace old ones. There will, therefore, be plenty of work for social scientists, probably more than ever. Social science will have its uses, plenty of them, provided that social scientists become really effective.

Let us therefore take a more prosaic view of the future. Let us try to forecast the future of social science by projecting recent rates of growth. Then one infers that social science will flourish, for since 1940 social science seemingly has grown remarkably in public esteem. For example, the number of members of the American Economic Association, a good index of the growth of the economics profession and a rough indicator of the growth of other social science professions, increased about 6.5 per cent per year between 1940 and 1967. This rate was higher than corresponding rates for other social science professions, in part because employment opportunities outside education, especially in business and government, are greater for economists.. Indeed, under the Kennedy regime, economists were charged with intellectual imperialism, with a desire to apply their "aggregate techniques and arithmetical methods . . . to the entire range of national problems," and with believing "that figures and statistics can illuminate the wordless aspirations and perplexities of American life."[4] The high post-1940 rate of increase in the number of social scientists, much above the low rate of the 1930's, also reflected both the multiplication of posts which social scientists could fill, and the continuing goodness of business conditions.[5]

The halcyon past three decades may not, however, be projectable very far into the future. Rates of increase of 6 to 7 per cent per year cannot long persist, since, if they did, the country would finally be overrun with economists and other social scientists. For example, should the population grow one per cent per year and the number of economists grow 6.5 per cent per year, after 50 years the ratio of economists to the population would be about 14 times as high as at the start. In the end the growth of the de-

---

[3] "Time, Leisure and the Computer: The Crisis of Modern Technology," *The Key Reporter* (Spring, 1967), p. 2.
[4] Theodore H. White, "Scholarly Impact on the Nation's Past," *Life*, 62 (June 16, 1967), p. 74B.
[5] After 1941 unemployment exceeded 6 per cent of the civilian labor force only twice, in 1958 and 1961.

mand for social scientists as for other scientists will be governed mainly
by the rate of growth of Gross National Product, a rate likely to fall in a
range of 4 to 5 per cent or even lower, should voluntary and enforced
leisure reduce the number of hours worked per year enough, along with
other deterrents, to counterbalance a good share of technical progress.
Some professions will grow less rapidly, others more rapidly, especially if
capable of competing effectively.

With respect to social science in particular we must ask, "Will the demand for social scientists continue to increase 5 or 6 per cent per year
while a population is growing (say) 1.5 per cent and its average income is
growing 2 per cent per year?" An income elasticity of demand for the
services of social scientists of nearly two would be called for. Whether
such elasticity, even if present initially, might persist would depend in the
end upon whether the population at large believed that the social scientists were "'delivering the goods expected of them."[6] After all, organized
social science is not to be compared to the Propaganda of the Faith whose
publicity-agents, Veblen observed, enjoyed the "high good fortune of the
perfect salesman . . . to promise everything and deliver nothing."[7] Only
the "military" and recent political risk-takers have proceeded as if they
would never be forced to deliver.[8] As a rule, delivery is required. Con-
trollers of the power of the purse demand results of social as well as of
natural scientists. They cannot long be put off by promises of serendipity,
by promises of the sort that have cushioned the financial impact of wasteful space-doggling and other federal potlatch. Unfortunately, the nature
of the social scientist's research is seldom if ever such as to yield more
than his *quaesitum* in the manner that natural science research often does.[9]

The power of the purse is already making itself felt. Inflation has been
reducing the purchasing power of university funds and the resulting short-
ages are not being made up by state legislatures or alumni who have become increasingly indisposed to finance institutions that seem to be
swamped by unwashed or alienated hooligans and administered by jerry-
built cretins. Of far greater significance, of course, is the failure of federal
support for research and development to grow after having expanded (in
terms of current dollars) about 225 times between 1940 and 1967. This
drying up of new support is especially painful to natural science practitioners who often seek $15–170 thousand per man per year and who
would like federal support to increase at a rate of 13–15 per cent per year,

---

[6] "Congress wants scientific research that gets results" declares the chairman of the
House Subcommittee which controls National-Science-Foundation and related financ-
ing. See Gene Bylinsky, "U.S. Science Enters A Not-So-Golden Era," *Fortune*, 78
(Nov., 1968), p. 206. See also J. P. Martino, "Science and Society in Equilibrium,"
Science, 165 (Aug. 22, 1969), pp. 769–772.

[7] Thorsten Veblen, *Absentee Ownership and Business Enterprise in Recent Times*
(New York: Viking, 1923), pp. 319–323.

[8] See Ralph E. Lapp's *The Weapons Culture* (New York: Norton, 1968), and
R. J. Barnet's review of this work in *Science*, 160 (April 19, 1968), pp. 293–294.

[9] Cf. V. J. Danilov, "The Spinoff Phenomenon," *Industrial Research* (May, 1969),
pp. 54–58.

enough to absorb the entire national income in a few decades.[10] Under the circumstances, spokesmen for the natural sciences will press for an even greater share of available funds than they have had during the recent honeymoon period when support of *all* science was growing rapidly and when therefore second-table privileges could safely be extended to the social sciences if they behaved non-politically. After all, in an age when nine-tenths of all federal research support is going to such agencies as NASA, AEC, and the Department of Defense,[11] those possessed of thermonuclear and related credentials must feel secure, enjoying as they do a great differential advantage when seeking governmental funds. One may apply in some measure to social science Machlup's comment on the disadvantage of the humanities when seeking support in competition with the natural sciences: "Humanistic studies . . . do not help beat the Russians either in peaceful competition or in cold or hot wars. Why spend money on such pure luxury?"[12] Spokesmen for natural science may also claim credit for much of the increase realized in average output per worker in recent decades. Furthermore, when seeking funds, these spokesmen usually can make a quantitatively convincing case supportive of the benefits to be expected from the specific projects under consideration. Finally, natural science spokesmen often have the support of well-financed and powerful business lobbies.

Two other conditions may prove less favorable to social science in the future than in the past. One source of demand for the services of particular disciplines is essentially phantom in character. Social scientists take in each other's wash. Within each discipline they thus generate a demand for the services of its members, they write mainly for each other, and they create each other's reputations on the basis of work, sometimes important and sometimes little better than the trivial.[13] "Matthew effects" may even be set in motion and Brahmins brought into existence.[14] Accompanying and accentuating this intradisciplinary reciprocity is differentiation and specialization which makes for the multiplication of "required courses" and hence for decrease in student-teacher load and increase in the employment of teaching personnel. This reciprocal process does not, how-

[10] Bylinsky, "U.S. Science," pp. 145ff. Scientific research may be very expensive. For example, see J. B. Adams, "Megaloscience," *Science*, 148 (June 18, 1965), pp. 1560–1564. For a detailed account see Fritz Machlup's splendid *The Production and Distribution of Knowledge in the United States* (Princeton: Princeton University Press, 1962).

[11] Bylinsky, "U.S. Science," p. 199. The three agencies named received 89 per cent of all support in 1958–1967. See also V. J. Danilov, "$26-Billion for Research," *Industrial Research* (Jan., 1969), pp. 62ff.

[12] Machlup, *Production and Distribution*, pp. 204–205. On some of the problems arising from the impact of science on military and civil affairs, see S. Zuckerman, *Scientists and War* (New York: Harper and Row, 1967).

[13] Gordon Tullock, *The Organization of Inquiry* (Durham, N.C.: Duke University Press, 1966), p. 191.

[14] See Robert K. Merton, "The Matthew Effect in Science," *Science*, 159 (Jan. 5, 1968), pp. 56–63; also Spencer Klaw, *The New Brahmins* (New York: Morrow, 1968).

ever, create much of its support which comes ultimately from legislatures, foundations, and university funds.

In the past, growth of post-secondary educational institutions accounted for much of the increase in demand for scientists of all sorts. This source will expand less rapidly in the future. Aggregate gross demand for university teaching personnel, consisting of *additions* to the stock of teachers and *replacements* (i.e., of retirees, decedents, and teachers transferring out of teaching), will no longer grow as in the 1960's when persons of college age increased about 48 per cent. For, given Bureau of the Census Projection C, persons of college age will increase only about 15 per cent in the 1970's and probably decrease slightly in the 1980's, a decade comparable to 1940–1960 when their number changed very little. In the 1980's, therefore, probably only replacement employment will be available since the ratio of persons enrolled in post-secondary educational institutions to those capable of doing college work will be close to unity. Persons of college age will increase again after 1990, perhaps 25 or more per cent in 1990–2000 and perhaps as much as 15 per cent in 2000–2015. Presumably the aggregate demand for social science teachers at the post-secondary-school level will follow the pattern described above even should college and university social science personnel increase in somewhat greater measure than the aggregate number of college and university teaching personnel. Of course, should the average student-teacher ratio increase, as is likely, given rising costs and new methods, the aggregate demand for personnel would increase more slowly than has been suggested above.

The upshot of what has been said in this section is that the demand for social scientists as a group is not likely to expand as in the recent past. Social scientists will have to meet market tests they have not been meeting and overcome obstacles they have not surmounted in the past. Does their past performance suggest that they can meet these difficulties? What can be done to put social science more nearly on a par with natural science in respect of public support? These issues will now be considered.

CURRENT PERSPECTIVES AND INTERVENTION

The business of the social scientist is to study himself though not necessarily in the tradition of Alexander Pope. He no longer takes his world as given, but as one modifiable through intervention, with his role that of *deus ex machina*. "Interventionist models are becoming dominant" and economists, political scientists, anthropologists, and sociologists "are operating on the basis of a meta-sociological principle of interventionism."[15] Increase in interventionism is, of course, the product of many forces, among them *hubris*; economically well-nourished think-tanks which supply scientism in the guise of science;[16] and emerging giant corporations whose

[15] Lewis S. Feuer, "Causality in the Social Sciences," in Daniel Lerner, ed., *Cause and Effect* (New York: The Free Press, 1965), p. 19.

[16] For example, see Leonard C. Lewis's popular account, "Those Super-Secret Think Tanks: Good or Evil," in *Family Weekly* (Dec. 29, 1968), p. 7.

highly paid senior executives, though in disagreement regarding social actions concerning which they are likely to be incompetent, talk as if corporate social responsibilities override all other corporate objectives.[17] Interventionism is the product also of the belief and discovery of social scientists (with the partial exception of historians)[18] that their wares not only may command good prices but must find sale if their disciplines are to flourish. Consequently, given the threat of deceleration described in the first part of this essay, interventionism is likely to be transmuted into the dominating objective of social scientists, particularly if foundation paymasters (who seldom doubt their capacities to determine what is best) or ill-informed legislators (alarmed at disorder but afraid to govern) call for prescription-ridden reports.

Three questions at once suggest themselves. Are the social scientists competent to intervene or to point to effective modes of intervention? Will the forms of intervention suggested by social scientists merely worsen the "evils" they are intended to alleviate? Or are solutions already at hand, but unaccompanied by the will to apply them?[19]

Capacity for effective intervention may flow naturally from a science, social or natural. After all, scientific inquiry has two immediate outcomes. First, it explains something, e.g., some sort of behavior.[20] Second, the knowledge of relationships underlying this explanation makes possible the power to predict and hence to intervene and redirect some course of events or man's response thereto. The social scientist is, however, at some disadvantage in that elements or relations composing an *explained* situation may undergo enough change to interfere with man's capacity to predict or intervene.[21]

[17] For example, see Fritz Machlup's delightful "Corporate Management, National Interest, and Behavior Theory," *Journal of Political Economy,* 75 (Oct., 1967), pp. 772–774; also Milton Friedman, *Capitalism and Freedom* (Chicago: University of Chicago Press, 1962), pp. 133–136.

[18] But see F. K. Ringer, *The Decline of the German Mandarins: The German Academic Community 1890–1933* (Cambridge: Harvard University Press, 1968).

[19] For example, see Garrett Hardin, "The Tragedy of the Commons," *Science,* 162 (Dec. 13, 1968), pp. 1243–1248.

[20] Robert Brown, having contrasted a generalization in the field of international trade with such physical laws as Henry's, concludes that "the conditions under which this law holds and does not hold have been more accurately determined than have the corresponding conditions of our economic equations. There is no difference in kind, however, for in both fields separate treatment must be given to the deviations." *Explanation in Social Science* (Chicago: Aldine Publishing Co., 1963), p. 157.

[21] A century ago, Alfred Marshall, having noted that economic science "requires the aid of an apparatus [e.g., calculus] which can grasp and handle quantitative relations on the assumption of which the theory is based," pointed to the significance of change in the economic environment. "In economics every event causes permanent alterations in the conditions under which future events can occur. This is, to some extent, the case in the physical world, but not to nearly so great an extent . . . . Every movement that takes place in the moral world alters the magnitude if not the character of the forces that govern succeeding movements. And economic forces belong to the moral world insofar as they depend upon habits and affections, upon man's knowledge and industrial skill." *Pure Theory of Foreign Trade* (London: London School of Economics, 1930), pp. 5, 26.

Social sciences differ somewhat from natural sciences in that they may embrace both a micro- and a macro-apparatus of analysis. For example, micro-economics proceeds from "generalizations about choices, decisions and actions of the individual" or the decision-maker analogous to the individual. Macro-economics "deals with aggregates and collectives, usually without regard to individual decision-units and individual choices."[22] Macro-economics thus is less well anchored in the universe of rewards and penalties embracing man, or in the motivational psychology employed to account for man's response to economic rewards and penalties. Macro-economics is interventionally oriented, focusing upon "improvement" of the environmental situation in which micro-economic behavior takes place. It is thus policy-oriented, collectivistic, and disposed to use the apparatus of state, whereas micro-economics tends to stress "economic and political individualism" and play down collectivist interventionism.[23] In each of the other social sciences we may identify both choosing decision-makers and environments within which these decision-makers perform. We may then break up the analytical apparatus of the science in question into that part focused on the behavior of decision-makers and that dealing with their embracing environment.

Interventionists find it much easier to deal with the environment embracing decision-makers. Such intervention is marked by economies of scale whereas interference with the activities of individual decision-makers is difficult, expensive, and probably subject to increasing cost. Accordingly, the influence of the intervening state and its agencies is exercised mainly in the macrosphere, upon the all-embracing environment. There the handles of power acquire leverage.

There is another reason for the intervening social scientist's inclination to stress the environment embracing decision-makers. Not much being known of the roles of the environment, environmentally-oriented intervention is not quickly shown to be scientifically untenable. "The power of the meta-sociological principle of interventionism guides social thought in regions where the criterion of verification grows tenuous," Feuer observes. He points to "how little verification had to do with" the reception of Keynes' views which, he believes, was traceable to "the will to intervene in economic processes" and perhaps avert the collapse of a capitalism threatened both internally and externally.[24]

While at first interventionism on a broad scale flourished only in the realm of economics, the advent of the computer is building up hope in the breast of the sociologist and the political scientist if not in that of the anthropologist engaged in modifying cultures in the Third World. I can do no better than quote from C. W. Churchman's review of Harold Sackman's *Computers, System Science, and Evolving Society*.[25]

[22] Fritz Machlup, *Essays on Economic Semantics* (Englewood Cliffs, N.J.: Prentice-Hall, 1963), p. 143.

[23] *Ibid.*, pp. 143–144.

[24] Feuer, "Causality," pp. 194–197.

[25] (New York: Wiley, 1967). Reviewed in *Science*, 159 (March 1, 1968), pp. 965–966.

The muddle of our age is implementation. There are those who believe that people of quality should study social problems and implement their findings in order to provide the "best" environment for all to live in. They want the experts to educate the uneducated, develop underdeveloped countries, employ the unemployed. The ultimate aim of the experts is to bring the under-privileged into a society where eventually all persons are qualified, all will share in designing better systems. Unfortunately, none of these modern do-gooders can tell us why he is especially qualified to do the job he has set out to do. Surely the privileged people outside of Watts need "retraining" as much as the people inside, because they have a distorted view of social reality.

It is not altogether ridiculous to say that social experimentation requires that there be no experts—or, if you wish, that everyone is an expert on some relevant aspect of planning. Indeed, one measure of performance of social planning might very well be the extent of contribution of all members of society. One of the most frustrating aspects of society today is the very little that most of us can contribute to the planning of social change; at best we have an occasional vote (often on undesirable alternatives) or an occasional letter to a representative. It would be a tragedy if all the good work of the earlier pragmatists produced a society ruled by "scientific" experts, no matter how elegant their experiments might be.

I'd feel a lot happier about the coming age of man-machine digital systems if I could more clearly understand a theory of implementation of the results of social experiment.

Churchman's doubts are reenforced by the underdeveloped state of our knowledge of the socialization of both children and adults, a subject neglected by the sociologists concerned with socializing organizations but not with the socialization process as such.[26]

Social sciences are unevenly adapted to assuming interventionist roles. There are differences in the universe of rewards and penalties with which each is suited to deal. Furthermore, the ease with which components of the relevant environment may be modified vary from science to science as well as in space and time. Social scientists as a group operate under greater handicaps than do physical scientists, under handicaps greater in some social sciences than in others. Of greatest importance is the weakness of the theoretical underpinning of the social sciences (with the partial exclusion of economics)[27], and their consequently reduced capacity to incorporate older theories as special and limiting cases in new theories. Moreover, the scientific environment in which the social scientist works is inferior to that of the natural scientist. The degree of validity attaching to findings often is unclear, and yet greater clarity may not be sought either because the results are likely to prove offensive, or because achieving clarity may be considered too costly. Professional discipline is weak, with the result that social scientists are not under strong compulsion to confirm or refute their own findings as well as those of others.[28] Hence fallacies may

26 John A. Clausen, et al., *Socialization and Society* (Boston: Little, Brown, 1968).
27 Brown, *Explanation*, chap. 11.
28 Tullock, *Organization*, chap. 7, esp. pp. 179–190. See also P. Abelson's essay, "Conditions for Discovery," in C. P. Haskins, ed., *The Search for Understanding* (Washington, D.C.: Carnegie Institution, 1967).

stay alive and ideological considerations may help give shape to the views of social scientists in respect even of their own specialties.[29]

While quantification is improving social science, it often is not adequately integrated with the underlying theoretical structure. Indeed, social scientists have increasingly followed Lord Kelvin's injunction to measure, though neglectful of Jacob Viner's advice that "when you express it in numbers, your knowledge is still of a meagre and unsatisfactory kind." Somewhat relevant is Hayek's observation that the social sciences deal not with objective phenomena but solely with subjective phenomena knowable to us because our minds are similar in structure to those which are objects of study.[30] This objection may be overcome, however, insofar as subjective phenomena have objective counterparts which lend themselves to quantification.[31] Of greater importance is the tendency of the social scientist to substitute quantitative matter for deeper analysis.

> Their chapters are a triumph of surveys over other methods; . . . of speed over depth . . .; of methodicalness over insightfulness; of sums over substance. They bring to mind Mannheim's observation about social scientists: "Instead of attempting to discover what is significant with the highest degree of precision possible under the existing circumstances . . . [they tend] to attribute importance to what is measurable merely because it happens to be measurable."[32]

Of a different order are the problems of verification that arise when computer simulation models are used to represent complex or relatively inaccessible real-world processes.[33]

Even granted that history is a social science rather than a branch of the humanities, its future is darkened by the rise of interventionism. The theoretical structure of history remains weak and its roles badly defined. More-

[29] "The social sciences today possess no wide-ranging systems of explanations, judged as adequate by a majority of professionally competent students, and they are characterized by serious disagreements on methodological as well as substantive questions." See E. Nagel, *The Structure of Science* (New York: Harcourt, Brace and World, 1961), p. 449. See also pp. 458–459 on misinterpreting causation. "In any event," Nagel later concludes, "it is not easy in most areas of inquiry to prevent our likes, aversions, hopes, and fears from coloring our conclusions. It has taken centuries of effort to develop habits and techniques of investigation which help safeguard inquiries in the natural sciences against the intrusion of irrelevant personal factors; and even in these disciplines the protection those procedures give is neither infallible nor complete. The problem is undoubtedly more acute in the study of human affairs, and the difficulties it creates for achieving reliable knowledge in the social sciences must be admitted." p. 488; see also pp. 490, 494–502.

[30] F. A. Hayek, *The Counter-Revolution of Science* (Glencoe, Ill.: The Free Press, 1952), pp. 28–31.

[31] For example, see Nagel, *Structure of Science*, pp. 473–485; or the literature on "revealed preference."

[32] Harold Orlans in his review of Bradley S. Greenberg and Edwin B. Parker, eds., *The Kennedy Assassination and the American Public: Communication in Crisis* (Stanford: Stanford University Press, 1965), in *Science*, 150 (Nov. 12, 1965), p. 872.

[33] For example, see T. H. Naylor and J. M. Finger, "Verification of Computer Simulation Models," *Management Science*, 14 (Oct., 1967), pp. B-92–101; also W. H. Starbuck, "Testing Case-Descriptive Models," *Behavioral Science*, 6 (July, 1961), pp. 191–199.

over, history in the sense of careful and disinterested search for the past, is threatened in several respects. Much of the interest in history is shallow. Furthermore, as Peter Gay points out, search for the past is under "persistent attack by the new myth-makers, by merchants of short-range practicality, and by nihilists without memory."[34] The historical profession itself remains in doubt respecting the main purpose of history, together with its methodology.[35] The cliometricians have, of course, blunted some of the criticism occasioned by the historian's past neglect of statistical matter. It is recognized also that historical as well as non-historical explanation entails application of Popper's hypothetico-deductive schema, with its emphasis upon the deductive character of explanation and the essentiality of universal hypotheses as well as initial, empirically testable conditions.[36] Unfortunately, social scientists tend to overlook the degree to which historical knowledge renders a scholar sceptical and guards him against a too easy acceptance of misleading models; and this oversight helps to reduce the importance attached to relevant history at the same time that it increases the gullibility component of other social sciences.

While it is possible that history will undergo a decline in relative importance, it should not suffer a plight so pronounced as that of the humanities. The humanities have undergone marked absolute growth in numbers, able students, and support, but less than that of the sciences. Their plight, if such it be, is traceable to the fact that knowledge has expanded more rapidly outside the area of the humanities than inside it. Presumably, as a result, the humanities are no longer quite so well-adapted to further their goals—goals to which less prestige attaches today than formerly.[37] It is possible, however, that growth in affluence will increase the importance of the goals espoused by the humanities. It may also be recognized that the humanities can be mobilized in defense of the worth of the individual and in support of "the extraordinary importance of the Life of the Mind," both of which are endangered in an interventionist world.[38]

A macro-approach is more favored by anthropologists than by sociologists, presumably because it lends itself to producing the cultural trans-

[34] See his review of John Lukacs's *Historical Consciousness, Or The Remembered Past* (New York: Harper & Row, 1968), in *New Republic* (Nov. 16, 1968), p. 20.
[35] Boyd C. Shafer, "The Study of History in the United States," *AAUP Bulletin*, 54 (Autumn, 1964), pp. 232–240.
[36] W. W. Bartley, III, "Achilles, the Tortoise, and Explanation in Science and History," *British Journal for the Philosophy of Science*, 13 (May, 1962), pp. 15–33; also Karl Popper, *The Logic of Scientific Discovery* (New York: Basic Books, 1959), sec. 12. See also F. M. Fisher, "On the Analysis of History and the Interdependence of the Social Sciences," *Philosophy of Science*, 27 (April, 1960), pp. 147–158; Nagel, *Structure of Science*, chap. 15.
[37] The above argument is put forward by W. D. Maxwell, "A Methodological Hypothesis for the Plight of the Humanities," *AAUP Bulletin*, 54 (Spring, 1968), pp. 78–84.
[38] C. P. Haskins, "The Humanities and the Natural Sciences: Partnership and Paradigm," *ACLS Newsletter*, 20 (Jan.–Feb., 1969), pp. 20–37. The entire Summer, 1969, number of *Daedalus* is devoted to the "future of the humanities." See also on the threats posed to the humanities by today's "barbarians of the exterior" and "the interior," Henri Peyre, "What is Wrong with the Humanities Today?" *The American Academy of Arts and Sciences Bulletin*, 23 (Oct., 1969), pp. 2–4.

formation essential to modernization of members of the Third World. A macro-approach is well adapted also to the study of national politico-administrative structures, a matter of great concern not only in developing countries but also in developed countries, most of which carry on with structures no younger than the steam railroad. Unfortunately, many political scientists have developed a taste for GIGO—i.e., Garbage-In, Garbage-Out—in the form of "political behavior" dear to computer jockeys.

A macro-approach is currently being fostered by the growing emphasis upon "systems analysis," practitioners of which, when displaying their wares, almost presume to possess Aladdin's lamp, a presumption often acquiesced in by governments and other customers.[39] Similar also is the effect of a belief—shared by sociologists and political scientists—in the supposed capacity of the state to resolve problems found difficult of solution at local levels even when financing is adequate. With the development of an annual social report paralleling the annual report of the President's Council of Economic Advisors, belief in the power of the state will be further strengthened even as it was in respect of economic policy after 1946.[40] Associated with the new emphasis upon the role of the state is a greater unwillingness to inquire scientifically into issues possibly involving challenge of current ideological shibboleths.

Tendencies of the sort enumerated are likely to be reenforced as tribally-minded graduate students settle upon social "science" as a career and as government and foundation bureaucrats, preferring elephantine to small undertakings, induce scholarly operators to stultify themselves "at the expense of what used to be called intellectual honesty."[41] Even now the "intellectual class" has ceased to remain independent as it should, "even of Intellect," having instead been "captivated by art, overawed by science, and seduced by philanthropy."[42]

What Barzun has to say is pertinent because it is social scientists far more than social science who are not ready to meet the challenges of an expanding interventionist role. One may, with Machlup, proceed from the properties of social phenomena to the complexities and difficulties faced by social scientists—properties that might present greater challenges than confront students of natural science phenomena. "There are more variety and change in social phenomena; . . . because of the large number of relevant variables and the impossibility of controlled experiments, hypotheses in the social sciences cannot be easily verified; . . . no numerical constants

---

[39] On the original intent of system theory see, for the views of one of its founders, Ludwig von Bertalanffy, *General System Theory. Foundations, Development* (New York: Braziller, 1969).

[40] On the present state of the emerging social report see U. S. Dept. of Health, Education, and Welfare, *Toward A Social Report* (Washington, D. C., 1968); also E. H. Sheldon and W. E. Moore, eds., *Indicators of Social Change* (New York: Russell Sage Foundation, 1968).

[41] Jacques Barzun, *The House of Intellect* (New York: Harper and Brothers, 1959), pp. 180, 183–184. See the whole of chap. 7, on "the folklore of philanthropy."

[42] *Ibid.*, p. 27.

can be detected in the social world."[43] The opportunity is greater, therefore, for disguised or latent values and ideological considerations to intrude into analysis, *not via the social sciences as such but via their practitioners.*

PAST PERFORMANCES

I turn now to reports on past interventionism of social scientists, among them Moynihan's reports.

Economics has long done quite well in the micro-realm where at least the direction of response to economic stimulus is clear, if not also its degree or the precise manner in which this response is related to other stimuli. Micro-economics has long been effective, for example, in demonstrating the welfare-reducing effects of various forms of governmental and collective intervention in price and wage determination. However, George Stigler, having contrasted the 1841 report of Nassau Senior and his associates on the English hand-loom weavers with comparable modern reports, and having noted that "perfection is not yet the signature of an economist," concluded that "modern economists at their best can write somewhat better reports" than Senior's group but "usually write inferior ones."[44]

Macro-economics commands more attention at the hands of policy-makers than does micro-economics which, as noted, is mainly adapted to the analysis and achievement of optimum resource use. Macro-economics is concerned, not with individual firms, industries, and other decision-makers, but with aggregates constituting the economic system, with their interrelations, and with the response of the system to events (e.g., change in the money supply, devaluation). From this response one can proceed roughly through its impact on the level and composition of the activity of aggregates to its impact on industries, households, etc. Difficulties have arisen less because of weaknesses in macro-theory than because it has been misapplied, usually in response to short-run political considerations (e.g., the reduction of residual, transitory unemployment, most of it connected with the price or wage structure, occupational shifts, physical and/or mental defects). Numerophilia has led to neglect of relevant variables which are not cardinally measurable, while in underdeveloped lands a penchant for irrelevant idiosyncratic macro-models has hidden the growth potential of agriculture from their authors.[45] Correction of these shortcomings would, of course, augment the relevance and improve the effectiveness of macro-theory and models.

At least until recently, much was being written of the success of the so-called New Economics to the neglect of its unfavorable impact. It has long

[43] Fritz Machlup, "Are the Social Sciences Really Inferior?" *Southern Economic Journal,* 27 (Jan., 1961), pp. 183–184.

[44] *Five Lectures on Economic Problems* (New York: Macmillan, 1949), p. 34. See also Fritz Machlup, "Do Economists Know Anything?" *American Scholar,* 22 (Spring, 1952–53), pp. 167–182.

[45] T. W. Schultz, *Transforming Traditional Agriculture* (New Haven: Yale University Press, 1964), p. 6.

been believed that if the money supply grows appropriately and those with access to this supply spend it, the economy will grow and prosper. This desired result can be accomplished, as Milton Friedman shows, through the Federal Reserve Board's allowing the supply of money to increase at a constant rate, commensurately with that of the output of goods and services, now about 4–5 per cent per year. Yet, as Paul McCracken points out, "the public sector has been the major source of cyclical instability and lapses from full employment." Fundamentally responsible has been deviation from correct policy, sometimes accentuated by supplementary policies intended to speed up or augment public and private spending. Before the New Deal, Federal Reserve policy was a principal source of instability. In and after the New Deal period, to the arsenal of Federal Reserve instruments were added pump-priming, tax and depreciation policy, and a federal budget conceived of as a stability-preserving balance wheel. In consequence we have had occasional periods of unemployment, creeping and now galloping inflation, and dissipation of expectations firm enough to support rational business policy and long-range commitments.[46] In sum, a combination of New Economics and badly chosen policy with Old Politics, has been responsible for some of our most troublesome economic problems as well as for the dollar-eroding methods employed to finance the most disastrous war in this nation's history.[47]

Not surprisingly, given their failures, economists have become subject to criticism far in excess of that implicit in the dictum that experts should be on tap but not on top. It is true that Postan's recent attack on British macro-economics, supported by Beloff's charge that British economists have neglected "the real causes of a society's successes and failures,"[48] has been rejected in the main. Yet, Harry Johnson, after pointing to the levelling philosophy underlying British economic policy and the barrister-like role of British government economists, has called attention to two sets of "counter-productive effects of the Keynesian revolution." The first is the assumption that economic problems are simple, often to be solved by mere gimmickry. The second and more important set, even as Postan re-

---

[46] On the issues raised in this paragraph see Paul W. McCracken, "Economic Policy in the Age of the Employment Act," in I. H. Siegel, ed., *Manpower Tomorrow: Prospects and Priorities* (New York: Augustus M. Kelley, 1967), pp. 73–86; Milton Friedman, *Capitalism and Freedom* (Chicago: University of Chicago Press, 1962), chaps. 3, 5; Yale Brozen, "Permanent Prosperity Through Permanent Deficits: The New Mythology of The New Economics," a paper delivered June 21, 1967; Gilbert Burck, "Must Full Employment Mean Inflation?" *Fortune* (Oct., 1966), pp. 120ff; Karl Brunner, "The Role of Money and Monetary Policy," Federal Reserve Bank of St. Louis *Review*, 50 (July, 1968), pp. 8–24; W. Wilson, "Fiscal Policy in the Sixties," Federal Reserve Bank of Richmond *Monthly Review* (Dec., 1968), pp. 2–5; E. R. Wicker, *Federal Reserve Monetary Policy, 1917–1933* (New York: Random House, 1966).

[47] Gilbert Burck, "The Deficit Comes Home to Roost," *Fortune*, 76 (Sept. 1, 1967), pp. 90–93; unsigned editorial, "The New Economics in an Old Box," *ibid.*, pp. 67–68. See also I. H. Siegel, *Fuller Employment with Less Inflation* (Kalamazoo: W. E. Upjohn Institute, 1969).

[48] Michael M. Postan, "A Plague of Economists?" *Encounter*, 30 (Jan., 1968), pp. 42–47, and Max Beloff's comments, *ibid.*, (March, 1968), p. 91.

marked, is concentration on short-run problems, neglect of micro-economics, overemphasis upon demand and investment, and underestimation of both shorter- and longer-run factors (e.g., entrepreneurs) important in economic growth and development.[49] More devastating than Johnson's assessment has been T. W. Hutchison's review and indictment of the contradictory views of Britain's economists respecting policy, of their shortage of knowledge, and of their subservience to ideology and dogmatism.[50] Others have observed that "practical" economists often ignore the findings of theoretical economists.[51] Dudley Seers has called attention also to the weaknesses of economists serving as advisers to governments in the underdeveloped world.[52] It has been noted, moreover, that large economic models (however remarkable), resting as they still do upon imperfect and sometimes incomplete data, remain prone to forecasting error, especially in the shorter run. It is not surprising, therefore, that Vaizey concedes "that running an economy to order may be beyond the power of analysis of present-day economists; just as one must conclude that the understanding of the roots of social inequality and of social pathology in general, is beyond the power of present-day sociology."[53]

Social scientists other than economists have come in for even more severe criticism. Joseph Alsop, reviewing the "cruelly false hopes" raised by the Supreme Court's 1954 decision desegregating the schools and based upon soft-minded social science preconceptions, refers to "the final bankruptcy of the social sciences, as they are currently studied and taught in American universities," with emphasis mainly upon what ought to be done to the neglect of what can be done.[54]

The social scientists, T. H. White suggests, seem finally to have learned that "they are not the mouthpieces of nature proclaiming oracular truth."[55] But they remain short on theory, long on clichés, inclined to depend upon computerizable survey data that may mislead, and unduly prone to generalize.[56] Jules Henry has described a recent famous summary of social science findings as providing convincing support of "a general theory of

[49] "A Catarrh of Economists?" *Encounter*, 30 (May, 1968), pp. 50–54. Whereas Johnson criticized only some economists, Michael Stewart traced Britain's troubles to politicians' neglect of the advice of economists. "A Plague of Politicians?" *ibid.*, pp. 54–56.

[50] *Economics and Economic Policy in Britain, 1946–66* (London: Allen & Unwin, 1968).

[51] For example, see W. J. Baumol, "Informed Judgment, Rigorous Theory, and Public Policy," *Southern Economic Journal*, 33 (Oct., 1965), pp. 137–145, and "Pitfalls in Contracyclical Policies: Some Tools and Results," *Review of Economics and Statistics*, 43 (Feb., 1961), pp. 21–26; Sidney Weintraub, "A Macro-Theory of Pricing, Income Distribution, and Employment," *Weltwirtschaftliches Archiv*, 102 (1) (1969), pp. 20–22.

[52] "Why Visiting Economists Fail," *Journal of Political Economy*, 70 (Aug., 1962), pp. 335–338, and "The Limitations of the Special Case," *Bulletin of Oxford Institute of Economics and Statistics*, 25 (May, 1963), pp. 77–98.

[53] John Vaizey, "Disenchanted Left," *Encounter*, 30 (Feb., 1968), p. 68.

[54] See his column in *Durham Morning Herald*, June 1, editorial page.

[55] "Chartmakers for Our Demanding Future," *Life*, 62 (June 23, 1967), p. 78D.

[56] *Ibid.*, pp. 77–83.

intellectual failure in the behavioral sciences."[57] He mentions as evidence: "(1) Inability to distinguish truism from discovery. (2) Insensitivity to platitude. (3) Insensitivity to tautology. (4) Confusion of causal sequence. ... (5) Misperception of variables. ... (6) The delusion of precision. ... (7) Issue avoidance. (8) The drawing of simple-minded parallels. ... (9) Multiparaphrasis. ... (10) Failure to observe the law of homologous extrapolation. ... (11) Lack of an existential concept of man." Henry may derive consolation from A. M. Weinberg's suggestion that many so-called social problems could be translated into technological terms and thus made much easier of solution. Yet great limitations exist,[58] and even computer learning could go the way of programmed learning.[59]

When a science is weak and lacking in predictive capacity and its practitioners are under little discipline, ideology, together with its coloration of the collection and interpretation of information, has considerable play. This is the case with social science other than economics. Illustrative is D. P. Moynihan's account of the "war" on poverty and unemployment under the Kennedy-Johnson regimes, mainly by means of acephalous community action designed to bring about results very speedily. Expectations were not realized. Indeed, the account recalls a theory that attributes the dinosaur's inability to adapt to new conditions, together with its extinction, to the smallness of the ratio of its brain to its body, a ratio much less than one-fiftieth of that of the elephant. With so small and lowly organized a brain, the dinosaur "could not meet new demands" occasioned by the Laramide revolution; "its vitality flickered, and was finally and irrevocably extinguished."[60] The role of well-meaning but unwitting dinosaur in Moynihan's Sartreian scenario is played by the Ford Foundation and the federal government. Neither of these shortsighted agencies anticipated the destructive outcome of the somewhat thoughtless policies which it set in motion, with the assistance of ideologically-oriented social scientists, some of whom seem to have been more interested in agitation than in accomplishing originally declared policy objectives.[61] Especially striking was the

[57] See his review of Bernard Berelson and Gary A. Steiner, *Human Behavior: An Inventory of Scientific Findings* (New York: Harcourt, Brace and World, 1964), in *Scientific American*, 211 (July, 1964), pp. 129–134.

[58] A. G. Oettinger, *Run, Computer, Run: The Mythology of Educational Innovation* (Cambridge: Harvard University Press, 1969), pp. 58–68, 215.

[59] *Ibid., passim;* see also P. W. Jackson, *The Teacher and The Machine* (Pittsburgh: University of Pittsburgh Press, 1968).

[60] W. E. Swinton, *The Dinosaurs* (London: Thomas Murby & Co., 1934), pp. 38, 187.

[61] Moynihan, *Maximum Feasible Misunderstanding* (New York: The Free Press, 1969), chaps. 2–7. Today, social workers, unsuccessful at reducing the number of persons on welfare, are working hard to increase both the number on welfare and average benefits and thus make dependency a satisfactory style of life. The welfare system itself is now functioning as a cornucopia of disaster. See Irving Kristol, "The Crisis Behind the Welfare Crisis," *Fortune*, 79 (June, 1969), pp. 227–228. In August, a draft copy of *A Trainer's Manual for Community Action Agency Boards* was distributed by OEO; among "legitimate" weapons of the poor it listed "demonstrations, economic boycotts and, ultimately, violence," according to Rowland Evans and Robert Novak, in

apparent neglect by both governmental and foundation personnel of the complex composition of the populations whose ills, of quite diverse genesis, were slated to be eased. Such uncritical behavior on the part of foundations and governments tends to be perpetuated by a current view that so long as money is spent on "doing good," the spender is to be complimented whether or not *good* results are achieved.[62]

Moynihan's inferences respecting the role of social science and social scientists in the formation of public policy are largely crowded into one chapter.[63] While he does not distinguish sharply between the problem-solving capacity of a social science and the behavior of its practitioners, he does infer the contribution of social science to be small though susceptible of considerable augmentation, especially if social scientists increase their own effectiveness. Social science is "at its worst, when it offers theories of individual or collective behavior which raise the possibility, by controlling certain inputs, of bringing about mass behavioral change. No such knowledge now exists." "Government, especially liberal government, . . . needs the discipline of skeptical and complex intelligence." While Moynihan's argument for a Devil's Advocate is very well taken, more is required. He seems to overlook that only the development of a better theory serves to dispose permanently of an inferior one. Quite untenable is his argument that "the role of social science lies not in the formulation of social policy, but in the measurement of its results." Even given a well-defined policy objective, its realization may have initially unrecognized side effects, good and bad, and so, in varying degree may each of the means available for realizing this objective. Only competent, non-ideological social scientists are likely to be able to identify these effects and weight them carefully enough to permit optimal selection of objective and means.

While it is possible to measure the effects of some economic legislation with considerable precision, it is much more difficult to measure the effects of social legislation. Evaluation procedures remain in their infancy. Much more help might be had from the creation of an institution homologous to the Brookings Institution, but designed to cover areas of legislation and policy other than such economic and governmental policy as is now dealt with by the Brookings Institution. Such an institution might also serve as an assembler and clearing house for diverse evaluative literature flowing from universities.[64] The formulation as well as the modifica-

---

their column on "OEO's Holdover Revolutionaries," *Durham Morning Herald* (Sept. 29, 1969), editorial page.

[62] E.g., in an article in defense of American foundations, a free-lance writer, Irwin Ross, declares that "the test is whether foundations are undertaking worthwhile projects that otherwise might not get done." See "Lets Not Fence in the Foundations," *Fortune*, 79 (June, 1969), p. 166. Not even the avowal of patriotic sentiment could provide a more encompassing protective robe for well-intentioned error. What is needed, of course, is continuing critical evaluation of foundation policy and performance.

[63] *Maximum Feasible*, chap. 8, on "social science and social policy," esp. pp. 190–195.

[64] I have discussed some of these matters in "Public Economic Policy in a Dynamic Society," in *Major Problems of the American Economy*, Special Publications Series,

tion of social policy would be both improved and accelerated as legislatures became more attuned to responding to intelligent extra-governmental
evaluations. Similar improvement in the area of foundation policy would
result if an independent institution were set up to assess periodically, say
yearly, the performance of foundations, given their increasing and often
misguided forays into the realm of social welfare.[65]

Moynihan may not have intended quite what the average reader gets
from his statement that "'all that is needed is a rough, but hopefully constantly refined, set of considerations as to what is associated with what."
For his favorable comments on J. S. Coleman's neglected report on educational opportunity suggests that Moynihan has in mind less rough measures
than his statement implies. In the realm of economic policy, action based
upon loose association can generate trouble. Presumably, it is advisable
that association be determined with as much precision as possible. In some
instances at least, these associations may be built into a simulation model
and the results of hypothetical policies examined. When this is not possible
(and probably when it is), it is desirable that sensitive feedback indicators
be built into policy to permit speedy ascertainment of the degree to which
expectations are being realized. Then administrators would find it more
difficult to cover up failures than at present. Whether it would be more
difficult for governmentally fostered monopolies to continue to take a toll
of $50 billion a year would remain to be seen.[66]

THE OUTLOOK FOR MEETING THE CHALLENGE

In what has gone before it is suggested that social science has not been
up to the demands made upon it and that social scientists have done much
less well than they might, given the analytical apparatus at their disposal.
It has also been argued that since funds for the support of science will grow
less rapidly in the future than in the past, competition for these funds will
be intensified. As a result social scientists may be tempted to promise more
than they can deliver to funding agencies, especially branches of government and omniscient foundations bent upon immediately removing society's persisting ills. Yet, what is needed is that practitioners of each social
science greatly improve its analytical apparatus, limit research commitments to what that apparatus is capable of doing, and so intensify internal
discipline as to minimize the influence of ideology and the persistence of
fallacy.[67]

Even given this corrective action, the outlook for science is not good. It

---

No. 16, of the National Academy of Economics and Political Science, American University, (Washington, D.C., 1960), pp. 12–18.

[65] It would be interesting to know how much peregrinating operators, financed by
foundations and international agencies, consume of the small amount of prime bureaucratic time available in the underdeveloped world—in junketing masquerading as
"research." Equally interesting would be the correlation between size of grant and
output per dollar.

[66] Yale Brozen, "Is Government the Source of Monopoly?" *Intercollegiate Review*,
5 (Winter, 1968–69), pp. 67–78.

[67] Cf. Tullock, *Organization of Inquiry*, chaps. 6–7.

may be asserted that "science serves society;" and yet, given the increasingly destabilizing effect of well-financed progress in natural science unmatched by progress in under-supported social science and public policy, a Luddite reaction may be waiting in the wings. "The rebels are right," Don K. Price writes, in being pessimistic in believing that an end has come to optimism and "blind faith in automatic progress." They are not "even pessimistic enough. . . . The new amount of technological power let loose in an overcrowded world may overload any system we might devise for its control; the possibility of a complete and apocalyptic end of civilization cannot be dismissed as a morbid fantasy."[68]

Social science could profit from this impasse. It may well hold the key to the future. For it there is no dearth of work. Indeed, society is confronted by a growing multitude of problems. Moreover, while technical change and progress will widen man's range of options,[69] it will also widen the gamut of social problems. For "when the era of universal prosperity dawns, mankind will at last be confronted," as will Marxism and Utopianism, "with the tragedy of its limitations."[70] It will be confronted also with the need to recognize the often great disparity between the real subjective world of individuals and groups and the incomplete picture of this world constructed by "scientific" observers on the basis of objective manifestations recorded, imputed, and measured.

Economic theory suggests that intervention may produce results quite other than those intended. When all relations but one are optimum, a correction of this one yields a Utopian solution. Only a second-best solution may be available, however, when many relations are sub-optimum. Even then, a correction of one relation may produce more harm than good.[71] The theory of the second-best needs to be incorporated in other social sciences than economics along with analogues, if any, of obstacles to the achievement of "economic welfare." Even then the yield of welfare economics is disturbingly small, as presumably would be the yield of "welfare social science."

> It requires an alarming degree of complacency to believe that a rising standard of living as commonly understood is the certain instrument of an expanding horizon of opportunities. . . . The concomitant subtopiasation of society involves a continual erosion of opportunities, at least for a sensitive

[68] D. K. Price, "Purists and Politicians," *Science*, 162 (Jan. 3, 1969), p. 31; also L. A. DuBridge, "Science Serves Society," *Science*, 164 (June 6, 1969), pp. 1137–1140, and Barry Commoner, *Science and Survival* (New York: Viking Press, 1966). But cf. D. S. Greenberg, "British AAS: Counterattack on Gloom about Science and Man," *Science*, 165 (Sept. 19, 1969), pp. 1239–1240.

[69] Emmanuel G. Mesthene, "How Technology Will Shape The Future," *Science*, 161 (July 12, 1968), pp. 135–143.

[70] Ignazio Silone, "Re-thinking Progress (II)," *Encounter*, 30 (April, 1968), p. 38; also Part I, *Encounter*, 30 (March, 1968), pp. 6–12.

[71] See J. E. Meade, *Trade and Welfare* (New York: Oxford University Press, 1955), chap. 7; also E. J. Mishan, "A Survey of Welfare Economics," in *Surveys of Economic Theory* (New York: St. Martin's Press, 1965), pp. 154–222, esp. pp. 202–203. These surveys were prepared for the American Economic Association and the Royal Economic Society.

minority. . . . A study of welfare which confines itself to the measurement of quantities of goods and their distribution is . . . positively misleading. For the things on which happiness ultimately depends, friendship, faith, the perception of beauty and so on, are outside its range: only the most obstinate pursuit of formalism would endeavor to bring them into relation with the measuring rod of money, and then to no practical effect. Thus, the triumphant achievements of modern technology, ever-swifter travel, round-the-clock synthetic entertainment, the annual cornucopia of slick and glossy gadgets, which rest perforce on the cult of efficiency, the single-minded pursuit of advancement, the craving for material success, may be exacting a fearful toll of human happiness. But the formal elegance of welfare economics will never reveal it.[72]

Nor will the expensive products of overpaid computer jockeys masquerading as social scientists.

There may be room, of course, for considerable governmental control when stochastic processes are at work, or there is great disparity between social costs and benefits, and solutions are not to be had from engineers[73] or through the establishment of extragenetic control mechanisms of the sort which order man's behavior and render it specific.[74]

If policy would augment welfare and free man of the tyranny of an emerging "welfare" or "consumer" state, it must escape a current paradox. In a Cybernetic Age, the range of options and choice-mixtures tends to increase markedly. As a result there is growing need for the decentralization of decision and choice. Meanwhile, however, macro-socioeconomic theory and its reenforing ideology, are exercising increasing pressure for the augmentation of information and the creation of institutional practices conducive to the centralization of decision-making until it already resembles that adapted to periods of crisis (e.g., war, induction of change in poverty-ridden lands). Yet, even in respect of public goods, the importance of which tends to rise with affluence, the role of the governmental apparatus must be limited, given its tendency to subdivide into essentially autonomous and self-serving enclaves of power. Decentralization does not, of course, come about automatically as some imply.[75] Countervailing theory is indicated (e.g., micro-social science, exchange theory, the theory of public choice and non-market decision making), together with dissipation of the current dogma of cultural homogenization.[76]

[72] *Ibid.*, pp. 212–213.

[73] For example, see Augustus B. Kinzel, "Engineering, Civilization, and Society," *Science*, 156 (June 9, 1967), pp. 1343–1345.

[74] See Clifford Geertz's paper in John R. Platt, ed., *New Views of the Nature of Man* (Chicago: University of Chicago Press, 1965), esp. pp. 106–107.

[75] For example, see W. G. Bennis and P. E. Slater, *The Temporary Society* (New York: Harper and Row, 1968).

[76] K. E. Boulding questions the "idea of a 'melting pot'" and "a uniform culture" which American society "has sought to create through public education." "With increased affluence and increased political skill, this ideal can now be called into question. Can we now invent a mosaic society composed of many small subcultures, each of which gives to its participants a sense of community and identity which is so desperately needed in a mass world, and which can at the same time remain at peace

Reduction of the immediate impact of the state as of the large foundation upon the shape and purpose of social science would conduce to its improvement. Bureaucratic simulation of papal infallibility would be reduced. Time horizons would be lengthened in keeping with reality instead of with short-run political considerations. Social scientists would perform under the watchful eyes of their fellows, with the result that there would be less room and reward for ideology, together with speedier extermination of fallacy. Social science would be on the way to becoming far more ready than now to meet the analytical and policy-oriented challenges that lie ahead. Its practitioners, moreover, would be on the way to becoming more ready than now to meet concrete challenges. There would then be less occasion for Henry Riecken to write "that we should be more concerned about unreasonable hopes of social science than about excessive fear of them as threats to human wellbeing."[77] Then the social sciences might get more of the support they need.

---

with its neighbors and not threaten to pull the society apart?" *Beyond Economics* (Ann Arbor: University of Michigan Press, 1968), p. 173. What this may amount to is the substitution of many small conformities for one large conformity. Cf. Walter B. Miller, "Implications of Urban Lower Class Culture for Social Work," *Social Service Review*, 33 (Sept., 1959), p. 225.

[77] "Government-Science Relations: The Physical and Social Sciences Compared," *American Psychologist*, 22 (March, 1967), p. 217. Even leading psychologists are now asserting that "society expects more than we have to provide." Bryce Nelson, "Psychologists: Searching for Social Relevance at APA Meeting," *Science*, 165 (Sept. 12, 1969), pp. 1101–1104.

·6·

NO GOOD IDEA GOES UNPUNISHED: MOYNIHAN'S MISUNDERSTANDINGS AND THE PROPER ROLE OF SOCIAL SCIENCE IN POLICY MAKING

PETER H. ROSSI

The Johns Hopkins University

A T LONG LAST, SOCIAL SCIENCE HAS COME ON CENTER STAGE IN AMERICAN society. Decades of being poised in the wings waiting for cues and polishing lines are over. Sociologists, psychologists, political scientists are wanted in government, industry and even religion. No longer do sociologists have to disguise themselves as economists to obtain civil service ratings. A few political scientists have managed to get themselves elected to office and a few sociologists have been appointed as presidents of universities. But, the final sign of acceptance is the appointment of a card-carrying social scientist as a presidential assistant. Variously described in the press as an "urbanologist," plain "social scientist," or "sociologist," but not very often as the "political scientist" he is by formal training, Daniel Patrick Moynihan serves as special assistant to Richard Nixon and as a powerful sign to the nation that social science is going to have some important impact on public policy.

All the more important, then, is *Maximum Feasible Misunderstanding*,[1] to which maximum feasible attention has been given in the press, not always, however, with maximum feasible understanding. Published shortly after his appointment as special assistant to the president and chairman of the newly formed White House Urban Affairs Council, Moynihan's slim volume has been reviewed widely. Moynihan's volume is an expanded essay dealing essentially with three main topics: (1) The political history of a set of ideas which led to the establishment of the Community Action Program of the Office of Economic Opportunity; (2) An evaluation of how CAP programs in fact worked out; and (3) a critique of the roles to be played by social scientists in the formulation of social policy. The stance from which the essay is written is not that of a social scientist *qua* social scientist but as policy maker. As such, Moynihan is more concerned with the political implications of intellectual matters than with their substantive character, a viewpoint which leads him to be obsessed with the problem of political consensus over programs rather than with whether the substantive goals of programs are being fulfilled.

The three major themes of Moynihan's volumes are not of equal interest in this discussion. A critique of his history of the links between the Ford Foundation, The President's Commission on Juvenile Delinquency and Crime, and the War on Poverty is best left either to other insiders who were party or close to the Kennedy and early Johnson administra-

---

[1] Daniel P. Moynihan, *Maximum Feasible Misunderstanding* (New York: The Free Press, 1969).

♦ First published in *Social Science Quarterly* 50, No. 3 (December, 1969).

tions or to professional historians. I have no reason to dispute his account: Indeed it jibes well with similar accounts written by other participants.[2] My main concern in this essay will be with his assessment of the Community Action Program and his remarks on the role of social science in the formulation of social policy.

THE PROCUREMENT OF SOCIAL SCIENCE

Moynihan's tracing of the history of the CAP program back to its beginning in the Ford Foundation's Public Affairs Program does raise an interesting issue to which I would like to devote some attention. In Moynihan's account social scientists and social science somehow manage to connect with policy makers but it is not clear by what routes. It is clear that the executive office did not procure its social science out on the open market. Nor did Presidents Kennedy and Johnson turn to the President's Scientific Advisory Council, the National Academy of Science, the National Science Foundation or the National Institutes of Health as ways of tying into the social science community.[3] Instead the underground railway led to the Ford Foundation and the social scientists who became involved were those who were associated with that enterprise. Indeed, it would be just as easy to characterize the group as social workers than as social scientists: Kravitz, Cloward and Ohlin were all based in schools of social work and only Ohlin had a degree in an academic social science, sociology. Paul Ylvisacker (then of the Ford Foundation) had been trained as a political scientist and Leonard Cottrell (mentioned by Moynihan as of some influence) was then head of the Russell Sage Foundation and was trained as a sociologist.[4] The intellectual leaders of the social science community of the time are barely mentioned in Moynihan's book and when noted are cited mainly as authorities off in the wings somewhere.[5]

Moynihan does mention that had policy makers taken the trouble to check around the social science community they would have learned that the Cloward-Ohlin thesis about the causation of delinquency was neither standard conventional doctrine nor without rival viewpoints. Apparently, however, policy makers acted as if they were competent to judge what was good social science, procuring their social science expertise through a sociometric network that ran through the New York private foundation

[2] See especially the essays by Sundquist, Yarmolinsky, Kravitz and Wofford in James L. Sundquist, ed., *On Fighting Poverty: Perspectives from Experience* (New York: Basic Books, 1969).

[3] Of course, neither PSAC or NAS at the time had any significant social science membership. But NSF and NIH were investing heavily in the social sciences at the time and had prominent social scientists on their staffs.

[4] For example, Robert K. Merton, whose seminal ideas lay behind the Cloward-Ohlin thesis of opportunity structure, is never mentioned except as providing some sort of authoritative support for the "theory." Merton played no role, apparently, either in PJDC or in the predecessor MFY or HARYOU-ACT.

[5] Richard Boone, who is cited as a University of Chicago sociologist, had also been undersheriff of Cook County and warden of Cook County's jail, an occupational citation which was not mentioned by Moynihan.

world into that portion of the social science community with which the foundations were then currently tied. The end result was the procurement of social science expertise and knowledge based on very shaky empirical bases, if any at all.

The procurement of other types of scientific advice often operates quite differently. The president's office has had, since World War II, a scientific advisor appointed from among very distinguished men in the physical sciences. The president's Scientific Advisory Committee also serves as an institution connecting the executive branch to the scientific communities in the physical and biological sciences. The National Academy of Sciences and the National Research Council, although not as intimately tied into the executive branch or the national legislature, is another well used avenue for government agencies to obtain scientific advice. The Council of Economic Advisors serves to provide the president with policy recommendations of a very prestigious group of economists.

Similar institutions have yet to be constructed to provide a bridge between the non-economic social sciences and the policy makers. There are some signs that the idea of constructing such institutions is beginning to catch on. A separate social science foundation has been proposed by Senators Harris and Mondale. Other public figures have proposed a "Council of Social Advisors" to function in a way analogous to the Council of Economic Advisors. Moynihan's appointment to the White House staff is in some ways similar to the appointment of a scientific advisor. It is too early to say what will come of these beginnings, although it is clear that there is concern that executive and legislative branches develop more efficient ways to obtain better social science advice and counsel.

The establishment of such connecting institutions running between the social science community and the federal government does not by itself totally insure that the best of social science advice is rendered unto the federal government. If the institutions function in the way their precedents do in the hard sciences, they will make it both easier to get the better social scientists into a more intimate relationship with policy and easier for policy makers to obtain evaluations of existing social science knowledge and personnel. The prestige of service on the governing boards of such institutions will make such positions attractive to social scientists who are now reluctant to take the temporary and sometimes anonymous posts offered by government commissions and agencies.[6] But, most important of all, policy makers need to be told that the route from social science knowledge to public policy is not a simple one, that instant results are not likely to be obtained and that social science still has a long way to go before it is thoroughly theoretical and empirical.

WHAT HAPPENED TO COMMUNITY ACTION?

The major portion of Moynihan's volume is devoted to accounts of what

[6] Witness the difficulties encountered by the Kerner Commission and by Milton Eisenhower's "Violence Commission" in obtaining help from the social science community on any but a parttime basis.

happened to the Community Action Program out in the hinterland. I wish it were the case that the content of his descriptions matched the labelling he gave to them. However, most of the descriptive accounts are *not* of CAP programs at all. A great deal of attention is paid to two programs. Mobilization for Youth and HARYOU-ACT, neither of which were part of the poverty program set up under the Economic Opportunity Act of 1964 (both preceded the CAP program). While a case might be made that they served as prototypes, in fact the major use in this instance that can be made of these cases is that they illustrate what might happen when local neighborhoods get organized enough to raise the level of demands directed at local political structures. The major example of a CAP program cited at any length by Moynihan is the program set up in Syracuse, New York, which came a cropper.

The fact of the matter is that good evaluations of CAP programs have yet to appear in forms which are easily available to the general public. Such evaluations were certainly not available to Moynihan at the time he wrote his volume.[7] What then were the failures of CAP to which Moynihan refers? The failures are political in character: CAP programs (exemplified mainly by MFY and HARYOU-ACT) tend to generate opposition among local public officials and in Congress. In volatile New York politics, accusations that MFY had been infiltrated by revolutionaries shook the regime of Mayor Wagner and in Syracuse CAP was dismantled by an irate city council. The denouncement arrived when Congress after considerable debate cut back on appropriations[8] for the CAP programs while giving support to the other parts of the poverty program. At the time Moynihan wrote his essay, the War on Poverty, and especially its CAP program, appeared to be headed for a demise in Congress. Nixon's recent (August 1969) statements about his welfare program indicate that OEO is slated to be reduced from an agency dispensing funds and controlling operating programs in the field to an experimenting and research agency. But, even now CAP is not dead: citizen participation is built into the Model Cities Program, administered by HUD, and more than one large urban school system are working out plans for decentralization.

For a "failure," the idea of citizen participation dies very hard. It is true that the CAP program did not always meet with joyful approval on the part of local government officials; it is also true that Congress will

---

[7] This is not to say that evaluations of the CAP programs did not exist in the files of the Office of Economic Opportunity at the time Moynihan wrote his volume; such did exist. However, with the possible exception of a report prepared by Daniel Yankelovitch (and cited by Moynihan) the evaluations were not worthy of the name. See my article "Practice, Method and Theory in Evaluating Social Action Programs" in James L. Sundquist, ed., *On Fighting Poverty*.

[8] Oddly enough, "maximum feasible participation" has not been eliminated from the legislation. Indeed, if anything, this provision has been strengthened by Congressional strictures that at least one third of the members of CAP governing boards be composed from among residents of the areas being served by the CAP programs. One would think that if "maximum feasible participation" were the bone that stuck in the Congressional craw, legislation passed in recent years would have eliminated rather than strengthened that feature of the CAP programs.

most likely put an end to the program as such. But, the general idea of the CAP program bids well to be incorporated into other parts of legislation dealing generally with welfare in urban areas. Nor did the CAP programs always give rise to trouble with local public officials. In Chicago, for example, Mayor Daley effectively incorporated CAP into the existing political machinery: indeed, community organization was not a major theme in a sizeable minority of CAP programs.

Leaving political acceptance aside, did the CAP programs actually achieve any appreciable change in the urban neighborhoods they were set up to serve? The evidence on this score is only now beginning to come in,[9] and appears to support the claims of the advocates of community organization. Vanecko finds that CAP programs which stress community organization (about 40 per cent of the 50 CAP programs studied by NORC) have had significant impact upon the organizations of social services, schools, and other municipal services provided in CAP areas.[10] Community organization has also had an impact upon employment and provided manpower retraining opportunities. The research cited is based upon interviews with officials in the affected organizations and is more in the way of an acknowledgement of influence than a direct measure of the impact upon the populations being served. Other researchers presently underway will be able to add data on this score.

So far community action has passed the test. It does work but not without some noise and friction. The friction and noise have not been as great in the last several years as in the early period of CAP and in the cases of MFY and HARYOU-ACT. Moynihan appears to have buried community action and "maximum feasible participation" prematurely.

It is hard to construct an image of what Moynihan would consider a successful social action program. It is clear that one important—if not overriding—criterion is that it should be acceptable to local public officials and national legislators. A program of public employment for the poor might fit the bill, assuming that such a program would receive the blessings of Congress. So would a wider and more generous program of income maintenance, providing again that Congress would go along. These are essentially programs which leave the existing institutional structures intact, or perhaps even strengthen their hands by providing more funds for their activities. They should also be programs which cut minimally into other benefits provided by government agencies to other sectors of

[9] One of the major faults of the CAP program was its failure to set up effective evaluation research programs from the outset. This occurred despite the willingness of prominent social scientists both to design and to carry out such research and despite the provision of specific appropriations in the 1964 Economic Opportunities Act for evaluation research. Even Head Start, the easiest of the programs to evaluate, has not been evaluated in anywhere near the optimum mode.

[10] James J. Vanecko, "National Evaluation of Urban Community Action Programs," Report # 1, National Opinion Research Center (Chicago, Ill.: Mimeographed, 1969), and Vanecko, "Community Mobilization and Institutional Change: The Influence of the Community Action Program in Large Cities," *Social Science Quarterly*, 50 (Dec. 1969), pp. 609–630.

the population. If only we could create a more equitable distribution of income and jobs by increasing the jobs and income going to the black poor without disturbing the levels of employment and income enjoyed by the rest of the population! Alas, for the past several years, the demands of the ugly war in Vietnam have eaten up so much of the GNP and the federal budget that this has not been possible (a point mentioned in passing by Moynihan).

The image of proper democratic politics underlying Moynihan's discussion is that of a polite gentleman's pluralism in which parties can dispute each other, but only within the framework of the existing party system and without hurting each other—a kind of powderpuff pluralism. The key role in such a system has to be played by those who are best equipped to ascertain what will "work," that is, what will be within the limits of the politically acceptable, a role best played by the practical, pragmatic professional politician.

THE PROPER ROLE OF SOCIAL SCIENCE IN PUBLIC POLICY

According to Moynihan, social science failed in the policy making surrounding the War on Poverty. The failure occurred on two levels: first, the social scientists advocated to the policy makers a viewpoint for which there was little empirical evidence and about which the social scientists themselves had little firm conviction. Second, the social scientists ignored (or were ignorant of) the political implications of the policies they were advocating. As a consequence, participatory democracy as a part of the poverty program failed to get over the thresholds of acceptance held by political leaders.

Leaving aside for the moment the important question of whether these two failures did ocur in fact and whether social scientists in general should be faulted for the Ford Foundation coterie's particular brand or variety of social science, what then should be the proper role of social science and social scientists in the formulation of social policy? Moynihan's answer is that social scientists should stick to what they know best: the measurement of social trends and the evaluation of the effectiveness of social action programs. In the last chapter of his book he advocates a number of specific tasks, all subordinate to the role of policy formulation and advocacy, which would be appropriate to social science. Moynihan is in favor of the social indicators "movement" to establish a set of measures monitoring social trends, much in the style of price indices and the measurement of unemployment. He also suggests that Congress set up an evaluation agency, analogous to the General Accounting Office, whose mission it would be to evaluate social action programs and to report and be responsible to the Congress. Coleman's study of equality of educational opportunity and the University of Wisconsin's current experimental study of income maintenance programs are pointed to as good examples of proper deployment of social science talents.

It should be understood that the roles assigned by Moynihan to social science are essentially conservative ones. Evaluation research is an activity which social scientists know how to do very well,[11] but all that can be evaluated is what has been tried. For example, Coleman finds that class size has little if any relationships to academic achievement once the socio-economic characteristics and scholastic aptitude of pupils are taken into account.[12] Although this finding, at first glance, appears to rule out class size as affecting academic achievement, it is important to note that this finding applies only to the range of class sizes to be found in American elementary and high schools at the time of his survey. It also applies only to the class sizes that students were currently experiencing and not to the experiences of students over the previous years of their education. Whether or not sizes of classes below or above the conventional range would have an appreciable effect on academic achievement is not ascertainable from Coleman's findings.

It is important to note that this is a limitation inherent in the definition of evaluation research which takes as given the existing (or projected) social action program and attempts to determine whether the program has an impact over and above what alternative treatments (or no treatment at all) would yield. The total set of conceivable programs lies beyond reach, as does that subset of programs which are reasonable alternatives to a given policy. To be more specific, an evaluation of the Job Corps Program, no matter how well done,[13] can only tell you whether sending a young man into the Job Corps yields more benefits to the Corpsman than leaving him in his native habitat. It does not tell you whether the Job Corps is worthwhile relative to alternative uses of the same amounts of money spent in other conceivable youth programs, for example subsidized apprenticeships in industry, money grants to take conventional high school and vocational school courses, subsidized trips around the world, or what-have-you.

Evaluation of existing social action programs will be especially conservative when the programs have been designed by the practical pragmatic professional politician. His vision of alternative treatments will be especially myopic, restricted to that range which he estimates to provide an acceptable amount of consensus and discord. Unless we grant to the

---

[11] Although they are not often given the opportunity to conduct evaluation research in the best possible manner. Despite the unique opportunities afforded by the programs established under either the Economic Opportunity Act of 1964 or the various titles of the Elementary and Secondary School Act of 1964, extremely few first-rate examples of evaluation researches can be found in connection with the large number of programs set up under either piece of legislation.

[12] James S. Coleman, Equality of Educational Opportunity (Washington, D.C.: U.S. Government Printing Office, 1966).

[13] The Job Corps Program has never been properly evaluated despite the fact that the program lent itself more than any other of the poverty programs to the controlled experiment design. Moynihan complains in the opening page of his chapter "Social Science and Public Policy" that the Labor Department searched in vain through government archives for evaluations of the Civilian Conservation Corps, a popular New Deal program which was the model for the Job Corps. The next time we rediscover the "poor," policy makers will be searching in vain through the archives to find the proper evaluation of the Job Corps.

policy maker an unusual degree of vision and Florentine cleverness it is likely that the programs advocated will be just a little different from current practices, different enough to appear that changes are being made and similar enough to garner support.[14] Because we can expect that policy makers' conventional vision will lead only to tinkering with existing social action programs, evaluation research tied to such programs can only be concerned with minor effects.

Somewhat more can be expected from the "social bookkeeping" role exemplified by the establishment of a set of social indicators or of social accounts. The continual monitoring of social trends is bound to bring to light unconventional ideas about what is happening to our society. For example, continual monitoring of drug usage would have brought to light earlier the fact that marijuana is fast approaching among young people the popularity of alcohol as a stimulant and would have provided us with more information than we have now on the effects of such drug usage on gross behavior features. But there is conservative bias in the social bookkeeping role as well. We can safely assume that social indicators will be more concerned with central tendencies than with changes in critical subgroups of the population. For example, opposition to the Vietnam war was in the earliest period a phenomenon restricted to so small a proportion of the population that President Johnson could safely ignore it. The fact that the opposition was heaviest among the better educated, among the young, and the more liberal parts of the population was something which could be safely ignored because these groups were so small a proportion of the total population. The ability of the dissidents to break down the appearance of consensus and to garner more and more support was apparently severely underestimated.

Of course, the success or failure of a program of social indicators depends very heavily on the social sciences being able to construct a reasonably sensible model of a modern complex society like that of the United States. To detect the beginnings of social changes requires being able to specify the important indicators that are sensitive to changes in the offing. Furthermore, to understand social change means to have a model of how changes in one area of social life are related to changes in another. Were it necessary to have a fully completed and fairly tight model of the society even to start such a program of social indicators, it is obvious that the social sciences would not yet be ready. Fortunately, it is only necessary to have a first approximation, which is better than having no information or ideas at all. Whatever the faults of social science and how grave its errors, it is still better than nothing.

The danger in initiating such a program of research at this stage lies in the ever-present possibility (or even likelihood) that a policy maker will seize on a given model—however unpretentiously set forth by its author—and proceed to base a monitoring system and a set of social policies upon that model. *This is indeed the lesson that comes through in the*

---

[14] The current (August 1969) changes in the social welfare program advocated by Prseident Nixon exemplify this statement all too well.

Moynihan volume; at the present time policy makers are not sufficiently aware of the fragile and tentative characteristics of contemporary social science knowledge and especially theory. To the social scientist it is almost laughable that presidential commissions are set up and given the mission to report within six months on the causes of civil disorders, or even three years on the causes of violence. It is almost laughable that serious and committed policy makers built a program around the notion of community action without being aware that the underlying social science notions were not by any means widely accepted and proven ideas.

Basic knowledge and theory in the social sciences have not progressed to the point where we can lay out a single model of a social system, however crudely formulated, to which the majority of social scientists would agree. The lesson that Moynihan would draw from this state of affairs is that social scientists should stay away from drawing any attention to the policy implications of the models which they have constructed. But, there is an alternative to this position which would be more likely to be to the benefit of society.

The fact that there is more than one social science model of our society, or even of some subsystem within the society, means that policy making ought to seek to test out the relative worths of alernative models. For example, there is a world of difference between the "culture of poverty" conceptions of the characteristics of the poor and the theories that claim the characteristics of the poor have been generated by lack of income. Only part of the controversy can be settled by empirical research on present day poor.[15] It would require a substantial commitment to experimentation with alternative social policies to settle whether or not the poor are "intrinsically different" or merely suffering from the effects of low income. Similarly, competing theories of juvenile delinquency (for example, the Cloward-Ohlin thesis of opportunity structures versus the "drift" hypothesis of David Matza) require similar programs of both experimentation with alternative social policies and research on existing delinquent and non-delinquent adolescents.

The experimental study of the effects of income maintenance programs run by the University of Wisconsin's Center for Poverty Research is the only existing prototype of the kind of policy-oriented research program I have in mind. This experiment involves subjecting a group of families in New Jersey to an income maintenance program similar to that which has been discussed in policy making quarters and comparing the effects of such a program on the families' employment patterns over time with the pattern of a similarly constituted "control group" of families. The end result of the experiment will be an evaluation of the effects of income maintenance on motivation to seek employment. The virtues of the experiment lie in its design; its faults lie in the relatively narrow range of income maintenance programs that it will test.

[15] See Zahava D. Blum and Peter H. Rossi "Images of the Poor" in Daniel P. Moynihan, ed., *On Understanding Poverty* (New York: Basic Books, 1969) for an exhaustive review of empirical studies of the poor.

At this historical juncture, the idea of large scale experimentation with social action programs is not very politically acceptable. (Indeed an attempt was made in Congress to incorporate into the budget of OEO for fiscal year 1969 a specific prohibition on income maintenance experiments.) The very term "experimentation" conjures up images of mad scientists wielding cruel scalpels on innocent victims. In addition, no one likes to be a member of the experimental group in an experiment that has failed. In large part, the problem lies in an incorrect understanding of the nature of experimental designs, a misunderstanding held by many social scientists as well as laymen. To evaluate a given experimental treatment it is not necessary that either the control group or the experimental group be deprived of all beneficial aid: All that is necessary is that the form of aid (or treatment) be systematically distributed among groups in accordance with the demands of the particular experimental design employed.[16]

If we begin to regard policy making in social action areas as providing prime opportunities for crucial experiments in social science, then the involvement of social science and social scientists in policy making becomes crucial. It is up to the social scientists to sift and cull through the competing theories concerning our social ills, picking those which it is worthwhile to set forth in experimental endeavours. It may well be that the range of particularly fruitful appearing theories in a given area often includes both those which are politically feasible and those which are not. Certainly those which appear as if they would generate immediate and certain opposition would best be eliminated from any experimental program. I would hope that the social scientists involved would spell out the full range. Of course, the decision about which policies should be tested experimentally is a political one; although I am not suggesting social scientists as philosopher kings, I am suggesting social scientists in as close an advisory capacity to policy makers as is presently the case for the physical, biological and medical sciences.

A program of experimentation in social action programs is particularly appropriate and important for narrowly defined areas of social action. Thus it is appropriate for such areas as the prevention of juvenile delinquency, the provision of support for the indigent, fostering academic achievement in schools, and so on. These areas have in common two characteristics: first, there is widespread consensus on the broad goals of the action involved—for all practical purposes, we are all in favor of reducing juvenile delinquency, increasing academic achievement in school children, and so forth. Second, these are programs which are directed at limited subsystems in the society (schools, neighborhoods) which are numerous enough to provide sufficient cases for experimentation.

There is another area of social policy to which social science and social scientists can make a contribution which is not as amenable to the kinds

---

[16] For an elaboration of this point along with several suggestions for the use of "placebos" in social action experimentation, see Peter H. Rossi, "Practice, Method and Theory in Evaluating Social Action Programs" in James L. Sundquist, ed., *On Fighting Poverty.*

of experimentation programs suggested above. The broad policy questions concerning the general direction in which the society should go do not lend themselves very well to experimentation. For example, how best to prevent war, what should be our national population policy, what are the forms of family life that should be recognized in our state and federal legislation, and so on? Here the major contribution of the social scientist should arise both from his understanding of the general empirical tendencies in the society and from his knowledge that conventional wisdom is not necessarily wise. The role of informed social critic is one which is particularly suited to the expertise of the social scientists.

I realize that social science struggled mightily to attain its present stance of *wertfreiheit*, to be free of the value biases of the surrounding society. But there is a point where we have to consider what lies beyond cultural relativity. In the effort to show that the diversity of human societies was not an expression of the diversity of human species, we took the stance that all societies (and by implication, all alternatives to our own society) had moral validity of their own. But as political men we deny cultural relativity; some societies are better than others and some social arrangements are better than others. At least on the fringes political men and social scientists converge; no one would deny that a society which would annihilate its members is morally invalid, and a social policy that would eliminate any status category within the society (for example, blacks or Jews) would also fall under that designation.

Social science and social scientists have not yet turned to the question of what is a good society and which social arrangements are to be preferred to others. I think we have reached the stage of maturity where we can turn again to these problems, for a completely value-free social science is a social science of little value.

RATIONALIZING THE POLICY PROCESS

RALPH K. HUITT

The University of Wisconsin[1]

THE APPROPRIATE ROLE OF SOCIAL SCIENCE IN POLICY-MAKING IS SUC-
cinctly by Daniel P. Moynihan in the closing pages of his book,
*Maximum Feasible Misunderstanding: "The role of social science
lies not in the formulation of social policy, but in the measurement of
results."*[2]

In his next paragraph he elaborates his conception of the policy process,
as it is and should be:

> The great questions of government have to do not with what *will* work,
> but with what *does* work. The best of behavioral sciences would in truth
> be of no very great utility in a genuine political democracy, where one
> opinion is as good as another, and where public policies emerging for
> legislative-executive collaboration will constantly move in one direction,
> then another, following such whim, fashion, or pressure that seems upper-
> most at the moment. What government and the public most need to know
> in the aftermath of this process is whether there was anything to show
> for the effort, and if so, what. Causal insights of the kind that can lead to
> the prediction of events are interesting, absorbing, but they are hardly
> necessary to the management of a large, open political system. All that
> is needed is a rough, but hopefully constantly refined, set of understand-
> ings as to what is associated with what. A good deal of medicine is no more
> than this, yet people are healthier as a result, and so might be the conse-
> quences for the body politic.[3]

This is cogent and forthright. It is true that Mr. Moynihan later puts
out feelers that suggest tentatively somewhat more that social *scientists*
may do, but he maintains consistently that "to proceed as if that which
might be so, was in fact so, was to misuse social science."[4]

Is this an adequate description of the policy process in this presumably
"genuine" democratic system? Is any opinion in fact as good as any other?
Can a method be fashioned which may enable us to decide better what
we want and proceed more directly to try to get it?

In order to suggest some answers to these difficult questions I will ignore Mr. Moynihan's special case, the community action program in the
war on poverty, and look first at the process through which new policy
usually is made.

THE LEGISLATIVE PROCESS

Most new policy requires the enactment of legislation and it generally
originates with the President. Whatever the original intent of the Con-

[1] On leave, as Guest Scholar at the Brookings Institution, Washington, D.C. Formerly
Assistant Secretary for Legislation, the Department of Health, Education, and Welfare.
[2] Daniel P. Moynihan, *Maximum Feasible Misunderstanding* (New York: The Free
Press, 1969), p. 193. The italics are Mr. Moynihan's.
[3] *Ibid.,* pp. 193–194.
[4] *Ibid.,* p. 189.

✦ First published in *Social Science Quarterly* 50, No. 3 (December, 1969).

stitution-makers, the President today is, in domestic affairs, preeminently a legislator. The public expects, indeed requires it, of him. His campaign promise is not that he will run the administrative agencies better, but that he will give the country some direction or inspiration through legislation. Congress waits upon his messages and bills, which furnish the point of departure for whatever Congress ultimately does. The press keeps a box-score on his legislative progress. If he does not try to lead Congress he is regarded by most people, expert and layman alike, as deficient in leadership to some degree. We begin then with him.

Inasmuch as the President never really is a superman (contrary to presidential mystique) and has a good deal more to do than send a hundred bills to Congress each year, he needs help. Policy advice must come from someone. The institutionalized devices for obtaining policy advice for the President are crucial to outcomes and deserve far more attention than has been paid them. To whom can he turn?

There is always the Cabinet.[5] This is an exciting and appealing picture: the President sitting at the long oval table, charting the nation's course with the help of his principal officers. Actually, the Cabinet is not much good for that. They are appointed for a variety of reasons—to get partisan, regional, and minority group balance; to pay off political debts; perhaps to co-opt a potential enemy—other than policy competence. Beyond that, the secretaries have constituencies—their departments—for which they must fight or risk impotence in their own establishments, and they often have political aspirations of their own. Consequently, Cabinet meetings generally serve internal morale-building and external public relations functions, but they do not make much policy.

Beginning with Harry Truman, the principal source of legislative proposals came to be the executive departments and agencies.[6] The invitation to submit proposals and the process of formulating them were formal. Agencies considered, first, old legislation which was expiring, then new ideas to be tried. What came to the President were the legislative "packages" of his principal administrative officers. There is much strength in such a process. Agencies run programs and should know what the logical next steps would be. This gives stability and predictability to policy. Secretaries can be relied on to fight for proposals initiated in their shops. On the other hand, proposals brought up from the bureaus tend to be parochial and self-serving, an incrementalism based on the notion that what is, is good, and more of the same would be better. Furthermore, bureaus add to their *own* programs, usually avoiding what might cause conflict within the department itself or (more to be dreaded) with other agencies.

[5] See Richard F. Fenno, Jr., *The President's Cabinet* (Cambridge, Mass.: Harvard University Press, 1959).

[6] See generally Thomas E. Cronin and Sanford D. Greenberg, eds., *The Presidential Advisory System* (New York: Harper and Row, 1969). In that volume, see especially Richard E. Neustadt, "Approaches to the Staffing of the Presidency," pp. 11–24; and Norman C. Thomas and Harold L. Wolman, "Policy Formulation in the Institutionalized Presidency: The Johnson Task Forces," pp. 124–143. The assessments generally are my own.

If a President wishes not to be a prisoner of the bureaus, he must find some way of making outside advice welcome and effective. A White House conference is one device, but it is hard to manage, unpredictable, and a one-shot effort at best. More useful is the public commission (or "task force"). The President appoints a prestigious chairman, then performs the usual feat of "balancing the ticket" among the regions, minorities and parties. The commission holds a few meetings (or many, in some cases), but the work usually is done by the chairman, a couple of active members, and the staff. The commission's report may be very helpful to the President, *if it recommends what he wants to do.* A good example is the task force on elementary and secondary education appointed by President Johnson, with John Gardner as chairman. Its report formed the basis of the celebrated Elementary and Secondary Education Act of 1965, part of the remarkable work of the President and the 89th Congress. Mr. Gardner became Secretary of Health, Education and Welfare (and so administrator of the Act) later in the year. Results are not always so felicitous, needless to say. One recalls Mr. Johnson's embarrassment at the report of his commission assigned to study the urban riots, chaired by Governor Otto Kerner of Illinois. When it was released Mr. Johnson was engaged in tortuous negotiations with Congress over the amount of savings he would have to make in current expenditures in order to get a surtax. It was hardly a good time to ask Congress to spend new billions on the cities, as the Commission recommended. In a case like this, the President is never allowed to forget that he "did not implement his own commission's report."

When John F. Kennedy won election he looked forward to the need to propose legislation which would distinguish his administration from its predecessors. He made good use of task forces between his election and inauguration, appointing 29 task forces in various areas of foreign and domestic policy, 24 of which reported before he took office. These were public task forces; their membership was announced and the reports published. There were disadvantages to their public character. Critics pointed to the disproportionate number of academic members and attacked their reports before Mr. Kennedy had even been sworn in. Mr. Johnson took careful note of these difficulties. His own task forces were anonymous and their reports secret. Sometimes even their existence was denied when they were most numerous and active. Mr. Johnson used them to initiate ideas and to analyze the proposals of others. His principal legislative staff visited major universities in the spring, brain-storming with policy-oriented professors. These ideas became grist for the task-force mill, along with those submitted by the agencies and others. By the end of 1966, the congeries of task forces under the direction of Joseph Califano, the President's special assistant in charge of legislative planning, had become the principal source of new legislation in the Johnson administration.

Like all other procedures, the anonymous task forces had both strengths and drawbacks. On the favorable side, they were free to consider and suggest literally anything. The President was free to accept or reject and he sometimes did both, more than once, to the same idea. They were remarkably flexible devices, springing into existence at a word from the White House and perishing without ado. Their handicap was the atmosphere of suspicion that grew up around them. A department head might theoretically be the chairman of all the task forces considering legislation that affected his department. The work actually was done by his principal staff, whom he had to trust to press vigorously for the adoption of his ideas. Those who were left out, who could not even find out with confidence what was going on—interest group staff, members and staff of congressional committees, bureaucrats involved in affected programs—resented the procedure and felt little obligation to fight loyally for legislation on which they had not been consulted.

The sentence one writes routinely at this point is that the legislation so formulated is "sent to Congress." Technically, it is. The President's messages on various categories of legislation, with accompanying bills, are sent to the Speaker of the House and the President of the Senate. Actually, they go to the appropriate committees in the two houses. What happens to them turns on committee action.[7] The strength and interest of the committee (and sub-committee) chairmen; the competition for committee time for hearings, markup, report and floor consideration; the settlement made by principal committee members of the respective houses who go to conference on the two versions of the bill—these are the elements of the system. The party leadership conceives its role (at least at present) as that of passing bills approved by committees and they take little interest in the bills before they are ready for the floor.

The congressional system, which parcels out power among so many feudal barons who chair standing committees with specialized jurisdiction, has made Congress a powerful body and kept it so. No organ of party leadership has proved capable of overriding the committee chairmen for very long at a time. The President must treat with the chairmen. The system does assure that most important bills, and especially those proposed by the administration, will get good consideration. Men long on a committee become expert; they know what is on the books and can assess new proposals in relation to existing legislation. But they are impotent if something which seriously affects their legislative concerns falls outside their committee's jurisdiction. The draft laws, to take an example, are crucial to higher education but they are outside the purview of the education committees; they are the work of the committees on armed services. The line is clear in law and precedent. Finally, it should be said that congressional strength—the capacity to give continuing informed attention to the details as well as the general character of legislation falling in specified categories—also is the source of an apparently irreparable congressional weakness: its inability to consider a legislative program (or even a budget) as a whole. The questions of national goals, priorities, and planning for

[7] See generally Ralph K. Huitt and Robert L. Peabody, *Congress: Two Decades of Analysis* (New York: Harper and Row, 1969) for the Senate, and Robert L. Peabody and Nelson W. Polsby, *New Perspectives on the House of Representatives* (Chicago: Rand McNally, rev. ed., 1969).

the future are outside its competence, not because its members are not equal to the tasks but because Congress has no institutional arrangements which would make that possible.

WHAT ABOUT SOCIAL SCIENCE?

This longish description of the policy process has had one purpose, to lead to the comment that it is hard to see what there is about it that Mr. Moynihan wants to protect from the contamination of social science.

Several summary statements might be made about it before attempting more evaluation.

1. It is not so much a policy system as a network of policy systems. Education policy, for example, is made in most important aspects by specialists in education—on the White House staff and in the Bureau of the Budget, in the Office of Education and DHEW, in the congressional committees, and in the education associations and professional writing circles. About the only generalist really concerned with it is the President.

2. Most time and money is spent on existing legislation. Authorizations, without which no money can be spent, usually are for two years at a time (for controversial programs, perhaps only one). Bureaucrats protest this practice; they contend that administrators ought to know what to count on. But programs are seldom killed. Given the pressures to have a legislative program every year, it is better for energy to be spent on basic programs than on gimmicks.

3. There is little consideration of goals for individual programs or of priorities among them. What are the goals of the federal government for higher education, for instance? It is possible to infer some goals from an examination of the programs, but the goals certainly were not set first. Only the President (with his staff and the Bureau of the Budget) is required to fix priorities, and there is no public statement of what went into their calculations.

4. Needless to say, long-range planning usually means next year. Making "five-year plans" is common in the executive branch but they do not mean much.

5. In consequence, there is not much real evaluation. How could there be? Programs must be planned with evaluation in mind—the problem assessed, goals set, methods agreed upon, and criteria for evaluation established (the Program Planning and Budgeting System aims at this, about which more later). Title I of the Elementary and Secondary Education Act, to take an example, pours a billion dollars a year into school districts to enrich the education of disadvantaged children. Does it work? Who can tell? One district may buy educational equipment, another hire teacher aides.

Now we must ask of this policy system (or network of systems) Mr. Moynihan's question: Does it work?

Of course it does. By many tests it works better than any other system in the world. But surely Mr. Moynihan's question is not adequate. Are there ways, consistent with the working of a "genuine political democracy," that some problems are more likely to be solved? There is no doubt that President Johnson and the 89th Congress demonstrated the responsiveness of the system and their own good will when they enacted dozens of items on the liberal legislative agenda. But some problems demonstrably were not solved. They are too stubborn to yield even to a storm of good things to do; perhaps they cannot be solved at all. This is the basic admission which must be made; then perhaps we will be ready to work on them with the persistence and social intelligence which might make success possible. The New Deal method of action on all fronts availed a society which needed to get a middle class back to work. It is not enough, say, for the problem of a third generation on welfare.

The first step in the construction of a method should be goal-setting. The most important thing to know about the federal government is that it cannot do everything and should not if it could. The basic mistake of the caption "Great Society" is the notion it conveys that the government can create a great society. It cannot. What it can do is to decide where it will put its limited resources to increase the chance that certain things will come about. Does it want to equalize educational opportunity—or what? Is this more important than something else? The questions should be asked explicitly and answered consciously. They should be put to the people by the President, in his speeches and messages to Congress and in every other way he can. The big questions belong to the people and, oddly enough, they are the only ones the public generally can handle.

Then some problem-solving methods must be tried, experimentally, on a small scale. The American way with an issue is to debate it fiercely for years on an abstract level, then plump billions into it the day after it is decided. But long before that day it should be possible to test alternative ways to get at a public objective. It is here that social science *does* have a part, or else it is nonsense indeed. Mr. Moynihan is quite right that huge ventures should not be launched on untested social science theory, but neither should they be on the notion of an assistant secretary or a Budget Bureau examiner. The trick is to start small. Any considerable commitment of money is the gift of life everlasting; the program gets a constituency which will not let it be stopped. Examples are as numerous as federal programs, but one will suffice: the program to subsidize school districts suffering "impact" from federal installations and the children of federal employees. Presidents have tried for years to cut back expenditures on the ground that there are now better ways to help education. But money from the program flows into roughly 400 congressional districts and Congress regularly appropriates more for impacted areas than it did the year before.

Happily, there is evidence that a better problem-solving method is in the making, albeit in an early stage. Mr. Johnson's order to all executive agencies to establish Program Planning and Budgeting Systems may well prove to be the most important contribution of his administration.[8] It must be admitted that PPBS was oversold at first and is no miracle-worker. Its road has been rocky and will continue to be. But PPBS has in it all the elements of a good social process and it will succeed, perhaps in another guise, because it must. It is a logical step in the development of governmental sophistication and responsibility, as the budget was. Furthermore, there are revolutionary process implications in the experiments of the Office of Economic Opportunity, through a contract with the University of Wisconsin, with the negative income tax involving a thousand low-income families in New Jersey. All these and more are cited by Mr. Moynihan as examples of progress.[9]

And social scientists themselves, "in their capacity as citizens, as interested, sentient beings" will be on hand "proferring proposals for universal improvements doubtless for all time to come." What of that? "And no bad thing," says Mr. Moynihan. How very right he is. And the model he provides by his own actions is as compelling as the text.

[8] See especially Charles L. Schultze, *The Politics and Economics of Public Spending* (Washington, D.C.: Brookings Institution, 1969). The literature on PPBS is extensive but Schultze is concerned about precisely the kind of problems Moynihan raises in relating planning to the political context of decisions.

[9] Moynihan, *Maximum Feasible Misunderstanding*, pp. 194–203.

·8·
SOME BROADER REALITY FRAMEWORKS FOR ANTI-POVERTY INTERVENTION

HAROLD L. SHEPPARD

Upjohn Institute for Employment Research and *American University*

IN DISCUSSING THE TOPIC OF SOCIAL SCIENCE AND SOCIAL INTERVENTION, I think it informative to go beyond the restricted preoccupation of so many students of current anti-poverty and community action policies and programs, and consider some wider frameworks of reality. For example, the very creation by government of an Economic Opportunity Act was itself an intervention strategy. We cannot ignore this fact. There is, of course, nothing new in legislative efforts to write class statutes benefitting one group more than another, or addressed directly to the problems of a stratum singled out more than others. Unlike other class-related laws, in this case the new law was only remotely—if at all—the result of lobbying or direct pressuring by the class intended to be positively affected. But this does not detract from the main point that the Economic Opportunity Act was a major form of social interventionism into a social and economic order that otherwise was functioning too slowly or too unevenly in reducing poverty, from the standpoint of selected organizations, groups, and persons.

The role of government as one, if not *the*, overwhelming agent of social intervention, insofar as poverty is concerned, cannot be exaggerated. That role goes beyond the enactment of any relatively small-scale specific piece of legislation and its appropriations-administrative resources (such as the community action component of the EOA). Take, for example, the wide variations in the average annual rates of decline in the proportions of American families with less than $3,000 income (in 1967 prices) in three different "political regimes," each with its own governmental fiscal and monetary policies regarding expansion and contraction of the economy. These data are presented in Table 1. The figures in the two right columns indicate clearly the impact an interventionist policy can have on family incomes.

I cite these types of figures because it is unimaginable to me that any discussion of social intervention on the level meant by advocates of "maximum feasible participation"—that is, on a localistic *micro*-level—can be intelligently carried on without a keen sensitivity to the broader, *macro*-context in which the poor, and representatives of the poor, participate in various degrees and forms presumably to reduce poverty.

Table 1 shows rather clearly that under political regimes which typically advocate and implement policies of government intervention into the broader socioeconomic process, greater progress has been made in the reduction of numbers of low-income families. *What is perhaps even more instructive is that in each Democratic political regime period, nonwhites did better than the general population, while under the Republican regime they fared worse than the general population!*

92   ♦ First published in *Social Science Quarterly* 50, No. 3 (December, 1969).

TABLE 1

Annual Rates of Decline in Percent of Families With Less
Than $3,000 Income, by Type of Political
Administration 1947–1967[a]

Period	Party in White House	Average Annual Rate of Decline in Percentage of Families With Less than $3,000 Income (1967 Prices)	
		All Families	Nonwhite Families
1947–1953	Democratic	—2.7[b]	—3.7[b]
1953–1961	Republican	—2.3	—1.5
1961–1967	Democratic	—5.5	—6.1

[a] Based on data from Table B-20, *Economic Report of the President*, 1969, p. 250.
[b] This figure and the two below it were calculated by dividing the number of years in each period into the *rate* of decline in proportion of families with less than $3,000. For example, from 1947 to 1953, the proportion declined from 27.4 to 23.0 per cent—a rate decline of 16 per cent which, when divided by the six years covered, yields an average annual decline rate of 2.7 per cent.

Further analysis shows that within the more narrow time period during which the "War on Poverty" was operating (1964–1967), the progress out of low income was greater than in the previous three years of Democratic rule, for both the general and the nonwhite population. It was only during the more recent 1964–1967 period that the out-of-poverty index for nonwhites exceeded that for the total, general population. This reveals that the intervention strategy takes a longer time to benefit previously neglected segments of the population. It also suggests, of course, that any government decision to retrench on those policies making for such progress will first adversely affect the same neglected segments.

It is critical to remind ourselves that the 1964–1967 period—during which the War on Poverty was conceived and began operations—was also (but *not* incidentally) the period during which a major tax-reduction took place, among other general programs, including capital investment credits, area economic development, and manpower training programs. These were all intervention strategies—structural, as well as aggregate-demand, efforts.

I doubt that the stress on community action programs and "maximum feasible participation" had very much to do with this sharp drop in the rate of low-income families in America. Along with some secular socioeconomic trends (notably the urban shift), the major contribution came from these more encompassing structural and aggregate-demand thrusts.[1]

Let me hasten to state that I am not arguing against community action

[1] And to some extent, from those OEO-funded programs that resulted in the creation of new, better paying jobs for the poor, in new career projects and local poverty agency staff positions, for example.

programs (CAP) and/or maximum feasible participation (MFP) in those programs. These efforts can perhaps be justified in terms of *other* criteria which—in the short run at least—may not be related to reducing the incidence of poverty.

But so far, if I am not too mistaken, there has been no evaluation, carried out under conditions acceptable to modern social science, of the effectiveness of CAP's and MFP in affecting the rate of poverty. Indeed, my major complaint has been that too *little*, and not too much, social science conceptualization and methodology went into the original legislation and subsequent administration of the Economic Opportunity Act. The almost ideological resistance to building in and applying careful *evaluation* procedures continues to characterize the staffs of CAP's and the indigenous poor. We still do not know with any degree of confidence what really works and doesn't work in the infinite number of community action approaches to combatting poverty. We still do not know what are the specific conditions and techniques that account for the successes and for the failures in Project Head Start.

It was one thing to have launched a war against poverty without first having a detailed multi-dimensional map of the terrain in which the war was to be conducted. It is even less defensible to have made a virtue out of not making that map as the generals, lieutenants, Sargents, and privates roamed and zig-zagged through the many unchanged fields, holes, mountains, and swamps, looking for the enemy.[2]

The attacks on the viewpoint expressed here can only be viewed as anti-intellectualism, and fear of putting one's ideas to a hard-nosed test. The much-to-be-desired expansion of anti-poverty expenditures will not be hastened by such attacks. They will instead serve to postpone the day when we will know much more surely where to place the additional funds.

The task still remains for social scientists and others to persuade Congress (and the Bureau of the Budget) to support the suggestion I made in a report prepared for the U.S. Senate Subcommittee on Employment, Manpower, and Poverty in 1968:

> There is a great need to make use of annually collected Census Bureau facts (based on an expanded sample when necessary) . . . in order to make more intelligent program-decision progress in the war against poverty. These facts can be organized in terms of age, family status and size, race, sex, region, work experience and occupation, etc. It is important that several of these variables be combined in order to be practical. Tables reporting age differences only, or white-nonwhite differences only, for example, tend to contribute spurious information for operating purposes. Furthermore, such data must be studied in the form of time trends, in order to detect degrees of progress for specific population categories.[3]

---

[2] This reminds me of the observation made by a former top advisor to Robert Kennedy, Adam Walinsky, that "the great failing of the community action program . . . was that it never had very much to organize about. . . ." in his review of D. P. Moynihan's *Maximum Feasible Misunderstanding*, in the *New York Times Book Review* (Feb. 2, 1969).

[3] *A Search for New Directions in the War Against Poverty*, an Appendix to *Toward*

I also pointed out in that report that through the same method it could be possible to determine the relative effectiveness of selected anti-poverty programs, by providing data on the degree and nature of participation by various population subgroupings in these programs and thereby comparing poverty-exit rates of participants vs. non-participants; of participation in one type of program vs. another, and so forth. Just as in the use of epidemiology in the fight against disease and illness, this type of research and knowledge is indispensable when determining if and to what degree any given technique, program, or policy is producing a poverty reduction in specifically identifiable population *subgroupings* (and not just in single, broad, sloppy categories such as age alone, sex alone, or race alone). How does anyone know where to intervene if there is no reliable concrete knowledge as to the detailed nature and distribution of "poverty" (and its trends)? Being poor oneself is not enough to stake a claim to absolute authority in deciding where and *how* to intervene. Unexamined experience has never been a reliable guide to effective action.

To be sure, it takes more than reports about a third party written for the hopefully careful attention of law makers, their staffs, and Executive Department chiefs. If social scientists are genuinely interested in making their academic craft a major input of statecraft, much more needs to be done to develop effective techniques of communication and impact on policy change. This requires not only persuasion of top policy makers, but also in certain circumstances, persuasion of the poor themselves that a given research finding calls for a certain range of social policy and program design.

As a small example of what I mean on the subject of specific subgroupings in the search for the "hard" and "soft" spots in the anti-poverty effort of our society, I want to present the following illustration of what one type of detailed analysis yields. The results, in turn, may raise some controversial questions concerning the intervention implications of social science findings.

A criterion such as changes in proportions of families with less than a given income figure, for example, the $3,000 used by the Council of Economic Advisers and cited earlier, is too crude a measure of progress, since it neglects considerations of such factors as family structure, family size, and place of family residence. The Social Security Administration measure, developed by Mollie Orshansky, seeks to overcome such a deficiency. In using this more sophisticated measure in an analysis of unpublished census data, I teased out the following changes in rates of poverty in our largest urban areas (Standard Metropolitan Statistical Areas of one million and larger), from 1960 to 1968. The data are conceptualized in terms of the

Economic Security for the Poor, Report of the Senate Subcommittee on Employment, Manpower, and Poverty, 90th Congress, 2nd Session, October, 1968; also reprinted separately by the W. E. Upjohn Institute for Employment Research (Kalamazoo, Michigan: Dec., 1968).

sex of the family head, along with the otherwise obscurantist, often misleading rubric of white vs. black.[4]

1. From 1960 to 1968, the greatest exit rate out of poverty occurred in
Negro families headed by a man: 47 per cent.

2. Running second were families headed by white males: 38 per cent.

3. As for the families in our big metros which were headed by females,
the rates of exit out of poverty were 18 per cent for whites, 15 per cent for
blacks.

In other words, the *relevant* conceptual framework for understanding
the phenomenon of urban poverty must include the usually neglected dimension of the nature of the urban family, in particular whether it is a
two-parent or single-parent (typically female-head) family. The data in
Table 2 indicate that the rate of progress out of poverty is related more to
the *sex* of the family head than to the *race* of the family head.

TABLE 2

Rates of Change, 1960–1968, in Poverty Incidence Among Families in SMSA's
of One Million or More Population, by Sex and Color of Head
(in percentages)

	Poverty incidence		% Change in incidence
Male heads	1960	1968	
Negro	24.5	13.0	—47
White	6.3	3.9	—38
Female heads			
Negro	54.0	46.1	—15
White	24.6	20.1	—18

Table 3 is similar to Table 2 except that it concentrates on children
(family members 21 or younger). It again reveals that *sex of family head*
is more "explanatory" than *race* in the 1960 to 1968 declines in the incidence of poverty in our large urban areas.

But more than that, it yields a greater gap between Negro children in
families with male heads and Negro children in families wtih a female
head than does Table 2.

Table 2 shows a gap of 32 (47–15), while Table 3 indicates a gap of 42
(57–15) in the rate of poverty exit over eight years.

Without presenting the details, it is also relevant to point out that (1)
in *smaller* metropolitan areas (under one million) the poverty exit rates
for children in families with female heads were higher than in "big metros"

[4] Twenty years ago, if any social scientist presented, for example, crime statistics
classified only according to whites and Negroes, we would have tarred and feathered
him and ridden him out of the professional community. But today, no eyebrows are
raised when social scientists do the same thing in the field of unemployment or poverty
statistics. It was wrong 20 years ago. It is wrong today. Or is it that I have failed to
keep up with the times?

TABLE 3

Rates of Change, 1960–68 in Poverty Incidence Among Family Members
Under 22 in SMSA's of One Million or More Population,
by Sex and Color of Family Head
(in percentages)

	Poverty incidence		% Change in incidence
	1960	1968	
With male heads			
Negro	36.9	15.8	—57
White	7.0	3.7	—47
With female heads			
Negro	73.5	62.4	—15
White	44.2	32.5	—26

—especially for those in Negro families; and (2) Negro children in big metro female-headed families have nearly doubled as a proportion of the nation's total number of Negro children, from 8 per cent to 15 per cent, during 1960–1968. The proportion who were in big metro male-headed families increased hardly at all: from 25 to 26 per cent. In absolute numbers, Negro children in big metro female-headed families increased by 138 per cent; for those in male-headed families only 35 per cent!

I cite this type of research finding because I want to call attention to the outstanding failure of intervention strategists of all sorts and varieties to come to grips with a more comprehensive reality framework of the problem—a failure that reveals how *little* social science knowledge or methodology was applied at the beginning of the Community Action Program, and (less excusably) subsequent to its creation.

That reality framework, especially in the large metropolitan urban environment, must reckon with the factors that make such an environment a much more viable and profitable economic one for families headed by males than for families with female heads, *regardless* of race; and the factors that make for, or maintain, such disadvantaged female-headed families.

But this immediately provokes the charge of the monster of "outsiders" sticking their noses into other people's affairs; the charge of imposition of middle-class—or academic—values upon a problem group which has the wisdom to solve its problems all by itself.

We must remember, however, that the notion of maximum feasible participation was a proposal that originated *outside* the poor themselves, that is, it was *imposed* on them. I am not against imposing externally-derived ideas and values upon other groups as long as it is not done through compulsion. And certainly the doctrine of maximum feasible participation was not imposed on the poor of America through compulsion. The critical point is that experts and others are always doing this. I won't cite the endless number of examples in which solutions to problems are derived from outside the population affected—such as in medicine, the origins of public education—and successfully adopted by that population. And in each and every instance, criticism of such impositions should be in terms of the merit of that which is being imposed. The criticism should *not* be that some alien intrusive element is imposing external values upon another group.

The function of the social scientist in this area is to assess as carefully as possible, through analysis of empirical data, the nature and etiology of a given problem; through careful evaluation of programs associated with policy-relevant issues; and through use of existing analyses, to help determine the effective solutions, the new directions for coping with that problem—including the best way, congruent with democratic values, to *implement* the program designed as the result of such a process.

Part III
HISTORICAL PERSPECTIVES ON
PLANNED SOCIAL INTERVENTION

Although most of this volume is concerned with current or very recent aspects of planned social intervention, the selections in this section describe politicians, social reformers, and social scientists as actors in historic large-scale intervention programs. They not only provide a context for the assessment of current efforts, but also reveal the contributions social scientists can make to intervention planning when they systematically review and analyze past planning efforts.

Huitt, in the preceding section of this anthology (contribution 7), impresses the reader with the labyrinthine nature of federal policy process. Opening Part III with contribution 9, a detailed and vivid account of the evolution of the first federal child-labor law, historian Walter I. Trattner describes in depth the tortuous path that intervention policy often takes on its way through formulation to implementation.

At first glance, the task of enacting child-labor legislation would seem relatively simple. Could anyone disagree that children should not be exploited? Would not the description of innocent youths trapped in ignorance and ill health, slaving sixteen hours a day in dark, airless "sweat shops," incite immediate remedial action? Clearly, such reform was "on the side of the angels." Surely, ameliorative intervention plans would speed through the policy process, overwhelmingly encouraged and supported by righteous legislators and executives. And Woodrow Wilson

—humanitarian and social scientist—was President! The intervention was needed; it was right; it could not fail. But Trattner demonstrates convincingly that "being on the side of angels" is not enough to open the corridors of the policy-process maze. The efforts of social workers, lawyers, ministers, and other citizens (even one social scientist—a sociologist) to influence child-labor legislation became enmeshed and bogged down in an enormous complex of political, economic, and systemic conflicts—North versus South, state versus state, federal versus state, industry versus government, Democrat versus Republican, House versus Senate, committee versus committee, personality versus personality, and so on. Even President Wilson, humanitarian and social scientist that he was, found himself unable at first to support actively a child-labor bill because of what he perceived to be constitutional complications and hazardous precedents.

Child-labor laws, according to Trattner, developed unevenly among the states, and their effectiveness was at best problematical. When the issue was elevated to the federal level, child-labor bills died in committee or were defeated for assorted political and economic reasons—reasons seemingly unrelated to the "merit" of the ameliorative intent. Finally, in 1916, again not without difficulty but with the open support of President Wilson, the first federal child-labor law was passed, though it was not to be implemented at the federal level until twenty years later.

Trattner indicates that it is erroneous to assume that the law was passed simply because it was perceived to be necessary for relieving a pressing social problem. It was passed primarily because arguments about the economic feasibility of the law became more tenable, because public opinion had coalesced in favor of it, and because a President concluded that the law's passing might be influential in a forthcoming election. Trattner quotes a response Wilson directed to reformers who had urged at an early point that the federal government take the lead in establishing a child-labor law. The government, according to Wilson, is "not so much an initiating agency as a responsive one, depending upon the vigorous action of its citizens." When citizen action became widespread and had crystallized to the point where a significant number of votes might be aligned accordingly, the policy process—indisputably a political process—responded.

Is the impact of publics upon the policy system any less today than it was in 1916? If not, then Mills' suggestion in contribution 1 of this anthology, that social scientists should create publics polarized toward salient planned social intervention, is well worth further consideration.

Probably at no point in the history of the United States did the political system respond with as many far-reaching innovative policies as during the Great Depression. Economist Eli Ginzberg and historian Hyman Berman offer a concise description of the immediate effects of the near collapse of the American economy and outline the major governmental efforts of the 1930's designed to stabilize the social and economic systems. Contribution 10 briefly describes New Deal efforts to provide employment, to alter the power of labor in the market, and to implement

a social-security system. This selection is offered to give the reader
a perspective on current intervention programs and current social policy
and to provide a context and sufficient background information for the
two selections which follow.

Historian Byrd L. Jones, in contribution 11, gives us an example of
successful participation by social scientists in the development of national
social policy. He describes the establishment and operations of the National Planning Board, which was inaugurated in 1933 under the New
Deal administration of Franklin D. Roosevelt. The board consisted of an
engineer–city planner (Frederic Delano), a political scientist (Charles
E. Merriam), and an economist (Wesley C. Mitchell), and was commissioned to develop "comprehensive and coordinated plans for regional
areas" based upon scientific surveys and analyses of federal projects.
Merriam and Mitchell's initial membership on the board reflects what
is still practice today: among social scientists, economists and political
scientists are easily the most active in the formulation of planned social
intervention at the federal level.

According to Jones, the National Planning Board wisely concentrated
on a plan for planning—establishing the requisite machinery and the
precedent whereby social scientists and social-science expertise might
be regularly drawn into government service. In good measure the board
members accomplished that task, having supported gainful social-science
research, demonstrated the usefulness of the published findings of social
scientists, written reform-oriented reports, and drawn a detailed agenda
of national social needs. Furthermore, several of the specific intervention
programs they suggested were implemented as part of the New Deal
package.

Why were these three men able to succeed in their intervention tasks?
Jones tells us that Merriam and Mitchell were academic social scientists, but had learned politics through experience, so that they were not
politically naive. The board had solid support from a strong President
(that Delano was the President's uncle was not unhelpful) and were on
the President's staff; thus, they were not isolated in a relatively powerless
commission or committee. But perhaps most important was the fact
that the board was able to recommend not only long-range planning
goals but also specific programs which could be implemented immediately.
In this way, the board was given the opportunity to demonstrate its
usefulness (and the usefulness of social science) to pragmatic politicians and voters.

Delano, Merriam, and Mitchell had their problems, however. Jones
recounts the often conflicting pressures visited upon the three men from
the President and from Congress, and the obstructions which were engendered by competition among various executive advisory groups. The
board (characteristically for social scientists in planned social intervention) was continually faced with dilemmas: How to employ scientific
expertise without contradicting manifest democratic choices; how to
reconcile the discontinuity between individual quality presumed by
democracy and the elitism of planning by experts. Jones reports that

in 1943 the board alienated Congress by the liberalism of its comprehensive plan for postwar America, and was disbanded—but not without first having set the precedent for the Council of Economic Advisers, which would be established in 1946 and remains effectively operating in 1970.

Jones cites the board's belief that national planning required agreement on at least three elements: the right mix of goals; the appropriate policies to be coordinated with those ends; and some social and economic theories which related the various parts. To maintain the continuity of those elements from the onset of planning through implementation is a most difficult endeavor, as we have learned from Trattner, Moynihan, and the symposium in Part II.

Gaston V. Rimlinger, an economist, reveals in contribution 12 the impact of cultural values upon the goals and strategies of planned social intervention. Paternalism in Germany, egalitarianism in England, individualism in the United States, and collectivism in the Soviet Union are discussed as the social perspectives influencing the diverse styles of economic protection of citizens in various countries.

Many of Rimlinger's insights are relevant to Moynihan's critique of the war on poverty. Rimlinger demonstrates that the United States, oriented toward individualism, has been slow to implement social reform unless that reform has been accompanied or rationalized by the promise of material gain. Thus, Rimlinger continues, workmen's compensation finally was enacted on a national level because it was widely perceived to be economically beneficial to employer and employee alike. The broad social-welfare programs of the New Deal were facilitated because they were expected to counter the material losses of the Depression.

It might be argued that intervention programs addressed to such problems as overpopulation and pollution will become functional only when a significant proportion of the polity accepts the programs as personally relevant or profitable. The strategy of personal relevance has, for example, been central to the Surgeon General's somewhat successful national antismoking campaign. Similarly, the Economic Opportunity Act often was supported with the argument that, in the long run, its impact would reduce the personal income tax by relieving the welfare rolls.

Another facet of American individualism is reflected in the widely accepted view that the poor are poor because of personal shortcomings. Early poor laws in the United States, as Rimlinger shows, implied that the poor should reform their character and modify their behavior—that the individual should prevent dependency through his own efforts. No less than in the poor laws of the early 1900's, the Economic Opportunity Act of 1964 espoused the "self-help" ethic. "Maximum feasible participation," though vaguely defined in the legislation, reflected at once a "self-help" and a social-therapy theme quite consistent with individualism. The poor were to "perform" their way out of poverty. Moynihan writes that the mandate for "maximum feasible participation" slipped through the policy process relatively unnoticed, and its implications for political conflict were overlooked. However, one wonders if the statement was perceived to be unremarkable precisely because it was so consistent with the individualism Rimlinger regards as a key American orientation. In fact, that section of the Economic Opportunity Act may actually have gained legislative support for the Act because it gave the war on poverty a nonwelfare look—it was not to be a "giveaway" program. The poor, as well as the rich, were to expend the effort demanded by planned social intervention.

Rimlinger's discussion stimulates the reader to speculate whether social scientists might effectively manipulate the profit motive in the social interest. To do so could be pragmatic, but the degree to which such a strategy would serve to perpetuate the value of individualism makes it imperative that the relevance of that value to contemporary American and world society be considered carefully and debated thoroughly.

THE FIRST FEDERAL CHILD LABOR LAW (1916)

WALTER I. TRATTNER

University of Wisconsin—Milwaukee

LIKE SOIL AND WATER AND FORESTS, THE CHILDREN OF AMERICA ARE A RE-
source that was sadly neglected in the past; each in its turn was exploited, with little regard for the eventual consequences. For the most
part, the lot of young children until the twentieth century was governed
more by economic expediency than by any widespread public concern for
the needs of the child. However, at each stage of America's history there
was a minority who fought to change the prevailing conception of human
as well as natural resources. And in the case of young children, these
efforts led to an eventual awakening of the public consciousness to the
humanitarian and economic, and thus also political, reasons for allowing
such children to be educated, not exploited. This, in turn, resulted in the
passage of the first federal child labor law, considered by some experts
to be one of "the most far-reaching and significant [pieces of] economic
and social legislation in American history before 1933."[1]

EARLY CHILD LABOR REFORM

On the whole, until the twentieth century, Americans not only tolerated
child labor, but looked favorably upon it; they assumed not only that
poor children had to work, but that within reason work was good for all
youngsters. Work removed boys and girls from the unwholesome influence
of the streets; it was, in other words, a cure for juvenile delinquency and
female promiscuity as well as the first rung on the ladder to success. In
addition, American economic conditions and the old Puritan notion, perpetuated by the Poor Richard-Horatio Alger-Gospel of Wealth tradition,
that hard work was virtuous and idleness sinful, reinforced the American
work ethic and approval of child labor. As a result, during the late nineteenth century, young children frequently toiled long hours under brutal-
izing and unhealthy conditions, six and sometimes even seven days a week,
particularly in the cotton textile mills, mines, glass factories, and tene-
ment ("homework") shops of the nation's larger cities.[2]

At this time, however, a ground swell of reform, often referred to as
the "progressive movement," began to sweep the nation. Many Americans
demanded government intervention, at the local, state, and even national
level, in behalf of the poor and the weak; one of their leading aims was
to put an end to the serious social problem of child labor.[3] An increased

[1] Arthur S. Link and William B. Catton, *American Epoch: A History of the United
States Since the 1890s* (New York: Alfred A. Knopf, 1963), pp. 135, 71.

[2] Josephine Goldmark, *Impatient Crusader: Florence Kelley's Life Story* (Urbana:
University of Illinois Press, 1953), p. 2; John Spargo, *The Bitter Cry of the Children*
(New York: The Macmillan Co., 1906), pp. 140–190; Jeremy P. Felt, *Hostages of
Fortune* (New York: Syracuse University Press, 1965), pp. 1–37.

[3] The literature on the "progressive movement" is voluminous, but for an excellent
brief account see, Link and Catton, *American Epoch*, pp. 17–45, 68–91.

♦ First published in *Social Science Quarterly* 50, No. 3 (December, 1969).   105

emphasis upon the importance of education helped create an awareness that the employment of children, for whatever reasons, allowed, and often forced youngsters to grow up in ignorance. The depression of the 1890's, too, brought growing concern over child labor; the anomaly of hundreds of thousands of unemployed adults alongside nearly two million working youngsters awakened many to the problem. Anxiety was also voiced over the effects of industrial accidents, often caused by the lack of dexterity and/or the poor working conditions to which children were exposed. Then there was the health problem; physicians examining working children found startling numbers of them undersized and consumptive. In addition, various reform groups and organizations created to combat specific social problems in the course of their other activities often found themselves confronted with the child labor problem. This was especially true of the settlement houses which were springing up in major American cities throughout the nation; residents seeking to treat the entire "culture of poverty," to use a current term, became increasingly concerned with child labor and its evil effects on the working child and society.

By 1900, 28 states had adopted at least some legislation to protect children working in factories, and ten more had laws regulating child labor in mines. But, as John Braeman has pointed out, most of these laws "were loosely drawn and . . . even more laxly enforced."[4] Moreover, although the problem was not merely a sectional one, the situation was incredible in the South: Alabama, North Carolina, South Carolina, and Georgia— the four leading cotton textile states—had no child labor or compulsory education laws at all. As a result, in 1900 there were nearly two million children between the ages of ten and fifteen gainfully employed in America.[5]

The National Consumers' League was one of the earliest and most important agencies working to impose legal restrictions on the employment of minors. Its general secretary and leading spirit was the fiery and well-known Florence Kelley, licensed attorney and former chief factory inspector of Illinois. As early as the 1890's she had advocated government responsibility for ending the callous exploitation of child labor.[6] She, and

---

[4] John Braeman, "Albert J. Beveridge and the First National Child Labor Bill," *Indiana Magazine of History*, 60 (March, 1964), p. 9; Robert Bremner, *From the Depths: The Discovery of Poverty in the United States* (New York: New York University Press, 1956), pp. 46–85, 123–163, 201–203, 212–217.

[5] The 1,750,178 working children between the ages of 10 and 15 made up approximately 18.2 per cent of the total child population between those ages. A comparison of these figures with those for 1880 shows that both the total number and the percentage of working children between the ages of 10 and 15 had increased during the 20 years, the former from 1,118,356 and the latter from 16.8 per cent. See U. S. Bureau of Census, *Twelfth Census of the United States: 1900* (Washington, D. C.: Government Printing Office, 1904), "Occupations," p. 142; Elizabeth Sands Johnson, "Child Labor Legislation," in John R. Commons *et al.*, *History of Labor in the United States* (4 Vols., New York: The Macmillan Co., 1926–1935), III, pp. 403–437. Earlier, Alabama had had a child labor law; it was repealed, however, in the 1890's.

[6] Goldmark, *Impatient Crusader, passim*. Florence Kelley's writings on child labor are staggering in number. For the best discussion of her views on the matter, see

others, including such prominent social workers as Jane Addams, Grace Abbott, and Julia Lathrop, embarked upon a campaign of public education to prepare the community to press for the passage and enforcement of factory laws. The reformers did not oppose child work, i.e., the performance of odd jobs or chores around the house or on the family farm. Nor did they even oppose employment for wages outside the home, so long as it was work that did not interfere with the child's proper physical, mental, and moral growth. They did oppose, however, what they termed child labor—the employment of children in any occupation at unfit ages, for unreasonable hours, under unhealthful conditions, or while the schools which they should be attending were in session.

Their prevalent message was that such labor was "cruel, stupid, and uneconomical," that it was harmful to the child, that it was unnecessary, and that to permit it to continue was contrary to the best interests of the community; that every dollar spent in preventing such labor and in promoting the health and education of children, was not only a humanitarian, charitable, and ethical gesture, but also essential for community health and welfare, social stability, and orderly progress. The reformers, in other words, were concerned with the bad economic and social consequences of child labor as well as with its inhumanity.[7]

In this respect, the reformers argued that "an ounce of prevention (or protection) was worth a pound of cure." Long hours of taxing labor by young children tended to prevent them from becoming fit for life; it injured their full development—it stifled their bodily and mental growth, as the high incidence of tuberculosis, heart strain, curvature of the spine, and permanent bone and muscle injury among child laborers verified. These things, in turn, often led to a purposeless life, one frequently plagued with delinquency and/or infirmity and dependency. And, as the reformers pointed out, to care for the sick and infirm, the delinquent and criminal, cost the taxpayers millions of dollars each year. It was, therefore, economical and in the public interest to abolish child labor.[8]

Ramona T. Mattson, "A Critical Evaluation of Florence Kelley's Speaking on the Child Labor Issue" (Doctoral Diss., State University of Iowa, 1956). For an understanding of the National Consumers' League see Louis Lee Athey, "The Consumers' Leagues and Social Reform, 1890–1923" (Doctoral Diss., University of Delaware, 1965); Maud Nathan, The Story of an Epoch-Making Movement (New York: Doubleday, Page Co., 1926).

[7] See, for example, Felix Adler, "The Attitude of Society Toward the Child as an Index of Civilization," Annals of the American Academy of Political and Social Science, 29 (Jan., 1907), pp. 135–141 (hereafter cited as Annals); Homer Folks, "The Charity Side of Child Labor," Charities, 10 (March 14, 1903), pp. 254–255, and "The Charity Side of the Child Labor Problem," Charities, 11 (March 19, 1904), pp. 293–294; New York Evening Post, May 19, 1904.

[8] Robert Hunter, Poverty (New York: The Macmillan Co., 1904), pp. 223, 233; Jane Addams, "Child Labor and Pauperism," Proceedings of the National Conference of Charities and Correction (Atlanta: National Conference of Charities and Correction, 1903), p. 117; Florence Kelley, "The Federal Government and the Working Children," Annals, 27 (March, 1906), pp. 289–292; Roy Lubove, The Progressives and the Slums (Pittsburgh: University of Pittsburgh Press, 1962), p. 210.

To the argument that it was essential for children of the poor to work in order to earn money to help support their families, the reformers replied that the burden of such financial responsibility should not be thrust upon the children. And although their studies proved that the number of poor widows supported by the pittances earned by their children was much smaller than was popularly supposed, they advocated—and in many places eventually implemented—"scholarships" or other forms of assistance to needy families in amounts either equivalent to the child's earnings or based on the family's needs, which would enable the child to attend school and allow the family in question to live in accordance with reasonable standards. In any event, the reformers contended that it would not be necessary for boys and girls to seek employment at an early age if the natural wage earner, the father, were paid a living wage. One of the main reasons he did not receive such a wage was child labor, for the presence of youngsters in the labor market depressed the wages of adults forced to compete with them for jobs.[9]

Despite these arguments, so widespread was the evil, and so powerful were the interests profiting from its continuance, that more individuals and other organizations were needed to help eliminate it. The campaign was taken up by concerned citizens all over the nation. Edgar Gardner Murphy, an Episcopal clergyman, shocked by conditions in Alabama's textile mills, became the leader of the fight in the South. Convinced of the need for a more informed public opinion, he formed the Alabama Child Labor Committee, the first such organization of its kind in the United States, in 1901.[10]

In the North, reformers in New York led the way. At the instigation of Miss Kelley, Lillian Wald, founder of New York's Nurses Settlement, and Robert Hunter, head resident at University Settlement, in November 1902 the New York Child Labor Committee was organized.[11] The New York and Alabama committees, and others being established elsewhere, were made up mainly of social workers, reformers, and academicians, who quickly enlisted the support of prominent and wealthy men and women, newspapers, and religious and civic groups. Despite violent opposition, largely from business interests, these organizations waged rather successful campaigns of education, propaganda, and legislation.[12]

[9] Homer Folks, "Poverty and Parental Dependence as an Obstacle to Child Labor Reform," *Annals*, 29 (Jan., 1907), pp. 3–6, and *Changes and Trends in Child Labor and its Control* (New York: National Child Labor Committee, 1938), p. 26; Mary Van Kleeck, "Child Labor in New York City Tenements," *Charities and the Commons*, 19 (Jan. 18, 1908), p. 1417.

[10] Maud King Murphy, *Edgar Gardner Murphy: From Records and Memories* (New York: G. P. Putnam's Sons, 1943), pp. 47–50; Braeman, "Beveridge," p. 10.

[11] Fred S. Hall, *Forty Years, 1902–1942: The Work of the New York Child Labor Committee* (New York: New York Child Labor Committee, 1943); Felt, *Hostages of Fortune*, pp. 38–62.

[12] The New York Child Labor Committee, for example, harmonized the state's incongruous factory and education laws, widened existing legislation, succeeded in partially regulating some previously unregulated areas, and strengthened the penal code dealing with violators of child labor legislation. In less than a year, the committee,

THE NATIONAL CHILD LABOR COMMITTEE AND THE BEVERIDGE BILL

Despite the successes of these committees, and in part because of them, reformers grew increasingly aware of the need for a larger organization that would spearhead a nationwide campaign against the evil and coordinate the activities of the various state and local groups. As a result, when Murphy presented a powerful address on "Child Labor as a National Problem" at the 1903 National Conference of Charities and Correction, it was enthusiastically received; a year later his suggestion was accepted and the National Child Labor Committee was organized.[13]

Under the leadership of Dr. Felix Adler, the noted educator and founder of the Ethical Culture Society (chairman of the board), Homer Folks, executive secretary of the New York State Charities Aid Association (vice chairman), and V. Everit Macy, philantropist-Director of the Title Guarantee Trust Co. (treasurer), the National Child Labor Committee won the support of eminent men and women all over America and secured so prominent and influential a national membership that it commanded a respectful hearing throughout the nation.[14]

At the outset, the real day-to-day work of the committee was in the hands of its general secretary, Dr. Samuel McCune Lindsay, professor of sociology at the University of Pennsylvania and acting Commissioner of Education of Puerto Rico when he accepted the position. Ably assisting Lindsay in carrying out the committee's work in the South was Alexander J. McKelway, Presbyterian clergyman-social worker, while Owen R. Lovejoy, who also gave up the ministry for social work, was named assistant secretary in charge of the organization's work in the North.[15]

The purpose of the NCLC was to supplement, not supplant, the work of local committees. In those states where such committees did not exist, it sought to encourage their creation and then help them "investigate and report the facts about child labor" and protect children by the passage and enforcement of "suitable legislation against premature or otherwise injurious employment." Through research, study, publicity, and legislation, the committee aimed to educate the public as to the sources and consequences of the social injustice and to eliminate it.[16]

To the consternation of some, early in its history the committee decided

---

through the passage of five bills, had brought about more significant changes in New York's child labor laws than had occurred in the entire preceding century. See Felt, *Hostages of Fortune*, pp. 38–62, and "Child Labor Then and Now," *The Independent*, 60 (March 29, 1906), pp. 746–747. For an example of some opposition to the committee's work, see the New York *Evening Post*, March 11, 1903.

[13] New York *Times*, June 4, 1904; Bremner, *From the Depths*, p. 219; Goldmark, *Impatient Crusader*, pp. 92–96; Braeman, "Beveridge," pp. 11–12.

[14] New York *Daily News*, June 5, 1904; *Charities*, 13 (Oct., 1904), p. 47; Braeman, "Beveridge," p. 12; Goldmark, *Impatient Crusader*, p. 92. On the committee were such prominent people as Gifford Pinchot, Lillian D. Wald, Graham Taylor, Paul N. and Paul M. Warburg, Robert W. deForest, Edward T. Devine, Grover Cleveland, Cardinal Gibbons, Hoke Smith, Ben Tillman, and Ben Lindsey.

[15] Braeman, "Beveridge," p. 13.

[16] *Ibid.*, p. 12.

against seeking or even supporting federal child labor legislation. In 1906 the first federal child labor bill was introduced in Congress. Sponsored by Senator Albert Beveridge, of Indiana, the measure was designed to prohibit the interstate transportation of articles produced in factories or mines that had not filed an affidavit that no children under 14 years of age were employed.[17] Some members of the committee ,including Lindsay, Miss Kelley, Folks, and Miss Addams, for example, felt that with the growth of industry on a nationwide basis, many of the problems created in its wake lay beyond the reach of individual states. Therefore, in their opinion, child labor was a national problem in need of uniform federal legislation. The majority, however, did not agree. Most NCLC members were convinced that a more effective and legally tenable means of regulation was through state legislation. Moreover, the National Committee contained many southerners, including Murphy, who were opposed, on constitutional and/or other grounds, to federal legislation in this area. In any event, they, and others felt bound by the committee's charter which called for a "non-federal" approach to the problem. They thought that to support federal legislation in a field previously considered the domain of the states would both handicap the committee in its work in the South, where the worst child labor abuses existed, and prevent it from achieving some of its other aims, such as the establishment of a federal children's bureau.[18] The NCLC, therefore, did not actively support the measure and the Beveridge bill was defeated.

Instead, the National Committee directed its early efforts at obtaining state laws with minimum age and maximum hour provisions, the prohibition of night work, and documentary proof of age for working youngsters. By 1909 it helped secure new child labor laws, or amendments to previous ones, in 43 states; the first ten years of its existence saw the greatest advance ever achieved in this country in the adoption of child labor laws.[19] Yet progress through state regulation was slow and uneven. Although the more progressive states passed relatively satisfactory laws, many of the southern states remained backward. As a result, states with high standards suffered from the competition of the low-standard southern states and every effort

[17] Ibid., pp. 16 ff.; New York Evening Post, Jan. 24, 1907; "A Bill to Prevent the Employment of Children in Factories and Mines," S. 6562 and H. R. 21404 (1906), reprinted in the Annals, 29 (1907), Child Labor Legislation Supplement. Stiff penalties were prescribed for violations by the carriers or for the filing of a false affidavit by the factories or the mines. Enforcement was left in the hands of local federal attorneys.

[18] Edgar Gardner Murphey, The Federal Regulation of Child Labor (Birmingham: Alabama Child Labor Committee, 1907), pp. 1–14; Braeman, "Beveridge," pp. 19–21, 28–30; Homer Folks, "Child Labor and the Law," Charities, 13 (Oct. 1, 1904), p. 1922; Jane Addams, "National Protection for Children," Annals, 29 (Jan., 1907), pp. 57–60; Samuel McCune Lindsay, "Child Labor as a National Problem," Charities, 27 (March, 1906), pp. 73–78; Goldmark, Impatient Crusader, pp. 94–100.

[19] Johnson, "Child Labor," p. 409. The standards the NCLC worked for were a minimum working age of 14 in manufacturing and 16 in mining; a maximum working day of eight hours; prohibition of night work; and documentary proof of age. When the committee was organized in 1904 no state had legislation that met all these requirements; many fell far below them.

to improve a state law brought objections from manufacturers who feared this substandard and "unfair" competition. Moreover, by expending its money and energy in securing the passage of laws, the national and local child labor committees often were unable to successfully follow up on their enforcement; in many places factory inspection was weak and corrupt. Having thus discovered that state regulation was an inadequate solution to the problem, especially after the 1910 census and the publication of a federal investigation into the condition of women and children wage-earners clearly showed that the wretched situation still prevailed and that the gap between the more progressive and more backward states was increasing, not diminishing, most members of the National Committee, and other supporters of child labor regulation, slowly shifted their opinion regarding the need for federal legislation.[20]

THE NATIONAL CHILD LABOR COMMITTEE SUPPORTS FEDERAL LEGISLATION

By 1912 a turning point in the child labor movement had been reached. After six years of concerted effort by the NCLC and other groups, the United States Children's Bureau was created. Directing the bureau to "investigate and report . . . upon all matters pertaining to the welfare of children and child life among all classes of our people," the federal government for the first time recognized the rights of children and the advisability of creating special machinery to study and protect them. This victory apparently freed many National Committee members from their reluctance to support federal child labor legislation lest their action jeopardize establishment of the bureau.[21] More importantly, the "climate of opinion" had shifted: publicity and the dissemination of information, especially during the 1912 presidential campaign, had done its work in opening the eyes of many national leaders and a growing segment of the general public to the existence of intolerable child labor conditions—and the need to do something effective about eliminating them.[22]

[20] The federal study, authorized by President Theodore Roosevelt in 1906, was conducted by the Secretary of Commerce and Labor. Published over three years, from 1910 to 1913, the 19-volume report disclosed that about two million children under 16 were at work in the United States, many under horrible conditions. See U. S. Senate, Document 645, *Report on the Condition of Women and Child Wage-Earners in the United States* (19 Vols., Washington, D. C.: Government Printing Office, 1910–1913), VI, p. 39; U. S. Bureau of Census, *Thirteenth Census of the United States: 1910* (Washington, D. C.: Government Printing Office, 1913), "Occupations," pp. 75, 302 ff.; E. N. Clopper, "The Extent of Child Labor Officially Measured," *Child Labor Bulletin*, 3 (Nov., 1914), pp. 30–36; Johnson, "Child Labor," pp. 439–444; Grace Abbott, "Federal Regulation of Child Labor, 1906–1938," *Social Service Review*, 13 (Sept., 1939), pp. 409–430; Frank J. Bruno, *Trends in Social Work, 1874–1956* (New York: Columbia University Press, 1957), p. 164.

[21] Florence Kelley, "The Federal Child Labor Law," *Survey*, 36 (Aug. 26, 1916), p. 533; "Act Establishing the Children's Bureau (42 U. S. C. Ch. 6) Approved April 9, 1912," in Dorothy E. Bradbury, *Five Decades of Action: A History of the Children's Bureau* (Washington, D. C.: Government Printing Office, 1962), p. 132.

[22] Extremely helpful in this respect was the 1912 presidential election, which educated millions of Americans to the need to put an end to the immense human waste. This was especially true of Theodore Roosevelt's Progressive party, whose platform,

Crucial for the future, however, was the new President's attitude toward solving the problem. Although many social workers supported Theodore Roosevelt in 1912,[23] a number of them met informally in February 1913 with President-elect Woodrow Wilson. During the meeting, characterized by *Survey* magazine as "something in the nature of a hearing on the state of the country,"[24] spokesmen for several reform groups proposed federal action in their respective fields. Although no one specifically presented the case for federal child labor legislation, Owen Lovejoy, who had become the general secretary and executive head of the NCLC, outlined the scope and purpose of the Children's Bureau, emphasizing the need for adequate information on the facts of childhood. To Lovejoy's dismay, Wilson replied that the government was "not so much an initiating agency as a responsive one, depending on the vigorous action of its citizens."[25] The President-elect believed that society was a living organism in which questions of morals and domestic social and economic relations were, at best, state matters which, in any event, would eventually adjust themselves through free competition.[26] His stand on federal regulation of child labor was unmistakable; apparently it had not changed since 1908 when, referring to the Beveridge bill, Wilson had written:

> The proposed federal legislation . . . affords a striking example of a tendency to carry Congressional power over interstate commerce beyond the utmost boundaries of reasonable and honest inference. If the power to regulate commerce between the states can be stretched to include the regulation of labor in mills and factories, it can be made to embrace every particular of the industrial organization and action of the country.[27]

To Lovejoy and the others who stood before him now, five years later, the President-elect declared, "My own party in some of its elements represents a very strong states' rights feeling. It is very plain that you would have to go much further than most interpretations of the Constitution would allow if you were to give the government general control over child

---

boiled down to a phrase, called upon the federal government to become an agency for human welfare by, among other things, abolishing child labor. See New York *Times,* Aug. 14, 1912; George E. Mowry, *Theodore Roosevelt and the Progressive Movement* (New York: Hill and Wang, 1960), p. 273; William Allen White, *The Autobiography of William Allen White* (New York: The Macmillan Co., 1946), pp. 487–488; Paul U. Kellogg, "The Industrial Platform of the New Party," *Survey,* 28 (Aug. 24, 1912), pp. 668–670.

[23] Allen F. Davis, "The Social Workers and the Progressive Party, 1912–1916," *American Historical Review,* 69 (April, 1964), pp. 671–679.

[24] "Governor Wilson and the Social Worker," *Survey,* 29 (Feb. 8, 1913), p. 639.

[25] *Ibid.,* p. 640.

[26] William Diamond, *Economic Thought of Woodrow Wilson* (Baltimore: The Johns Hopkins University Press, 1943), p. 75; John M. Blum, *Woodrow Wilson and the Politics of Morality* (Boston: Little, Brown and Co., 1956), p. 39.

[27] Woodrow Wilson, *Constitutional Government in the United States* (New York: Columbia University Press, 1908), p. 179.

labor throughout the country."[28] Wilson's faith in the free individual did not permit him to fully understand the dynamics of industrial growth, nor that the actions of some men created the need for federal intervention in some areas.

In contrast to the Presidential attitude, however, there were increasing signs of congressional readiness to consider child labor legislation. Senator Ira Copley, of Illinois, and Representative Miles Poindexter, of Washington, Roosevelt supporters in 1912, introduced a bill to fulfill the Progressive party's campaign pledge for federal child labor legislation. And, at the request of the International Child Welfare League, Senator William Kenyon, of Iowa, introduced a similar measure which prohibited the shipment in interstate commerce of goods manufactured in whole or in part by children under 14 years of age and of products of mines or quarries where children under 16 were employed.[29]

Social workers heartily supported these and similar measures. Without officially endorsing any specific proposal, the delegates to the 1913 National Conference of Charities and Correction went on record in favor of cooperating in the battle to control child labor through federal legislation.[30] Lindsay and Miss Kelley, always staunch advocates of federal action, continued to urge the NCLC to work for a "Federal Child Labor Law of some kind."[31] McKelway also stated publicly that the only answer lay with "Uncle Sam," and Felix Adler, after much consideration and hesitation, concurred.[32]

As a result, in April 1913 the NCLC began to reconsider its official policy regarding federal legislation. In December a special three-man committee was appointed to prepare a report summarizing the child labor bills before Congress and to make recommendations to the board of trustees for appropriate action. A month later, after careful study and much debate, the board not only reversed its earlier stand agianst federal legislation, but also endorsed the draft of a new federal bill drawn up by the special committee in consultation with legal experts, the principal provisions of which were similar to the measures already before Congress, but which differed

[28] "Governor Wilson and the Social Worker," *Survey*, 29 (Feb. 8, 1913), p. 640.

[29] "Federal Control Over Anti-Social Labor," *Survey*, 30 (Aug. 16, 1913), p. 615.

[30] Alexander J. McKelway, "Child Labor and Poverty," *Survey*, 30 (April 12, 1913), pp. 60–62.

[31] *Minutes* of the Meetings of the Board of Trustees of the National Child Labor Committee, Jan. 22, 1914, *Minute Books*, National Child Labor Committee Papers, Manuscripts Division, Library of Congress, Washington, D. C. (hereafter cited as *NCLC Minutes*).

[32] Alexander J. McKelway, "Ten Years of Child Labor Reform in the South," *Child Labor Bulletin*, 1 (Feb., 1913), p. 35; Felix Adler, "The Abolition of Child Labor, A National Duty," *Child Labor Bulletin*, 3 (May, 1914), p. 20. By 1914 only nine states had met all the standards recommended by the committee ten years earlier. Twenty-two states still permitted children under 14 years of age to work in factories; 16 demanded no documentary proof of age; 28 allowed children under 16 years to work more than eight hours a day; and 23 states had failed to adopt adequate restrictions on night work for minors.

from them in its enforcement procedures and by specifying the number of hours per day and days per week any child could work.[33] In addition to endorsing the proposed bill, the board resolved that "the officers of the Committee be authorized to take measures to secure its enactment," including the designation of a senator and a representative to introduce it in Congress. Wasting no time, another committee, consisting of Lovejoy and board members Folks, Miss Kelley, Adler, Edward T. Devine, secretary of the Charity Organization Society of New York, and Dr. Stephen Wise, Rabbi of the Free Synagogue of New York City, was created to carry the board's action into effect. The committee immediately requested an appointment with President Wilson and asked Representative A. Mitchell Palmer (Dem.–Pa.) to introduce the bill in the House. Robert L. Owen (Dem.–Okla.) was urged to sponsor the proposal in the Senate.

Wilson met with Adler, McKelway, Devine, and Lovejoy on February 2, 1914. Speaking for the group, Adler reviewed for the President the steps by which the committee had arrived at its decision to seek federal legislation. Then, after referring to Wilson's earlier statement that federal child labor legislation was unconstitutional, Adler asked the President to withhold any adverse comment on the matter so that an educational campaign planned by the committee could be carried forward.[34] Wilson reiterated his conviction that the proposed measure was unconstitutional and would, if passed. open the door to virtually unlimited national economic regulation, but he agreed not "to say anything that might impede the campaign."[35]

Thus, with at least the guarantee of presidential neutrality, the legislative battle began. The Palmer-Owen bill was introduced in Congress, public hearings were held, and the measure was endorsed by a large number of state and local child labor committees and numerous other organizations, including the American Federation of Labor, the American Medical Association, the Farmers' Educational and Cooperative Union of America, the International Child League, and many state federations of women's clubs, church conferences, temperance unions, health officers, and the like.[36]

The only opponents of the measure, at the public hearings, were three

---

[33] NCLC Minutes, Jan. 22, 1914; Owen R. Lovejoy, "Federal Government and Child Labor," Child Labor Bulletin, 2 (Feb., 1914), pp. 19–25. Briefly, the bill forbade the employment of children under 14 years of age in manufacturing and limited the employment of children under 16 to eight hours a day. For mines and quarries, the age limit was fixed at 16. A permanent administrative board, composed of the Secretaries of Labor and Commerce and the Attorney General, was authorized to establish rules and regulations; the Secretary of Labor was to inspect and prosecute violations. Each individual shipment of prescribed articles in violation of the law was to be considered a separate offense with punishment for the first infraction to be a fine of not less than $100 or more than $1,000, or imprisonment of not more than one year nor less than one month, at the discretion of the court. See "Memorandum to the Board of Trustees," NCLC Minutes, April 20, 1914.

[34] "Report of the General Secretary to the Fortieth Meeting of the Board of Trustees," NCLC Minutes, April 20, 1914.

[35] Ibid. Also see Arthur S. Link, Wilson: The New Freedom (Princeton: Princeton University Press, 1956), pp. 256–257.

[36] Bremner, From the Depths, p. 225; Child Labor Bulletin, 3 (May, 1914), p. 3.

representatives of southern cotton textile manufacturers—Lewis Parker, president of the Parker Cotton Mills Co. of South Carolina; Samuel F. Patterson, treasurer of both the Roanoke Mills and the Rose-Mary Manufacturing Co., Roanoke Rapids, North Carolina; and David Clark, editor of the *Southern Textile Bulletin*. They denounced the movement for federal child labor legislation as unconstitutional and an effort by northern agitators to kill the infant industries of the South; they also argued that children had to learn to spin when they were young in order to become skilled laborers and, in any event, youngsters were better off in the mills than they had been on the mountain farms from which they and their parents were brought by the mill owners.[37]

Despite the overwhelming support for the measure, the relatively little overt opposition to it, and its passage in the House by a vote of 233–55, the Palmer-Owen bill did not become law. The Senate Committee on Interstate and Foreign Commerce, to which the bill had gone for consideration, had reported the measure favorably, but the chairman of the committee had the power to keep it from being placed before the full Senate. And while the President remained silent, Senator Lee Overman, of North Carolina, a state which had one of the worst child labor laws in America and had thousands of children working in its cotton mills, exercised that power. As a result, the Palmer-Owen bill was never even debated or voted upon in the upper House.[38] It was perfectly clear that without the aggressive support of the President, a federal child labor bill could not get through the Senate.

Disappointed but undaunted, on March 15, 1915, the NCLC's board of trustees voted to reintroduce the bill at the next congressional session: "promoting of a bill in Congress to forbid interstate commerce in the products of child labor," it resolved, "should continue without hesitation."[39]

1916—THE KEATING-OWEN BILL

Although by this time the President was increasingly concerned with foreign affairs (in Mexico and in Europe), barely mentioning a word about social legislation in a recent address to Congress and the nation,[40] the NCLC remained firm in its determination to press for a federal child labor law; it had Representative Edward Keating (Dem.–Colo.) and Senator Robert Owen (Dem.–Okla.) reintroduce its bill at the start of the next congressional session. At public hearings held by the House Committee on Labor, Lovejoy, McKelway, and Thomas Parkinson of Columbia University's Legislative Reference Bureau, one of the bill's chief authors, urged

---

[37] Testimony of Lewis W. Parker before the Committee on Labor, House of Representatives, 63rd Congress, 2nd Session, May 22, 1914, reprinted in Grace Abbott, ed., *The Child and the State* (2 Vols., Chicago: University of Chicago Press, 1938), I, pp. 477–480; David Clark, "A Demand for a Square Deal," *Child Labor Bulletin*, 4 (May, 1915), p. 37.

[38] *NCLC Minutes*, March 15, 1915; National Child Labor Committee Press Release, March 16, 1915, *NCLC Papers*.

[39] *NCLC Minutes*, March 15, 1915; *Child Labor Bulletin*, 4 (Nov., 1915), p. 1.

[40] *Survey*, 35 (Dec. 11, 1915), p. 281.

passage of the measure. Once again, representatives of southern cotton textile manufacturers opposed the bill; they were, however, joined this time by James A. Emery, chief attorney for the National Association of Manufacturers who, after admitting that his appearance had not been directly authorized by the association, nevertheless claimed to speak for its more than four thousand members.[41]

Legal counsel for the cotton manufacturers was W. W. Kitchen, former governor of North Carolina and brother of Claude Kitchen, the House floor leader. As usual, opposition to the proposed measure rested on the argument that such a law would severely limit the growth of the southern cotton textile industry. It would, as a result, prove detrimental to poor parents and their children whose "inherent right" to work was being abridged. Finally, it was an invasion of the domain of local self-government; its passage would prove to be a deplorable error opening the way for eventual extensive interference with states' rights.[42]

Despite the opposition, more vociferous this time than in the past, after issuing 317 pages of testimony and a 41-page report, on January 15, 1916, the House Labor Committee recommended passage of the bill and placed it on the order of the day for January 26. Supporters of the measure were optimistic, although cautious not to become too complacent when, several days later, the final vote was taken. With the help of Republican minority leader James R. Mann, of Illinois, the Keating-Owen bill passed the House by a 343–46 vote that crossed party lines.

As feared, however, action in the Senate was not as rapid. No new arguments were heard in opposition, but, as a *Survey* editor acidly commented, "the same undertakers who officiated so successfully last year [at the burial] are again proceeding with the funeral arrangements."[43] Nevertheless, in April, the Senate Committee on Interstate and Foreign Commerce recommended passage of a slightly amended version of the bill, one which the NCLC and its legal counsel found acceptable.[44] Republican minority leader Jacob H. Gallinger, of New Hampshire, reported that his party was solidly behind the measure, and it was believed that a majority of Democrats also favored its enactment. Once again, however, Senator Overman

---

[41] Arthur S. Link, *Wilson: Campaigns for Progressivism and Peace, 1916–1917* (Princeton: Princeton University Press, 1965), p. 57; Abbott, *The Child and the State, I*, pp. 480–481.

[42] *Outlook*, 112 (Jan. 26, 1916), p. 169; *New Republic*, 6 (Feb., 1916), p. 9. Last minute opposition also appeared in the form of testimony before the House Committee on Labor by Mrs. A. A. Birney and Miss Mary S. Garrett who, claiming to represent the 100,000 members of the National Congress of Mothers, objected to the 14-year minimum as too high a limitation on children needing or wanting to work. Immediately, mothers' clubs of Pennsylvania (which, interestingly, was the only northern state whose Senators were to vote against the Keating-Owen bill) rallied at least 15 other state clubs in favor of the measure, urging their members to communicate to congressmen their support of the bill. The battle between clubs raged for a time in the "Letters to the Editor" column of *Survey*, but appears to have had little effect on congressional action.

[43] "Working Children and the Senate," *Survey*, 36 (April 15, 1916), p. 69.

[44] *Ibid.*

controlled the fate of the bill. Moreover, even if he allowed it out of committee, the Democratic caucus, which controlled the order in which bills were considered, was dominated by southerners who were strongly opposed to the measure. As a result, the situation looked bad for the reformers early in the summer of 1916 when attention turned to national party conventions and the approaching presidential election.

PRESIDENT WILSON AND THE FEDERAL CHILD LABOR LAW

Early in June President Wilson pondered possible planks for his party's platform, to be written a couple of weeks later. Among the domestic issues, a major question concerned Democratic endorsement of social legislation, including, of course, a federal child labor bill. In the hope of attracting some Progressives to the Democratic party, Senator Owen, co-sponsor of the child labor bill before Congress, suggested that the party adopt the social justice plank of the 1912 Progressive party platform.[45] Wilson, however, expressed the fear that many of the Progressive party platform principles existed "merely in thesis, because they affected matters controlled by the state and not by the national government."[46]

At the President's request for a memorandum outlining issues which "we could all agree upon," Owen drew up a general plank that endorsed all the popular social justice proposals and at the same time managed to evade the states' rights question. Among its provisions was a pledge for "the harmonious exercise of the public authority of State and Nation in . . . the prohibition of child labor."[47] This rather vague proposal, which Wilson supported, was, however, replaced in the party platform adopted on June 16 by a definite commitment to *federal* legislation which read: "We favor the speedy enactment of an effective Federal Child Labor Law." The Republican party also adopted a plank favoring the enactment of federal child labor legislation.[48]

When Congress reconvened, the Democratic senatorial caucus, pledged to support federal child labor legislation sometime in the next four years, under pressure from its southern members decided not to consider the Keating-Owen bill (still before the Senate Committee on Interstate and Foreign Commerce) during the remainder of the current session. McKelway, whose headquarters had been moved to Washington so that he could more effectively lobby for the bill, lost no time warning the President that failure to enact a child labor bill would cost the Democrats a great deal of support in the coming election. Pointedly reminding Wilson that Republicans in Congress had agreed to facilitate the passage of such a measure and that his opponent for the presidency, former Chief Justice Charles Evans Hughes, was expected to endorse their action and a compre-

[45] Link, *Wilson: Campaigns*, p. 39.
[46] *Ibid.*
[47] *Ibid.*, p. 40.
[48] The Republican party platform went further, stating, "We favor . . . the enactment and rigid enforcement of a Federal child labor law." See, Kirk H. Porter and Donald B. Johnson, eds., *National Party Platforms, 1840–1964* (Urbana: University of Illinois Press, 1966), pp. 207, 199.

hensive social justice program, McKelway expressed fear that "in spite of the progressive record of the Democratic Party . . . the action on the child labor bill will be regarded as [the] . . . test of [the party's] genuine interest in humane measures opposed by commercial interests."[49]

Wilson, who had never actively opposed the child labor bill, but rather in the past had merely refused to support it, apparently concluded that McKelway (together with Secretary of the Navy Josephus Daniels, who had written in a similar vein) was right: victory could be achieved only by convincing progressives that the Democratic party was the party of reform.[50] With political astuteness, the President assessed both the public pressure for the immediate enactment of a federal child labor law and the means by which he could transmit that pressure to his own party leaders. After much thought, he decided to postpone acceptance of his renomination for the presidency by the Democratic party until he received assurance from party leaders that the child labor bill would be pushed through to enactment during the current session.[51] That assurance came on July 18 when, to their surprise, Democratic leaders were summoned to the President's room in the Capitol to meet personally with Wilson, who had secretly ascended the Hill to remind them of the political realities of the situation.[52] Apparently the exigencies of political expediency convinced them, as indeed they had convinced Wilson, that it was "of the utmost importance that the child labor bill . . . be passed at this session."[53] "I am encouraged to believe that the situation has changed considerably," the President wrote to McKelway after his trip to Capitol Hill.[54] And, indeed, it had; one week later the Democratic caucus placed the Keating-Owen bill on its priority list.

On August 3, 1916, Senator Joe T. Robinson (Dem.–Ark.), rose on the floor of the U.S. Senate and moved that the child labor bill be considered. Supporting and opposing arguments followed, with the debate revolving largely about the issue of constitutionality. Senators Thomas W. Hardwick (Dem.–Ga.) and Ellison Smith (Dem.–S. C.) led the opposition. Standing firmly on traditional states' rights grounds, they questioned both the right of the federal government to enter the sphere of child labor and the need

49 Alexander J. McKelway to Woodrow Wilson, July 17, 1916, McKelway Papers, Manuscript Division, Library of Congress, Washington, D. C. (hereafter cited as McKelway Papers). Also see, Link, Wilson: Campaigns, p. 58, and Woodrow Wilson and the Progressive Era (New York: Harper and Row, 1954), p. 227.

50 Wilson, of course, was aware that the incident presented to the American public "the spectacle of the President of the United States fighting the minority of his party with the aid of leaders of the opposition." See "The President and the Mill-Child," Literary Digest, 53 (Aug. 5, 1916), p. 290.

51 Link, Wilson: Campaigns, pp. 58–59; "President Urges Child Labor Bill," Independent, 87 (July 31, 1916), p. 150.

52 "Passing the Federal Child Labor Law," Child Labor Bulletin, 5 (Aug., 1916), pp. 91–93; Link, Woodrow Wilson and the Progressive Era, p. 277, and Wilson: Campaigns, p. 59.

53 Survey, 36 (July 22, 1916), p. 424.

54 Woodrow Wilson to Alexander J. McKelway, July 19, 1916, McKelway Papers; Link, Wilson: Campaigns, p. 59, and Woodrow Wilson and the Progressive Era, p. 227.

for further legislation to supplement what they felt was sufficient and effective state regulation. As Senator Smith put it, "I am concerned with the Federal Government interfering with my domestic affairs. . . . What I am opposed to in this bill is its hypocritical plea that it is for the child. . . . I do not propose to jeopardize State rights by opening this Pandora's box and allowing the Federal Government to say who shall work and under what conditions they shall work, provided the product of that work enters interstate commerce. . . ."[55] Senator Ben Tillman (Dem.–S. C.), another staunch opponent of the measure, also took the floor and suggested that a

> national child-labor law, . . . [even if] it accomplished nothing, would still be notice to the world that the United States Government had assumed the right to enter the homes of the people and tell them how they must rear their children, and how, when, and where they must work them. That right once established, [the Senator feared,] all the evils of centralization would inevitably follow.[56]

Proponents of the bill were led by Senators Robinson, Albert B. Cummins (Rep.–Iowa), LeBaren B. Colt (Rep.–R. I.), and Charles Townsend (Rep.–Mich.). Their case rested largely on recent Supreme Court decisions, particularly those upholding the so-called Lottery and White Slave Acts, which they felt lent legal support to the Keating-Owen bill.[57] Reflecting what proved to be the majority's sentiment, Senator Townsend affirmed "that Congress has the right to determine what matters are considered of sufficient importance to bring them under the wide scope of the commerce provisions of the Constitution." And although he admitted that "it is perhaps the longest step that has thus far been taken," he concluded nevertheless that "it is in the same direction of established precedents."[58] When the measure came to a vote, most Senators obviously agreed. A last minute attempt by Senator Overman to weaken the bill by adding an amendment that would have delayed the date of its implementation by three years was rejected. Final roll call showed that 52 Senators favored the Keating-Owen bill, while 12 opposed it; there were 31 abstentions. Ten southern Democrats and the two Republican Senators from Pennsylvania

---

[55] U. S. Congressional Record, 64th Congress, 3rd Session, 1916, 53, Part 12, p. 12288.
[56] Ibid., p. 12294.
[57] In both of these instances the U. S. Supreme Court recognized an increasing sphere of federal police power under the congressional power to regulate interstate commerce. Specifically, in Champion v. Ames [188 U. S. 321 (1903)] the Supreme Court, by a 5–4 vote, upheld a federal law forbidding the shipment of lottery tickets in interstate commerce. In doing so, the Court dwelt at length upon the supreme and plenary powers of Congress in the field of interstate commerce, stating that such power, which could rightfully touch upon any problem that could be correctly construed as interstate commerce, was absolute. In Hoke v. United States [227 U. S. 308 (1913)] the Court upheld the constitutionality of the (Mann) White Slave Traffic Act of 1910 which, by making it a felony to transport a woman from one state to another for immoral purposes, was another instance of the congressional use of the police power to regulate interstate commerce.
[58] U. S. Congressional Record, 64th Congress, 3rd Session, 1916, 53, Part 12, p. 12284.

(a state which had more child laborers than all the southern states combined) had voted for its defeat.[59]

On September 1, 1916, President Wilson signed the Keating-Owen bill into law. "I want to say with what real emotion I sign this bill," he remarked to a group of reformers present at the signing, "because I know how long the struggle has been to secure legislation of this sort and what it is going to mean to the health and to the vigor of the country, and also to the happiness of those whom it affects. It is with genuine pride," the President concluded, "that I play my part in completing this legislation. I congratulate the country and felicitate myself."[60]

There appears to be little evidence to suggest that Wilson had shifted his political philosophy to accept, in principle, widespread use of federal authority to benefit special, underprivileged classes, including children.[61] His insistence that the Democratic party pass the Keating-Owen bill in the summer of 1916 was chiefly a belated but effective recognition of the demands of political expedience, a move perceptively summed up by Senator Hardwick, a staunch opponent of the measure who, during the Senate debate on it stated, "I am not sure that the President has changed his mind on this question, even if he has . . . changed his position."[62]

Nevertheless, whatever his motivation, Wilson's responsibility for passage of the act did not go unheeded. "If President Wilson was seeking political credit when he insisted on the passage of this measure, he is entitled to it now," editorialized the New York *Tribune*, a consistent Republican critic of the administration. "While he was merely taking up near its end the campaign carried on by reformers for years, he gave aid when it was much needed and he took his stand regardless of offending wealthy Southerners whose political support he may need."[63]

Or, as Judge Ben B. Lindsey, a member of the National Child Labor

[59] The bill, as finally approved, stipulated that
> No producer, manufacturer, or dealer shall ship or deliver for shipment in interstate or foreign commerce any article or commodity the product of any mine or quarry, situated in the United States, in which within thirty days prior to the time of removal of such product therefrom children under the age of sixteen years have been employed or permitted to work, or any article or commodity the product of any mill, cannery, workshop, factory, or manufacturing establishment . . . in which within thirty days prior to the removal of such product therefrom children under the age of fourteen years have been employed or permitted to work. . . .

In addition, the measure included hours provisions and specified administrative details and penalties for violations. While it provided less severe penalties than the Beveridge bill of a decade earlier, the Keating-Owen bill set higher age limits and also spelled out more carefully the administrative apparatus for implementing the statute than did the earlier proposal. For the full text of the measure ("An Act to Prevent Interstate Commerce in the Products of Child Labor and for Other Purposes") see Abbott, *The Child and the State*, I, pp. 483–486.

[60] New York *Times*, Sept. 2, 1916.

[61] Diamond, *Economic Thought*, p. 73.

[62] U. S. *Congressional Record*, 64th Congress, 3rd Session, 1916, 53, Part 12, p. 12070.

[63] Quoted in "The Democrat's Child-Labor Law," *Literary Digest*, 53 (Sept. 2, 1916), p. 547.

Committee, put it: "Your splendid attitude on this question and willingness to change from your former position with the states' rights Democrats to Federal or National control when it became clearly apparent that it is the best method to put an end to certain evils or advance certain rights," he wrote to Wilson, "should be sufficient proof to wavering Progressives that the Democratic Party is as willing as the Republican Party in proper cases to put the National welfare above state considerations."[64] Apparently it was, for although the peace issue no doubt helped Wilson achieve his narrow victory in 1916, he certainly would not have recaptured the White House had it not been for the fact that the child labor law (and other social justice measures) won for him the support of many progressive Republicans and independents who had followed Theodore Roosevelt in 1912.[65]

CONCLUSION—THE LEGACY

However happy the reformers were over what they expected to be the immediate effect of the new law—they estimated that the lives of from 100,000 to 150,000 children would be brightened by it—they also, of course, recognized that the statute only affected those laboring in industries engaged in interstate commerce, leaving approximately 1,850,000 youngsters untouched by federal jurisdiction.[66] The measure, then, they felt, marked not the end, but in many ways a fresh start in efforts to control child labor. But, as the reformers pointed out, it was precisely here where the principle value of the law lay, for by establishing a minimum standard of protection, by standardizing the machinery and methods of enforcement, and, above all, by putting federal authority behind the principle of the abolition of child labor, the reformers expected it to lead to the ultimate extinction of child labor.[67]

Unfortunately, the law's potential effectiveness was never fully demonstrated. On the grounds that it deprived his two sons (both under 16) of their constitutional rights to liberty and property, specifically their right to work an 11-hour day, three days before the act went into effect Roland Dagenhart of North Carolina obtained a permanent injunction against its enforcement. And on June 3, 1918, in a 5-4 decision, the United States Supreme Court ruled that the law was unconstitutional. Pointing out that the previously cited lottery case concerned interstate shipment of goods in themselves harmful, the majority in the famous *Hammer v. Dagenhart* case held that the child labor law both transcended the delegated authority

[64] Quoted in Link, *Wilson: Campaigns*, p. 60.
[65] *New York Post*, Oct. 14, 1916; Jane Addams, *Second Twenty Years at Hull House* (New York: The Macmillan Co., 1930), p. 46; E. David Cronon, *The Political Thought of Woodrow Wilson* (Indianapolis: The Bobbs-Merrill Co., 1965), Intro., p. lv; Davis, "Social Workers," p. 688.
[66] *NCLC Minutes*, Sept. 30, 1916, and Oct. 3, 1917; *Survey*, 38 (July 21, 1917), p. 357.
[67] Helen C. Dwight, "Beyond the Reach of the Law," *Survey*, 37 (Jan. 6, 1917), p. 397; *Survey*, 40 (June 8, 1918), p. 283.

of Congress over commerce and exacted power over a purely local matter to which federal authority did not extend.[68]

Although the issue was dead for the time being,[69] the fight had not been in vain. The national campaign which resulted in the passage of the federal law did much to awaken the general public to the necessity of protecting children against premature employment and to raise the legal standards of many state laws.[70] Moreover, the act remained a symbol of the changing role of the federal government in providing for the welfare of its citizens. Most importantly, however, it provided a firm foundation for some of the most significant elements of the larger social justice movement that came to fruition during the Great Depression.[71] More than 20 years later, those who had fought so hard for the Keating-Owen Act were vindicated when the U.S. Supreme Court, in ruling upon the Fair Labor Standards Act (1938), which, among other things, forbade the shipment in interstate commerce of any goods manufactured in whole or in part by children under 16, ruled:

> The conclusion is inescapable that *Hammer v. Dagenhart* was a departure from the principles which have prevailed in the interpretation of the commerce clause both before and since the decision and that such vitality, as a precedent, as it then had has long since been exhausted. It should be and now is overruled.[72]

[68] *Hammer v. Dagenhart* [247 U. S. 251 (1918)]; Alpheus T. Mason and William M. Beaney, *American Constitutional Law* (Englewood Cliffs, N. J.: Prentice-Hall, Inc., 1958), pp. 277–281. For an excellent account of the Supreme Court and the constitutional issues involved in the first, and second, federal child labor laws, see a work published after this article was completed: Stephen B. Wood, *Constitutional Politics in the Progressive Era* (Chicago: University of Chicago Press, 1968).

[69] A second attempt at federal action against child labor was made in 1919, this time through the use of the taxing power; Congress levied a prohibitive tax on products manufactured in whole or in part by children. This, too, was declared unconstitutional by the U. S. Supreme Court when, in 1922, by an 8–1 decision in the case of *Bailey v. Drexel Furniture Co.* [259 U. S. 42 (1922)], the majority declared that Congress could not use the taxing power to accomplish an unconstitutional regulation. See, Mason and Beaney, *American Constitutional Law*, pp. 327–329.

With the defeat of this measure, the reformers then resorted to an attempt to enact a constitutional amendment which gave to Congress, without impairing the states' authority in the area, the "power to limit, regulate, and prohibit the labor of persons under eighteen years of age." Although the proposal received nonpartisan backing and overwhelmingly passed through both houses of Congress, by June 1924, when it came before the states for ratification a bitter campaign to defeat it was launched; as a result, it was never ratified by the requisite number of states. See Richard B. Sherman, "The Rejection of the Child Labor Amendment," *Mid-America*, 45 (Jan., 1963), pp. 3–17.

[70] U. S. Children's Bureau, *Administration of the First Federal Child-Labor Law* (Washington, D.C.: Government Printing Office, 1921).

[71] Link and Catton, *American Epoch*, pp. 429–430.

[72] *United States v. Darby*, [312 U. S. 100 (1941)]; Mason and Beaney, *American Constitutional Law*, pp. 305–307.

·10·
THE GREAT DEPRESSION

ELI GINZBERG
Columbia University

HYMAN BERMAN
University of Minnesota

J
UST AS IT WAS DIFFICULT FOR CONTEMPORARIES TO RECOGNIZE THE END
of the New Era it is difficult even now to reach agreement as to when
in the 1930's the forces unleashed by the Great Depression had spent
themselves. Some contend that in the all-important matter of employment the depression failed to lift throughout the whole of the decade
—although it was mitigated after Mr. Roosevelt took office. They say
that the major upward movement in the economy, at least as measured
by the full recovery in employment, did not begin until the war mobilization boom of the early 1940's. The student of business fluctuations
dates the Great Depression from 1929 to 1933; he notes that the recovery
in the following years left large numbers of the labor force still on the
unemployment rolls; he calls attention to the sharp depression of 1937–38
but he insists that a strikingly rapid recovery followed 1938.

The economic historian has an alternative interpretation: his reading that the whole of the 1930's was a period of poor economic performance is underscored by the fact that the basic indices for 1939 showed
no significant gains over 1929. The most telling support for this appraisal
is the fact that a high level of unemployment persisted, the key measure
of the performance of a modern industrial economy.

The index of common stocks—the important harbinger of the prosperous twenties—had risen from about 8.5 per cent in 1923 to over 26.0
in 1929, or a gain of more than 300 per cent. By 1932 it had fallen to
under 7, a decline of over 70 per cent within a period of three years.[1]
An interesting point to recall is the failure of so many to acknowledge
that the economy had run into stormy weather.

There was a decline of almost 26 billion dollars in the value of securi-
ties listed on the Stock Exchange in the fall of 1929. Irving Fisher, an
economist of international repute, commented on this tremendous drop
as being "so full of sound and fury, signifies little." He argued that since
only about 1 per cent of the population earned over $9000 per annum,
the vast majority of the population would not be affected by the vagaries
of the stock market.[2] Henry Ford, an early apostle of the doctrine of
high wages as a lever to economic prosperity, publicly reaffirmed his

[1] *Historical Statistics of the United States*, U.S. Dept. of Commerce, 1960, p. 573.
[2] Ginzberg, Eli, *The Illusion of Economic Stability*, Harper & Bros., 1939, p. 146.

✦ Reprinted with permission of The Macmillan Company from *The American
Worker in the Twentieth Century: A History through Autobiographies* by Eli Ginzberg
and Hyman Berman. © by The Free Press of Glencoe, a Division of The Macmillan
Company, 1963. The footnotes have been renumbered to run in sequence throughout the selection.

faith in his theory shortly after the stock market broke by recommending that: "Wages must not come down, they must not even stay at their present level; they must go up."[3]

Since the seven good years of the 1920's had been preceded by the expansion of World War I and the immediate postwar years—marred only by the sharp liquidation of 1921–22; and since, in the much larger sweep of time from the recovery of the economy after the depression of the mid-1890's until the outbreak of World War I, business had escaped any serious period of liquidation (for the panic of 1907 was quickly contained)—it is not surprising that the country's leadership remained optimistic after the stock market collapse of 1929. They had good reason to hope and expect that at the worst there would be some radical re-adjustments in financial markets and possibly even in commodity prices. But in light of their experience, and more particularly because of the absence of overt inflationary trends during the 1920's, they did not anticipate a major falling off in production, employment, or income.

But as it turned out they were completely wrong. President Roosevelt stated that "the almost complete collapse of the American economic system marked the beginning of my administration."[4]

A few figures can go far to substantiate the correctness of the President's judgment. The number unemployed in 1929 was about 1.5 million, just over 3 per cent of the labor force; in 1933 the total number out of work was just under 13 million, approximately 25 per cent of the entire labor force. At no time during the rest of the decade did the total drop below 7 million or 14 per cent; in three years—1934, 1935, and 1938—the total fluctuated around 10 to 11 million, or in the neighborhood of 20 per cent.[5]

But even these figures understate the plight of the working man during these years. If the work force is defined in terms of non-farm employees, then at the height of the depression more than one out of every three workers was out of a job and at no time throughout the rest of the decade did the percentage drop below one in five.[6]

While, of course, those who lost their jobs suffered the most, many who held them also endured privation. There was for instance a decline in the average weekly hours of work for production workers from over 44 in 1929 to under 35 in 1934, a reduction of about 20 per cent. Average hourly earnings declined during this same period by about the same percentage, with a resulting drop in average weekly earnings of almost 33 per cent. While the price index of consumer goods also declined during those years, many workers were attempting to pay off debts that they accumulated earlier with dollars that had become more valuable.[7]

---

[3] *Ibid.*, p. 153.

[4] *Ibid.*, p. 172.

[5] *Historical Statistics, op. cit.*, p. 73.

[6] Lebergott, Stanley, "Annual Estimates of Unemployment in the United States, 1900–54," in *The Measurement and Behavior of Unemployment*, A Conference of the Universities, National Bureau for Economic Research, Princeton, 1957, p. 215.

[7] *Historical Statistics, op. cit.*, p. 92.

These averages hide about as much as they disclose. In a decade in which many more were seeking work than there was work available, a great many in the laboring population were hardly able to support their families. Some employers paid as little as 5 cents an hour; others were unable to meet their payrolls at all; many could offer only a few days of employment a month to the few members of their work force for whom they felt a special obligation.

In recognition of the enormity of the problem, particularly the inadequacy of the job market, the New Deal was established to provide income and to put people to work on projects financed and operated by the federal government. Between 1934 and 1940 there were approximately 300,000 young men at all times in the Civilian Conservation Corps. The National Youth Administration provided part-time employment for between 500,000 and 750,000 students during those five years. Thus, more than a million young people directly benefited from these two programs. Between 2 and 3 million men and women were on the rolls of the Work Projects Administration, which spent in the neighborhood of 1.5 billion dollars annually. Other federal programs provided employment for an additional half million persons or so.[8]

In the depression years the various programs of the federal government gave direct employment to almost 4.5 million persons. This represented almost half of the total employment provided by manufacturing.

In addition to the New Deal's direct efforts to provide employment, it acted on two other fronts which had tremendous impact in the long run: it altered the power of labor in the market and provided a large number of new benefits to the working man through the development of a social security system.

As might have been expected, the trade union movement, which had been losing ground steadily since the end of the World War I boom, was all but extinguished in the collapse of the economy during the years of the Great Depression. Reported membership declined from about 3.6 million to 2.9 million in the four years 1929 to 1933, but many who were carried on the rolls had long before stopped paying their dues. The American Federation of Labor, with a membership of only slightly above 2 million in 1933, was back to the level where it had been on the eve of World War I, two decades previously. In the interim, of course, there had been a marked expansion of the industrial sector, which means that organized labor's relative position had worsened appreciably.[9]

When President Roosevelt established the National Industrial Recovery Act in 1933, a section was inserted which provided "that employees shall have the right to organize and bargain collectively . . . free from interference, restraint and coercion of employers of labor. . . ." In large part, this provision was made in order to balance the opportunities offered industry under the NIRA codes to establish prices through joint action.

[8] *Ibid.*, p. 200.
[9] *Ibid.*, p. 97.

Two years later Congress was ready to incorporate into permanent legislation the right of workers to join unions of their own choosing. The National Labor Relations Act went far to alter the relative power of employer and employees in the struggle of the marketplace. Among the potent factors operating in this direction was the National Labor Relations Board, established under the provisions of the Act, which through interpretation and administration reinforced the expanding strength of organized labor.

A friendly President, supportive legislation, and administrative agencies that were inclined to be sympathetic to its claims all contributed to the truly spectacular gains made by organized labor in the latter part of the decade. The ranks of organized labor swelled from under 3 million members in 1933 to over 8 million in 1938—a gain of 170 per cent in five years.[10] It is probable that an important precipitant of the sharp business depression of 1938–39, which reinforced the effect of the drop in governmental spending, was the immobilization and frustration which beset the business community as it watched the ever-greater accretion of power by the trade union movement. Except for two unusual years—1919, which marked the postwar inflation, and 1934, which marked the beginning of the recovery from the depth of the Great Depression— wages rose more in 1936–37 than in any previous year in American history: average earnings per hour of work in manufacturing rose almost 7 cents on a base of 54 cents or by approximately 13 per cent in a single year.[11] Much of the momentum which helped to increase membership and improve conditions came from the industrial unions, old and new, which had formed themselves into the Congress of Industrial Organizations under the leadership of John L. Lewis.

The year 1935 was significant beyond all other years in American labor history because it saw the passage not only of the Wagner Act but also of the Social Security Act. It is ironic but nevertheless revealing of the ideological orientation of American labor that as late as 1932 the Convention of the American Federation of Labor looked askance at governmental programs of unemployment insurance. Labor was almost as wary of governmental action as was management. Nevertheless the lesson of the Great Depression and its aftermath of continuing high-level unemployment was finally learned. One important segment of the legislation passed in 1935 was the establishment of a federal-state unemployment insurance system.

The Act also set up the first system of general benefits for workers who were no longer able or willing to work. Benefits were paid to workers after they reached 65, on a sliding scale depending on their previous earnings and contributions. Later amendments, in 1939, made benefits available to certain dependents of the wage earner after his retirement or death.

Unemployment and old age benefits were based on the contribution

[10] *Ibid.*, p. 98.

[11] Rees, Albert, *New Measures of Wage-Earner Compensation in Manufacturing,* Occ. Paper 73, National Bureau of Economic Research, New York, 1960, p. 3.

principle, but the Social Security Act also provided for public assistance programs financed by federal, state, and local governments to provide essential assistance to persons on the basis of need without reference to their past earnings or contributions. While several states had been providing various types of assistance to needy persons for some years, their programs had been very uneven and a great many persons in want had been receiving nothing or very little.[12]

The impact of the new federal legislation in the area of labor relations was immediate; more time was required before the economic and social implications of the new social security system became manifest.

The position of the American worker had been reduced in the 1930's to a theretofore unknown low. Millions lost their jobs and homes, and the prospects were dim for many ever again to improve their positions. Their hopes were shattered. But at the very same time, organized labor gained a new lease on life, and government acted to insure that in the future the working man would never again have to bear so much of the costs of the instability that are characteristic of a dynamic industrial economy.

[12] *The American Worker's Fact Book*, U.S. Dept. of Labor, 1960.

·11·
A PLAN FOR PLANNING IN THE NEW DEAL

BYRD L. JONES
University of Massachusetts at Amherst

F OR A BRIEF PERIOD DURING THE EARLY NEW DEAL, AMERICANS SEEMED
ready for planning as a cure for economic imbalances. Conventional
accounts have explained the rapid collapse of that support. President
Roosevelt staffed an alphabet soup of agencies with professors—each with
a scheme to remake America. Despite repeated efforts, however, the
planners' basic impracticality brought failure. Declared unconstitutional,
the National Industrial Recovery Act (NRA) and the Agricultural Adjustment Act (AAA) left not a plan behind them. Thus, the story usually continues, Roosevelt turned toward restoring competition; and effective management of the national economy awaited the Keynesian revolution. Certainly the NRA industrial codes failed, yet the account has missed much
of the significance of the planning function in the New Deal. In 1933 and
1934 the National Planning Board adapted that function to the American
government with its tradition of laissez-faire. Its success should cast some
light on what happened to planning during the New Deal.[1]

In the preface to the NRA authorizing public works, Congress had stated
its intention to encourage cooperation among firms and between labor and
management, to stimulate recovery by increasing employment and purchasing power, "and otherwise to rehabilitate industry and to conserve
natural resources." That responsibility for a healthy economy implied intelligent foresight—a commitment to national planning seldom evident
during the experimental hurly-burly of the early New Deal. On July 20,
1933, Harold Ickes, as head of the Emergency Administration of Public
Works, appointed the National Planning Board. Specifically, the Board
was to develop "comprehensive and coordinated plans for regional areas"
based upon scientific surveys and analyses of federal projects.[2]

Realistically assessing their problems and limitations, the Board worked
on "a plan for planning." Not proponents of some blueprint for recovery,
the Board sought an institutional arrangement which would bring planners
into government service. Presumably, men trained in various social sciences would advise the President about future trends, institute research,
help coordinate executive programs, and generally apply their knowledge
to problems of government at all levels. In spite of weak support in Con-

[1] For examples of the conventional account, see James M. Burns, *Roosevelt: The
Lion and the Fox* (New York: Harcourt, Brace & World, 1956), pp. 472–477; the
clearest exposition of Arthur Schlesinger's views is his chapter in John M. Blum, *et al.*,
The National Experience (New York: Harcourt, Brace & World, 1963), pp. 649–672,
esp. pp. 660–661; and Ellis W. Hawley, *The New Deal and the Problem of Monopoly*
(Princeton: Princeton University Press, 1966), pp. 133–134, 139, 186.

[2] Congressional intent for NRA cited in Merle Fainsod, *et al.*, *Government and the
American Economy* (New York: W. W. Norton, 1959), p. 530; executive order given
in National Planning Board, *Final Report—1933–34* (Washington, D.C.: Government
Printing Office, 1934), p. 1.

gress and opposition from Secretary Dern and the Army Engineers, the Board flourished for a decade. In 1934, 1935, and 1939, new executive orders brought changes in the title of the planning Board, but two of the three members and its staff served until 1943 (when its liberal and comprehensive plan for postwar America alienated Congress). Its record for durability measured its success.[3]

BACKGROUND OF THE BOARD

The Board—Chairman Frederic A. Delano, Charles E. Merriam, and Wesley C. Mitchell—represented three traditions of planning ideas. Delano, an engineer and railroad president, had become involved with city planning in 1904 when he sought a consolidated terminal in Chicago. Later he widened his scope as chairman of the Committee on the Regional Plan of New York and Its Environs and as organizer of the Joint Committee on Bases of Sound Land Policy. Merriam, a political scientist at the University of Chicago and candidate for mayor during the progressive era, had increasingly sought urban reform through scientific public administration—in city managers, accounting budgets, and more efficient staff arrangements. Mitchell, an economist at Columbia University and a leading expert on business cycles, had worked through the National Bureau of Economic Research to develop comprehensive data on business instability. Such information, he trusted, would assist both private and government efforts at economic stabilization.[4]

Sharing an emphasis upon professional expertise which had infused (and divided) reform movements during the 1920's, the Board members had learned politics through experience. Delano had petitioned Congress for a National Capital Park and Planning Commission which he later headed.

[3] In 1934 the three-man Board became members of a larger cabinet level National Resources Board, which a year later became the National Resources Committee. The same three men also formed an Advisory Committee which continued to act as they had earlier. Then with executive reorganization in 1939, the Board served the President as the National Resources Planning Board.

[4] For Delano, see the Delano papers in F. D. Roosevelt Library at Hyde Park, New York; D. C. Coyle, "Frederic A. Delano, Catalyst," *Survey Graphic*, 35 (July, 1946), pp. 252–254; 269–270; *Regional Plan of New York and Its Environs* (8 vols., New York: Regional Plan of New York and Its Environs, 1929); and Committee on Bases of Sound Land Policy, *What about the Year 2000?* (Washington: Federated Societies, 1929). For Merriam, see Charles E. Merriam, "The Education of Charles E. Merriam," in Leonard D. White, ed., *The Future of Government in the United States* (Chicago: University of Chicago Press, 1942), pp. 1–24; Merriam, "Planning Agencies in America," *American Political Science Review*, 29 (April, 1935), pp. 197–211; Merriam, "The National Resources Planning Board: A Chapter in American Planning Experience," *American Political Science Review*, 38 (Dec., 1944), pp. 1075–1088. For Mitchell, see Lucy Sprague Mitchell, *Two Lives: The Story of Wesley Clair Mitchell and Myself* (New York: Simon and Schuster, 1953); Arthur F. Burns, ed., *Wesley Clair Mitchell: The Economic Scientist* (New York: National Bureau of Economic Research, 1952), esp. the essay by Alvin Hansen; Forest G. Hill, "Wesley Mitchell's Theory of Planning," *Political Science Quarterly*, 72 (March, 1957), pp. 100–118; and Wesley Mitchell, *The Backward Art of Spending Money and Other Essays* (New York: McGraw-Hill, 1937). Also the Wesley C. Mitchell papers in Special Collections, Columbia University Library, although most of the interesting letters are cited in his wife's biography.

He had worked with businessmen and government officials, as well as reformers. Although Roosevelt worried that his uncle's appointment might arouse an outcry of nepotism, Delano had demonstrated his ability to run a planning group. Harold Ickes, who had managed Merriam's mayoralty campaign, also provided strong political support. Ickes respected Merriam's ideas on public administration and trusted him not to undermine the Interior Department. As an adviser for the Rockefeller-supported Spelman Fund and an organizer of the Social Science Research Council (SSRC), Merriam had influence within academic establishments. Mitchell had directed research for the National Bureau, also worked closely with the SSRC, and served as chairman of the President's Research Committee on Social Trends. A friend both of Hoover and of economic reformers, Mitchell had earned a high reputation for scientific work and a political acceptability rare among economists in 1933.

Also the Board members shared certain beliefs common among planners. The failure of laissez-faire had seemed obvious even during the prosperous 1920's. In summarizing *Recent Social Trends*, Mitchell had well expressed a common justification for planning among social scientists. After commenting briefly upon the bewildering array of unresolved social issues in the United States, he described the key issue "as that of bringing about a realization of the interdependence of the factors of our complicated social structure. . . ." Presumably "a comprehensive study of social movements and social tendencies" would direct "attention to the importance of balance among the factors of change." Empirical studies, however, promised no panaceas. "To deal with the central problem of balance, or with any of its ramifications, economic planning is called for," Mitchell wrote. But he saw it as a "social need" not as a "social capacity."[5]

AN ADVISORY ROLE

As of July, 1933, the three men had an opportunity to define their places in the government. Their backgrounds, which made them acceptable appointees, indicated they would neither remain content with insignificant tasks nor would they urge some pre-packaged five-year plan. They had to create a demand for their services and to compete with other planning groups and agencies. They might have insured their survival by functioning as part of Secretary Ickes' staff—operating within the bureaucracy to administer established activities more efficiently. Or, they might seek a more pervasive, independent, and professionally-oriented role by acting as presidential advisers. The latter ambition required not only political astuteness but also the best of scientific expertise.[6]

From the first the Board hoped for a national advisory role rather than a

[5] President's Research Committee on Social Trends, *Recent Social Trends in the United States*, I (New York: McGraw-Hill, 1933), pp. xii, xiii, xxxi. Also see Merriam's chapter on "Government and Society," II, pp. 1489–1541.

[6] For an analysis which confirms the validity of that choice see Edward S. Flash, *Economic Advice and Presidential Leadership: The Council of Economic Advisers* (New York: Columbia University Press, 1965), pp. 336–338.

bureaucratic one. Delano, who wanted tangible results more than the other two men, had proposed that "intelligent nationwide planning presupposes as a primary consideration, the thorough study of our land resources, the topography, soil conditions, . . ." He urged surveys of trends in industry and population; but Delano offered no detailed comments on how to select immediate public works projects, which was the Board's ostensible purpose. Happily, the Board could rely upon the Deputy Administrator, an engineer and former city manager, to allocate projects equitably and to avoid waste.[7]

The organization and expenditures of the National Planning Board reflected its advisory function. The three men met for 16 sessions lasting two or three days each time, except for a nine-day meeting on their *Final Report*. The Board spent half of its $100,000 budget to support local planning agencies which were urged "to demonstrate the practical value of well prepared comprehensive plans." About $30,000 went for research projects and the rest for the central office. The secretariat under Charles Eliot, Jr., handled most routine matters, drafted statements, arranged for meetings, disbursed funds and pep talks to local groups, and left the three-man Board free to work on "a continued National plan."[8]

Fortunately, the Board members' diverse interests fitted into a mutually complementary pattern. Mitchell and Merriam hammered out a scheme of "three converging types of planning." They agreed "that Dr. Merriam would prepare an outline on problems of government or administrative planning, Dr. Mitchell one on economic planning problems, and Mr. Delano and Mr. Eliot one on city and regional planning. . . ." Economists should plan public works expenditures in order to dampen business cycles; conservationists and engineers should devise projects consonant with local and national needs. Administrative problems involved an immediate need for economists and engineers to work with Congress in eliminating wasteful projects. For the long run, Merriam sought some reorganization of executive agencies which would incorpirate planning procedures. No other group in the New Deal so effectively joined the two major traditions of progressive reforms—resource conservation and government procedures —with the newer work on business cycles.[9]

But as the Board discovered, long-range planning by experts had slight relevance for immediate administrative problems. On October 22, Mitchell again asked "what the function of the Board might be in relation to a plan for public works, plan for a national plan, etc." They discussed the "interrelation of physical, administrative and economic planning, experience with planning survey in New York State, etc." Delano recommended starting with a good physical geography textbook. Merriam hoped that *Recent*

[7] Delano's memo filed with Minutes of National Planning Board, Central Office Correspondence 106, Central Office Records of the National Resources Planning Board, The National Archives. Hereafter referred to as NPB Minutes with the date.

[8] F. A. Delano to "Members of Planning Boards of Towns, Cities, and Regions," Aug. 17, 1933, Daily File of Central Office Correspondence. Reference to a continued plan from NPB Minutes, July 30, 1933.

[9] NPB Minutes, Sept. 7, 1933.

Social Trends had "provided background up to the point of preparing a plan." Mitchell, who had initiated the question, then ended the discussion by contrasting Hoover's "fact-finding emphasis" with Roosevelt's "demand for action."[10]

Until the Board agreed that they should work toward a permanent planning agency, they had seemed torn between the immediate and the long run, between their technical skills and their political situation. The three men wanted more power than came from volumes of researches or from planning priorities among public works. As a compromise between their advisory possibilities and their need to be useful, the Board happily endorsed Ickes' suggestion of a "Plan for a continuing National Planning Activity" which Merriam labelled "a plan for planning."[11]

But if they were to expand their advisory influence they had to satisfy a double constituency: Roosevelt with his administrative heads and Congress with its hypersensitivity to executive power. Winning support from Ickes and Roosevelt required a demonstration of administrative usefulness. On the other hand they had to convince Congress and the public that they would not regiment, dictate, or otherwise limit freedom of choice. Thus they had to show the practicality of science and at the same time reveal how such expertise could be used without contradicting democratic choices.

PRACTICAL WORK

The Board worked along two lines useful for the administration of a national government: coordination of policies and initiating research for publication. Direct efforts to get an executive order making the Board "a clearing-house of all planning agencies" failed as other groups jealously guarded their own chances to become the key presidential advisory board. The National Emergency Council with its Central Statistical Board probably offered the most serious competition; but neither they nor the Board could disturb Isador Lubin in the Bureau of Labor Statistics. Secretary Dern and the Army Engineers refused to join a national conservation plan, and Secretary Wallace's support for planning grew confused in his struggle with Ickes for control of conservation. Yet much could be achieved without formal authority.[12]

In one major instance, the Board moved to iron out some difficulties in the submarginal land program under which the government bought infertile, isolated, or otherwise poor land. Former owners found more productive work, while the government used the land for watershed protection, forest recreation, grazing lease, or whatever seemed suitable. As governor of New York, Roosevelt had supported a similar program, and he remained interested in the combined goals of conservation, recreation, re-

[10] NPB Minutes, Oct. 22–23, 1933.

[11] *Ibid.*

[12] Delano, Merriam, and Mitchell to Administrator [Ickes], Oct. 23, 1933, Central Office Correspondence, 455–451.1. For dispute with Dern, see transcript of meeting on Nov. 28, 1935 of the National Resources Board.

lief, and regional planning. Responding to conflicts among government agencies involved with those overlapping purposes, the Board organized an interdepartmental Land Use Committee composed of experts. In addition, the Board asked Congress to end homesteading rights, requested its state and area planning groups to sell the program locally, and considered connections between submarginal lands and the reforestation provisions of the Lumber Industry code.

Also the Board looked into the coordination of government projects for the Mississippi Valley. The staff assigned relief workers to such tasks as recording daily river flows and door-to-door polling. Meeting in different parts of the country, the Board discussed programs with various groups such as the New England Council and the Tennessee Valley Authority. Often acting individually on ad hoc issues, Board members investigated methods of flood control, adequate geological survey maps, standardization of government data, and other cases where their knowledge seemed relevant to problems of government organization and innovation.

As administrative procedures settled into normal patterns, the Board increasingly attended to publication of basic studies on public works planning, the structure of the economy, population trends, land classification, and other topics. Their budgets for research and publication grew. Between 1935 and 1939, the National Resources Committee published many of the studies initiated or approved by Delano, Merriam, and Mitchell. Such economists as Arthur Gayer, John M. Clark, John Kenneth Galbraith, Thomas Blaisdell, Gardiner Means, Everett Hagen, and Paul Samuelson worked for the Board's successors. Their works justified the use of trained scholars in government service.

Both the *Final Report* finished in June, 1934 and the *Report* of December 1, which the three men prepared as the Advisory Committee to the National Resources Board, established a high standard for subsequent publications. The Board's editorial skills received full play when Roosevelt allowed five months for a major report "on national planning and public works in relation to natural resources and including land use and water resources with findings and recommendations." Working quickly, the Board organized widely scattered information about the question of how the government could improve the national environment. Even critics who favored laissez-faire found little to complain about in those factual, but reform-oriented reports to the President.[13]

The Board described sufficient projects for any foreseeable public works programs. Among a long series of recommendations they included such things as state and county zoning for better land use and open spaces, compensation for farm tenants and consolidation of commercial agricultural units, tax reforms to encourage reforestation, federal cooperation and aid in preserving historical sites, better treatment for Indians both on and off reservations, a time table for erosion control by areas, limitations on water and air pollution, consideration of river basins as a unit for flood

---

[13] National Resources Board, *A Report on National Planning . . . December 1, 1934* (Washington, D.C.: Government Printing Office, 1934), pp. 2–6.

control and hydroelectric power, connection of electric systems for efficiency and to prevent area-wide blackouts, and a permanent PWA with
provision for a six-year shelf of public works. Thirty-five years later it
would still be an impressive agenda of national needs. If the Board had
not succeeded on that practical level, its case for ongoing national planning would have been much weaker.

A PLAN FOR PLANNING

Both the *Final Report* and the *Report* of December 1, 1934, included the
Board's "plan for planning." In drafting that section five times, the three
men balanced their desire for orderly national planning against their fears
that political opposition might destroy the gains already made by the
New Deal. The Board reviewed past and present planning in the United
States for half of its 22 large double-columned pages in order to "make it
clear that national planning is not an 'untried experiment' in the United
States." Despite some stretching of labels, the Board corrected a common
historical myth that the invisible hand had always guided the American
economy. Hoping to mute one source of criticism, the *Report* cited business
as "the stronghold of economic planning and the 'center of diffusion' from
which the practice has spread. . . ."[14]

At times the Board retreated into superficial generalizations. After hiring Lewis Lorwin, then an economist with the Brookings Institution, to
prepare a history of planning, the Board peppered him with suggestions.
Merriam objected to "an unfortunate emphasis upon control and coercion . . . which might better be rephrased to present the idea of planning
as release." Mitchell referred to laissez-faire as a "plan for no planning."
In one compendium of words, the Board called for "a continuing effort
to analyze and interpret the broad trends and possibilities of the life of
our nation; and somewhat after the manner of a General Staff, consider
critically the most important situations and indicate alternative possibilities, to the end that programs of action adaped to changing situations
may be developed by those responsible for official decisions and actions."
But what did it mean?[15]

In functional terms, national planning required general agreement upon
at least three elements: the right mix of goals, the appropriate policies to
be coordinated to those ends, and some social and economic theories which
related the various parts. Accordingly, the core of planning lay in balancing
competing aims and policies in order to maximize the national welfare
within a general equilibrium of social and economic forces. Hence, the
detail possible in a plan depended upon the preciseness of goals and the
definiteness of knowledge about social interrelationships. Planning in the
modern world required measurable guidelines, quantitative knowledge

---

[14] *Final Report—1933–34*, p. 21. Also see Minutes for June 27, 1934.

[15] For Lorwin's work see especially Minutes, Jan. 7, 1934, Feb. 18, 1934, and April 22,
1934. These discussions helped produce agreement on the meaning of planning. Last
citation included in "Memo to Ickes" on "Program for a National Plan," Minutes of
Nov. 13, 1933. Also see Rexford Tugwell to Charles Eliot, Nov. 21, 1934, Central Office
Correspondence, 103.4.

about current conditions, projections, and repeated refinements of statistical and analytic practices. America's traditional goal of individual freedom precluded planning until it was related to a measurable standard such as efficient output during the 1920's or economic security during the 1930's. Thus, New Deal planning had to be vague and imprecise, concerned with goals as well as means, involved in accumulating the skills needed for even rough prediction and control.[16]

Assuming those skills were scientific, the Board asked the National Academy of Science and the Social Science Research Council how their disciplines could contribute toward planning. Their answers, prepared for the *Final Report*, betrayed some uneasiness. Scientists wanted government support for research, but they feared possible interference. Somewhat myopically, academic scholars believed work of their own choosing served the national interest while federal-directed research might not. Charging that "the material aspects of American culture have developed at a faster rate than social adjustments," some social scientists favored a moratorium on funds for their colleagues in physics and chemistry. Nevertheless, both groups of scientists wanted to be useful (and to have influence). They agreed that "as the fund of knowledge increases, arbitrary choices are less likely, and the range of choice is narrowed."[17]

The expectation that most planners would be experts from universities helped shape the Board's recommendations about a permanent organization. A secretariat should supervise a staff, provide a framework for bringing in other government personnel for special studies, and prepare drafts of annual reports. In addition to providing information and coordinating government programs, a planning board should initiate research "to apprehend more clearly and promptly the emerging trends and problems of the Nation, and should contribute to the formulation of sound national policies adapted to the technological, economic, and social change in the American life." It should consult a panel of distinguished dedicated scholars which might draw into government service some dedicated scholars who shied away from broader responsibilities.[18]

Finally the plan for planning called for the Board to be "'directly responsible to the country's Chief Executive." Its three to five members would serve as part of the President's staff. As an institutionalized brain trust, it would bring scientific training—both analytic techniques and a body of information about society—into the government. That position met the President's need for a larger staff and the social scientists' desire for influence. The President had an incentive to appoint the best men—not only able scholars but also persons who understood the possibilities of executive decision-making. While the arrangement did not free experts

---

[16] See Jan Tinbergen, *Central Planning* (New Haven: Yale University Press, 1964), esp. p. 10, for a functional definition of national planning.

[17] *Final Report—1933–34*, pp. 55, 56.

[18] *Ibid.*, pp. 35–37.

from political pressures, it gave them as national and as comprehensive an outlook as any post in government.[19]

The Planning Board had particular reason to appreciate the genius of Merriam's idea for placing planners on the presidential staff. During the 1920's, they had served on independent commissions without power, but they recognized that the influence they sought required some responsibility to the people—a responsibility which inhered only in elected officials. Also, they had experienced the gap between the generalizations of economics and political science and the immediate, often minor, situations confronting administrators. On the other hand they saw little purpose in scholars becoming mere bureaucrats. Merriam's success in solving the twin problems of a responsible national outlook for planners and of some responsibility to the electorate was attested to in 1946 when Congress established the Council of Economic Advisers after the pattern set down a dozen years earlier.

SOME CONCLUDING REMARKS

On a more philosophical level, the Board's plan for planning went beyond institutional arrangements for using experts in government. However treated, there existed a gap between the individual quality presumed by democracy and the elitism of planning by experts. Social scientists had fought hard for professional standing in universities so they could pursue their researches and publish whatever seemed scientifically true. Unlike military officers, social scientists could not proclaim their subordination to the President and maintain the respect of their colleagues. On the other hand, the American public has not often tolerated arrogance among scientific planners—no matter how sound their ideas. Probably that tension was unresolvable, but at least the Board recognized the issue.

Indeed the Board showed a way to reconcile the differences. The Board adopted as goals the purposes which social scientists had long cited to justify their reform activities. Rephrasing the equality of men into quantifiable form, the Board stated that American "democracy has been based upon the principle that the gains of civilization are essentially mass gains and should be distributed through the community as rapidly as possible." Then, the Board qualified that radical commitment with a second goal— national consensus: "While our lines of national policy are directed toward [equality], we are committed to democratic procedure in this process, and to evolutionary rather than revolutionary methods of advance."[20]

In the United States, democratic equality seemed possible through peaceful means. Natural science would create new and better products. Social science would prevent such dislocations as depression. Mass production and mass education promised a middle class society. Prosperity allowed increasing equality without forced redistribution of wealth. Education, the Board believed, might bring about the necessary consensus

[19] *Ibid.*, pp. 35–37. See Barry Karl, *Executive Reorganization and Reform in the New Deal* (Cambridge: Harvard University Press, 1963).
[20] *Final Report—1933–34*, p. 28.

for national action upon plans recommended by experts. Whatever its flaws, that vision of America has proven its attraction—particularly to college-educated liberals.

At times the ideology of planning as expressed by the National Planning Board in 1933–1934 lacked sophistication and range. The Board had little to say about irrational elements such as Hitler or war in general. Its views ignored the power of the wealthy and the attitudes of the poor. The Board assumed that economics, political science, and sociology might be handled with first-year algebra. Instead, the social sciences have grown increasingly baffling to the uninitiated. Further, the Board relied—to a dangerous degree perhaps—upon the disinterested good faith of social scientists to judge the national interests. Too often scientific truth has proven neither plain enough nor compelling enough to establish a consensus for social reforms. Once recovered from depression, America's material plenty has vitiated the urgency of planning for the efficient use of resources.

Not surprisingly Delano, Merriam, and Mitchell expressed a view of planning remarkably consonant with the strengths and weaknesses of the American reform movement in the twentieth century. Since agreement upon goals and means had to precede planning, the success of the Board depended upon fitting its work into the existing pattern. As Mitchell noted in 1935, the National Planning Board had not brought startling changes. It had provided a national outlook which helped recognize "the interrelationships among social processes" and a long-range interest which encouraged identification of "social problems before they have produced national emergencies."[21]

Neither the National Planning Board nor its successors revolutionized government through their systematic appraisal of the long-run national interest; but the Board had shown how such a function could fit into the federal government. That lesson kept its successors going and indicated how to establish a Council of Economic Advisers which could both function with professional expertise and maintain responsibility in the President. In time the Council would use sophisticated tools of forecasting and specific targets for various components. It would gain power and prestige in the executive establishment. But Americans would accept planning only after it demonstrated its usefulness. Thus the quiescence of political debate over planning ideas during the late New Deal did not indicate their final defeat, but reflected a shift from propaganda to the hard tasks of planning. Far from abandoning its use of expert advice to balance its goals in an efficient administration, the New Deal assimilated that function into the bureaucracy.

[21] Wesley C. Mitchell, "The Social Sciences and National Planning," in Mitchell, *Backward Art*, p. 100.

·12·
SOCIAL SECURITY AND SOCIETY: AN EAST-WEST COMPARISON[1]

GASTON V. RIMLINGER
Rice University

S OCIAL SECURITY IS SHAPED BY AN INTERPLAY OF FORCES WHICH VARY OVER time and between countries. Recent studies have analyzed the role of some of these factors in the development of social security systems.[2] This paper takes a broad comparative view of the interplay of forces, with the hope of identifying the patterns that have emerged in different environments.

ECONOMIC PROTECTION AS A SOCIAL RIGHT

It might be appropriate to begin with a look at alternative economic guarantees a society may offer. These includes the right to earn an income, the right to income maintenance, the right to opportunity, and the right to defend one's economic interest. The right to earn an income may be in the form of the right to work or the right to own land and capital. Socialist countries tend to guarantee the right to work but severely restrict the right to own income-producing property. The right to opporunity is a more general way to look upon the right to earn an income. Today, the right to opportunity includes certainly the right to education, training, health care, rehabilitation, counseling, placement, and so forth. The right of individuals to defend their economic interests, especially through group action, has been seen as an alternative to protection provided by society. Before Bismarck turned to social insurance, he promoted the workers' right to organize in the hope that this might provide some protection against the bourgeoisie. Until the 1930's, American trade unions were opposed to social insurance on the grounds that it was their function, not the state's, to protect the American worker.

A few words may be added regarding the right to work. One of the knottiest problems in the development of income maintenance programs has always been the handling of the able-bodied worker. Historically, his right to relief has been tied to his duty to work, insofar as work was usually made a condition of relief. Relief for the able-bodied worker therefore

[1] This paper was read at the annual meetings of the American Sociological Association in Boston, August 27, 1968. Support for its preparation was received from the Center for Social Change and Economic Development at Rice University under ARPA Order No. 738, monitored by the Office of Naval Research, Group Psychology Branch, Contract Number N00014–67–A–0145–0001, NR 177–909. I am indebted to my colleague, Dr. Louis Galambos, for critical comments. Responsibility for the content is solely mine.

[2] Phillips Cutright, "Political Structure, Economic Development, and National Security Programs," *American Journal of Sociology*, 70 (March, 1965), pp. 537–548; Gaston V. Rimlinger, "Welfare Policy and Economic Development," *Journal of Economic History*, 24 (Dec., 1966), pp. 556–571; Walter Galenson, "Social Security and Economic Development: A Quantitative Approach," *Industrial and Labor Relations Review*, 21 (July, 1968), pp. 559–569.

implied recognition of his right to work. This conception of the right to work, in the sense of *droit au travail*, was strongly supported by the left wing during the French revolutions of 1789 and 1848.[3] It has also figured prominently in socialist ideology since then and has become enshrined in the Soviet Constitution as one of the basic rights of Soviet citizens. Not by accident does the same Constitution prolaim the duty to work, in terms of the Biblical principle: "He who does not work, neither shall he eat."[4] Another conception of the right to work, the *droit de travailler*, in effect access to work, is part of the liberal heritage of the eighteenth century. Its main support at that time was again in France, where it served as a weapon against restrictive guilds and the absolutism of the Crown. Today, this same conception of the right to work is contained in the famous Section 14(b) of the Taft-Hartley Act, where it is intended to limit trade-union restrictions on the free labor market.

These two conceptions of the right to work—that of the Soviet Union and that of the United States—illustrate one of the fundamental differences in the provision of social rights in a free enterprise market economy and a socialist planned economy. In the market economy, the emphasis is on freedom of contract. Ideally, the freely competitive market distributes income in a manner that is consistent with the most efficient allocation of resources, which tends to maximize aggregate income. Unfortunately, the market mechanism does not provide for nonparticipants in the productive process. It is necessary therefore to supplement the primary income distribution of the market with a secondary system of redistribution and transfers. This raises the possibility of a conflict of distributive principles. Market distribution is based on contract, but contract-based distribution has only limited applicability to those who are not actively in the labor market. It applies only to the extent that secondary distribution consists of transfers derived from previous contractual relationships or of advances based on future contractual commitments. Within these limits, it is usually impossible to provide the full array of social rights a modern state deems desirable. It becomes a question therefore of how far a society is willing to deviate from contractual rights and distribute income on the basis of rights associated with status.

Since the eighteenth century, the Anglo-American-French tradition has emphasized individualistic contractual rights, consistent with the political philosophy of the "Social Contract." The German tradition of paternalistic government, on the other hand, was more congenial to the development of income distribution based on social status.[5] This tradition, which emphasizes the collective over the individual interest, is also dominant in the socialist state. In theory, a centrally planned command economy can concen-

---

[3] For a discussion of the history of the "right to work" idea, see Joseph J. Spengler, "Right to Work: A Backward Glance," *Journal of Economic History*, 28 (June, 1968), pp. 171–196.

[4] There are some obvious similarities between the Christian tradition of the duty to work and the Communist position. For a discussion of the Catholic conception, see Carlos Marti-Bufill, *Tratado Comparado de Seguridad Social* (Madrid, 1951), p. 128.

[5] Marti-Bufill, *Tratado*, pp. 47ff.

trate on collective goals and achieve the most efficient allocation of resorces quite independently of the returns to the owners of productice factors. It could therefore allocate income as it pleases to meet whatever social objectives it chooses. In practice, of course, the ultimate communist distribution principle "to each according to his needs" cannot be met so long as people are more responsive to material incentives than to ideological exhortation. While this limits the authorities' freedom of income distribution in the Soviet Union, they are at least not hampered by individualistic traditions. The absence of any contractual ties, in fact, gives the Soviet planners great leeway to adjust the distribution of social income to meet the needs of the state, the party, or the economy, as they see them.

POOR LAWS

It was in response to the social and economic changes engendered by industrialization that one country after another found it necessary to shift from the old systems of poor relief to modern programs of social insurance and public assistance. With advancing industralism and the democratization of political power, the old poor laws had become inappropriate. It has to be understood that even in countries like England, where there was a recognized "right to relief" under the Poor Laws, this meant only that the national state had imposed upon the local community a duty to provide relief. The emphasis of the Poor Laws was not on the rights of the individual but on the welfare of the community: poor relief was a sanitation measure. The strong deterrents attached to the receipt of relief made the Poor Laws an instrument which the ruling groups used to inculcate habits of work and industry among the needy.[6]

The poor law in the West (and for that matter, in Russia, too) was an attempt to reform if not the character at least the behavior of those in need.[7] It looked upon poverty, especially in the case of able-bodied individuals, as evidence of some personal shortcomings which needed to be corrected. The ruling group's perception of these shortcomings and of the anticipated consequences of relief changed over time, but there was always an argument as to why it was harmful for society to make the poor comfortable. The arguments have not died. Perhaps there is some truth in them. But they have lost their conviction in today's industrial society. The poor laws, after

[6] In their monumental study the Webbs characterize the English Poor Laws as a system of relief within a framework of repression. Sidney and Beatrice Webb, *English Poor Law History* (London: Longmans, Green and Co., 1927), 1, p. 396. Professor Titmus writes: "The poor law, with its quasi-disciplinary functions, rested on assumptions about how people ought to behave. It only went into action if people behaved in a certain way and the services it provided were based on conditions that people should thereafter behave in a certain way." Richard M. Titmus, *Essays on the Welfare State* (London: Allen and Unwin, 1948), p. 18. For a discussion of relief in Imperial Russia, see Direction Générale de l'Economie Locale du Ministère de l'Interieur, *L'Assistance Publique et Privée en Russie* (St. Petersburg, 1906).

[7] In spite of the mercantilistic origins of state regulations of relief in Russia, the repressive emphasis was soon eroded, no doubt partly as a consequence of the strong traditions of begging and alms giving. See Direction Générale, *L'Assistance Publique, passim.*

all, were expected to apply only to a small minority living at the margin of society. They were ill-suited to deal with the problems of economic insecurity of large groups of normally self-supporting individuals who may be temporarily disabled or unemployed, or have become too old to compete in the labor market. When social investigations showed that age, illness, and involuntary unemployment were the greatest causes of poverty among a wage-working population, social means of protection that were free from the punitive stigma of the poor law became inevitable.

GERMANY: THE PATERNALISTIC HERITAGE

Germany was the first country to introduce large-scale social insurance programs. Bismarck's dominant concerns were to woo the workers away from socialism and to preserve the country's authoritarian monarchy. The creation of social security rights was a response to pressure from below; but the rights were justified and shaped from above. Bismarck had a genuine paternalistic interest in the welfare of the workers. His emphasis, however, was on the duty of those who rule to protect the ruled, rather than on the rights of the ruled.[8] Bismarck and the feudalized upper bourgeoisie who supported his welfare program thought of the workers' rights to protection mainly as a counterpart of the laborers' duty of obedience and deference. It is somewhat ironic that the initiators of modern social rights were looking backwards to the duties of the loyal subject rather than to the privileges of modern citizenship. Social rights were introduced partly as a compensation for the weakness of political rights.

This frame of reference naturally had an impact on the nature of the rights that were granted. The thrust of the program was to protect the "economically weak" who were also politically dangerous. It was a program primarily for the industrial workingman. Initially, it had little or nothing to offer the salaried employee, the artisan, the agricultural laborer, and the peasant. Some of them were in great need of protection, but they were neither organized nor dangerous. The level of protection aimed at in the early German system was barely sufficient to alleviate hardship. It was not intended to maintain a customary standard of living or a designated national minimum. This aim was consistent with Bismarck's political objectives. With regard to financing and adminstraton, Bismarck argued strongly for state financing and for administrative control in the hands of a centralized state bureaucracy.[9] He feared that if the workers had to pay, the desired impact on them would be lost. On both the financing and the administrative issues Bismarck had to accept compromises as his bills went through the Reichstag. The state, the employers, and the workers shared in the cost and the administration of the health and old-age programs. With the exception of the Social Democrats and the feudalized big industrialists, there was a general feeling that workers ought to share in the cost of social insurance.

[8] For an analysis of his views see Friedrich Lütge, "Die Grundprinzipien der Bismarckschen Sozialpolitik," *Jahrbuch für Nationalökonomie und Statistik*, 134:1 (1931).

[9] For an analysis of these issues, see Walter Vogel, *Bismarcks Arbeiterversicherung; ihre Entstehung im Kräftespiel der Zeit* (Braunschweig: G. Westermann, 1951).

The Social Democrats, who had mixed feelings about the attempt to bribe the working class, demanded benefits equal to full wages, to be paid for completely by the employers but administered by the workers. In reality, they did not expect these demands to be met, nor did they think genuine economic security would be provided for the workers until socialism replaced the existing order.[10]

In subsequent years the character of the original programs changed considerably. Already, before World War I, the system had lost its strict industrial working class orientation. Coverage was extended to include salaried employees, and benefits were improved. But it remained a system of social rights which had its limits set by an authoritarian regime. The passing of the old order and the upsurge of popular political forces after World War I led to reform demands. During the mid-1920's the whole system of social rights was the subject of lively debate, with reform proposals ranging from complete and universal protection to complete abolition of social protection.[11] As a result, social rights were expanded, especially through protection of the unemployed, but the burden of social income redistribution now became a politically divisive issue. It is significant that it was the financing of unemployment insurance that broke the back of the right-left political coalition in 1930—a break which opened the road to the Nazi regime.[12] Hitler used social insurance to support his political objectives, but the major reforms that were planned were never introduced.

After World War II a complete reformulation of social rights had become inevitable. East Germany followed the Soviet path. West Germany put its economic faith in the Social Market Economy, a system which tries to blend the stimuli of the market with the social concerns of the state. The new West German social security system reflects these tendencies, as well as a new concern with equality.[13] It is a cradle-to-grave system for everybody, but it has shed the old paternalism. It emphasizes the individualistic insurance principle of relating benefit levels to contributions. The ideological emphasis is no longer on the state's but on the individual's contribution. The stress is not on redistribution from rich to poor, but on transfer from productive to nonproductive citizens according to previous performance. Benefit levels are geared not to mere alleviation of hardships, or attainment of a minimum standard, but to the maintenance of whatever standard an individual may have achieved through his own work. Solidarity between generations is a keynote. It is highlighted through systematic pension adjustments to the growth in national income. The system tries to solidify not to alter the stratification derived from the division of labor.

[10] For more detail see Hertha Wolf, *Die Stellung der Sozialdemokratie zur deutschen Arbeiterversicherungsgesetzgebung von ihrer Entstehung an bis zur Reichsversicherungsordnung.* (Ph.D. diss., University of Freiburg i. B., 1933).

[11] See Ludwig Preller, *Sozialpolitik in der Weimarer Republik* (Stuttgart: Franz Mittelbach Verlag, 1949), pp. 330 ff.

[12] Helga Timm, *Die deutsche Sozialpolitik und der Bruch der grossen Koalition im März 1930* (Düsseldorf: Droste-Verlag, 1952).

[13] See Gaston V. Rimlinger, "The Economics of Postwar German Social Policy," *Industrial Relations,* 6 (Feb., 1967), pp. 184–204.

BRITAIN: THE EGALITARIAN TRADITION

Differentiated benefits and contributions have always characterized German social security. In this respect it presents a sharp contrast to the British system, which has a tradition of flat benefits and flat contributions. This latter tradition, which emphasizes equal social rights regardless of individual economic merit, goes back to the beginnings of the modern British welfare state. The movement which led to the 1908 Old-Age Pension Act had its roots in the late nineteenth century struggle for greater social equality. In 1885 the extension of the franchise further democratized political power, there was a new militancy of the less skilled elements of the working class, and a new social consciousness became evident among elements of the upper and middle classes; as a consequence, reform of the poor law had become irresistible. Yet, the mood of reform was hardly revolutionary; its main insistence was on the "national minimum," the right to a minimum standard of existence. This social egalitarian orientation, as well as the precedents of the poor law and private charitable organizations, established the pattern of flat minimum benefits.[14] Another factor which helped to promote the idea of a national minimum was the mounting concern in the early twentieth century with national efficiency. The maintenance of a national minimum of health and vigor was believed to be essential to the preservation of the country's economic and political position.

On the matter of financing there was considerable division of opinion. The Socialists demanded that all programs be made universal and noncontributory, but there was resistance from those who feared encroachment of the state upon individual freedom and from those who were concerned with protecting the Exchequer against seemingly boundless fiscal responsibilities. There has always been a widespread feeling in Britain, and for that matter in Germany, that the individual ought to contribute at least part of the cost in order to preserve a sense of social responsibility. Nevertheless, the 1908 Pension Act was made noncontributory, partly because its purpose was to rescue the aged poor from the curse of the poor law, and partly to placate the friendly societies which feared state competition for the workers' meager savings. On the other hand, the health and unemployment insurance programs of the 1911 National Insurance Act were made contributory. The Liberal leaders, David Lloyd-George and Winston Churchill, who pushed these reforms were more concerned with national efficiency than with philanthropy or social reform.

The egalitarian and national minimum concepts established by these early programs received their fullest formulation in the famous Beveridge Report of 1942.[15] This was a comprehensive statement of the citizen's social right to freedom from want and of the means to implement it. Its central

[14] The best discussion of this period is in Bentley B. Gilbert, *The Evolution of National Insurance in Great Britain* (London: Michael Joseph, 1966); see also Samuel Mencher, *Poor Law to Poverty Program* (Pittsburgh: University of Pittsburgh Press, 1967), chap. 10.

[15] *Social Insurance and Allied Services*, Report by Sir William Beveridge (Am. ed., New York: Macmillan, 1942).

idea was the national minimum: "Social insurance should aim at guaranteeing the minimum income needed for subsistence," Beveridge declared.[16] He strongly advocated egalitarian social insurance, regardless of earnings. "All insured persons, rich or poor, will pay the same contributions for the same security; those with larger means will pay more to the National Exchequer and so to the State share of the Social Insurance Fund."[17] This approach, he argued, "has been found to accord best with the sentiments of British people." He added that there was growing support for the principle that "in compulsory insurance all men should stand together on equal terms, that no individual should be allowed to claim better terms because he is healthier or in more regular employment."[18] Along with this Dunkirk-inspired posture and an emphasis on society's responsibility for the welfare of the individual, Beveridge expressed the traditional British concern for individual freedom and responsibility. This concern was behind his insistence on providing only minimum benefits and keeping the system contributory. "Management of one's income," he observed, "is an essential element of a citizen's freedom."[19] He believed that guaranteeing the minimum would give the citizen both the freedom and the incentive to provide more for himself and his family. With regard to worker contributions, he noted that "insured persons should not feel that income for idleness, however caused, can come from a bottomless purse."[20]

The fundamental features of the Beveridge proposals were enacted into law between 1945 and 1948. At that time these laws gave Britain one of the most comprehensive health and social security systems in the world. Since then one of its fundamental features, the egalitarian benefit, has been discarded. With growing affluence during the post-war years, there arose increasing dissatisfaction with a system that almost necessarily tied benefits to a level somewhat below the lowest common wages. In 1959 Britain introduced a second layer of wage-related pensions to supplement the national minimum. It may be worth noting that during the same year Sweden also altered her traditional, egalitarian system in favor of wage-related pension and cash sickness benefits.[21]

THE UNITED STATES: THE INDIVIDUALISTIC TRADITION

In Europe we have seen a varying balance between individual and social interests. In the United States the balance has been heavily weighted in favor of individual interests. The traditional emphasis on self-help and individual achievement, the identification of state intervention with loss of freedom and destruction of economic vitality, the lack of class solidarity, the hostility of organized labor to governmental competition, and an optimistic faith in boundless opportunities—all of these factors created an

[16] *Ibid.*, p. 14.
[17] *Ibid.*, p. 121.
[18] *Ibid.*, p. 30.
[19] *Ibid.*, p. 12.
[20] *Ibid.*

[21] Albert H. Rosenthal, *The Social Programs of Sweden* (Minneapolis: University of Minnesota Press, 1967), chaps. 2 and 3.

environment in which advocating compulsory social protection of the individual was more likely to invite political retribution than reward.

It is significant that until the 1930's the only kind of nondeterrent social protection that had gained general acceptance was compensation for industrial injuries. Workmen's compensation was supported by all the major parties in the 1912 campaign, and was even before then officially endorsed by the National Association of Manufacturers and many trade and employer associations.[22] The reason for this exception is rather simple. Workmen's compensation, even though compulsory, could easily be treated as a police and profits problem, rather than a social welfare problem. It could be divorced from social rights and duties and presented as a matter of industrial efficiency. The accident prevention programs which were induced by workmen's compensation appealed to employer self-interest. John R. Commons, one of the guiding lights of the early compensation movement, explained that the "appeal was made to a new kind of 'efficiency,' efficiency in preventing accidents, by which the cost of production could be reduced, with the result that prices need not be increased."[23] The success of the workmen's compensation campaign in the second decade of the century gave false hope to the social insurance advocates, mainly social workers and intellectuals, that the efficiency theme could serve as a vehicle for introducing other forms of social insurance, especially health insurance. Economists and statisticians, like Irving Fisher and I. M. Rubinow, calculated the returns in productivity that improved health care through health insurance would provide. This was an appeal for social protection not for the sake of social rights but for the sake of productivity. Unfortunately, the economic gains from better general health are primarily social rather than private. In this sense, the effects of health insurance are unlike those of workmen's compensation. In the individualistic American environment the absence of demonstrable private gains made compulsory action difficult.

During the 1920's the efficiency theme was applied to old-age pensions and unemployment insurance. The emphasis now was on the private gains, through improved efficiency made possible by timely retirements and through regularization of employment. To the extent that the arguments had validity, they could justify voluntary private measures but not compulsory governmental action. Quite a few private schemes were introduced with the enthusiastic support of the American Management Association. Their significance lies not in what they achieved, but in the models they provided when social action on a large scale became unavoidable in the 1930's.

The main programs of the Social Security Act of 1935, pensions and unemployment benefits, were patterned after plans that had been tested in a private interest setting. The underlying idea was to violate in the least possible way the market principle of an exchange of benefits for contributions.

22 For the position of the NAM, see F. C. Schwedtman and J. A. Emery, *Accident Prevention and Relief* (New York: National Association of Manufacturers, 1911).

23 John R. Commons, *Institutional Economics* (Madison: University of Wisconsin Press, 1959), 2, p. 857.

The system had to be as consistent as possible with the principle of efficiency maximization through profits. In the case of unemployment insurance this led to the adoption of the Wisconsin plan (similar to the "American Plan" supported by the American Association for Labor Legislation), which put the entire cost of the employer and made his tax a function of the amount of unemployment he caused. This was exactly parallel to workmen's compensation, and a similar result was expected in the form of a reduction of unemployment. The unemployment tax was expected to induce improved management. Moreover, in this manner, it was argued, each employer would pay for *his* unemployment, not for that of other employers. Benefits were based on wages and the length of previous employment. The economic merits of the scheme were and still are controversial, but its advocates had no doubt that it was highly suitable for America. Commons, whose life-long goal was to build institutions that would utilize the profit motive in the social interest, declared: "It is extraordinarily an individualistic and capitalistic scheme."[24] Another member of the Wisconsin school described the plan as "enlighted individualism," which involved "the least change in private business consistent with the government's vital interest in steadier employment and income. . . ."[25]

The individualistic element was even more pronounced in the structure of the old-age pension program. The crucial concept here was the *contributory-contractual principle*. Even in the depth of the depression, the spokesmen for the program found it necessary to emphasize again and again that protection for the aged was not to be a matter of governmental benevolence but a matter of individual, contractual rights. Such rights protect freedom, they felt, while government benevolence threatens it. The emphasis, therefore, had to be on contractual equity rather than social justice, which meant that benefits had to be geared as closely as possible to contributions by and for the worker, with a minimum of redistribution. In testimony on behalf of the social security bill, J. Douglas Brown, then a member of the technical staff, explained that "a contributory-contractual plan uses the method of thrift to protect workers" and that "by contributing the individual worker establishes an earned contractual right."[26] As should be clear, this idea of an *earned contractual right* as a rationale for a contributory system is quite different from Beveridge's concern with the maintenance of a sense of individual responsibility. In spite of Franklin D. Roosevelt's oratory about freedom from want, the idea of social rights was still suspect in America. One way out was to make social security appear as a kind of self-help scheme, which would threaten neither individual initiative nor individual freedom. In Brown's words, "We wanted our government to provide a mechanism whereby the individual could prevent

[24] John R. Commons, "The Groves Unemployment Reserve Law," *American Labor Legislation Review*, 22 (March, 1932), p. 9.
[25] Paul A. Raushenbush, "Wisconsin's Unemployment Compensation Act," *American Labor Legislation Review*, 22 (March, 1932), p. 18.
[26] *Hearings before the Committee on Ways and Means on H. R. 4120*, 74th Congress, 1st Sess. (1935), pp. 241, 242.

dependency through his own efforts."[27] The government was to provide merely the mechanism for self-help, not a new conception of the citizen's social rights.

It was not possible, of course, to adhere completely to the logic of the contributory-contractual principle and to the precedents of private welfare plans. Some redistribution in favor of low income receivers and people near retirement was unavoidable. But in America (unlike Europe), the government did not make any contribution from general revenue toward the cost of social insurance. Since contributions were from the beginning levied only on the lowest part of earnings, there has always been a regressive element in the American system. When benefits were liberalized in 1939, by adding survivorship and dependents' benefits, the tendency toward regressiveness was increased. The recent substantial raises of the tax base have reduced, but by no means eliminated, all of the regressive features of the system. So long as there is no contribution from progressive taxes, we will have a system in which the poor and the rich bear the same financial burden for the protection of the poor. Its great "virtue" is that it forces the poor to protect themselves and thereby protects the more affluent members of our society.[28]

U.S.S.R.: THE COLLECTIVE APPROACH

The contrast between East and West has been most emphasized by Soviet writers. One of them notes the following differences: in the U.S.S.R., social security "is a factor in the improvement of life and of the material and cultural position of the working class; it is one of the levers for the uplifting of all those who work." In the West, on the other hand: "Its substance lies in the use of pacifiers . . . to protect capitalist property against encroachment from the poor." And he goes on: "What underlies social security in Capitalist countries is not the needs of man, nor the right to secure old age, but the interest in profits, the interest in strengthening the capitalist mode of production by way of partial concessions to the worker."[29] Wrong-headed as this interpretation may be, it is nevertheless partially correct. In the West we have found varying degrees of individual and social responsibility for protection from want; in the U.S.S.R. the emphasis is exclusively on social responsibility. Reliance on the state rather than self-help is the keynote of Soviet welfare.

This difference is closely associated with the differing explanations of poverty in the Western tradition and in Marxist thought. The former concentrated on the shortcomings of the individual while the latter focused exclusively on the failures of the economic system. Before coming to power,

[27] J. Douglas Brown, "The American Philosophy of Social Insurance," *Social Service Review*, 30 (March, 1956), p. 3.

[28] For a more extended discussion along these lines, see Gaston V. Rimlinger, "American Social Security in a European Perspective," in W. G. Bowen *et al.*, eds., *The American System of Social Insurance* (New York: McGraw-Hill, 1968), chap. 8.

[29] M. Lantsev, "Sotsial'noe Obespechenie v SSSR i v Kapitalisticheskikh Stranakh," *Sotsialisticheskii Trud* (Sept., 1958), p. 30. See also V. S. Andreev, *Material'noe Obespechenie Grazhdan SSSR* (Moscow, 1963), chap. 2.

the Bolsheviks, like other Socialists, insisted on the principle that it was the Capitalist system that was the cause of insecurity; therefore, it was up to the ruling class to provide and pay for the workers' protection. Their right to comprehensive, free protection derived from the fact that they were being exploited by the Capitalists. The kind of social security system that this implied was spelled out by Lenin at the 1912 Prague Conference of the Russian Social Democratic Workers' Party. He cited the following principles: (1) state social security had to protect against all risks of income loss, (2) it had to cover all workers and their families, (3) it had to pay full compensation of lost earnings, (4) all costs had to be borne by employers and the state, and (5) there had to be a unified system of administration (as opposed to separate programs for separate risks) under the complete control of the insured workers.[30] These principles have remained the touchstone of Soviet social insurance. They were embodied in a bill prepared by the Bolsheviks in 1914 and in the social security proclamation issued by the Bolshevik leaders only five days after the seizure of power. In 1936, the right to comprehensive social protection for all Soviet citizens was incorporated into the Constitution.

In the development of Soviet social security these principles have been adapted to the economic and political needs of the hour. While Soviet writers charge that under capitalism social security serves mainly the purposes of the ruling class, there is no country in which welfare programs have been so closely tailored to the needs of those in power as they have in the Soviet Union. The promise of November, 1917 to establish without delay a comprehensive program of social insurance for all workers and for all urban and rural poor was soon pushed into the background under the impact of civil strife. Soviet social insurance began, effectively, in 1921 on a less than comprehensive scale. It applied only to wage and salary earners. The self-employed were excluded. It was not until 1964 that the mass of agricultural workers, the *kolkhoz* members, were included in the state pension and temporary disability programs.

While it is not possible to review here the details of the Soviet social security system, some of its outstanding characteristics should be noted. One aspect which Soviet spokesmen often point to with naïve pride is the absence of contributions by the workers. The official ideology stresses the fact that benefits are a gift from the state, an expression of its deep concern for the average citizen. Soviet legal experts note that there is no contractual relationship in their social insurance; only the state has an obligation, not the worker.[31] A worker is entitled to social insurance because of his status as a worker, not because he or his employer paid contributions. Initially, there was not even a test of an individual's attachment to the work force.

[30] V. I. Lenin, *Collected Works* (Moscow: Foreign Languages Publishing House, 1963), 17, p. 476.
[31] A. S. Krasnopol'skii, "On the Nature of Soviet State Social Insurance," *Current Digest of the Soviet Press,* 3 (Dec. 29, 1951), p. 6; for a more extensive discussion see his *Osnovnye Printsipy Sovetskogo Gosudarstvennogo Sotsial'nogo Strakhovaniia* (Moscow, 1951).

The idea of a service requirement was gradually introduced during the 1920's—at first, mainly to determine the eligible status group.[32] With the beginning of the five-year plan era, the service requirement became a determining factor in the granting of benefits.

In 1929, the social insurance agencies were ordered to reorganize their work in order "to achieve every possible support for the growth of labor productivity and every encouragement for shock work and socialist competition, to heighten the struggle against absenteeism and labor turnover, and to aid in the formation of cadres and the strengthening of labor discipline."[33] In 1930, unemployment benefits were summarily abolished, and the unemployed sent to any available jobs. In the following years the service requirments were considerably tightened, with particular emphasis being placed on the length of unbroken service in the same establishment. Workers who moved from job to job were penalized with lower benefits and denied benefits altogether during the first six months on a job. Workers in important industries and shock workers were given preferential treatment.[34] In 1933, the trade unions were given the dominant role in the day-to-day administration of social insurance for active members of the work force.[35] While most workers belong to a trade union, those who do not are entitled to temporary disability at a rate of 50 per cent of what is paid to union members. The unions were ordered to use social insurance in a manner which would strengthen labor discipline, reward the zealous and punish the loafers. This certainly was an ironic development for workers in a country which had accepted the principle of management by the insured.

The disciplinary character which Soviet social insurance acquired during the Stalin five-year plans was relaxed after his demise, although its productivity objectives were retained. The vast improvement of pensions in 1956 gives the country a system with a better balance between productivity and welfare objectives. Until then the maximum pension for the vast majority of pensioners was below a minimum subsistence level, which forced most of them to continue to work. Today the Soviet pension scale provides benefits which are a higher percentage of wages for most workers than in the United States. Like almost all Soviet benefits, pensions are still highly differentiated and incentive oriented; they offer special bonuses for long and steady work and higher rates and lower retirement ages for dangerous or difficult work. Workers in the Far East and Far North are singled out for privileged treatment. Since 1930, the Soviet authorities have emphasized, and sometimes pushed to extremes, the differentiation of benefits. Only

[32] The development of the work requirement is discussed at length in L. Ia. Gintsburg, *Trudovoi Stazh Rabochikh i Sluzhashchikh* (Moscow, 1958).

[33] *Ibid.*, p. 66.

[34] Seee Gaston V. Rimlinger, "Social Security, Incentives, and Controls in the U.S. and U.S.S.R.," *Comparative Studies in Society and History*, 4 (Nov., 1961), pp. 116–118.

[35] On the role of the trade unions, see Gaston V. Rimlinger, "The Trade Union in Soviet Social Insurance: Historical Development and Present Functions," *Industrial and Labor Relations Review* 24 (April, 1961), pp. 397–418.

since 1956 are pensions weighted in favor of low income receivers. In their rejection of egalitarian rewards, the Russians are like the Americans, and very much unlike the British and the Swedes.

Today Soviet citizens enjoy a comprehensive and unified system of health care and social security rights. According to studies by the International Labor Office, the Soviet Union in 1963 spent 10.2 per cent of its Gross National Product on social security, which is substantially more (relative to GNP) than the 6.2 per cent spent by the United States. On the other hand, the U.S.S.R. rates behind countries like West Germany (15.3 per cent), France (14.6 per cent), Sweden (13.5 per cent), and the United Kingdom (11.2 per cent).[36]

CONCLUDING COMMENTS

In comparative analysis there are two opposite dangers: one is to over-stress differences in order to bring out contrasts, the other is to exaggerate similarities in order to highlight unity. Keeping these pitfalls in mind, we must take note of a remarkable convergence. In spite of vastly different starting points in terms of ideologies, social, economic, and political conditions, the countries surveyed have ended up wth remarkably similar systems of income protection. The American, German, or Soviet pensioners waiting for the postman to bring their monthly social security benefit certainly have something important in common. But as we look beyond the technical similarities of the programs, as we examine their social and economic context, we find that significant differences remain. These are embedded in the degree of protection, the conditions under which rights are awarded, and the meaning attached to them.

One decisive factor in the historical process by which social rights are granted is the emphasis society places on individual versus collective interests. Whether a government is more or less representative does not necessarily affect the extent of social rights granted but has a great deal to do with the structure of these rights. The less representative a government, the more it is inclined to manipulate the rights to suit the objectives of the ruling group. Social rights have inherent limitations; they extend certain dimensions of freedom but necessarily curtail others; they may increase social equality, but beyond a point only at the cost of economic incentive. These are the considerations which account for both differences and similarities in the patterns of East and West.

[36] For data on other countries, see Galenson, "Social Security and Economic Development," pp. 568–569.

Part IV
REFLECTION AND CRITIQUE
AS SOCIAL INTERVENTION

Stockbrokers not so jokingly tell the tale that economists on the President's Council of Economic Advisers can influence the market by facial expression alone: If they smile, the market inclines; if they frown, it declines. The exaggeration of influence by physiognomy does not belie the fact that the economic advisers to the President *do* have very considerable impact. Very few social scientists by their offices have so much potential for direct social intervention. However, some social scientists do by their offices and through their oral and written works have the capacity at least indirectly to affect the direction or intensity of social planning and program implementation. Examples of such work are presented in this section, in which five economists, four sociologists, a political scientist, and a legal scholar reflect on and critique some status-quo social systems and policies at various levels of abstraction. The kind of evidence and the range of opinions presented with different degrees of subjectivity and objectivity by the authors exemplify how, as evidence and opinion summate, social scientists can provoke and support planned social intervention.

In contribution 13 sociologist Elliott A. Krause directs attention to the fact that dynamic interaction among macrolevel social institutions can either promote or thwart planned intervention. Krause suggests that comparative research on the military-industrial complex and on

antipoverty organizations should be done in the areas of budgetary politics, the use of ideologies by bureaucracies, "complexing" phenomena,
and societal evolution based on technological development. In the Mills
tradition, Krause advises that before major strategic decisions are made
to expand the power and resources of antipoverty bureaucracies (or any
social-intervention organizations) and their affiliates, the extent to which
they contribute to the military-industrial complex should be ascertained.
Further, he demonstrates that the federal government, especially the
Department of Defense, is particularly adept at planned intervention.
He suggests that important lessons might be learned from analyses of
that expertise, and the lessons applied to salutory strategies for overcoming social problems.

Krause's list of research needs goes beyond the military-industrial
complex, and more or less serves to categorize the remaining contributions in this section. Political scientist Robert L. Lineberry addresses his
research to the issue of budgetary politics in contribution 14. Considering planning as a dependent variable operationalized by the allocation
of funds, Lineberry shows that the allocation is *not* related to community
needs, demographic characteristics, governmental reformism, or party
strength. Rather, budgets are assigned and planning implemented according to the interplay of group forces and community ecology. Lineberry
concludes that planning agencies are not well integrated into community
ecological structure.

Sociologist Eleanor P. Wolf, in contribution 15, is concerned with an
issue which is related to Krause's suggested research on the role of
ideology in organizational action. Wolf notes that previous long-term
programs to improve the academic performance of low-income black
pupils have proved very difficult to attain, have been uncertain as to
outcome, and have often been glibly supported by research data which
appeared to threaten black self-esteem. She suggests that an ideology of
community control, with its potential for community social integration,
could be instrumental in encouraging group pride and assertiveness and
thereby would serve to enhance the preparation of black children for the
educational system.

Several articles in this section are related to Krause's recommendation
for research into "complexing" phenomena, which he defines in part as a
progressive divorce of a set of institutional relationships from the aims
and goals of the wider society. In contribution 16, sociologist Mayer N.
Zald outlines the emergence of new social-service programs in a manner
that seems generally applicable to planned social intervention. He traces
the process from societal change and increasing social differentiation,
through the labeling of new social categories as social problems, and
finally to the components which define intervention and create new organizations to deal with the problems as defined. Zald demonstrates that
as the social problems are defined and the intervention organizations
proliferate, questions of integration and coordination arise. Documenting
his analysis with specific cases, he assesses the cost and the benefits of
organizational integration and concludes that integration is *not* always in

the best interest of social-intervention goals. Each case of planned social intervention must be individually appraised according to economic, political, and social criteria.

In his discussion, Zald comments that, as a rule, intervention organizations have carefully detailed budgets, but their formal goals are often vaguely written. As an example, he cites the diffuse goal set for correctional institutions—"rehabilitate inmates." There is another example of this kind of diffuse goal in Part II—the vagueness and resultant complications of the Community Action Program's commission to eradicate poverty with the "maximum feasible participation" of the poor.

In contribution 17, law professor Michael Katz warns that the incorporation of insights from social-science theory into legal codes can result in what Krause might call "complexing"—the impact of legislation serves goals quite disparate from the interventionist's intention. Katz more specifically advises that, should the legal system and the population-planning process prove to be compatible, there is a danger that social-science hypotheses will become legal norms without having first been adequately tested empirically. The articles in Part II concerning the theoretical bases for "maximum feasible participation" testify to that possibility. Katz observes that legal principles effectively narrow the range of alternatives open to the planner and concludes that failures to calculate the legal implications of population policy decisions might nullify even the best-constructed models.

Economists Richard X. Chase and Gene Laber, in contribution 18, provide evidence which suggests that change in the level of economic activity in and of itself will tend to bring about a greater concentration of poverty among certain "backwash" subgroupings of the population. Their article argues that "smaller" demographic subgroups (for example, aged, farm, female-headed families) are unable to escape from poverty by exploiting the opportunities created by general economic advances. Consequently, they are left behind, in the backwash, and are in relative terms even more economically disadvantaged as a result. To Krause, this phenomenon probably would represent the absence of an effective societal complex acting in the interests of all the poor. Chase and Laber conclude that since the amelioration of poverty cannot be left solely to the general progress of the economy, selective and specific antipoverty interventions should be aimed at "smaller" target subgroups.

Contributions 19 and 20 offer examples of "complexing" as it relates to the character of military manpower. Economist Robert Evans, Jr., describes some social and economic relationships in the conscripted military and suggests that they are analogous to slavery. He indicates that attempted intervention—that is, raising the wages of draftees to comparable civilian levels—would meet with resistance from inside and outside the military and would disturb long-standing fiscal relationships between governmental and civilian pay structures.

Evans suggests that only an emancipation can end the draft-slave system—a complete upsetting of the social and economic relations, the "complexes" which maintain the system. That emancipation may become possible, according to Evans, when citizens perceive the cost of the draft to be too high, particularly the cost of lost civilian opportunity. The lottery draft system was adopted after Evans had written his article, and can be interpreted as a governmental effort to neutralize citizen discontent with unequally distributed opportunity loss under the previous selective-service procedure.

In contribution 20, economists William Freithaler Ford and Robert Tollison offer a preliminary analysis of theoretical issues and empirical data in which they argue that it is improbable that a volunteer army would be, as critics charge, primarily black. Ford and Tollison acknowledge that government intervention creating a volunteer army would necessarily increase soldiers' pay. That increase, and other resultant structural changes, would entice whites as well as blacks into the army. Like Evans, Ford and Tollison reveal the potential social, economic, and political repercussions of intervention into systems linked in "complexes."

Contribution 21, by sociologist Amitai Etzioni, is appropriate to Krause's suggestion for the analysis of societal evolution based on technology. To Etzioni, the capacity of societies to treat their own social problems effectively and to effect change in themselves seems rather limited. Societies need guidance. Drawing from a cybernetic model, Etzioni relates knowledge units, decision-making strategies, and the distribution of power, as elements of societal guidance, to directed social change. In commenting on knowledge units, he feels—as do other authors in this anthology—that the work of most social scientists has been neither policy-oriented nor accessible to key decision makers, and he thinks that communication efforts should be intensified.

Etzioni remarks that decision making in the Anglo-Saxon world is adequate under conditions of stability, but is lacking in periods of marked social change. It can be assumed that social change will very likely continue to accelerate in highly technical societies, bringing new challenges for guidance and adaptation. Discussing power, the third element of societal guidance, Etzioni advises that the society which provides for the reduction of power differences among its various collectivities is better able to treat its problems. Mills, Krause, Rimlinger, Trattner, Zald—in fact, the majority of authors in this anthology—remind the reader that power is relinquished by its holders begrudgingly, if at all.

13

POVERTY, HUMAN RESOURCES, AND THE MILITARY-INDUSTRIAL COMPLEX: SOME RESEARCH ISSUES

ELLIOTT A. KRAUSE
Northeastern University

RESEARCH CAN BE VIEWED AS A PRELUDE TO POLITICAL ACTION AS WELL as to further research. But a major problem for intervention-directed research lies in gaining insights sufficient for informed action, without taking so long that the process to be intervened in is already a part of history. Priorities must be set. This article argues that research on the causes, actions, and consequences of the military-industrial complex should be a top priority item for those interested in mobilizing support for the poor and in affecting the general directions of change in our present society. We will suggest a series of general research issues and conclude with types of action possible once more information is available.

More basic information is needed on American society's relation to the military-industrial complex, in order to understand the degree to which present plans are realistic. To what extent is the military-industrial complex an actual competitor for funds which might otherwise go to the poor, or is the military-industrial complex merely a symptom of more basic structural alignments in a society which would spare none of its resources for the poor, regardless of the existence of such a complex? A series of research issues which comprehend the above problem would include: budgetary politics, the role of ideologies in organizational action, complexing phenomena, and general trends of societal evolution based on technology. With more information in these areas, and using the military-industrial complex as a research subject because of its central involvement in these issues, it may be more possible to anticipate blocks to antipoverty movements and conversely to anticipate opportunities of reallocation of societal resources.

BUDGETARY POLITICS AND THE ALLOCATION OF RESOURCES

Wildavsky, in *The Politics of the Budgetary Process,* isolates a set of factors which enter into the decisions made by governments, especially at the federal level, as to what kinds of commitments are made to various programs and organizations.[1] He points out that all organizations demand a considerable backing for their own programs, expecting in the heat of battle to be cut back on requested funds. How much is asked for—the original size of the slice of pie—is a consequence of present aims, actual needs, and capacity to mobilize outside power. Research is needed for a more recent appraisal of the precise inside and outside pressures which can successfully mobilize support in this struggle, and the extent to which

[1] Aaron Wildavsky, *The Politics of the Budgetary Process* (Boston: Little-Brown, 1964).

♦ First published in *Social Science Quarterly* 50, No. 3 (December, 1969).

there is any generalizability from MIC strategy to that used by the anti-poverty groups. C. Wright Mills's hypothesis was that, in part, the apathy of an unorganized mass resulted in the last 15 years of growth of the MIC, and that failure to control the complexing was due in part to lack of knowledge of it and lack of political organization in the electorate to fight it.[2] Perhaps the ABM controversy in 1969 is illustrating basic changes in the average level of citizen political activism—on any issue and on any side of any issue—not relevant to the time of Mills's analysis. Another issue in research would be the extent to which informal congressional procedures have been the cause of part of the problem, with a change in procedure itself resulting in major changes in the power of a particular complex. To ask a basic question of Mills: to what extent is the strategy of budgetary infighting generalizable from situation to situation or historical period to period?[3]

If we knew more about how political attitudes in the general public could be mobilized and focused on the budgetary process, through differential evaluation of the successes of different techniques on specific issues, we might have a better idea as to how to proceed on a particular budgetary issue. To date this knowledge is informal, existing as the political expertise or "savvy" of professionals in politics, but it needn't remain so. Along the lines of mobilization of support of budgetary struggles, it could be valuable to research the reasons why some federal agencies, such as the Department of Defense, allocate the sums they do for public relations and congressional liaison, in contrast to the lower percentages (and concretely far lower sums) used for lobbying by most health and welfare bureaus. Along these lines, further research would inquire as to why the heavy expenditure of time and funds by OEO was unsuccessful in proportion to the sums and time spent by the other HEW agencies in their lobbying activities. Is it the amount of time and effort or the nature of the cause and the population which benefits which is dominant in predicting the outcome?

A more general study of this process will consider the critical question: to what degree would dollars diverted from military spending go to the poor? Historical evidence such as that marshaled by Lubove indicates that during 1900–1930 the private voluntary agencies, the insurance companies, and organized medicine collaborated and conspired to fight any attempt at social insurance or compensation for disability or illness which they could not turn to their own advantage.[4] During this period, the welfare state was politically unacceptable to these groups, even in a most attenuated form. These same forces are presently in action. To what degree will interest-based political opposition today, as in the early decades of the twentieth century, make significant social legislation—such as a guar-

---

[2] C. Wright Mills, *The Power Elite* (New York: Oxford University Press, 1956), pp. 269–297.

[3] C. Wright Mills, *The Sociological Imagination* (New York: Oxford University Press, 1959).

[4] Roy Lubove, *The Struggle for Social Security 1900–1930* (Cambridge, Mass.: Harvard University Press, 1968).

anteed annual income—impossible? Given the political climate, what effect does such a climate have on the aims of groups engaged in budgetary
struggles?

Titmuss, in his research on the English welfare state,[5] considers another
aspect of this issue, and ultimately arrives at the most basic issue. While
the welfare state legislation in theory profited all, it did not involve a redistribution of income sufficient to change class lines, and with the passage
of time the amendments and administration of these programs has tended
to favor the English middle class at the expense of the poor, the way our
social security program is essentially for the steady blue-collar or white-
collar worker, not for the poor. In the last decade, as England has developed a racial issue superimposed on the welfare state, the reaction has
accelerated. To what extent do racial and class interests stand behind any
budgetary struggle in a western democracy, and therefore to what extent
is it realistic at all to talk about influencing budgetary struggles through
the use of programs which do not change the power alignments of these
basic interests?

THE ROLE OF IDEOLOGY IN ACTION ORGANIZATIONS

An ideology can be defined as any word, set of phrases, or text which is
used by one group—the proponents—and directed at another group for
the purpose of politically organizing and activating the target group to
behave in a way which will be in the basic self-interest of the proponents.[6]
The topic of ideology has traditionally been reserved for political parties
or national movements. In the use of the term here, the role of ideologies
in the striving of action organizations can profitably be inspected, with
special interest placed on the ideologies of highly successful action organizations such as the DOD. Success here simply means ideologies which
have been used by the organization with wide enough acceptance to
achieve acquisition of a significant share of national resources. We might
begin by enumerating a set of ideologies used by the DOD, and ask about
the degree to which each of the proposed ideologies has a basis in fact, in
that they are relevant to the concrete needs of the entire society and not
just to the aims and interests of the MIC. To what extent is each ideology
politically effective with each subgroup in the society? What determines,
over time, the degree to which an ideology remains successful or finds
refutation by the society or key opposition groups within it?

At present, one can make a tentative classification of the types of ideologies used by the MIC into those appealing to the emotions (statements,
slogans, and imprecations relating to fear and patriotism), to rationality
(the Department of Defense as improver of manpower skills, as preserver
of the peace, as a developer of technological breakthroughs valuable to
civilian society), to the professional capability and responsibility of the

[5] Richard M. Titmuss, *Essays on the Welfare State* (London: Unwin University
Books, 1958).
[6] Elliott A. Krause, "Functions of a Bureaucratic Ideology: Citizen Participation,"
Social Problems, 21 (Fall, 1968), p. 132.

military (security classification with its sociopolitical implications), and
finally, to self-interest in economic terms. The last is most clearly seen in
the campaign billboards of congressmen such as Mendel Rivers of South
Carolina, who lists a series of defense projects and new military bases in
his district, over his picture, with the slogan, "Rivers Delivers."

Each of these ideologies and selling strategies has some basis in the factual needs of the social system. But the research needs to be done as to the
extent to which the statements and claims of the Department of Defense
are based on fact or are primarily ideological and used to gain a greater
share of resources. Another related issue is the political effectiveness of
ideologies, regardless of their factual basis. If one by research found that
a specific ideology used by the MIC was extremely effective politically,
the morality of its use as well as its scientific relevance to antipoverty
intervention would have to be raised. In any case, research on the concrete
uses of the MIC's ideologies could perhaps provide a more effective ideological armamentarium for those in antipoverty work.

A major question which falls within the topic of ideology has to do with
the interests of those proposing the ideologies and those toward whom the
ideologies are directed. A more extensive comparison needs to be made between the ideologies of the military-industrial complex, a mutually rein-
forcing and mutually supporting arrangement between defense contractors,
politicians, a federal bureaucracy, and voters in the community—on the one
hand—and the ideology of the OEO, on the other hand. OEO could not
use its ideologies to the point of organizing or maintaining a *complex* in
the sense of the MIC. As Zurcher points out, even its supporters on the side
of the poor were forced to a marginal position as they could not deliver
anything to their fellows.[7] The action agencies often were instead co-opted
by local conservative forces, and acquisition of power by the poor was
fought through political channels which eventually reached back to the
local community action agency through the federal OEO headquarters. To
what extent was this situation due to the kinds of arguments or ideologies
which the OEO used, and to what extent was it due instead to the groups
toward whom the ideologies were directed? "Maximum feasible participation" was an ideology with a venerable Jeffersonian ancestry, but it was
directed by OEO primarily at the poor and the group Moynihan has called
the "professional reformers."[8] They accepted it and acted on it, at least at
first. But if we compare this single main ideology with the several ideologies in use by the DOD, we note that those of the DOD have a wider set
of targets: the public at large (appealing to fear or patriotism), the manpower resources professionals (the DOD as skill developer), the engineering world (the DOD as employer, major contractor, and market for inven-
tions), and organized labor (the DOD as job developer). The broader

[7] Louis A. Zurcher, Jr., "Functional Marginality: The Dynamics of a Poverty Intervention Organization," (*Southwestern*) *Social Science Quarterly*, 48 (Dec., 1967),
pp. 411–421.

[8] Daniel P. Moynihan, *Maximum Feasible Misunderstanding* (New York: The Free
Press, 1969).

spectrum of targets and the broader set of ideologies used by Defense is illuminating in comparison to the rather narrow band of groups toward whom the single major action ideology of OEO was directed. More research needs to be done on the factors resulting in the decision to create ideologies, and the decisions on the target groups to be singled out in each case.

To sum up, research on the role of ideologies in use by government bureaucracies such as the DOD may give us clues as to what has worked, what is vulnerable in the present MIC ideological area, and what, moral issues aside, could be a successful ideology in gaining general political support for programs for the poor, and for legislation directed at the betterment of their living conditions and life chances.

COMPLEXING PHENOMENA: ARE THE LESSONS RELEVANT?

In any discussion of the "complexing" phenomenon, the allocation of resources is a central research topic. The phenomenon involves the breakdown in the older boundaries between the public and private sectors of the economy and the weakening of older systems of checks and balances. Complexing can be defined as a progressive divorce of a set of institutional relationships from the aims and goals of the wider society, brought about by political apathy on the part of the public with respect to controlling these institutional relations, in a situation where it is to the benefit of the involved institutions to divert the society's overall resources toward their ends. Complexing can be observed in any public-private institutional interaction, such as for example the relation between judges, lawyers who support their election, and legislatures made up of lawyers also in practice.[9] Huntington notes that the relation between industries and regulatory government agencies such as the FAA can develop a form of complexing, or to use his term, "clientalism," which defeats the purpose of the government's regulatory role.[10] Complexing is socially important to the extent that the involved institutions are strategically central to the life of the society and are potentially in command of significant societal resources. The study of complexing phenomena displayed by the military-industrial complex is important because of the knowledge it can yield on the way institutional relationships are constructed, maintained, or destroyed. As we noted above in the discussion on ideology research, the past absence of a societal complex acting in the interests of the poor may be significant in explaining why these programs have met with so little success.

The MIC gives us a valuable area for research on the weak and strong elements inherent in a complexing situation. For example, is is important to note the difference between (a) those industries involved in defense contracting, (b) those industries in no way involved in such work, and (c) those industries in a trend away from military to civilian customers. The nature of the complex, and ascertaining whether long-term trends are

---

[9] Murray T. Bloom, *The Trouble with Lawyers* (New York: Doubleday, 1968), pp. 157–191.

[10] Samuel P. Huntington, *Clientalism, A Study in Administrative Politics* (Harvard University: Ph.D. diss., 1951).

or are not in the same direction as the present short-term gains by those in group (a), deserve far more complete study by economists, sociologists, and political scientists. On the other hand, to what extent does there already exist a "domestic industry complex" and a "computer-technological-university" complex in process of formation? Would these latter be of any greater long-term benefit to the poor than the MIC? Otherwise put, can a profitable complex to aid the poor be constructed of organizations and industries built on the profit motive? The same question can be asked about non-profit voluntary agencies and public service. As Marris and Rein point out in their critique of the Ford Foundation Gray Areas program and the poverty program,

> Bureaucracy, as the instrument of power, can be taken to reflect the interests of the dominant social classes. The apparent irrelevance of social serices, judged by the needs of the poor, could have a harsher explanation than the devotion to ritual of organization men. It may suit the needs of the middle classes, whose well-being would be threatened by more generous and effective service to the poor.[11]

In this way, we can see that a health-and-welfare complex, an industry-education complex, or an interlocking action directorate of public and private agencies (with or without the participation of the poor) could be a conservative force in a community, and might be no more willing than the MIC to allow its resources to fall directly into the hands of the poor. Indeed, the primary focus of most public and private agencies, including most of the OEO Community Action Agencies, has not involved political mobilization for national legislation on social insurance, guaranteed income, or any other form of redistributive legislaton which would benefit the poor. One must note, therefore, that a study of the factors which go to maintain the MIC may simply be one aspect of the interests of all types of organization in maintaining a status quo from which they benefit. In intervention terms, will action aimed at changing the MIC's power and use of resources be fruitful without simultaneous intervention in aspects of the total human service system, where it, too, is engaging in complexing behavior? In addition to the question of whether there are parallels between the MIC and human service complexes (with both defined) we must ascertain whether the *poor* will benefit from greater complexing in the service field. Added power and control over resources by a strong health-welfare complex may not automatically improve conditions or opportunities for the poor.

SOCIETAL EVOLUTION: PLANNED AND UNPLANNED

The technological revolution has created many factors which must be considered in any long-run attempt to change the nature of the society. To what extent, in Meynaud's phrase, are we evolving into a technocracy, and what are the implications of this technocracy for our intervention stra-

---

[11] Peter Marris and Martin Rein, *Dilemmas of Social Reform* (New York: Atherton Press, 1968), p. 45.

tegies?[12] The MIC is presently the most evident example of the growth of technocracy—the ascendance of technical experts and bureaucrats to positions of power at the expense of democratic processes and as a consequence of the nature of production and the problem of organizing a complex society. This general issue, studied with respect to the MIC, could also be of great importance in evaluating past procedures and future strategies in antipoverty fields.

Three main consequences of the technological-scientific evolution are (a) the role of the educational processes of the society in producing technologists, (b) the ascendance of scientific and social-planning elites, and (c) the political consequences of an unstable nuclear balance of power in a multi-nation arms race.

It can be proven that the production of military and industrial technologists is proceeding at a more rapid pace than the production of human services personnel, although far greater needs exist for the latter than the former, especially in the health fields. The demands made upon the service professions seem to be such that training is required beyond the level of the case aide. Therefore, to what extent is this basic social trend reversed by the importation or enlistment of a large number of hastily trained aides? An inefficient program (with or without community aides) usually is politically vulnerable, and the extensive use of auxiliary personnel can hand ammunition to a conservative opposition, if these people are allowed too many mistakes or unchecked enthusiasms. From this point of view, is "citizen participation" a short-run palliative while being the perpetuator of a long-run problem? Or is political participation and power the heart of the matter?[13]

We need to consider another implication of demand exceeding supply of trained service personnel: the increased power of those presently in the positions, with a consequent disinterest in significantly increasing the pool of trained individuals with loyalty to the poor. Here we can view citizen participation in the opposite way. If the citizens, especially the poor, are allowed to participate only peripherally, and not in the *technical* areas of decision-making, we have a parallel to laymen being barred from debates and decisions made by the DOD. Can we not hypothesize that both the MIC and the welfare-planning elites are unwilling to expand the numbers of those in command of key technical skills? Why then are such people turned out anyway by the MIC, but not by the health and welfare fields?

What will be the long-term political and economic implications of the rise of technocratic, social-planning elites? Price has written extensively on the added political influence which the scientific elite has gained as a consequence of the technological evolution of the society.[14] The problem must be considered for social planners as well. Indeed, the existence of a special

---

[12] Jean Meynaud, *Technocracy* (New York: The Free Press, 1968).

[13] Stephan Thernstrom, *Poverty, Politics, and Planning: The Origins of ABCD* (New York: Basic Books, 1969).

[14] Don K. Price, *The Scientific Estate* (Cambridge, Mass.: Harvard University Press, 1968), pp. 15–17.

issue of the *Social Science Quarterly* on "intervention" basically assumes that the social scientist *ought* to have a central role as a planning and intervention expert. Yet are social scientists a disinterested or class-detached group? The surface impartiality of planning efforts is often a mask for the justification of interest groups. The MIT-Harvard Joint Center for Urban Studies, a few years ago, accepted a contract to design *where*, not *if*, Cambridge should have a high-speed belt parkway. Unsurprisingly, they recommended that it be built halfway between Harvard and MIT—right through the poverty areas of Cambridge. Why has Boston's black community refused to allow the Center, or its students, into its home territory? One clue may be a new publication of the Center by Forrester, which constructs a computer model of cities for projection over 50 years or more.[15] Forrester concludes that his model demonstrates that it is to the long-run economic benefit of a city to demolish low-cost housing and replace it with industry.[16] Perhaps this is so, perhaps not, but one cannot expect Roxbury to view the new urban technologists as politically neutral, disinterested research planners. The political and class-conflict implications of increased power on the part of planners needs more research. A most strategic way to begin would be a comparative political and occupational study of two work groups in relation to their society: defense strategists and the new breed of urban technologists.

Finally, one aspect of our society's, and the world's, present social evolution, is that the escalation of military spending creates its own self-fulfilling prophecy. As the international uncertainty related to multiple nuclear power-holders increases, the possibility of accidental or deliberate nuclear war escalates as well. Boulding shows that the "threat system" of international relations is far more unstable than the "exchange system" of economic interest groups in competition for world markets.[17] In an unstable situation, ideologies of the fear and emotion-based type may have an almost limitless power over a segment of the population. Research needs to be done on the psychological-political consequences of this type of international situation. Since Stouffer's classic work on attitudes toward communism as these relate to the concept of civil liberty, very little of this type of work is available.[18] Also, more economic research of the type done by Leontief and his co-workers needs to be done to prove what is suspected by economists of widely varying political persuasions: that military spending promotes inflation while it slows the rate of economic growth, and both have major consequences for the perpetuation of poverty.[19]

---

[15] Jay Forrester, *Urban Dynamics* (Cambridge, Mass.: MIT Press, 1969).

[16] *Ibid.*, pp. 1–25.

[17] Kenneth Boulding, "The Role of the War Industry in International Conflict," *Journal of Social Issues*, 23 (Jan., 1967), pp. 47–61.

[18] Samuel Stouffer, *Communism, Conformity, and Civil Liberty.* (Garden City: Doubleday, 1955).

[19] Wassily Leontief and Marvin Hoffenberg, "The Economic Effects of Disarmament," in Wassily Leontief, *Input-Output Economics* (New York: Oxford University Press, 1966), pp. 167–183.

SUMMARY

We have considered a series of research issues related to basic assumptions of antipoverty intervention. The military-industrial complex can be seen as a useful example for parallel comparison to presently existing antipoverty organizations and activities. Budgetary politics, organizational ideologies, complexing phenomena, and the technological evolution of the society are topics on which the parallels between defense and antipoverty need further research to more clearly understand whether the military-industrial complex is a basic cause of the society's poverty, or a symptom. Are conflicts of interests between haves and have-nots almost as frequently seen in antipoverty programs? The questions of what kind of intervention, and by whom, are at this time still open. Until it can be ascertained that the poverty warriors will not behave as the other kind, direct political action involving confrontation and social legislation may be a wiser course. The research might provide valuable information as to whether specific interventions and planning by action professionals, or broad-scale political action, is more likely to advance the interests of the poor.

14

COMMUNITY STRUCTURE AND PLANNING COMMITMENT: A NOTE ON THE CORRELATES OF AGENCY EXPENDITURES

ROBERT L. LINEBERRY

The University of Texas at Austin

O NE OF THE MOST STRIKING CHANGES ACCOMPANYING THE URBANIZATION of the American population is the growth of municipal planning. Because of the increasing recognition of the importance of rationally constructed urban growth, both state governments and the federal government are increasing their support for planning at the local level. Today, only a handful of cities of more than 10,000 persons lack some kind of planning program. Metropolitan-wide planning is the newest and most controversial development, with 142 of the 212 Standard Metropolitan Statistical Areas having some form of area-wide program by 1963.[1] With the passage of the Intergovernmental Cooperation Act of 1968, and the emergence of regional Councils of Government,[2] the amount of area-wide planning activity is likely to increase still further in the next decade.

For many years, teachers of city planning, like teachers of public administration, operated upon the comfortable, but largely undemonstrated, assumption that theirs was principally a technical enterprise, safely insulated from municipal politics by the dichotomy between "politics" and "administration." Concepts such as "rationality," "efficiency," and "the public interest" were the hallmark of the planning profession. It is interesting in this respect to note that the classic work advocating a "master plan" for the municipality gave no attention whatsoever to planning as a part of the political process.[3]

More recently, however, both practitioners of planning and students of the planning process have argued persuasively that the decisions of planners are neither formulated nor executed in a vacuum and that political realities are viable subjects for inquiry by both planners and other social scientists. Both Meyerson and Banfield's study of Chicago and Altshuler's study of the Twin Cities[4] concluded that the planning process was inex-

---

[1] Joint Center for Urban Studies, "The Effectivness of Metropolitan Planning," prepared for the Subcommittee on Inter-Governmental Relations of the Senate Committee on Government Operations, 1964, p. 1. For current information on municipal planning programs, see the annual issues of *The Municipal Year Book* (Chicago: International City Managers' Association, annual).

[2] By April 1968, according to a report of the Local Government Studies Center of the State University of New York at Albany, 88 metropolitan Councils of Government were in operation.

[3] Edward M. Bassett, *The Master Plan* (New York: The Russell Sage Foundation, 1938).

[4] Martin Meyerson and Edward C. Banfield, *Politics, Planning and the Public Interest* (New York: The Free Press, 1955); and Alan Altshuler, *The City Planning Process* (Ithaca, New York: Cornell University Press, 1965). For a more recent treatment, which utilizes data on six New Jersey communities, see Francine Rabinovitz, *City Politics and Planning* (New York: Atherton Press, 1969).

♦ First published in *Social Science Quarterly* 50, No. 3 (December, 1969).

tricably tied up with political considerations. Indeed, both studies concluded that planners suffered in their effectiveness because of their inattention to political phenomena.

This study will undertake an analysis of planning expenditures in American cities with 1960 populations greater than 50,000, in an effort to identify the socioeconomic and political correlates of planning budgets. We thus assume that the datum of size of planning budget is a meaningful indicator of a municipality's valuation of planning activities, an assumption which, while imperfect, does not do great violence to the canons of common sense. Indeed, both ordinary language and social scientific research make similar assumptions about the importance of family and national budgeting in reflecting basic value choices. As Masotti and Bowen argue, "The community budget may be viewed as public policy spelled out in dollars and cents. . . . [b]udget decisions represent the allocations of certain kinds of values."[5] . . .

METHODOLOGY

Sample. The usual research technique for studying the politics of planning has hitherto been the case-study method, as typified by both the Chicago and the Twin Cities examples. However much the case study has to recommend it (and we happen to think that it is a very productive tool), it inevitably suffers from a limited generalizability. The present research will use data on 190 American municipalities whose planning expenditures for fiscal year 1964 were reported by the American Society of Planning Officials, and whose 1960 populations were greater than 50,000. Unfortunately, these 190 cities are only a part of the 310 cities of this size range in that year, but data availability, of necessity, limited the scale of the inquiry.

The Planning Variable. The measure of planning expenditures as provided in the American Society of Planning Officials' publication *Expenditures, Staff and Salaries of Local Planning Agencies*[6] is the agency expenditure per capita. The figures represent only the amount spent by each municipality's[7] planning agency for the previous fiscal year. Thus, whatever planning is done in other departments is excluded from consideration.

Other Variables. Data on 24 other variables were collected for each of the 190 municipalities. These included:

1. Manufacturing ratio.
2. Percentage of elementary school children enrolled in private schools.
3. Percentage of dwelling units owner occupied.

---

[5] Louis H. Masotti and Don R. Bowen, "Communities and Budgets: The Sociology of Municipal Expenditures," *Urban Affairs Quarterly*, 1 (Dec., 1965), p. 39. variety of socioeconomic and political variables.

[6] American Society of Planning Officials, Report No. 196, March, 1965.

[7] In a very few cases, city and county planning offices were combined and the fiscal report included only this total. In those cases, the combined city-county figure was coded.

4. "Bureaucratization," i.e., level of civil service coverage.
5. "Party Strength," i.e., the method of nominations.
6. Turnout in the "most recent" municipal election before 1962.
7. Percentage Roman Catholic in Metropolitan Area, 1950.
8. Reformism score.
9. Population size, 1960.
10. Population density, 1960.
11. Population gain or loss, 1950–1960.
12. Percentage nonwhite, 1960.
13. Median age of population, 1960.
14. "Ethnicity," i.e., proportion native-born of foreign-born or mixed parentage, 1960.
15. Median family income, 1959.
16. Percentage of family incomes less than $3,000, 1959.
17. Percentage of family incomes over $10,000, 1959.
18. Median education of adult population, 1960.
19. Percentage of adults with college educations, 1960.
20. Population mobility, 1955–1960.
21. Percentage of working force in white collar jobs, 1960.
22. Percentage of housing units in standard condition, 1960.
23. Percentage Republican vote in county, 1960 Presidential election.
24. Size of municipal budget, excluding educational expenditures, 1963–1964.[8]

PLANNING AS A DEPENDENT VARIABLE

David Easton originally formulated the heuristically useful model of a "political system" in which *outputs* were seen as the end-product of the *input process* and *conversion mechanisms*.[9] A variety of studies of state and local expenditure patterns have relied heavily upon Easton's theoretical formulations, beginning with Dawson and Robinson's study of state welfare policies. They began "with the assumption that public policy is the major

[8] A very brief note on the sources of these variables is in order. Variables 2, 3, and 9–24 are taken directly from various publications of the United States Bureau of the Census, particularly from *County and City Data Book, 1962* (Washington, D.C.: U.S. Government Printing Office, 1962). Variable 1, Manufacturing Ratio, is the percentage which manufacturing employment is of total employment, derived from Richard S. Forstall *et al.*, "Economic and Social Characteristics of Urban Places," *Municipal Year Book 1963*, pp. 85–157. Variable 4, taken to be a rough index of the professionalization of a city's bureaucracy, is also from the *Municipal Year Book 1963*. Variables 5 and 6 are from Eugene C. Lee's survey of municipal elections, which collected data on various electoral characteristics of American cities for the "most recent" election prior to his survey in 1962. I am indebted to Professor Lee and to Mrs. Ruth Dixon for making these data available to me. Variable 7, Percentage Roman Catholic, is derived from a survey made by the National Council of Churches of Christ of the United States and published in their *Churches and Church Membership in the United States*, Series D, No. 1, 1957. The index of governmental reformism, variable 8, is taken from Robert L. Lineberry and Edmund P. Fowler, "Reformism and Public Policies in American Cities," *American Political Science Review*, 61 (Sept., 1967), pp. 701–716.

[9] See David Easton, "An Approach to the Analysis of Political Systems," *World Politics*, 9 (Apr., 1957), pp. 383–400.

dependent variable which political science seeks to explain. The task of political science, then, is to find and explain the independent and intervening variables which account for policy differences."[10] Our task here is to specify which, if any, community structural variables are associated with variations in planning expenditures.

From previous research on the politics of city planning, we have developed several hypotheses which can be tested with the available data. First, and perhaps most obviously, it might be assumed that planning commitment would vary directly with indicators of community "needs" for planning. Although several of our 24 variables might be taken as indicators of need, two of them, the municipal growth rate and the incidence of poverty in the community, should provide reasonable indicators of the kinds of public problems that planners might be expected to grapple with. Thus, it was hypothesized:

1. *The greater the need for planning, as measured by the incidence of community poverty and the rate of municipal growth, the higher a city's planning expenditures.*

The Pearsonian correlations reported in Table 1 for variables 11 and 15 suggest that the data do not support the hypothesis. Neither independent variable taken as an indicator of community need is even positively related to the level of planning commitment, much less significantly so. Perhaps it seems incongruous to the liberal-minded social scientist to discover that observer-defined "needs" are only minimally reflected in public policies purportedly designed to rectify public problems. Dawson and Robinson, for example, concluded that "the greater the need [for welfare expenditures], the less effort was put out by the state to meet the need."[11] If our indicators are reasonable ones, then much the same story is told about municipal planning policies. It would have made little difference, by the way, if we had used other indices of need, such as variables 10, 12, or 22.

Perhaps, however, variations in planning commitment are not explained by abstract considerations of community need, but by the interplay of group forces and by community ecology. Most students of urban planning have observed that planning agencies are ordinarily supported by upper middle-class elements in the population and opposed by persons of ethnic and working-class backgrounds. A study prepared for the Senate Subcom-

---

[10] Richard E. Dawson and James A. Robinson, "Inter-Party Competition, Economic Variables, and Welfare Policies in the American States," *Journal of Politics*, 25 (1963), p. 266. Other research on state and local fiscal policy includes Thomas R. Dye, *Politics, Economics, and the Public* (Chicago: Rand McNally, 1966); Alan K. Campbell and Seymour Sacks, *Metropolitan America* (New York: The Free Press, 1967); Otto Davis and George H. Harris, Jr., "A Political Approach to a Theory of Public Expenditures: The Case of Municipalities," *National Tax Journal*, 19 (Sept., 1966), pp. 259–275; Masotti and Bowen, "Communities and Budgets;" and Lineberry and Fowler, "Reformism."

[11] Richard E. Dawson and James A. Robinson, "The Politics of Welfare," in Herbert Jacob and Kenneth N. Vines, eds., *Politics in the American States* (Boston: Little, Brown and Co., 1965), p. 403.

TABLE 1

Simple Correlations Between 24 Variables and Planning
Expenditures in 190 American Cities Over
50,000 Population in 1960

Variable	r
1. Manufacturing ratio	.042
2. Private school attendance	—.237
3. Owner occupancy	—.152
4. Bureaucratization	.056
5. Party strength	.147
6. Electoral turnout	—.137
7. Percentage Catholic	—.083
8. Reformism score	—.018
9. Population size	—.075
10. Density	—.096
11. Population change, 1950–1960	—.155
12. Percentage Negro	—.063
13. Median age	—.165
14. Ethnicity	.002
15. Percentage incomes under $3,000	—.046
16. Percentage incomes over $10,000	.120
17. Median family income	—.086
18. Median education in years	.094
19. Percentage college educated	—.003
20. Mobility	.080
21. Percentage white collar	.203
22. Percentage housing units standard	.036
23. County Republican vote, 1960	.109
24. City noneducational expenditures	—.166

mittee on Inter-Governmental Relations by the Joint Center for Urban
Studies points to the "unconscious reflection of middle class values shared
by professional planners" and suggests that "business and middle class
groups have recognized their interest in voicing their ideas to the
planners."[12] Meyerson and Banfield found in Chicago that planning officials, representing as they did a middle class, "public-regarding" interest,
were ordinarily supported by business interests and opposed by ethnic and
working-class interests.[13] Altshuler's study of planning in the Twin Cities
notes that "businessmen have been the primary patrons of the urban planning movement since its beginnings."[14] Conversely, Banfield and Wilson's
imaginative theory about the "private-regarding" values of ethnic and
working-class elements might suggest the opposition of the latter to plan-

[12] Joint Center for Urban Studies, "Effectiveness of Municipal Planning," p. 27.
[13] Meyerson and Banfield, *Politics, Planning*, Ch. 9–11, *passim*.
[14] Altshuler, *City Planning Process*, p. 323.

ning policy.[15] While we have warned elsewhere against the simplistic ecological fallacy which equates the size of a group in the population with its control over policy variations,[16] it will still be useful to see if there is any relationship between the class and interest structure of a community and its planning commitment.

We thus hypothesize:

2. *Cities with larger middle- and upper-class groups in the population are more likely to spend heavily on planning than cities with fewer middle- or upper-class persons.*

And, similarly:

3. *Cities with heavy concentrations of ethnic and religious minorities are less likely to spend heavily on planning activities than cities with fewer ethnic and religious minorities.*

If we take variables 16–19 and 21 (pertaining to income, education, and occupation) as indicators of socioeconomic status and variables 7 and 14 (pertaining to ethnicity and Catholicism) as indicators of ethnicity, then we have some basis for testing the hypotheses. Although there are some weak correlations on two variables (16 and 21) supporting Hypothesis 2, the evidence probably is best weighed against it. There is almost no relationship between our measures of ethnicity and planning variations.

The paucity of political data available for large samples of cities makes it difficult to assess the interaction of planning and politics. We have collected data on six political characteristics of these cities (variables 4, 5, 6, 8, 23, and 24), which should permit at least some general observations. In this connection, the historic and ideological linkages between planning and the municipal reform movement, together with the political asceticism of both reformers and planners,[17] might suggest that:

4a. *Indicators of bureaucratization and governmental reformism are positively associated with planning commitment, and*

4b. *Party strength is negatively associated with planning commitment.*

But either the direction or the strength of the relationships between these indicators and planning expenditures compels a rejection of both 4a and

---

[15] Edward C. Banfield and James Q. Wilson, *City Politics* (Cambridge, Mass.: Harvard University Press and the M.I.T. Press, 1963), pp. 234–240. Raymond Wolfinger and John O. Field tested the hypothesis that planning expenditures and the ethnic proportion of the population were negatively related and found evidence to reject the hypothesis. See their "Political Ethos and the Structure of City Government," *American Political Science Review*, 60 (June, 1966), esp. pp. 322–324.

[16] Lineberry and Fowler, "Reformism," p. 707.

[17] A survey of planning directors by Rabinovitz and Pottinger conducted in 1965 concluded that the great majority of directors viewed their role as something more than that of a technical specialist. But 60 per cent saw their role as one of informing city officials on technical aspects only. No more than a quarter reported that they tried to persuade as well as inform city officials. See Francine Rabinovitz and J. Stanley Pottinger, "Organization for Local Planning: The Attitudes of Directors," *Journal of the American Institute of Planners*, 33 (Jan., 1967), p. 28. Spokesmen for "advocacy planning" like Paul Davidoff and Lisa Peattie urge planners to take more overtly political roles. This argument is articulated in Davidoff, "Advocacy and Pluralism in Planning," *Journal of the American Institute of Planners*, 31 (Dec., 1965), pp. 331–338.

4b. Moreover, given the image of planners as having a "professional bias in favor of bigger and bigger government,[18] it is interesting to note that general noneducational spending and planning expenditures are negatively, albeit slightly, related.

TABLE 2

Stepwise Correlations Between Independent Variables
with Greatest Explanatory Power
and Planning Expenditures[a]

Independent Variables	Cumulative R^2
Private school attendance	.056
Owner occupancy	.085
Electoral turnout	.100
Percentage white collar	.107
Reformism score	.112
Cumulative R^2 with all 24 variables	.140

[a] A stepwise correlation takes the most highly correlated independent variable, controls for it, and, in a process of cumulative multiple partial correlations, continues until all independent variables have been included.

More generally, as the correlations in Table 1 indicate, there are only the most tenuous of linkages between community ecology and variations in the dependent variable. The highest correlation attained is an unimpressive —.237 and most hover around zero. Indeed, Table 2, which reports the partial results of a stepwise correlation, indicates that all 24 independent variables can explain only 14 per cent of the variation in urban planning costs. Community ecology is, then, only modestly predictive of variations in planning commitment.

DISCUSSION

Perhaps we should not make too much of negative findings. We think, however, that these negative findings point up the ecological distance between planning agencies and the sociopolitical structure of municipalities. Studies of state and local finance explain and predict a very large proportion of the variation in fiscal policies,[19] the implication being that community variables such as income distribution or political structure in some sense "determine" the level of fiscal outputs. Planning expenditures, on the other hand, have only the most tenuous linkages to these community structural variables. Perhaps this is an indication of the distance which planning stands from the larger process of community decision-making, with planners operating in at least a partial political vacuum. Indeed, planners have often been criticized for their relative naïveté concerning the political aspects of their profession.[20] While planners are often the victims of poli-

[18] Altshuler, *City Planning Process*, p. 313.
[19] See the studies cited in fn. 10.
[20] See, e.g., Banfield and Wilson, *City Politics*, Ch. 14.

tics, they may be insufficiently integrated into the community's ecological structure to gain political resources from intimate ties to relevant groups and individuals. If that is the case, then plans may be more a symbolic than a material output of the political system,[21] functioning primarily as "civic New Year's resolutions."[22] The kind of impact that can be made by the output of planning policy thus becomes problematic.

[21] Murray Edelman, *The Symbolic Uses of Politics* (Urbana: University of Illinois Press, 1964).

[22] Norton E. Long, *The Polity* (Chicago: Rand McNally, 1962), p. 192.

·15·
COMMUNITY CONTROL OF SCHOOLS AS AN IDEOLOGY AND SOCIAL MECHANISM[1]

ELEANOR P. WOLF
Wayne State University

ALL-OUT FROM THE CONFLICT WITHIN THE NEW YORK CITY SCHOOL system last winter received especially wide coverage in the Sunday issue of the *New York Times* on January 26, 1969. At one point Francis Keppel, former Commissioner of Education, in the course of responding to a reporter's question about the increase in Negro-Jewish tensions as a by-product of the decentralization experiment, said: "If those social science fellows were so right and smart about what we did wrong, why didn't they say so at the time?"[2]

Keppel's question is a good one and we note a number of attempts by academics to explore various aspects of the movement for community control as it gathers momentum across the nation. In this paper we will consider: (1) the "ideology" or assertions of belief which serve as rationale for the community control movement and (2) some of the social effects or consequences of this effort to relocate the control of urban schools. It should be noted at the outset however, that despite Keppel's plea for enlightenment, what social scientists say is not likely to be a very important factor in this struggle. By contrast, the attempts of the recent past to improve the racial balance of Northern schools made very extensive use of research findings, often, unfortunately, much exaggerated or seriously misinterpreted.[3] Pressure for proposals involving bussing, pairing, educational parks and other means of improving racial balance came largely from middle-class liberals in the civil rights movement and their allies in intellectual circles. Both the content of the supporting ideology and the training and background of many of its leaders and supporters encouraged heavy use of social science data. In addition, since there was, and still is, considerable doubt concerning any legal or constitutional right to have a racially-mixed pupil population, such proposals had to be justified on the basis of educational policy. The fact that there was often little grass-roots support (and indeed often widespread opposition from white parents) contributed to the somewhat elitist character of these efforts in many communities. Superintendents and boards of education were urged to "exercise leadership" in promulgating such programs as "sound educational policy."

The emphasis on the necessity for racial balance and the repeated assertion that education in its absence could not possibly be successful helped to generate a social climate which seemed to set the stage for this latest

[1] This is a slightly revised version of a paper presented at the meetings of the Society for the Study of Social Problems, September 1, 1969, in San Francisco.

[2] *New York Times*, Jan. 26, 1969, p. 59.

[3] Eleanor P. Wolf, "Using Research Data to Support Civil Rights Propositions," paper presented at the meetings of the Society for the Study of Social Problems, Aug. 30, 1964, Montreal. (Mimeographed)

♦ First published in *Social Science Quarterly* 50, No. 3 (December, 1969).

strategy. Certainly the message to Negro parents conveyed in that earlier campaign (which seemed to this writer then and now a major strategic blunder) was this: Our evidence proves that your children cannot learn unless they are in racially mixed schools. If black parents believed this assertion, they must have concluded that not having achieved such class-rooms, their children were doomed to failure. And if such were the case, any alternative, however drastic or doubtful, might appear worth trying.

Not very much use is being made of research materials in the current campaigns for community control of schools. Data previously used to demonstrate the need for better racial balance are ignored or rejected by implication; research materials which relate under-achievement to social and economic disadvantage are often explicitly repudiated. The Bundy Report (outlining the plan for New York City school decentralization) while resting its case largely on educational grounds, does not cite evidence to show that a greater degree of neighborhood control will of itself upgrade the educational performance of children.[4] In fact, there is the implicit rejection of such a claim in the Report's warning that no system of reorganization is a substitute for the "massive infusion of funds."[5]

At the neighborhood level in many cities, the major emphasis, in keeping with the current mood of increased black assertiveness, is on the *right* of citizens to control their own institutions. In addition, however, some use is being made of arguments to support the contention that local control and direct "accountability" to neighborhood residents would upgrade pupil performance. An examination of the content of a sampling of this literature reveals widespread use of the following themes:[6]

1. The educational achievement of Negro pupils is deteriorating.
2. This failure is not caused by inadequate financial support ("After vast increases in public expenditures for education . . . still—Johnny can't read.")[7]
3. Nor is it caused by the social background of pupils. (". . . school personnel shift the blame for their failure to educate our children . . . [they] are 'culturally deprived', they alibi").[8]

[4] *Reconnection for Learning*, Advisory Panel on Decentralization of New York City Schools Report, (Nov. 9, 1967).

[5] *Ibid.*, Letter of transmittal to Mayor Lindsay.

[6] Since the literature of a movement has no clear boundaries, these citations are merely illustrative: "Why the New York Urban League backs the Ocean Hill-Brownsville governing board without reservation" (adv.), *New York Times*, (Oct. 11, 1968), p. 30; E. Sell, "Viewpoint," *Detroit Teacher* (Feb. 10, 1969), p. 10; Community Action Neighbors Northwest, *Newsletter* 1:2 (Jan., 1969); Detroit Citizens for Community Control of Schools, Leaflets (undated), P. O. Box 494; Miller High School District Advisory Council Position Statement (undated), Detroit. Reference to arguments made by extremist groups (e.g., charges of educational genocide) have been omitted on the supposition that they are unrepresentative of substantial segments of supporting opinion. For a sympathetic treatment reporting on and interpreting the views and rationale of both leaders and grass-roots supporters in the Ocean Hill area, see Agee Ward, "Ocean Hill: Education, Community Power, and the Media," *The Center Forum*, 3 (Nov. 13, 1968), Center for Urban Education.

[7] CANN, Newsletter.

[8] Detroit Citizens for Community Control of Schools, Leaflet.

4. Local participation in educational decision-making (ranging from some degree of involvement to complete neighborhood control) will improve the educational performance of pupils. The implied chain of causation is not specified. There are varying degrees of emphasis on the need for curriculum to reflect "black culture" and neighborhood preferences, but the main contention seems to be that if the population using the schools holds power over personnel, their greater effort and responsiveness will produce educational success.

Those familiar with the professional literature in this field will note that there is little evidence to support these propositions. The under-achievement of Negro children from low-income families is not a new social phenomenon. What is new is that beginning about ten years ago this condition began to receive widespread attention and was defined as an urgent social problem. There are no data to suggest that children from the lowest stratum in the urban community do worse in school now than they did in the past, although in terms of their need for educational competence the question is hardly relevant. The lowered average achievement scores, however, which are usually used as evidence of educational "decline" are produced by an alteration in the social class mix of the pupil population.

The contention that there have been vast increases in the financial resources made available to big city school systems is misleading. Urban schools, simply as a consequence of rising costs and shrinking tax base, are in deep financial difficulty.[9] Their per capita expenditure is, on the average, below that of prosperous suburban communities where pupil needs are much less. This knowledge, however, should not obscure the fact that we have as yet no adequate body of evidence to indicate what effect—if any— various types and levels of expenditures would have upon the academic performance of disadvantaged pupils. (What is reasonably clear, however, is that if such programs were to have the desired impact they would have to be unequally distributed, in favor of low-achieving groups. If we raise the level of educational performance of all, the gap remains.) While the Coleman data do not reveal much impact on performance as a consequence of school-input factors, it has been pointed out that both the choice of unit and the probability that variation in school factors would need to be greater in order to show their effects *may* be responsible for this. We do not know. It is strange that after years of controversy and the funding of a large amount of educational research we still have no field experiment whereby the impact of very substantial increases in school factors might be tested.[10]

[9] See Alan K. Campbell, "Inequities of School Finance," *Saturday Review* (Jan. 11, 1969), pp. 44–48 for materials on the current fiscal crisis. For discussion of the estimated costs of a serious but not at all grandiose program of compensatory education see David K. Cohen, "Teachers Want What Children Need . . . or Do They?" *The Urban Review*, 2 (June, 1968), pp. 25–29.

[10] Perhaps the most ambitious of these has been the "More Effective Schools Program" in New York City. See the special supplement of *Urban Review*, 2 (May, 1968) for a discussion of its impact. See also E. B. Sheldon and Raymond Glazier, "*Pupils and Schools in New York City*" (New York: Russell Sage Foundation, 1965).

The contention that the social background of pupils is no explanation for substandard educational performance, but is merely an alibi for failure, is a challenge to social science, and to rational discussion of a crucial national problem. We have, of course, much evidence to show that not only in the United States but in many other societies life-circumstances and life-styles do affect academic achievement. We have, moreover, a steadily increasing array of research which is beginning to specify more precisely the variables involved, and to trace the causal linkages between them and school learning.[11] One notes, for example, recent studies which reveal the relationship between sub-cultural "ethos" and scholastic abilities at similar social class levels. Nevertheless, the emphasis on disadvantage as an "explanation" arouses resentment in some groups and contributes to sentiment in favor of community control of schools, which offers a competing ideology.

Some liberal and many radical intellectuals reveal a chronic ambivalence in their attitude toward poverty and low social status as they shift from presenting evidence showing the destructive effects of these conditions to the assertion that somehow, the victims have been—miraculously—unharmed. Thus for example, so able a scholar as Kenneth Clark once insisted:

> Let us not teach these children as if they were different . . . there is no psychological or educational evidence . . . that so-called low socio-economic background children have any greater difficulty learning to read than other children will have. . . . *There is no evidence that there is any cultural factor that is relevant to the complexity of the learning process.*[12] (My emphasis)

[11] Among the many contributors to this research are Anne Anastasi, David Ausubel, Basil Bernstein, Benjamin Bloom, Urie Bronfenbrenner, Martin Deutsch, Miriam Goldberg, Robert Hess, P. Levenstein, Benjamin Passamanick, A. H. Passow, Irving Sigel, J. McV. Hunt and Virginia Shipman. Recent research on the relationship between specific components of intellectual functioning and ethnicity is exemplified by Gerald Lesser, G. Fifer and D. H. Clark, *The Mental Abilities of Children from Different Social-Class and Cultural Groups* (Chicago: The University of Chicago Press, 1965), and Morris Gross, *Learning Readiness in Two Jewish Groups* (comparing children, all Jewish, from Sephardic and Ashkenazic background), Center for Urban Education. Ethnic studies, such as N. Glazer and D. P. Moynihan, *Beyond the Melting Pot* (Cambridge, Mass.: MIT Press, 1963), and Herbert Gans, *The Urban Villagers* (New York: The Free Press, 1962) have revealed important differences in cultural emphasis which their authors believe affect educational achievement; the same applies to Bernard Rosen's work on achievement motivation. In addition, the field of national character and culture-personality studies makes at least by inference, important contributions to our understanding of the relationship of ethnicity to academic performance; see for example, William Caudill, "Japanese-American Personality and Acculturation," *Genetic Psychology Monographs*, 1952; Harry Kitano, *Japanese-Americans* (New York: Prentice-Hall, 1969), esp. Chaps. 5 and 7; Charles Keil's appreciative treatment of the lower-class black urban community as a subculture, *Urban Blues* (Chicago: The University of Chicago Press, 1967).

[12] Kenneth Clark, "Clash of Cultures in the Classroom," *Integrated Education*, 1 (Aug., 1963), pp. 11–12.

Persons bent on school reforms are, understandably, wary of causal explanations which may have the latent function of excusing inaction or encouraging complacency. (Similarly, those wishing to improve the effectiveness of the police are impatient with sociocultural explanations of criminal behavior, despite the fact that these were not offered as substitutes for police protection.) And those wanting schools to make maximum efforts to overcome the dismally consistent relationship between social background and academic performance fear that to emphasize this might blunt the force of educational reform.

There is yet another aspect of this matter which those who lack direct contact with inner-city schools may not recognize, and it is this: No one has yet found a way to tell parents what most social scientists believe to be the fundamental reasons for their children's educational problems. To capture the essence of this dilemma, you must imagine yourself addressing a meeting of parents in an inner-city school. They are looking at a chart of reading scores made by fourth graders in that school over the past 20 years, and the curve moves down as the percentage of Negro children goes up. (If the school was once occupied, and this is not infrequent, by Jewish children, the contrast is startling.) Speak, if you can, in plain English, of life-circumstances and social class, subcultural emphasis, and linguistic development to troubled and deeply concerned parents whose pride has suffered many injuries, and who are so vulnerable to offense regardless of pure intentions. It is in these encounters that much of the impetus for community control is being generated.

In the past, groups allied with efforts to improve the education of disadvantaged children (for example some locals of the American Federation of Teachers) could focus such discussions on the undeniable facts of discrimination in the allocation of resources.[13] As resource allocation approached equality within some city school systems, this explanation became less persuasive. As parent groups became more knowledgeable about tests of achievement they learned that serious educational difficulties emerge in the early grades. This means that whereas all other levels of education can attribute failure to the "poor preparation" of those who come to them, the primary school must confront the fact of initial disadvantage, with its painful implication that (no matter what caused it) parents have somehow been unable to give their children a good start in life.

The wish to avoid discussions of this kind explains much of the evasiveness and attempts at concealment often practiced by school personnel, a strategy which often escalates citizen annoyance into rage. It is a truism that when the basic causes of failure are not clear, or if made clear are unacceptable, there is a tendency for substitutive responses—scapegoating—to be generated. Further, it might well be that even if concerned citizens made their diagnosis of the reasons for educational under-achievement with the greatest objectivity, the programs which constitute a more rational re-

[13] For an example of this emphasis see Patricia C. Sexton, *Education and Income* (New York: Viking, 1961).

sponse might appear so long-range and difficult to secure that it would seem quite reasonable to reject them.

In the ideology of community control, attention is directed away from humiliating explanations of low achievement as the product of disadvantage or deprivation. The earlier contention, which also contains humiliating implications, that the presence of white pupils is a necessary condition for the educational success of black children, is for the most part, merely ignored. Low achievement is re-defined, in some of the movement's literature, as failure to learn the "white man's culture" and thus not failure at all. The demand for "curriculum relevant to the Black Community"[14] or for "education from a black perspective" is vague enough not to directly challenge the overwhelming evidence that Negro Americans do not have goals and aspirations for their children's success different from those of whites. Drawing upon the growing sense of distinctive ethnicity, educational difficulties can be re-defined as the result of the imposition of alien standards which can and must be rejected.

If achievement is accepted as being low, it is attributed to the faulty attitude of school personnel. In the early sixties under-achievement was often attributed to the (undeniably) larger proportion of academically less-qualified teachers working in ghetto areas; at present, the class or racial bias of personnel is more commonly emphasized. This bias is often characterized as "unconscious" or so subtle as to defy empirical verification: ("How many witnesses are needed to convict teachers of their failure to love their children?").[15] It is in this aspect of the ideology of the community control movement that there has been some recourse to "what research says," drawing largely on the work of Robert Rosenthal and his associates, especially in *Pygmalion in the Classroom*.[16] *Pygmalion* has many inconsistent findings and the data presented do not reveal very much about the impact of teacher-expectancy upon academic achievement. It would be difficult indeed to draw from it the conclusion that this variable intervenes with an effect sufficient to upset the relationship between social background and school performance.[17] However, this claim is typical of literature now widely circulated in support of community control: "As we all know from the research studies, when a teacher expects students to fail, they fail; when a teacher expects students to succeed, they succeed."[18] Thus the power of positive thinking replaces all of the expensive and complex strategies designed to intervene in one of the most persistent relationships known to social science: the tendency for children reared in marked inequality of condition to be at a competitive disadvantage.

In situations where there are large numbers of Negro teachers, pupil

---

[14] Detroit Committee for Community Control of Schools, Leaflet.

[15] From "Why the Urban League."

[16] R. Rosenthal and L. Jacobson, *Pygmalion in the Classroom* (New York: Holt, Rinehart and Winston, 1968).

[17] For a discussion of this relationship see James S. Coleman, "Equal Schools or Equal Students?" *The Public Interest*, 4 (Summer, 1966), pp. 70–75.

[18] E. Sell, "Viewpoint," *Detroit Teacher* (Feb., 1969), p. 10.

•

failure may be attributed to the nature of the relationship between school and neighborhood. Stressed, in varying degrees, are: the need for "accountability" of the local school to the neighborhood it serves; the dysfunctional interference of "administration" and "bureaucracy;" and the necessity for direct citizen participation in educational decision-making. These arguments contain a mixture of elements involving some (implicit) hypotheses about the impact of parental involvement upon children's educational performance, as well as the assertion that controlling power, regardless of its educational consequences, is a right which citizens possess.

Reduced to its simplest terms, the principle of accountability seems to declare that if power rests with neighborhood residents, school staff would "try harder," and if they did, pupil achievement would not be substandard. (College professors might ponder the application of this principle to their own students whose work is unsatisfactory.) The emphasis on more localized control reflects not only a bid for increased power of the black community, but the generalized resentment against bureaucracies in many institutional areas.[19] As such it strikes a responsive note in the present climate of opinion, although the relationship between bureaucratic defects and social class variations in school achievement is not clear. Research is rarely invoked to support claims that direct citizen participation in educational decisions and processes would enhance pupil performance. The United States already has a rather decentralized system of public education, and direct citizen involvement in school affairs has, in the past, often been associated with fundamentalist and other anti-liberal pressures from the grass roots.[20]

The creation and preservation of adequate social space between professionals and the public, and the demarcation of a line (often unclear) between the former's prerogatives and the rights of citizens has been considered essential. The anti-professional bias and vaguely populist antagonism to "the experts" expressed as "We know what is best for our own schools" has had perennial appeal to many low-status groups.[21] At present, however, and especially if espoused by Negroes, this anti-professionalism

[19] After this paper was written an article by Nathan Glazer stressing this theme appeared in the New York Times, Sunday Magazine Section, "For White and Black, Community Control is the Issue," April 27, 1969.

[20] A large body of research tends to support the view that: "It is deferential respect for the elite rather than tolerant popular opinion which underlies the vaunted freedom of dissent in countries like Britain and Sweden." See S. M. Lipset, "Value Patterns, Class and the Democratic Polity," in R. Bendix and S. M. Lipset, eds., Class, Status and Power (New York: The Free Press, 1966) which discusses the problems of populist vs. elitist styles of pluralistic democracy. Some ways in which various forms of parent and citizen participation have affected schools is discussed by David Reisman in his Constraint and Variety in American Education (New York: Doubleday Anchor, 1957), esp. pp. 123–134. See also Samuel Stouffer, Communism, Conformity and Civil Liberties (New York: Doubleday, 1955), which, like most other research data, supports the generalization that intolerance of dissent, lack of concern for due process, etc. are more characteristic of the less educated. See also S. M. Lipset, Political Man (New York: Doubleday, 1963), pp. 92–108.

[21] This was a major theme in the Wallace campaign literature and speeches in 1968.

receives support from some intellectuals in and out of academic life. (In view of the usual response of the academic community to intrusion or scrutiny by laymen it is interesting to note the support some have given to this kind of activity within the public schools.)

Some segments of middle-class opinion tend to view participation and citizen-action as ends desirable in themselves. The facts that middle-class parents have been active participants in school affairs in the United States and their children have fewer educational difficulties than those of the poor are seen by some as cause and effect. It would be difficult to assert this causal relationship as established, in view of a rather large amount of contrary evidence.[22] Finally, although it would not be possible to support the claim that the relocation of control alone would improve the educational performance of poor black children, many groups in this country have demanded and won institutional change with as little or less verification of their assertions from the social sciences.

The immediate rewards of community control. Kenneth Haskins, principal of Morgan School in Washington, D.C., has said that "community control has emerged not because of the great promise it holds for the education of black children, but because of the failure of what has taken place so far."[23] It would be more accurate to say that programs which might have been expected to improve educational performance have *not* taken place. Not enough support has been mustered for sustained and substantial programs of compensatory education nor for anti-poverty efforts of sufficient magnitude to make significant reductions in economic inequality. Our best evidence suggests both would be necessary. Social change of this magnitude depends on success in the development of national coalition politics; present prospects are not very encouraging. By contrast, the movement for community control of schools meets some immediate needs and incorporates elements attractive to a variety of key groups.

Pressures for community control, by generating a climate which many whites find uncomfortable, have already created additional employment opportunities for Negroes. It is difficult to disentangle the impact of these new pressures from the influence of other factors which make jobs in inner-city schools difficult for whites, but the notion of "accountability" plus the emphasis on the danger of "unconscious" bias held by whites is felt as

[22] We have already noted that the inverse relationship between social class and academic performance exists in other societies where parental participation and citizen involvement in school affairs is virtually unknown. We know that in the United States, children of the very prosperous often attend private boarding schools where, following the British pattern, education is left to the "experts" and the parent rarely enters the school. It is interesting to note that the Plowden Report, while offering a wide variety of educational reforms, does not even consider the possibility that parents might be participants in staff selection or curriculum planning. See *Children and Their Primary Schools*, A Report of the Central Advisory Council for Education in England (London, Her Majesty's Stationery Office, 1967), 1, Chap. 4. What the effect of parental involvement in educational decision-making would be on children's achievement at various social class levels is, unfortunately, not known; it would be valuable to design an experiment where this factor alone was manipulated.

[23] K. Haskins, "The Case for Local Control," *Saturday Review* (Jan. 11, 1969), p. 53.

threatening. In addition, some school systems have become more flexible in their selection procedures, bypassing seniority and other traditional promotion criteria in order to upgrade black personnel to fill sensitive administrative positions. The impact of these changes, plus their estimate of what the future holds in store, has tended to discourage the entrance of new white recruits and has.hastened the gradual movement of white staff to suburban school systems. It should be noted that some of these reactions to more aggressive lay participation and accountability for school failures are felt by black teachers and administrators as well; they, however, have fewer employment alternatives.

All movement toward a greater degree of community control which involves the creation of neighborhood boards or advisory committees distributes varying amounts of power and prestige within the black community. Even the publicity attached to such positions is helpful in the development of political careers. Further, although the extent to which pupils will benefit educationally from these developments is debatable, they are surely a valuable learning experience for adult participants. (If, as has been suggested, claims for the impact of community control upon academic achievement are based on inadequate or non-rational grounds, it is hard to think of a more effective way for its supporters to be persuaded of this.) Both the struggle for community control and its operation, if enacted, offer new opportunities for the development of Negro leadership and organizational expertise.

Community control has considerable appeal for local government officials as a means of handling discontent. City officials, lacking as they are in the power to make effective responses to demands in the realms of employment, health, housing, public assistance and police protection, are under constant attack. The effort to relocate control of schools appears to channel some of this turbulence onto the educational establishment. It is one program with significant support within the black community in northern cities which makes few demands upon city funds.

Most middle-class white households with children, and large segments of the white working-class as well, now live outside city boundaries and are thus not threatened by these developments. Within the city at the present time few schools serve biracial populations stable enough to predict that such racial mixtures will continue to exist. It would appear, then, that there may not be many situations where struggles concerning community control will divide parents on a racial basis. In cities such as Detroit, where a large proportion of the school staff is black, much of the conflict may be played out within the Negro community.

The movement for community control of schools gives its leaders and supporters a cause which offers promise of speedy success. While the extent and intensity of grass-roots support is hard to estimate, it is difficult to see any force which is both able and willing to block its enactment.[24]

[24] The numbers involved may be smaller than might be expected, however. In a Detroit experiment, the "Neighborhood Education Center Project," a rather widely publicized election to name representatives to two citizen boards resulted in 37 votes cast

Black leaders, then, will be able to demonstrate their ability to "make something happen," to offer visible evidence of the power to achieve change. Such victories, which resemble some of the civil rights triumphs of the South, have been rare indeed in northern cities, where the struggle against the problems of poverty has been slow and arduous, requiring drastic alterations in the distribution of rewards and the allocation of resources.

In conclusion. The current efforts to secure varying degrees of neighborhood control of schools present an ideology which, in contrast to the usual sociological explanations for under-achievement is gratifying to self-esteem and contributes to positive ethnic identification. The movement serves as a mechanism for the discharge of hostility and a focal point for the emerging organization of the black community. It can be a testing-ground for its capacity and power and a means of developing its cohesion and leadership although it also seems likely that in the process segments of the populations may be mobilized and "radicalized" for ends as yet unclear.

This movement confronts a somewhat vulnerable institution whose basic task involves compelling the participation of masses of children and youth in an enterprise where too many, under present conditions, cannot succeed, at a time when their success is a requirement for upward mobility. Although schools are often described as removed or remote from the public this is not quite the case; rather, the social space between parents and school operations is insufficient to afford the insulation and privacy enjoyed (for good or ill) by most other professions. The short-comings, failures, defects and inadequacies of any large group of professionals are inexhaustible; in the public schools, they are more visible than in most other bureaucratic settings. This suggests the possibility that in cities such as Detroit, with its large and rapidly growing proportion of Negro school personnel, and in other cities as this process develops, the conflicting interests of layman and professional will reassert themselves. There is also some evidence to suggest that many Negro parents are wary of a localism which they fear may involve too much turbulence and disorder in the schools their children attend. It is possible that the movement called "community control," having discharged some of the functions we have described, will be a rather shortlived stage in the transition to predominantly Negro leadership in some American cities. But this is speculation.

(from a potential electorate of 800) in one area and 40 (from a potential electorate of 4,000) in another. From Detroit Board of Education, *Proceedings* (May 13, 1969). See also G. Rothbell and J. Eisler, "Community Opinion: Who is Speaking for Whom?" *The Center Forum*, 3 (Nov. 13, 1968).

16

THE STRUCTURE OF SOCIETY AND SOCIAL SERVICE INTEGRATION[1]

MAYER N. ZALD

Vanderbilt University

A S AMERICA BECAME AN URBANIZED SOCIETY IN THE SECOND HALF OF THE nineteenth century, its churches, governments, women of compassion, and social movement leaders began to recognize that the streets of gold had gutters of slime; that the open road of opportunity also contained dead ends of despair, disease, injury, isolation and poverty.[2] The response to perceived social problems was the creation, in the public and private sectors, of a plethora of programs, services, and organizations. Almost as soon as those early entrepreneurial agents of mercy defined and organized services to meet the needs, they began to recognize the problems of coordination and integration of services. The Social Services Exchange (now almost dead) and Welfare councils are not a product of the post-World War II era, but were products of the very first large-scale welfare efforts in our cities.

The proliferation of services in our own times has intensified the demands for coordination and integration and there have been recurring attempts to achieve better coordination. The modern emphasis on comprehensive planning has had two main goals: the provision of an adequate level and range of service and program elements and the effective *integration* of the elements of the service or program network, both within and between communities. Yet often the earlier attempts failed to solve problems of fragmentation, and no one viewing the present scene can be sanguine about the orderly relations among our attempts to solve major social problems. Problems of coordinating urban development and service also have preoccupied political scientists and public administrators. Although this essay focuses on the social welfare agency, much of its analysis applies to the coordination and integration of other urban services as well.[3]

Since so many of the modern day intervention strategies do involve comprehensive service plans and integrative networks, it is well worth our while to understand the sources of resistance to coordination and integration. Especially since in the world of public officials and social service executives, "coordination" and "integration" are much like the words "competi-

[1] This article is a revised version of a paper read at the Joint Public Meeting, Josephine Baird Children's Center, Elizabeth Lund Home, Vermont Catholic Charities, and Vermont Children's Aid Society, Burlington, Vermont, October 30, 1968. The author holds a Public Health Service Research Scientist Development Award (K–MH–34, 919) from the National Institute of Mental Health. John Tropman critically read an earlier draft.

[2] For a good historical account see Robert Bremner, *From the Depths: The Discovery of Poverty in the United States* (New York: New York University Press, 1956).

[3] William L. C. Wheaton, "Integration at the Urban Level: Political Influence and the Decision Process," in Philip E. Jacobs and James V. Toscano, eds., *The Integration of Political Communities* (New York: Lippincott, 1964), pp. 120–142.

tive marketplace" to the business executive. In both cases they are treasured words, but the actual conditions they represent are hardly pursued with vigor. It is easily understandable why the business executive would want to avoid the rigors of the competitive marketplace: in a fully competitive market he would not make much profit. But it is less clear why executives of agencies for the public weal would attempt to avoid coordination and integration. After all, is not that the route to efficient and effective service?

Instead of analysing why executives and their organizations resist bringing nirvana to the welfare world, we have typically impugned their motives—they are empire builders, or conservatives (read "fuddy-duddies"), or they are trying to protect their own jobs. In particular instances each of these charges might be correct, but a serious examination will indicate, in many cases, a sound logic behind the resistance to integration and coordination. No argument is made *for* fragmentation and low coordination; instead, there are costs and benefits to *both* integration of services and autonomy of services. Only if these costs and benefits are seriously weighed can anyone estimate the value of different *degrees* of coordination and integration under varying *structural* arrangements.

Our largely theoretical analysis attempts to link up several threads of recent sociological analysis, theories of social differentiation, the "new look" in social problem analysis, and interorganizational analysis. First, we analyze the relationship of changes in social structure and societal differentiation to the perception and definition of "social categories at risk," the target of social problems solutions. Second, the perception and definition of social problems leads to the creation of agencies and programs to cope with them. Each differentiated agency or program presents a new interface for coordination and integration. Third, agencies develop a character and set of commitments that lead to a shifting set of enmities, alliances, and coalitions. With this as our background framework we then turn to a crude, qualitative cost and benefit analysis of various integrative and coordinating mechanisms.

SOCIAL STRUCTURE AND THE EMERGENCE OF SOCIAL SERVICE PROGRAMS

There are many kinds of programs that few would have imagined a century ago, or even, in some cases, 30 years ago: crisis (suicide) prevention centers, comprehensive neighborhood health units, community mental health clinics, group treatment units in our prisons, half-way houses, street workers' programs in our largest cities, Medicare, Medicaid, consumer education leagues, and so on.

Where do these programs come from? How are they related to the changing social structure of modern society? There are three, partially interrelated, processes involved. First, the changing composition and structure of society divides the society into social categories. Second, processes within society and within relevant professions lead to definitions of social categories as social problems, creating the potential for new services or changes in existing ones. Third, new technologies, knowledge, and beliefs about how to treat or handle specific problems create the need for new organizations and structures to utilize them.

Changing composition and social structure. For organized services to come into existence there must be a perception of a fairly wide-spread social category requiring a service. A certain (undefined) minimum population mass must be in a specific category. Thus, only as the society differentiates into recognizable and sizeable groups—e.g., divorcees, adolescents, alcoholics, senior citizens—can a social problem even begin to be defined. The greater the differentiation, by definition, the greater the number of social categories.

These social categories become potential service receivers as groups within the society begin to define categories as "deficit," as not measuring up to some standard of performance. The changing social structure creates and makes salient the definition of a social category as being in some sense deficient. For example, no one thought of school dropouts as a group or, for that matter, as a problem in the nineteenth century. Only as the age of voluntary school leaving was raised did the category called "dropout" emerge. Furthermore, only as schooling was perceived as a key route to occupational success did the category become defined as a social problem. Similarly, defining old age as a social problem is caused by a combination of mortality rates, changing family structure and retirement policies, not by changing mortality rates alone. The point is that, in conjunction with values or standards of "adequate" living, it is the changing structure of society that creates social categories needing service.[4]

Social definitions of problems. Not only are the social categories for service created by the structure of the society, but the very definitions of a social problem, of deficit, are determined by the processes of organizational and professional growth and interaction. The "new look" in deviance research has focused on the way in which members of society, professional groups and "moral entrepreneurs" create the definition of deficient functioning.[5] Moral entrepreneurs have a "stake" in the perception of deficient operation. Problems are created by societal rules—"bookmaking" becomes a crime when the society decides to regulate gambling. No regulation, no crime. (Marijuana usage as a social problem is exactly of this created kind.) Different groups with different values "create" social problems.[6] The problem of positive mental health exists only to the extent that professional groups convince others to spend money to attempt to achieve positive mental health in the society. The general sociological point is that increasing differentiation leads to not only a greater range of social categories at

[4] Richard M. Titmuss, *Essays on the Welfare State* (New Haven: Yale University Press, 1959), esp. Ch. 2.

[5] Howard S. Becker, *Outsiders: Studies in the Sociology of Deviance* (Glencoe, Ill.: Free Press, 1963), and Thomas J. Scheff, *Becoming Mentally Ill* (Chicago: Aldine Publishing Co., 1967).

[6] Joseph R. Gusfield, *Symbolic Crusade: Status Politics and the American Temperance Movement* (Urbana: University of Illinois Press, 1963), and Joseph R. Gusfield, "Moral Passage: The Symbolic Process in Public Designations of Deviance," *Social Problems,* 15 (Fall, 1967), pp. 175–188.

risk, but to an increasing number of groups and organizations having a stake in defining groups at risk.

Changes in technology, knowledge, and beliefs. Finally, new organizations and services are created as a variety of solutions are proposed based on beliefs and knowledge about how to solve problems. Half-way houses are created as mental health and penological practitioners come to believe that people who are not fully incapacitated are better off outside our institutions. Adoption agencies are made regulated services when it is believed that children can have better lives this way than when placed in homes through unregulated services. A behavioral conditioning unit is introduced in a hospital when these techniques are believed to be more efficacious for certain disorders than other techniques.

The general thrust of this argument is that the creation of new large and definable categories in society, the growth and change of professional groups, and changing technology create the ever-growing possibility of new organizations and services. (Note, however, that these same processes, though more rarely, can lead to the elimination of "need" for a given type of service. For instance, the need for orphanages declined as a result of: (1) increasing longevity, (2) welfare provisions to support single parents, and (3) the emergence of adoption services.)

Thus, the fragmentation of services and the lack of integration of services is, ultimately, a result of some of the basic processes of modern society creating literally hundreds of specific purpose programs. Each new program is a planned intervention to affect some problematic category. The addition of each new program or agency multiplies the problem of coordination with every related funding, governmental and civic organization serving similar or related clientele groups. Each interface shared between organizations becomes a potential coordination area.

ORGANIZATIONS AND THEIR ENVIRONMENT

Of course, if all agencies existed in a world of sweetness and light, in a world without scarcity of time, money, and motivation, in a world of consensus on values and priorities, the problems created by the existence of hundreds of agencies might easily be overcome. If organizations were machines, complete in themselves and made up of mechanized parts, their inter-adjustment might be relatively easy. Turn a screw here, adjust an interagency linkage there. But it is precisely because they are made up of a number of groups of people with different conceptions of purpose and commitment and because they are in a constant state of flux asking for support from the multiple constituencies of the larger society that they do not lend themselves to easy integration. Essentially, the argument is that organizations are dynamic entities operating in a world of scarcity and more or less constantly faced with problems of motivating support in the community, and within themselves.[7]

[7] The approach to organizations used here, often called "Organizational Analysis," is best exemplified in the works of Philip Selznick and his students. For Selznick, see his *TVA and the Grass Roots; a Study in the Sociology of Formal Organizations* (Berkeley:

As each new organization comes into existence, it must define its goals and opening procedures. Although some social service organizations come into existence with clear-cut goals, target populations, and operating procedures, for most organizations each one of these aspects requires definition. For both public and private organizations, official charters are phrased in ambiguous or general language; scope of mission remains to be determined. A correctional institution is told to "rehabiliate inmates," a children's psychiatric service is given preventive goals and told to have residential and out-patient service. Note that relative priorities and financial allocations are rarely considered. Even in a governmental program like Medicare, although the financial base was specified by law, operating procedures were worked out through an administrative give-and-take. These goals, priorities, and target groups are worked out between executive and staff, other agencies and key board members and constituencies.[8] There is an organizational give-and-take as, over time, "turf" is defined, and programs are adjusted to perceived need and to organizational competence.

If these evolving goals and programs were value-neutral, that is, if the people did not have strong feelings about the social worth and importance of these programs, there would be much less problem in changing and coordinating social service progress. But social welfare programs are not like a line of groceries; various groups inside and outside of the specific agencies have strong feelings about the purposes of different agencies, the client to be served, and the procedures or technologies of the organization. Attempts to change them often run into stiff opposition based on these strong values and attachments.

Furthermore, the funding patterns of service-welfare organizations contribute to the maintenance of organizational autonomy. Most, if not all, social service organizations, unlike businesses, depend for most of their finances on getting funds and general support from groups who are not the direct recipients of services. Whether they are public or private agencies, they are dependent on the good will of funding agencies. Since good will is a sometimes tenuous thing, social service agencies often attempt to "lock in" good will by developing external constituencies and alliances that will work for them and with the various funding agencies. These constituencies (which in specific cases may be board members, the local mental health association, key members of legislative committees, associations of judges or of police chiefs) also develop commitments supporting various goals and modes of operation. Thus, to change organizations in the social service arena is also to neutralize or change the perspectives and operations of a lot of other groups related to the organization.

The discussion of funding arrangements leads to another point: Although social service organizations are usually not thought of as operating

---

University of California Press, 1949). See also Burton Clark, *Open Door College* (New York: McGraw–Hill, 1960).

[8] James D. Thompson and William J. McEwen, "Organization Goals and Environment: Goal Setting as an Interaction Process," *American Sociological Review*, 23 (Feb., 1958), pp. 23–31.

in a competitive marketplace, because they do not price their products to meet a competitor's price, in fact they operate in an extremely competitive environment (sometimes disguised) in which they compete for the allegiance and financial support of key groups. Unlike the competition of business, the competition is frowned upon in our public rhetoric, yet within and without government, the competition goes on.

What is the consequence of all this for the coordination and integration of agencies? It comes to this: The process of organizational formation and development leads to a host of agencies and services, each with partisans within and without the organization. These organizations may collaborate with others for some specific purposes, but not for other purposes.[9] Given our earlier argument about the increasing differentiation of organizations and social categories, comprehensive planning emerges as an attempt to establish guidelines and integrative nets for the operation of an increasingly fragmented (differentiated) agency-program scene. Whether it or any integration-coordination mechanism is successful depends upon its reckoning with the realities of organizational dynamics and operation.

COORDINATION AND INTEGRATION: COSTS AND BENEFITS

The words "coordination" and "integration" apply to a wide variety of proposals for changing the authority structure, communication channels and synchronization of programs and purposes. These proposals run from major structural reforms in which previously separate, private organizations become part of one "super-agency," to units of government being given a common central authority, to common fund-raising efforts, to relatively minor exchanges of information about a particular case or project.

A dramatic example of the problem of one kind of agency coordination has been presented by Miller.[10] Miller observed a continuing situation in which increasing delinquency in Roxbury, Mass., led to calls for a coordinated preventive program. Although several ad hoc community committees proposed a program, and finally a committee representing concerned agencies was appointed, the committee rarely met. Following the slaying of a Rabbi, the Jewish community groups started pushing for a program; the committee began to meet regularly and a program was funded and in operation. Yet, within two years the program fell apart. Miller explained the failure of the program in terms of differences among the agencies in their conceptions of the *etiology* of delinquency; of the *disposition* of the delinquent; of the *approach priority*; of the appropriate *organizational method*; and of the proper *status of personnel*.

This example, while extreme, indicates the multitude of commitments that leads to difficulty in coordination and integration of services. Overcoming each commitment and conception costs time, energy, and even organizational integrity. The costs are often too high. But there are cases

[9] Norton Long, "Local Community as an Ecology of Games," *American Journal of Sociology*, 64 (Nov., 1958), pp. 251–261.

[10] Walter Miller, "Inter-Institutional Conflict as a Major Impediment to Delinquency Prevention," *Human Organization*, 17 (Fall, 1958).

where coordination and integration do operate successfully. The problem is to specify the costs and benefits of different levels of coordination and integration.

There are two major classes of argument used in arguing for integration and coordination. One involves issues of *efficiency*—savings in money, time, and personnel—and the other involves *effectiveness*—the ability to accomplish ends.

Efficiency arguments have been involved in several major integration movements in recent times. Two of the most prominent examples are the development of state commissions of higher education and the development of coordinated fund-raising in the private sector (UGF, Red Feather). The development of state commissions (boards) of higher education has come about as the growth of mass higher education has placed an increasing strain on state finances and as the complexity of the system has made it difficult to evaluate alternatives. Often the commissions have been imposed on the universities by the legislature and taxpayer groups seeking efficiency or by a coalition of the weaker and less prestigious schools who want a larger share of the pie. In some cases, the established institutions want to be protected from newer ones. In any case, the commission often insulates the legislature from the job of establishing priorities and weighing multiple appeals. The commission does this by formalizing criteria and rules for allocational incisions.[11]

While the development of commissions helps the legislature solve *its* decision-making problems, there is no evidence that it leads to better education. It may stop duplication of facilities, but it also may lead to a slower rise in the quality of education as intra-university competition within a state is cut down. The commissions do not lead to smaller educational budgets, though they may lead to a more efficient use of the money that is allocated.

In our time, one of the other major cases of integration has been the federated fund-raising drives of UGF (variously called Red Feather Drive, Community Fund, and so forth). There are two sources of efficiency here. First, administrative costs in raising money are reduced for each agency. Second, businessmen were saved the time and effort of their own personnel who were involved in the multiple solicitations within the business.[12]

Note, however, the costs. Individual agencies participating in the drives have not been able to raise their own dollar volume as fast as those agencies with specialized appeals (e.g., national health groups like the Cancer Society) which have refused to participate. Furthermore, involvement and lay support has to some extent been lessened.

(This should not be read as an argument for the demise of the joint drive. Many people would resent violently a return to the old system. A return to the old system would also hurt newer groups that have muscled

---

[11] Lyman A. Glenny, *Autonomy of Public Colleges: The Challenge of Coordination* (New York: McGraw-Hill, 1959).

[12] Richard Carter, *Gentle Legions* (Garden City, N. Y.: Doubleday, 1961), esp. Ch. 9.

in with their own campaigns, and the new groups—including civil rights groups as well as the health associations—deserve attention.)

The efficiency principle is seen in a negative case, the decline of Social Services Exchanges. The Social Services Exchanges were established early in the century to coordinate services among private agencies. Each agency listed its cases and the services, including money, that were being given. Ostensibly such a service would still be valuable for the information exchanged. As public welfare increase, however, the real reason for the exchanges declined. The exchanges had stopped beneficiaries from obtaining grants from several agencies. As money was no longer saved by the service, most communities have dismantled their Social Services Exchanges.[13] (It may be that today modern computers, sharing of information would be less costly.)

Effectiveness argument. In the social welfare arena there are three major effectiveness problems that are supposed to be solved by increased coordination and integration. The first is the problem of uniform services, the second may be labeled the pin-ball problem, and the third is the problem of partial solutions.

The problem of uniformity of services is a false issue for, in almost every case, people arguing for better integration of services to achieve uniformity of standards are talking about uniform higher standards. For instance no one argues that New York's welfare payments should be uniformly reduced to Mississippi's. Except for a few people who think rule standardization is a good in itself regardless of the *quality* of the rules, few would pay the cost of lowering some persons' welfare to achieve uniformity.

The pin-ball problem is that with so many agencies and individuals offering services, the clients may bounce from agency to agency without getting "proper" service. Cumming described this well in the mental health field.[14] People with problems become "pin-balls" which are bounced from friend to minister, to doctor, to one agency or another, without being "properly" treated. If there were only one agency, would not the services be allocated more effectively? The answer is, No! On the one hand, there is no possibility of eliminating the interpersonal and informal network of friends, doctor, and minister. On the other hand, each new agency, private and public, has identified a new set of needs. One only has to note that without significantly affecting suicide rates the development of Suicide Prevention Centers has provided important services to troubled people. Frightened and anxious people who were not calling the police and who were not going directly to established agencies have a new route into the system.

The argument about partial solutions concerns the multi-problem family or client. A host of agencies deal on a fragmented basis with one client or group; would they not be more effective if there were one organization?

---

[13] The example of the Social Services Exchange is drawn from Eugene Litwak and Lydia Hylton, "Inter-Organizational Analysis: A Hypothesis on Coordinating Agencies," *Administrative Science Quarterly*, 6 (March, 1962), pp. 395–420.

[14] Elaine Cumming, in "Allocation of Care to the Mentally Ill, American Style," in Mayer N. Zald, ed., *Organizing for Community Welfare* (Chicago: Quadrangle Books, 1967), pp. 109–159.

Let us note that this problem applies as well between the range of government agencies as between private agencies. Robb, for instance, has discussed this very problem in New Zealand where the various units of the Public Service relate on an individual basis to families.[15] If one had just one unit, all of the benefits of specialization and commitment would disappear. It may be that for that section of the population that is multi-problemed, special units are needed. But the largest part of our total social service potential does not really fall into this category. Handling the simple case through one elaborate coordinated service structure would be fantastically costly in money and time. The problem becomes one of finding mechanisms of integration and coordination in which costs are low relative to benefits.

Coordination proposals, as noted earlier, range from simple and ad hoc arrangements to the total reshuffling of organizations.[16] Ad hoc case coordination involves a decision by a worker in one agency to contact another agency concerning a shared client. Just as long as an agency policy does not forbid such contact (if the agencies have a history of enmity such contact may be forbidden), if both workers are willing and have the time and inclination, one-shot coordination may take place. Agency policy may even encourage such sharing, but there is a cost to the workers involved. There are costs in communications time and the workers may end up picking up new responsibilities.

Information exchanges are also relatively simple coordinating devices usually handled through meetings of top executives or, where a large audience is to be reached, through formal newsletters.

If two agencies share a large common case load or interests, two integrating devices may be proposed: liaison teams or procedural integration. Procedural integration requires developing a formal set of rules and decision criteria; it is more costly than ad hoc case relations because it requires overall organizational adjustment and commitment—records have to be changed, routing procedures adjusted, and the like. At some point, procedural integration will usually involve upper level executives and the weighing of consequences of the new procedures from the point of view of overall organization as well as for the specialized clientele.

Liaison personnel or teams are likely to be proposed when the volume of agency exchange is high and the exchange involves continuous interagency adjustments and communications about specific cases.[17] This solution leads to increased role specialization within each agency. (For instance, in one case a social service agency that had considerable court work turned one worker into a fulltime court liaison person.[18] All agency cases involving the

[15] J. H. Robb, "Family Structure and Agency Coordination: Decentralization and the Citizen," in J. L. Roberts, ed., *Decentralization in New Zealand Government Administration* (New York: Oxford University Press, 1961), pp. 33–55.

[16] The line of analysis in the remainder of this section parallels that of Litwak and Hylton, "Inter-Organizational Analysis."

[17] The relation of liaison teams to organizational structure on an intra- and inter-organizational basis has been discussed by James D. Thompson in *Organizations in Action* (New York: McGraw-Hill, 1967), pp. 51–82.

court were channelled through this person.)

A fifth type of coordination is program integration which involves the joint administration of coordinated staffs.[19] A coordinated program of this type is quite costly in manpower and time. Since we can assume that most personnel are already engaged in organizationally meaningful tasks, it is most likely to come about either when new finances are made available or under duress.[20]

New programs at the federal level have had a real impact on program coordination and integration. These programs often require joint community planning. Part of this emphasis on comprehensive planning stems from bureaucratic reasons: (1) the federal agencies would find themselves faced with a fantastic number of applications to evaluate if joint applications were not encouraged, and (2) insisting upon comprehensive planning forces the collecting of data which helps the federal agencies in evaluating need. From the local community side, this emphasis represents a cost. Time and money are spent on collecting data and demonstrating need; however, the cost is usually more than matched by the benefits of money that allow better services, programs, and organizational expansion. But it is not necessarily accompanied by greater actual integration of service. Each new government program in itself contributes to the differentiation of social categories and the creation of new organizational interfaces.

Finally, organizational integration may take place through the creation of one super-agency, the placing of separate organizations under one head. For instance, several cities have created Human Resources administrations. If the major goals and perspectives of the various organizations included are quite different, the costs of such integration may be very high, at least as perceived by respective constituencies, executives, and the like. Usually, such integration will be achieved only if the integration is seen as part of a larger social movement in which large numbers of people are involved and power is mobilized.[21] On the other hand, if goals and norms are similar, if large cost efficiencies are possible, integration may be more easily achieved.

[18] Oral communication with Roger Lind.

[19] Ad hoc coordination, procedural integration, and program integration have been discussed in similar terms by William Reid, "Interagency Coordination in Delinquency Prevention and Control," *Social Service Review*, 38 (Dec., 1964). It is reprinted in Mayer N. Zald, ed., *Social Welfare Institutions: A Sociological Reader* (New York: John Wiley and Sons, 1965), pp. 355–367.

[20] Miller, "Inter-Institutional Conflict."

[21] Here may be found one of the reasons why the movement to metropolitan forms of government has largely failed while advisory regional development groups and specific problem compacts (such as sewage disposal) have been created between cities. On the one hand, the broad mass of population is not highly dissatisfied with their own governmental forms and many people are positively attached to present forms. On the other hand, office holders have vested interests in preserving the status quo. Purely technical criteria can be used in specific problem areas, and regional development boards do not directly attack either the office holders or value-identities of their constituents.

CONCLUSION

We have stressed that there are a number of hidden costs to integration and coordination that are often ignored. The growth and development of agencies and services in modern society is related to basic changes in the social structure of the society, increasing differentiation of social categories, emerging professions and new definitions of service needs and means. Organizations develop commitments and internal and external constituencies to support their goals, territories, and procedures. As a consequence they relate to each other like semi-autonomous states and engage in coalitions and alliances for specific purposes. Coordination and integration have both benefits and costs and coordination proposals can be compared in terms of these costs and benefits.

In weighing costs and benefits, it is necessary to use both economic, political, and social standards. Many coordination and integration programs have high overall dollar benefits while being extremely costly to specific groups or organizations. Analysts of costs and benefits have to examine the organizational, political and professional costs as well. Thus, in American society it is easier to add new services than to eliminate old ones, to create new compacts than eliminate total structures.

There is a deep, pervasive strain between the search for equity and equal treatment of all citizens and the increasingly complex, differentiated, and interdependent structure of urbanized and industrialized society. Coordination and integration mechanisms are in part aimed at providing equitable, uniform and effective services. But, on the one hand, they often entail costs which make them prohibitive and, on the other, the underlying processes of specialization and technological changes create new facets of interdependence and new interfaces of service. Leviathan and a fantastic computer system might solve the problem. But, in the meantime, we shall continue to add categories and devices dealing with the problematic categories and to worry about means to control and integrate the devices.

17

LEGAL DIMENSIONS OF POPULATION POLICY[1]

MICHAEL KATZ

The University of North Carolina at Chapel Hill

L ESTER WARD ONCE OBSERVED THAT "THE IMPROVEMENT OF SOCIETY BY cold calculation"[2] is the only proper end for social science research. The decision to formulate a model population policy is a manifestation of this philosophy and demonstrates a confidence on the part of social scientists that would probably have been considered presumptuous only 30 years ago. There appear to be three major assumptions implicit in the decision to undertake this effort: first, that such a policy is feasible and that social scientists are equal to the task; second, that such a policy is necessary, and third, that the end product, if implemented by reasonable decision-makers, will prove to be a significant improvement over existing social arrangements.[3]

The decision to formulate a population policy at the state level represents a singularly important manifestation of the rapidly changing relationship between social science research and the traditional democratic process.[4] It reflects the growing dependence of decision-makers on expert advisers who have been thoroughly trained in the new disciplines of the social sciences. It has become increasingly apparent in recent years that, in order to develop and coordinate plans for the continued improvement of society, and the optimum development of social values, rational decision-making requires craftsmen skilled in the techniques of economics, sociology, information science, demography, ecology and political science. Nowhere is this need greater than in the development of an overall population policy. Population planning might best be understood therefore, as the development of models premised on one fundamental assumption: that the most productive use of natural resources and the maximum development of sociopolitical groups is most appropriately determined by

[1] The author wishes to thank Steven Polgar, Associate Director of the Carolina Population Center, for his assistance in the preparation of this article.

[2] Lester Ward, *Dynamic Sociology* (Boston: Ginn and Co., 1906), Vol. 1, p. 468.

[3] Raymond A. Bauer and Kenneth J. Gergen, eds., *The Study of Policy Formation* (New York: Free Press, 1968); Charles E. Lindblom, *The Policy Making Process* (Englewood Cliffs, N. J.: Prentice-Hall, 1968); William J. Ewald, Jr., ed., *Environment and Change: The Next Fifty Years* (Bloomington: Indiana University Press, 1968); S. M. Miller and Frank Riessman, *Social Class and Social Policy* (New York: Basic Books, 1968).

[4] As part of its continuing efforts to explore the problems and theoretical dimensions of policy formulation in the area of population planning the Carolina Population Center established the North Carolina Population Policy Council and entrusted it with responsibility for investigating the feasibility of constructing a population policy at the state level. A different version of this paper was read at a seminar held by the Council on January 5, 1969. For an overview of the policy problems with which the Carolina Population Center has concerned itself in recent years, see Carolina Population Center, *Approaches to the Human Fertility Problem* (Chapel Hill, 1968), prepared for the United Nations Advisory Committee on the Application of Science and Technology to Development.

calculating an optimum population size that is conducive to a full enjoyment of all available facilities, without imposing a strain on the productive capacities of the economy.

In the initial stages of its work, any planning group operating at the state level will find itself confronted by the need to cope with a number of conceptual and analytical problems. The ultimate success or failure of its exertions will to a large degree be dependent upon its ability to overcome or circumvent these obstacles. One problem that will require the group's immediate attention is the presence of a variety of statutory enactments bearing on various facets of population policy. The overall impression derived from a scrutiny of the statute laws of a typical American jurisdiction is one of inconsistent application of diverse policies, reflecting an absence of systematic thought on questions of population growth, size and distribution. The continued existence of these laws may well pre-empt efforts to devise an integrated population policy, since some of these provisions may reflect decisions antithetical to the goals postulated by the group.[5] In sum, the confused state of the law might well operate to neutralize the group's efforts to develop a coherent, orderly population policy.

Clearly, the formulation of a coherent state population policy requires something in addition to a general revision or repeal of the offending statutes; for the policy to succeed, it is important that social scientists take into consideration the effects of subsequent additions to or changes in the law. It is necessary, therefore, that they understand the relationship between law and population policy planning.

It is the thesis of this article that law shapes the process by which population policy is formulated and institutionalized in two ways: to begin with, the most important function that legal analysis performs for the planning process itself is to demarcate the limitations on the planner, and to define the boundaries of permissible decision-making. Abstract though it might be, the law represents as much a limitation on the planner as do the more concrete restrictions imposed by limited time, space, resources or political reality. In short, by defining the line between permissible decision-making and impermissible decision-making, the law marks the outer perimeter of

[5] The ultimate goals of population reduction programs have been variously formulated in the literature. In its Report to the United Nations Advisory Committee, the Carolina Population Center has suggested that one of the immediate tasks confronting planners is "to obtain a reasonably sound estimate of the pattern to which demographic patterns, including fertility patterns, should move for optimal social benefit. . . ." (*Approaches to the Human Fertility Problem*, p. 63). A less dramatic goal is the elimination of "excess" births. The elimination of "excess" births would ". . . improve the overall quality of life and the human dividend" enjoyed by its population. See C. Horace Hamilton, "The Need for Family Planning in North Carolina," *The University of North Carolina News Letter*, 53 (Sept., 1968). A third goal is the elimination of poverty: See A. A. Campbell, "The Role of Family Planning in the Reduction of Poverty," *Journal of Marriage and the Family*, 30 (May, 1968), p. 236. However formulated, it is clear that program development must be adapted to contemporary political limitations. The relative popularity of family planning is due in part to its political acceptability. (See Bernard Berelson, "Beyond Family Planning," *Studies in Family Planning*, 38 (Feb., 1969).

any policy that the state may ultimately adopt. In this manner, the legal system serves to maintain the vitality and validity of the concepts of due process, equal protection, fundamental fairness and human dignity in the American political process.

Law shapes the outcome of policy judgments in another, less perceptible but equally significant way. Quite frequently incorporation of a policy recommendation into the framework of the law leads to unanticipated and unwanted consequences. It is a not uncommon occurrence for rules of law to demonstrate what Mr. Justice Cardozo once described as "the tendency of a principle to expand itself to the limit of its logic."[6] Once a theory advanced by social scientists has been incorporated into the "seamless web" of the law, it takes on a life of its own and might well be expanded to cover a variety of circumstances contemplated by neither its originator nor its proponents, and which are connected to the initial point of entry into the law by the most tenuous strands of logic. The process by which the courts or legislatures expand established principles or doctrines to cover new situations has been described by legal scholars as "reasoning by example"[7] and is among the most highly prized professional skills that lawyers possess. Proficiency in the art of argument by analogy is considered by members of the legal profession to comprise an indispensable constituent of that thought process referred to as "thinking like a lawyer."

Buck v. Bell[8] provides a classic illustration of this method of reasoning at work. In that case, Justice Holmes upheld the Virginia Compulsory Sterilization Statute on the grounds that "The principle that sustains compulsory vaccination is broad enough to cover cutting the Fallopian tubes,"[9] and cited in support of this proposition *Jacobsen v. Massachusetts.*[10] *Jacobsen*, however, merely decided that the state's interest in the preservation of the public health and safety entitled it to require compulsory vaccination against smallpox, despite objections by a few individuals that this represented an unwarranted intrusion into their personal liberties and that they were perfectly able to provide for their own health themselves.

The lesson for policy planners is obvious: it is necessary for them to guard against the likelihood that many of their suggestions will be adopted

---

[6] Benjamin N. Cardozo, *The Nature of the Judicial Process* (New Haven: Yale University Press, 1921), p. 51.

[7] Edward H. Levi, *An Introduction to Legal Reasoning* (Chicago: The University of Chicago Press, 1963), p. 1: Although this work is essentially an apology for the weaknesses in the process of "legal reasoning" Levi does acknowledge that as a mode of analysis it is not without its difficulties: "The basic pattern of legal reasoning is by example. It is reasoning from case to case. It is a three-step process described by the doctrine of precedent in which a proposition descriptive of the first case is made into a rule of law and then applied to a next similar situation. The steps are these: similarity is seen between cases; next the rule of law inherent in the first case is announced; then the rule of law is made applicable to the second. *This is a method of reasoning necessary for the law, but it has characteristics which under other circumstances might be considered imperfections.*" (My emphasis)

[8] United States Supreme Court Reports, 274 (1927) at 200.

[9] *Ibid.*, at 207.

[10] United States Supreme Court Reports, 197 (1904) at 11.

as the law in a variety of unrelated areas by carefully defining their terms and specifying precisely the social conditions for which they consider their recommendations to be valid.

LAW AND POPULATION POLICY: THE MORAL PERSPECTIVE

To speak of policy decisions as rules of law is to assume two things about them: first, that they have qualified under the constitutive process, which means, very simply, that they have been enacted by a political agency constitutionally competent to do so; and second, that such policies resemble laws in form. Policies are, after all, to be found in a variety of places. But laws are found in statute books and court decisions, and are identified by the shapes that they take. Laws are neither precatory, hortatory nor commendatory; they are either prescriptive, proscriptive, directive or compulsory. In form they either forbid or require action, they are usually general in their application, and they are intended to bind all persons subject to their jurisdiction.

Whether it is considered as a coherent, systematic body of rules or as a series of analytic techniques for the resolution of conflicts, the law does not provide from within itself policies adequate to the immense problems of a rapidly expanding and complex society. The sources of such policy lie elsewhere, but need to be translated into law for effective action. The law, therefore, serves not only as a limiting factor in the policy process, but provides, in addition, a necessary and integral dimension of a humane population policy. Without it, policies, no matter how carefully designed, would remain no more than moral norms or scientific models abstractly conceived. Although the legal system does not serve as a source or framework for policy formulation and development, it provides a humanizing element, as well as serving as the instrument by which authority and legitimacy are extended to the work-product of other disciplines. In this sense, law functions as a corrective mechanism. It provides a perspective from which the proposals of other, more relevant disciplines and frameworks can be subjected to critical scrutiny, in order first to humanize them and then to translate them into binding rules of decision.

An illustration of the humanizing influence that legal analysis can exert on the process of population policy formation is provided by Mr. Justice Goldberg's concurring opinion in *Griswold v. Connecticut.*[11] In that case the petitioners, the executive director of the Connecticut Planned Parenthood League and its medical director, challenged the constitutionality of their convictions under two Connecticut statutes. The first statute declared the use of any artificial contraceptive device "for the purpose of preventing contraception" to be a criminal offense[12] and the second provided that "Any person who assists, abets, counsels, causes, hires or commands" another to use such devices was to be punished "as if he were a principal offender."[13] The United States Supreme Court struck the former statute, better known

[11] United States Supreme Court Reports, 381 (1964) at 479.
[12] Connecticut General Statutes, No. 55–32 (1958 edition).
[13] *Ibid.*, at No. 54–196.

as the "Connecticut Birth Control Statute," as an impermissible intrusion by the state into the constitutionally protected area of "marital privacy."[14]

In his concurrence, Goldberg started from the premise that the "right of marital privacy" was of so fundamental a nature that, although it was nowhere specifically mentioned in the Bill of Rights, it was nevertheless one of the rights "retained by the people" as guaranteed by the Ninth Amendment, and that the silence of the first eight Amendments on the matter could not be "construed to deny or disparage" the existence of so profoundly important an element in the concept of liberty:

> The entire fabric of the Constitution and the purposes that clearly underlie its specific guarantees demonstrate that the rights to marital privacy and to marry and raise a family are of similar order and magnitude as the fundamental rights specifically protected.[15]

Thus far, so good. But the question remained, whether the Connecticut statute could be defended on the grounds that it was a rational means by which the state could protect or advance a legitimate interest in the welfare of its inhabitants. The state sought to argue that this was indeed the case, that the statute operated to reduce the amount and frequency of extra-marital sexual intercourse because it increased the risk of unwanted pregnancies. This argument could, of course, be easily countered by the argument that, even conceding that the quantity of illicit sexual activity had in fact been diminished, this was not an argument that the state had stamped out the practice entirely. Therefore, the diminution in frequency of acts of extra-marital sexual intercourse would be counterbalanced by the increased number of pregnancies which the unavailability of preventive devices would almost certainly produce. It is significant however, to note that this was not the argument that Mr. Justice Goldberg relied upon. He chose to dismiss the state's argument on the simple ground that "the rationality of (such a) justification is dubious"[16] but without advancing any contradicting arguments, primarily because the countervailing arguments contained implications which were not without constitutional difficulties of their own. In his view, the difficulty with this approach was that:

> The logic of the dissents would sanction federal or state legislation that seems to me even more plainly unconstitutional than the statute before us. Surely the Government, absent a showing of a compelling subordinating state interest, could not decree that all husbands and wives must be sterilized after two children have been born to them. Yet by their reasoning such an invasion of marital privacy would not be subject to constitutional challenge because, while it might seem "silly," no provision of the Constitution specifically prevents the Government from curtailing the marital right to bear children and raise a family. While it may shock some of my Brethren that the Court holds today that the Constitution protects the right of marital privacy, in my view it is far more shocking to believe that the personal liberty guaranteed by the Constitution does not include protection

[14] United States Supreme Court Reports 381 (1964) at 486.
[15] *Ibid.*, at 497.
[16] *Ibid.*, at 498.

against such totalitarian limitation of family size, which is at complete variance with our constitutional concepts. Yet, if upon a showing of a slender basis of rationality, a law outlawing voluntary birth control by married persons is valid, then by the same reasoning a law requiring compulsory birth control also would seem to be valid. In my view, however, both types of law would unjustifiably intrude upon rights of marital privacy which are constitutionally protected.[17]

For Mr. Justice Goldberg, it is clear, the paradigm "family" is the end product of a series of willed choices and decisions by its members, and the determination of such questions as its size and distribution over time can never be matters for the state. The lesson for population planners in Goldberg's concurrence is clear and simple: "What is specifically not wanted are State-imposed population controls."[18] While it remains possible for the state to resort to indirect measures, such as manipulation of its fiscal and tax policies, programs designed to change public attitudes and opinions, and incentive programs, the institution of the "family" must be kept immune from the application of direct measures by the state. However, since the immunity of the family from the coercive pressures of state action has been elevated by the *Griswold* Court to the level of a fundamental liberty, guaranteed by the Bill of Rights, the question of state regulation of family size is, for all practical purposes, no longer open for debate.

LAW AND POPULATION POLICY: TWO CASE STUDIES IN CONFLICT AND
COOPERATION

The Conflict Model. Another illustration of legal analysis serving to humanize population policies can be found in current efforts to eliminate the use of residence requirements in determining welfare eligibility. In this situation lawyers, by performing an adversary function, have sought to challenge the decisions of policy-makers, and to restrict the range of possible alternatives available to state officials.

Posed in its largest terms, every state is always confronted with the need to define its population. The problem is one central to all efforts at formulating a meaningful population policy, for it is surely a precondition of any rationally conceived policy that (1) the state should have a legitimate interest in the people affected by its decisions, which in turn requires that some pragmatic nexus exists on which this judgment can be based, and (2) that the people affected by the state's decisions will remain within its jurisdiction long enough for the investment of services and resources to produce some beneficial effect. An obvious example of this problem is presented by the student attending college out of his state of residence. Questions such as his eligibility to vote in local elections, his liability for state and local taxes, and his obligation to qualify under the state's driver licensing laws all present administrators with the need to define his status. Frequently, however, such administrative classifications appear incongruous or ano-

---

[17] *Ibid.*, at 496–497.

[18] Albert Blaustein, "Arguendo: The Legal Challenge of Population Control," *Law and Society Review*, 3 (Aug., 1968), pp. 107–114.

molous. The precise resolution of such questions has rarely been accomplished by any bureaucracy, and in all probability never will be. It is in the nature of the phenomenon—lines are blurred, distinctions difficult to sustain, and there is no way to resolve the ambiguities to the satisfaction to everyone.

A more serious problem is that presented by the contemporary pattern of migration from the rural southern states towards the industrial areas of the northeast.[19] Welfare administrators of population-importing states are particularly affected by the need to formulate a rational yet equitable definition of who constitutes the population of the state. In this they have been given very little guidance. The Social Security Act merely provides that the Secretary of Health, Education and Welfare in granting federal aid to a state program, shall not approve a plan requiring more than one year's residence in the state.[20] Such requirements are routinely imposed by the great majority of states, a situation currently under challenge in the United States Supreme Court. In *Shapiro v. Thompson*,[21] which was recently argued before the Supreme Court for the second time,[22] the welfare directors of Connecticut, Pennsylvania and the District of Columbia appealed lower court rulings that residence requirements for welfare assistance are unconstitutional. In each case a three-judge federal court of appeal held that the imposition of a residence requirement as a qualifying condition for the receipt of welfare benefits violates the Equal Protection clause of the Fourteenth Amendment, as well as the Privileges and Immunities and Commerce clauses of the Constitution.[23] In seeking to obtain reversal of these decisions, the states seek to justify their policies on a number of grounds. Thus counsel for the State of Connecticut urged that the rule ". . . prevented subsidized travel"![24] and a similar Iowa statute was said to be required by ". . . reasons of fiscal necessity and administrative convenience."[25] All three states defended their residence policies ". . . as a discrimination validly based on recipients' investment in the community, as providing an objective test of residency and as keeping a state's liberal welfare program from serving as a magnet for out-of-state indigents to the detriment of the

[19] U. S. Dept. of Commerce, Bureau of the Census: *Current Population Reports: Population Characteristics*, Series P.-20, No. 156 (Washington, D. C.: U. S. Government Printing Office, 1966); No. 171 (Washington, D. C.: U. S. Government Printing Office, 1968). In general, see Karl E. Taeuber and Alma F. Taeuber," The Changing Character of Negro Migration," *American Journal of Sociology*, 70 (Jan., 1965), pp. 429–441.

[20] United States Code, Title 42, No. 602(b)(1964 edition).

[21] United States Supreme Court, Docket No. 9 (1968 Term). See *United States Law Week*, 37, p. 3015. (Hereafter cited as *USLW*.)

[22] Oral argument was first heard during the 1967 Term: *USLW*, 36, p. 3421; the case was restored to the Calendar for reargument on June 17, 1968 (*USLW*, 36, p. 3483) and reargued during the 1968 Term on October 23 and 24, 1968 (*USLW*, 37, p. 3153).

[23] *Shapiro v. Thompson*, 270 F. Supp. 331 (1967); *Harrell, et al. v. Tobriner, et al.*, 279 F. Supp. 22 (1968); *Smith v. Reynolds*, 277 F. Supp. 65 (1968).

[24] *USLW*, 36, p. 3421.

[25] *Ibid.*

state fisc."[26] The essence of their position emerges from the argument of counsel for the State of Iowa: "this is a program for residents; it isn't a program for transients. . . . We want them to feel that they're ours. . . . It isn't a program that you can offer to someone coming in for only a few weeks or so."[27]

The states argue that the imposition of a qualifying condition on welfare benefits is both necessary and justified. First, they claim, it is reasonable for the states to select recipients of a state service (such as welfare benefits) on the basis of their relationshop to the state. Thus, states may properly limit the disbursement of benefits to "permanent" residents of the state. Essentially, this is an argument that while the states are obliged to provide for their own residents, or citizens, they may properly reserve to themselves the right to define the terms on which citizenship is obtained, or residence is established. There is some surface plausibility to this argument. While the Fourteenth Amendment provides that "All persons born or naturalized in the United States, and subject to the jurisdiction thereof, are citizens of the United States, and of the State wherein they reside,"[28] it nowhere explicitly defines who is to be regarded as a "resident" of a state, or what the permissible criteria for making such a determination are to be. Establishing the criteria for residence, it is at least arguable, is a matter for the states themselves, and thus a residency requirement of general application would presumably not violate the terms of this constitutional provision.

Furthermore, the states argue, the presence of such a requirement removes the need for administrative determination on a case-by-case basis. The residence requirement operates to benefit both parties: the state is spared the cost of establishing an administrative structure for the determination of the eligibility of individual claimants in each and every case while the claimant is served by knowing in advance what the criteria for eligibility are that he must meet; that the relevant rule is uniform, and consistently applied, and that he is thereby afforded a measure of protection against arbitrary action by lower level state employees. Furthermore, as counsel for the District of Columbia urged, the policy relieves him of the burden of demonstrating a fixed and settled intention to acquire residence in the jurisdiction. The policy, the argument ran, provides an objective test for determining residency, and was eminently practical:

> Many indigent people honestly cannot say whether they intend to reside in a state where they happen to arrive, because their staying depends on so many contingencies—such as contacting relatives or finding a job. Therefore, the statute is really beneficial by arbitrarily granting resident status after one year of presence in the state without respect to certainty or intention.[29]

The second argument is perhaps more dubious: the states argue that the imposition of such a restriction operates to "discourage" indigent persons

---

[26] *Ibid.*, 37, p. 315s.
[27] *Ibid.*
[28] United States Constitution, 14th Amendment.
[29] *USLW*, 37, pp. 3153–3154.

from moving to other states in search of higher welfare benefits, and is required by the population-importing states of the northeast to prevent their welfare rolls from being overrun by indigent immigrants from less affluent regions of the country. Such a policy, the State of Connecticut argued, "poses no threat to impoverished persons without means of support who contemplate coming to Connecticut for support, but merely discourages them from doing so."[30]

The short answer to these arguments was simple. Counsel for the welfare claimants rested his argument on the proposition that by adopting such a policy, the states have imposed an unfair burden upon a class of persons defined by the lack of economic resources, and thrusts upon them (1) the requirement of a year's residence in order to qualify for a state-supported service, and (2) the duty to establish that they are entitled to receive benefits under state-supported welfare programs. These policies, which counsel likened to "the medieval idea that 'our parish takes care of its own and only its own' "[31] discriminate against the welfare poor by applying a criterion not reasonably related to any relevant governmental interest which might be involved. The "contribution to the community" theory on which the states had so heavily relied was dismissed as no more than ". . . a euphemistic way of expressing that same discrimination against strangers."[32]

This, apparently, was the viewpoint that prevailed. On April 21, 1969, the Supreme Court handed down its decision.[33] By a vote of six to three the Court upheld the decisions of the lower courts, and affirmed that state residence requirements imposed as qualifications for welfare benefits are unconstitutional. In this manner, the Court took advantage of the opportunity presented it by the case to introduce an element of humanity into the procedure by which states determine who is to be considered a "resident" or "citizen" for purposes of obtaining access to benefits provided through publicly-funded welfare programs.

THE COOPERATION MODEL

There are eugenic sterilization laws on the statute books of 26 states today.[34] These laws, the result of an unusually high degree of collaboration between lawyers, legislators and social scientists, were originally enacted to eliminate feeblemindedness from the population. The original rationale of eugenic sterilization was that retardation and other similar mental defects were hereditary characteristics, and thus transmissible. Therefore, it was argued, the most effective method by which to eliminate this trait from the population was to prevent mentally retarded or defective people from reproducing by sterilizing them. The eugenic sterilization movement ap-

---

[30] *Ibid.*, 36, p. 3421.

[31] *Ibid.*, 37, p. 3154.

[32] *Ibid.*

[33] *New York Times*, April 22, 1969, p. 15, col. 3.

[34] Patrick J. McKinley, "Compulsory Eugenic Sterilization: For Whom Does the 'Bell' Toll?" *Duquesne University Law Review*, 6:2 (1967), p. 145; The Statutory provisions are compiled in footnote 2. See also Regina Bligh, "Sterilization and Mental Retardation," *American Bar Association Journal*, 51 (Nov., 1965), pp. 1059–1063.

pears to have reached its zenith in 1927. In that year Mr. Justice Holmes, writing for a unanimous Court, granted such legislation the imprimatur of constitutional validity on the theory that "three generations of imbeciles are enough."[35] By 1932 some 24 states had adopted such legislation.[36] Julius Paul reports that these enactments contained at least 34 "sterilizable" categories, many of which (such as epilepsy) bore no relationship whatsoever to the avowed legislative policy of protecting future generations against feeblemindedness and retardation.[37] Moreover, he continues, although the eugenic sterilization movement underwent a minor recession during World War II, state legislatures have shown a revived interest in the possibilities of this technique in recent years.

Among the purposes for which it has been suggested that this operation is particularly well adapted is the sterilization of unmarried mothers. The argument justifying this application of the technique stresses the large number of illegitimate children receiving public welfare assistance, and the high cost to the taxpayer of this continued burden on the public fisc.[38] To date the pressure for adoption of such measures has been countered with fair success,[39] but there is a salutary lesson to be drawn by population planners from the entire history of eugenic sterilization legislation. It provides the clearest possible illustration of the "tendency of a principle to expand itself to the limit of its logic" that Cardozo found to be so distinctive a feature of the growth of the law.[40] Futhermore, the expansion of the scope of sterilization laws and the emergence of the doctrine of "punitive sterilization" demonstrate that theories adduced in order to effect reforms may well be reinterpreted and turned against their proponents—a danger which several writers have drawn attention to in recent years.[41]

CONCLUSION

This article has been concerned with the relationship between law and the process of population policy formation, particularly at the level of state government. This relationship can be either of a collaborative, supportive

[35] United States Supreme Court Reports, 274 (1927) at 207.

[36] Julius Paul, "Population 'Quality' and 'Fitness for Parenthood' in the Light of State Eugenic Sterilization Experience, 1907–1966," *Population Studies*, 21 (Nov., 1967), p. 295–299.

[37] *Ibid.*, p. 296.

[38] Julius Paul, "The Return of Punitive Sterilization Proposals: Current Attacks on Illegitimacy and the AFDC Program," *Law and Society Review*, 3 (Aug., 1968), p. 77–106.

[39] *Ibid.*

[40] Benjamin N. Cardozo, *Nature*, p. 51.

[41] "It behooves us then, not only to study significant problems and report our findings accurately, but also to be sensitive to the way these findings are used, particularly to whether or not they are used in ways that seem illegitimate, given the findings," Lee Rainwater and D. J. Pittman, "Ethical Problems in Studying a Politically Sensitive and Deviant Community," *Social Problems*, 14 (Spring, 1967), pp. 362–363. See also: Frederick S. Jaffe and Steven Polgar, "Family Planning and Public Policy: Is the 'Culture of Poverty' the New Cop-Out?" *Journal of Marriage and the Family*, 30 (May, 1968), pp. 230–231.

nature, or one of an adversary nature; the terms of the relationship depend, apparently, upon whether the values underlying the sought-after policy are consistent with or antithetical to the fundamental values of the legal system. If these values are compatible, it is possible that the social science concepts involved will become part of "the seamless web" of the law too rapidly, with the concomitant danger that they will not have been sufficiently tested prior to their becoming legally valid principles of action. Again, these concepts may be extended, through the process of legal analogy, into areas of social concern far removed from their original area of application and validity. The net result of this process might be to cause more harm than good.

Finally, it is part of the thesis of this article that legal principles are methodologically relevant to population planners, particularly those operating at the level of state government. Law operates to reduce the number and range of options available to policy makers, and failure on their part to calculate the costs and limitations imposed by the contours of the legal system may result in the defeat of the entire product of the planning enterprise.

·18·

ECONOMIC GROWTH AS AN ANTI-POVERTY TOOL: A FURTHER CONSIDERATION OF THE BACKWASH DEBATE

RICHARD X. CHASE
University of Vermont

GENE LABER
University of Vermont

THE COUNCIL OF ECONOMIC ADVISERS OBSERVED IN ITS 1964 *Economic Report* that the postwar rate of reduction in the percentage incidence of poverty for American families was less during 1956–62 than it had been during 1947–56.[1] The Council took the position that, while this slower decline in poverty incidence was caused in part by a slower intertemporal rate of economic growth in the 1956–62 period, on the whole families in the poverty category apparently were becoming less able to exploit the opportunities created by general economic advance to escape from poverty. "We cannot," the Council stated, "leave the further wearing away of poverty solely to the general progress of the economy."[2] This position has been called the "backwash thesis"—i.e., that a substantial part of the 1956–1962 deceleration in the rate of poverty reduction among American families is attributable to the presence of a "hardcore" group among the poor who are basically not affected by the normal processes of economic growth. The backwash proposition has been debated in the recent economic literature,[3] with a substantial burden of the argument, both pro and con, resting on statistical estimations derived from regression analyses. In this paper, we report the results of a multivariate regression model, in double log form, of poverty incidence (regressed) on median family income and unemployment for eight poverty subgroups of American families for the time series 1947 to 1966.[4]

[1] Council of Economic Advisers, *Economic Report of The President* (Washington, D.C.: U.S. Government Printing Office, 1964), p. 64.

[2] *Ibid.*, p. 60.

[3] See, for example: W. H. Locke-Anderson, "Trickling Down: The Relationship Between Economic Growth and The Extent of Poverty Among American Families," *Quarterly Journal of Economics*, 78 (Nov., 1964), pp. 511–524; Lowell E. Gallaway, "The Foundations of the 'War on Poverty'," *American Economic Review*, 55 (March, 1965), pp. 122–131; Henry Aaron, "The Foundations of the 'War on Poverty' Reexamined," *American Economic Review*, 57 (Dec., 1967), pp. 1229–1240; Gallaway, "The Foundations of the 'War on Poverty': Reply," *Ibid.*, pp. 1241–1243; Richard X. Chase, "Structural and Aggregative Empases in Anti-Poverty Policy," *American Journal of Economics and Sociology*, 27 (Jan., 1968), pp. 9–25; and Richard X. Chase, "Unrelated Individuals: A 'Backwash' Poverty Population," *Ibid.*, (Oct., 1968), pp. 337–345.

[4] These groups are the demographic categories for which the Bureau of the Census reports annual family income data. See Bureau of the Census, U.S. Department of Commerce, *Current Population Reports*, Consumer Income, Series P-60, 1947 through 1966 (Washington, D.C.: U.S. Government Printing Office, 1967).

♦ First published in *Social Science Quarterly* 50, No. 3 (December, 1969).

THE MODEL AND THE RESULTS

A crucial question in examining the backwash proposition is the comparative, intertemporal responsiveness to some measure of economic well-being of the poverty-incidence rates of various identifiable demographic groups into which the population can be subdivided. Among the groupings for which the Bureau of the Census reports annual income data are: nonfarm and farm, white and nonwhite, male and female headed households, and age categories.[5] It is for these subgroups that we report results of a regression model that employs the aggregate (annual) unemployment rate and deflated median family income as estimators (the independent variables) for general economic growth and progress.

Regression coefficients estimated from a double log model can be interpreted as elasticities; and in Table 1 are listed the resultant elasticities estimated from the double log form of the following equation:

$$P = AU^b M^{-c} e, \text{ where}$$
P = poverty (family income less than $3000 in 1962 dollars) incidence rate for each family subgroup;
U = overall annual unemployment rate;
M = overall median family income (1962 dollars).

As can be seen from Table 1 the regression coefficients for the unemployment variable are all substantially less than one, and in four out of the nine cases (nonfarm, farm, 65+ and female) are not statistically significant.[6] The unemployment coefficient for nonwhites, however, is worthy of some note. Nonwhites is the only "smaller"[7] demographic subgrouping

---

Poverty incidence rates are derived from the above cited income data, and are the percentage of families in each reported category with annual incomes below $3,000 deflated to 1962 dollars. Median family income is also deflated to 1962 dollars.

[5] The *Current Population Survey* (Series P-60) reports annual income data for six age groups: 14–24, 25–34, 35–44, 45–54, 55–64, and 65 and over. For ease of exposition the subgroups have been aggregated into two: the nonaged (14–64) and the aged (65 and over).

[6] In passing, it is worth noting that unemployment changes have a more important effect on poverty incidence than is perhaps at first indicated by the regression coefficients estimated in our equations. For example, our coefficient of .055 for aggregate unemployment means that if the unemployment rate falls *one percentage point* from, say, a 5 per cent level (the average for our time series) to, say, the defined "full employment" level of 4 per cent (a 20 per cent decrease in unemployment), the aggregate level of poverty incidence will, according to the equation, fall about 1.1 per cent (.055 · 20 per cent). Substituting the *employment* rate (1–U) for the unemployment variable (U) in our equation for all families yields results that are in accordance with the preceding calculation—i.e., the coefficient for the employment rate exceeds 1.0, while the coefficient of median family income and the fit of the equation remain essentially the same. Substituting the employment rate variable into the equations for the remaining demographic groups yields results that are consistent with the foregoing illustration.

[7] The term "smaller" is used here to refer to those subgroupings that comprise the smaller population total within any of the given population categories, i.e., nonwhites, aged, farm and female headed families. "Larger" subgroupings are conversely the larger population subtotals within any given population category, i.e., whites, nonaged, nonfarm and male headed families.

TABLE 1

Logarithmic Regressions Relating Group Poverty Incidence to the Aggregate
Unemployment Rate and to Deflated[a] Median Family Income, 1947–1966

| Family group | Intercept log a | Regression Coefficients[b] | | | | Adjusted R^2 | Durbin-Watson |
		Unemployment (std. error)		Median family income (std. error)			
All	6.17499	.05539*	(.01731)	−1.30188*	(.02200)	.995	2.208[c]
Nonfarm	5.33180	.06793	(.04255)	−1.0945*	(.05409)	.960	.579
Farm	4.97822	.09887	(.09060)	−0.89747*	(.11517)	.771	.654
Under 65	7.47048	.06692†	(.02448)	−1.67686*	(.03112)	.994	1.953[c]
65+	3.80793	.01370	(.03336)	−0.56510*	(.04241)	.914	0.801
White	6.42579	.06068‡	(.02657)	−1.38501*	(.03378)	.990	2.021[c]
Nonwhite	5.90024	.10892*	(.03755)	−1.14849*	(.04774)	.971	1.647[c]
Male	6.99872	.05596†	(.02064)	−1.53976*	(.02623)	.995	2.104[c]
Female	3.52887	.08273	(.04989)	−0.50588*	(.06342)	.776	.871

[a] Deflated to 1962 dollars.
[b] Asterisk indicates level of significance of coefficient: * = .01; † = .02; ‡ = .05.
[c] The null hypothesis of random disturbance terms cannot be rejected.

where this coefficient is not only statistically significant (and highly so in this case) but is also substantially larger in relation to the coefficient for the corresponding "larger" family subgrouping (i.e., white). This indicates, of course, that a decrease in the aggregate unemployment rate has a relatively more powerful salutary effect on nonwhite family poverty than on poverty among white families.

The regression coefficients for median family income are analytically more interesting. Not only are they all highly statistically significant, but in each case the elasticity of response for the "larger" population subdivision is both greater than unity as well as higher than it is for its corresponding "smaller" subdivision.[8] The implication of this is that economic growth, measured by rising median family income, has a relatively much more powerful effect on reducing poverty among the "larger" subdivisions of each population aggregate than among the corresponding "smaller" sub-divisions, thereby tending to leave poverty increasingly more concentrated among the latter. This is to say that each "smaller" population subgrouping constitutes a poverty backwash *in relation* to the corresponding "larger" subgrouping.[9]

The nonwhite category is again worthy of some additional note. It is the only "smaller" population subdivision for which the elasticity of responsiveness of P to M (though less than the elasticity for the corresponding "larger" population category) is greater than unity. This indicates that— even though nonwhites constitute a relative poverty backwash in that economic growth will tend to leave poverty more concentrated among them— a given percentage increase in median family income will tend to bring about a greater percentage decrease in nonwhite poverty incidence. Also worthy of note is the point that the regression fit for nonwhites (.971) is the highest for any of the "smaller" population categories.

In passing we should also mention that the regression fits for all "smaller" population subdivisions other than nonwhites are probably overstated. A Durbin-Watson test on each of these groups indicates a high likelihood of autocorrelation. The existence of autocorrelation suggests the existence of a variable(s) *other than M and U*—our measure of economic growth—for explaining poverty reduction among these demographic groups.

CONCLUSIONS

The regression estimates reported in this paper are highlighted by the following findings:

[8] This latter point is not to be confused with and is in addition to an important point developed by another contributor to the backwash debate that *within* each population group there are theoretical as well as empirical reasons for believing that there exists a group of hardcore poor. See Aaron, "The Foundations," pp. 1229–1240.

[9] The coefficients of median income are likely upward-biased for farm poverty and downward-biased for nonfarm. The shift of families from farm to nonfarm, for instance, has probably added some poverty-level families to the nonfarm group. Since overall median family income and the number of nonfarm families would be positively correlated in the 1947–66 time series, the effect of omitting the number of nonfarm families from the regression is to lower the coefficient of median income for this group. The opposite would be the case for the coefficient for median income for farm families.

(1) there are sharp differences in the responsiveness of poverty inci-
     dence rates to income growth and unemployment variables among
     the various poverty subgroups; and

(2) poverty incidence in the nonwhite subgroup, while lagging behind
     the response of overall poverty incidence, responds elastically to
     overall median income.

These findings lead us to advance what may be termed a *relative* backwash proposition. That is, when the poor family population is grouped
according to "larger" and "smaller" population classifications, the "smaller"
categories show: (1) a lesser rate of poverty reduction in response to income growth (even though one "smaller" subdivision, nonwhites, does
respond elastically) and (2) for the "smaller" population categories, in all
cases except nonwhites, there is a good probability that the rate of poverty
reduction responds significantly to some unspecified independent vari-
able(s).[10] Thus, changes in the level of economic activity (i.e., economic
growth) in and of itself as an anti-poverty policy tool likely will tend to
bring about a greater concentration of poverty among the "smaller" population subgroupings, and if poverty comes to be progressively more concentrated among such relative "backwash" groups, one might expect the
linkage between change in the overall level of poverty incidence and the
growth income to become weaker with the passage of time.[11] In short, this
paper may be viewed as support for the soundness of increasing public
policy emphasis on selective and specific anti-poverty programs aimed at
those problems and characteristics that act to insulate some poor families
more than others from the salutary effects of general economic advance.

[10] In these cases the Durbin-Watson statistic indicates the high probability of omitted
explanatory variables.

[11] For a theoretical development and another empirical test of a similar point see
Locke-Anderson, "Trickling Down: The Relationship," pp. 511–524.

19

THE MILITARY DRAFT AS A SLAVE SYSTEM: AN ECONOMIC VIEW

ROBERT EVANS, JR.
Brandeis University

T HE MILITARY RECRUITMENT PROBLEM IS AN APPROPRIATE SUBJECT FOR an economist to analyze, combining as it does elements of micro- and macroeconomic analysis, having distributive and allocative implications, and containing profound ethical difficulties.[1] Only recently, however, has professional attention been given to some implications of our system of military manpower procurement.[2] These analyses have largely tended to view the problem in purely economic terms, and therefore have utilized the assumption that they are dealing with a free market institution which is merely subject to an imperfection; namely, that the price of a significant portion of its labor force is too low. Thus their analysis of the specific problems can proceed in the same spirit, and with many of the same conclusions, as would a study of rent control or wage and price guidelines.

The military draft is also a social system with characteristics and implications which go far beyond formal economics. The essence of this article is that, for many aspects of public policy, especially those associated with ending the draft, the draft system can best be understod in a broader social context. Since the draft is a system of involuntary labor, the appropriate context would seem to be a forced labor or slave system.

The usefulness and implications of the slave system analogy are developed in three sections. The first presents the necessary conditions for slavery and some of its operational characteristics. The second section illustrates the degree to which the military draft is consistent with a slave system. The final section discusses some of the implications of the analysis. The parallels between the draft and all aspects of the slave systems may not be perfect. It is sufficient if they are exact enough for this approach to heighten our understanding of the military manpower situation.[3]

NECESSARY CONDITIONS FOR SLAVERY

In general, there are four conditions which are necessary and sufficient in order for a system of forced labor to develop. These are: (1) surplus of labor, (2) a marked difference between the supply and demand prices for

---

[1] George H. Hildebrand, "Discussion," *Papers and Proceedings of the American Economic Association*, 57 (May, 1967), pp. 63–66.

[2] See the following and the literature cited therein: Stuart H. Altman and Alan E. Fechter, "The Supply of Military Personnel in the Absence of a Draft," *Papers and Proceedings of the American Economic Association*, 57 (May, 1967), pp. 19–31; W. Lee Hansen and Burton A. Weisbrod, "Economics of the Military Draft," *Quarterly Journal of Economics*, 81 (Aug., 1967), pp. 395–421, and Walter W. Oi, "The Economic Cost of the Draft," *Papers and Proceedings of the American Economic Association*, 57 (May, 1967), pp. 39–62.

[3] See the discussion of analogy and evidence in Stanley M. Elkins, *Slavery* (New York: Grosset and Dunlap, 1963), pp. 225–226.

♦ First published in *Social Science Quarterly* 50, No. 3 (December, 1969).

labor at some "desired" level of output, with the difference primarily due to a high disutility associated with the work, (3) an enslavable population, and (4) a political and moral basis for enslaving the subject population.

A general labor surplus is necessary in order to reduce opposition from employers who would otherwise object to losing their employees into slavery. The excess supply also strengthens the moral basis for the enslavement, since under these conditions, the potential slaves ought to have been willing to accept the lower wage and employment. The need for the difference in demand and supply prices is obvious since if people were willing to work at the price offered there would be no reason to incur the costs of enslavement. The imbalance must be largely due to worker disutility rather than skill requirements in order for the quality of labor not to be a problem. An enslavable population is clearly required, and since to be a slave is not a desirable status, it is essential that the slave population be distinguishable from the free population on the basis of social, cultural, or political characteristics. Lastly, since enslavement is ultimately carried out with the approval of the government, those with a will to enslave must have political power and be able to provide some moral rationale for the slavery.

In addition to these necessary conditions all slave systems have a number of special characteristics which are associated with their operation. A few of these will be discussed here in order to strengthen the analogy. One of the most important characteristics is segregation of the slaves from too great an interaction with free persons. To achieve this, the slaves are usually forced to live apart from the rest of society and they are made to wear distinctive clothing or to otherwise make clear their second-class status. Their status is also manifest in the slaves' being subject to a separate legal code, one which provides for fewer civil rights and protections of due process. Slave compensation (housing, food, clothes, and perhaps small sums of money) is both meager and largely undifferentiated on the basis of skills or economic contribution.

All historical slave systems have shared a common characteristic in the long run: the slaves have been emancipated. The conditions under which liberation has taken place can be grouped into two situations: (a) those in which the system has become inefficient, and (b) those where major political changes have taken place. Inefficiency may take a variety of forms but it is usually related to the costs of enslavement or the secondary consequences of slavery upon the whole society rather than simple economic inefficiency at the workplace. The failure of early attempts to enslave the American Indians because it was too easy for them to melt into the forests, or the termination of early slavery in Japan because intermarriage had erased the racial distinctions, would be examples of the former. The Russian emacipation of the serfs in the aftermath of the Crimean War because the feudal system was seen as a danger to the economic and political viability of the Russian state illustrates the latter. Moral revulsion may assist in the emancipation process but it is unlikely that it would be sufficient in itself. The sole historical exception would seem to be the British emancipation in the West Indies but this affected only a handful of Englishmen miles from the seat of political power. Thus we can conclude that emancipation is not a marginal change but rather is a part of a dramatic upheaval within society.

There are three forced labor systems whose existence and characteristics are at least casually known to most Americans. These are the USSR's forced labor camps of the 1930's, German use of forced labor during World War II, and our own Negro slavery. A brief review of these three will illustrate the points presented above.

All began in periods of general labor surplus: the Soviet Union had surplus agricultural labor when the Kulaks (well-to-do peasants) were sent to forced labor camps, the Germans found massive unemployment in Poland and western Russia following their brief but highly successful military campaigns, and the American planters had the resources of the unemployed and underemployed millions of Africa and Europe to draw upon. The success of each system generated a demand for an increased number of slaves. These demands were met by the political prisoners of Stalin's purges of the 1930's, the impressment of employed Eastern Europeans, and more extensive slave hunting in the interior of Africa by African slave suppliers. In each case, the argument was made that the necessary labor for the particular tasks was not forthcoming at an "appropriate" wage level, primarily because of the nonpecuniary aspects of the employment. The enslaved were all drawn from "inferior" populations. The Soviets considered the Kulaks to be politically inferior, the Germans thought the Poles and Russians were racially inferior, while the planters of the South viewed the Negro as less than human. It might be argued that the inferiority of the subject people was the most important reason for their enslavement, but the evidence is not consistent with such a view. The political and economic values of removing the Kulaks could have been obtained by confiscation of assets and exile from their home communities. The Germans initially recruited Eastern Europeans as voluntary contract labor and turned to force only when an adequate supply was not forthcoming.[4] A concern over having a large number of free Negroes in their midst may have had some influence on the enslavement decision in the South, but the early planter clearly preferred white labor to black.[5]

The three forced labor systems also exhibited the operating conditions which were given above. In the Soviet case the living and employment locations were separated, largely geographically, from those of free workers. In Germany, the slave laborers worked alongside free Germans, but their living quarters and recreational areas were separated. Negro slaves, especially on plantations, worked apart from free labor and were housed in

---

[4] Three days after the Germans crossed the frontier, labor recruitment offices were opened in the Polish cities of Rybnik and Dirshau and by May of 1940 some 700,000–800,000 Poles were working in Germany. One-third to one-half of those workers were civilians; the remainder were POW's. By the middle of 1940, pressure from Berlin to increase the flow of labor from Poland at current wages left the occupation authorities with no alternative but to utilize force. Edward L. Homze, *Foreign Labor in Nazi Germany* (Princeton: Princeton University Press, 1967), pp. 25–35.

[5] Elkins, *Slavery*, pp. 37–52.

their own areas. The slaves in each system were subject to separate legal systems which lacked most of the safeguards available to the free populations. Additional examples of the slaves' second-class citizenship could be given. For example, in Germany it was a crime punishable by death for a German to have sexual relations with a female forced-laborer. In the USSR the laundry of laborers and guards was done separately in order to avoid "contamination." And in the South, miscegenation was looked upon with horror.

The termination of these three systems and the emancipation of the slaves fall into our situation (b), major political change. In the latter two, German and Negro slavery, the political change came after military defeat and the installation of new governments. In the Soviet Union the freedom came within the context of the political changes attendant upon Stalin's death.

From a purely economic point of view it is difficult to estimate the inefficiencies of these three systems, though none who write of them suggest that they were as efficient as a free labor system. In the Soviet Union, it seems clear that the labor camp productivity level was below that of free labor, though whether it was as low as the 50 per cent estimate of one author[6] is open to question. Indeed, another author[7] argues that, due to the longer hours per day and days per year, high work norms, fear, and a graduated feeding program, the average product of the forced laborer was equal to that of the free worker, though this takes no account of the costs of administration and surveillance, which were very high. In the case of Germany, it was noted that by 1943 the foreign workers were becoming sullen, indifferent, and hostile. Absenteeism and illness rose sharply to a rate of 12 to 14 per cent for Eastern workers, about double the rate for German nationals. For the same period it was also estimated that foreign labor might be as low as only 65 per cent as effective as German labor.[8] Nor is American slavery more easily assessed. Quotations from individual employers suggest that the slave[9] was anywhere from much less to 150 per cent more effective than available white labor. Daily wage data from naval shipyards and large-scale construction projects suggest that slaves were about 70–85 per cent as effective as free labor.[10] Alternatively, slaves em-

[6] David J. Dallin and B. I. Nilolaevsky, *Forced Labor in Soviet Russia* (New Haven: Yale University Press, 1947), p. 137.

[7] Michael Romanenko, in United Nations Economic and Social Council, *Slave Labor in Russia: The Case Presented by the American Federation of Labor to the United Nations* (New York: UN Economic and Social Council, 1949), pp. 58–60.

[8] Homze, *Foreign Labor*, pp. 249–259.

[9] *Southern Planter* (Richmond, Virginia), 3 (Sept., 1843), pp. 205–206, as cited in Eugene D. Genovese, *The Political Economy of Slavery* (New York: Vintage Books, 1967), p. 54. Yet the Engineer of the State of Louisiana was quoted as saying, "I think 20 Negroes will perform as much hard work as 30 whites," in James D. B. DeBow, ed., *The Commercial Review of the South and West* (*DeBow's Review*), 9 (1850), p. 153.

[10] Relative efficiency is determined by the ratio of wages for similar occupations. Data are from the National Archives, Washington, D.C., United States Navy Bureau of

ployed in Petersburg tobacco factories earned incentive wages up to an amount equal to the rent (net of subsistance) which the factory was paying their owners.[11]

In summary, the Soviet, German, and American Negro slave systems largely conformed to the precondition requirements, contained the typical characteristics, including large-scale inefficiency,[12] and were terminated in conformity with the principles outlined.

THE MILITARY DRAFT AS A SLAVE SYSTEM

It will be legitimate to analyze the military draft as a slave system to the extent that it generally fulfills the conditions and characteristics described above. It is to this question of conformity that we now turn.

The American military draft was instituted at a time when official government policy was opposed to a foreign war and when many people sincerely believed that such a war could be avoided. Initially service was limited to one year and to a maximum of 900,000 men, though budgetary limitations kept the number drafted below the maximum.

In 1940 there were 8 million unemployed, 14.6 per cent of the labor force, surely a large enough pool from which to draw 900,000 men by the usual free market mechanisms of vigorous recruitment and higher wages. Thus the draft fulfills the requirement of being instituted in a period of labor surplus. The inability to equate supply and demand prices was not due to skill problems, for no provisions were made for any special labor quality. The political and moral basis for the enslavement was that it was necessary for the preservation of the national freedom. A weak point in the analogy is that the enslavable population did not differ extensively from the general population, though, since it was to be applied only to those who were single and the age restriction of under 27 was soon added, it was certainly applied to a minority group. The apparent cultural, racial, and social inferiority of the enslaved population, however, has become even more evident in recent years as income and educational provisions have been added to the de-facto draft law, so that the probability of being drafted or coerced to serve as a reluctant volunteer has been much higher for groups such as Negroes

Yards and Docks, Payrolls of Mechanics and Laborers for Gosport, Virginia, 1852–1859, and Pensacola, Florida, 1848–1859; and from the South Carolina State Archives, Columbia, for State House Payrolls, 1856–1860.

[11] Frederick Lewis Olmstead, *A Journey in the Seaboard Slave States* (New York: Mason Brothers, 1856), p. 103. Other instances of incentive wages are given in Clement Eaton, "Slave Hiring in the Upper South: A Step Toward Freedom," *Mississippi Valley Historical Review,* 46 (March, 1960), p. 670.

[12] A more complete analysis of the level of efficiency is difficult because of the lack of essential data and the problem of correctly specifying the alternative. For data on the Soviet case see N. Jasny, "Labor and Output in Soviet Concentration Camps," *Journal of Political Economy,* 59 (Oct., 1951), pp. 405–419; and A. David Redding, "Reliability of Estimates of Unfree Labor in the USSR," *Journal of Political Economy,* 60 (Aug., 1952), pp. 337–340. On Negro slavery see Genovese, *Political Economy of Slavery,* pp. 43–69.

and for low education and income groups, which are considered to be socially inferior.[13]

The article's basic argument is that given certain conditions, slavery will result. Thus it is unnecessary to ask why the United States adopted conscription in specific historical contexts. Nor would it be an easy question to answer. One author has suggested that it was the conscript army of Prussia's easy victory over the professional army of France in the Franco-Prussian War that led other countries to adopt conscript armies.[14] In the case of Japan there was some emulation of "modern" Prussia, but of greater importance was the fact that conscription made the modern Japanese army representative of the nation as a whole and not one of class, the *bushi* (warrior caste), as had historically been the case. This argument of social balance, perhaps heightened by England's experience in the early years of World War I, appears to have been important in Congress' thinking during the debate over conscription in the First World War. In all probability, though, the use of conscript armies and the high casualty rates of the major World War I powers were the convincing elements, for the "success and necessity" of conscription in World War I appears to have dominated the 1940 decision.

In operation the draft system demonstrated those characteristics of segregation, separate legal systems, distinctive dress, and other features which are typical of slave economies. The second-class nature of the new slaves is also evident in the poor housing available to families, high insurance and loan rates, and exclusion from the social life of the camp communities. Moreover, from 1952 to 1965, while the general level of wages was rising about 60 per cent, from $1.52 an hour to $2.45 an hour, the wages of enlisted men with less than two years of service were not increased at all. Thus we can conclude that, because the military draft is consistent with the preconditions for slavery and exhibits the operational characteristics of slavery, its basic characteristics are more slave than free and it can be analyzed accordingly.

[13] An assessment of the degree of discrimination involved in the draft depends upon how one treats men who are rejected for service on the basis of health and mental ability. When only those who meet military standards are included, the discrimination of the draft is relatively clear. According to a 1961 census sample, the ratio of whites aged 26–34 who had been inducted into the military to those who were deferred or exempt was 1.7; for nonwhites the ratio was 3.0. The data are shown in David B. Johnson, "The Alternatives in Military Manpower Procurement," in James C. Miller, ed., *Why the Draft* (Baltimore: Penguin, 1968), p. 29. It has been estimated that annually between fiscal year 1970 and 1975, at normal (non-Vietnam) levels of military manpower, 177,700 men will be inducted or become draft-induced volunteers into the enlisted forces. About 21.5 per cent of these men will have between 1 and 3 years of high school education. Yet, in 1975 only 15.0 per cent of the males aged 25–34 will have completed only 1–3 years of high school. In the same period, 2 per cent of the men drafted into enlisted ranks will have at least completed college, compared to 19.8 per cent of the males 25–34 in 1975. The military figures are from Oi, "Economic Cost of the Draft," p. 56, and the population education data are from Denis F. Johnston, "Education of Adult Workers in 1975," *Monthly Labor Review*, 91 (April, 1968), p. 12.

[14] Cotton M. Lindsay, "Our National Tradition of Conscription: Experience with the Draft," in Miller, ed., *Why the Draft*, pp. 138–139.

SOME IMPLICATIONS

A traditional economic analysis of the draft will conclude that it will result in some lost civilian output because the men drafted will probably not be those with the relatively highest military productivity and the relatively lowest civilian productivity. The additional insight of the slave analysis is that military output is primarily diminished because the draftee, like slaves everywhere, lacks the motivation and interest of the free laborer.

The low social position of the draftee and his inadequate compensation tend to lower the compensation and prestige of those free laborers who are employed with him. As a consequence, the slave works in collaboration with a low quality work force. The present extent of this low quality can be seen in the fact that about 40 per cent of the military's true volunteers who were 18 to 24 years of age had less than a high school education,[15] but only 27.4 per cent of the 1966 male labor force aged 20–24 were not high school graduates. The fact that the military's proportion of low quality free labor is almost 80 per cent greater than for the economy as a whole is eloquent testimony to the negative impact upon complementary factors of production.

Several studies of military manpower[16] in a market context have concluded that either a completely voluntary army or a partially drafted military force of about 3,000,000 men in a non-war situation, with men compensated at something approximating their foregone civilian earnings, could be obtained with modest increases in budgetary costs. (In other words, a slightly higher military wage rate would attract enough qualified volunteers.) In the context of our slave perspective, such optimistic events appear unlikely. The freeing of the slaves through the elimination of the draft or the payment of adequate compensation is not merely a simple increase in relative wages, such as, for example, has been enjoyed by the over-the-road truck drivers in the postwar years. Rather, it would be emancipation, the complete upsetting of social and economic relationships which have grown up over the last 30 years. Consequently, its costs and problems must be seen in the broader social context.

While certain present costs due to rapid turnover would be avoided under a free army, it would lack the present system's great flexibility of size due to high flow-through rates, large training sections, the freezing of discharges, higher draft calls, and if necessary, as in the Korean War, the call-back of veterans. The staffing of the reserves would also be more difficult since it is estimated that 70 per cent of the total accessions to the National Guard and the reserves are draft-motivated.[17]

Emancipation on the basis of paying military men their alternative foregone civilian earnings would probably involve relatively modest budgetary costs. Even so, it is not clear that the public would be willing to incur

[15] These were calculated from Table 3 of Altman and Fechter, "Supply of Military Personnel," p. 23; and Table 2 of Oi, "Economic Cost of the Draft," p. 44.
[16] See Altman and Fechter, "Supply of Military Personnel," p. 30; Oi, "Economic Cost of the Draft," p. 60; Hansen and Weisbrod, "Economics of the Draft," p. 417.
[17] Oi, "Economic Cost of the Draft," p. 60.

these increased costs because so many households are headed by men who were once drafted or coerced into volunteering. It is highly probable that many of the more than 23 million veterans would feel that, since they served at low wages, it is appropriate for this generation's young men to serve at low wages. Some support for this view of the unwillingness of veterans to incur these double costs (their own tax in kind and the new higher money cost associated with emancipation) may be found in the fact that between 1952 and 1965 federal civilian pay was increased 46.3 per cent, but military pay by only 36.6 per cent, and educational benefits for post-January, 1955 servicemen had to await the Vietnam War for Congressional passage.

It is unlikely that new pay schedules could be designed to attract additional volunteers and also eliminate higher compensation for those who even now would volunteer. This would mean that all military pay levels would have to be increased in order to preserve the internal wage structure. The large general increase would in turn drastically alter the historic relationships between military and civilian government pay structure. The experience of private employers and governments (New York City, for example) with altered relative pay levels suggests that substantial increases in military wages would have to be followed by substantial increases in federal civilian payrolls.[18]

At present, internal allocation of labor within the military, as in any slave system, is largely done by command and not by market forces. Under a voluntary army this would probably have to be changed since there are marked differences between being in the Quartermaster Corps and in the Infantry or between being a company clerk an hour from London and being one in a tent along the Korean DMZ. A change-over to an internal market system would not only entail shifts in prestige and pay within the military, but would also introduce the uncertainties of a market as opposed to a command system. The near impossibility of obtaining such changes is suggested by the current resistance within the Soviet bloc countries to modest shifts between command and market forces and by the intense resistance within the American military to the introduction of continuous-aim firing in the Navy and the retirement of the cavalry in the Army.[19]

The slave analogy provides a basis for assessing the probabilities associated with ending the draft and some insights concerning the conditions under which it might occur. The German and the American Negro slave systems ended as a result of unconditional military defeat and the displacement of the enslaving government, a possibility which appears unlikely in the current case. The Soviet system ended under the twin pres-

[18] Certainly the unwillingness of Congress to be guided by market forces and its reliance upon preservation of historic patterns in the government's civilian wage structure lend support to this view.

[19] These are discussed in Edward L. Katzenbach, Jr., "The Horse Cavalry in the Twentieth Century: A Study in Policy," in Carl S. Friedrich and Seymour E. Harris, eds., *Public Policy*, 8 (Cambridge, Mass.: Harvard Graduate School of Public Administration, 1958), pp. 120–150; and Elting E. Morison, "A Case Study of Innovation," *Engineering and Science Monthly* (April, 1950), pp. 5–11.

sures of the basic political changes which followed Stalin's death and the realization that the slaves represented an un-economic utilization of labor which was then in short supply. A political change in this country equivalent to that of de-Stalinization would appear unlikely, but the high opportunity cost of the slave system to the society as a whole may be relevant. Its relevance is strengthened when one recalls that it was a similar excessive opportunity cost which was instrumental in freeing the serfs in nineteenth-century Russia and in fundamentally altering economic relationships in Japan at the time of the Restoration (1868). Society's opportunity cost is probably also the principal factor which would have led to the freeing of the American Negro slaves in the absence of the Civil War. From this we conclude that only if future conditions dramatize the inefficiencies and foregone valuable opportunities which are associated with our military slave system can there be an expectation that the society will emancipate its own slaves voluntarily.

It is instructive to note that the slave analogy and traditional economics yield dramatically different conclusions on the relationship between the draft and unemployment. The conventional economic analysis inversely relates the level of unemployment with the volunteer rate, which means low unemployment and high draft calls, and vice versa. Slave systems, however, are established, as was the draft, in surplus labor situations, and only in times of acute labor shortage are they apt to be ended. This difference in expectation stems from the fact that the conventional analysis concerns itself with the opportunity cost to individuals, while the slave system analysis concentrates upon the opportunity cost to the entire society. Therefore, only when the opportunity cost to the society of maintaining slavery is very great, as would be the case under a severe labor shortage,[20] is the draft apt to be ended.

CONCLUSION

The American military draft is not a free market institution with a disequilibrium wage. It is a forced labor system and exhibits most of the characteristics, save length of service, of other modern slave systems, such as those in Stalinist Russia, Nazi Germany, and American Negro slavery. As a slave system, it is inefficient because of a misallocation of labor, but primarily it is inefficient due to lack of proper motivation and morale. In addition, the slave analogy allows one to understand very clearly that an end to the draft is not a simple increase in a wage level, but that it is emancipation with all that it means in terms of upsetting countless economic and social relationships. The analogy has also allowed us to suggest that it is only when the opportunity cost to society of having a military slave system becomes onerous that the draft is apt to be ended.

[20] If the shortage of labor were to be associated with a general war of the magnitude of World War II, it is possible that the inefficiencies associated with transfer of funds from civilian to military personnel sufficient in magnitude to obtain a voluntary army would more than counterbalance the gains from abandoning the draft. The general use of direct controls in place of market forces as well as the social pressure to do "one's part" which was characteristic of World War II makes it difficult to estimate which cost would be apt to be the greater.

20

NOTES ON THE COLOR OF THE VOLUNTEER ARMY[1]

WILLIAM FREITHALER FORD
Texas Tech University

ROBERT TOLLISON
Cornell University

IN RECENT MONTHS THE VOLUNTEER ARMY CONCEPT HAS MOVED FROM THE realm of polemics to the national policy arena. It is therefore imperative that the major issues involved in the debate over this proposal be carefully scrutinized to clarify their implications. This paper examines the widely publicized argument that a volunteer army would be manned primarily by economically disadvantaged minorities, especially Negroes.[2]

SUPPLY PROSPECTS

Critics of the volunteer concept imply that volunteers would come primarily from lower income groups in which Negroes are disproportionately represented. It should be noted, however, that even in the lowest income brackets (that is, under $3,000), white families outnumber black families by very substantial margins, and these margins expand rapidly as one ascends the income scale. For example, in 1966, 32 per cent of all Negro families had incomes of less than $3,000 while only 13 per cent of all white families fell in that category. Nevertheless, the number of white families in this income bracket outweighed that of Negroes by a factor of approximately 5.72 to 1.57 million. Moreover, in the $3,000–4,999 category, the ratio of white to Negro families (6.16–1.18 million) was even higher.[3] These data, although stated in terms of family units, would seem to indicate that the *potential* supply of white volunteers is significantly larger than that of their black counterparts in the lower income groups of the economy.[4]

[1] Thanks should be extended to Donald L. Martin, and Roland N. McKean of the University of Virginia, and Thomas D. Willett of Harvard University for helpful advice and criticism. Any errors are, of course, ours.

[2] For representative statements of this argument see Harry A. Marmion, *Selective Service: Conflict and Compromise* (New York: John Wiley and Sons, 1968), pp. 64–65; Morris Janowitz, "American Democracy and Military Service," *Trans-action,* 4 (March, 1967), p. 9; Editorial, *Wall Street Journal* (February 24, 1969), p. 14.

[3] Roughly similar disparities appear if one considers only the racial composition of unemployed adults. These findings are derived from data presented in a joint publication of the U.S. Department of Commerce, Bureau of the Census, and the U.S. Department of Labor, Bureau of Labor Statistics, entitled, "Social and Economic Conditions of Negroes in the United States," *Current Population Reports,* Series P-23, No. 24, and BLS Report No. 332 (Washington, D.C.: U.S. Government Printing Office, Oct., 1967), pp. 18, 22.

[4] As of March, 1967, the racial composition of the adult male population living below the "poverty level" (as defined by the Social Security Administration) consisted of approximately 2,164,000 white and 808,000 nonwhite individuals. See U.S. Bureau of the Census, *Statistical Abstracts of the United States, 1968* (89th ed.), (Washington, D.C.: U.S. Government Printing Office, 1969), p. 330.

 ◆ First published in *Social Science Quarterly* 50, No. 3 (December, 1969).

In spite of this preponderance of potential white volunteers a predominantly black army could still emerge under the volunteer system if the propensity of Negroes to enlist was much greater than that of whites. Recent data on the racial composition of first-term enlistees provide the best available evidence bearing on this issue. These data indicate that 5.7 per cent of draft-age whites relative to 3.7 per cent of draft-age Negroes are volunteering to serve at current wage levels.[5] The higher proportion of white enlistees may, in part, reflect a higher propensity among whites than Negroes to enlist under the threat of the draft. The facts, however, are not clear on this, and the discrepancy in unadjusted rates is so large that "true" volunteer rates would probably still show a somewhat higher proportion of draft-age white enlistees. These figures also reflect in part the fact that a higher percentage of Negroes than whites (58 per cent vis-à-vis 25 per cent) fails to qualify for military service in pre-induction examinations.[6] Moreover, the higher pay scales for the volunteer army would probably attract proportionately greater numbers of whites than Negroes into military job markets.[7]

In any case, the available data indicate that qualified Negroes would face substantial competition for jobs in a volunteer army from a much larger group of qualified whites.

DEMAND FACTORS

This analysis would be inadequate if some attempt were not made to consider the reaction of the military to free labor market conditions. Various studies of military manpower policies have asserted that the armed forces tend to employ labor-intensive processes over a wide range of their activities.[8] This represents a rational adjustment to the present economic situation since the draft provides labor to the armed forces at below market wages. Thus, one would expect a military warehouse, cafeteria, motor pool or maintenance facility to employ a greater amount of labor (and lesser quantities of other resources) than a private firm would use to produce the same services.

Abolishing the draft would eliminate this labor cost advantage and should tend to promote the adoption of labor-saving processes throughout the military establishment. Capital equipment, in particular, would dis-

---

[5] "Social and Economic Conditions of Negroes," p. 81.

[6] Ibid., p. 82.

[7] Milton Friedman has asserted that in this regard present levels of pay are *comparatively* more attractive to Negroes than the higher levels of pay of a volunteer system would be. This indicates that the majority of Negroes who would be affected by a wage differential between the civilian and military sectors have already responded to the differential and are already in the armed services. If Friedman's hypothesis is correct, the above analysis is further strengthened because the response of Negroes to the higher levels of pay in a volunteer system would be proportionately less than whites. Milton Friedman, "An All Volunteer Army," *New York Times Magazine* (May 14, 1967), p. 118.

[8] For example, see W. L. Hansen and B. A. Weisbrod, "Economics of the Military Draft," *Quarterly Journal of Economics*, 81 (Aug., 1967), p. 402.

place labor in many military activities.[9] The ubiquitous box-lifting trench-digging, foot-weary infantryman, for example, would be replaced by a corps of space age warriors employing fork lift trucks, trench-digging machines, and more sophisticated weapons systems. In short, a well-managed volunteer army could not afford "Beetle Bailey."

This adjustment to higher priced labor would obviously affect both the number and kinds of job openings available in the military establishment. It would imply a general reduction in total military employment to achieve a given overall level of defense capability.[10] In addition, it would probably result in an upward revision of the minimal labor skills and educational achievements demanded of recruits by the military. A proportionately greater number of jobs would exist, for example, for operators and maintainers of modern military equipment. Fewer jobs would be available to high school dropouts and unskilled and undereducated workers. Negroes, of course, are over-represented in the ranks of our unskilled and under-educated workers. This factor would further reduce their chances of successfully competing for a disproportionate share of the jobs in a peacetime volunteer army.

Under the current system of military manpower procurement, the proportion of Negroes in the armed services is on the order of 9 per cent, while their representation in the total population is about 11 per cent.[11] However, because of their generally disadvantaged background, Negroes, once in the military, tend to be allocated in disproportionate numbers to low skill jobs such as combat operations.[12] If a settlement should be reached in Southeast Asia, it seems reasonable to assume that combat units of the armed forces would be deactivated most rapidly. Military employment opportunities for relatively unskilled Negroes would therefore probably be reduced in a post-Viet Nam context even if the draft were not abolished. Indeed, the military's use of the draft system has traditionally been more selective in periods of peace. This effect would be compounded by a shift to a volunteer basis since, as noted above, such a system would require a smaller and more highly skilled military labor force.

[9] See Armen A. Alchian and William R. Allen, *Exchange and Production Theory in Use* (Belmont, California: Wadsworth, 1969), p. 525, for a statement of this point in a different context. Also, the labor-saving tendency would be accentuated if the volunteer army enjoyed more success than its predecessor in procuring capital equipment at truly competitive prices.

[10] Complementing this relative movement away from labor-intensive processes would be the various manpower economies which could be achieved under the volunteer system in its training operations. These economies would result because the lower personnel turnover of the volunteer army implies a smaller commitment of manpower to training functions. On this point, see Hansen and Weisbrod, "Economics of the Military Draft," p. 402.

[11] These data, reflecting conditions in June, 1967, are drawn from "Social and Economic Conditions of Negroes in the United States."

[12] As of June, 1967, Negroes accounted for approximately 9 per cent of the total manpower in our armed forces, but only about 2 per cent of the officers on active duty. The fact that 15 per cent of our men killed in action in Viet Nam (as of mid-1967) were Negroes further illustrates this point. *Ibid.*, pp. 83–84.

CONCLUSION

An exhaustive manpower study would have to be made to predict precisely the racial and socioeconomic composition of our armed forces if the draft were replaced by a peacetime volunteer army. Critics of the volunteer concept have simply asserted that an "all black" (or predominantly black) army would emerge. Our preliminary analysis of the relevant theoretical issues and empirical data indicates that this assertion is implausible. Two complementary lines of reasoning have led us to this conclusion.

One concerns the nature of manpower requirements that would evolve under an all-volunteer system. As the wages of military labor rose toward competitive levels, the rational economic reaction of the armed forces would be to mechanize and reduce the labor intensivity of their various productive processes. Smaller numbers of more highly skilled servicemen would be sought by the military establishment.

The second line of reasoning pursued the question of how the Negro job seeker would fare in these restructured military job markets. The data and arguments we presented indicate that job competition in these markets might well be intensified by shifting to a volunteer system, with predicted detrimental effects to the military employment prospects of Negroes and other disadvantaged groups. If this should develop in practice, critics of the volunteer army concept might still find themselves in the position of objecting to its racial composition, but on the grounds that it is "too white" rather than "all black."

21

TOWARD A THEORY OF GUIDED SOCIETAL CHANGE[1]

AMITAI ETZIONI

Columbia University

I F WE OBSERVE A SOCIETY FACED WITH A PROBLEM—POVERTY, RIOTS, UN-safe cars—and formulating a program to deal with it, we can be sure that nine times out of ten the problem will not be solved. If we look again, ten or twenty years later, we shall find that the problem may have been trimmed, redefined, or redistributed, but only infrequently will it have been treated to anyone's satisfaction. Thus, we flatly predict that 15 years from now there will still be massive poverty in the United States (despite the "total war" devoted to its eradication), there will still be out-breaks of violence in the streets during hot summers, and there probably will still be tens of thousands of casualties on the highways each year.

Other societies do not score much better in their systematic attempts to deal with their problems, although the differences in symptom and treat-ment, we shall see, are not without interest. Nine out of ten underdeveloped countries which as recently as a decade ago optimistically spun master plans for their own development are still underdeveloped.[2] Even countries which knew a revolution (for example, Bolivia in 1952) or a government oriented toward development and democratization (for example, Bosch's government in the Dominican Republic) did not score much better.[3] The Soviet Union's achievements over the last 50 years are impressive, but it has not achieved the goals it set for itself in 1917: to eliminate the state, sharp economic differences and privileges, religion, and maybe the family.[4] Israel, which set out in 1949 to absorb a massive wave of immigrants, seems instead to be slowly being absorbed by them. In short, the capacity of societies to treat their own problems and to change themselves seems rather limited.

[1] This article is based on a project conducted for the National Science Foundation (GS-1475). The main report of this project is included in my *The Active Society: A Theory of Societal and Political Processes* (New York: The Free Press, 1968).

[2] On the difficulties see Albert Waterston, *Development Planning: Lessons of Ex-perience* (Baltimore: Johns Hopkins University Press, 1965); A. G. Ganson, *The Process of Planning: A Study of India's Five-year Plans, 1950–1964* (London: Oxford University Press, 1966), esp. pp. 525–538. See also various reports in Bertram M. Gross, ed., *Action Under Planning: the Guidance of Economic Development* (New York: McGraw-Hill, 1967); Fred G. Burke, *Tanganyika: Preplanning* (Syracuse: Syracuse University Press, 1965), pp. 53–57.

[3] See Abraham F. Lowenthal, "Foreign Aid as a Political Instrument, the Case of the Dominican Republic," in John D. Montgomery and Arthur Smithes, eds., *Public Policy*, 14 (Cambridge, Mass.: Harvard Graduate School of Public Administration, 1966), pp. 141–160; and John Bartlow Martin, *Overtaken by Events* (Garden City, N.Y.: Doubleday, 1966).

[4] Barrington Moore, Jr., *Soviet Politics: The Dilemma of Power* (New York: Harper and Row, 1965); Adam B. Ulam, *The Unfinished Revolution* (New York: Random House, 1960).

 ♦ First published in *Social Science Quarterly* 50, No. 3 (December, 1969).

SOCIETAL CYBERNETICS

Our purpose is to outline the main sociopolitical factors which, as we see it, significantly affect the relative capacity of a society to act. Our effort is not based on a specific study but is a "theoretical effort," attempting to analyze the factors involved by drawing on a large variety of studies conducted by others, on abstract assumptions about what the relations among factors may or may not be, and on distilled common sense. Above all, we draw on an analogue, from cybernetics.[5]

Cybernetics is the study of steering, of the ways groups of machines, of persons, or combinations of machines and persons, are guided to work jointly to realize goals set by the cybernetic overlayer. Cybernetics is most highly developed in mechanical and electrical systems, where it consists of (1) one or more centers which issue instructions to the units which do the work, and (2) communication lines which carry the instructions from the center(s) to the working units, and return "feedback" information and responses from the subject units. While many cybernetic models omit power, we see it as a third main factor. If the steering units cannot back up their signals with rewards or sanctions, they will frequently be disregarded. A further subtlety is to distinguish, within the centers, between sub-units which absorb and analyze the incoming information and those which make decisions.

When all these elements are available and functioning effectively—communication lines are well "hooked up;" information and decision-making units speak freely to each other—we have an effective *control* system. Some engineers and managers think that a social system—be it a corporation or a society—can also be run in this manner. As we see it, however, when a cybernetic model is applied to a social unit, it must be taken into account that, for both practical and ethical reasons, the member unit which does the work cannot be coerced to follow "signals" unless they are, at least to some extent, responsive to the member's values and interests. Hence, the downward flow of control signals must be accompanied by an upward flow and a "lateral" (intermember) flow which express what the members wish or are willing to do. We refer to these flows as consensus-building, and to the combination of control and consensus-building, the societal cybernatorial mechanisms, as social guidance.

THE ELEMENTS OF SOCIETAL GUIDANCE

The differences between active and passive societies, between those more and those less able to handle their problems, are best studied by examining one cybernatorial factor at a time, although effective guidance requires their combination.

Knowledge-units. The main guidance mechanism of societies, whether we like it or not, is the state. When we examine the amount of its funds,

[5] For basic works on cybernetics, see Norbert Wiener, *Cybernetics* (Cambridge, Mass.: MIT Press, 1961), and his *Human Use of Human Beings* (New York: Avon, 1967).

the size of its manpower resources and the extent to which its experts are devoted to the collection and processing of knowledge as compared to other activities, we get an impression of how "knowledgeable" the particular state will be. In looking at contemporary societies, we are immediately struck with one reason they are doing so poorly in their self-management: they spend relatively very little on knowledge and much more on "doing." And, most of the funds that go into the production of knowledge go into natural sciences—the study of the non-social environment. When societies attempt to deal with poverty, riots, and urban problems they often know little about the underlying factors. Blue ribbon commissions appointed to study these factors are composed of prestigious citizens, not experts, and even they can give only a small part of their time. Most social scientists' work, as Herbert Gans recently pointed out, is not policy-oriented and is not readily accessible to key decision-makers.[6] Few corporations would open an overseas branch on the basis of so little and unsophisticated study as goes into the launching of major national programs of social guidance.

Knowledge that is available must be communicated to the decision-makers. Even in corporations, the planning or R&D unit often has a hard time gaining the ear of the executive board. In society, the sociodistance between the campus, where many of the best experts reside, and Washington, D.C., is often gigantic, with burned-out scientists, academic statesmen and "operators" frequently blocking the passage. Federal agencies which have their own "think-tanks," such as RAND for the Air Force, do better, at least in terms of their particular goals.

Decision-making. The decision-making strategies followed by the "cybernetic" centers, either explicitly or implicitly, affect the quality of the societal efforts. Anglo-Saxon societies are inclined to be "pragmatic," to "muddle through," making one small decision at a time; they abhor long-range and encompassing planning. Their approach works well when the environment is relatively stable and the system is basically sound. Then, minor revisions do quite nicely. But when basic turnabouts are required, something more than "muddling through," they have a hard time.

Totalitarian societies often err in the opposite direction. They tend to assume that they possess a greater capacity to control the society from one center, over more matters, and for a longer period of time than they actually do. Thus, they overplan and often launch major projects, "Great Leaps," only to be forced to scale them down or recast them at great economic and human cost.

It would be tempting to state that the most effective decision-making strategy is a happy medium. It seems more precise to suggest that the capacity of both pluralistic and totalitarian societies to plan, and hence to make encompassing and anticipatory decisions, rises with improvement in the technology of communication, knowledge storing and retrieval, computation, and research, as has been rapidly occurring since about 1955.

As it is, each society, to some degree, has the decision-making it deserves.

[6] "Where Sociologists have Failed," Editorial in *Trans-Action*, 4 (Oct., 1967), p. 2.

Decision-making strategies are not chosen in a vacuum but reflect the political structure of the society. Pluralistic societies tend toward muddling through because no central authority—not even the presidency—can impose a set of centrally-made decisions. The decisions reached are affected significantly by the pulling and pushing of a large variety of interest groups. No consistent direction seems possible; zig-zagging is the natural course. Totalitarian societies are more able to travel a straight track, but also tend to run roughshod over the feelings and interests of most of their members.

The conditions under which a "middling" pattern of decision-making may evolve, more encompassing and "deep" than democratic decision-making, and less inhuman than totalitarian decision-making, depend not only on the availability of new technologies but also on the proper power configuration.

Power. All societies may be viewed as compositions of groupings (by class, ethnic group, region) that differ in their share of societal assets and power. The distribution of power to any one community significantly affects its capacity to treat its problems and to change, if necessary. It is useful to consider the distribution of power from two viewpoints: (1) between the members of the society and the state; (2) among the members of the society.

The state may overpower the society; this occurs either when the state bureaucracies themselves checkmate all other power centers (especially in "pure" military regimes), or—more commonly—in conjunction with some other organization (the Party, the Church) or certain social groupings (such as the landed aristocracy). Or, the state may be weak, overpowered by the society, and fragmented along the same lines as the society. This has occurred in highly feudal societies (e.g., fifth century Europe or ninth century France) and in contemporary tribal societies such as Nigeria (at least up to the time of the recent civil war). When the state is overpowering, societal guidance tends to be unresponsive to most members' needs and values; when it is overpowered, the major agencies for planning and action and union are knocked out. Only a balanced tension between society and state, each one guarding its autonomy, allows the operation of relatively responsive and active societal guidance. Democracy itself requires such a power distribution: the power of the state to limit conflicts among members to non-violent confrontations and to prevent the overpowering of some members by others; and the autonomous power of the members, to sustain the political give-and-take and to replace those who guide the state if they cease to be responsive to the plurality of the members. Thus, the closer the distribution of power among the members approximates equality the more fully is democracy realized. As the needs of no one group of members are superior to those of others, the only way to make a society responsive to the membership is to give every group an equal hand in guidance. The Scandinavian countries are more democratic than most societies, precisely because they are relatively less inegalitarian.[7]

---

[7] Studies which offer evidence relevant to the three preceeding points include:

226

21. *Etzioni*

MOBILIZATION AND SOCIETAL CHANGE

The distribution of assets and power in most societies is highly inegalitarian. Consequently some members are able to slant the societal efforts in directions desirable to them. This basic fact is at the root of many societal problems. There is much we could do to eradicate poverty, desegregate, and establish a just and stable peace, but that would cost those who are more powerful part of their worldly goods and—even more important— some of their power.

A society better able to treat its problems thus requires some reduction of power differences. This can be achieved by mobilization of the weaker and underprivileged collectivities. That is the way the working classes made their way into Western societies, and the way Negro-Americans are trying now. The question may be asked: are not those groupings which "hog" the "goodies" and power also those which prevent—by their influence over education, television, jobs, police forces, and so forth—the mobilization of the weaker collectivities? Does not the power to be at the top include the power to keep others at the bottom?

Our answer is that while those at the top do have disproportionate political resources and skills, they cannot prevent the mobilization of the weak for several reasons: (a) processes which they cannot stop if the needs of the economy are to be served (e.g., the spread of education) are assisting the mobilization of the weak; (b) those at the top subscribe to democratic values and make some concessions because of these commitments; and (c) most important, each grouping is free to choose—within the limits of its societal station—how to use whatever resources and skills it commands. Will it be drinking, interpersonal violence, and search for consumer goods, or political organization and action? The transformation which Negro-Americans are now undergoing illustrates both the possibilities and the limits of such self-mobilization. One thing is sure: unless society's guidance mechanism proves responsive to its black members, the transformation of Negro-Americans will not be accomplished. They will not acquire their share of the power, and their problems will not be solved.

There is much more that needs to be said on the subject. (It takes us over

226

James W. Prothro and C. M. Grigg, "Fundamental Principles of Democracy: Bases of Agreement and Disagreement," *Journal of Politics*, 22 (May, 1960), pp. 276–294, where evidence is presented that agreement on "fundamentals" does not exist in the United States on many issues. See also Herbert McClosky, "Consensus and Ideology in American Politics," in Joseph R. Fiszman, *The American Political Arena*, 2nd ed. (Boston: Little, Brown and Co., 1966), pp. 39–70, and Herbert McClosky, Paul J. Hoffmann, and Rosemary O'Hara, "Issue Conflict and Consensus Among Party Leaders and Followers," *American Political Science Review*, 54 (June, 1960), pp. 406–427. For data on the homogeneity of social characteristics and values among American elite groups, see James N. Rosenau, "Consensus-Building in the American National Community: Hypotheses and Supporting Data," *Journal of Politics*, 24 (Nov., 1962), pp. 639–661; Warren E. Miller and Donald E. Stokes, "Constituency and Influence on Congress," *American Political Science Review*, 57 (March, 1963), pp. 45–56.

seven hundred pages to indicate our viewpoint in *The Active Society*.)[8] The details are less important than the over-all perspective:society viewed not as a pre-ordained, natural, or rigid structure, but subject to self-directed change by its members, for its members. The social sciences, especially the study of societal guidance, can contribute much to the growth of an active orientation of the society toward itself.

[8] Amitai Etzioni, *The Active Society: A Theory of Societal and Political Processes* (New York: The Free Press, 1968).

Part V

PROGRAM EVALUATION AS SOCIAL INTERVENTION

One way that social scientists can contribute directly to planned social intervention is by contracting with intervention agencies to evaluate the impact of ongoing programs. In this section nine sociologists, two social psychologists, two political scientists, an anthropologist, and a scholar in community organization and social planning report and/or reflect on portions of their recent research evaluations of intervention programs. Most of the authors were funded at least in part for their evaluation endeavors by contracts or grants from the federal government.

At the time this anthology was being prepared, the massive intervention and evaluation projects of OEO's war on poverty were actively operating. Many social scientists felt that the scope and intensity of the program provided them with the finest opportunity ever for developing and conducting intervention research. Whether or not they have risen to the occasion remains to be seen.

Since one goal of this anthology is to present current work of intervention researchers, most of the articles in this section are concerned with OEO programs—ten of them specifically with Community Action Programs. Several of the articles report preliminary findings or only fragments of large-scale studies. Contributions 27, 28, and 31, for example, are excerpts from three of the OEO national evaluation projects.

In contribution 22, sociologist John W. Evans, formerly Chief of the

Evaluation Division of OEO's Office of Research, Plans, Programs, and Evaluations, discusses the evaluation of social-action programs. Evans notes that useful empirical evaluations of major planned social-intervention programs have been few and late, but like Rossi (contribution 6) and Sheppard (contribution 8), he does not believe that inadequate methodology may be held accountable. Though the evaluative research techniques now in hand are admittedly limited, they are not being adequately utilized by enough social scientists. Evans observes that there is a marked shortage of interested, capable, and pragmatically oriented social scientists to perform adequate evaluations of intervention programs. Evaluative research reports that are submitted to funding agencies are often esoteric and not in time to be of use for program deliberations.

Evans also points to systemic conditions within the agencies which are impediments to the effective utilization of evaluative research. Program administrators, who must be program advocates, are not usually empirically oriented. They generally prefer to have "softer" research material since it affords more flexibility of interpretation. Earlier articles by Huitt (contribution 7), Trattner (contribution 9) Lineberry (contribution 14), and Zald (contribution 16) also attested to the impact of political considerations upon policy recommendations.

Nevertheless, Evans is hopeful about the future of intervention research. He sees the implementation of the federal Planning, Programming, and Budgeting System (PPBS) as a beneficial trend, countering the pressures of partisan politics. Social-science research, he suggests, will better serve to improve policy decisions if evaluation is made a central part of the management process by giving it a superordinate location within the government bureaucracy. Jones (contribution 11) demonstrated the impact of the National Planning Board's social scientists, who as advisers to the President were indeed in a superordinate position. Capable and dedicated professional staff and an invulnerable budget are further conditions which Evans sees as essential for the improvement of evaluative research.

Evans presents a paradigm for the evaluation of social-action programs, and suggests that there is a threefold scheme into which all evaluations can be categorized: Type I, over-all national program impact; Type II, effectiveness of alternative strategies and techniques for carrying out a program; Type III, evaluation of individual projects, with emphasis on managerial and operational efficiency. Evaluation Types I, II, and III answer, respectively: What programs? What techniques? What projects? Evans assigns the types on the basis of functions of different levels of the agency's evaluation mission and warns that they are arbitrary and overlapping.

Since several of the remaining articles in this section are partial reports of broader evaluation research, it is difficult to categorize them neatly according to Evans' types. With the possible exception of contribution 34, none of the articles in themselves represents the national impact measures of Type I. Rather, the selections represent evaluations of either Type II or Type III, assessments of alternative strategies and individual projects or some mixture of the two. The research is not as sweeping as is found for Type I, but the reports of suitable length that were available are revealing not only of specific forms of planned social intervention, but also of social scientists' evaluations and subsequent program recommendations.

In contribution 23, sociologist James J. Vanecko presents data from fifty cities, evaluating OEO Community Action Programs in terms of their success in influencing other institutions to become more responsive to the poor. Vanecko reports that those programs oriented toward mobilization of the poor were more effective in changing institutions than in changing programs oriented toward the provision of services. Vanecko has taken one of the goals of community organization, the transformation of existing institutions, as an hypothesis set. After devising a classificatory scheme for Community Action Programs, deriving a more refined typology from field data, and controlling for relevant demographic variables, he found that the effective Community Action Program is one which has central-office support for community organization, has neighborhood centers actively involved in community organization and uninvolved in militant activities, and does not spend time pressing specific demands on other institutions. These criteria reflect some of the aspects of social-service integration as outlined by Zald in contribution 16.

In contribution 24, sociologists Walter Gove and Herbert Costner present data pertaining to several major problems that contributed to the failure of an effort to develop neighborhood self-improvement associations among the residents of a poverty area through the efforts of paid, indigenous community organizers. Their article describes differences between successful and unsuccessful low-income neighborhood "clubs" intended to deal with neighborhood social and physical problems. The differences are relatively inconsequential, since the clubs as a group showed little specific accomplishment.

Gove and Costner assess the program's problems to have included the following: the indigenous organizers were insufficiently skilled; the relatively advantaged rather than the "hard core" poor were attracted to the clubs; even small and limited goals were rarely accomplished by the clubs; immediate concrete rewards were not provided to neighborhood residents for participation in the clubs; and the neighborhood-based clubs were too small to be effective. They recommend that strategies for organizing the poor which can overcome these difficulties might be more successful. Specifically, Gove and Costner suggest that community organization focused around a common problem rather than a shared locality would provide a more realistic basis for organizing the poor and that contributions of the poor to goal attainment can best be achieved if the poor work closely with citizens who have the skills which they lack. Their conclusions demonstrate some of the potential impediments to community-organization strategy such as that advised by Wolf in contribution 15.

In their article, Gove and Costner cite as an alternative strategy for organizing the poor the "overlap model." Contributions 25 and 26 by social psychologist Louis A. Zurcher, Jr., explain the overlap model, and submit it to an empirical test. Contribution 25 describes the dilemmas and the staff stress that result when a poverty-intervention organization attempts to implement the "maximum feasible participation" mandate of the Economic Opportunity Act. The strategy for social change assumed by the organization is labeled the "overlap model." This model is operationalized by the "functional marginality" of the poverty-intervention organization—a "middle-ground" position between the community poor and the community nonpoor intended to facilitate their beneficial interaction.

Functional marginality, Zurcher reports, is difficult to maintain. Challenges to the organization's marginality are recurrent and severe, stimulated by conflicts ranging from participants' varying perceptions of the poverty program to national OEO's varying criteria for program success. Zurcher recommends that the poverty-intervention organization attempting functional marginality must, along with its staff, be flexible, durable, considered to be temporary, and capable of accommodating the change it purports to engender. To borrow Krause's term (contribution 13), whatever "complexing" it engages should serve the poor and relevant social change, not merely the perpetuation of the organization itself.

In contribution 26, Zurcher translates the assumptions of participation-related social-psychological change (that is, the "overlap model") into a set of hypotheses, and tests them in the setting of the Community Action Program's board of directors. He concludes that the poor and the nonpoor participants on the poverty board had quite different program-associated attitudes and values, that those differences influenced the decision-making process of the board, and that the poor did indeed change in social-psychological characteristics as a result of "maximum feasible participation," with the direction and intensity of the change influenced by the kind of participation.

Zurcher recommends that the diversity of poverty-board membership can be a strength, that the *process* of board experience is often more important than the content, and that at least as much attention should be given to careful planning concerning the kinds of participation experienced by the members (and the training they receive) as typically is given to their proportional representation.

Contribution 27 also presents data on the participation of poor and nonpoor representatives in a Community Action Program's board of directors, and documents changes in the social character of the board over time. Political scientists Fremont James Lyden and Jerry V. Thomas show that the active participation of representatives of the poor on the poverty board depends upon the agenda items. Using the Bales Interaction Process Analysis technique and Parsons' typology of functional group problems, Lyden and Thomas demonstrate that a workable division of labor was evolving in the poverty board during their period of research observation. Community-leader representatives, agency representatives, and poverty representatives had accepted the responsibility, according to Lyden and Thomas, to join in common effort and make policy decisions. Each subgroup of representatives provided leadership toward board pattern maintenance, seeing to it that decisions made by the organization would incorporate the values of its constituents. Similarly, each subgroup provided board integration, emotional supports necessary for the containment of conflict. The community-leader and agency representatives assumed major responsibility for goal attainment and adaptation—task-oriented development and facilitation—with the poverty representatives playing a strong supporting role in adaptation.

Lyden and Thomas agree with Zurcher (contribution 26) that heterogeneity of orientations among the members of a poverty board can be functional for effective group development and accomplishment (although Zald's warning in contribution 16 about the possible costs of integration must be heeded). It would appear that the poverty representatives on the board studied by Zurcher had greater opportunity to evolve what Lyden and Thomas would classify as skills in goal attainment and adaptation.

Both contributions 26 and 27 reveal that boards of directors of Community Action Programs, and perhaps other decision-making bodies having poor and nonpoor representation, are complex and evolving groups, with wide ranges of role sets, in which volatile but constructive interpersonal dynamics might obtain.

Lyden and Thomas (and Zurcher in contribution 26) note the impact of change in board leadership upon group development. Such occurrences are not only relevant to the evaluation of board activities, but demonstrate a fact of life in intervention research: new intervening variables can and do emerge, sometimes with disconcerting suddenness.

In contribution 28, sociologist Charles M. Bonjean and social psychologist Wayman J. Crow discuss the impact of antipoverty activities upon community-leadership networks. The article presents data from the city studied which indicate that, as a result of involvement in the poverty program, there has been increased task-oriented interaction among Mexican-American, black, and establishment leaders (in that order). Bonjean and Crow further report that program participation has been a major catalyst in developing leadership in the Mexican-American community and in strengthening its ties with other community-leadership groups. Thus, the evidence suggests that intervention programs may produce leadership structures as well as be the product of them.

Frederick L. Ahearn, Jr., an expert in community organization and social planning, describes in contribution 29 some correlates of job status among indigenous nonprofessionals in Community Action Programs. The study explores the relationship between high and low job status in Community Action Programs and the social background, job experiences, attitudes, and perceptions of indigenous nonprofessionals.

Ahearn reports the indigenous nonprofessionals in two Community Action Programs to be better off in quality of job and rate of pay than they were before participating in the program. However, the high-status employees are seen to reflect a "cream of the crop" selection phenomenon —to have been relatively well off before employment in the program and perhaps hired less because of personal need than because they could contribute to organizational maintenance without receiving training. Ahearn indicates that the high-status employees had the potential to move up the promotion ladder, and actually were not markedly dependent upon the program for jobs. The low-status nonprofessionals, on the other hand, were worse off prior to their jobs in the Community Action Program, and in fact were in need of jobs when hired. But their positions in the program are among those demanding minimum skills, are of short tenure, and are dead-end. Many of the low-status employees depend upon the Community Action Program for employment, and could not find jobs elsewhere. Ahearn concludes that the entire concept of career ladders for the poor may have been too ambitious an undertaking for Community Action Programs. He recommends that in order to be minimally effective with new career endeavors, Community Action Programs must cease promising more than they can deliver. Furthermore, they should closely analyze the jobs they do have available, provide adequate training programs for the jobs, and carefully establish a visible and workable career ladder for indigenous nonprofessionals.

Ahearn puzzles over the finding that the high-status employees had lower job aspirations than did the low-status employees. He concludes that the high-status nonprofessionals, being more familiar with the program, might be much more realistic about their future. This interpretation fits with alternative explanations offered by Zurcher (contribution 26) to explain the feelings of powerlessness among active indigenous leaders, and by Sutton (contribution 31) to explain the unfavorable perceptions of the directional impact of the poverty program by persons most actively involved in it.

In contribution 30, anthropologist Robert L. Bee describes historical aspects of tribal leadership as these relate to the difficulties experienced by a group of American Indians placed in leadership roles in an intervention program. When the tribal council Bee studied became the sponsoring agency for four poverty-intervention projects, council members were caught in conflicts amid differing "client" and agency project perceptions and expectations, and were confused and harassed in the "self-help" leadership role.

Bee recommends that program planners consider the culture, and particularly the leadership patterns, of the community for which intervention is intended. He further suggests that indigenous attitudes toward planned social intervention might be quite different at the time of program proposal than they are after the beginning of intervention. Those attitude shifts can considerably affect program progress.

Sociologist Willis A. Sutton, Jr., in contribution 31, observes that the Community Action Program he evaluated in a rural antipoverty campaign was perceived as helping to provide services (education, health, job opportunity, and income) rather than as affecting the area's institutional structure. Few respondents felt that the poor had been mobilized or their power increased. According to Vanecko's criteria (contribution 23), this Community Action Program had not succeeded: it had not supported mobilization of the poor and stimulated institutional change.

Sutton notes that those participants directly involved in the activities of the program, who were emotionally committed to the interests of the poor and less concerned than other groups with general county conditions, evaluated the program's directional impact (on the target population) less favorably than its general effectiveness (on the county). The dissatisfaction quite possibly reflected participant disappointment with an apparent deemphasis on meaningful involvement of the poor and on constructive social change among the community institutions. Whereas Vanecko (contribution 23) suggests that which a Community Action Program's orientation should be, perhaps Sutton suggests what that orientation should not be.

According to sociologist Patrick H. McNamara, effective participation of churches in planned social intervention depends on the interaction of pastoral leadership, denominational policy, church traditions, and theological doctrine. Contribution 32 indicates that the successful priest-led poverty-intervention organizations he studied had the support of (or at least no overt opposition from) church hierarchy. In addition, effective intervention in urban settings assumed the priest's (and his church's) alliance with secular and other religious institutions; in small-town settings the priest had to appear as a unique spokesman for the poor, and the prospect of receiving federal funds had to be perceived as attractive by the community.

Field-worker priests engaged in organizations using militant action, observes McNamara, received no hierarchial support, and usually were perceived as a threat by the community. Consequently, they had great difficulty in successfully implementing social or institutional change relevant to the poor. In the urban and small-town settings described by McNamara, intervention efforts had central-office support (see contribution 23), were nonmilitant, and were essentially unabrasive. They were, in McNamara's view, successful. The nonsupported, militant intervention efforts of the field-worker priests were, by contrast, fraught with difficulty.

McNamara recommends that priests may be among the most appropriate initial leaders of the poor. They have a protected career line, can slip aside when indigenous leaders emerge, and have an ideology for serving the poor. Perhaps they are well suited to maintain the "functional marginality" which Zurcher (contribution 25) indicates may be an assumption of many organizations involved in planned social intervention. However, the priests' potential effectiveness in that role cannot be considered without an assessment of the behavioral restrictions placed upon them by church organization.

In contribution 33, sociologist J. Allen Williams, Jr., presents data indicating that four of the five major goals of the urban-renewal program were not adequately fulfilled in the project he evaluated. Williams suggests that after relocation, the low-income black residents did not acquire more decent housing, a more suitable living environment, desegregation, or the alleviation of social and personal problems by increased availability of agency services.

Williams implies the existence of "complexing" (see contribution 13) in the urban-renewal program and recommends that the program reorder its priorities, considering first the rehabilitation and preservation of communities. If families must be relocated, he further advises, their moves should be staged so that adequate and affordable housing becomes available prior to displacement.

The last selection in Part V is perhaps of more interest for its demonstration of the impact of program vagaries upon evaluation research than it is for the research findings themselves. Sociologist Joseph M. Conforti, in contribution 34, assesses the attitudes toward health care among low-income youth and concludes that the attitudes were not as unfavorable as expected in the Neighborhood Youth Corps sample he evaluated. Among low-income persons, he adds, alienation and negativism vis-à-vis social institutions may not crystallize until adulthood. Conforti recommends that intervention planners pay as much attention to the situational bases of attitudes among the poor as they do to the assumption that such attitudes exist.

Conforti reports that when officials of the local department of health tried to acquire funds for the provision of health services to Neighborhood Youth Corps enrollees, they were informed by OEO that money was available not for service but for demonstration projects. The health officials thereupon shifted their concern (at least on paper) from the provision of health service per se to a consideration of the implications of such services—and an evaluative research project was born. The officials reasoned that the Neighborhood Youth Corps program was intended to overcome young persons' alienation from major social institutions. Such institutions included health-service organizations. The modification of negative attitudes toward health services could contribute, therefore, to the over-all goal of the youth corps program. The health officials then concluded that comprehensive medical examination and treatment in the most attractive possible setting, including private patient-physician interaction, would be an appropriate attitude-modifying intervention strategy. But OEO would not allow the private patient-physician strategy, insisting that all medical services be provided by local public facilities. These facilities were, according to evaluator Conforti, the same community hospitals and clinics judged responsible for the enrollees' alleged alienation in the first place. The officials were then faced with the problem of finding nonalienating facilities within the assumed alienating health organizations. However, during the gathering of baseline data, Neighborhood Youth Corps enrollees were found, contrary to expectations—*not* to be remarkably alienated from health services. The project directors subsequently "deemphasized" this phase of the program. It was even suggested by way of hypothesis that the experimental conditions themselves, defined as they were by program reality, might actually *increase* the alienation and negativism of enrollees concerning health services.

To these mercurial designs and hypotheses were added additional program-related evaluation problems. A host of the enrollees were "noncooperative" throughout the examination and treatment phases of the program. Large percentages of enrollees dropped out of the youth corps or simply declined to show up for questionnaires, examinations, and treatment. Gottlieb (contribution 4) notes similar attrition and testing problems in the evaluation of Job Corps programs.

Conforti's study indicates that the researcher can be at the mercy of program vagaries during his evaluation of planned social intervention. Often he will be able effectively to isolate and label an unexpected program shift or modification as another independent, intervening, or dependent variable. Sometimes, though, he may only be able to meditate about his misfortune—and perhaps wish for a moment that he had chosen other than intervention research.

22

EVALUATING SOCIAL ACTION PROGRAMS

JOHN W. EVANS
Office of Economic Opportunity

NOTHING IS MORE IMPORTANT TO THE *actual* SUCCESS OF SOCIAL ACTION programs than that we know whether or not they work. If we are sensibly to alter or terminate programs which are not achieving their objectives, or continue and expand those that are, we must have some decent evidence of how effective and efficient these programs are.

All of this should go without saying. Yet odd as it may seem, despite the billions of dollars we have spent in such areas as manpower training, compensatory education, and welfare, and despite the fact that the decision to spend these staggering sums is made in a society known for its hard nosed practicality, rationality, and scientific research, we in fact know relatively little about the effectiveness of many of the social action programs which the government has initiated.[1]

There are a number of reasons for this lack of objective, empirical evaluations and it is well to examine them before looking at the present situation and what the future may hold.

The reason most often given as to why we have not produced useful empirical evaluations of large-scale social action programs is that we do not know how. That is, we lack adequate social science methodology, our measuring instruments are too primitive, the real world environment is too complex to sort out cause-effect relationships, and so forth. There is no question that the "state of the art" is a very important factor contributing to the underdeveloped state of evaluation, and there is no question that the long catalogue of deficiencies and complexities, recited with hand-wringing despair by both administrators and social scientists, is all true. Our measuring instruments—in the area of cognitive and affective development in children, for example—are far from what we would like to have. The methodological task of sorting out the influence of an education or manpower training program from all the other relevant influences in its participants' lives is indeed so formidable that many say it simply can't be done with any confidence.

In my own view, as true and as formidable as these considerations are, they are not sufficient to account for or justify the dearth of adequate program evaluations. I believe we can greatly improve our basis for assessing social action programs by utilizing the admittedly limited techniques we now have in hand, and I shall have more to say on this below.

One of the most important reasons why objective and empirical evalua-

---

[1] In a preliminary draft (June 9, 1969) of a *Study of Federal Program Evaluation Practices,* Joseph S. Wholey at the Urban Institute remarks that, "a large number of major social programs ought to be viewed as quasi-experimental. They were designed on the assumption that certain courses of action would improve education, increase employment, improve housing, or the like. Generally, however, the Federal Government has made no real attempt to evaluate the effectiveness of social programs or local projects within the programs."

♦ First published in *Social Science Quarterly* 50, No. 3 (December, 1969).

tions have not become an established, organic part of the decision-making process in the federal government is that empirical evaluation is a mode of thinking that is foreign to the kind of people who have traditionally found themselves in the role of government administrators and program directors. Cabinet members, assistant secretaries, and program directors do not typically come from either a physical or social science background. As a result, when faced with their own and others' concerns about the effectiveness of their programs their thinking does not naturally turn to the existence and quality of empirical evidence—to matters of criteria, measures, control groups, and the like. This mode of thinking is something which becomes natural only as a result of formal scientific training. Without such thinking, however, the analysis and assessment process must suffer. Sincerity of motivation is confused with effectiveness of results, and inputs (such as dollars and program size) are substituted for outputs as indicators of program success. Even in the defense area, where hardware problems and the more evaluation-accustomed physical sciences prevail, it took a McNamara to bring this kind of thinking to the top decision levels of the Defense Department.

A second important reason is that the role of program administration and the role of objective evaluation involve conflicting interests. We have not yet arrived at that ideal (and unreal) point in the conduct of affairs in our government where agency heads and program directors see their role as an impartial custodian or overseer of the public interest. It is hard to imagine, for example, the secretary of one of the major departments going to the Congress, reporting that one of his major programs does not appear to be producing any appreciable effect, and recommending that Congress take back the several billion dollars devoted to this program and abolish part of his department. Rather, the program administrator's role seems inevitably to be that of program advocate. To a very considerable extent it is desirable that this should be the case. But the typical process which takes place annually within government agencies preparing for Congressional hearings is not one of developing an even handed presentation of the successes and advantages vs. the failures and difficulties of a program, but rather one of collecting and displaying those things (with limited scrutiny of their validity) which show the program and its accomplishments in a favorable light. This is a situation and a process for which program administrators are not to blame. They know full well from past experience—or at least they believe it to be the case—that if they go before Congress with a report that their program is not working they can expect a cry to go up for their scalp. An admission of program failure will be taken as an admission of personal failure. In this context it does not take the perceptive program administrator long to become wary of hard, clear cut, empirical evaluations, for they are a two-edged sword. The more attractive course is to go with softer information that is more subject to manipulation.

As a result of all these factors and the pressures they generate (as well as the imperatives of day-to-day operations), it has often been the case that research and evaluation get shunted aside and play second fiddle to program administration and operation. This means, for example, that research and evaluation are organizationally often off to one side in a weaker bureaucratic position relative to the program elements and that funds and staff for the evaluation are allocated sparingly. Within the organization the strong testimonials of the program managers often drown out the weaker and "negative" sounding voices of the research and evaluation staff who are calling for quantitative and objective assessment of program outcomes. In this situation, it is easy to let the political considerations— which are often totally overriding anyway—be the dominant factors in deciding how good a program is and what should be done about it.

Finally, apart from the weaknesses in social science methodology and the foreign and sometimes threatening character of evaluation, there is also the fact that social scientists themselves have shown only limited interest in becoming evaluators. More often than not when they have undertaken evaluation studies they have not performed well. The problem seems to center around the practical and policy character of the evaluator's role. The socializing experience of graduate school instills in the majority of social scientists a negative definition of practical or applied careers. These are defined as sell-outs of one kind or another and something to be avoided in favor of careers which stress academic, theoretical, and disciplinary goals. When program evaluations are undertaken by academic social scientists, there is a tendency to convert them from a practical or policy task into a theoretical research project or retreat to a focus on models and methodology. The social scientist's scholarly habit of following the analysis where it leads makes him insensitive to and impatient with deadlines and schedules, with the frequent result that by the time he feels his final report is ready, the problem it addressed has been overtaken by events.

Faced with a theoretically oriented study which he did not want, reaching him too late to be useful and in such voluminous and technically esoteric form that neither he nor his policy people can understand it, the harried administrator throws up his hands. The experience adds to his stereotype of social science as useless to real world decisions, and pushes him a little further if reluctantly toward the conclusion that the only evaluations he can count on are the informal and partisan ones he receives from his program staffs.

Quite apart, then, from the internal organizational considerations, one of the factors contributing to the lack of adequate empirical evaluations of social action programs is the shortage of interested, capable, and practically oriented social scientists to perform them.

EVALUATION AT OEO

The situation I have outlined above is more of a constructed type than an accurate description of any particular government agency. Indeed, in the last few years considerable progress has been made. Based on the dramatic changes made by McNamara in the Defense Department, President Johnson ordered the Bureau of the Budget to implement a similar Planning, Programming and Budgeting System (PPBS) throughout the federal government.[2] The essence of this new system is nothing short of a radically different approach to federal decision-making and resource allocation at the highest level. In the defense area, where there has been the greatest effort to apply the PPB System, the intention has been to get away from the traditional interservice power struggle and other ad hoc considerations as the main basis for deciding, for example, whether the Navy should get two new aircraft carriers, the Air Force should get a new bomber, or the Army should be increased by two divisions. Instead, the PPB System requires that we specify precisely what our military objective is, (say, the defense of a certain area), what the various alternative means for achieving it are (remotely located missiles, mobile naval or troop forces, or whatever) and finally what the relative cost and effectiveness of each of these alternative means is. Thus, in this type of decision-making, resource allocation system, the primary focus is taken off of the means and put where it should be on the objectives, with each means, or program, being assessed in terms of its comparative ability to achieve an objective. Obviously, rigorous evaluation of program effectiveness is central to this kind of decision-making system.

While considerable progress has been made, and the domestic arms of the government are now struggling with the implementation of the PPB System, it is nevertheless still the case that in most government agencies empirical evaluation is not yet the automatic and organic part of the decision-making process that it should be and could be.

Probably one of the better beginnings has been made at the Office of Economic Opportunity (OEO). From its early days, OEO had a unit which functioned as an extension of the Director's office called the Office of Research, Plans, Programs, and Evaluation (RPP&E). This office carried out basic research on poverty, prepared short- and long-range plans for the poverty program, and was used by the Director and Deputy Director for advice on major program and policy questions. It eventually acquired the all important budgeting function which allowed its analyses and studies to be more directly influential in important resource allocation decisions (within the limited latitude, of course, which political considerations allowed).

Up until 1968, however, the RPP&E office carried out few formal, empirical evaluations of OEO programs. There were a number of reasons for this, among them the fact that during the early years of the War on Poverty most programs were struggling to become operational and overall assessment of their effectiveness did not make much sense at that time. In addition, an early organization decision had created small research and evaluation offices in each of the major program elements (that is, within Job

[2] See *The Analysis and Evaluation of Public Expenditures: The PPB System. A Compendium of Papers Submitted to the Sub-committee on Economy in Government of the Joint Economic Committee* (Congress of the United States, 91st Congress, 1969), vols. 1–3.

Corps, Head Start, VISTA, and others), and at that time it seemed these offices would collectively provide the needed program evaluations.

By the summer of 1967, however, the then director of RPP&E, Robert A. Levine, an economist, had concluded that depending upon the program offices to produce the needed evaluations of the effectiveness of their programs was not working and that his own office should develop a capability to evaluate the impact of all OEO programs.[3] I was asked to come to OEO in the fall of 1967 and develop the new evaluation function.

After a general review, my small staff and I concluded, as Levine had, that despite the fact that a great deal of money had been spent on evaluation studies by the various program offices, it was not possible to get from these studies a useful answer to the question, "How effective has the program been in achieving its objectives?" We also concluded that it seemed unlikely that the existing organizational arrangement would produce methodologically sophisticated evaluations that focused on the tough questions.

We finally decided that some fairly radical changes would have to be made if the antipoverty programs were to be evaluated in a useful way. We therefore made a number of far reaching recommendations to Bertrand Harding, the then Acting Director of OEO.

We began by proposing a three-fold scheme into which all evaluations be categorized:

Type I. The assessment of overall program impact and effectiveness where the emphasis is on determining the extent to which programs are successful in achieving basic objectives.

Type II. The evaluation of the relative effectiveness of different program strategies and variables where the emphasis is on determining which alternative techniques for carrying out a program are most productive (for example, determining whether one type of curriculum is more effective than another for teaching Head Start children).

Type III. The evaluation of individual projects through site visits and other monitoring activities where the emphasis is on assessing managerial and operational efficiency.

We recommended that primary responsibility for the Type I evaluation of all OEO programs be assigned to the newly created RPP&E Evaluation Division; and that the research and evaluation units in the program offices (Job Corps, Head Start, VISTA, and the others) be responsible for the Type II and Type III evaluations of their respective programs.

There is nothing intellectually elegant about this three-fold distinction. Indeed, it can be argued that separating Type I and Type II evaluations creates an artificial distinction between studies focusing on effectiveness and those focusing on the factors which do or do not contribute to effectiveness. But it seemed clear that if the responsibility for Type I evaluations were left to the programs they would not get done. As noted earlier, there are just too many built in pressures at the program level that militate

---

[3] See the critical but accurate assessment of early OEO evaluation efforts by Peter Rossi, "Practice, Method, and Theory in Evaluating Social Action Programs," in James L. Sundquist, ed., *On Fighting Poverty* (New York: Basic Books, 1969), pp. 221–223.

against the overall effectiveness question getting properly asked or answered. It seemed important that this type of evaluation be removed from the program level and made an overview function of a staff office which would not be faced with the budgetary choice of reducing program activity in order to fund such evaluations, and which could take an impartial view of all programs. On the other hand, we felt it was important that the Type II evaluations not be removed from the program level because of the need for intimate program knowledge in determining what program variables should be investigated. These considerations led us to make the three-fold distinction and recommend the division of responsibility between RPP&E and the program offices. Clearly, there were as many practical as conceptual considerations involved.

It should also be pointed out that the three types of evaluation parallel three major organization levels and the different kinds of decisions required at each. At the top level—Congress, the Bureau of the Budget, and the agency director—the question is "What programs?" (Type I); at the level of the program director the question is "What techniques?" (Type II); and at the regional or local level the question is "What projects?" (Type III).

We recommended that the agency set aside as much as 1 per cent of its total appropriation for evaluation of all three types and that one-sixth of this 1 per cent (about $2.8 million) be set aside for the new Evaluation Division to fund priority Type I evaluations.

We further recommended that the new Evaluation Division be given several additional senior level positions to allow the hiring of Ph.D. level professionals and that the program offices be required to submit an annual evaluation plan covering their Type II and Type III evaluations for approval by the new RPP&E Evaluation Division.

These proposals were not greeted with enthusiasm by most of the program heads. Many of them were, understandably, opposed to the idea of outside evaluations of their programs and they protested the levy on their program budgets to fund such evaluations. Numerous meetings were held and memoranda exchanged, but Harding's final decision was to approve all the recommendations. In March of 1968 an official order went out formally establishing the new evaluation division, indicating the division of responsibility between it and the various program offices for the different types of evaluation, and setting aside the necessary funds.[4] In the following months, six professionals were recruited (from the fields of sociology, psychology, mathematics, and systems analysis) and national evaluations were designed and initiated on Head Start, the Community Action Program, five manpower programs (Job Corps, NYC out-of-school, MDTA institutional, New Careers, and the JOBS program), the Neighborhood Health Centers, the Family Planning Program, Upward Bound, and the Title I-D Special Impact programs.

The Type I evaluation process is intended to provide answers to four fundamental, almost common sense, questions.

1. *Is the program reasonably addressed to the needs of those towards whom*

[4] OEO Instruction 72–8, March 6, 1968.

it is aimed? This question merely points up that before launching a training program, for example, we should be sure that the people to be trained
are capable of acquiring the skills to be taught, that there is a need for such
skills in the labor market, and so forth. As obvious as this point is, it is possible to find examples of programs ill-suited to the needs of the people they
were supposed to serve—not necessarily because of misdirection by program managers but because making an accurate assessment of human and
social needs requires detailed data on the target population that are often
not available.[5] The point here is simply that one of the key steps in evaluating a program is to determine whether or not it really addresses the needs
of the population at which it is directed, and this requires not only clear
policy but detailed data on the target population as well.

2. *To what extent does the program reach the intended population?* In
the absence of information on how well a program achieves its objectives,
it is possible to make an evaluative judgment of a program's potential effectiveness on the basis of the extent of its reach. Other things equal, a
program which reaches a large proportion of the intended population is
more effective than if it reaches only a small proportion. To make even this
level of evaluative judgment, however, requires detailed and extensive data
on both the universe of need and the number of people the program is
serving.

3. *How successful is the program in achieving its objectives?* Answering
this question is getting directly to the problem of determining how well
the program is accomplishing what it set out to do. Such an assessment
should, of course, be based upon carefully designed and controlled research; but, as I have indicated, in actual practice it is usually based on
much less—often little more than impressionistic and subjective judgments.
The essence of evaluation is attribution. Therefore the prototypic evaluation should approximate the classic model of experimental design, in
which before-after measures are made on a representative sample of program participants and on a comparable control sample of non-participants,
preferably randomly assigned. The evaluations we have designed do approximate this model, but many compromises are necessary and approxi-
mations are the best we are ever going to get. For example, the requirement
of random assignment to program and control groups will, in my opinion,
only rarely be feasible for national studies of ongoing programs.

---

[5] The War on Poverty itself provides such examples. One of the basic purposes of the
In-School component of the Neighborhood Youth Corps was to supply some kind of
employment to poverty kids in order to deter them from dropping out of school. But it
appears that economic reasons may not be a major factor in deciding to leave school.
There is even some suggestion that by supplying employment and money the program
may in fact be counter-productive by encouraging some kids to leave school. There is
also the early form of the Small Business Development Program where the qualification
requirements resulted in it being nearly impossible to make loans to the group for
which the program was intended. Similarly, the basic skills component of several manpower programs, the type of teachers used, the scheduling of classes, and the seeming
irrelevance of the material resulted in these programs failing to attract poor, unemployed males—the group at which they were aimed.

4. How does the cost of the program compare with the value of its benefits?
Even if we know how well a program fits the needs of its target population,
how completely it is reaching that population, and how effectively it is
accomplishing its objectives, in order to fully evaluate that program we
must still determine whether the benefits of the program are greater than
its cost or vice versa. This phase of evaluation also requires sophisticated
data on both the costs and the benefits of the program—data that are usually not routinely available for most programs.

In sum, if we can answer these four questions about any social action
program we will know whether in a general way the program makes sense,
how far it is reaching, what effect it is having on those it does reach, and
what it is costing to achieve this effect.

Chart 1 provides a general paradigm for the evaluation of antipoverty
programs based on the acquisition of data relating to universe of need, program reach, program effectiveness and program cost for each antipoverty
program.

Going down the left-hand Evaluation Data column from A through H
will indicate how the completed paradigm would be useful in overall planning and programming. With dependable data for each program on universe of need (A) and program reach (B), we can calculate, and compare
programs on, the extent to which they are reaching their target populations
(C). A solid figure on program coverage (C) would be useful in planning
and budgeting both within a given program and across the total array of
programs. Bringing together for all programs the information on their total
costs (D) (on which we usually have good data) and information on the
number of people they reach (B) (on which we usually don't) would allow
us to compute, and compare programs on, the cost per person reached (E).
With information on program costs (D), the total universe of need (A),
and the present program reach (B), we could determine for each program
what the cost of total coverage would be and how much of an increment
over present budget outlays this would require (F).

Of course the paradigm oversimplifies some very complex issues. In the
first place, some of the cells in the table will turn out to be inappropriate.
For example, in evaluating the extent to which the Community Action Program achieves institutional change, such concepts as universe of need and
program reach are not very meaningful. Secondly, some programs are not
aimed so much at individuals as they are at groups, communities, or families, which means that individual measures such as cost per person reached
are not relevant. Third, the programs are treated individually, and no provision is made in the chart for the cumulative or interactive impact of several programs operating together, though some effort to assess this will
have to be made. Finally, meaningful comparisons of the effectiveness of
different programs in different functional areas will probably remain essentially intuitive unless a standard measure like the benefit-cost ratio can be
developed for all programs. Otherwise, we find ourselves trying to compare the relative values of an educated youth from Job Corps with an improved child from Head Start, with a potential drop-out sent on to college

CHART 1

Paradigm for the Evaluation of Antipoverty Programs

Evaluation Data	Antipoverty Programs[a]								
	Job Corps	VISTA	Community Action Agencies	Legal Services	Head Start	Follow Through	Upward Bound	Health Services	etc.
A. Universe of Need									
B. Program Reach									
C. Program Coverage ($\frac{A}{B}$)									
D. Program Cost									
E. Cost per Person Reached ($\frac{D}{B}$)									
F. Cost of Total $\therefore$ Coverage (E) (A)[b]									
G. Measures of Program Effectiveness: 1. Immediate Objectives 2. Poverty Reduction									
H. Benefit-Cost Ratio ($\frac{G}{D}$)									

[a] This array of programs is for illustration. It does not reflect the recent organizational changes in OEO or the fact that some programs, e.g., Upward Bound, have been transferred to other agencies.

[b] A correct computation would not be this simple but would take into account the marginal cost required to expand programs at different levels.

by Upward Bound, with a medically cured mother by Health Services. Assembling program costs is comparatively easy. Ascertaining or even estimating the total individual and social benefits of any program is very difficult, and assigning dollar values to all these benefits may be impossible.

These considerations make it quite clear that we will never achieve a purely mechanical decision-making system. Nevertheless, it is equally clear that developing as much reliable data as we can for each program on its universe of need, its reach, its cost, and its effectiveness will allow us to make much better assessments of our various efforts to move people out of poverty, and to make more rational decisions about the allocation of our limited resources than we are able to do now.

As this is being written most of the evaluations we have initiated are still in process, so it remains to be seen what impact both the organizational changes and the results of these studies will have. The one major evaluation which has been completed, the one on Head Start, found, to the disappointment of many and the disbelief of some, that Head Start appeared to have few if any lasting cognitive or motivational effects on the children who went through the program. The study has occasioned considerable debate along predictably partisan lines but the well-documented general conclusions of the study are hard to dismiss, and it seems likely the results will have an important influence on the larger decisions yet to be made about Head Start's future.[6]

SOME THOUGHTS ABOUT THE FUTURE

Out of this entire experience, there are several major conclusions I have come to and I pass them on to others interested in evaluation in the hope that they may comprise a number of lessons which it will not be necessary for us all to learn separately over and over again.

1. My experiences lead me to disagree with the cynic's view that evaluation is generally a waste of time—that partisan political considerations are the overwhelming factor in determining what happens to government social action programs and that empirical evaluation and rational analysis can never hope to be more than an insignificant input in the decision-making process. Irrelevant and often irrational factors still do play a distressingly large role in the assessment of our programs and in the decisions about their future, but my experience in the government leads me to believe—and I think not naively—that the long run trend is in the other direction. Such a trend is becoming established within the government itself with the Planning, Programming, Budgeting System being pushed strongly by the

---

[6] *The Impact of Head Start: An Evaluation of the Effects of Head Start on Children's Cognitive and Affective Development* (The Westinghouse Learning Corporation and Ohio University, June 1969). On the debate over the study see the forthcoming paper by Sheldon White, "The National Impact Study of Head Start," the three-part piece in the Fall 1969 edition of the *Britannica Review of American Education* by Victor Cicirelli, William Madow, and John W. Evans; and Walter Williams and John W. Evans, *Evaluating the War on Poverty,* "The Politics of Evaluation: The Case of Head Start," *The Annals of the American Academy of Political and Social Science* (Sept., 1969).

Bureau of the Budget and increasingly becoming a fixture, if indeed an imperfect one, in most government agencies. But also in the Congress, the press, and the public as well, there is both an increasing demand that judgments and decisions be founded on the best kind of empirical evidence possible and, though it is somewhat more slow in coming, a willingness to accept distasteful judgments about one's favorite (or most hated) program if they appear to be based upon some evidence.

2. An important lesson we must all learn is that our task in evaluating social action programs in the real world is not to produce methodologically perfect studies but rather to *improve decisions* by doing the best that can be done in a timely and relevant way. Evaluation, every bit as much as politics, is the art of the possible. And those of us who practice it and wish to have an impact upon the important events of our time must realize that decisions are going to be made either in the presence or absence of information. This is the nature of the political process and I do not think it is likely to change much in our lifetime if ever. Putting aside important decisions to await the design and completion of an ideal study is not the way Congress and the executive branch work, or indeed the way any program can long operate. Therefore, the task of the evaluator is to bring the best possible information he can to the decision-making point at a time when it can be expected to have some impact. The argument against this position is that some information can be worse than none. Even though this is an obvious and valid point, I believe we should normally assume the reverse. There is no question that in some cases imperfect evaluations and incomplete information will be misleading; but as a general rule, imperfect and incomplete analyses are going to be better than none at all—which is what the alternative is and which, unfortunately, is the basis on which many important decisions have been made.

3. For the reasons cited above, the most important instrumental problem in program evaluation today is not the "poor state of the art"—the inadequacy of measurement techniques, the absence of comprehensive and valid program data systems, or the need for other technical "breakthroughs" in the social sciences. These are very severe problems, which all of us in both the academic and applied areas must continue our efforts to solve. But there is a great deal that can be done with existing admittedly imperfect research and evaluation techniques which can greatly improve our current mode of assessing program effectiveness. There is in my judgment a large gap between the way programs are currently being evaluated and what could be done by a wider application of the research and evaluation techniques we now have in hand. I think we have a long way to go in putting present-day techniques to work before we can legitimately complain that we are stymied in our efforts to improve rational decision-making because of inadequate methodology. Continuing to belabor the point of the "poor state of the art," as so many of us do, is a poor excuse for not getting at the task at hand and it serves only to delay, not to accelerate, the contribution that social science can make to program assessment and policy determination.

4. The single most important step that can be taken to accelerate useful evaluations of government social action programs and insure that such evaluations have impact on decisions is to make evaluation a central part of the management process by giving it a superordinate location within government agencies. As I indicated above, progress along these lines is being made in some agencies, but we still have a long way to go.

It is part of the chronic special pleading of every government bureaucrat that in the next reorganization his element should be "attached to the Director's office." The argument for evaluation, however, is quite different because it rests on the fact that the determination of program effectiveness is a key executive function. Consequently, evaluation is—or should be—a central part of the decision-making and resource allocation process. It is in this respect quite different from the line or operation function of the programs themselves.

The ideal type of organizational arrangement is, in my opinion, one which combines the key executive functions of planning, programming, evaluation (Type I), and *budgeting* in a single staff office which serves as the agency director's key advisor and implementing arm.[7]

There are different ways to categorize types of evaluation and assign organization responsibilities for seeing that they are carried out. My threefold scheme is only one. But regardless of what distinctions and divisions are made, one principle which I believe must be followed is that the responsibility for what I have called Type I evaluations must be removed from the program level.

5. Equal in importance to the organizational location of the evaluation function, is the need for it to be staffed with professionally qualified people. As I noted above, one of the principal reasons for the lack of evaluations and their poor quality has been the shortage of technically competent social scientists within the government to insure that evaluations are methodologically well-designed, relevant to policy and program issues, carried out properly and in a timely fashion by the contracting organization doing the actual work, and reported in a way which allows their results to be understood and used by those at the top levels of the executive and legislative branches who are going to make the actual decisions. Too often well-meaning administrators have attempted to initiate evaluations but their lack of technical expertise has caused the evaluation to run afoul of all of the problems just listed. The result has been worse than just useless studies and wasted money because it has discredited social science and

---

[7] This is ideal when we are talking about individual agencies. The logic for separating the assessment functions from the program can be extended to arguing that the Type I evaluation function should be taken out of individual agencies altogether and placed at the supra-agency level. A number of proposals have been made to create a government-wide evaluation function (for domestic programs) in the executive office of the President, in the Bureau of the Budget, in the Urban Affairs Council, and—to serve the Congress—in the General Accounting Office. This idea has great merit and, in my opinion, will eventually be adopted. But, as of this writing, its time has not yet come.

led to the belief that useful empirical evaluations are not practically possible.

If conditions are developing to the point where objective, empirical evaluations are going to play an increasingly important role in government decision-making—as I believe they are—then the problem of the necessary professional manpower must be solved. Increasing numbers of social scientists are going to be needed if methodologically adequate and professionally guided evaluations are actually going to get designed, carried out, and fed into the government decision-making process. I do not believe this can be accomplished by using academically based social scientists on a consulting or short-term contractual basis, though the widespread effort to do this will doubtless continue. Program evaluation and academic research are two different things. They have different goals, they are likely to utilize different methods, they call for different time schedules, and they yield different kinds of results. It is rarely possible to make one the by-product of the other. For this reason, we can continue to expect that social scientists who are primarily interested in theoretical and discipline oriented research are not likely to be interested in the kind of program evaluations that are useful to the government; and as occasionally happens, if they do undertake such studies they are not likely to do a good job from the government's standpoint. What is needed as we look to the future is an increased number of top-notch social scientists who emerge from their graduate studies with a desire to put their skills to work in the applied setting of social action programs. Despite all the talk these days about "relevance," relatively few social scientists with this kind of orientation are emerging from our graduate schools. If we want our disciplines to have the impact on public policy that we continually argue they should, this is a serious problem which must somehow be solved. Otherwise, as things stand now, we as social scientists are in the untenable position of continually criticizing the government for not basing its judgments and decisions on social science research while at the same time being unwilling to provide the practically oriented professional talent necessary for this to occur.

6. In addition to the requirement for professional staff it is essential that the evaluation function have an invulnerable source of funds. There are different ways this can be accomplished. At OEO we have done it by setting aside a fixed percentage of the total OEO appropriation. This, in my opinion, is better than either designating a fixed amount of money for evaluation or the still more unreliable system of promising that "adequate funds for evaluation will be made available on a project-by-project basis." When budget crises arise, as they always do in all agencies every fiscal year, the research and evaluation budgets are often the first to be raided.

7. Finally, it should be clear that the lot of the evaluator is destined to be a harassed and controversial one and those who contemplate a career in this field should be fully aware of this. The evaluator's problems begin at the beginning of an evaluation but do not end at the end. He can expect opposition from the program staffs at the outset because "our programs are not ready to be evaluated yet," "the evaluation does not focus on the right

objectives," "there is no way to properly measure success or failure on the objectives of our program," "the evaluation study will not yield definitive conclusions," and so forth.[8] When the evaluation is completed, he can expect to be attacked from both sides regardless of what the findings are. If the findings show the program to be generally successful, the program people will point out that a great deal of money has been spent merely to find out what everyone knew from the beginning anyway. The program detractors will attack the study as unreliable and inconclusive pointing out all its methodological flaws. If the results show the program to be generally unsuccessful, the same charges will be made but from the opposite sides of the fence. Harry Truman's warning, "If you can't stand the heat, stay out of the kitchen," applies to evaluation as well as politics. But for those who can stand the heat, there is an unparalleled professional gratification to be found in the satisfaction that one's work can have an important influence on the key problems of the day.

In sum, there seems little doubt that evaluation is the wave of the future. Powerful forces inside and outside government are no longer content to take argument, exhortation, and anecdotes as the main basis for deciding how billions of dollars should be spent. They have been told by social scientists and others that a more scientific and objective basis for making decisions is possible and they are demanding that it be used. But before objective and empirical evaluations can become a truly influential part of the decision-making process, two things must occur. Within government agencies the evaluation function must be placed in a central location and be given the necessary funds, authority, and professional staff to accomplish its mission. If the necessary number of social science professionals is to be forthcoming to fill these key roles there must be a markedly increased emphasis and interest within the various branches of social science in the practical and policy orientation required for evaluation. While there are considerable pressures and changes inside the federal government that I think are likely to accomplish the first of these changes in the reasonably near future; it is hard to be as optimistic on the second. Most social scientists emerging from their graduate training today eschew this type of professional role.

If social science is to have the impact upon national policy that all of us think it should, this stands a far better chance of achievement, in my opinion, through the application of social science methods to policy problems and program evaluation and through the direct involvement of social scientists in these activities than it does through the continued and largely one-sided emphasis in our respective disciplines on exclusively theoretical and disciplinary concerns.

---

[8] See the discussion of this problem in Edward A. Suchman's excellent book, *Evaluative Research* (New York: Russell Sage Foundation, 1967), pp. 144–145.

23

COMMUNITY MOBILIZATION AND INSTITUTIONAL CHANGE: THE INFLUENCE OF THE COMMUNITY ACTION PROGRAM IN LARGE CITIES[1]

JAMES J. VANECKO

National Opinion Research Center and
University of Illinois at Chicago Circle

SOCIAL APPLICATION OF THE ART OF JUJITSU"[2] WHICH IS AT ONCE "POLITI-cally viable, radically democratic, and scientifically rational"[3] is a description of the Community Action Program of the Office of Economic Opportunity which would send a prudent empirical social researcher off to look for another problem. Such a definition clearly indicates why so much paper and so many printed words have been generated concerning community action with so little understanding, comprehension, and agreement resulting. Although the concept, not to mention the practice and operation, of community action is diffuse and elusive, nevertheless there has emerged in the past two years, a reasonable consensus on its meaning,[4] a large stock of empirical information about its practice,[5] and at

[1] The evaluation reported herein was performed pursuant to contract #B89–4645 with the Office of Economic Opportunity, Executive Office of the President, Washington, D.C. 20506. The opinions expressed herein are those of the author and should not be construed as representing the opinions or policy of any agency of the United States Government. The author would like to thank Sidney Hollander and Susan Orden who have contributed greatly throughout the research reported here and also Robert L. Crain and Laura L. Morlock who conceived much of the analysis presented here. Jonathan Lane of OEO has been a stern but just critic. Barbara Gubbins provided invaluable typing and editing assistance under considerable pressure.

[2] Paul Ylvisaker, "Private Philanthropy in America," an address to the National Council on Community Foundations, May 1964.

[3] Peter Marris and Martin Rein, *Dilemmas of Social Reform* (New York: Atherton Press, 1967), p. 9.

[4] See the following works for description and typologies which are largely similar: John Donovan, *The Politics of Poverty* (New York: Pegasus, 1967); Daniel Patrick Moynihan, "What is 'Community Action'?" *The Public Interest*, 5 (Fall, 1966); Sar A. Levitan, "Community Action Program: Concepts and Operations," mimeographed, 1969; Sanford Kravitz, "The Community Action Program: Past, Present, and Its Future?" in James L. Sundquist, ed., *On Fighting Poverty* (New York: Basic Books, 1969).

[5] See the works cited in note 4 and the following: Ralph M. Kramer, *Participation of the Poor* (Englewood Cliffs, N. J.: Prentice-Hall, 1969); Sar A. Levitan, *The Great Society's Poor Law* (Baltimore: Johns Hopkins University Press, 1969); David Austin, *Community Representation in Community Action Programs*, five reports: Feb., 1968; Aug., 1968; Jan., 1969; Nov., 1968; March, 1969 (Waltham Mass.: Brandeis University for OEO); Resource Management Corporation, "Evaluation of the War on Poverty," monograph prepared for the General Accounting Office, 1969; Daniel Yankelovich, "The Community Action Program," summary of a research report prepared for the Office of Economic Opportunity, April, 1967; Kirschner Associates, "A Description and Evaluation of Neighborhood Centers," a report for the Office of Economic Opportunity, 1966.

♦ First published in *Social Science Quarterly* 50, No. 3 (December, 1969).   253

least some clearly defined disagreements over the political questions involved.[6] Thus, it has been possible in the past year to launch the first national evaluation of the Community Action Program. This paper reports some preliminary results of that evaluation.

The theoretical basis of the Community Action Program is the proposition that poverty in an affluent society is neither lack of individual economic resources nor "relative deprivation," but the lack of control by poor people over the institutions which serve them. The theory holds that this power vacuum has come about in a wide variety of ways—the increasing scale of society, the elimination of ethnic politics and/or urban political bosses, the concentration of the poor black population in the northern urban ghettoes —but the critical fact is that all of these processes together are producing increasing detachment of the poor population and thus strengthening the cycle of poverty.[7] To break the cycle both power itself and self-awareness of power are necessary. The implication of this theoretical perspective is that intervention into this process must take one of two courses. Either the poor must attain political power so that they can influence the institutions affecting them or the institutions themselves must be changed so that they are more responsive to the needs and demands of the poor. Community action in theory and practice aims at both targets.

The translation of this theory into practice has been, to say the least, complicated by a wide variety of constraints and modifications—administrative, practical, political, and even theoretical. In general however, the theory in the simple form stated above forms the backdrop for the formation of the Community Action Program. It has resulted in what Moynihan describes as four concepts of community action:

1. The Bureau of the Budget Concept. The guiding principle of this concept is efficiency. Community action under this rubric is seen as a device to coordinate services.

2. The Alinsky Concept. Named after Saul Alinsky, patriarch of the Back of the Yards Council, the Woodlawn Organization, FIGHT, and several other conflict-oriented community organizations, this concept saw the need of the poor to acquire political power as the central and overriding theme.

3. The Peace Corps Concept. The guiding principles in this idea are the provision of services and, more explicitly, the delivery and decentralization of services.

4. The Task Force Concept. The guiding principle here is political effec-

[6] For examples see: Daniel Patrick Moynihan, *Maximum Feasible Misunderstanding* (New York: The Free Press, 1969), and also reviews of this book: Adam Walinsky in *The New York Times Book Review*, Feb. 2, 1969, and Robert Levine in *The Washington Post*, Jan. 26, 1969.

[7] The more neutral word "detached" is used here in preference to the more common and graphic word, "alienated." This statement is a rather simple summary of some complicated theoretical arguments. See, for example, Richard Cloward and Lloyd Ohlin, *Delinquency and Opportunity* (New York: The Free Press, 1963).

tiveness and the participation of the poor in the Community Action Agencies themselves. This concept, of course, produced the "maximum feasible participation" clause.[8]

Other writers have characterized the idea of community action as involving all or some of these aspects.[9] Concretely, these concepts are Community Action Program goals which individual Community Action Agencies emphasize to greater or lesser degrees:

A. Community action aimed at organizing and mobilizing the poor or, more precisely, the residents of the poor neighborhood (items 2 and 4 in Moynihan's scheme).

B. Community action aimed directly at the transformation of institutions serving the poor and direct service of the poor. This kind of community action aims at:
   (1) Better coordination of services (item 1 under Moynihan's scheme).
   (2) Better delivery of services (item 3 under Moynihan's scheme).
   (3) The development of innovations in services or service mixes (item 3 under Moynihan's scheme).

The legislation creating the Community Action Program is, in fact, open and flexible enough to allow a local CAA to concentrate on achieving any one or a combination of these goals. Administrative practice, Congressional appropriation, and the earmarking of funds by Congress and OEO do not allow such complete local autonomy, but a wide range of actual programs and informal practices are permitted. Thus, it is possible to evaluate Community Action Programs from the perspective of the kinds of goal and program orientations they maintain and the kinds of results they achieve. This paper presents such an evaluation.

The research reported is guided by one central and three corollary hypotheses. The central hypothesis will be stated in the most neutral way possible, but it should be noted that the test of this hypothesis implies answers to dramatic political arguments. It questions the importance of the "maximum feasible participation" provision and the necessity of political mobilization for the success of the Community Action program. The hypotheses are the following:

Main Hypothesis: If Community Action Agencies emphasize community organization and mobilization, the institutions serving the poor are more likely to become responsive to the needs and demands of the poor than if the Community Action Agencies emphasize educational, welfare, and employment services.

Corollary Hypothesis 1: If Community Action Agencies emphasize community organization and mobilization, change in the institutions serving the poor is more likely to come about from pressure exerted by the poor themselves than through direct intervention of the CAA.

[8] Moynihan, "What is 'Community Action'?"
[9] Donovan, *Politics of Poverty*; Kravitz, "The Community Action Program."

Corollary Hypothesis 2: If Community Action Agencies emphasize community organization and mobilization, the types of changes which institutions serving the poor are likely to undergo are those concerning involvement of the poor rather than increased service.

Corollary Hypothesis 3: If Community Action Agencies emphasize community organization and mobilization, change in the institutions serving the poor is more likely to come about from the involvement of the neighborhood centers with community organizations.

METHODOLOGY

The project reported in this paper is a large scale investigation of urban Community Action Programs using survey procedures. The entire study encompasses a probability sample of one hundred U.S. cities of 50,000 or greater population. The analysis reported here includes 50 of those cities since the interviewing was done in two stages of 50 cities each. The study is part of a program of research utilizing the Permanent Community Sample of the National Opinion Research Center.[10]

The interviews were designed to obtain information on different aspects of the CAA such as activities, goals, and organization; to obtain information on the characteristics of the cities and neighborhoods expected to be important factors in the changes being studied, and to uncover changes. Interviewed in each city were the following:

   I. Five members of the CAA board (selected from members of executive committee if possible): the president; a representative of the public, closely associated with the mayor; a representative of the private sector; a representative of the poor not associated with the civil rights movement; a representative of the poor associated with the civil rights movement

  II. The CAA executive director

 III. The director of the neighborhood center program

 IV. The director of the employment program

  V. Three directors of neighborhood centers (randomly selected)

 VI. Presidents of three PTA's in a target neighborhood chosen randomly from among the three mentioned in V

VII. Directors of three private social service agencies in the same target neighborhood

---

[10] The sample of one hundred cities was constructed by selecting two probability samples (probability proportionate to size) of fifty cities each, which together amount to a single probability sample. The sampling was done in this way to cover the contingencies of either halting the effort after beginning analysis of fifty cities or going on to one hundred cities. The decision has been made to include one hundred cities but the data from the second fifty cities are not yet ready for analysis. It will be possible to do a split sample test of the hypotheses developed in this initial analysis of fifty cities using the second fifty cities and also to do more elaborate multi-variate analysis of the entire sample of one hundred cases. For a description see Peter H. Rossi and Robert L. Crain, "The NORC Permanent Community Sample," *Public Opinion Quarterly*, 32 (Summer, 1968), pp. 261–272.

VIII. Personnel officers of the three largest potential employers for persons living in the same target neighborhood

IX. Three political leaders involved in the same neighborhood

Each of the Roman numerals above represents a different interview schedule. The overall response rate from these interviews was 96 per cent. The political leaders had the lowest response rate—84 per cent.

MAIN HYPOTHESIS

The goal and program orientation of the Community Action Agencies were measured in an admittedly crude but, we think, reliable manner. Each of the board members and the executive directors were given a fixed choice question on the four most emphasized goals of the CAA and the one of those four which is best developed in the programs of the agency. Then they were asked what the programs aimed at achieving these goals are. On the basis of these questions, CAA's can be classified on a scale of the degree to which they emphasize each of four goals:[11] (1) education goals, (2) social service goals, (3) employment goals, and (4) community organization and mobilization goals.

On the basis of the interviews with the persons not in the CAA we can measure several dimensions of institutional change. We have chosen 18 of these measures for presentation here because they are concrete and therefore probably both valid and reliable and also because they are dimensions of change which most people would agree were desirable. For example, there is considerable disagreement over the importance and legitimacy of protest actions as political participation, but there are very few who would argue that the poor should not vote and present testimony before elected and appointed public bodies such as school boards and city councils. The latter two forms of political participation are the two used here.

Each of the dimensions of institutional change used is measured by asking each of the three respondents in the specific institutional sector involved for a report of the characteristic in 1964 and in 1968. Then change from 1964 to 1968 was calculated and the answers of the respondents from a given city averaged. Thus, the data presented are primarily "hard" but the method of gathering them is "soft."

[11] There is some bias in the measurement of these four variables caused by the use of the same items in different variables. The bias is not so strong as to rule out the analysis of these variables separately. They have been combined into a typology of goal orientation which shall be used in future analysis. The particular coefficient used in this study to measure the strength of association between CAA characteristics and outputs is called the "gamma coefficient" and was developed by Professor Leo Goodman of the University of Chicago. See L. A. Goodman and W. H. Kruskal, "Measures of Association for Cross Classifications," *Journal of the American Statistical Association,* 49 (1954), pp. 732–764. Readers interested in the mathematics of gamma should consult the Goodman article as well as J. A. Davis, "A Net Partial and Multiple Coefficient for Goodman and Kruskal's Gamma," unpublished MS (National Opinion Research Center, 1964), which develops the notion of the net partial gamma also used in the present study.

ANALYSIS

Table 1 presents the gamma coefficients[12] between the four goal orienta-

TABLE 1

Zero Order Gamma Coefficients[a] between Community Action Program
Goal Orientation and Institutional Change Toward Increased
Responsiveness to the Poor

Institutional Change	Education	Goal Orientation Social Service	Organi- zation	Employ- ment
1. Increased number of people served by social service agencies.		—.28	.40	
2. Change in the per cent of social service agency clients who are poor.		—.11	.37	
3. Change in the per cent of social service agency clients who are minority group members.		—.45	.39	
4. Increased involvement of the poor in decision-making within social service agencies.		—.13	.63	
5. Increased availability of the physical facilities of social service agencies.		—.20	.31	
6. Increased number of employees working for social service agencies.		—.53	.59	
7. Increased number of volunteers working for social service agencies.		—.20	—.02	
8. Increased number of referrals to and from social service agencies.		—.62	.68	
9. Increased efforts to hire hard-core unemployed by employers.				.19
10. Increased hiring of graduates of vocational programs by employers.				.40
11. Increased per cent of school staff minority group members.	—.04		—.53	

[12] When the variables are dichotomized at the medians, a gamma or Q correlation coefficient of .40 is significant at the .01 level.

12. Decreased student-teacher ratio in public school.	—.22		.33
13. Decreased crowding of schools.	—.35		—.01
14. Increased auxiliary staff in schools.	—.30		.27
15. Increased participation of residents of the target neighborhoods in schools.	—.41		.09
16. Increased promotion of participation by public schools.	—.19		.30
17. Increased level of political organization and increased presentation of demands to public bodies by residents of target neighborhood.			.74
18. Increased participation in electoral politics by residents of target neighborhoods.			—.41
Average gamma	—.25	—.32	.26	.29

a In all except three cases, the correlation coefficient is a Q (Q is a gamma of two dichotomies). The exceptions are due to the pattern of the data which did not permit a reasonable distribution for dichotomization or to the meaning of the categories into which the data was distributed, e.g., a case in which we did not wish to put decreases and small increases into the same category. The variables are dichotomized as close to the median as possible.

tions of Community Action Agencies outlined above and eighteen dependent variables describing dimensions of institutional change among public schools, private social service agencies, private employers, and neighborhood political organizations. The matrix is not completely filled because only those cases in which there is an *a priori* logical relationship between CAA goal orientation and change were examined. The most striking aspect of the matrix is the community organization column. The gammas in this column are overwhelmingly positive—12 of 16—and predominantly high.[13] These correlations are more striking when contrasted with the correlations between educational goals and the dependent variables and the correlations between social service goals and the dependent variables. The very clear pattern emerging is that cities in which the CAA emphasizes community organization have a great deal of institutional change and those in which the CAA emphasizes more traditional service goals

[13] The dissatisfaction with this presentation is that the gammas are not strictly comparable given differences in distribution for the variables and that it disguises curvilinear relationships and interaction effects.

show very little institutional change. One might argue that we would expect this, except that supposedly all CAA's try to achieve institutional change. In fact, we are only talking about institutions with which we would expect the CAA to have contact—education oriented CAA's with public schools, social service oriented Community Action Agencies with private social service agencies. We have no specific reason to assume that community organization CAA's would have contact with these institutions. Furthermore, the correlations of educational and social service orientation with institutional change are negative; in fact, the presence of this kind of Community Action Program seems to inhibit institutional change. The compelling pattern of the matrix is to indicate that when CAA's emphasize community organization, institutional change occurs, and when CAA's emphasize education and social service, institutional change does not occur. This is reflected in the average gammas: —.25 for education, —.32 for social service, .26 for community organization. An employment orientation shows an average gamma of .29, but this is only for two change dimensions. These will not be treated further in this paper.

Table 1 clearly confirms the major hypothesis presented above. Community organization goal orientation is positively associated with institutional change. Social service and educational goal orientation are negatively associated with institutional change. Employment goal orientation is the only exception.

CONTROLS FOR CITY CHARACTERISTICS

We must now examine what is probably the most important objection which can be raised to interpreting these associations as causal. This is the objection that the associations observed are spurious and due to characteristics of the city which account for these changes and for the kind of CAA a city has as well. If this is the case, then the characteristics of the Community Action Agencies and the institutional changes observed are caused by the relevant characteristics of the city and no conclusion can be made about the influence of the CAA. This objection has added weight given the small scope of Community Action Programs relative to the other characteristics of a city which might be influential. Thus, in Table 2 we examine the association between community organization goal orientation of CAA's and institutional change, while holding constant several characteristics of cities which could account for the changes. The data are presented as net partial gammas, which are not totally satisfactory, but which do allow one to summarize a great deal of data in a relatively brief presentation.

Column A shows the net partial gammas between community organization goal orientation and institutional change with the size of city controlled. Size of city is dichotomized at 250,000. The association between community organization goal orientation and increased participation in electoral politics goes from a —.41 to a —.27. This is not a case in which the control variable suppresses or eliminates an observed positive relationship, but one in which the control variable actually suppresses observed

Net Partial Gamma Coefficients between Community Organization Goal Orientation and Institutional Change Toward Increased Responsiveness to the Poor Controlling for City Characteristics

Institutional Change	Control Variables					
	City Size (A)	Percent Nonwhite (B)	Percent Poor (C)	Region (D)	CAP Expenditures (E)	Level of Political Activity (F)
Social Service Agency						
1. Number of clients	.36	.45	.33	.40	.50	.48
2. Poor clients	.33	.36	.37	.41	.47	.36
3. Minority clients	.49	.45	.69	.64	.55	.58
4. Participation of poor	.67	.63	.67	.70	.54	.61
5. Facilities	.32	.27	.33	.48	.33	.33
6. Number of Employees	.54	.58	.63	.49	.78	.72
7. Number of volunteers	-.02	-.02	.03	-.05	-.08	-.21
8. Number of referrals	.73	.71	.57	.68	.83	.62
Employer						
9. Hiring Hard-core	—	—	—	—	—	—
10. Program grads	—	—	—	—	—	—
Public school						
11. Minority staff	-.43	-.64	-.50	-.64	-.67	-.64
12. Student/teacher	.35	.33	.40	.28	.23	.47
13. Crowding	-.04	-.04	.02	-.02	.14	-.15
14. Auxiliary staff	.30	.30	.20	.45	.40	.42
15. Participation of poor	.12	.02	.10	.09	.17	-.13
16. Promotion of partic.	.33	.28	.28	.32	.13	.27
Political						
17. Political organization	.76	.73	.65	.84	.67	.59
18. Electoral participation	-.27	-.45	-.31	-.63	-.33	-.41
Average gamma	.28	.25	.28	.28	.29	.24

negative relationships. The reason for the difference between the zero order and the net partial correlation is that size of city is negatively correlated with community organization goal orientation ($Q = -.36$) and positively associated with increased participation in electoral policies. Within this pattern, the relationship between community organization and electoral participation is actually .00 for small cities and —.55 for large cities. Thus, it is in those cities which are most likely to have a community organization goal orientation that the relationship is actually zero. This suggests that a community organization orientation does not prevent electoral participation while promoting organized petitioning of public bodies, except by retarding the increase in large cities. It is clear that controlling for city size does not wash out and, in fact, does not significantly alter the positive associations observed between community organization orientation and institutional change.

In column B, the control variable is the per cent of the population nonwhite. This is dichotomized at the median, 15 per cent. We would expect cities with large Negro populations to have undergone more institutional change because of the work of the civil rights movement and the general increasing political participation of Negroes. In addition, we would expect the Community Action Programs in the cities with large Negro populations to be oriented towards community organization. The latter expectation is empirically validated. The Q coefficient between per cent nonwhite and community organization goal orientation is .23.

The comparison of column B with Table 1 shows that there are only two coefficients which change .10 or more. We may be simply observing the effects of an increase in the Negro population during the 1950's and the subsequent recruitment of more Negro teachers. It is again very important to note that the positive association between the community organization goal orientation and institutional change remains intact.

Again the most important finding in column C is that per cent poor does not wash out the effects of a community organization goal orientation on the part of CAA's. Indeed, the only correlation which is substantially altered is enhanced rather than diminished by controlling for this variable. This is the association between community organization goal orientation and per cent of the clientele of social service agencies who are members of a minority group. This correlation goes from a .39 to a .69. This change is due to the eccentricities of the gamma correlation coefficient. In the category—high percentage poor—the gamma correlation coefficient is 1.00 due to the fact that there is an empty cell.

Column D shows the net partial gamma correlation coefficients between community organization goal orientation of the Community Action Agencies and institutional change with region controlled. Region is divided into four categories—northeast, south, midwest, west. It does not make sense to speak of a correlation between region and goal orientation using a gamma coefficient since region is not an ordinal variable. We can point out that cities in the northeast and the west are more likely to have a community organization goal orientation than cities in the south and the midwest.

When we compare column D with Table 1 we find four cells in which there is a substantial change from the zero order gamma to the net partial gamma. These are number three, change in the per cent of social service agency clients who are minority group members; number eleven, increased per cent of school staff who are minority group members; number fourteen, increased auxiliary staff in schools; and number eighteen, increased participation in electoral politics by residents of target neighborhoods. There is no consistent pattern in the gamma relationships within region for these four variables.

The closest we can come to portraying a pattern in the effects of region on the previously observed correlation is to observe that cities in the midwest which have a community organization goal orientation are more likely to behave differently than cities in other regions. However, the difference is not great nor are there enough cases for a conclusive argument nor does this substantially change the overall pattern and the average gamma coefficient between community organization goal orientation and institutional change. Once again, on the basis of column D we must conclude that the findings in Table 1 stand the test of a control variable and are not spurious.

It could be argued that any association we observed between characteristics of CAA's and institutional change are really functions of the overall scope of community action efforts. This argument would contend that whatever the characteristic is, it is positively associated with the scope of effort. In this particular case, the argument would contend that community organization goal orientation is positively associated with scope of community action efforts. The best way to answer this argument is to measure the size of the effort and observe its effect on the associations we have previously presented. Size of effort has been simply measured by the per capita amount of federal funds for the Community Action Program in each city. When this variable is dichotomized at $100 per capita the association with community organization goal orientation is negative ($Q = -.25$). This is presented in column E.

Column E shows much more change from the zero order coefficients we observed in Table 1 than any of the columns we have examined so far. Seven out of sixteen associations between community organization goal orientation and institutional change show a difference of more than .10. Although controlling for the level of federal funds does not lead us to conclude that our original findings were spurious, it certainly requires further interpretation of those findings. If we look at this pattern simply in terms of whether cities in which CAP funding is low or high show more of a tendency towards positive association between goal orientation and institutional change, we find that in five out of seven cases where the association between community organization and institutional change is substantially modified, it is in those cities with a low level of funding that the association is more positive.

The final column showing the gamma coefficients between community organization goal orientation and institutional change controls for the general level of political activity within the target area. This variable is constructed from data provided by the interview with the neighborhood political leader and involves a mixture of protest activity, direct petitioning of government agencies, and other efforts on the part of community organizations. While this variable may include within it some activity of the CAA, it is not in any way limited to this nor does it explicitly ask for this. Thus, it is a good independent measure of the amount of political activity in a neighborhood which we could expect to be very closely associated with community organization goal emphasis. In fact, community organization goal orientation is positively associated with general level of political activity in the target area (Q = .61). Thus, we might expect that the associations between community organization and institutional change would be a spurious function of the level of political activity in the neighborhood.

When we turn to column F in Table 2 and compare it with Table 1 we find that nine out of the sixteen associations are substantially altered. Again, the overall result is balanced, with four changes in the direction of a stronger positive association and five in the direction of either a greater negative association or a decreased positive association. The four associations which are stronger in Table 2 than in Table 1 are per cent social service agency clients who are minority group members, number of employees working for social service agencies, student-teacher ratio, and auxiliary staff in the public schools. Three associations become more strongly negative. These are number of volunteers working for social service agencies, per cent school staff who are minority group members, and crowding of the public schools. One association actually reverses, that between community organization and participation of residents of the target neighborhood in the public schools. Finally, one association, that between community organization and political organization and presentation of demands, decreases in the strength of its positive association. It is interesting to note that the four variables which change in a positive direction are all concrete aspects of service delivery and for all four of them we find that the positive association is stronger in cities with a low level of political activity. This would suggest that a community organization goal orientation helps to influence institutional change in cities with low levels of political activity above and beyond the effect of the mere presence of the CAA.

It is also interesting to note in regard to column F of Table 2 that two of the variables which show positive zero order associations and decrease with level of political activity controlled are variables which we would expect to be very strongly associated with level of political activity in the neighborhood. These are increased participation of residents in the public schools and increased political organization and presentation of demands. The participation of residents in public schools is actually reversed for cities with both low and high levels of political activity. CAA's seem unable to produce or create participation where it doesn't exist and unable to increase it very much where it already does exist. The increased level of political organization and presentation of demands is slightly lower than the zero order for cities with low levels of political activity and it is practically zero for cities with high levels of political activity. Thus, it seems that more political activity can be generated with a community organization emphasis by the CAA, but the CAA is unable to increase political activity where it is already relatively high.[14]

The overwhelming conclusion that can be drawn from Table 2 is that the goal orientation of the CAA is an important predictor of institutional change regardless of the kind of city in which the CAA operates. Community Action Agencies which emphasize community organization goals are much more likely to influence institutional change than are agencies which emphasize educational and social service goals. Not one of the columns shows an average gamma for community organization goal orientation that is more than .03 different from the zero order correlation. The evidence for the corollary hypotheses presented above is much less clear, although there are some suggestions in the findings discussed that these also are confirmed.

COROLLARY HYPOTHESES

The pursuit of the corollary hypotheses presented above requires the introduction of additional variables. The first of these hypotheses concerns the source of pressure exerted on the institutions for change. The hypothesis suggests that citizen pressure will be more characteristic of CAA's oriented toward community organization than will direct CAA pressure. Thus, we must measure citizen pressure. The second hypothesis involves the dimensions of institutional change which have been discussed above, but about which we can say more as we discuss activities of the CAA. It does not require the introduction of additional variables. The third hypothesis suggests that the effectiveness of CAA's oriented toward community organization is a function of the neighborhood centers' involvement with community organizations. Thus, we need to measure that involvement.

In the interviews with the 12 respondents who were not associated with the Community Action Programs, there were questions about certain aspects of the organizations' operations which asked for direct reports of change between 1964 and 1968. Whenever there was a change, respondents were asked who, if anyone, outside of the organization was seeking a change. In several instances, they were asked directly if the CAA neighborhood center was seeking change and in some cases were asked if groups of citizens were seeking change. The variables used here to measure citizen pressure and neighborhood center pressure were obtained in the interview with the neighborhood political leader. The variables are constructed separately for the social service agencies and for the public schools, which are the two institutions with which we are primarily concerned here. Since

---

[14] Since political activity is measured for 1968, it is not absolutely clear that the interpretation offered is accurate. We have to measure political activity in 1964, to make this argument firm.

the variable is linked to institutional change one might suspect that it would be a function of the overall amount of change; but it is not.[15] Thus, pressure is operationalized in terms of seeking and getting change.

Since there has been great concern with whether or not CAA's are radical political organizations and whether or not militancy on the part of CAA's is an effective strategy for bringing about institutional change, involvement with community organizations and in political activity is measured separately from involvement in militant activities. Involvement with community organizations is ascertained by asking the neighborhood political leader whether staff and board members meet with representatives of welfare rights organizations, tenants unions, nationality organizations, civil rights organizations, and PTA's, and whether the two most important and active community organizations are both involved in organizing the poor and work with the neighborhood center. The variable on support for militant activities is constructed by asking whether the neighborhood center has supported demonstrations or similar programs demanding welfare rights, tenants' rights, and community control of schools.

Table 3 is a diagram showing the gamma correlation coefficient between various characteristics of CAA's pressure exerted on schools and social service agencies, and the general level of political activity in the target neighborhood. It presents a model from which we can construct the appropriate analysis of the activities of Community Action Agencies and institutional change. The model flows from left to right beginning with the general context within which neighborhood centers operate—the goal orientation of Community Action Agencies and the level of political activity in the neighborhood, to the activities of the neighborhod, to the activities of the neighborhood center, to the pressures exerted on schools and social service agencies. The model does not provide an exact description of CAA's but does allow a rather helpful typology from which to further the analysis. There are four types of CAA's which emphasize a community organization goal orientation.

The first type exists in neighborhoods which have a high level of political activity. These agencies provide a high level of support for militant activities. This type is projected from the neighborhood center's positive associations with community organization activity and with militant activities, in addition to the positive correlation of community organization activity by the neighborhood center with general political activity and with support for militant issues, plus the positive association between support for militant activity within the neighborhood center and community organization orientation. This type of Community Action Agency is thus the predominant one among those oriented toward community organization. The kind of pressure which we would expect to come from this type of agency can be constructed by looking at the gamma correlation coeffi-

---

[15] It should be remembered that questions concerning actors responsible for changes and whether the CAA was influential are only asked after change is reported. The fact that these variables are not a function or not highly correlated with overall amount of change is partially because the level of reported influence is low.

TABLE 3

Diagram of Gamma Coefficients Among Community Action Agency Characteristics and
Pressure Exerted on Schools and Social Service Agencies

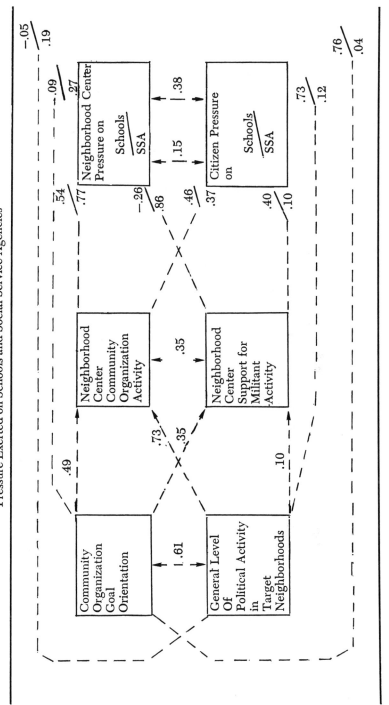

cients in the part of the table farthest to the right. There are two kinds of pressures with which each of the four characteristics outlined above are positively and rather strongly associated, neighborhood center pressure on social service agencies and citizen pressure on schools.

The second type of CAA emphasizing community organization goals is projected from the observation that the positive associations of general level of political activity and of neighborhood center community organization activity with neighborhood center support for militant issues are not very strong—.10 and .35 respectively. This type then is one which also exists in cities where there is a high level of political activity and there is a high level of community organization in the neighborhood center, but the agencies do not show much support for militant activity. If we then look at the four dimensions of pressure, selecting those which show a positive association with activity level and neighborhood center community organization activity, while showing no association or a negative association with neighborhood center support for militant activity, we see that the dimension of pressure produced by this type of agency is citizen pressure on the social service agencies.

The third type of Community Action Agency exists in neighborhoods where the level of political activity is low. These are community organization oriented agencies with a low level of community organization activity and a high level of support for militant activity. The level of community organization activity would be low because of the very high correlation between general level of political activity and neighborhood center community organizing, $Q = .73$. It is possible to have a high level of support for militant activity and a low level of community organization activity since the correlation between them is not too high, .35. There would obviously not be very many agencies of this type. There are apparently no components of observed pressure generated by this type of agency. This means that any influence exerted towards institutional change from this kind of agency must flow directly from the militant activity which it supports.

The fourth and least prevalent type is one in which there is little community organization activity and little support for militant activity by the neighborhood center. This kind of agency does not generate pressures either. Thus, its effects must derive solely from the community organization purposes of its board and executive director. The effects of these agencies have been observed above as well as they can be.

One final note needs to be added to our interpretation of the diagram of community action activities presented in Table 3. Neighborhood center community organization activity is so highly correlated with the general level of political activity in the target neighborhood that it is not appropriate to project a type of agency which exists in a city with a low activity and one which has a high level of community organizing activity by the neighborhood center. However, it should be noted that neighborhood center community organizing activity generates neighborhood center pressure on schools in spite of the effects of general level of political activity in the neighborhood. The correlation coefficient between general political activity and neighborhood center pressure on schools is actually negative, —.05. This pressure is also negatively associated with militant activity, $Q = -.26$. Thus, it comes closest to fitting into the second type of agency described above.

DISCUSSION

The interpretation of Table 3 presented above has described each of these four types of Community Action Agencies as projections from the data offered. It is clear that the typology cannot be constructed from the data at hand since the case base is too small. There are only 20 agencies which we score high on community organization emphasis and thus at best we could have five cases within each type. In fact, since most of these agencies would fall into the first type, the skew of the distribution would preclude analysis. The best that can be done at this point is to offer the types as projections of the findings and within the context to assess the effectiveness of these types in producing institutional change.

Table 4 offers a beginning of this assessment. This table shows the gamma between each of the variables presented in Table 3 and institutional change. Rather than go into a detailed discussion of the complex set of relationships presented, we will limit the discussion to the average coefficients at the bottom of the page. The detailed breakdown of the dimensions of institutional change are presented so that the reader can make his own assessment if he so desires.

The first type of agency projected from Table 3 is marked by community organization activity and support for militant issues by the neighborhood center which leads to neighborhood center pressure on social service agencies and citizen pressure on the schools. Table 4 shows that neighborhood center pressure on the social service agencies is unlikely to produce any change, $Q = -.01$. Citizen pressure on the schools is only a little bit more likely to produce any change, $Q = .07$. Thus, the kinds of pressures which these agencies generate are not factors in institutional change. What then of the activity of the neighborhood centers? Since we have already seen the clear and strong influence of community organization goal orientation on institutional change, we would expect to find some intervening process contributing to such change. Neighborhood center community organization activity is that process. The average Q between this variable and changes in the social service agencies is .22. Between it and changes in the schools it is .36. The same coefficients for support of militant activity are —.11 and .07. Thus, this type of Community Action Agency is effective not because of the generation of direct pressures on these institutions but because of general organizational involvement. Schools and social service agencies do change in such cities. Why they change is less clear. They may change in anticipation of demands or pressures being directed at them, because the organizational density of such neighborhoods creates a culture ture defining such changes as desirable, or simply because organizational activity makes change a viable alternative to the status quo by the dis-

TABLE 4

Gamma[a] Coefficients of Selected Community Action Agency Activities and General Level of Political Activity with Institutional Change

Institutional Change	Selected CAA Activities				
	Neighborhood Center Pressure	Citizen Pressure	General Political Activity Level of Target Neighborhood	Community Organization Activity	Neighborhood Center Support for Militant Activity
Social service agency					
1. Number of clients	.10	—.13	.02	—.07	.62
2. Poor clients	.23	.65	.40	.64	.35
3. Minority clients	—.07	.55	.09	.08	—.55
4. Participation of poor	—.22	.62	.21	.34	—.59
5. Facilities	—.23	.48	.31	.20	—.02
6. Number of employees	.24	.45	.10	.08	—.19
7. Number of volunteers	—.42	.14	.47	.45	—.37
8. Number of referrals	.26	.48	.67	.07	—.14
Public schools					
11. Minority staff	—.12	—.28	—.03	.57	.00
12. Student/teacher	.33	.36	—.04	.53	—.26
13. Crowding	—.10	.32	.20	—.08	—.02
14. Auxiliary staff	.28	.31	—.12	.42	.33
15. Participation of poor	.05	—.18	.28	.45	.43
16. Promotion of partic.	.16	—.10	.14	.29	—.05
Political					
17. Political organization	—	—	1.00	.82	—.25
18. Electoral participation	—	—	—.11	—.03	—.27
Average Gamma, excluding pol. change	.04 (14)	.26 (14)	.19 (14)	.28 (14)	.03 (14)
Average Gamma, including pol. change	—	—	.22 (16)	.30 (16)	—.06 (16)
Av. Gamma, SSA	—.01	.41	.28	.22	—.11
Av. Gamma, Schools	.10	.07	.07	.36	.07

[a] Each of these variables are dichotomies so the statistic is a Q coefficient, which is a species of gamma.

cussion of issues without the presentation of demands. The surprising fact seems to be that such change takes place in spite of the support given to militant activity by the neighborhood center.

This leads us into the second type of Community Action Agency—one having community organization activity and not giving support for militant activity through the neighborhood center. These agencies are equally likely to produce change through community organization activity and are apparently not burdened with the need to overcome the negative effect of support for militant activity on changes in the social service agencies where the coefficient is —.11.

This interpretation can be empirically analyzed by looking at the association between community organization activity and institutional change with support for militant activity controlled. Table 5 presents the zero order gamma coefficients, the net partial gamma coefficient, and each of the partial gamma coefficients between neighborhood center community organization activity and institutional change. The evidence in Table 5 is

TABLE 5

Gamma Coefficients Between Neighborhood Center Community Organization Activity and Institutional Change: Zero Order, Net Partial Controlling for Neighborhood Center Support for Militant Activity, Partial for Weak Support for Militant Activity and Partial for Strong Support for Militant Activity

Institutional Change	Zero Order	Net Partial	Partial When Militant Support Is Weak	Partial When Militant Support Is Strong
Social service agency				
1. Number of clients	—.07	—.16	—.45	—.09
2. Poor clients	.64	.52	1.00	.60
3. Minority clients	.08	—.12	—.18	.60
4. Participation of poor	.34	.31	.20	1.00
5. Facilities	.20	.18	.14	.11
6. Number of employees	.08	.04	—.65	1.00
7. Number of volunteers	.45	.28	.71	1.00
8. Number of referrals	.07	—.06	.00	.20
Public Schools				
11. Minority staff	.57	.73	1.00	1.00
12. Student/teacher	.53	.65	.67	.20
13. Crowding	—.08	.04	—.11	—1.00
14. Auxiliary staff	.42	.50	.67	—1.00
15. Participation of poor	.45	.44	.37	.45
16. Promotion of partic.	.29	.55	.49	.20
Average gamma	.28	.28	.28	.30
Average gamma, social service agency	.22	.12	.10	.55
Average gamma, schools	.36	.48	.52	—.02

mixed. The average partial gamma between community organization activity and change does not differ among the zero order, the net partial or either of the partial coefficients. Thus, the effect of community organization activity overall is not a function of the absence or presence of miiltant activities. However, when we look within institutional areas, we see that there are substantial shifts. For social service agencies the effect of community organization activity is much greater when accompanied by support for militant activities than when not. For the schools it is just the opposite. The overall effect of these controls is to decrease the level of association for social service agencies and to increase the level of association for schools. Thus, the contribution of militant activity is apparently more threatening to social service agencies and more effective in changing them. This effect is at least partially generated through direct pressure exerted by the neighborhood center which is what develops when there is little support for militant activity. Schools are less susceptible to the threat of militant activity and the pressures of citizens. They are most likely to change simply because the neighborhood is organized. Militant activity is a substitute for citizen pressure on social science agencies but prevents the effects of community organizing on the schools.

The other interesting feature to be noted about Community Action Aegncies of the second type is that the kind of direct pressure they tend to generate—citizen pressure on social service agencies—is also very likely to produce change (see Table 4). Thus, these agencies seem to have two fronts operating to produce change. Additionally it should be noted that neighborhood center pressure on the schools which is not necessarily a component process of this type of agency but is more likely to be found here than anywhere else is positively, though not very strongly, associated with change in the schools. These types of agencies are most likely to be effective from each of these aspects.

The third type of CAA with a low level of community organization activity and a high level of support for militant activity without generation of direct pressures can quite simply be seen on the basis of Table 4 to have little or no effect since the only path to institutional change is through militant activity which we have already noted is not positively associated with change. However, one note of caution should be entered here. When we look at the effects of support for militant activity with the general political activity level of the neighborhood controlled, we find that in 12 of 14 cases there is a positive association between support for militant activity and institutional change when the general political activity level of the neighborhood is low. Militant activity as a last recourse does seem to be effective in encouraging institutional change, but it is so unlikely that such an inactive city will produce a community organization oriented Community Action Agency and militant activity that the contribution of support for militant activity by the CAA seems minimal.

What can now be said concerning the corollary hypotheses presented at the beginning of this paper? First, we can say that community organization oriented Community Action Agencies are more likely to produce change through citizen activity than through direct pressure only in private social service agencies. For schools, neither course is too likely to produce change. However, we can add to this finding the observation that general level of political activity and neighborhood center community organization activity are also both associated with change in both schools and social service agencies. Thus, while direct citizen pressure and demands are not especially effective paths to change, citizen activity does seem to be. The first corollary hypothesis offered is confirmed by this set of findings.

The second hypothesis is not confirmed. It is interesting to note that at least one reason why it is not confirmed is that change apparently is associated with citizen activity, but not with citizen demands or pressures, on schools. Institutions, especially the public schools, are apparently most effected by CAA's when these agencies do not present a direct challenge to the schools' or educators' autonomy, authority, and accuracy. When there is activity without demand the schools will change and will probably choose what and how to change. It is informative to note that the schools' promotion of resident participation withstood the test of control variables better than residents' actual participation. The social service agencies are influenced by activity but pressure also influences them. They fit the second corollary hypothesis more closely.

The third corollary hypothesis is directly and strongly confirmed. Neighborhood center community organization activity is the strongest predictor of institutional change.

CONCLUSION

The conclusion of this analysis is clear. It is a simple description of the effective Community Action Program. The effective Community Action Program is one which has central office support for community organization, which has neighborhood centers actively involved in community organizing, which has neighborhood centers uninvolved in militant activities, and which does not spend time pressing specific demands on other institutions. Since such agencies exist primarily in cities with relatively high levels of political activity in poor neighborhoods, their effectiveness is in extending or complementing the activity and involvement of the residents of poor neighborhoods. We can only speculate at this point, but the critical additions that CAA's provide may be protection from active resistance to the efforts of neighborhood residents, integration of the activities which may be somewhat diffuse, legitimacy for suspect activities, moral support, and perhaps simplest of all, financial backing. These interpretations can be tested with further analysis.

The Peace Corps and the Task Force concepts seem to come closest to describing the effective Community Action Agency. It is different from the Peace Corps concept in that the involvement is not so much with economic technical assistance but with political technical assistance. It is different from the Task Force concept in that the participation and involvement of the poor which we have analyzed is not in the Community Action Agency itself but in other institutions and organizations. It will be possible to see to what extent participation in the CAA itself will be associated with such participation in other organizations.

It can be concluded additionally that the absence of a relatively high level of general political activity in the target neighborhood does not provide much opportunity for community organization activity by the neighborhood center and the complementary role described above. In this event, it seems that militant activity can be effective in inducing institutional change, especially in social service agencies. As a last recourse in an inactive city, militancy can get some results.

Finally, we can add that there are evidently two critical stages in the development of Community Action Agencies which lead to their effectiveness. One is obtaining support from the board and the executive director for community organization emphasis. The second is developing community organization activities within the neighborhood center. To the extent that Community Action Programs are able to do this, they are effective in bringing about change in the institutions serving the poor. They are as likely to bring about change in concrete service as in the more ephemeral areas of participation in decision-making.

24

ORGANIZING THE POOR: AN EVALUATION OF A STRATEGY[1]

WALTER GOVE
Vanderbilt University

HERBERT COSTNER
University of Washington

M OST SOCIAL SCIENTISTS, AS HAGGSTROM HAS NOTED, HAVE AGREED THAT the poor (1) live on a moment-to-moment basis and rarely plan their activities; (2) perceive the world from a concrete personal perspective, being largely limited to self, family and neighborhood; and (3) typically feel envious and hostile towards the more affluent.[2] The poor are also typically perceived as fatalistic in their outlook on life and as lacking in social and instrumental skills.[3] It is now recognized that the lifestyle and perspective of the poor are attributable not only to their financial impoverishment, but also to a poverty culture[4] which is produced, at least in part, by a feeling of powerlessness.[5]

A traditional way of resolving problems in the United States has been through the development of local self-improvement associations.[6] In spite of the fact that the above characteristics of the poor suggest that they would not participate effectively in voluntary associations, many intervention programs reflect the belief that self-help associations constitute an important, if not an indispensable, ingredient for breaking the poverty culture.[7] There appear to be two main goals sought through local self-help

[1] The research reported in this paper was performed pursuant to Contract # 1375 with the Office of Economic Opportunity, Washington, D.C. 20506.

[2] Warren C. Haggstrom, "The Power of the Poor" in Frank Riessman, Jerome Cohen, and Arthur Pearl, eds., *Mental Health of the Poor* (New York: The Free Press, 1964).

[3] See, for example, Oscar Lewis, *The Children of Sanchez: Autobiography of a Mexican Family* (Vintage, N.Y.: Alfred A. Knopf, 1963); Walter Miller, "Focal Concerns of Lower Class Cultures," and Murray Hausknecht, "The Blue Collar Joiner," in Arthur Shostak and William Gomberg, eds., *Blue Collar World: Studies of the American Worker* (Englewood Cliffs, N.J.: Prentice-Hall, Inc., 1964).

[4] Michael Harrington, *The Other America: Poverty in the United States* (Baltimore, Md.: Penquin Books, 1962).

[5] See, for example, Marshall B. Clinard, *Slums and Community Development: Experiments in Self-Help* (New York: The Free Press, 1966); Haggstrom, "Power of the Poor," and Patricia C. Sexton, *Spanish Harlem: Anatomy of Poverty* (New York: Harper and Row, 1965).

[6] For example, Alexis de Tocqueville, in his classic commentary on life in the United States in the early nineteenth century noted the prominence of the "principle of association" in the resolution of collective problems in America as compared to alternative forms of resolving problems in Europe. Bradford Smith in *A Dangerous Freedom* (New York: J. B. Lippincott, Co., 1952), has chronicled the successes of dozens of special-purpose associations in the United States from the nineteenth to the middle of the twentieth century, many representing attempts of local citizens to solve local problems.

[7] For example, Warner Bloomberg, "Notes on Poverty and Dependency," unpublished paper, sees the organization of the poor as an effective strategy in com-

✦ First published in *Social Science Quarterly* 50, No. 3 (December, 1969).   275

organizations of the poor. First, it is believed that participation in self-help associations will help alleviate feelings of powerlessness which will lead to other changes in perspective and behavior and ultimately to a break with the poverty culture. This assumption remains largely untested, although Levens[8] has provided evidence that participants in self-help organizations do have a stronger feeling of destiny control than non-participants. Second, it is assumed that such organizations will be helpful in bringing about institutional changes that will benefit the poor. This may be a more important goal, for the proportion of poor involved in self-help organizations will typically be small, and if the sole accomplishment of a self-help organization is the improved self-concept of those involved, the majority of the poor may remain unaffected by such organizations. To change the orientation of nonparticipants, it is probably necessary to implement concrete changes in the world they encounter.

Organizing the poor on their own behalf can be attempted either in conjunction with the prevailing social order, as in the community action programs sponsored by the Office of Economic Opportunity, or in opposition to the prevailing order, as in programs associated with Saul Alinsky or the new student left.[9] Organizing the poor in opposition to the prevailing social order does not elicit support from established social institutions,[10] but may provide the drama and the emotional appeal that will motivate participation by a substantial segment of the poor population. On the other hand, organizing within the framework of the existing social order may produce strong institutional support, but it limits the targets and tactics of organizational strategy. Local neighborhood self-improvement associations seem to provide a "safe" type of organization whose goals—neighborhood improvement, improved public services for the area, playgrounds for children, and so forth—would elicit broad support from established institutions. A concern with relatively small, concrete goals would presumably enhance the likelihood of successful accomplishments and hence maximize the po-

---

batting feelings of dependency, while Nathan Cohen in "A National Program for the Improvement of Welfare Services and the Reduction of Welfare Dependency" in Margaret S. Gordon, ed., *Poverty in America* (San Francisco, Calif.: Chandler Publishing Co., 1965) maintains that the way to alleviate a feeling of powerlessness is by socially and politically organizing the poor to deal with the problems that directly confront them. Haggstrom, "Power of the Poor," suggests that participation in powerful neighborhood conflict organizations will enhance the poor's conception of their own worth and will overcome their feeling of powerlessness.

[8] Helene Levens, "Organizational Affiliations and Powerlessness: A Case Study of the Welfare Poor," *Social Problems*, 16 (Summer, 1968), pp. 18–32. Her finding of greater degree of destiny control among participants, however, may be a consequence of the selection process involved in becoming a member of such an organization. Although Levens attempts to control for this possibility, she is unable to rule out the selectivity hypothesis as she only has cross-sectional data.

[9] Frank Riessman, "A Comparison of Two Social Action Approaches: Saul Alinsky and the New Student Left," unpublished paper.

[10] Warren Haggstrom, "On Eliminating Poverty: What We Have Learned," in Warren Bloomberg, Jr., and Henry Schmandt, eds., *Power, Poverty and Urban Policy*, (Beverly Hills, Calif.: Sage Publications, 1968).

tential for alleviating feelings of powerlessness. Furthermore, the focus on the immediate neighborhood would seem to be in accord with the concrete personal perspective that characterizes the poor. On the other hand, the main problems perceived by the impoverished seem to extend beyond the confines of the immediate neighborhood, and the diffuse unrest of such a population may be difficult to focus on neighborhood problems.

The remainder of this paper describes one attempt to develop neighborhood self-help associations among the poor and the fate of this attempt. An evaluation of this attempt leads to a summary of general problems encountered in organizing the poor.

THE NEIGHBORHOOD ORGANIZATIONS

Late in 1965, the Central Area Motivational Program (CAMP), a part of OEO in Seattle, began a program of organizing neighborhood clubs in its service area. Nineteen such neighborhood clubs were eventually listed, along with their membership, in the records of CAMP. The clubs were given names indicative of their intended focus and purpose—"Neighborhood Concern," "Trinity Motivation Council," "Coleman Community Club," "Willing Workers," "27th Avenue Improvement Club," and so on. Each listing represented the effort of a community organizer, a paid member of the CAMP staff, whose responsibilities included organizing a neighborhood group for a specific geographic area and providing assistance to the group in identifying and resolving neighborhood problems. The geographic base of each club was comprised of a few blocks rather than a broad geographic area of the city.

CAMP anticipated that, as the clubs became established, the members would assume the major responsibility for the operation of the club activities and that the community organizer would serve primarily as an adviser and as liaison with the parent organization, CAMP. As CAMP envisioned the program, the clubs would discuss neighborhood problems, devise projects to alleviate these problems (e.g., build playgrounds on vacant lots, press for improved public services in their area, and so forth), stage small fund-raising events to support their projects, assist in resolving the problems of individual families in the neighborhood and cooperate with other clubs and agencies in the area in matters of common interest.

The community organizers were "indigenous workers," that is, residents of the general impoverished area (though not necessarily of the immediate neighborhood served by the club they advised) who were recruited from those not gainfully employed. Most were housewives before becoming community organizers. Formal training or experience in similar roles was not required, although one consideration in selection was the potential for working effectively with such neighborhood groups, and an attempt was made to provide on-the-job training. All of the community organizers and almost all of the club members were Negro women.

STUDY DESIGN

The study was aimed at making an evaluation of the effectiveness of this particular strategy of organizing the poor. In particular, it was concerned with: (1) the extent of participation in the clubs, especially by those who constitute the "hard core" poor, (2) the goals and actual accomplishments of the clubs, and (3) the characteristics that distinguished effective clubs from ineffective clubs.

The data for this study were collected in interviews with a sample of 112 adult residents of the CAMP service area and with *all* interviewable persons on the available membership lists of *all* the neighborhood clubs sponsored by CAMP. Five community organizers were also interviewed. Club members were asked the same series of questions asked of nonmembers, and, in addition, a series of questions pertaining to their own neighborhood club. Interviews were conducted by a team of nine paid student interviewers, eight of whom were black.

The sample of nonmembers was actually a sample of households, one from each of 112 randomly selected blocks. In six of these households no respondent was found at home, and in four, the respondent refused to be interviewed. Each of these ten missing respondents was then replaced by another draw. Hence, a total of 122 interviews were attempted with 112 completions for a completion rate of 92 per cent.

All listed members of the neighborhood clubs were target respondents. The membership lists obtained from CAMP contained the names of 132 persons. CAMP was unable to supply the addresses for seven of these persons and attempts to locate them by another means proved fruitless, leaving 125 to be interviewed.

CLUB MEMBERSHIP

The study was initiated with the assumption that all of the neighborhood clubs listed in the CAMP records were operating, and that they had been operating since their initiation several months previously. That assumption was erroneous; some of the clubs were operating, many were not. Table 1 shows the results of attempts to interview persons on the membership lists and the responses pertaining to club identification and participation among those who were interviewed. Table 2 shows other aspects of these same data tabulated for each club separately. Several features of the tables require comment.

First, approximately one out of every four persons listed as club members had moved since the listing approximately 18 months previously. The data from the community sample indicates that the overall mobility rate for persons living in the area serviced by CAMP is even higher than this: of those interviewed in the sample, 47 per cent indicated that they had changed their residence at least once during the past two years. Such a high rate of mobility implies that almost any association which is based on the local neighborhood, as these clubs were, will experience a heavy and rapid attrition of members. Since many of these movers undoubtedly move to other parts of the general area served by CAMP, the attrition rate due to moving would probably be less for a special-interest group than for a geographically based association.

Second, at least one out of every four persons listed as a club member,

TABLE 1
Results of Attempts to Contact Persons Listed as Club Members

	N	Per cent	N	Per cent
Not Interviewed			52	39
Moved, no new address	31	23		
Never an address available	7	5		
Not at home on any of five contact attempts	7	5		
Refused to be interviewed	4	3		
Ineligible[a]	3	2		
Interviewed			80	61
Stated that they were at present a member of one of the clubs (3 did not know the name of club)	20	15		
Stated that they were at present a member of one of the clubs but named a club whose name did not approximate any on CAMP list	12	9		
Stated that they had been but no longer were a member of one of the clubs (8 did not know the name of club)	14	11		
Stated that they had been but no longer were a member of one of the clubs but named a club whose name did not approximate any on the CAMP list	3	2		
Stated that they had never been a member of one of the CAMP neighborhood clubs	31	23		
Total			132	100

[a] Persons who could not have been club members, e.g., a seven-year-old boy, a senile, 85-year-old woman cared for by her daughter.

had, in fact, never been a club member, and the proportion may well be higher. Many persons listed as members denied having ever been affiliated with the clubs, while a few others were obviously ineligible for membership. The only reasonable interpretation for the inclusion of the "ineligibles" is that the membership lists were "padded"; the most generous interpretation of the inclusion of persons who denied ever having been affiliated with any such club is that in some contact with the community organizer they made remarks that indicated that they might be interested in participating. The conclusion seems unmistakable that the efforts of the community organizers to bring together neighborhood residents to form a club were frequently casual. Apparently for some of the community organizers, the assignment was beyond their experience and they did not know how to go about it.

Third, at the time of the interviews only half of the clubs gave any evidence of continuing to operate and only four of the clubs (A, H, O and R) were clearly active at the time of the interviews. Of the 49 persons who apparently started as members of the clubs (i.e., all those interviewed except those who denied ever having been affiliated with any of the clubs), approximately one out of three remain in the neighborhood but do not remain active members for as long as 18 months. Among the 32 persons who identified themselves as current members at the time of the interview, one-third reported that they had not participated in any club activities for over one month. It would appear that the clubs were generally unable to sustain the initial interest of their members.

Taken together, these results indicate that the general program of neighborhood clubs was never fully activated. A more intensive organizing effort than that undertaken in this program would be required, and it seems highly doubtful that housewives recruited primarily because they need employment are well suited to the task.

CHARACTERISTICS OF THE CLUB MEMBERS

The contribution of self-help associations toward breaking the poverty culture presumably can be realized only if participants include the carriers of that culture. With some exceptions, areas of a city that are designated "poverty areas" are not populated by residents who are uniformly poor, and such areas frequently include a minority rather than a majority of "hard core" poverty cases who are the primary carriers of the poverty culture. Consequently, neighborhood associations in poverty areas may fail to include the very persons to whom participation would presumably be of the greatest benefit. Carriers of the poverty culture typically are concentrated among those who have a low income and who frequently are unemployed and supported by welfare. We would expect them to have a high proportion of broken homes and to participate in voluntary associations only infrequently. Furthermore, it might be anticipated that the hard core poor would have a distinctive perception of the problems of their area that would set them apart from the more advantaged. We turn now to a description of those characteristics of the club participants that serve as indicators of their status as carriers or non-carriers of the poverty culture.

As indicated by Table 3, there is little basis for assuming that the club participants were typically hard core poverty cases embedded in the poverty culture. Most were employed, married with spouse present, and had incomes greater than $4,000 a year. The most striking difference between club members and nonmembers is that fact that almost all (94 per cent) of the club members were black, while the area population was just slightly more than half black (57 per cent). The heavy predominance of Negroes in the clubs seems to be a result of the fact that the community organizers

TABLE 2

Selected Characteristics of 19 Neighborhood Clubs

Club	Number of Members on Original List	Number Interviewed	Number Interviewed Who Claimed Membership at time of Interview[a]	Inferred Status of Club at Time of Interviews
A	10	8	7	active
B	3	1	0	not active
C	4	3	1[b]	not active
D	7	5	3	active
E	6	2	0	not active
F	5	5	1[b]	not active
G	7	3	2	active
H	8	8	4	active
I	8	6	1[c]	not active
J	5	4	1	(?) active
K	4	3	1	(?) active
L	4	1	0	not active
M	5	2	1[c]	not active
N	6	3	1[d]	not active
O	10	8	4	active
P	7	5	0	not active
Q	9	7	2	active
R	15	6	3	active
S[e]	9	0	0	not active
Total	112	80	32	

[a] Includes those who claim membership but who do not know the name of the club or who give a club name not correspondent to name in CAMP record.

[b] Respondent listed as "acting chairman" or "president" did not know the club name.

[c] Respondent listed as "president" denied ever having been a member.

[d] Although one person claimed current membership the community organizer reported it to be inactive.

[e] A community organizer informed us that club "S" was not a neighborhood club (although it was listed as such) but was an alliance of state employees and students, which had never functioned. None of the listed members could be located.

were themselves black and the parent organization, CAMP, was largely oriented to the blacks in the area. Other differences between members and nonmembers are less striking. They do, however, indicate that the club members, far from being the least affluent in the area, were somewhat advantaged in comparison to the area as a whole. Club members were more likely to be between 30 and 50 years old, to be married, and to have children in the household. The general picture of the neighborhood serviced by CAMP is that of a relatively poor working-class area, but one in which the majority of persons are not hard core poverty cases. Furthermore, the club members have been drawn primarily from those who are slightly more favorably situated than their neighbors and they are in the middle years of a relatively stable family life cycle.

Members of the neighborhood clubs were much more frequently involved in voluntary associations than nonmembers (see Table 3). The most common voluntary association was church membership, with club members belonging much more frequently than nonmembers. Church-affiliated groups (e.g., a missionary society), civil rights and labor organizations predominated among the other associational memberships. For purposes of summarizing participation in voluntary associations other than churches and CAMP, each respondent was classified as to (1) regular attendance in one or more organizations, (2) occasional attendance in one or more organizations, and (3) never attends. The data in Table 3 indicate that, even omitting church membership and attendance, the members of neighborhood clubs were more likely to be "joiners" than were the nonmembers of the area.

The respondents were asked to indicate if they were satisfied or dissatisfied with 14 different conditions in their own neighborhood—play space for children, housing, police protection, public transportation, and so forth. Club members indicated more dissatisfaction than the nonmembers on every condition, suggesting a greater sensitivity to or awareness of neighborhood problems. Only "play space for children" elicited a response indicating dissatisfaction by as many as half of the nonmembers. In contrast, six of the fourteen conditions—housing, play space, appearance of the area, traffic safety, police protection, condition of streets—elicited a response of dissatisfaction by half or more of the club members.

In addition, respondents were asked what they felt was the "most important community problem" facing the residents of their general area; responses to this open-ended question suggest there is no general consensus since no single problem was named by more than 17 per cent of the respondents. Among the club members, however, 47 per cent named housing. In contrast, the very poor nonmembers (incomes less than $4,000) most frequently named crime and employment. Club members, then, appear to view the problems of the area from a somewhat different perspective than do the hard core poverty cases. A further illustration of this tendency comes from an interview with a community organizer who reported that one of her clubs was composed entirely of home owners. The focus of a series of club meetings was how to force three or four of their renting neighbors to clean up the property they were renting, as their behavior was forcing down the financial values of other property in the neighborhood.

The general characteristics of the club members indicate that club membership was not concentrated among the very poor and that club members were not likely to be carriers of the poverty culture. Furthermore, our data indicate that the clubs were not comprised primarily of persons who would otherwise have been lacking in voluntary association participation; indeed it appears that members of the neighborhood clubs were already rather heavily involved in voluntary associations. Finally, there is

TABLE 3

Comparison of Neighborhood Club Members and Nonmembers
on Selected Characterisitcs (in per cent)

	Neighborhood Club Members (N = 49)	Nonmembers (N = 112)
Race		
Negro	94	57
Caucasian	6	39
Oriental	0	4
Marital status		
Married	71	56
Separated or divorced	8	20
Widowed	10	7
Never married	10	13
Children		
No children in household	10	32
Age		
Under 30	22	26
30–50	59	38
Over 50	19	36
Education		
Complete high school	49	54
Amount of income		
$4,000 or more/yr.[a]	81	73
Main source of income		
Wage or salaries	76	71
Welfare	10	10
Other	14	19
Occupation class		
White collar	20	17
Blue collar	63	53
Unemployed	2	9
Housewife	8	6
Student or retired	6	10
Not ascertained	0	5
Church[b]		
Member, attends regularly	61	39
Member, attends occasionally or never	25	28
Not a member	14	33
Voluntary organizations other than church or CAMP[b]		
Regular attendance in one or more organizations	49	39
Occasional attendance in one or more organizations	37	29
Never attends (including nonmembers)	14	31

[a] Twelve of the club members and 28 persons in the community sample did not reply to this question.

[b] For four persons in the community sample, this information was not ascertained.

some evidence that club members have a different view of the "most important problem of the area" than the very poor.

ACCOMPLISHMENTS OF THE CLUBS AND FACTORS RELATED TO CLUB SUCCESS

Even though the neighborhood clubs varied in their degrees of success over a very limited range, the existence of this variation permits a preliminary exploration of some of the factors that contribute to success or failure. Success may be judged either in terms of the benefits presumably accruing from the concrete accomplishments of the clubs or in terms of the self-perceived achievement of club goals.

Each club member interviewed (who did not deny club affiliation) was asked to name the goals sought by his own club, to describe the activities undertaken in an attempt to achieve these goals, and to indicate if he felt the goal had been accomplished. The lack of consensus in many clubs suggested that they had not developed clear goals. Furthermore, for many of the club members, successful accomplishment of a goal meant that the club had discussed a problem on a particular occasion, or that a telephone call had been made, or a letter written. These interviews, as well as those with the community organizers, indicated that most of the club members had no conception of the type of activities necessary to put pressure upon governmental or commercial agencies, to say nothing of knowing how to organize and implement such activities.

The ratio of goals perceived as accomplished to goals named was low—even with the very liberal meaning of "accomplish" used by the respondents. Members named 107 goals for their respective clubs; in 37 cases (34 per cent) the respondent naming the goal indicated that it had been accomplished. The low rate of perceived success may have been one of the reasons for the high dropout rate.

The concrete accomplishments of the clubs were, if anything, even less spectacular, and they can be listed in their entirety very briefly. One club succeeded in establishing a "tot lot" playground on land donated by a club member. Another club painted one building, while a different club, with the aid of their community organizer, obtained a donation of paint which they attempted to give to others in the neighborhood who needed it. (They reported plaintively, however, that no one would accept it.) Two clubs, in an attempt to provide assistance to the needy, staged small fund-raising events (a rummage sale and a raffle). The most spectacular accomplishment of any neighborhood club was the role one club played in the establishment of a crosstown bus route. The idea for the route initially came from the club; however, implementation required CAMP officials and other important community leaders to organize and carry out the campaign eventually leading to the bus route establishment.

Two members of the research team independently made a "dichotomized" judgment of the relative success of each club based on the information available. These judges agreed on the placement of all but two of the clubs, and these disagreements were resolved by discussing the characteristics of these clubs and arriving at a common decision.[11] Six clubs (A, H, K, N, O, and R in Table 2) were categorized "more successful" while the remainder were categorized "less successful."

The members of the more successful and less successful clubs were compared with only trivial differences between the two sets of club members in terms of age, socioeconomic status, other organizational memberships, or in attitudes toward the community or toward CAMP. Although the differences are not great enough to rule out random variation as a source of difference, the members of the more successful clubs had fewer children, fewer persons in the household, and were less likely to be employed outside the home. These differences, although slight, suggest that members of more successful clubs may have had more time available to devote to club activities. Members of the more successful clubs also tended to be slightly more personally "optimistic" (i.e., more anticipated that five years from now they would occupy a more favorable position).

Probably the most significant difference between successful and unsuccessful clubs was club size. The average size of the initial membership listed for the more successful clubs was 8.8 persons as contrasted to an initial membership of 5.8 persons for the unsuccessful clubs. The less successful clubs were only slightly more likely to have listed members who moved away or who denied ever belonging to the club.[12] However, the loss of any particular club member was more of a serious threat to a small club than to a large one.

Very small clubs appear to be disadvantageous for a number of reasons.[13] First, when mobility is high and dropouts are likely, as in this case, a larger

[11] These judgments were then compared against four objective indicators of success: (a) number of tasks attempted, (b) ratio of tasks accomplished to tasks attempted, (c) proportion of members on the membership list who could be identified as active members, and (d) the ratio of all attendances at club meetings during the month preceeding the interview to the number of members. The judgments had a higher association with each of the other indicators than these other indicators had with each other.

[12] Twenty-one per cent of those appearing on the membership lists of the "more successful" clubs had moved by the time of the interviews, as compared to 25 per cent of those on the lists for the "less successful" clubs. The percentage denying ever belonging to the club was 23 per cent in the "more successful" and 27 per cent in the "less successful" clubs. Eight per cent of the membership list of the "more successful" clubs were dropouts, as compared to 19 per cent in the "less successful" clubs.

[13] Since the community organizers assumed the responsibility for assembling the club members initially and also for continuing to work with the clubs, the possibility arises that the more energetic community organizers had both larger and more successful clubs, membership size itself making no contribution to club success. We do not have a detailed record of the activities of the community organizers, but the meager evidence available on this point suggests that this interpretation of the relation between club size and success is untenable. Approximately one-third of the members of the "less successful" clubs, as compared to only one-sixth of the members of the "more successful" clubs reported that the community organizers had focused the problem for the club. This suggests that, if there were any differences in community organizer activity between the more and the less successful clubs, the community organizer was more dominant in those clubs that were less successful.

membership can sustain some losses from these sources without diminishing the membership to one or two lone survivors. Second, it is difficult to undertake projects of any consequence, and thereby sustain motivation and interest through activity and accomplishment, if the membership is too small. It is difficult, for example, for a club of three or four members to muster the courage to go to city hall or the energy to start a clean-up campaign because the social support from within the group for such an undertaking is so limited. Third, it is probably difficult for a club of three or four members to develop a sense of being a club at all; in a club with only three or four members the absence or inactivity of one or two members turn the "club meeting" into a tête-a-tête, and any feeling of accomplishment is difficult to muster under such circumstances.

More than one-third of the neighborhood clubs organized by CAMP community organizers had an initial membership list of five or fewer members, and with one exception these very small clubs had ceased to be active by the time of the interviews. Allowing for the possibility of people moving and dropping out, almost all of the neighborhood clubs started with a precariously small membership which may have been a major source of their difficulty. It is conceivable that the "local neighborhood" is simply too small an area to provide a population base for workable self-improvement associations among the poor.

Discussion and Conclusions

The strategy of organizing the poor described in this paper—an attempt to develop local neighborhood self-improvement associations through the efforts of an indigenous community organizer—was a failure. The types of problems encountered appear to be common, and other attempts based on a similar strategy will probably be similarly unsuccessful. The major problems are these:

1. Indigenous community organizers working without close expert guidance and supervision are likely to find the task of organizing difficult and frustrating. As a consequence, their efforts may be perfunctory and records may exaggerate the degree of organization accomplished.

2. Community residents most easily recruited and most likely to continue as participants seem to be the relatively advantaged residents of the area who are already participating in other associations, rather than the "hard core" poor. Whatever the presumed benefits of participation, the unaffiliated and unintegrated are not likely to be reached, nor are their viewpoints necessarily well represented by their slightly more advantaged neighbors.

3. Although residents of poverty areas, and especially club members, respond to questions about area problems in ways that suggest moderately high dissatisfaction with prevailing neighborhood conditions, they apparently lack knowledge of how to deal effectively with the sources of dissatisfaction. Even very small and limited goals are rarely accomplished.

4. Residents of poverty areas typically have pressing personal concerns

and are particularly geared to immediate concrete rewards.[14] The slow processes of accomplishing ends through organization seem to provide little satisfaction and dropouts are frequent. Club participation seems to be lacking in any zeal and, if it has any effect on psychological outlook, probably adds to a sense of frustration rather than imparting any feeling of accomplishment and power.

5. Associations with a neighborhood base are likely to be too small to make for organizational continuity in the face of mobility and dropouts, too small to generate and sustain a feeling of being a real organization, and too small to undertake some of the tasks that would presumably be necessary to alleviate sources of dissatisfaction. The larger neighborhood clubs had a better chance of achieving some success than the smaller ones, but the local neighborhood seems to be an inappropriate unit for dealing with many of the problems of the impoverished.

Strategies for organizing the poor that can overcome these difficulties should enjoy a more favorable prognosis for success than would a repetition of the strategy described here. An organizational focus around a common problem rather than a shared locality might provide a more realistic base for organizing the poor, and might also assist in recruiting a higher proportion of the hard core poor and a larger membership base. Involvement of professionals in relevant specialties and citizens other than the poor and near poor might assist in overcoming some of the other organizational problems (listed above) by providing information and guidance as well as encouragement in the face of delayed achievement.

A strategy embodying such points has recently been described by Zurcher and Key.[15] In such a program the poor act as experts on what goals need to be accomplished, while persons already skilled in the intricacies of community activity play a major role in achieving these goals. This "Overlap Model," as Zurcher and Key have named it, when viewed from the standpoint of the now conventional objectives of organizing the poor, appears to present a dilemma of its own: How can an organizational "model" that is built in part around the dependency of the poor help reduce the feeling of powerlessness of the poor? The feeling of powerlessness among the poor, however, is reality, not illusion, and its significance for the poor may lie not so much in the psychological adaptions that emerge from the *feeling* of powerlessness as in the limited life chances that emerge from the *reality* of powerlessness. In the long run, organization among the poor may be most effective if participation by the poor is viewed

---

[14] See, for example, Elizabeth Herzog, "Some Assumptions About the Poor," *Social Service Review*, 37 (Dec., 1963), pp. 391–400; Lawrence L. LeShan, "Time Orientation and Social Class," *Journal of Abnormal and Social Psychology*, 47 (June, 1952), pp. 589–592; S. M. Miller, Frank Riessman, and Arthur A. Seagull, "Poverty and Self-Indulgence: A Critique of Non-Deferred Gratification Pattern," in Louis Ferman, Joyce Kornbluh, and Alan Haber, eds., *Poverty in America* (Ann Arbor: University of Michigan Press, 1965), pp. 285–302.

[15] Louis Zurcher and William Key, "The Overlap Model: A Comparison of Strategies for Social Change," *Sociological Quarterly*, 10 (Winter, 1968), pp. 85–96.

in terms of its instrumental contributions to goal achievement rather than in terms of its social-emotional contributions to psychological change. The program discussed in this paper suggests that the contributions of the poor to goal attainment can be best achieved if they work closely with others who have the skills which the poor lack. The fate of this program also suggests that neighborhood-based associations are ill-suited for changing the reality of powerlessness.

25

FUNCTIONAL MARGINALITY: DYNAMICS OF A POVERTY INTERVENTION ORGANIZATION[1]

LOUIS A. ZURCHER, JR.
The University of Texas at Austin

T HE ECONOMIC OPPORTUNITY ACT OF 1964 ESTABLISHED THE OFFICE of Economic Opportunity, declared the "War Against Poverty" and provided for the funding of poverty intervention organizations (PIO's) to be established in applicant communities throughout the United States. The PIO's were intended to stimulate or accelerate change in the socioeconomic and opportunity structures of communities by going beyond the traditional expedient of mechanically supplying material resources to the poor and involving them, through "maximum feasible participation," in the decisions and processes which led to their acquisition of the resources.[2] The strategy of funds and active involvement was designated with the hope of disrupting the perpetuated cycle of poverty.

At this writing (July, 1966) over seven-hundred PIO's have under a wide variety of names been funded by the Office of Economic Opportunity. The proliferation of those potential agents for social change challenges both practitioner and theorist—the former to implement the innovation of beneficiary participation, the latter to determine the utility of formal organization and community action theories to accommodate PIO phenomena. With glimpses at challenges to practitioner and theorist, this paper presents some of the dynamics and dilemmas of one PIO as it attempted to enact the expectations and approach the goals of the War Against Poverty.

SETTING AND METHOD

The subject PIO, the Topeka Office of Economic Opportunity (Topeka OEO), was funded and staffed with a director, assistant director and secretary on May 1, 1965. Topeka is the capital city of Kansas and has a population of approximately 120,000. It is a quiet community, lightly-industrialized, politically conservative and is not experiencing the pressures for social change extant in large urban centers. Poverty clearly exists, but is less apparent than in larger cities because of the relative absence of ghettos, multiple family dwellings and organized protest.[3]

[1] Revision of a paper read in the Community Research and Development Session, Joint Meeting of the Society for the Study of Social Problems and the Rural Sociological Society, Miami Beach, Florida, August 28, 1966. Research upon which the paper was based was supported by the Office of Economic Opportunity (Grant 66–9744). The author gratefully acknowledges the helpful comments of Drs. Gardner Murphy, William Key, James Taylor and Robert Harder.

[2] Economic Opportunity Act of 1964, 78 Stat. 508, Title II, Sec. 202 (a).

[3] Topeka-Shawnee Regional Planning Commission, *Neighborhood Analysis for the Topeka-Shawnee County Regional Planning Area* (Topeka: Master Plan Report Number 5, 1965).

♦ Reprinted by permission from *(Southwestern) Social Science Quarterly* 48 (December, 1967), pp. 411–421.

The Topeka OEO staff designated twelve "Target Neighborhoods" in the community, each of which had comparatively high indices of poverty and blight. Ten of the Target Neighborhoods subsequently were represented by "Target Neighborhood Committees" of low-income people. The Target Neighborhood Committees had elected chairmen, vice-chairmen and secretaries, and met at least monthly to discuss the formulation and implementation of various OEO community action proposals. A second set of committees, called "Study Committees," was established by the Topeka OEO staff in order to provide a flow of resource data between the Target Neighborhood Committees and other interested community members. Each of the eleven Study Committees dealt with a specific community problem (*e.g.*, housing, education, employment, *etc.*), had its own chairman, vice-chairman and secretary, met monthly, and was composed of approximately one-third professionals in a related field, one-third citizens from the community-at-large, and one-third residents from the Target Neighborhoods. The third and major committee established by the Topeka OEO staff was the "Economic Opportunity Board," which met at least quarterly and was composed of a maximum of seventy-five voting members—the chairmen and vice-chairmen of the Target Neighborhood Committees, the chairmen of the Study Committees, representatives from all of the community's major agencies and representatives from business, organized religion, civil rights groups and local government. Over one-third of the voting members of the Board were Target Neighborhood residents. In October, 1966, the Economic Opportunity Board was legally incorporated and was empowered to approve OEO community action proposals, make contracts, set budgets and hire or fire the staff of the Topeka OEO. The Topeka OEO nonetheless remained the managing and coordinating center for the program and will be the referent in this paper for the term "PIO."

The research methods used in this study were participant observation[4] (in the committee complex and in Topeka OEO staff activities) and unstructured interviews (with Topeka OEO staff and poor and not-poor members of the committee complex). The sensitivity of the participants, the fragility of the newly formed PIO and its component parts and the determination of the research staff not to interfere with the development of the poverty program dictated the choice of methods.[5] At this writing

[4] The participant observation was similar to Gold's type "observer-as-participant"—that is, the observers attended the meetings and sat with the members but did not take an active part and remained as inconspicuous as possible (Raymond L. Gold, "Roles in Sociological Field Observations," *Social Forces*, 36 [March, 1958], pp. 217–223).

[5] The author was particularly influenced toward the methods employed in this study by the work of Richard N. Adams and Jack J. Preiss (eds.), *Human Organization Research: Field Relations and Techniques* (Homewood, Illinois: Dorsey Press, 1960), pp. 290–431; Oscar Lewis, *The Children of Sanchez* (New York: Vintage Books, 1961); and William W. Whyte, *Street Corner Society* (Chicago: University of Chicago Press, 1943). For an exposition of the research staff's techniques for gaining access to meetings and interviewees, see Louis A. Zurcher, "The Leader and the Lost: A Case Study of Indigenous Leadership in a Poverty Program Community Action Committee," *Genetic Psychology Monographs* 76 (Aug., 1967), pp. 23–93.

the study has been conducted for nine months (September, 1965–June, 1966) and includes over two-hundred interviews and observation in seventy meetings. Significant events prior to September, 1965, were reconstructed from in-depth interviews with Topeka OEO staff and Board members and from analysis of PIO records and reports. The research field office was located in the same set of buildings as the Topeka OEO; daily discussions were thus possible between research and Topeka OEO staff. Besides field contact with indigenous leaders, the research staff was able to sound leaders' opinions in the Research Study Committee—a monthly meeting, open only to Target Neighborhood officers and research staff, during which opinions were freely expressed concerning topics relevant to the local poverty program.

DYNAMICS AND DILEMMAS

PIO rationale. The Topeka OEO staff developed the committee complex on the assumptions: (1) that the overall structure would best implement the mandate of the Economic Opportunity Act and would provide meaningful participation of the poor; (2) that the *process experience* of the indigent participants would increase their repertoire of social roles and skills whereby they might acquire more power and control *vis-à-vis* those community elements which affect their lives; and (3) that the equal status pursuit of mutual goals (OEO community action proposals) by members from disparate socioeconomic levels working together in structured social situations (Board and Study Committee meetings) would break down stereotypes, encourage communication, broaden understanding and engender social change. These assumptions were conceptualized in an earlier paper as the "Overlap Model" for social change.[6]

The PIO thus planned to occupy and sustain a marginal position between the community poor and not-poor, providing a vehicle for their functional interaction. The first Annual Report of the Topeka OEO pronounced that "The Topeka Program rests on middle ground, reaching out and including all actions and efforts for social change."[7] But what does being "on middle ground" mean, and does that position readily permit "reaching out and including *all* actions and efforts for social change"?

Initial community reaction. The pervading reaction of the Topeka OEO's early efforts was community indifference. The first response of

[6] Louis A. Zurcher and William H. Key, "The Overlap Model: A Comparison of Strategies for Social Change," *Sociological Quarterly*, 8 (Winter, 1968), pp. 85–97. This model as conceived is similar in intent to the "Co-Determination" strategy advocated by Shostak and the third party antipoverty intervention suggested by Rein and Riessman (Arthur B. Shostak, "Promoting Participation of the Poor: Philadelphia's Anti-poverty Program," *Social Work*, 11 [Jan., 1966], pp. 65–72; Arthur B. Shostak, "Containment, Co-Optation, or Co-Determination?" *American Child* [Nov., 1965], pp. 1–5; Martin Rein and Frank Riessman, "A Strategy for Antipoverty Community Action Programs," *Social Work*, 11 [April, 1966], pp. 3–12). For a critique of the War against Poverty and an alternative, "outside-the-system" model for poverty intervention, see Saul D. Alinsky, "The War on Poverty: Political Pornography," *Journal of Social Issues*, 21 (Jan., 1965), pp. 41–47.

[7] Topeka Office of Economic Opportunity, *Annual Report for 1965–1966* (Topeka: Topeka Office of Economic Opportunity, 1966), p. 10.

FIGURE 1

Functional Schematic of the Topeka Poverty Program

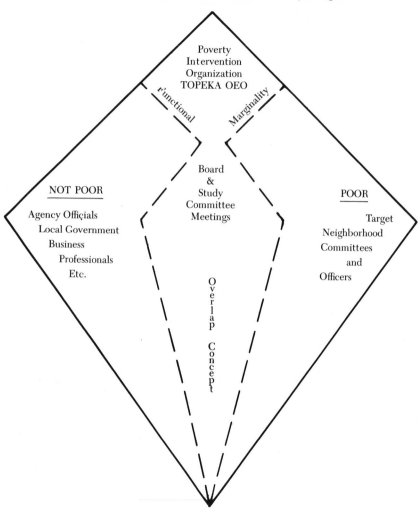

several of those individuals who did show interest was concern with the *intervention* quality of the PIO. The Topeka OEO, intervening into the "quasi-stationary equilibrium" of the community,[8] was warily viewed: 1) by some local government officials who perceived it to be a potential "Federal power grab"; 2) by a few Welfare professionals who saw it as a threat to their competencies; 3) by a number of traditional mediators for

[8] Kurt Lewin, "Quasi-Stationary Social Equilibria and the Problem of Permanent Change," in Warren G. Bennis, Kenneth D. Benne and Robert Chin (eds.), *The Planning of Change* (New York: Holt, Rinehart and Winston, 1962), pp. 235–238.

the poor (*e.g.*, ministers, civil rights' group officers) who perceived it to be a threat to their mediation role; 4) by some not-poor members of the community who saw it potentially "stirring up trouble" and "turning loose *those* people on the community"; and 5) by many of the poor themselves, who suspected a "con job" and perceived it to be nothing different from nor less manipulative than any other agency in which they had no say. At the onset, therefore, the Topeka OEO found itself faced with the task of explaining its reasons for existence and demonstrating why it should be allowed to "rock the boat" in a community that was essentially self-satisfied, resistant to change and generally unaware of the prevalence and chronicity of its poverty.[9]

Recruiting participants. As the Topeka OEO director and assistant director attempted to populate the committee complex with community members, they discovered a recruitment dilemma. Those strategies which often convinced agency, business or government officials to cooperate with the PIO seemed to be those which discouraged the poor from becoming involved. To get representatives from the community power structure "aboard," the PIO staff talked of policy, guidelines, "paced" social change, standardized procedures, spheres of operation, *etc.* The staff represented themselves as competent *agency* officials who knew and used the language and practices of bureaucracy.[10] The impersonality, abstract rationales and distant policies seemed, however, mainly to convince the poor that the PIO would be "just another one of those agencies that tell us what we can have and what we can do." On the other hand, the Target Neighborhood residents seemed to respond when the staff

---

[9] Community action theorists often postulate a prerequisite of goal concurrence before action can occur. Bruyn, for example, writes that "community sentiment" and a consensually validated "set of beliefs" is necessary "for any association to survive in effective operation in the community" (Severyn T. Bruyn, *Communities in Action* [New Haven: College and University Press, 1963], pp. 128–129). Holland, Tiedke and Miller state that "in order for action to take place at all, there must be some convergence of interests of those actors in the social system who had appropriate sentiments, beliefs, and/or rationally calculated purposes with references to a problem" (John B. Holland, Kenneth E. Tiedke and Paul A. Miller, "A Theoretical Model for Health Action," *Rural Sociology*, 22 [June, 1957], pp. 149–155). See also: Floyd Hunter, Ruth C. Schaffer and Cecil G. Sheps, *Community Organization: Action and Inaction* (Chapel Hill: University of North Carolina Press, 1956), pp. 226–240; James W. Green and Selz C. Mayo, "A Framework for Research in the Actions of Community Groups," *Social Forces*, 31 (May, 1953), pp. 323–326; and Paul A. Miller, *Community Health Action* (East Lansing: Michigan State College Press, 1953).

The PIO striving to operationalize the Economic Opportunity Act introduces two distinct goal-sets for which it seeks community consensus: the program *content* available through OEO community action proposals, and the "maximum feasible participation" *process* experience for the poor. Both of these goal-sets may be foreign to established patterns of community action. In such a case the consensus-then-action-then-change model is not an accurate theoretical sequence for the PIO. Consensus seeking for innovative content and process goal-sets impinges upon entrenched attitudes, role expectations, social habits and organizational policies and is *in itself* action with potential for social change.

[10] A "universalistic" approach (Talcott Parsons and Edward A. Shils [eds.], *Toward a General Theory of Action* [Cambridge: Harvard University Press, 1959], pp. 76–79).

made an effort to become known to them as persons rather than as titled officials.[11]

The Topeka OEO director and assistant director met the recruitment dilemma with a division of labor. The director, a white Methodist minister with three terms' experience in the House of Representatives of the Kansas State Legislature, concentrated primarily upon the community's power structure. His political ability and bureaucratic expertise eventually won the cooperation and participation of most of the city's key agency and governmental officials.[12] The assistant director, a Mexican-American former factory worker and union organizer, gradually gained the confidence and participation of Target Neighborhood residents because "he was a regular guy, just like us, and we got to know him as a *person*."

The division of labor engendered staff stresses within the functionally marginal PIO. If the Target Neighborhood residents made an autonomous program move that was perceived by an agency to be inappropriate, the PIO director often would be criticized by that agency for "not being able to control the program." If a Target Neighborhood Committee felt their plans had been restricted by an agency, the PIO Assistant Director usually was accused by the members of "being more interested in pleasing the agencies than in working with us." The strategies which appeared to stimulate initial participation of the poor and not-poor seemed also, until new roles were more clearly understood, to develop unrealistic expectations for program power and control among both poor and not-poor alike. The frustration of unfulfilled expectations typically was vented upon the PIO staff.[13]

---

[11] A "particularistic" approach (*Ibid.*, pp. 76–79).

[12] In contrast to PIO's in other communities, the Topeka OEO was not a "city hall" operation—partly because the conservative local government preferred not to be identified with a "Great Society" program, partly because it was felt that the director "knew the score" politically (though he was not a member of the majority political party).

[13] During their efforts to attract participants to the developing PIO committee complex both the director and assistant director manifested considerable charismatic behavior. The assistant director more closely enacted classic Weberian charisma when recruiting Target Neighborhood residents. He eschewed confining organization and rigid rules, preached the urgency of "changing times" and the "Great Society," enthusiastically and dramatically pronounced the new cause heralded by "maximum feasible participation," admonished all to "get on the bandwagon," and emphasized the *process* goals of the PIO. The director, though he appealed to the not-poor with such bureaucratic abstractions as "increased agency outreach" and "maximization of services" and emphasized the *content* goals of the PIO, was nonetheless charismatic in his interactions with agency and local government officials. The author suggests that the director's behavior might be representative of a leadership or authority type generated in and by modern bureaucracy, and that one might call the type-behavior *bureaucharisma*. For a discussion of the characteristics of charisma see Hans H. Gerth and C. Wright Mills (trans. and eds.), *From Max Weber: Essays in Sociology* (New York: Oxford University Press, 1946), pp. 196–204.

It was impossible for the PIO director and assistant director continually to maintain their contrived division of labor (*e.g.*, at Board meetings they had to interact simultaneously with both poor and not-poor participants). Merton noted that any single position involves the individual in not one but a whole set of role relations and expectations, and that inherent in such a role-set is a possibility for conflicting expectations. Merton further observes that a person usually is spared conflicting demands

Organizational style. When an organization is young, changing or relatively informal, its day-to-day operating procedures are more likely to be
influenced by the personal managerial philosophy of key staff.[14] The organizational style of the Topeka OEO was primarily determined by the
director's political experience. The director wrote that the Topeka OEO
was "styled along the lines of grass roots democracy, combining a New
England Town Meeting with the Kansas House of Representatives . . .
The study and neighborhood committees sift ideas as do the standing
committees in the Kansas House of Representatives."[15] The "Key Words"
for the program, reflecting "an all-out effort to keep everyone aboard,"
were: "compromise, communication, negotiation, cooperation, evolution
and representative democracy."[16]

The "political" organizational style of the PIO seemed to fit well with
the "Overlap Model" for social change, and provided Target Neighborhood representatives with a chance to experience participative democracy.
However, as the PIO grew, some incongruities could be perceived between participant democracy as might be seen in the Kansas Legislature
and participant democracy as it was in the PIO committee complex. Most
apparent was the fact that the poor were not politicians. Arguments and
debates were not so abstract nor affectively neutral in the committee
meetings as they usually are in legislatures. Conflict centered around
powers and controls that were meaningful to the poor in terms of their
everyday lives and not some distant constituency. The PIO Director's
own experiences with the developing program prompted him to comment: "It's not really working like the Legislature, as I had hoped. There,
proposals are presented, discussed, voted upon and we move on. Here,
proposals often become less important than the debate itself. The participants stay worked up even after an issue is voted upon and off the
agenda. The road always seems bumpy!"

If the PIO was enacting its purported functional marginality, it
should   be expected that the content of a specific community action

by the fact that he does not have contacts with all members of his role-set at once—
thus he can live up to the expectations of some at one time and others at another
time (Robert K. Merton, "The Role Set," *British Journal of Sociology,* 8 [1957], pp.
106–120). Clearly the positions of PIO director and assistant director support role-
sets which contain conflicting expectations of the various publics served. Further, the
PIO rationale of bringing together members from disparate socioeconomic components
of the community encourages opportunities for the staff's experiencing of conflicting
expectations. Goldner reports that "boundary roles" (like those of the PIO director and
assistant director) can facilitate the individual's ability to "bridge" disparate publics,
but also can result in the individual's being held suspect by those publics (Fred H.
Goldner, "Organizations and Their Environment: Roles at Their Boundary," paper
read at the meetings of the American Sociological Association, New York, 1960). See
also Robert L. Kahn, Donald M. Wolfe, Robert P. Quinn, J. Diedrick Snoek, and Robert
A. Rosenthal, *Organizational Stress: Studies in Role Conflict and Ambiguity* (New
York: Wiley, 1964).

14 Peter M. Blau and W. Richard Scott, *Formal Organizations* (San Francisco:
Chandler Publishing Company, 1962), p. 6. See also Joseph A. Litterer, *Organizations:
Structure and Behavior* (New York: Wiley, 1963), p. 34.

15 Topeka OEO, *Annual Report,* p. 8.

16 *Ibid.,* p. 10.

proposal often would appear secondary, especially for the poor, to the participative and power experiencing process of developing and implementing it. To sustain an organizational style which permits the "road to be bumpy" is stressful to the PIO staff, particularly at the beginning and if that style was based upon prior experiences with more conventional kinds of organizations.

Action now! The not-poor who were participating in the Topeka OEO committee complex were accustomed to long-range planning and the slow but systematic processing of proposals through bureaucratic machinery. The PIO staff saw its major material task to be the winning of federal funds through community action programming—a task which also demanded long-range planning and patient processing. In contrast, the Target Neighborhood residents generally insisted upon immediate results and were vociferously impatient with delays. The poor's demands for action *now* indicated more than a desire for programs or funds, *per se.* Their behavior seemed to manifest an indifference to future orientation[17] and an urgency *quickly to achieve results for which they themselves were at least somewhat responsible.* The Target Neighborhood residents had continually been told that the "poverty program is *your* program," and many of them were eager to test the promise.

The Topeka OEO's functional marginality was severely challenged during arguments between the poor and not-poor participants concerning action-timing. If community action proposals (particularly those involving delegate agencies) moved more quickly than the agencies could comfortably accommodate, the PIO staff would be pressured to "keep things in line." If the proposals bogged down for any reasons beyond their control, the Target Neighborhood residents would become angry or, worse, disillusioned and the PIO would be held accountable for "selling them out."

From "clients" to colleagues. As the poor increasingly exercised their prerogative to participate in decision-making concerning the conduct of the Topeka poverty program, some of the representatives from agencies traditionally accustomed to doing *for* the poor were challenged to shift, at least during committee meetings, their perception of the poor from "clients" to colleagues. In order to be consistent with its proclamations for equal status interaction among the participants, the PIO had to encourage agency officials to decrease their role distance from the poor, sometimes with the result that jealously guarded professional statuses were threatened. Further, the PIO staff on occasion suggested that an agency make formal or informal policy changes to accommodate the poor's program

---

[17] Present rather than future orientation is often cited as a characteristic of lower socioeconomic life style. See, for example, Elizabeth Herzog, "Some Assumptions About the Poor," *Social Service Review,* 37 (Dec., 1963), pp. 391–400; Lawrence L. LeShan, "Time Orientation and Social Class," *Journal of Abnormal and Social Psychology,* 47 (June, 1952), pp. 589–592; Lewis, *Children,* pp. xxvi–xxvii; and S. M. Miller, Frank Riessman and Arthur A. Seagull, "Poverty and Self-Indulgence: A Critique of the Non-Deferred Gratification Pattern," in Louis A. Ferman, Joyce L. Kornbluh and Alan Haber (eds.), *Poverty in America* (Ann Arbor: University of Michigan Press, 1965), pp. 285–302.

and participation expectations. Such encouragements and suggestions often brought "interloper" criticisms from officials who felt they had been dealing with social problems and the poor much longer than the PIO staff.[18]

How much power? As the Target Neighborhood participants became more comfortable with and practiced in new social roles in the committee complex, the issue of power introduced another PIO dilemma. Specifically, how much power could the poor have within the poverty program? What were the limits of "maximum feasible participation"? Who set the ceiling of power for the poor, and who re-sets that ceiling when inevitably it is reached? The Topeka OEO chose a particular structure and style, determined the balance of votes on the Board, and thus set the degree of organizational control available to the poor. But what if the power and control available to the indigent participants cannot keep pace with the growing skills, confidences and desires anticipated by the "Overlap Model"? Will the poor be forced to leave the program and form splinter groups or stay with it but "keep their place"? Will the participating poor pressure the PIO to restructure, yielding more formal control to them? What would be the not-poor participants' reaction to increased power for the poor? Paradoxically, the Topeka OEO may, over time, grow more bureaucratic, more identified with agencies and government, and become less favorable toward "participative democracy."[19] It is assumed that the "Overlap" experience will allow power shifts within the poverty program—the not-poor increasingly yielding to the more clearly focused and presented desires of the poor. But if that assumption is incorrect, or if the "Overlap Model" demands more time than the participants are

---

[18] The PIO's dual goal-sets (program *content* and participation *process*) and the diversity of membership in its committee complex make it difficult to isolate as a specific formal organization type. The PIO does, however, seem to fall into Etzioni's loose category of "multipurpose" organizations, and manifests the goal conflicts and staff-role strain he sees as unavoidable in that type (Amitai Etzioni, *Modern Organizations* [New Jersey: Prentice-Hall, 1964], pp. 14–16). Perhaps the complexity of the PIO as a formal organization type is best revealed by considering Blau and Scott's four classifications based upon "prime beneficiary": (1) "mutual benefit associations," where the prime beneficiary is the membership; (2) "business concerns," where the owners are prime beneficiary; (3) "service organizations," where the client group is the prime beneficiary; and (4) "commonweal organizations," where the prime beneficiary is the public-at-large (Blau and Scott, *Formal Organization*, p. 43). If one considers the process experience of the poor when participating in decisions which determine the conduct of the PIO, it becomes a "mutual benefit association." When one observes the do-*for*-the-poor inclinations of agency and local government participants, or the services rendered to the poor not participating in the committee complex the PIO becomes a "sevice organization." If one considers the staff rewards for management efficiency and positive cost-benefit analysis, the PIO loosely becomes a "business concern." Finally, if the poverty program is seen to be a benefit to the entire community, the PIO becomes a "commonweal organization." The chameleon quality of the PIO indicates the need for comparative research toward the more adequate typing of the PIO and other contemporary social intervention organizations.

[19] The PIO may follow the means-end goal displacement described in Sheldon L. Messinger, "Organizational Transformation," *American Sociological Review*, 20 (Feb., 1955), pp. 3–10.

willing to wait, then the Topeka OEO will be hard pressed to remain "on middle ground." At this writing, the question "How much power?" is gently being asked by some of the Target Neighborhood participants. The answers given by the Topeka OEO staff may be crucial for the future of the PIO.

Growth toward autonomy. The PIO's political style implied an attempt toward organizational solidarity. The director felt that all components of the committee complex should remain "within the fold." Thus the Target Neighborhood Committees were to consult with the Topeka OEO staff concerning scheduling of meetings, elections, agenda, developing of community action proposals, *etc.* But as the participating poor became more familiar with the poverty program, some of them felt the need to act, in small ways at first, more independently and to be less accountable to the PIO. The conflict between what is perceived by PIO staff to be "organizational integrity" and potentially increasing Target Neighborhood Committee push for autonomy could develop into a dilemma which, like the ceiling of power problem, might become a recurring dynamic.

The paradox of PIO success. Like any organization that must be funded externally and recurrently, the Topeka OEO was concerned with *demonstrating* its efficiency. The most tangible evidence for efficiency was the technically correct and successful preparation and implementation of OEO community action proposals. An extension of that criterion, one stimulated by the political style of the organization, was the rapid passing of a proposal through the PIO committee complex. But proposal producing is a wordy business. According to the *Annual Report,* the written information materials distributed to participants are "not measured by the sheet but by the inch."[20] The participating poor, not so practiced as the not-poor in skimming over such materials but nonetheless wanting to know what was happening in "their program" often impeded the "efficiency" of the proposal machinery. The poor's desire for "action now" does not mean action to the exclusion of their "say" in program determinations. Therefore, another dilemma faced the PIO—on the one hand, a commitment was made to involve the poor in the decision-making process; on the other hand, their involvement decreased the PIO's major measurable index of efficiency.[21] The Topeka OEO generally favored the former horn of the dilemma and consequently often was prompted by higher levels of OEO management to "get more programs going."

Community evaluation of the PIO's activities may also present paradoxical criteria for success. When the PIO accomplishes no social change (and thus actually is failing) the worst the staff usually can expect is community indifference. When change is engendered and consequently some anxieties and resistances aroused, the PIO may be negatively evaluated by community members. Ironically, the mark of the PIO's success for social change might be unpopularity—a situation that can be

[20] Topeka OEO, *Annual Report,* p. 5.
[21] Blau points out that an organization overconcerned with efficiency easily becomes impatient with the slowness of the democratic process (Peter M. Blau, *Bureaucracy in Modern Society* [New York: Random House, 1956], pp. 105–110).

extremely stressful to staff members who identify with or have "roots" in the community.

CONCLUSION

The Topeka OEO is a specific PIO in a specific community—thus generalizations are left to the discretion of the reader. Differing from the Alinsky[22] approach (which generally excludes community agencies) and the "city hall" approach (which generally excludes the poor), the Topeka OEO has been shown to be a PIO striving to maintain a "functional marginality" between the poor and not-poor and, employing a political organizational style, attempting to bring poor and not-poor together in order to implement an "Overlap Model" for social change.[23]

To maintain functional marginality and keep the "Overlap Model" operating demands rather unique organizational dynamics. The PIO must be durable under recurring stress and crises, and must remain flexible and innovative—adaptable in its expectations and assumptions so that it may accommodate social change. If operating as planned, it must expect to be a vortex of community controversy and be able to resist resultant pressures and temptations to identify exclusively either with the poor or with the power structure. The PIO must be considered temporary, someday to be obsolete, and therefore it must attempt to avoid the goal displacement that usually accompanies longevity and expansion. In short, the PIO as considered in this paper must be an atypical organization, as changeable as the change it hopes to stimulate. Whether or not such an organization can endure toward its defined goals, whether or not it can remain functionally marginal without becoming marginally functional, is at this point still an hypothesis being tested.

[22] Alinsky, *op. cit.*

[23] The logistics of the Topeka OEO have not been within the scope of this paper. It should be mentioned, however, that the PIO presently coordinates ten assorted federally funded programs totalling $800,000 and has employed two hundred full and part-time employees from the Target Neighborhoods.

26

THE POVERTY BOARD: SOME CONSEQUENCES OF "MAXIMUM FEASIBLE PARTICIPATION"*

LOUIS A. ZURCHER, JR.
The University of Texas at Austin

THE ECONOMIC OPPORTUNITY ACT OF 1964, under a section providing for the development of local Community Action Programs, stated that such programs were to be "developed, conducted, and administered with the maximum feasible participation of residents of the areas and members of the groups to be served."[1] Both the origin and the meaning of that mandate were, at least initially, rather unclear.[2] As the act was implemented across the Nation, ad-hoc interpretations of the degree and kind of participation open to the poor engendered dramatic controversy, particularly concerning the representation, selection, and decision-making power of the poor on the policy-formulating "poverty boards" which governed local Community Action Programs.[3] Congress subsequently attempted to resolve how many poor constituted "maximum feasi-

* This research was supported by the Office of Economic Opportunity (Grant 66–9744) and was conducted while the author was a staff member of the Division of Social Science Research, the Menninger Foundation, Topeka, Kansas. The cooperation of Robert C. Harder and Simon Martinez, both formerly with the Topeka Office of Economic Opportunity, is gratefully acknowledged. The author also expresses his appreciation to William Simons, Susan Zurcher, Fred Hill, Rosanne Barnhill, Basil Keiser, and Janice Boldridge for their research assistance, and to Drs. William Key, James Taylor, Gardner Muphy, Ivan Belknap, Charles Bonjean, and Norval Glenn for their helpful comments. Final analysis of the data and manuscript preparation were supported by a grant from the Hogg Foundation for Mental Health, the University of Texas, Dr. Robert Sutherland, Director. Without the generous cooperation of the members of the Economic Opportunity Board of Shawnee County, Kansas, Incorporated, the study would not have been possible.

[1] Economic Opportunity Act of 1964, 78 Stat. 508, Sec. 202 (a).

[2] Lillian Rubin, "Maximum Feasible Participation: The Origins, Implications, and Present Status," *Poverty and Human Resources Abstracts*, 2 (November–December, 1967), pp. 5–18.

[3] See, for example: Richard A. Cloward, "The War on Poverty: Are the Poor Left Out?" *Nation* 201 (August 2, 1965), pp. 55–60; Barbara Carter, "Sargent Shriver and the Role of the Poor," *Reporter*, 35 (May 5, 1966), pp. 18–19; William C. Selover, "Federal Pressure Felt: U.S. Poor Gain Foothold in Local Programs," *Christian Science Monitor* (August 2, 1966), p. 10; Erwin Knoll and Jules Whitcover, "Fighting Poverty—and City Hall," *Reporter*, 32 (June 3, 1965), pp. 19–22; Erwin Knoll and Jules Whitcover, "Policies and the Poor: Shriver's Second Thoughts," *Reporter*, 33 (December 30, 1965), pp. 23–25; Woody Klein, "People vs. Politicians: Defeat in Harlem," *Nation*, 199 (July 27, 1964), pp. 27–29; William C. Selover, "Old Ways Bind Poverty Drive," *Christian Science Monitor* (August 3, 1966), p. 1; David Sanford, "The Poor in Their Place," *New Republic*, 153 (November 20, 1965), pp. 5–6; and "The Controversy over the Federal Antipoverty Program: Pro and Con," *Congressional Digest*, 45 (March, 1966).

† Published in this volume, by permission of the Society for the Psychological Study of Social Issues, from duplicate manuscript prepared by the author for publication in the *Journal of Social Issues* 26 (Summer, 1970).

ble participation" by amending the Economic Opportunity Act, and declaring that no Community Action Program would be funded unless at least one-third of its board membership were representatives of the poor.[4] At the same time, Congress attempted to clarify criteria for board membership, specifying that "the representatives of the poor shall be selected by the residents of areas of concentration of poverty, with special emphasis on participation by residents of the area who are poor."[5]

Rubin suggests that the "maximum feasible participation" idea had a social history prior to its becoming a legislative mandate.[6] Involvement of the beneficiaries in program determination, emphasis upon "self-help," and the importance of local autonomy and responsibility were all conceptual cornerstones and practical realities in, for example: the U.S. projects for underdeveloped countries,[7] the militant civil-rights movement,[8] and domestic community-development programs such as those of Saul Alinsky,[9] the Ford Foundation,[10] Harlem Youth Opportunities Unlimited,[11] and Mobilization for Youth.[12]

The framers of the Economic Opportunity Act, several of whom had been associated with programs listed above, at least implicitly assumed that "maximum feasible participation" of the poor in OEO Community Action Programs would have both *instrumental* and *social-psychological* results over and above the benefits of expanded and improved services. The impact of participation would be instrumental in the sense that numbers of the poor united in social action would provide the political and strategic leverage necessary to open closed opportunity structures. The impact would be social-psychological in the sense that active and meaningful involvement in programs which get results would foster changes in participant self-concept, motivational structure, and in fact "change the poor who were produced by the system."[13] This paper will be concerned

[4] Economic Opportunity Amendments of 1966, 80 Stat. 1451, Sec. 203 (c) 2.

[5] Economic Opportunity Amendments of 1966, 80 Stat. 1451, Sec. 203 (c) 3.

[6] Rubin, *op. cit.*, pp. 7–9.

[7] Peter Kuenstler, "Urban Community Center Work in Underdeveloped Countries," *Community Development*, 1 (1958), pp. 27–31; Ibrahim Shamin, "The Role of Lay Leaders," *Community Development*, 3 (1959), pp. 81–87.

[8] John H. Wheeler, "Civil Rights Groups—Their Impact Upon the War on Poverty," *Law and Contemporary Problems*, 31 (Winter, 1966), pp. 152–158.

[9] James Ridgeway, "Saul Alinsky in Smugtown," *New Republic*, 152 (June 26, 1965), pp. 15–17; Charles E. Silberman, *Crisis in Black and White* (New York: Vintage Books, 1964), pp. 308–355; Frank Riessman, "A Comparison of Two Social Action Approaches: Saul Alinsky and the New Student Left," Department of Psychiatry, Albert Einstein College of Medicine, New York, September, 1965, Mimeographed.

[10] *American Community Development: Preliminary Reports by Directors of Projects Assisted by the Ford Foundation in Four Cities and a State* (New York: Ford Foundation, Office of Reports, 1964); *Stirrings in the Big Cities: The Great Cities Projects* (New York: Ford Foundation, Office of Reports, 1964).

[11] *The Federal Delinquency Program: Objectives and Operation under the President's Committee on Juvenile Delinquency and Youth Crime* (Washington, D.C.: U.S. Government Printing Office, 1962).

[12] *Ibid.*

[13] Daniel P. Moynihan, "Three Problems in Combatting Poverty," in Margaret S. Gordon, ed., *Poverty in America* (Scranton: Chandler Publishing Company, 1965), pp. 41–53.

with the latter of the two assumptions—with hypotheses generated from the expectation for social-psychological changes among participants in OEO Community Action Programs.

A number of experimental small-group studies, not directly concerned with the poor or poverty intervention, have demonstrated in general that a member's experience of meaningful influence in group decision tends to strengthen his satisfaction with membership, enhance his self-image, and facilitate changes in his attitudes.[14]

Recently, a paper by Gottesfeld and Dozier reported an empirical measurement of social-psychological change among a cohort of poor as a function of their active participation in an OEO Community Action Program. The authors found a statistically significant decrease in feelings of powerlessness as measured by Rotter's I-E Scale,[15] showed an association of that decrease with length of service as an indigenous community organizer, and interpreted their over-all findings to indicate "that the aims of community action programs in making the poor more hopeful and ambitious about what they can do in their own behalf are being realized."[16]

The research upon which the present paper is based included as subjects the members of an OEO poverty board and tested two primary hypotheses. First, that board members who were representatives of the poor would differ significantly from members who were not representatives of the poor in social-psychological variables, often associated with socioeconomic status, which are indicative of their general sense of competence and confidence vis-à-vis society, broadly defined. Second, that as a result of their participation in the decision-making processes of the board and its associated committees, the representatives of the poor would show significant changes in those social-psychological variables.

More specifically, it was hypothesized that board members who were representatives of the poor would be significantly *lower* than the other board members in annual family income, membership in voluntary associations, formal education, activism, achievement orientation, and future orientation—and significantly *higher* in anomie, integration with relatives, isolation, normlessness, powerlessness, alienation, and particu-

[14] See, for example: Kurt Lewin, "Group Decision and Social Change," in T. H. Newcomb and E. L. Hartley, eds., *Readings in Social Psychology* (New York: Holt, 1947), pp. 330–344; L. Coch and J. R. P. French, "Overcoming Resistance to Change," *Human Relations*, 1 (1948), pp. 512–532; J. Levine and J. Butler, "Lecture versus Group Discussion in Changing Behavior," *Journal of Applied Psychology*, 36 (1952), pp. 29–33; N. R. F. Maier, "The Quality of Group Decisions as Influenced by the Discussion Leader," *Human Relations*, 3 (1950), pp. 155–174; M. G. Preston and R. K. Heintz, "Effects of Participatory versus Supervisory Leadership on Group Judgment," *Journal of Abnormal and Social Psychology*, 44 (1949), pp. 345–355; Kurt Lewin, *Field Theory in Social Science* (New York: Harper, 1951).

[15] J. B. Rotter, "Generalized Expectancies of Internal versus External Control of Reinforcement," *Psychological Monographs*, 80 (1966), No. 609.

[16] Harry Gottesfeld and Gerterlyn Dozier, "Changes in Feelings of Powerlessness in a Community Action Program," *Psychological Reports*, 19 (1966), p. 978.

larism.[17] It was also hypothesized that, for representatives of the poor, participation would be associated with significant *increases* in activism, achievement orientation, and future orientation—and with significant *decreases* in anomie, integration with relatives, isolation, normlessness, powerlessness, alienation, and particularism. No significant changes were hypothesized for the participating board members who were not representatives of the poor.

It was further hypothesized that for the poor the degree of change on the variables to be measured would be related to the quality of participation, length of participation, and willingness to continue participation.

SETTING FOR THE STUDY

On May 1, 1965, the Topeka (Kansas) Welfare Planning Council, a volunteer citizens' group with a demonstrated interest in local social problems, was awarded a community-action planning grant by the Office of Economic Opportunity, Washington, D.C. (OEO). The council summarily established and staffed the Topeka Office of Economic Opportunity (TOEO), which was to be the "community-action agency" responsible for developing and administering assorted poverty projects available under the Economic Opportunity Act.

The Welfare Planning Council and the Topeka OEO staff together designed a committee complex intended to involve a wide representation of the Topeka citizenry, poor and nonpoor. The committee complex in-

[17] Some previous studies which illustrate various social-psychological characteristics of the poor are: M. Beiser, "Poverty, Social Disintegration and Personality," *Journal of Social Issues,* 21 (1965), pp. 56–78; B. J. Boose and S. S. Boose, "Some Personality Characteristics of the Culturally Disadvantaged," *Journal of Psychology,* 66 (1967), pp. 157–162; W. Bell, "Anomie, Social Isolation and Class Structure," *Sociometry,* 20 (1957), pp. 105–116; W. C. Haggstrom, "The Power of the Poor," in F. Riessman, J. Cohen, and A. Pearl, eds., *Mental Health of the Poor* (Glencoe, Ill.: Free Press, 1964), pp. 205–223; E. Herzog, "Some Assumptions About the Poor," *Social Service Review,* 37 (1963), pp. 391–400; L. LeShan, "Time Orientation and Social Class," *Journal of Abnormal and Social Psychology,* 47 (1952), pp. 589–592; O. Lewis, *The Children of Sanchez* (New York: Random House, 1961), and *La Vida* (New York: Random House, 1966); H. McClosky and J. Schaar, "Psychological Dimensions of Anomie," *American Sociological Review,* 30 (1965), pp. 14–40; W. B. Miller, "Focal Concerns of Lower Class Culture," in L. Ferman, J. Kornbluh, and A. Haber, eds., *Poverty in America* (Ann Arbor: University of Michigan Press, 1965), pp. 261–270; F. Riessman, "The Strengths of the Poor," in A. Shostak and W. Gomberg, eds., *New Perspectives on Poverty* (Englewood Cliffs, N.J.: Prentice-Hall, 1966), pp. 40–47; B. Rosen and A. D'Andrade, "Psychosocial Origins of Achievement Motivation," *Sociometry,* 22 (1959), pp. 185–218; R. L. Simpson and M. Miller, "Social Status and Alienation," *Social Problems,* 10 (1963), pp. 256–264; G. Sjoberg, R. Brymer, and B. Farris, "Bureaucracy and the Lower Class," *Sociology and Social Research,* 50 (1966), pp. 325–337; I. Stone, D. Leighton, and A. H. Leighton, "Poverty and the Individual," in L. Fishman, ed., *Poverty Amid Affluence* (New Haven: Yale University Press, 1966), pp. 72–97; M. Strauss, "Deferred Gratification, Social Class, and the Achievement Syndrome," *American Sociological Review,* 27 (1962), pp. 326–335; C. Wright and H. Hyman, "Voluntary Association Memberships of American Adults," *American Sociological Review,* 23 (1958), pp. 284–294.

cluded three major types: Study Committees, Target Neighborhood Committees, and the Economic Opportunity Board.

Eleven Study Committees, each dealing with a specific topic (for example, employment, housing, recreation), were to assess community needs and resources and to make appropriate recommendations concerning future poverty programing. Committee members were to be topic specialists and low-income area representatives, and each committee was to have its own officers.

The council and the Topeka OEO staff had designated twelve "target neighborhoods" in sections of the city which manifested indices of poverty. Each target neighborhood was to have a Target Neighborhood Committee, whose members and elected officers would be area residents. The Target Neighborhood Committees were to serve as forums for the expression of neighborhood needs and problems.

The third committee component was to be the Economic Opportunity Board, and would be the central decision-making body for the Topeka poverty program. The voting members of the board were to be: the chairmen of Study Committees; the chairmen and vice-chairmen of Target Neighborhood Committees; representatives from local government, agencies, businesses, and professions; and representatives from religious, civic, and civil-rights groups. As initially structured, the board was to have a maximum of seventy-five voting members, of whom at least one-third were to be representatives of the poor. When functionally possible, the board was to be incorporated, the Topeka OEO staff were to become its employees, and the Welfare Planning Council was to terminate its role as a steering body. The board then would have general responsibility for planning, developing, implementing, and coordinating subsequent OEO poverty projects.[18]

By October, 1965, the committee complex was functioning, sixty-four member slots had been allotted, the board had been incorporated, and several poverty projects were being formulated.

The planners of the Topeka poverty program had deliberately designed the committee complex to attract diverse community representation and particularly to provide opportunity for involvement of the poor in all aspects of the program. They anticipated that "community action programs would be generated and articulated *by* the low income person, not *for* the low income person" and that such participation would develop "leadership and confidence" among the participating poor, who should consequently "begin to assume a more active and creative part in society."[19] Participation in the program, especially in the decision-mak-

[18] For a more complete report of the development of the Topeka poverty program, see: Louis A. Zurcher, "Implementing a Community Action Agency," in Milton Shore and F. V. Mannino, eds., *Community Mental Health: Problems, Programs, and Strategies* (New York: Behavioral Publications, 1969). A detailed description of the Topeka OEO organizational structure is presented in the *Topeka OEO Annual Report for 1965–1966*, Topeka, Kansas, Office of Economic Opportunity, 1966, Mimeographed.

[19] *Topeka OEO Annual Report for 1965–1966, op. cit.*, pp. 6-8.

ing processes of the Economic Opportunity Board, was viewed by the planners as an "important means" for the poor "to become middle-class," not only in material resources but in attitudes and orientations as well.[20]

METHOD OF STUDY

The author began a study of the Topeka OEO poverty-intervention organization, and its impact for individual and social change, in September, 1965. As part of that broader research, the author and a minimum of three research-staff members attended as nonparticipating observers all of the board's meetings (nineteen regular and seventeen executive sessions) from its incorporation in October, 1965, until the completion of the study in May, 1967. Member statements, interactions, and emotional tones were independently noted by each observer, and his record subsequently compared with those of the other observers and with official board records for accuracy, validity, and reliability. Formal, open-ended interviews were conducted at least twice with all board members, and the key participants were informally interviewed as many as one hundred times. Research staff had ample opportunity for close and sustained contact with board members, particularly with the Target Neighborhood officers, both in and out of board sessions.

In November, 1966, after the research staff agreed that more noticeable research intervention would not be disruptive to board dynamics, a questionnaire was administered individually to board members. In addition to biographical items and questions assessing extent of program participation, the questionnaire included the following scales:

(a) *Kahl Activism Scale*—sense of mastery over the physical and social environment[21]
(b) *Srole Anomie Scale*—social malintegration; the internalized counterpart of social dysfunction[22]
(c) *Kahl Integration with Relatives Scale*—degree of dependence upon family[23]
(d) *Rosen Achievement Value Orientation Scale*—value for and motivation toward academic and occupational achievement, particularly regarding striving for status through social mobility[24]
(e) *Future Orientation Items*—Three items drawn from the Kahl

---

[20] *Ibid.*, p. 73. The assumptions of the planners of the Topeka poverty program concerning the impact of committee participation upon the representatives of the poor have earlier been conceptualized as "The Overlap Model for Social Change." See: Louis A. Zurcher and William H. Key, "The Overlap Model: A Comparison of Strategies for Social Change," *Sociological Quarterly*, 8 (Winter, 1968), pp. 85–97.

[21] Joseph A. Kahl, "Some Measurements of Achievement Motivation," *American Journal of Sociology*, 70 (1965), pp. 669–681.

[22] Leo Srole, "Social Integration and Certain Corollaries: An Exploratory Study," *American Sociological Review*, 21 (December, 1956), pp. 709–717.

[23] Kahl, *op. cit.*, p. 674.

[24] Bernard C. Rosen, "The Achievement Syndrome: A Psychocultural Dimension of Social Stratification," *American Sociological Review*, 21 (April, 1956), pp. 203–211.

Activism Scale which, based upon face validity, were taken to indicate willingness to plan for the future: (1) Nowadays a person has to live pretty much for today and let tomorrow take care of itself. (2) How important is it to know clearly in advance your plans for the future? (3) Planning only makes a person unhappy since your plans hardly ever work out anyway.[25]

(f) *Dean Isolation Subscale*—feeling of separation from the majority group or its standards[26]

(g) *Dean Normlessness Subscale*—feeling of purposelessness; absence of values that might give direction to life[27]

(h) *Dean Powerlessness Subscale*—feeling of helplessness; inability to understand or influence the events upon which one depends[28]

(i) *Dean Alienation Scale*—sum total of isolation, normlessness, and powerlessness subscales; taken to indicate a general syndrome of alienation[29]

(j) *Stouffer-Toby Role Conflict Scale*—value orientation toward institutionalized obligations of friendship (particularism) versus value orientation toward institutionalized obligations to society (universalism)[30]

A few of the items measuring activism, anomie, achievement orientation, or future orientation were indentical on two or more of those scales. In the present study, such items appeared only once on the questionnaire, but were scored as appropriate for each scale. All questionnaire items were randomly ordered. Administration I responses were analyzed for significant differences between members who were representatives of the poor and those who were not.

To test the hypotheses of participation-stimulated member change in variables measured by the scales, the questionnaire was readministered (Administration II) in May, 1967, to board members who had responded to Administration I. Scale scores resulting from the two administrations were compared for significant indices of change.

Based upon observational and interview data, the quality of member participation (that is, attendance, activity, leadership, offices held) in board and associated meetings was assessed. Upon concurrence by research staff, board members were classified as either "active" or "inactive" participants, and respondents in those categories were compared for differences and changes in scale scores. Since some of the Administration I respondents who had resigned or been eliminated from board membership nonetheless agreed to respond to Administration II, "stayers" were compared with "leavers" for differences and changes in scale scores.

25 Kahl, *op. cit.*, p. 680.
26 Dwight G. Dean, "Alienation: Its Meaning and Measurement," *American Sociological Review*, 26 (October, 1961), pp. 753–758.
27 *Ibid.*, pp. 755–756.
28 *Ibid.*, pp. 754–755.
29 *Ibid.*, pp. 756–757.
30 Samuel A. Stouffer and Jackson Toby, "Role Conflict and Personality," *American Journal of Sociology*, 56 (March, 1951), pp. 395–406.

Analyses of Administration I and Administration II versus I responses by sex, ethnic group, and board-member subtype were performed and are introduced when relevant. Scale scores were intercorrelated, and the matrices are presented.

RESULTS AND DISCUSSION

Administration I: portrait of the poverty board. Sixty-one board members completed questionnaires for Administration I. Of the respondents, twenty-three were Target Neighborhood Committee Officers (representatives of the poor; hereafter TNOs); thirty-eight were government or agency officials, businessmen, professionals, religious and civic leaders, and the like (Non-TNOs). Of the TNOs, twelve were male and eleven were female; eight were Anglo-American, ten were Negro-American, three were Mexican-American, and two were American Indian. The median annual family income for TNOs was from $3,000 to $5,000, with 44% earning less than $3,000 annually. Median level of formal education was high-school graduate, with 40% being high-school dropouts. Of the Non-TNOs, thirty-four were male and four were female; thirty-two were Anglo-American, three were Negro-American, and three were Mexican-American. The median annual family income was $7,000+, and the median level of formal education was college graduate, with 45% having done graduate work. Differences between TNO and Non-TNO median annual family income, level of formal education, and membership in voluntary associations (TNO = 2; Non-TNO = 4) were statistically significant ($p <$ .01).[31] TNO medians for age (46 yrs), board attendance (4 meetings), length of Topeka residency (29 yrs), and time as board member (8 months) did not differ significantly from Non-TNO medians for age (43 yrs), board attendance (4 meetings), length of Topeka residency (21 yrs), and time as board member (10 months).[32]

Table 1 reveals striking and consistent differences between TNOs and Non-TNOs in the social-psychological variables measured by Administration I. The differences are statistically significant in the directions expected. That is, TNOs scored lower than Non-TNOs in activism, achievement orientation, and future orientation, but higher than Non-TNOs in anomie, isolation, normlessness, powerlessness, alienation, and particularism.

There are more than one thousand OEO poverty boards distributed throughout the United States. Topeka's Economic Opportunity Board is assumed to be fairly typical of the others, though it has a larger membership than most. At minimum, boards are similar in that they all *must* have no less than one-third of their members representative of and selected by residents in poverty areas. Since the balance of members usually is drawn from higher socioeconomic strata, it can be hypothesized that

---

31 Wilcoxon Rank Sum Test, one-tailed. See: Frank Wilcoxon, S. K. Katti, and Roberta A. Wilcox, *Critical Values and Probability Levels for the Wilcoxon Rank Sum Test and the Wilcoxon Signed Rank Test*, American Cyanamid Company and Florida State University, August, 1963.
32 Wilcoxon Rank Sum Test, two-tailed. *Ibid.*

TABLE 1

Comparison of TNO and Non-TNO Median Scale Scores
for Administration I (N = 61)

Scale[a]	TNO (N = 23)	Non-TNO (N = 38)	Sig. of Difference[b]
Activism	17.0	18.5	$p < .01$
Anomie	6.0	4.0	$p < .01$
Integration with relatives	2.5	2.0	NS
Achievement orientation	15.0	17.0	$p < .01$
Future orientation	9.0	10.0	$p < .05$
Isolation	16.0	13.0	$p < .01$
Normlessness	10.0	6.0	$p < .01$
Powerlessness	15.0	12.0	$p < .01$
Alienation	40.0	32.0	$p < .01$
Particularism	1.5	0.0	$p < .02$

[a] Not used as Guttman Scales.
[b] Wilcoxon Rank Sum Test, one-tailed. See footnote 31.

social-psychological differences, paralleling those manifested in the Topeka Economic Opportunity Board and presented in Table 1, will exist among the total membership of a given board. What effects would such differences have upon board dynamics, particularly upon the processes of decision making? How might such differences influence members' perceptions of one another and of the board's means and ends? Poverty boards have been characterized as "conflict-ridden." To what extent is such conflict a function of members' disparate definitions of the situation, influenced by differing attitudes toward self-in-society?

Observations of meetings of the Economic Opportunity Board and interviews with the participants revealed patterns of member behavior which reflected TNO/Non-TNO differences in scale variables. The following are some examples of issues around which debate, sometimes heated, centered during early board meetings. The scale variable which seems most closely related to each issue is indicated in parentheses.

Non-TNOs tended to view the local poverty program as they might any organized community program—optimistically, and confident that their efforts would bring results beneficial to the community. They took their participation, and the fact that such participation would be meaningful, for granted. TNOs initially seemed pessimistic about the meaningfulness of their participation, and expressed the feeling that their efforts would most likely not bring results (activism). Non-TNOs appeared convinced that community officials wanted to help with the programs, and they wanted to invite their cooperation. TNOs seemed to feel that most local officials actually didn't care about the poor and that officials in general were guilty until proven innocent (anomie). Non-TNOs appeared influenced by a conviction that, with dedicated and concerted work, those community factors which perpetuated poverty could be changed and that the local program could be made into the best in the country. TNOs at first did not seem as certain that the system could be changed, nor that it would be judicious to exert as much energy as the program was calling for, since the rewards were at that time rather unclear (achievement orientation). Non-TNOs appeared quite tolerant of program delays endemic to bureaucratic process and argued for the importance of "long-range programing," "feasibility studies," and the like. TNOs seemed markedly impatient with such delays and insisted upon "action now" (future orientation). Non-TNOs tended to identify with the community as a whole and wanted to link the board with as many other community components as would be workable. TNOs seemed often to indicate perception of a "have versus have-not" or an "us versus them" struggle, and at the onset they seemed to avoid identifying with the community (isolation). Non-TNOs tended to believe that if the board conformed to OEO standards, if they met the criteria for community need, and if their applications were prepared according to rules and regulations specified by OEO, they could with some confidence expect grants for additional local poverty projects (contingent upon the availability of federal funds). TNOs, on the other hand, did not initially seem willing to invest the rules, regulations, criteria, or procedures with purposeful value nor to accept the relative predictability of outcome from conformity to those norms (normlessness). Non-TNOs appeared to be satisfied with their degree of individual influence in board decision-making processes and with the potential impact of those decisions for community change. TNOs did not seem to feel that board action would change much for the poor nor that their own influence within board decision-making processes was significant (powerlessness). Non-TNOs tended to accept other board members or cooperating officials on the basis of title and to encourage the impartial and objective hiring of program staff. TNOs tended to favor evaluation of others not on the basis of title but rather according to "what kind of guy he was" and to insist that one should give jobs to people he knew or to whom he was related (particularism).[33]

Similar issues pivotal to controversy and debate might be expected in other poverty boards in which TNOs (or their counterparts) and Non-TNOs significantly differ in social-psychological variables such as those measured in this study. Also, it might be anticipated that, as was the case in the Economic Opportunity Board, Non-TNOs will tend to dominate the early meetings—perhaps not advertently but by virtue of their familiarity with, and skills and attitudes related to, the structure and functions of formal meetings.

The differences between TNOs and Non-TNOs presented in Table 1

---

[33] More detailed descriptions of issues that were sources of debate, and their relationships to scale variables, are presented in Louis A. Zurcher, *Poverty Warriors: The Human Experience of Planned Social Intervention* (Austin and London: University of Texas Press, 1970). For another view of conflict in a poverty program, see: Ralph Segalman, "Dramatis Personae of the Community Action Program: A 'Built-In' Conflict Situation," *Rocky Mountain Social Science Journal*, 4 (October, 1967), pp. 140–150.

illustrate the complex task confronting an OEO community-action agency like the Topeka OEO. If the agency has implemented the federal mandate, it will have populated its poverty board with poor and nonpoor and thus probably will have established a social situation in which conflict is inevitable. Such conflict certainly is intended to have social benefit and to have potential for engendering social change.[34] But it is nonetheless conflict, and the community-action agency is expected to be the mediator. The agency, as did the Topeka OEO, would purport to be a "bridge" between the TNOs and Non-TNOs, would attempt to coordinate their efforts in the board, and would acquire consensus concerning ways and means of poverty programing. Thus, particularly in the beginning phases of board operation, the staff of a community-action agency may find themselves attempting to relate to and satisfy the demands of both poor and nonpoor members, possibly to the satisfaction of neither.[35]

Finally, TNO/Non-TNO differences highlight the fact that board dynamics can represent much more than the manifest aspects of program content. The dynamics can reflect a fission or a fusion of world views, and the travails of socialization. The experience of board *process*, particularly for TNOs, may be more meaningful (or frustrating) than the *content* of board proceedings.

OEO training programs for the staff of community-action agencies and for board members might profit from including in their curricula not only discussions of the content of poverty programs and of the formal roles for participants, but discussions of participant interaction, perceptions, and process experiences. Another point for training discussion, and a research hypothesis as well, would be that the kinds of social-psychological differences which exist between TNOs and Non-TNOs might obtain between TNOs and those poverty-area residents who are not OEO indigenous leaders or who are not participating in OEO activities. Patterns of issue-related conflicts among those groups might parallel conflicts seen between TNO and Non-TNO board members.[36]

Further analyses revealed that TNO males differed significantly ($p <$ .05)[37] from TNO females only in isolation (male median = 14; female median = 18.5) and in annual family income (male median = \$3/5,000; female median = \$0/3,000.) There were no significant differences between male and female Non-TNOs. Significant ($p < .05$)[38] ethnic dif-

[34] See, for example: Lewis Coser, *The Social Functions of Conflict* (Glencoe, Ill.: Free Press, 1956); and Ralph Lane, Jr., "Sociological Aspects of Mental Well-Being," in *Mental Health in a Changing Community* (New York: Grune and Stratton, 1966), pp. 43–45.

[35] The complexity of a community-action agency's task is further detailed in Louis A. Zurcher, "Functional Marginality: Dynamics of a Poverty Intervention Organization," *Southwestern Social Science Quarterly*, 48 (December, 1967), pp. 411–421.

[36] Louis A. Zurcher, "Walking the Tightrope: Some Role and Value Conflicts Experienced by a Poverty Program's Indigenous Leaders," paper presented at the meetings of the American Sociological Association, Miami Beach, Florida, August, 1966.

[37] Wilcoxon Rank Sum Test, two-tailed. See footnote 31.

[38] Kruskal-Wallis One-Way Analysis of Variance. See: Sidney Seigel, *Nonparametric Statistics for the Behavioral Sciences* (New York: McGraw-Hill, 1956), pp. 184-194.

ferences were found among TNO medians for activism (A = 17.5; NA = 16.0; MA = 16.5; I = 14),[39] normlessness (A = 8; NA = 10; MA = 13; I = 14.5), and powerlessness (A = 15; NA = 17.5; MA = 15; I = 12). No significant ethnic differences were found among Non-TNO medians. Though the number of subjects was quite small within each ethnic sub-division, there was enough variation among scale scores among the sub-divisions to hypothesize for further research that median TNO scale scores may be influenced by the proportion of ethnic representation. The same hypothesis may be offered for the proportion of TNO males and fe-males. If TNO sex and ethnic factors are broadly related to social-psy-chological variables such as those measured here, then poverty boards might expect such differences to stimulate controversy over program issues among TNOs themselves, as well as between TNOs and Non-TNOs. It has been observed that no significant sex or ethnic differences existed among the Non-TNOs. Again, though the number of subjects was very small, it might cautiously be concluded that the differences in social-psychological variables reported here are more closely related to socio-economic factors than to sex or ethnic factors, but that the influence of sex and ethnic factors becomes more apparent among the TNO group.

Table 2 presents correlations among scale variables, age, income, educa-tion, and voluntary associations for all board members in Administration I. As might be expected, activism, achievement orientation, future orienta-tion, annual family income, formal education, and membership in volun-tary associations are positively related to one another and negatively related to anomie, integration with relatives, isolation, normlessness, powerlessness, alienation, and particularism. The latter variables are all positively related. The correlation coefficients among anomie, achievement orientation, and future orientation are escalated by those items which the scales have in common. Similarly, the correlation coefficient signifying the relationship of alienation to each of its subscales (isolation, normlessness, and powerlessness) reflects the representation of the subscale items in the total alienation-scale score. Respondents' age was not notably related to the other variables.

These data support findings of the scales' authors concerning the inter-relationships among the specific variables measured, and the relationships of the variables to socioeconomic level. The data further illustrate the directions of differences between TNO and Non-TNO board members.

Though the correlations were not statistically significant and were of a very low order, TNO board attendance and time as member were posi-tively related to activism, achievement orientation, and future orientation, and were negatively related to isolation, normlessness, and alienation. The relations cannot be considered change data, but may have indicated the direction of changes which were taking place as a result of subsequent program participation.

Administration II: indices of change. In May, 1967, the questionnaire was again given to all of the Administration I respondents who were ac-

[39] A=Anglo-American; NA=Negro-American; MA=Mexican-American; I=Amer-ican Indian.

TABLE 2

Correlations among Scale Variables, Age, Income, Education, and Voluntary Associations (Administration I)[a]

	Age	Act.	Ano.	Rel.	Ach.	Fut.	Iso.	Nor.	Pow.	Ali.	Par.	Inc.	Edu.
Age	—												
Activism	-.04	—											
Anomie	.10	-.71*	—										
Integration with relatives	.02	-.21	.20	—									
Achievement orientation	-.16	.73*	-.72*	-.34*	—								
Future orientation	.07	.79*	-.80*	-.28**	.72*	—							
Isolation	.02	-.35*	.52*	.30**	-.46*	-.46*	—						
Normlessness	-.01	-.57*	.54*	.25**	-.56*	-.51*	.35*	—					
Powerlessness	.03	-.47*	.57*	.24	-.53*	-.48*	.65*	.62*	—				
Alienation	.02	-.55*	.65*	.31**	-.62*	-.57*	.80*	.77*	.92*	—			
Particularism	.22	-.10	.06	.14	-.13	-.04	.09	.20	.21	.20	—		
Annual family income	-.19	.49*	-.48*	.04	.55*	.42*	-.31**	-.29**	-.42*	-.41*	-.16	—	
Formal education	-.19	.30**	-.27**	-.01	.41*	.23	-.19	-.25**	-.16	-.23	-.17	.51*	—
Voluntary-association membership	-.03	.13	-.22	-.06	.12	.11	-.19	-.11	-.10	-.16	.05	.20	.40*

[a] Pearson r; $N = 61$; $df = 59$.
* $p < .01$
** $p < .05$

cessible and willing. Forty-three Administration I respondents completed questionnaires for Administration II—eighteen TNOs and twenty-five Non-TNOs. Of the TNOs, seven were male and eleven were female; three were Anglo-American, ten were Negro-American, three were Mexican-American, and two were American Indian. Of the Non-TNOs, twenty-one were male and four were female; twenty-three were Anglo-American, and two were Mexican-American. TNO and Non-TNO differences in annual family income, level of formal education, membership in voluntary associations, age, and length of Topeka residency were virtually identical to the differences found in Administration I. Non-TNOs again were significantly higher than TNOs in income, education, and voluntary-association membership. The medians for board attendance (TNO = 10 meetings; Non-TNO = 11 meetings) and time as board member (TNO = 17 months; Non-TNO = 20 months) of course increased, but still without significant differences between the two groups.

The board, particularly the Non-TNO representation, had been restructured by March, 1967, as required in amendments to the Economic Opportunity Act. The restructuring at least in part explains the decrease in respondents from among the Non-TNO group. Among the forty-three Administration II respondents were eight TNOs and thirteen Non-TNOs who had terminated board membership at some time subsequent to their having completed Administration I.

Administration II was conducted to provide indices of change and, unlike Administration I (which included all but three of the board members), cannot be considered a "portrait" of the poverty board. Administration II did not include new board members for whom Administration I data were missing, and thus did not include all of the then current board members.

During the seven months between Administration I and Administration II, twelve board meetings were held, supported by ten meetings of the board's Executive Committee (all TNO chairmen, all Study Committee chairmen). Each Target Neighborhood Committee met at least monthly, and several of the Study Committees held three or more meetings. Many board members, particularly TNOs, formally and informally discussed and formulated poverty projects with an assortment of local officials. The board's agenda included such issues as Head Start, Neighborhood Youth Corps, Day Care Centers, a Beautification Project, an Extension Worker Program, and a Neighborhood Center. Considerable debate and concentrated member interaction focused around the development, implementation, or maintenance of those and other programs, whose total budget approached $1 million. During the seven months between Administration I and Administration II, therefore, TNOs and Non-TNOs were continually and often deeply involved in board and related activities. More than twice as many board meetings were held during that period than in the previous thirteen months of the board's corporate status. TNO verbal participation in the meetings, as indicated by a statement count, increased steadily throughout the seven months.

Table 3 presents and compares TNO and Non-TNO median scale

TABLE 3

Comparison of TNO and Non-TNO Administration II Median Scale Scores with Administration I Median Scale Scores for the Same Respondents (N = 43)

Scale[a]	TNO (N=18)			Non-TNO (N=25)		
	Admin. II	Admin. I	Sig. of Diff.[b]	Admin. II	Admin. I	Sig. of Diff.[c]
Activism	18.0	16.0	$p < .05$	19.0	19.0	NS
Anomie	5.0	6.0	NS	4.0	3.0	NS
Integration with relatives	2.5	3.0	NS	2.0	2.0	NS
Achievement orientation	16.0	14.5	$p < .05$	17.0	17.0	NS
Future orientation	9.0	9.0	NS	10.0	10.0	NS
Isolation	15.5	16.0	NS	14.0	15.0	NS
Normlessness	9.0	10.0	NS	6.0	6.0	NS
Powerlessness	16.0	15.0	NS	12.0	12.0	NS
Alienation	41.0	41.5	NS	31.0	32.0	NS
Particularism	0.0	2.0	$p < .05$	0.0	0.0	NS

[a] Not used as Guttman Scales.
[b] Wilcoxon Rank Sum Test, one-tailed. See footnote 31.
[c] Wilcoxon Rank Sum Test, two-tailed. See footnote 31.

scores on Administration II with median scale scores for the same respondents on Administration I. As hypothesized, there were no significant changes among Non-TNOs in the social-psychological variables measured. On the other hand, the directional changes hypothesized for TNOs seem, with some exceptions, to have been supported. As indicated in Table 3, activism and achievement orientation increased, and particularism decreased significantly. Anomie, integration with relatives, isolation, normlessness, and alienation decreased, though not significantly. Future orientation remained unchanged. Powerlessness ran counter to the trend of results and increased, though not significantly. The latter finding seems to conflict with Gottesfeld and Dozier's report of decreased powerlessness among indigenous community organizers, but it must be emphasized that neither the participant experience nor the powerlessness measures used in Gottesfeld's study and in the present study are necessarily comparable. Dean, the author of the alienation scale of which powerlessness is a component, reminds his reader that alienation may be situationally influenced.[40] At Administration II, TNOs were in general favorably disposed toward the board and its related activities. They had seen some accomplishments, recognized program potentials, were aware of and generally agreed with board goals, and felt very much a part of the board. Such experiences certainly influenced their hypotheses-supporting responses in Administration II. However, they were not content

[40] Dean, op. cit., p. 757.

with the director of the local community-action agency, whom they felt was "making too many decisions without us having our say." Several TNOs were actively attempting to influence or replace the director, without much success and with accompanying feelings of frustration. That experience, since it was current with Administration II, might account for the increased powerlessness score. It might further be speculated that TNO increases in the kinds of knowledge, competency, and confidence which moved scale scores in the hypothesized directions developed more quickly than the poverty program's capacity to accommodate them. The disparity between increased skills/motivations and the opportunity to use them as fully as desired could have generated an increased sense of powerlessness. If that speculation is even partially accurate, the message for poverty-intervention organizations is clear: to stimulate aspirations and inculcate skills without providing an outlet for their use can compound frustration.

When TNOs were arbitrarily divided (by consensus of research staff) into "active" and "inactive" categories (on the bases of meetings attended, offices held, observed performance, and so on), the changes in scale scores became more apparent. As shown in Table 4, active TNOs followed the same pattern of change as TNOs in general (Table 3), but with increases in activism and achievement orientation and with decreases in normlessness, alienation, and particularism attaining statistical significance. As did TNOs in general, active TNOs showed a not-significant increase in powerlessness and no change in future orientation.

The pattern of changes for inactive TNOs varied considerably from those of actives and TNOs in general. Inactives, as indicated in Table 4, showed significant increases in integration with relatives, isolation, powerlessness, and alienation and a significant decrease in particularism. Achievement orientation, future orientation, and normlessness remained unchanged, while activism decreased and anomie increased not-significantly. These results may be interpreted to indicate that the quality of participation in poverty programs is related to the consequent social-psychological impact upon participants. The experience apparently was not neutral for the TNO; either he found opportunity for active participation and subsequently manifested changes in the hypothesized directions, or he for some reason was an inactive participant and manifested changes in directions opposite to those hypothesized.[41] Participation can, therefore, have an impact upon some individuals that is the reverse of poverty-program expectations.

A comparison of actives and inactives on Administration I (see Table 4) yields no consistent initial differences which could explain the variations in change. It may be that the opportunity for active participation is limited for some TNOs, with the development of increased personal

[41] For a detailed description of TNO participation which resulted in frustration, see: Louis A. Zurcher, "The Leader and the Lost: A Case Study of Indigenous Leadership in a Poverty Program Community Action Committee," (*Genetic Psychology Monographs*, 76 (August, 1967), pp. 23–93. For a detailed description of positive TNO experience, see: Louis A. Zurcher and Alvin E. Green, *From Dependency to Dignity: Some Individual and Social Consequences of a Neighborhood House* (New York: Behavioral Publications, 1969).

TABLE 4

Comparison of Administration II Median Scale Scores with Administration I Median Scale Scores for TNO Categories: Actives, Inactives, Stayers, and Leavers

Scale[a]	Actives (N = 13)			Inactives (N = 5)			Stayers (N = 10)			Leavers (N = 8)		
	II	I	p^b	II	I	p	II	I	p	II	I	p
Activism	18.0	16.0	< .05	16.0	17.0	NS	18.5	17.0	< .05	17.0	16.5	NS
Anomie	5.0	6.0	NS	6.0	5.0	NS	5.0	6.0	NS	5.5	6.0	NS
Integration with relatives	2.0	2.0	NS	3.0	1.0	< .05	2.0	2.5	NS	3.0	3.0	NS
Achievement orientation	16.0	14.0	< .05	15.0	15.0	NS	16.0	14.5	< .05	15.0	14.0	NS
Future orientation	9.0	9.0	NS	9.0	9.0	NS	10.0	9.0	NS	9.0	9.0	NS
Isolation	15.5	15.5	NS	19.0	16.0	< .05	15.5	15.0	NS	16.0	16.5	NS
Normlessness	8.0	10.0	< .05	8.0	8.0	NS	9.0	9.0	NS	8.0	11.5	< .05
Powerlessness	16.0	15.0	NS	19.0	15.0	< .05	16.0	18.0	< .05	16.5	15.0	< .05
Alienation	38.0	43.0	< .05	45.0	39.0	< .05	41.0	41.5	NS	40.0	40.5	NS
Particularism	0.0	2.0	< .05	0.0	2.0	< .05	0.0	1.5	< .05	0.5	2.5	< .05

[a] Not used as Guttman Scales.
[b] Statistical analyses reported in Table 4 were Wilcoxon Rank Sum Tests. See footnote 31.

frustration. Observational data at least partially support that interpretation: three of the inactive TNOs felt they did not have the "skills" to become effective participants and thus hesitated to make themselves "look stupid." To the degree that these findings are valid and can be generalized, they underscore the obligation of community-action agencies to eliminate, by organizational flexibility and continuous training programs, factors which might prevent representatives of the poor from experiencing active participation.

Analysis of active and inactive Non-TNO categories produced only one notable change. Non-TNO actives (N = 18) showed a significant ($p <$ .05) increase in particularism. This result, buttressed by observational data, may indicate that active Non-TNOs tended to shift to a more personalistic view of events and individuals, possibly as a result of board experience and interaction with the TNOs. TNOs, as indicated in Tables 3 and 4, tended to become less particularistic. One might speculate that TNO/Non-TNO influence, at least on this variable, was mutual.

Eight TNOs terminated their participation in the poverty program between Administration I and Administration II. Some of those "leavers" quit after becoming disillusioned, some "no longer had time" for participation, and some were not reelected to TNO positions. As indicated in Table 4, those who remained, the "stayers," revealed a change pattern quite similar to TNOs in general (Table 3), with one striking exception—a significant decrease in powerlessness. By contrast, leavers showed significant decreases in normlessness and particularism, a significant increase in powerlessness, and no significant changes in the remaining variables. These findings again highlight the fact that participation is not a neutral experience for the TNO, and indicate that to a considerable extent the powerlessness increase for TNOs in general was concentrated among the leavers. One wonders what course of behavior TNO leavers might take now, since their perception of norms is clearer but their sense of powerlessness more acute. At least two of the leavers have become outspoken and somewhat militant opponents of the poverty program.

Over-all, time as a TNO and number of attendances at board meetings (Administration II) showed low and not-significant negative correlations with anomie, isolation, normlessness, and particularism, and positive correlations with activism and achievement orientation. These relationships are consistent with indices of over-all TNO change in variables measured. There was a slight increase in the number of TNO voluntary-association memberships, and a slight increase in mean (but not median) level of income—neither change approaching significance.

The patterns of change for male TNOs (N = 7) were similar to those of female TNOs (N = 11). Males did, however, show a greater decrease in normlessness (Administration II, median = 9; Administration I, median = 12; $p <$ .03) than females.

Patterns of TNO changes were observed to vary for different ethnic groups, though the validity of interpretations is mitigated by the small number of respondents distributed among the ethnic categories. Anglo-Americans (N = 3) showed increases in activism, integration with relatives, achievement orientation, isolation, powerlessness, and alienation; a decrease in particularism; and no changes in anomie, future orientation, and normlessness. Negro-Americans ($N = 10$) showed an increase in achievement orientation; decreases in integration with relatives, isolation, normlessness, and particularism; and no changes in activism, anomie, future orientation, powerlessness, and alienation. Mexican-Americans ($N = 3$) showed increases in anomie, isolation, powerlessness, and alienation; and decreases in activism, integration with relatives, achievement orientation, isolation, normlessness, and particularism. American Indians ($N = 2$) showed increases in activism, achievement orientation, future orientation, powerlessness, and particularism; and decreases in anomie, integration with relatives, isolation, normlessness, and alienation. It might appear that Negro-Americans and American Indians manifested changes more in line with the hypotheses than did Anglo-Americans and Mexican-Americans. However, this is not clearly a cultural phenomenon, since nine Negro-Americans and both American Indians were among the active TNOs, and all but one Anglo-American and one Mexican-American were inactives. The key variable for changes in the direction of the hypotheses thus may be the quality of participation rather than ethnicity. This interpretation is supported by the fact that eight Negro-American TNOs, but only one Anglo-American and one Mexican-American TNO were among the stayers. On the other hand, neither American Indian TNO was a stayer, and yet their changes tended to fit those hypothesized. These tenuous findings call for further research on cultural predispositions toward participation in poverty programs and on the impact of different kinds of participative experiences upon representatives from different ethnic groups.

CONCLUSION

Data from Administration I supported the hypothesis that TNOs would differ significantly from Non-TNOs in social-psychological variables indicative of a sense of competence and confidence vis-à-vis society, broadly defined. Those differences, and the corollary differences by sex and ethnic membership, suggest the potential heterogeneity of other poverty boards and indicate the probable impact of such heterogeneity upon board dynamics and decision-making processes. This is not to argue that membership mix is dysfunctional; on the contrary, the varying values and perceptions of a diverse membership may yield significant program innovations through participant democracy. Rather, the point is emphasized that conflicts and their resolution are apt to be facts of board life. Community-action agencies who support or are supported by such boards thus would need to maintain enough organizational flexibility to accommodate the give-and-take of membership mix. Also, the agency would need to be concerned with developing staff and member understanding of the processes as well as the contents of program participation.

Administration I data further supported the view that the scaled variables—activism, anomie, integration with relatives, achievement orientation, future orientation, isolation, normlessness, powerlessness, alienation, and particularism—are related to one another and to indices of socio-economic status.

Comparisons of Administration II with Administration I scale scores for those respondents who completed both administrations generally supported the hypotheses for directional, participation-related TNO change among the scaled social-psychological variables. Correlations among the variables, time as a TNO, and number of attendances at board meetings were congruent with the change data. One might conclude, therefore, that program participation generally had the impact upon representatives of the poor anticipated nationally by the Office of Economic Opportunity and locally by the TOEO. Such a conclusion concurs with the findings of others who have studied individual and social consequences of low-income members' participation in community-action programs.[42]

The impact of participation upon TNOs, indeed the directions of change in variables, appeared to be importantly related to the quality of the participation and to the TNO's perception of his experience with the program. That finding, and the indication that participation is not in any case a neutral experience for TNOs, suggests to community-action agencies that at least as much attention should be given to careful planning concerning the kinds of participation representatives of the poor will experience as is typically given to determining their proportional representation. Similarly, the data suggest that attention be given to the possibility that opportunities for participation might be more accessible to or differentially responded to by males and females and by members of different ethnic groups.

The degree to which findings presented in this study can be generalized to other poverty programs is problematical and left to the discretion of the reader. Clearly, there is need for comparative research involving poverty programs representative of different geographical locations, organizational styles, and member characteristics. The relationships among specific kinds of participation by specific kinds of individuals in specific kinds of programs—and the associations of those factors with social-psychological change—need to be more precisely detailed.

A broader question remains concerning the degree to which changes in the social-psychological variables measured in this study are associated with behavioral changes and modification in life style. Furthermore, this study has not questioned the positive value placed by OEO in general and the TOEO in particular upon transitions of the poor to a more "middle-class" way of believing and behaving. Rather, the purpose has been to translate the assumption of participation-related change into a set of hypotheses, to operationalize the hypotheses with scale-measured variables, and then to test the assumption in a limited fashion with a single case.

[42] M. Beiser, "Poverty, Social Disorganization, and Personality," *Journal of Social Issues*, 21 (1963), pp. 56–78; Haggstrom, *op. cit.*; A. Leighton, "Poverty and Social Change," *Scientific American*, 212 (1965), pp. 21–27; Helen Pearlman, "Self-Determination: Reality or Illusion?" *Social Service Review*, 39 (1965), pp. 410–422; Stone, Leighton, and Leighton, *op. cit.*

27

CITIZEN PARTICIPATION IN POLICY-MAKING: A STUDY OF A COMMUNITY ACTION PROGRAM*

FREMONT JAMES LYDEN
University of Washington

JERRY V. THOMAS
University of Washington

T HE PARTICIPATION OF THE PUBLIC IN FORMULATION OF PUBLIC POLICY has been invited, encouraged, and even urged by governmental agencies for many years. A measure of the public response can be seen in the advisory boards serving federal, state, and local agencies today. There are literally hundreds of such boards, concerned with a variety of public programs and the agencies that administer them. The agency-clientele relationships represented have a range of policy impacts, but to categorize them as merely legitimizing instruments for agency-defined policy is to underestimate many of them. Philip Selznick's study of the TVA demonstrates the influence that co-opted leaders of clientele groups can have on an agency's course of action.[1] In some instances, indeed, these influences become so powerful that they impede agency coordination of effort.[2]

But welfare agencies seem to have been less successful than other governmental agencies in bringing their clientele groups into participation in defining and articulating needs, and in developing programs to meet these needs. In a recent study of Mexican-Americans in San Antonio, Sjoberg, Brymer, and Farris[3] found that lower-class clientele were unable to communicate their needs through the bureaucratic mechanisms provided for this purpose. The impersonal mechanics utilized by bureaucracy are accepted and well understood by most members of society. But they are alien and confusing to the disadvantaged, who tend to relate to one another on a personal basis. Bureaucracy to them is cold and unfeeling, and its language is strange and unintelligible.

The Economic Opportunity Act passed by Congress in 1964 represented, among other things, an effort to overcome this alienation. The crux of the effort was in the provision for Community Action Programs, locally developed for local needs, and directed by local boards, composed of representatives of local government, community leadership, and the poor. This approach has been controversial before and since its adoption.[4]

---

* This study was supported by Contract No. 1375 with the Office of Economic Opportunity.

[1] Philip Selznick, *TVA and the Grass Roots* (Berkeley: University of California Press, 1949).

[2] Phillip O. Foss, *Politics and Grass* (Seattle: University of Washington Press, 1960).

[3] Gideon Sjoberg, Richard A. Brymer and Buford Farris, "Bureaucracy and the Lower Class," *Sociology and Social Research*, 50 (April, 1966), pp. 325–337.

[4] Hans B. C. Spiegel, ed., *Citizen Participation in Urban Development* (Washington, D.C.: National Institute for Applied Behavioral Science, 1968); Edmund M. Burke,

♦ First published in *Social Science Quarterly* 50, No. 3 (December, 1969).

The workability of the policy board, in particular, has been a subject of debate. To realize its role, the board would have to evolve into a social entity capable of accommodating the diverse orientations of its members, and of insuring that the interests of their constituencies were faithfully represented.[5]

This paper reports upon a 19-month study of one Community Action Program board. The study was aimed at determining whether the representatives of the poor were able to contribute effectively to policy making in this context, and whether members representing the diverse interests and values of community leaders, public officials and the poor could develop a viable decision-making entity.

THE SETTING

The Seattle-King County Economic Opportunity Board (henceforth referred to as SKCEOB), was legally incorporated under Washington state law in July 1965. This CAP for the Seattle metropolitan area, like most CAP's, resulted from the joint efforts of a number of local business, citizen, and governmental organizations.

The board consisted of thirty members.[6] Ten were designated public officials (or their representatives), ten were community leaders jointly appointed by public officials, and ten were representatives of the poor

---

"Citizen Participation Strategies," *American Institute of Planners Journal* (Sept., 1968), pp. 287–294; "Participation of the Poor: Section 202 (a) (3) Organizations Under the Economic Opportunity Act of 1964," *Yale Law Journal*, 74 (March, 1966), pp. 599–629; E. A. Krause, "Functions of a Bureaucratic Ideology: 'Citizen Participation'," *Social Problems*, 16 (Fall, 1968), pp. 129–143; H. Kaufman, "Administrative Decentralization and Political Power," *Public Administration Review*, 29 (Jan./Feb., 1969), pp. 3–15; S. M. Miller, "Participation, Poverty and Administration," *Public Administration Review*, 29 (Jan./Feb., 1969), pp. 15–25; Michael P. Smith, "Self-Fulfillment in a Bureaucratic Society," *Public Administration Review*, 29 (Jan./Feb., 1969), pp. 25–32; O. F. White, "The Dialectical Organization: An Alternative to Bureaucracy," *Public Administration Review*, 29 (Jan./Feb., 1969), pp. 32–42; W. G. Scott, "Organization Government: The Prospects for a Truly Participative System," *Public Administration Review*, 29 (Jan./Feb., 1969), pp. 43–53; H. G. Wilcox, "Hierarchy, Human Nature, and the Participative Panacea," *Public Administration Review*, 29 (Jan./Feb., 1969), pp. 53–63.

[5] L. A. Zurcher, "Stages of Development in Poverty Program Neighborhood Action Committees," *Journal of Applied Behavioral Science*, 5 (Apr./May/Je., 1969), pp. 223–257; Zurcher, "The Leader and the Lost: A Case Study of Indigenous Leadership in a Poverty Program Community Action Committee," *Genetic Psychological Monographs*, 76 (Aug., 1967), pp. 23–93; Zurcher, "Functional Marginality: The Dynamics of a Poverty Intervention Organization," (*Southwestern*) *Social Science Quarterly*, 48 (Dec., 1967), pp. 411–421; Zurcher, "The Overlap Model: A Comparison of Strategies for Social Change," *Sociological Quarterly*, 8 (Winter, 1968), pp. 85–97; Zurcher, "Poverty Program Indigenous Leaders: A Study of Marginality," *Sociology and Social Research*, 53 (Jan., 1969), pp. 147–162; H. W. Reynolds, "Placing the Poor in the Poverty Program," *Midwest Review of Public Administration*, 1 (Aug., 1967), pp. 87–94; Ralph M. Kramer, *Participation of the Poor* (New York: Prentice-Hall, 1969); Ralph Segalman, "Dramatis Personae of the Community Action Program: A 'Built-in' Conflict Situation," *Rocky Mountain Social Science Journal*, 4 (Oct., 1967), pp. 140–150.

[6] Increased to 33 members in June 1967.

appointed by the board. Ethnic identification, occupational background, and institutional association were all considered in selecting members.[7] Any groups or organizations believing themselves to be inadequately represented could petition for membership[8]

At a relatively early stage the board decided to carry out its program by contracting with existing governmental and nongovernmental agencies in the community. These agencies were encouraged to apply for program grants. The board decided which applications should be funded, and, upon OEO approval, entered into contracts. Agencies receiving contracts were so-called delegate agencies. A CAP staff headed by an executive director was formed to assist applicants in preparing grant requests, advise and assist the board in grant evaluation, and monitor the grants awarded.

METHOD OF STUDY

Study of the SKCEOB was begun in December 1966 as part of a larger evaluation study by a group of researchers at the University of Washington for the Office of Economic Opportunity. The board, in operation several months, appeared to be still in its formative stage. A longitudinal study was projected to cover 19 months of board operations.

The method of study selected was a modification of Bales' Interaction Process Analysis.[9] The authors' primary interest was in an approach that would yield reliable information on the developmental growth of the board as a policy-making organization.[10] Thus they sought a method of study that would center on the goal orientation of the board. A governing body is a purposive organization designed to solve specific kinds of problems. Although this involves both the cognitive and affective participa-

[7] The ethnic composition of the board, as of July 1967, was 19 Caucasians, 11 Negroes, 2 Orientals, and 1 Indian-Eskimo. From an occupational perspective 19 were professional, 2 managerial, 2 technical, 2 laboring, and 8 retired or housewives. Predictably, the professionals were associated primarily with the public representation group; the technical, laboring, and retired or housewives primarily with the poverty representation group. In terms of institutional affiliation, 6 members were from government, 4 from the public schools, 4 from private welfare, 4 from churches, 2 from business, 4 from unions, 1 from the medical profession and 8 were indigenous. Representation from government and the public schools apart, most community institutions had fairly even representation in the community and poverty groups.

[8] The SKCEOB bylaws were amended in 1968 to include additional provisions for the "maximum feasible participation" of the poor in accordance with the requirements of the Green Amendment: Pub. L. 90–222 Title I 104, 42 USCA 2790, 2791 as amended. See F. J. Lyden, A *Study of Organizational and Institutional Change* (Research Report No. 10, Part 2, Social Change Evaluation Project, Seattle: University of Washington, 1968), Appendix 9.

[9] R. F. Bales, *Interaction Process Analysis* (Cambridge: Addison-Wesley Press, Inc., 1950). For applications of this method to the study of organizational decision-making, see J. D. Barber, *Power in Committees: An Experiment in the Governmental Process*, (Chicago: Rand McNally, 1966); W. Caudill, *The Psychiatric Hospital as a Small Society* (Cambridge: Harvard University Press, 1958).

[10] B. W. Tuckman, "Developmental Sequence in Small Groups," *Psychological Bulletin*, 63 (June, 1965), pp. 384–399; R. F. Bales, and F. L. Strodtbeck, "Phases in Group Problem-Solving," *Journal of Abnormal and Social Psychology*, 46 (1951), pp. 485–495.

tion of its members, attention is focused on the goal direction of the organization. Bales' Interaction Process Analysis, which distinguishes between task and socioemotional acts in a problem-solving context, appeared to be a particularly appropriate instrument for quantifying board members' participation.[11]

The Bales schema was employed to study the regular monthly meetings of SKCEOB from December 1966 to June 1968.[12] One researcher, the junior author of the paper, attended every regular meeting of the board during this period of time, recording all acts observed, according to the Bales Classification System.[13]

The twelve categories under which data are assembled in the Bales schema are usually collapsed into four major categories for analytical purposes: (A) positive reactions (showing solidarity, tension release, or agreement): (B) answers (giving suggestions, opinions, or information); (C) questions (asking for suggestions, opinions, or information); and (D) negative reactions (showing disagreement, tension, or antagonism). Categories C and B, asking questions and giving answers, are task oriented, while categories A and D, showing positive or negative reactions, are socioemotional oriented.

The four categories can also be related, in general terms, to Parsons' four functional problems:[14]

Bales' Category	Parsons' Problem
A. Positive reactions	Integration
B. Giving answers	Goal attainment
C. Asking questions	Adaptation
D. Negative reactions	Pattern maintenance

Parsons' postulate, that any organization or institution must cope with these four problems in maintaining itself as an ongoing viable body, appears to be a productive focus for analyzing the operations of the board.

[11] The Bales technique attempts to identify and quantify each "act" initiated. An "act" was defined as any verbal behavior which is communicated to at least one other person in the group and which has an observable beginning and end. Each act was scored as to its originator and its type designation under the Bales twelve-fold classification. In addition each act was classified according to the organizational problem—program, budget, or personnel—with which it could be most readily identified. For details, see Lyden, *Organizational and Institutional Change*, Appendix 10.

[12] Except during February, March, and July 1967, when either no meeting was held or the meeting was collapsed into a training session.

[13] Although the use of two observers is usually recommended, it was not possible to retain two researchers trained in the use of the Bales technique for a study of this duration. A second observer was utilized for a seven month period (1112 acts) to test the reliability of the first observer's work. Overall interobserver reliability averaged between 84 per cent and 87 per cent after the second observer had become fully skilled in the application of the technique. See Lyden, *Organizational and Institutional Change*.

[14] T. Parsons, R. F. Bales, and E. A. Shils, *Working Papers in the Theory of Action* (Glencoe: The Free Press, 1953). It is true, of course, that context as well as content is involved in classifying acts according to Parsons' functional problems. Checks made against the context of acts recorded, though, strongly reinforced the validity of the Bales-Parsons cross classification.

As a purposive organization, the board must identify its goals, and means for evaluating goal accomplishment (goal attainment problem). It must undertake those facilitative actions which will set a context for goal oriented activity. That is, the right questions must be asked (adaptation problem). Positive reinforcement must be provided by members if an approach is to be agreed upon for solving the goal attainment and adaptation problems (integration problem). Finally, the process of integrating divergent orientations of members will produce tensions, unless the group is willing to discuss the bases for its points of disagreement, and search for a solution compatible to all (pattern maintenance problem). The organization of this paper follows this interpretive arrangement of the recorded data.

RESULTS AND DISCUSSION

The monthly board meetings held from December 1966 to June 1968 averaged 133 minutes in length. An average of 15 members and 4 alternates attended each meeting. Approximately 9 formal votes were acted upon per meeting. Of these votes, 44 per cent dealt with internal organization and 56 per cent with programmatic questions (14 per cent education, 11 per cent social rehabilitation, 8 per cent employment-training, and 23 per cent multiple issues).

A much higher proportion of poverty representatives (77 per cent) attended the average meeting than did representatives of the other two groups (community representatives, 51 per cent; public representatives, 54 per cent). But a much higher proportion of community and public representatives who did attend, participated actively[15] in the board discussion (52 per cent for community and public representatives respectively as compared with 21 per cent for poverty representatives).

During the period studied, community and public representation groups each contributed about twice as many acts as the poverty group. The largest proportion of acts contributed by the poverty and public representatives (55 per cent and 57 per cent respectively) had to do with substantive program issues (e.g., number of students to be tutored, types of training to be initiated, etc.) rather than with budget or personnel (staffing) questions (Table 1). The community representatives, on the other hand, were about equally concerned with all three types of matters. This difference is probably attributable to the expertise many of the community representives had developed in dealing with budgetary and personnel problems in connection with their work in community organizations. The other two groups were more attracted to the program issues as those about which they could exercise more generalized judgment.

Analyzing the aggregate acts contributed by the three representation groups in terms of the four functional problems, we find, in Table 1, that the majority of the community and public representatives' acts were directed to goal attainment, while the poverty representatives had as high

[15] Only those representatives who contributed five or more acts during a meeting were included in the tabulation of acts.

TABLE 1

Percentage of Board Acts by Representation Groups Classified
by Organizational and Functional Problems

	Representation Groups (Total number of acts contributed by each group in parenthesis)		
	Community Group (1046)	Public Group (946)	Poverty Group (571)
Organizational			
Program	39	57	55
Personnel	26	10	22
Budget	35	33	23
	100%	100%	100%
Functional			
Adaptation (C)[a]	20	21	27
Goal attainment (B)	54	62	30
Integration (A)	7	6	13
Pattern maintenance (D)	19	11	30
	100%	100%	100%

[a] Letters designate Bales categories.

a proportion of acts directed to integration and pattern maintenance as the other two groups combined. This is to be expected. The middle-class orientations of the community and public groups led them to structure actions for solving the problems at hand. The poverty representatives had less confidence that purposive action designed in a bureaucratic mode would really solve problems as they were perceived by the poor. But these aggregate data tell us nothing about the dynamic development of the board over time. Perhaps some conclusion could be drawn from them with respect to an established, well-accepted organization. But SKCEOB was an experiment in institution building. The body's development into a viable organization necessitated accommodation of divergent cultural orientations. The trends indicated by the month-by-month performance of the board must be considered for any real insight into the dynamics of its operation.

Table 2 shows the marked changes in attendance and participation occurring in the last five months of the observation period.

From December 1966 to January 1968, 67 per cent of the members were attending meetings, but during the last five months less than 50 per cent attended. All representation groups contributed to this drop. On the other hand, the proportion of attending members who participated actively in discussions increased, for the board as a whole, from 35 per cent to 49 per cent. But the increased participation came primarily from the community

TABLE 2

Percentage of Board Members Attending and Participating in Board Meetings

Representation Group	Per Cent Attending			Per Cent Participating		
	Dec. 1966– June 1968	Dec. 1966– Jan. 1968	Feb. 1968– June 1968	Dec. 1966– June 1968	Dec. 1966– Jan. 1968	Feb. 1968– June 1968
All Groups	61	67	47	39	35	49
Poverty	77	86	58	21	21	22
Public	54	59	44	52	46	67
Community	51	56	38	52	46	71

and public groups. Since fewer community and public representatives were attending than previously, their increased rate of participation indicates that the absent members were those whose participation during the earlier period had been minimal.

A change in CAP leadership, occurring in January 1968 may account in part for this change in the attendance and participation of members. The executive director who served from December 1966 to January 1968 had been with the organization since its inception. He was a Caucasian, trained in social work (MSW), and had had considerable settlement house and fund organization experience. He resisted taking a strong leadership role in his relations with the board for fear of creating a dependency relationship which could undercut the maturation of the board as a self-sustaining social entity.[16] The results of this orientation may be seen in Figure 1. From December 1966 through October 1967, we see a gradually increasing number of task acts and a consistently low level of socioemotional acts by the executive director. (The same pattern of action was followed by the chairman.) In response, the board's socioemotional acts decreased and its task oriented acts increased consistently.

The second executive director was a Negro, with a business major in college, and experience in purchasing and insurance. Congress' increasing emphasis on educational and employment programs and de-emphasis on community involvement activities appealed to this executive director. During his first meeting with the board he suggested that the organization had established its community involvement orientation and more purposive action toward coping with workforce problems was now timely. Figure 1 shows dramatic rises in the executive director's acts in both the task-oriented and socioemotional areas in the early months of 1968. The board's task-oriented acts declined, and its socioemotional acts increased in a sporadic fashion. It might be argued from these data that the board, while it had matured considerably as a task-oriented body by the end of 1967, had not yet reached the stage where it could cope with strong leadership inputs from a new, forceful advisor. Therefore, the board's immediate responses were decreased attendance, increased socioemotional acts and a decline in task-oriented acts. A counter argument may be proposed: the

[16] Indicated in conversations with the senior author.

FIGURE 1

Number of Task and Socio-Emotional Acts by Rep. Groups and Leaders
December 1966–June 1968

(a) Task acts

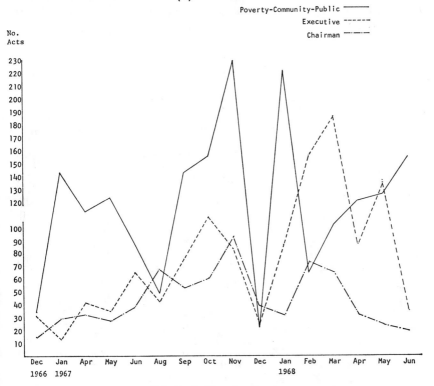

(b) Socio-Emotional acts

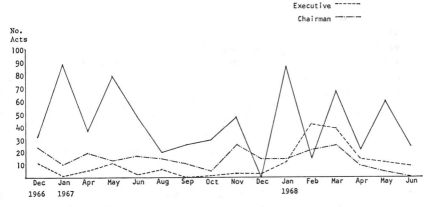

Months

participation of the most active public and community representatives did not decline during the period; it increased. The same, however, cannot be said for the poverty representatives. Twenty-one per cent of the attending poverty members participated from December 1966 to January 1968, as compared to 22 per cent participating from February to June 1968.

Perhaps the participation of the three groups should be examined more closely over time. Table 3 shows the proportion of program, budget, and personnel acts contributed by each group on a month-by-month basis.

TABLE 3

Percentage of Monthly Program, Personnel, and Budget Acts Contributed by Each of Representation Groups, January 1966–June 1968[a]

	Program Acts			Personnel Acts			Budget Acts		
	Com.	Pub.	Pov.	Com.	Pub.	Pov.	Com.	Pub.	Pov.
Dec. 1966	62	0	38	0	92	8	0	0	100
Jan. 1967	62	38	0	75	15	10	63	23	14
Apr.	75	13	12	66	34	0	0	30	70
May	31	54	15	72	5	23	50	28	22
June	32	23	45	60	19	21	68	23	9
Aug.	8	48	44	79	0	21	54	46	0
Sept.	30	34	36	93	7	0	80	17	3
Oct.	5	62	33	0	47	53	0	20	80
Nov.	21	51	28	39	26	35	20	55	25
Dec.	47	53	0	0	0	0	67	33	0
Jan. 1968	11	58	31	23	7	70	20	64	16
Feb.	29	70	1	0	0	100	100	0	0
Mar.	16	71	13	100	0	0	22	73	5
Apr.	31	31	38	0	0	0	80	10	10
May	38	48	14	100	0	0	58	38	7
June	47	27	26	0	0	0	7	85	8

[a] Boxed percentages show groups contributing majority of each type of acts during each month.

During the first five to seven months, community representatives were clearly dominant in matters dealing with programs and personnel. As the community representatives' involvement in program matters declined after April, the public representatives took on a more dominant role. This increased participation of public representatives parallels the development of a Model Cities grant application by the City of Seattle.[17] While the community representatives gave way to the public representatives on program matters, however, they participated actively in budgetary issues throughout the period studied. The participation of poverty representatives was sporadic on all three types of organizational issues, but their develop-

[17] Seattle applied for a Model Cities grant April 28, 1967. Preliminary approval was received in November and the action proposal was submitted December 23.

ing participation in program issues from December 1966 through October 1967 shows that this group, too, was becoming more consistently involved in the body's work up to the time the first executive director left.

The question of how each group contributed to the board's development as an organizational entity may be looked at from the perspective of Parsons' four functional problems. Acts relating to goal attainment were dominated throughout the observation period by community and public representatives (Table 4).

TABLE 4

Percentage of Monthly Adaptation, Goal Attainment, Integration, and Pattern Maintenance Acts Contributed by each of Representation Groups, January 1966–June 1968[a]

	Adaptation (C)[b] Com. Pub. Pov.			Goal Attain.(B)[b] Com. Pub. Pov.			Integration (A)[b] Com. Pub. Pov.			Patt. Maint. (D)[b] Com. Pub. Pov.		
Dec. 1966	27	9	[64]	[57]	39	4	[50]	0	[50]	0	4	[96]
Jan. 1967	35	39	26	[68]	28	4	[56]	0	44	[70]	16	14
Apr.	[71]	11	18	64	33	3	42	25	33	[75]	4	21
May	31	47	22	60	37	3	29	0	[71]	48	13	39
June	[50]	17	33	55	23	23	[56]	44	0	[72]	6	22
Aug.	26	44	30	[69]	0	31	63	0	37	17	[50]	33
Sept.	[53]	8	39	49	37	14	[82]	0	18	[67]	20	13
Oct.	2	27	[71]	5	[60]	35	0	43	[57]	0	[80]	20
Nov.	33	40	27	31	[56]	13	10	28	[62]	0	0	[100]
Dec.	[54]	46	0	46	[54]	0	0	0	0	0	0	0
Jan. 1968	[50]	[50]	0	14	[60]	26	[67]	28	5	5	23	[72]
Feb.	0	[100]	0	36	[54]	10	40	[53]	7	0	0	0
Mar.	[50]	39	11	43	[55]	2	33	45	22	29	[71]	0
Apr.	30	33	37	[64]	18	19	0	0	[100]	[100]	0	0
May	41	44	15	[68]	32	0	33	[67]	0	41	34	25
June	21	47	32	46	[51]	3	15	46	39	0	0	[100]

[a] Boxed percentages show groups contributing majority of each type of acts during any month.
[b] Letters indicate the Bales categories used.

Concern for goal attainment could be expected of both of these groups, but one might also expect some shared leadership in this area in individual meetings. Not so, however; in all but one meeting either one group or the other contributed more than 50 per cent of the goal attainment acts. This may be accounted for in part by the consistently small contribution of the poverty representatives to goal attainment. Thus the public, or community, representatives could contribute 50 per cent or more of the acts, and a sizeable number would still be left to the other group.

In the second task area, adaptation, the poverty group performed better. They contributed one-third or more of the adaptation acts in six out of the sixteen monthly meetings observed. Since adaptation acts are intended to provide a facilitative environment for the consideration of task-oriented problems, poverty representatives were evidently cognizant of the task responsibility of the board. It should be noted, however, that the group's rate of contributions to adaptation acts was consistently higher from December 1966 through November 1967 than from December 1967 through June 1968. This pattern of behavior may reflect, in part, a response of this group to the board's change in executive director in January 1968. The community group was apparently not similarly affected by this change. These members played the dominant role in the consideration of adaptation problems throughout the 19-month period, undoubtedly due in large part to the institutionalized orientation of their primary frame of reference —the voluntary community agency.

The appropriate consideration of the socioemotional problems of integration and pattern maintenance is critical for the development of an organization operating in a complicated cultural milieu. The integration problem was dealt with primarily by the community representatives during the early months of observation, but after October 1967 the other two groups became equally involved. Pattern maintenance appears to have been a concern of all three groups. The majority of acts in this area was contributed in five meetings by community representatives, in four meetings by poverty representatives, and in three meetings by the public representatives. Although the community representatives were consistently dominant in the early months, the other two groups assumed increasing leadership responsibilities in the consideration of these problems for the remaining months.

In summary, the community and the public representatives assumed leadership roles in dealing with goal attainment problems of the organization. The contributions of the poverty representatives to goal attainment were minimal. The community representatives took the lead in the consideration of facilitative actions (adaptation) but the other two groups played consistently supportive roles in this problem area. All three groups alternately assumed the leadership role in dealing with integration and pattern maintenance problems.

CONCLUSIONS

A viable decision-making entity did evolve out of the representation schema developed for SKCEOB. Each group exercised leadership in assuring that decisions made by the organization would incorporate the values of its constituents (pattern maintenance). All groups played leadership roles in providing the emotional supports necessary for the containment of conflict (integration). The community and public groups assumed the major leadership responsibilities for the task-oriented development of the organization (goal attainment and adaptation), but the poverty representatives played a strong supportive role in adaptation.

Since each of the representation groups reflects values of a different subcultural environment, one would expect that each group would have its own unique contribution to make to the solution of the functional problems of the organization. The data reveal the nature of the contribution made by each group. It is evident that none of the groups had "nothing to say" on any of the problems; and therefore all accepted the responsibility of joining in a common effort to create organizational products (policy decisions). To the extent that this phenomenon is demonstrated, one can say that the maturation of the board as a discrete social entity did occur during the period the board was under study. The proportion of poverty representatives who became active participants remained small, and thus the board probably did not fully incorporate the views of this constituency. Those poverty members who were active, however, reflected a wide variety of interests (ethnic, occupational, and institutional) and participated in a wide variety of contexts.

The interjection of an executive director who elected to play a much more substantive role than his predecessor in board deliberations had effects which, in the short run, appear to have complicated the developmental course of the board. Whether, in the longer run, the board will regain its task-oriented momentum will undoubtedly depend upon how the executive director and the board accommodate to each other and how federal support to Community Action effort evolves.

From a research perspective, it would appear that Bales' Interaction Process Analysis can be a useful tool for examining the dynamics in the developmental process of a public policy-making body. Its use in this study suggests that increased research attention needs to be given to the nature of the maturation process of a newly created body such as the poverty board and to the role played by leader catalysts (in this case, executive directors) in its development.

28

THE WAR ON POVERTY AND COMMUNITY LEADERSHIP: AN EXPLORATORY NOTE[1]

CHARLES M. BONJEAN
The University of Texas at Austin

WAYMAN J. CROW
Western Behavioral Sciences Institute, La Jolla, California

A CONCERN WITH THE RELATIONSHIP BETWEEN THE NATURE OF community leadership and aspects of local programs or policies has, for the most part, been only implicit or incidental in the now vast literature on community power structure.[2] Where this focus can be found, the usual orientation has been to view leadership characteristics as independent variables and programs or policies as dependent variables.[3] Relatively little attention has been given to the opposite relationship—the possibility that programs or policies may influence the structure of leadership.[4] Thus, the major purposes of this exploratory

[1] The research reported was performed pursuant to OEO Contract B89-4352 awarded to the Western Behavioral Sciences Institute, La Jolla, California. Another report of these data and the others referred to in the text of this note is Charles M. Bonjean and Wayman J. Crow, *Voices That Count: Establishment, Brown, and Black Influentials in San Diego County, California,* Technical Report No. 20, Western Behavioral Sciences Institute, La Jolla, California. Opinions based on the research are those of the authors and should not be construed as representing the opinions or policy of any agency of the United States Government. The authors acknowledge with gratitude important contributions made to the research design and execution of the study by Rosemary J. Erickson, LeRoy A. Grissom, June A. Rucker, Carolyn S. Alkire, and Jessie R. Rohrbough of WBSI. Assistance was also provided by Michael D. Grimes and Paula Jean Miller of the University of Texas. We are grateful for the useful suggestions made by Robert L. Lineberry and Louis A. Zurcher, who read an earlier draft of the report.

[2] More than 300 items are presented in Roland J. Pellegrin, "Selected Bibliography on Community Power Structure," (*Southwestern*) *Social Science Quarterly,* 48 (December, 1967), pp. 451–465.

[3] The perspective is implicit in much of the research literature employing the decisional approach. Robert A. Dahl, *Who Governs? Democracy and Power in an American City* (New Haven: Yale University Press, 1961), notes, for example in discussing urban redevelopment (p. 124): "One way to decide the matter is to reconstruct all the important decisions on development and renewal between 1950–1958 and determine which individuals (or in some cases agencies) most often initiated the proposals that were finally adopted . . ." The perspective is treated incidentally in much of the elitist literature. See, for example, the chapter "Projects, Issues, and Policy" in Floyd Hunter, *Community Power Structure* (Chapel Hill: University of North Carolina Press, 1953). A few recent studies have focused explicitly on the relationship. See, for example, Terry N. Clark, "Community Structure, Decision-Making, Budget Expenditures and Urban Renewal in 51 American Communities," *American Sociological Review,* 33 (August, 1968), pp. 576–593.

[4] Exceptions are rare. One, also dealing with a federally imposed program, is Phillip Edward Present, "Defense Contracting and Community Leadership: A Comparative Analysis," (*Southwestern*) *Social Science Quarterly,* 48 (December, 1967), pp. 399–410.

♦ First published in this volume.

note are to suggest one means—sociometric data—for the analysis of this reverse relationship and to present data from one community suggesting the utility of the perspective and method. An ancillary purpose is to report one of the most impressive results of the war on poverty in San Diego, California.

METHOD OF INVESTIGATION

Leadership in ethnically pluralistic communities such as San Diego is likely to be somewhat more complex than the structure of leadership in homogeneous communities. Previous studies have indicated that a majority power structure is likely to be dominant in such communities and that it may, more or less, react to the demands or requests of minority communities which may or may not have their own leadership structures.[5] A 1965 power-structure study of San Diego provided sufficient evidence to suggest that this assumption was a reasonable point of departure for the current study.[6] Thus, a variation on the reputational approach was used to identify the top leadership personnel in San Diego (hereafter termed the "establishment" power structure), while at the same time separate studies were conducted to identify key leaders in the Negro and Mexican-American subcommunities.[7]

Three panels of six judges each, assumed to be especially knowledgeable in regard to key decision making in their own community, were selected from among known establishment Negro and Mexican-American leaders. The final selection of judges was the result of an attempt not only to gain the cooperation of individuals who were active themselves, but to select judges who also adhered to different political ideologies and who were oriented toward different institutional sectors of their communities or subcommunities.[8]

Each judge was presented with a deck of cards on which were placed

[5] See, for example, Hunter, *Community Power Structure*, pp. 114–150; M. Elaine Burgess, *Negro Leadership in a Southern City* (Chapel Hill: University of North Carolina Press, 1960), and, for a description of a less well developed but separate structure of leadership in a Negro subcommunity, Ernest A. T. Barth and Baha Abu-Laban, "Power Structure and the Negro Sub-Community," *American Sociological Review*, 24 (February, 1959), pp. 69–76.

[6] Aubrey Wendling of San Diego State College made relevant data available in a communication of January 28, 1969.

[7] The shortcomings (as well as the advantages) of the reputational approach are acknowledged. For a summary of them, see Charles M. Bonjean and David M. Olson, "Community Leadership: Directions of Research," *Administrative Science Quarterly*, 9 (December, 1964), pp. 278–300.

[8] Three of the establishment judges were businessmen, one was a staff member of a voluntary agency, one was a representative of the mass media, and the sixth was an attorney. Mexican-American judges represented most of the organizations active in the local Mexican-American subcommunity, ranged in education from a college professor to respondents who had not completed high school, and included four members who supported the Delano grape strike as well as two who were actively against it. The Negro judges represented the old middle class as well as new leaders, professional and nonprofessional personnel, militants and moderates. Two judges were directors of human-relations agencies of San Diego, two directed Community Action Programs, one was a businessman, and one was an active Black Nationalist.

names of influentials identified by previous studies, the research staff, and the judges themselves (as later judges added names, earlier ones were contacted again to rate those nominees not previously rated).[9] Each judge was asked to sort the cards into four piles: first-level influentials, second-level influentials, third-level influentials, and names not recognized. It was explained to the judges that influence in policy *making* as opposed to involvement in implementation should be used as the basic criterion in rating. Including nominations made by the judges themselves, 72 establishment, 67 Mexican-American, and 87 Negroes were rated by the respective panels of judges. Top leaders were arbitrarily identified as those individuals rated as first-level influentials by four or more of the six judges. This level of agreement among judges yielded 12 establishment, 10 Mexican-American, and 8 Negro leaders. All nominees were ranked by assigning weights to the judges' ratings.

The assumption dictating the research design appeared to be a valid one since no overlap was found among the three sets of top leaders. With one exception, the establishment power structure was an Anglo political-economic elite.[10] Of its 12 members, 4 held public office, and most of the rest were business or industrial leaders.

Attempts were made to interview all three sets of first-level leaders identified. Among the 12 establishment leaders, there were 4 refusals and 3 unsuccessful contacts due to poor health and travel. An additional 4 interviews were obtained from high-ranking second-level influentials, but only after additional refusals and vacations were encountered. Finally, interviews were completed with 9 of the top 22 establishment leaders. Response rates among minority leaders were more satisfactory. Of the top 10 Mexican-American leaders, 8 were interviewed. Also, 2 high-ranking second-level influentials were interviewed, but only after 3 others were found to be unavailable (only 1 of the 15 top leaders refused to be interviewed). Of the 8 top leaders in the Negro community, 7 were interviewed, as were 3 high-ranking second-level leaders. In summary, 10 of the top 13 Negro leaders were interviewed (1 refused and 2 were out of town).

Leaders were identified in February and March of 1969, and the 29 interviews were conducted during July and August. All leaders were administered the same interview schedule, which consisted of 22 open-ended and structured questions. In addition to demographic data, questions concerned a variety of phenomena including knowledge of and attitudes toward the war on poverty and its specific programs, the salience of poverty compared with other community problems, the respondents'

[9] In addition to the Wendling study, lists were compiled from an earlier WBSI-OEO survey in which Negro respondents were asked to name three individuals in the community who had "the most to say about what gets done" from lists of leaders of social, fraternal, and service organizations and from Mexican-American collaborators.

[10] Although a comparison of the 1965 study results with the 1969 findings revealed considerable turnover in leadership (for example, 11 of the top 30 in 1965 were deceased or had left the community by 1969), both studies indicate that minority representation was nonexistent (in 1965) or minimal (in 1969 the top leaders included one minority member).

beliefs in regard to the causes of poverty and their preferred means for its amelioration, evaluations of the war on poverty in general as well as its specific programs, and a number of questions concerning leaders' relationships to one another and to the war-on-poverty programs. Only data from the latter questions will be presented here. Specifically, each respondent was presented with a list of all top-level establishment, Negro, and Mexican-American leaders and was asked which of the leaders (1) he knew of, (2) he knew personally, (3) he had worked with on community or business projects, (4) he had worked with, formally or informally, on war-on-poverty programs, and (5) he had met because of their association with war-on-poverty programs. Comparison of responses to various sets of questions permits an assessment of the influence of one general program—the war on poverty—on interaction patterns within and between leadership groups. Although findings in regard to the establishment leaders are incomplete because of the low response rate, the relatively high response rates for Negroes and Mexican-Americans permit some degree of confidence in regard to descriptions of interaction patterns within both of these leadership groups as well as between *all* groups.[11] At the same time, the data offer the opportunity to assess the degree to which one of the goals of the war on poverty's Community Action Programs has been achieved in one community: "Development and strengthening of indigenous leadership in the low-income community."[12]

FINDINGS

Data presented in items 2 and 3 of Table 1 support conventional wisdom concerning leaders' knowledge of and interaction with one another. All establishment leaders know of one another, and the same is true of Mexican-American and Negro leaders. Establishment knowledge of Mexican-American leaders is quite low, and Mexican-American knowledge of establishment leaders is relatively low, suggesting somewhat less mutual attention and concern than is the case among other combinations of groupings. The percentages shown in the table cells are based on the number of positive responses made by all leaders in each category compared with the total possible number of positive responses (see item 1). Thus, while the number of establishment respondents in the first column is only 9, the number of responses used to compute percentages is 103 when the object is other establishment leaders, 90 for Mexican-Americans, and 72 for Negroes. Thus, it can be seen that all but one of the establishment respondents reported personal acquaintanceship with all listed establishment leaders. The exception reported personal acquaintanceship with all but one leader. Personal-acquaintance patterns parallel, with one exception, the knowledge patterns. Although 78 per cent of the

[11] There is no reason to assume that establishment responses to acquaintance-interaction questions are more valid than minority responses to the same questions. In fact, in the present case, generalizations based on the minority responses are probably more valid since it is likely that the Anglo leadership sample is biased in the direction of poverty-program participation.

[12] Office of Economic Opportunity, RFP No. CAP-9128.

Mexican-Americans' "knowledge of" responses were positive, only 28 per cent represented personal contacts.

These data, as well as the data reporting the percentage of individuals who have worked with one another, show (1) a very high level of knowledge, acquaintanceship, and task-oriented interaction *among* members of each leadership category, (2) a relatively high degree of knowledge, acquaintanceship, and task-oriented interaction between establishment and Negro leaders and between Negro and Mexican-American

TABLE 1

Sociometrics of the San Diego Leadership Structures

	Number and Per Cent of Responses from					
	Establishment Leaders (N = 9)		Mexican-American Leaders (N = 10)		Negro Leaders (N = 10)	
	N	%	N	%	N	%
1. Who could know[a]						
a. 12 establishment leaders	103	100	120	100	120	100
b. 10 Mexican-American leaders	90	100	92	100	100	100
c. 8 Negro leaders	72	100	80	100	73	100
2. Who knew of						
a. 12 establishment leaders	103	100	93	78	117	98
b. 10 Mexican-American leaders	47	52	92	100	83	83
c. 8 Negro leaders	66	92	77	96	73	100
3. Who knew personally						
a. 12 establishment leaders	102	99	33	28	95	79
b. 10 Mexican-American leaders	37	41	87	95	69	69
c. 8 Negro leaders	64	89	69	86	73	100
4. Who had worked with						
a. 12 establishment leaders	99	96	14	12	72	60
b. 10 Mexican-American leaders	36	40	84	91	64	64
c. 8 Negro leaders	60	83	53	66	70	96
5. Who had worked with on war-on-poverty activities						
a. 12 establishment leaders	33	32	3	3	16	13
b. 10 Mexican-American leaders	14	16	53	58	39	39
c. 8 Negro leaders	25	35	31	39	37	51
6. Who had met through war-on-poverty activities						
a. 12 establishment leaders	1	1	10	8	1	1
b. 10 Mexican-American leaders	12	13	38	41	23	23
c. 8 Negro leaders	11	15	29	36	1	1

[a] Ns listed here are used as the base figures for computing the percentages in items 2–6. Ns for this item were determined by multiplying the number of respondents by the number of items (individuals) rated and subtracting the number of possible self-ratings (for example, an establishment respondent on the list of establishment leaders rated only 11 rather than 12 individuals).

leaders, and (3) a much lower degree of knowledge, acquaintanceship, and task-oriented interaction between establishment and Mexican-American leaders. The absence of longitudinal data makes it impossible to assess the reasons for the gap between establishment and Mexican-American leadership relative to other combinations, but relevant literature and recent events suggest some plausible explanations. Certainly the most obvious has been the civil-rights movement and organized Negro politics which have initiated contacts with establishment leaders and to which responses could not be ignored by establishment leaders.[13] A similar movement among Mexican-Americans has been neither as intense nor as extensive and, to the degree that it exists, has been of shorter duration. It has been suggested that one reason for this may be the fact that potential leaders in the Mexican-American community, rather than choosing ethnic leadership roles, have accepted second- or third-level leadership positions in the establishment community.[14] In short, in San Diego and probably elsewhere, establishment/Mexican-American interaction is low because a leadership structure in the latter community is a relatively recent or emerging phenomenon. The data discussed below lend some support to this interpretation.

Table 1 indicates that from a number of standpoints, war-on-poverty programs played an important role in bringing community leaders into contact wtih one another. The most striking data concern the Mexican-American leaders. Asked when they had first met other leaders, 38 new contacts were reported *within* the subcommunity context as a result of war-on-poverty programs. Thus, 44 per cent of all acquaintances among Mexican-American leaders were a consequence of this specific program. The data imply that leadership in this subcommunity was not well structured before the implementation of war-on-poverty activities. These data are in contrast with those for the establishment and Negro power structures, most of whose members knew one another or had met one another in other contexts.

Interaction between leaders in the different communities was also facilitated by the war on poverty, and again the Mexican-American data are most striking. Of the 33 contacts with establishment leaders reported by Mexican-American leaders, 10 were initiated by war-on-poverty activities. Similarly, 29 of the 69 contacts with Negro leaders apparently had the same stimulus. By contrast, Negroes reported only 1 of their 79 contacts with establishment leaders was a result of war-on-poverty programs, implying that previous issues (probably the civil-rights movement) were the stimuli for contact.

<hr>

[13] Recent political advancements made by Negroes in the South are summarized in Joe R. Feagin and Harlan Hahn, "The Second Reconstruction: Black Political Strength in the South," *Social Science Quarterly*, 51 (June, 1970), pp. 42–56.

[14] This and other reasons for a relative absence of leadership in one Mexican-American subcommunity are discussed by James B. Watson and Julian Samora, "Subordinate Leadership in a Bicultural Community: An Analysis," *American Sociological Review*, 19 (August, 1954), pp. 413–424.

SUMMARY AND CONCLUSIONS

The data presented above suggest that the war on poverty modified the structure of leadership in San Diego in two important ways: it increased task-oriented interaction among Mexican-American, Negro, and establishment leaders (in that order); and it also brought leaders from the sub-communities into contact with one another and with establishment leaders. It does not seem to be out of line to suggest that this program may have been the major catalyst in developing leadership in the Mexican-American community and in strengthening its ties with other community leadership groups.

Beyond reporting the relative success of the Community Action Program in meeting one of its goals in San Diego and, at the same time, illustrating how this type of goal attainment may be evaluated, the method, mode of analysis, and findings are suggestive for leadership studies in other contexts. First, they suggest that just as leaders may influence the selection and direction of programs, these programs may in turn modify the knowledge, acquaintanceships, and interaction patterns of leaders. Second, the utility of sociometric and interaction data for leadership studies in general is demonstrated. In addition to the relevance of the data for the specific problem presented, data from one set of respondents may be compared with data on the same phenomenon from another set of respondents as an internal validity check. Similarly, the data may be used to verify or question the results of the method used to identify leaders (for example, one would be suspicious if those individuals nominated as top leaders did not know of one another or if they did not interact with one another).[15] Finally, because the program studied (although locally administered) had its origins at the federal level of government, the findings presented here lend further support to the growing body of literature suggesting that, increasingly, the sources of local change may be found in the relationships between community and extracommunity institutions.[16]

[15] Sociometric checks have been suggested by previous studies but have appeared infrequently in the relevant literature. See Charles M. Bonjean, "Community Leadership: A Case Study and Conceptual Refinement," *American Journal of Sociology*, 68 (May, 1963), pp. 672–681.
[16] See especially John Walton, "The Vertical Axis of Community Organization and the Structure of Power," (*Southwestern*) *Social Science Quarterly*, 48 (December 1967), pp. 353–368.

29

CORRELATES OF JOB STATUS AMONG INDIGENOUS NONPROFESSIONALS IN COMMUNITY ACTION PROGRAMS

FREDERICK L. AHEARN, JR.
Boston College

THIS STUDY EXPLORES THE RELATIONSHIP BETWEEN HIGH AND LOW JOB status in community action programs (CAP) and the social backgrounds, job experiences, attitudes and perceptions of indigenous nonprofessionals.[1] Such an analysis may prove useful in describing the degree to which poor individuals have benefited from the poverty program and may have implications for the employment and use of indigenous workers.

In recent years, sociologists and social workers have paid considerable attention to the use of indigenous personnel in a variety of social programs.[2] One of the more popular suggestions, the proposal to develop "new careers" for the poor,[3] recommends that the poor be provided with employment mobility through the acquisition of new skills, training, and education. Such

[1] Individuals from a poor neighborhood or ghetto who are employed in some service capacity in the CAP; and also those in higher positions who are linked to a specific target neighborhood and do not have the usual professional requirements for the position but have been selected for the job based on performance.

[2] The roles proposed for the indigenous nonprofessional include that of case aide, specialist, social work technician, social work associate, organizer, helper, and mediator. Among the reasons given for assigning these roles are (a) the shortage of professionally trained social workers; (b) the ability of the nonprofessional to bridge the cultural gap between the agency and the poor neighborhood; (c) the therapeutic result of helping others enables the nonprofessional to handle better some of his own problems; (d) more effective service by agencies; and, (e) the use of indigenous personnel provides one of several meaningful forms of resident participation in community action programs. For additional information concerning these roles, see Verne Weed and William H. Denham, "Toward More Effective Use of the Nonprofessional Worker: A Recent Experiment," *Social Work*, 6 (Oct., 1961), pp. 29–36; Fergus T. Monahan, "A Study of Nonprofessional Personnel in Social Work—The Army Social Work Specialist," (Unpublished D.S.W. diss., The Catholic University of America, 1960); Willard C. Richan, "A Theoretical Scheme for Determining Roles of Professional and Nonprofessional Personnel," *Social Work*, 6 (Oct., 1961), pp. 22–28; Bertram M. Beck, "Wanted Now: Social Work Associates," *The Social Welfare Forum* (New York: Columbia University Press, 1963), pp. 195–205; Laura Epstein, "Differential Use of Staff: A Method to Expand Social Services," *Social Work*, 7 (Oct., 1962), pp. 66–72; Gertrude Goldberg, "Untrained Neighborhood Workers in a Social Work Program," (New York: Mobilization For Youth, 1964) (Mimeographed); Perry Levinson and Jerry Schiller, "Role Analysis of the Indigenous Nonprofessional," *Social Work*, 11 (July, 1966), p. 96; Melvin B. Mogulof, "Involving the Low-Income Neighborhoods in Anti-Poverty Programs," *Social Work*, 10 (Oct., 1965), p. 55; George Brager, "The Indigenous Worker: A New Approach to Social Work Technicians," *Social Work*, 10 (Apr., 1965), p. 34; Frank Riessman, "The 'Helper' Therapy Principle," *Social Work*, 10 (Apr., 1965), p. 28; and *Youth in the Ghetto* (New York: Harlem Youth Opportunities Unlimited, 1964), p. 609.

[3] Arthur Pearl and Frank Riessman, *New Careers for the Poor* (New York: Free Press, 1965), pp. 13–15.

✦ First published in *Social Science Quarterly* 50, No. 3 (December, 1969).

mobility is assumed to provide either (1) a career line to the top of the system, or (2) the upgrading of the poor one level within the system. The need, then, as one author put it, is for imperative action in using CAP employment opportunities for mobility into new careers both within the CAP employment system and also in other employment systems.[4]

Initial expectations were high that the new program to abolish poverty would, indeed, create new employment opportunities for the poor. However, Yankelovich reported in his study of nine CAP's that most employment opportunities available to the poor were one-level jobs—jobs not very different from the old dead-end jobs previously available to this group.[5] More recent cutbacks in funds to the local CAP's have necessitated curtailment of programming and, in some cases, forced lay-offs of poverty employees.

If the attempt to create job opportunities of "new careers" for the poor is thwarted by dead-end jobs or funding cutbacks, it would seem that these strains would have some effect upon the aspirations of the indigenous worker, his value orientation, his loyalty to the agency, his degree of work alienation, and his perception of the CAP's efficacy. Although this study does not purport to measure attitudinal changes over time, it is hoped that nonprofessionals with high and low job status in the CAP can be differentiated on the basis of their attitudes, their CAP-related job experiences, and social backgrounds. Specific policy questions concern the issues of who is recruited by the CAP for high and low level nonprofessional jobs, and how job training programs are used to upgrade nonprofessionals within the CAP system.

DATA AND METHODS

The data upon which this study is based were gathered in early 1968 from two large New England CAP's. Both agencies were in existence prior to the Office of Economic Opportunity legislation, having been created in response to the President's Committee on Juvenile Delinquency in one case, and the Ford Foundation's "grey areas" projects in the other. Each agency was created through the efforts of various city and organizational leaders with considerable influence and control exerted by the mayor. Soon after their establishment, each agency began to hire indigenous workers as aides and neighborhood workers and later as counselors, program directors, and community organizers. The sizes of the two agencies were comparable in fiscal 1967–68 with each having a budget of approximately five million dollars after having sustained federal cutbacks of 8 per cent and 15 per cent, respectively.

The sample consisted of an equal number of randomly selected black nonprofessionals, both male and female, from each program who were employed at least half time. It excluded blacks of Puerto Rican and Cape

---

[4] Paula Atkeson, "Alternative Career Opportunities for the Neighborhood Worker," *Social Work*, 12 (Oct., 1967), p. 81.

[5] Daniel Yankelovich, *A Study of the Nonprofessional in CAP* (New York: Office of Economic Opportunity, 1966).

Verdian (Portuguese) descent because it was felt that recent immigrants to mainland America might not reflect the attitudes of American-born blacks. Women who were not the main support of their families were also excluded, so that the sample would consist of breadwinners who would be concerned about career possibilities within the CAP. Finally, the sample excluded nonprofessionals who were under 21 years of age or over 50 years because they might be too young or too old to consider the career possibilities of their employment.

From a roster of 28 black females and 33 black males in CAP agency A, 26 women and 30 men were interviewed. Five individuals were not interviewed: two refused to participate; two terminated employment before they were interviewed; and one woman was discovered not to be the main support of her family. In CAP agency B, 30 black females and 26 black males were randomly selected from a roster of 62 black women and 32 black men. There were no refusals from this CAP program. In all, the total number interviewed was 112 black nonprofessionals—equally divided between men and women and between the two CAP programs.

Insofar as availability sampling of different CAP agencies posed potential problems of bias, it was necessary to control for this by partialing CAP agency differences from all the rest of the correlates reported in this study.

To operationalize the concept of the indigenous worker's status in CAP, measures of CAP income and CAP job status[6] were standardized and summed. This variable is called CAP socioeconomic status (SES) index. Similarly, an index of past SES was devised by standardizing and combining measures of education, income, and job status[7] prior to CAP employment.

Background variables utilized in the study were age, sex, marital status, and a measure of whether the nonprofessional was employed prior to coming to his present job. Variables pertaining to CAP-related job experiences were measures of length of employment, whether the indigenous worker held other jobs in CAP, and whether he received any training for his position.

Several attitudinal and perceptual variables were also operationalized. There were measures of anomie,[8] conventionalism (a measure of acceptance of middle-class values),[9] work alienation,[10] aspirations,[11] and agency-neighborhood orientation (a five-item adaptation of Zurcher's Marginality

[6] Albert J. Reiss, *Occupations and Social Status* (New York: The Free Press of Glencoe, Inc., 1961), pp. 263–275.

[7] *Ibid.*

[8] Edward L. McDill, "Anomie, Authoritarianism, Prejudice, and Socio-Economic Status," *Social Forces*, 39 (Mar., 1961), p. 243.

[9] T. W. Adorno, *et al.*, *The Authoritarian Personality* (New York: Harper and Row, 1950), p. 255.

[10] Melvin Seeman, "On the Personal Consequences of Alienation in Work," *American Sociological Review*, 32 (Apr., 1967), p. 275.

[11] Charles F. Grosser, "Characteristics of Middle Class Professional and Local Indigenous Workers vis à vis Their Lower Class Clients," (Unpublished D.S.W. dissertation, Columbia University School of Social Work, 1965), App. II.

Scale,[12] which refers to an individual's orientation to either agency or neighborhood goals). In addition, a four-item "CAP efficacy scale" was created and pretested to tap the nonprofessional's perceptions of the CAP effectiveness in serving others. Finally, an "aspiration-expectation differential index" was constructed to measure the indigenous employee's perceived inaccessibility to future jobs and income. This was accomplished by standardizing and summing difference scores on the measures of aspirations and expectations of job status and salary five years hence.

In order to analyse the differences between high status and low status nonprofessionals, partial correlation coefficients were computed, thereby removing CAP agency differences. Although not all the data were interval or ratio scales, as technically required for the use of product-moment correlation, they were ordinal scales. Such heuristic use of interval statistical measures has been rationalized on the grounds that, in the social sciences, few, if any, truly interval scales exist, most actually being ordinal scales.[13]

FINDINGS

As Table 1 indicates, those nonprofessionals with high CAP SES are most likely to be married, to have had a high socioeconomic status prior to coming to their CAP positions, to have been employed prior to CAP, to be males, and, finally, to have a relatively large number of dependents. Conversely, those indigenous workers with low CAP SES are most likely to be unmarried, to have had a low socioeconomic status prior to coming to their CAP positions, to have been unemployed prior to CAP, to be women, and, finally, to have relatively few dependents.

TABLE 1

Background Correlates of CAP SES
(Low to High)

Variable	Partial r[a]
Marital status (not married vs. married)	.35[b]
Past SES (low to high)	.34[b]
Employment status prior to CAP (employed vs. unemployed)	—.33[b]
Sex (male vs. female)	—.30[b]
Number of dependents (low to high)	.26[b]

[a] CAP Agency A vs. B differences partialed.
[b] $p < .01$

These findings appear to indicate that CAP agencies recruit nonprofessionals with good past employment histories and education (reflected in past SES), as well as stable family backgrounds, for the higher status posi-

[12] Louis A. Zurcher, "Poverty Program Indigenous Leaders: A Study of Marginality," *Sociology and Social Research,* 53 (Jan., 1969), pp. 147–162.
[13] Fred N. Kerlinger, *Foundation of Behavioral Research* (New York: Holt, Rinehart and Winston, Inc., 1965), pp. 425–428.

tions available to indigenous employees in CAP. Workers with poor work histories and less education and who lack a stable family life tend to be given low status jobs in CAP, such as aides or trainees. More often than not, this second category is likely to be women, many of whom were previously on welfare or unemployed.

Once employed in the CAP, certain job-related experiences may or may not alter the nonprofessional's opportunity to advance to higher-status positions. Table 2 shows that indigenous personnel with high CAP SES have been employed a long period of time, did not receive any job training from the agency, and had held other jobs before their present one in the CAP. On the other hand, low status nonprofessionals tended to have a short tenure with the program, had received some training for CAP duties, and had not held other jobs within the agency.

TABLE 2

CAP-Related Job Correlates of CAP SES
(Low to High)

Variable	Partial r^a
Length of employment in CAP (low to high)	.29^c
CAP job training (no vs. yes)	—.26^c
Other jobs in CAP (no vs. yes)	.21^b

[a] CAP Agency A vs. B differences partialed.
[b] $p < .05$
[c] $p < .01$

These relationships imply that CAP agencies have tended to promote the high status nonprofessionals over time without the benefit of additional job training. No doubt, this is because these individuals, although living in poverty, come to the agency with the ability and skills to advance to higher positions without benefit of a time-consuming and expensive training program. Low status workers enter job-training programs but, possibly due to a host of factors, e.g., failure of training programs, poor employment histories, or short tenure, have not in most instances received promotions.

The relationship of indigenous workers' attitudes and perceptions with CAP socioeconomic status is shown in Table 3. The significant correlations indicate that those non-professionals with high CAP status are likely to have low aspirations and expectations of job status and employment five years hence, and to believe the CAP to be doing a poor job in serving the poor. Conversely, low status workers tend to have the opposite attitudes and perceptions—high aspirations, optimistic aspirations but pessimistic expectations of their future jobs and salaries, and a favorable opinion of the CAP's efficacy in helping others.

The negative correlate of CAP SES with aspirations is somewhat surprising. Most likely, high status nonprofessionals are much more realistic in their future hopes than low status workers. This notion is supported, in

TABLE 3

Attitudinal and Perceptual Correlates of CAP SES
(Low to High)

Variable	Partial r^a
Aspiration scale (low to high)	—.28[c]
Aspiration-expectation discrepancy index (low to high)	—.27[c]
CAP efficacy scale (low to high)	—.24[b]

[a] CAP Agency A vs. B differences partialed.
[b] $p < .05$
[c] $p < .01$

part, by the association of the aspiration-expectation discrepancy index and CAP SES where high status indigenous personnel have a significantly lower discrepancy between what they hope for and what they expect to get in the future. Of course, another possibility is that high status workers, having achieved relatively good jobs in CAP, have scaled down their future aspirations to match their future expectations. In any case, low status workers are hoping for "the moon" but do not really expect it. Perhaps this is a psychological defense employed by individuals who have experienced considerable hardship and failure in life.

Another interesting finding is that high status workers do not think the CAP is adequately serving the poor. It can be speculated that they are keenly aware and critical of programmatic limitations in the agency. On the other hand, low status workers who strongly believe in the CAP's efficacy in helping the poor most likely are demonstrating their appreciation in being off the unemployment or welfare rolls and having the opportunity to be trained for a new career, even though their positions may not provide them with access to other and better positions.

Several other variables hypothesized to be significantly correlated with CAP SES were not. The anomie and conventionalism scales, although significantly associated at the zero-order level, were not significantly related after partialing out CAP-agency differences. The work alienation and agency-neighborhood orientation scales were not significantly correlated with CAP SES.

CONCLUSIONS AND IMPLICATIONS

In spite of the limitations of the measures used and the generalizability of these findings to other nonprofessional populations, the results do have implications for employment policies of the poor as well as for additional research. Nonprofessionals studied were in better positions and earned more money than they did prior to the CAP program. In many cases, individuals were removed from unemployment and dependence on welfare by the employment opportunities in CAP.

The question of who does well in CAP and why is clarified, to some degree, by the analysis. As previously indicated, a major factor in doing well in CAP is having done well before CAP. This would suggest that CAP agencies attempt to recruit "the cream of the crop" from the ranks of the poor. Marris and Rein state that oftentimes this results from the agency's desire to insure success in their employment of indigenous personnel.[14] Also, as indicated by the high negative correlation between CAP SES and job training, agencies do not have to spend extra time and resources in training nonprofessionals with previous stable employment histories and useful skills. This may explain why workers with high CAP status had long job tenures as it is most likely they were among the first to be hired.

Low status nonprofessionals who come to the agency with poor employment, educational, and financial histories are indeed better off than they were before, but the question remains whether these individuals, many of whom could be referred to as "the hard-core unemployed," can expect a new career within the CAP program. Workers with poor backgrounds receive some job training from the CAP, but seldom are promoted and usually have the shortest tenure with the program. It is quite possible that agencies recruit these persons from the unemployment and welfare rolls for a variety of dead-end jobs, as Yankelovich[15] suggests, or that these individuals do not stay a sufficient duration of time to be promoted. It would seem, then, that these findings do not completely sustain the notion that the poverty program is providing viable new careers with the prospect of not only a job but also upward movement within the CAP employment system.

These findings also indicate that the nonprofessionals' attitudes and perceptions vary according to their statuses in the CAP. The high status worker seems realistic and self-assured in his aspirations and expectations of future employment and income undoubtedly reflecting the fact that he has skills and knowledge which are more likely to be marketable outside the CAP system. The low status worker, on the other hand, appears to have incorporated the many promises of the poverty program into his aspirations for the future, although, in reality, he expects little. His faith in the CAP's efficacy may reflect his hopes that some of his aspirations will be realized, or it might be a psychological defense against the recognition that few poverty program promises have been fulfilled.

These findings suggest the question of whether or not the entire concept of career ladders for the poor is too ambitious an undertaking for CAP agencies and the host community social agencies to implement successfully. In many respects, agencies have avoided confronting the problem either by recruiting poor individuals who have already been relatively successful in competing for good jobs or by their lack of sound training programs and additional educational opportunities for those nonprofessionals with unstable employment histories. Too often CAP agencies have promised much but have delivered little.

Any viable employment program must, as Pearl and Riessman recom-

[14] Peter Marris and Martin Rein, *Dilemmas of Social Reform* (New York: Atherton Press, 1967), pp. 72–73.
[15] Yankelovich, *The Nonprofessional in CAP*.

mend, first provide meaningful and worthwhile jobs which can serve as paths to new careers.[16] To do this, many agencies may have to evaluate and alter specific duties and functions which the nonprofessional can perform. Once viable jobs are available, useful training and educational opportunities for the indigenous worker are crucial. Anything less will, no doubt, contribute to the frustration and alienation of many nonprofessionals. Hopefully, additional suggestions and answers will be forthcoming when researchers undertake further representative studies in order to assess the effectiveness and consequences of new career programs for the poor.

[16] Pearl and Riessman, *New Careers,* p. 13.

30

TRIBAL LEADERSHIP IN THE WAR ON POVERTY: A CASE STUDY[1]

ROBERT L. BEE

University of Connecticut

A S SEVERAL "SELF-HELP" DEVELOPMENT PROGRAMS GAINED MOMENTUM on the Fort Yuma Indian Reservation, it became apparent that the behavior of the local tribal council members was deviating from the enthusiasm and cooperation anticipated both in the formal provisions of the development schemes and by some government officials assigned to work with the Indians. The following discussion argues that such behavior was not at all inconsistent with the conditions of "pre-program" reservation leadership or the formal requirements of the leaders' participation in the programs, and that therefore such behavior could have been predicted. Specifically, the leadership behavior is placed within a context of three interrelated causal factors. The first is the persistence of a heritage of authority[2] struggles at two levels: between the council as a unit and the non-tribal administration; and among individual council members themselves. The second is the persistence of a tendency for several formal leadership statuses simultaneously to be vested in a single individual. The third factor is the dual nature of the leaders' involvement in the development effort. They were at once program administrators, ideally impartial, and recipients of lucrative program benefits. Given the presence of these factors, it is argued, the leaders' behavior can be viewed as a rational effort to maximize the political and material potential of the programs for their personal satisfaction.[3]

THE SOCIOCULTURAL SETTING AND TRIBAL LEADERSHIP

The Fort Yuma Indian Reservation is located in the extreme southeastern corner of the state of California, just across the Colorado River from Yuma, Arizona. There are about 1,000 Indians living on, or directly adjacent to, the 8,766-acre reservation. The remaining 500 or so individuals listed on the tribal roll have moved to urban areas such as San Francisco or Los Angeles. Once the Yuma were subsistence horticulturalists, using the fertile bottomlands of the Colorado to grow crops with relatively little effort or

[1] Funds for the research upon which this report is based were provided by a National Institute of Mental Health Pre-Doctoral Fellowship and a Wenner-Gren Foundation for Anthropological Research Pre-Doctoral Research Grant. The author wishes to express his gratitude to both these agencies, and to James A. Clifton, Murray Wax, Eric Larson and Larry Carney for their patient reading and criticism of earlier drafts of the case study.

[2] Following Swartz *et al.*, "authority" refers to "the right to use and acquire power vested in a status . . ."; power ". . . is the capacity to secure compliance with binding decisions." Marc J. Swartz, Victor W. Turner, and Arthur Tuden, *Political Anthropology* (Chicago: Aldine Publishing Co., 1966), pp. 17–18.

[3] This same basic perspective has been adopted by F. G. Bailey in his *Tribe, Caste and Nation* (Manchester: University of Manchester Press, 1960), a masterful analysis of politics and social change in India.

anxiety. Today there is little subsistence or cash-cropping performed by the people. Some have chosen to work for Anglo farmers who have leased Indian lands, but most of those employed work at various unskilled jobs in the town of Yuma or at one of the nearby government installations. According to one estimate, only ten of the reservation's 180 families had an annual income in excess of $4,000 in 1965.[4] The physical presence of government authority on the reservation is provided by a small subagency of the Bureau of Indian Affairs (BIA), and by a 14-bed Public Health Service hospital.

After subjection to intervention by the Spanish in the 18th century and the Anglos in the 19th century, the traditional tribal leadership patterns were well into a process of transformation by 1900. Tribal "chief" had become a status validated by written government certification, rather than by achievement through "dream power."[5] The chief was expected to convey the wishes of the government to his people, and to assist the government administrators in securing compliance. Those who refused to perform such roles were formally deposed by the external authorities.[6] Deposed chiefs, would-be chiefs, and their followers retaliated against the regime by convening informal "councils" to air protests, and by bombarding the higher government echelons with petitions.

The tenor of the petitions reflected the two levels at which authority struggles were waged. One type of petition-protest pitted the tribe (specifically, its "spokesmen") against the government over such issues as the forceful removal of children to boarding school and the inequities of the land-leasing procedures. A second type included attempts by politically active individuals and their supporters to discredit the activities of their opponents within the tribe, and to gain official government validation of their own claims to influential statuses.[7] Contents of this latter type of petition and recollections of informants indicate that, as in other similar situations,[8] alliances were made and broken between politicians, allegiance was shifting among individuals beyond the diffuse boundaries of the bilateral kinship support group, and the positions on vaguely conceived issues were characteristically subject to radical alteration. Petitions of both types were incapable themselves of producing lasting rearrangements of the authority structure.

[4] Program Proposal, Fort Yuma Community Action Program, April 27, 1965.

[5] C. Daryll Forde, "Ethnography of the Yuma Indians," *University of California Publications in American Archaeology and Ethnology*, 28 (1930–1931), p. 134.

[6] Letter from J. A. Leonard, Special Investigator, United States Indian Service, to the Commissioner of Indian Affairs, March 22, 1893.

[7] One series of letters and petitions protested the activities of a prominent political activist who had embarked on a mission to Washington to "talk with the Commissioner," a venture financed by collections from the tribal members. The mission mysteriously ended up in Philadelphia. These and other petitions of protest have been preserved in the National Archives in Washington, D.C.

[8] Situations which are generally labelled as "factionalism." See, for example, James A. Clifton's illuminating study of "Culture Change, Structural Stability and Factionalism in the Prairie Potawatomi Reservation Community," *Midcontinent American Studies Journal*, 6 (Fall, 1965), pp. 101–123.

The Yuma apparently perceived some hope for enhanced tribal authori-ty vis-à-vis the government in the creation of a federally-sanctioned tribal council in 1938. Community enthusiasm was reflected in large voter turn-outs for the first two council elections. The new council optimistically drafted a comprehensive proposal for community agricultural development in 1940, and forwarded it through government channels for approval. Yet the final reaction of the government was indifference, forced by the fiscal demands of World War II. The project never passed beyond the proposal stage. Furthermore, government control at the local level was eased only slightly, if at all, with the election of the new council. The BIA maintained its control of the tribal budget, acting under advice from Washington to be watchful for evidence of fiscal irresponsibility on the part of local Yuma leaders.[9] A tribal court was created to hear cases of (only minor) offenses, but it was abolished with the passage of Public Law 280 in 1953.

Coupled with this persistence of government control after 1938 was the persistence of political haggling among councilmen, backed by their sup-port groups. Members introduced resolutions in meetings calling for the impeachment of rivals; the rivals retaliated with written countercharges, liberally laced with rhetorical flourishes. The apparent aim was the en-hancement of individual authority.

The combined effect of all these circumstances, and others, at the com-munity level was the erosion of confidence in the council's ability to bring meaningful change. Councilmen were well aware of this erosion. Their awareness was one goad in their short-lived attempt in 1960 to seize, uni-laterally, the power to blockade reservation roads against non-Indian tres-passers (the issue involving in part the government's reluctance in return-ing land adjacent to the reservation to tribal control). Significantly, the tribal court abolished in 1953 was briefly and unilaterally re-constituted by the council to handle cases resulting from incidents at the blockades. The council held press conferences, capitalizing on the publicity created by the blockade to air their grievances against the government. Popular support for the council's action among tribesmen temporarily fused the haggling groups into a more or less united front against a common external threat. But five days after the blockade had begun, the action was deemed illegal by the BIA, and the bid for enhanced council authority versus the government was squelched.[10] Haggling resumed between councilmen, and the community's beliefs about council impotence were reinforced.

The second relevant factor in this case, the tendency for one person to occupy more than one leadership status, can be attributed to several con-ditions existing prior to the advent of the programs. Typically, the leader-ship statuses have involved roles requiring a speaking ability, either in native Quechan or in English, which must be demonstrated in public gatherings. Frequently there is also a necessity to interact with non-Indians: religious functionaries, veterans' leaders, newspapermen, BIA

[9] Letter, F. H. Daiker of the Office of Indian Affairs to C. H. Gensler, Superintendent of the Colorado River Agency, 1938 (no month or day listed).
[10] *Yuma Daily Sun*, April 25 to May 1, 1960.

representatives, and the like. There are few in the community who are willing to perform such roles, fearing public criticism for "not getting things right" or for "trying to be the big shot." Thus those seeking office in the tribal government, which involves such role behavior, tend also to be favored as leaders of reservation voluntary associations[11] because of their willingness to speak before an audience or to interact, as leaders, with outsiders.

Tribal leadership is also affected by the unattractiveness of the reservation community for highly acculturated Yumas. It is not an environment luring the individuals who, by Anglo standards, are the most educated and upwardly-mobile members of the tribe.[12] Such individuals have moved into nearby towns, or to Los Angeles or San Francisco, and return only for celebrations and visits with relatives and friends. In general, the most educated, upwardly-mobile individuals who choose to remain on the reservation seek membership in the tribal government, or other positions of leadership (typically in voluntary associations which are not "traditional" in organization or function).

Finally, in keeping with the tendency to personal authority enhancement, at least one council president simply appointed himself to serve in several leadership statuses. This incurred ample criticism, but no impeachment.

These several conditions have combined to produce a relatively small pool of individuals willing to assume the status of leaders, and therefore a multiplicity of leadership statuses held by a single individual. With an increase in available statuses brought by the development programs, and without an enlargement of the size of the tribal leadership pool, the feature has persisted.

THE DEVELOPMENT PROGRAMS

In the period 1963–1965, the Yuma tribe became the beneficiaries of:

1. A mutual-help housing program designed to provide low-income families with new cinder-brick homes, in return for volunteer labor in their construction and modest monthly payments;

2. A water and sanitation project which would eventually bring running water and indoor bathrooms to those willing to pay monthly water bills;

3. A Community Action Program aimed at providing vocational training with wages, as well as improving public health, educational achievement, domestic planning and skills, and recreation facilities for the community and adjacent areas;

---

[11] Voluntary associations were surprisingly numerous, relative to the population of the reservation community. They included several Christian mission groups, a veterans' organization, various athletic teams, women's clubs, dancing clubs (to revive or perpetuate traditional dances), and others.

[12] This same condition was reported in a Mexican community undergoing developmental change. See George Foster, *Tzintzuntzan: Mexican Peasants in a Changing World* (Boston: Little, Brown and Co., 1967), p. 274.

4. A Neighborhood Youth Corps program to provide part-time employment for students who needed money to stay in school.

All of the programs were administered according to policy dictated by the federal government, and all involved a coordination of activities between local government representatives and tribal members. The tribal council was a signatory to the formal acceptance of each program. In part because it was also a ready-made coordinating committee, it was designated the "sponsoring agency" of both the Community Action Program and the Neighborhood Youth Corps. The assumption of this new status was heralded by the council and outside administrators alike as a breakthrough in the path toward eventual self-determination, providing the council with needed experience in previously unencountered problems of administration. Among other things, the status carried with it the responsibility for seeing that the tribe fulfilled its portion of the agreements, and, of greater immediate concern to the councilmen, it granted them the authority to hire and fire personnel involved.[13]

The council had no such formal status in the housing or water programs, however, aside from the appointment of members to the water program coordinating committee and the final approval of agreements between the water committee and the Public Health Service (the government agency involved). Coordination on the housing program was effected by a "housing authority" consisting of two highly acculturated Yumas[14] and three Anglos. The chairman of the authority was an Anglo woman.

THE COURSE OF EVENTS

During the planning phases of the water and housing programs, informants recalled some wariness on the part of councilmen, but the general attitude reported was one of enthusiasm and willingness to cooperate with the government. The attitudes which emerged after the projects were underway were not apparently foreshadowed in the council's reaction in these earliest steps of the development effort. The same salutary attitudes were reported during the planning phases of the Community Action Program and the Neighborhood Youth Corps. Had the hostility and suspicion subsequently manifested by the council been anticipated, it is unlikely it would have been designated the sponsoring agency of either program at the outset.

Then the programs were funded, and government personnel, other hired supervisors, equipment, and construction materials began to arrive on the

[13] The hiring authority was circumscribed, however. Applicants for key supervisory positions in the CAP and NYC were first screened by "advisory committees" composed of Yumas and local Anglo educators, businessmen, and government personnel, whose recommendations were then approved by the council. During my stay in the community, the council hired no key personnel without the prior approval of the appropriate advisory committee.

[14] One had formerly served as tribal council president; the other was a successful candidate for the council in a special election in 1966. The individual tendency to serve in more than one leadership status is apparent.

reservation. Even though its members lacked administrative sophistication and exhaustive knowledge about the provisions of the programs, the council seemed most anxious to assume some sort of role behavior appropriate to their statuses as members of the sponsoring agency and governing body. But what would their behavior be, and from which reference groups[15] would it be derived? The council had never been a sponsoring agency before. And, although their formal status in the water and housing programs was not specified, individual councilmen and their friends and relatives were participating in both, adding an element of personal interest to the council's behavior. These friends and relatives came to individual councilmen with problems and questions about the program, rather than to the external government experts and administrators. To satisfy their supporters, the councilmen had to relay the problems to the appropriate expert and receive appropriate answers.

Thus the council's role in the programs, as perceived by the councilmen themselves, came to be that of a monitoring body for *all* the development agencies. That is, councilmen heard local citizens' complaints, conducted inquiries into the managment of specific program activities when the situation seemed serious enough, and stated repeatedly that they wanted to make sure that the community members (including themselves) were receiving all the benefits to which they were entitled. Even in the two programs in which they were not designated the sponsoring agency, the councilmen nonetheless justified their inquiries as members of the elected government of the reservation community.

Within months, the council's monitor role became infused with suspicion and hostility toward those project administrators who either failed to keep the council informed, or did so only after important program developments had already become the subject of community conversation. The suspicion was less apparent in relationships with the director of the Community Action Program, an Anglo, who conscientiously prepared timely reports for presentation in council meetings. Such action served to validate the status of the council as the sponsoring agency in this case, and thus to ameliorate some of the tension. In the other programs, however, it had become evident that the councilmen were most sensitive to perceived circumventions or diminutions of their authority.

Some examples: by June, 1966, the relationship between some councilmen and key personnel involved in the water program was characterized by mutual antipathy. The councilmen claimed they had not been kept informed about developments on the project. They believed (mistakenly) that the Public Health Service had been making plans unilaterally to withdraw its support prior to the terminal date agreed upon by both the PHS and the tribe. Project personnel, on the other hand, privately charged the

---

[15] As used here, "a reference group is a group, collectivity, or person which the actor takes into account in some manner in the course of selecting a behavior from among a set of alternatives, or in making a judgment about a problematic issue." Theodore D. Kemper, "Reference Groups, Socialization and Achievement," *American Sociological Review*, 33 (Feb., 1968), pp. 31–45.

council with "playing a game of pretense" by assuming that the project was a *council* project, with councilmen, not the PHS personnel, as directors. The majority of the interaction on the water project took place between PHS authorities and the water program planning committee, rather than the council as a unit. This was in keeping with the terms of the formal agreement between the tribe and the PHS.

In the housing program, the housing authority held policy meetings with individual homeowners, some of whom were council members. But the council as a unit did not participate. On one occasion, the authority chairman cancelled a meeting with homeowners allegedly because she learned the council planned to attend the meeting *en masse* to get answers to grievances.[16] This, at least, was the councilmen's interpretation of the cancellation, and their suspicion was thereby intensified.

The council was soon to learn that even the status of sponsoring agency did not carry with it the authority its members had initially considered their own. This disconcerting message was conveyed through a series of interrelated episodes involving both the general authority of the tribal council acting in its sponsor status, and the interpersonal struggle for influence among council members.

The focal figure in the episodes was a woman, highly acculturated, who had recently returned to the reservation after several years' absence. Because of her experience in various bureaucratic jobs, her obvious interest in reservation affairs, and her willingness to assume leadership roles, she was in demand as a leader. Her several statuses included (but were not limited to) chairman of the water planning committee, director of the Neighborhood Youth Corps (the council officially "hired" her), and member of the tribal council.[17]

Her tenure on the council had been marked by political haggling between herself and other council members, primarily over her alleged failure to keep the council informed of changes taking place in the Neighborhood Youth Corps program. Finally, in June, 1966, she was asked to resign from the council because she had moved to a home just outside the reservation boundary (an automatic disqualification from council membership according to the tribal constitution). She chose to resist the ouster on the grounds that the residence rule was being arbitrarily enforced in her case.

Tempers flared, and the council was inspired to take further and more punitive action to reassert its authority: acting in the status of sponsoring agency, it passed a resolution to fire her as director of the Neighborhood Youth Corps.

[16] Their grievances included a perceived incompetence of technical experts on the project and charges that inferior materials were being used in house construction, to mention only a few.

[17] For a time the woman served simultaneously as a member of the tribal council, chairman of the water planning committee, president of the Catholic women's club, president of the local Home and School Association, president of the San Pasqual Welfare Council, and director of the Neighborhood Youth Corps. One of her political rivals served as president of the tribal council, commander of the veterans' group, band manager, and funeral director (one of two in the community).

However, this action was nullified by administrative fluctuations in the regional NYC structure. At the time the resolution was passed, the status of the council *itself* as sponsoring agency of the local NYC was about to be terminated and the responsibility shifted to the county.[18] The woman was advised by higher NYC authority *not* to step down on the basis of the council's resolution. Political supporters of the woman were meanwhile marshalling community sentiment against the council's high-handed tactics: how, it was asked, could the Yuma ever hope to develop real leadership if ambitious persons were to be thus thwarted by their own people? The sentiment was unambiguously communicated to the council during a particularly heated public meeting.

The council had believed that it had the authority to fire the woman as NYC director, and was chagrined at the action of the higher NYC echelons. The woman resigned from the council, but she maintained her status as NYC director, and for a time following this incident maintained her office on the reservation—while the council yielded its own office space to the burgeoning Community Action Program and set up temporary quarters in the BIA subagency.

So the struggle ostensibly over the tenure of a council position spread into a different structural entity, the Neighborhood Youth Corps. But because the woman held several leadership statuses simultaneously, the repercussions of the haggling did not end there. They diffused into the water program as well.

The local Public Health Service officials had been anxiously prodding the council to approve plans for the establishment of a corporation to manage the new water system. Councilmen had hedged, saying they needed to study the plans more carefully. The woman, while still on the council, agreed to make copies for each councilman to read, but she had not distributed them at the time of her dismissal. An impasse of several weeks then ensued, during which the council and the woman each accused the other of abrogation of responsibility. It was broken when a NYC worker carried the copies across the old Fort Yuma quadrangle and placed them on the council president's desk.

In the meantime, the local PHS authorities were being frustrated in their attempts to gain some sort of concrete reaction to the plans from the council, and several families were already using water from the new system although billing procedures had not been worked out. The plans were still not approved two months after this incident. (As of December, 1967—a year and a half later—the water corporation was not yet formed.)

LEADERSHIP BEHAVIOR IN ITS CONTEXT

It is evident that in the course of the programs the tribal council was faced with several variables in its attempt to forge some sort of role behavior appropriate to its status as sponsoring agency and governing body. First, individual councilmen were not merely by-standers with an aloof or

[18] The council had been apprised of this possibility some weeks earlier, but apparently had no clear notion of when the shift would take place.

impartial interest in program benefits. They were themselves beneficiaries: six of the ten new houses being built were their own, or those of close kinsmen, for example. To ensure that the full provisions of the government's commitment were being met was of the greatest personal concern.

As tribal politicians, they were also concerned about maintaining their voter support, characteristically given by kinsmen and close friends. In the course of the progression of the programs from the proposal-writing stage into the stage of implementation,[19] there were inevitably misunderstandings and re-adjustments forced by unanticipated developments, *Constituents seldom came to the councilmen to tell them they were satisfied.* Instead, they confronted their councilmen with their difficulties or misunderstandings, and demanded council action. There was the lurking danger, regardless of the fact that the supporters were kinsmen, that a councilman's failure to take steps to alleviate the misunderstanding would spell his political doom at the next election.[20]

Against these two demanding considerations was that of the tenor of council participation expected by the government agencies involved. Objectively considered, this cue for expected behavior had to be less compelling than the others. It was the community, not the government, who elected the council. And the leadership statuses in the development programs were matters of written agreement between the tribe and the government, they could not easily be eradicated by less-than-ideal role performance (or so it seemed before the attempted dismissal of the NYC director).

Thus the best interests of the councilmen were served by their wary behavior and their demands for information: they thereby satisfied themselves that their personal benefits were not being affected by some sort of bureaucratic folderol; and by satisfying their personal doubts they were at the same time engaging in action which would ensure their continued political viability.

But while the nature of councilmen's participation and their behavioral alternatives can be invoked in order to understand better the wariness in councilmen's behavior, they cannot alone account for the hostility which became manifest toward project personnel representing government agencies. Thus it is necessary to reconsider the issue of tribal council authority.

The two different levels of authority enhancement in which leaders had been perennially involved resulted in contradictory tendencies. First, as a unit, the council wished to enhance its authority in the programs, with the result that the council's role appropriate to its sponsoring agency status was generalized into programs in which it enjoyed no such formal status.

Validation of the claim to enhanced authority could, however, ultimately come only from the external government agencies themselves, much as the validation of the status of chief over half a century earlier. No such

---

[19] That is, the actual commencement of the programs within the community, marked by the arrival of personnel, materials and funds.

[20] Kinship support was in fact withdrawn from an individual in one election in the 1950's, but because there were so few candidates for council positions, he was elected with an extremely small vote total.

validation, in terms the council was willing to recognize, came from officials in either the housing program or the water program. And none came from the Neighborhood Youth Corps director.

The NYC case introduces the second, and contradictory, level of the authority problem: the enhancement of individual authority over one's political opponents. The NYC director's multifarious and important statuses chafed her ambitious rivals, and her resistance against their actions could only have exacerbated their hostility. Add to her resistance the veto of higher external authorities and some blunt criticism from their own constituency, and the councilmen's hostility becomes all the more intelligible, if in part illegitimate.

The speed with which the NYC dismissal resolution was passed, relative to the extensive deliberation required for action on the plans for the water corporation, indicates that the council was quick to act on matters involving authority, but rather slow to formulate decisive action on important procedural details.

Finally, it is obvious that the multifaceted commitment of the woman in community affairs contributed to a diffusion or generalization of the conflict. In other communities, such as "Springdale" described by Vidich and Bensman,[21] the simultaneous occupation of many leadership statuses by a few individuals could result in the successful coordination of community activities. But among the Yuma leaders it appears that the means of conflict resolution were less effective and the pattern of superior-subordinate relationships less well established.

CONCLUSION

This paper has offered an analysis of "self-help" programs at the grass roots level by portraying the tribal council both as a group whose political ideologies have been molded by a tradition of what Robert Thomas has called "powerless politics,"[22] and as a body of individuals perfectly capable of making rational choices between different behavioral alternatives. That their choices have not always coincided with those anticipated by Anglo planners at the policy-making level is self-evident. The point is that policy-makers should have anticipated this incongruity, rather than cheerful acquiesence and apolitical altruism. This case further suggests that even when the latter attitudes are manifested during the proposal-writing stages, they are not necessarily reliable indicators of how leaders will behave once the programs are underway.

Patterns of community leadership behavior in the context of newly-created development programs might be anticipated by careful study of leadership in the pre-program community, with particular attention to the way in which authority squabbles are handled, the degree of past authority granted indigenous leaders relative to that anticipated in new programs,

---

[21] Arthur J. Vidich and Joseph Bensman, *Small Town in Mass Society* (Garden City, N.Y.: Doubleday Anchor Books, 1960).
[22] "Powerless Politics," *New University Thought*, 4 (Winter, 1966–1967), pp. 44–53.

and the processes of leadership selection (including the availability of local personnel willing and able to perform necessary leadership functions).

None of the conditions sketched above seems unique to the Yuma Indian community. Zurcher,[23] for example, describes the dilemma of Indian poverty program leaders caught between the expectations of their people and those of external administrative agencies in an urban setting. Authority squabbles are widely reported in American Indian materials.[24] Aside from the "Springdale" study and some passing references by Walker,[25] overlapping leadership statuses in small leadership pools are less explicitly described, but do not seem atypical. The Waxes[26] note the shrewd calculations of potential program benefits on the part of Indian leaders.

Additional comparative research may reveal that these factors exist elsewhere in the same or similar combinations, with similar effects. If so, this knowledge could then be used in the adjustment of expectations and policies for future "self-help" programs, resulting in their greater effectiveness from the perspective of both the administrators and the recipients.

[23] Louis A. Zurcher, "The Leader and the Lost: a Case Study of Indigenous Leadership in a Poverty Program Community Action Committee," *Genetic Psychology Monographs,* 76 (Aug., 1967), pp. 23–93.

[24] See, for example, Mary Shepardson, *Navajo Ways in Government* (American Anthropological Association Memoir 96, 1963), pp. 68–69, 94–95; Edward Spicer, *Cycles of Conquest* (Tucson: University of Arizona Press, 1962), pp. 491–501; and Deward Walker, *Conflict and Schism in Nez Perce Acculturation* (Pullman: Washington State University Press, 1968), p. 143.

[25] Walker, *Conflict and Schism,* p. 123.

[26] Murray and Rosalie Wax, "Enemies of the People," in H. S. Becker *et al.,* eds., *Institutions and the Person* (Chicago: Aldine Publishing Co., 1968), pp. 101–118.

31

DIFFERENTIAL PERCEPTIONS OF IMPACT
OF A RURAL ANTI-POVERTY CAMPAIGN[1]

WILLIS A. SUTTON, JR.

University of Kentucky

E VALUATIONS OF COMMUNITY ACTION PROGRAMS HAVE GIVEN LITTLE AT-
tention to the differential perceptions of impact held by different
segments of the communities involved.[2] Of course group perceptions
prove neither the effectiveness nor the ineffectiveness of such programs,
but whether most persons toward whom such a program is aimed feel
it is helpful or hurtful, whether those working in the program feel it accomplishes little or much, whether those volunteering their time to policy
boards feel it is worthy or unworthy, and whether community leaders
generally view it favorably or unfavorably are all data significant for program policy and for social action generalization and theory.

The purpose of this paper is to describe the perceptions of impact of a
rural community action program held by several different components of
the population and to comment briefly on the factors related to these variations.

THE STUDY SETTING AND RESPONDENTS

Knox County, Kentucky, has had one of the country's major rural community action programs operating under the Office of Economic Opportunity. Starting with one staff person in February, 1965, its operation was
quickly expanded. In each of the next three years, its annual budget was
something over $700,000. Operated through more than a dozen community
centers, all but two located in one of the more isolated sections of the
county, this program carried on a wide range of activities including pre-
school and adult education, youth and recreation activities, health services,
vocational and job training, consumer and citizen participation programs.

Six sets of Knox County respondents were asked their impressions of the
local OEO programs in spring, 1968:

1. A 1966 random sample of 727 persons in 12 rural neighborhoods[3] yielded

---

[1] A revision of a paper presented at the 1968 meetings of the American Sociological
Association. The data on which this paper is based were collected under auspices of
the University of Kentucky's Center for Developmental Change and within Contract
693 between the University of Kentucky Research Foundation and the Office of
Economic Opportunity. The author wishes to acknowledge his debt to the CDC which
supported additional analysis and to express special appreciation to Mrs. Vibha Saiyed
for her able assistance in data processing.

[2] A search of the literature since the Economic Opportunity Act was passed in 1964
failed to yield any study dealing specifically with such differential perceptions. Perceptions by the staff of several urban neighborhood centers are treated in a study by
Sidney J. Kaplan and Andre Delbecq, "Perceived Hindrance to Social Change in a
Poverty Program," *Sociology and Social Research*, 52 (Jan., 1968), pp. 269–278.

[3] This sample was drawn in the following fashion. The 12 neighborhoods were
purposively selected. They included four where community centers operated and eight
others selected so that altogether they had a population of size and social characteristics

♦ First published in Social Science Quarterly 50, No. 3 (December, 1969).

618 respondents who still lived in the county in 1968. Of these, 539 had never been members of several OEO "local action groups" and were thus considered to have the least knowledge of and connection with the program.

2. The 79 respondents in the 12 neighborhood sample who at any time had been members of one of these main citizen organizations were defined as participants and labelled "LAG members."

3. The original 727 sample respondents and 37 community leaders were asked to nominate county leaders. Those 29 who were nominated four or more times by the sample respondents or two or more times by the community leaders, and who were *not* members of the community action agency board of directors, are designated as county leaders. They might be expected, because of their civic participation, to have some impression of a program as large as this one, but, like the non-LAG members, they had no direct contact with the work of the agency.

4. More closely related to the program were 36 respondents designated "leaders of the poor." These were a two-thirds random sample of persons holding non-paying leadership positions either on the policy board of the community action agency or on the neighborhood or county level citizen organizations created by the program as forums and action groups to represent the poor.[4]

5. To represent the community action agency board of directors a two-thirds sample of the 53 board members who had served three months or longer was drawn. The application of other pertinent criteria, however, reduced the number of respondents in the category to 23.[5]

---

comparable to the four center neighborhoods. Within each of these neighborhoods a total census of households was secured. The sample consisted of all heads of households and homemakers in a randomly selected 50 per cent of each neighborhood's households.

[4] From a list of 40 "officers," of the four local action groups in the neighborhoods used in the larger sample, a two-thirds random sample was selected. Another two-thirds sample was drawn from a list of 29 persons who were either officers of the Association (the county-level organization) of Local Action Groups, or were community action agency board of directors members who also were poor. The 36 "leaders of the poor" derive then from both these "local" and "county" samples.

"Officers" here include both the chairman, vice-chairman, secretary and treasurer, and the three representatives to the county-level Association of Local Action Groups which each local group elected. In some instances one person filled more than one of these positions.

Actually, if all persons drawn in these two two-thirds samples could have been used, the respondents would have numbered about 50. It was later found, however, that a number of these "leaders of the poor" had become paid staff members, and hence had to be classed as staff personnel and not as volunteer citizen leaders.

[5] Of the original 38 persons drawn, one was discovered not to have been a member of the board, one refused to be interviewed, one had moved from the county, nine were more appropriately classed as "leaders of the poor," and three had become employees in the program and hence, had to be classed as staff members.

Six of the remaining 23 board members also qualified as "county leaders," but since their board status was more salient to their program orientation than their community position, they were retained as part of the "board" set of respondents rather than classed among the county leaders.

6. Those closest to the program were persons having full- or part-time employment with the agency. The 28 "staff" employees interviewed in the study included all ten of the people in the top supervisory posts in the program and all neighborhood center personnel in each of the four neighborhoods originally selected for study.[6]

THE NATURE OF THE DATA

Each of these six sets of respondents was asked two main questions. The first had to do with their perceptions of the program's effect on each of a number of aspects of community life:

> As you know, we are seeking to learn what the Knox County Economic Opportunity Program has meant to this county. We are going to mention several different aspects of life now, and, FOR EACH ONE, we would like you to tell us whether you think Knox County's Economic Opportunity Program—(Community Action Program)—has IMPROVED THINGS, has MADE THINGS WORSE, or has had NO SIGNIFICANT EFFECT EITHER WAY. Now, what would you say its effect has been on _____ (inserting the first item)? Would you say the KCEOC program *improved this, made this worse, or had no significant or appreciable effect?*

Each respondent was asked this question for the 17 items listed in Table 1.

After inspection of a sample of the responses disclosed that a considerable majority of respondents viewed the program as having improved most items, the categories of "made worse" and "had no effect" were "collapsed," both being considered responses *unfavorable* to the program. A dichotomized code of either "favorable" or "unfavorable" to the program for each answer was thus established.[7]

The other question was designed to secure respondents' impressions of how well the community action program had reached the target population:

> Whatever your opinions about the KCEOC program's over-all or specific effects we would like to know your feeling about

---

It should be noted, in addition, that several members of the CAA Board—those who were themselves poor—are not here classed as board respondents. They are included among the "leaders of the poor" along with other officers of the organizations set up for and with the poor.

[6] The major supervisory personnel included were the Executive Director, two Center Program Directors, Personnel Officer, Director of Technical Services, Special Assistant to the Executive Director, Training Officer, Director of Early Childhood Program, Assistant Community Center Director and Director of Manpower Programs. At the four community centers all persons in the positions of Center Director, Early Childhood Program Teacher, Teacher Aide and Community Aide were included.

[7] Respondents were permitted a "don't know" or "no opinion" answer as a last resort. Not many of these were found, but, in coding, these, also, were counted as unfavorable responses.

TABLE 1

Extent of Favorable Perception of Impact on Seventeen Selected Items

(Per Cent of Respondents in Each of Six Sets Who Perceived the KCEOC Community Action Program as Having Helped or Improved Each of 17 Items, and Rank Order of Favorability Toward Items.)

Favorable Responses on:	All Respondents (N=734)		TYPES OF RESPONDENTS										
			Staff (N=28)		Board (N=23)		Leaders of Poor (N=36)		County Leaders (N=29)		LAG Members (N=79)		Non-LAG Members (N=539)	
	Per Cent	Rank	Per Cent	Rank	Per Cent	Rank	Per Cent	Rank	Per Cent	Rank	Per Cent	Rank	Per Cent	Rank
1) Educational Opportunities	84.5	1	100.0	2.5	95.7	2	91.7	1.5	79.3	4	94.4	1	81.6	2
2) Health Services	84.3	2	100.0	2.5	95.7	2	88.9	4	75.9	5.5	93.7	2	81.8	1
3) Level of Income	76.8	3	92.9	10	91.3	4	91.7	1.5	93.1	1	88.6	3	71.7	4
4) Job Opportunities	76.2	4	88.9	13	82.6	6	86.1	5	65.5	8.5	83.5	6.5	74.2	3
5) Life in General Here	71.9	5	100.0	2.5	78.3	7.5	75.0	9	82.8	3	84.4	4	67.6	5.5
6) Work Skills of the Poor	70.5	6	96.4	6	60.9	13	71.4	12.5	65.5	8.5	84.6	5	67.6	5.5
7) Opportunities of the Poor to Get Together More and Talk About Their Problems	69.5	7	100.0	2.5	95.7	2	91.4	3	86.2	2	82.3	8	62.6	8
8) Hopefulness of the People	68.1	8	92.9	10	69.6	10	74.3	10	65.5	8.5	83.5	6.5	64.2	7

9) Opportunities Poor Have for Organized Group Action	58.7	9	96.4	6	87.0	5	80.0	8	75.9	5.5	80.8	10	49.9	11
10) Talk Between Poor and Local Officials	57.5	10	92.9	10	65.9	11	80.6	7	58.6	11	72.2	14	51.5	10
11) Organization for Economic Development of County	56.4	11	96.4	6	73.9	9	72.2	11	51.7	12	73.4	13	50.5	9
12) The "Say-so" the Poor Have on Important Matters	55.6	12	92.9	10	63.9	12	66.7	14	48.3	13	81.0	9	49.3	12
13) Neighborhood Leadership	55.0	13	92.9	10	78.3	7.5	82.9	6	65.5	8.5	75.6	12	46.6	13
14) The Way Important Things Get Decided	49.8	14	85.7	14	47.8	14.5	71.4	12.5	41.4	14.5	64.6	16	44.9	15
15) Confidence in Government	49.5	15	57.1	17	34.8	16.5	58.2	15	41.4	14.5	78.2	11	45.3	14
16) County Leadership	46.5	16	78.6	15	47.8	14.5	55.6	16	34.5	16	65.8	15	42.0	16
17) The Way Welfare is Handled	44.0	17	75.4	16	34.8	16.5	47.2	17	31.0	17	53.2	17	41.9	17

WHICH part, if any, of all the people of Knox County it has helped the most. Of these four groups: a) the poorest people in the county; b) the poor, but not the very poorest; c) the middle income group; and d) the well-to-do, which, if any, do you think have been most helped by the KCEOC program?

Anyone checking either the poor or poorest was classed as perceiving the program to be directed at its target population while those checking any other response (including "don't know") were classed as perceiving the program not to be directed at its appropriate population. Classification from this question provides data on what will, later in the paper, be termed "directional," in contrast to "general," impact.

FINDINGS ON THE 17 CONTENT ITEMS

The number and per cent of all respondents giving a favorable reaction on each of the 17 items are presented in Table 1. The items judged to have been helped or improved by the program by more people than any others were "educational opportunities," "health services," "level of income," and "job opportunities." More than 75 per cent of all the Knox countians interviewed said the community action program had improved each of these. On the other hand, items perceived to have been improved by less than half of the respondents were: "the way important things get decided in the county," "confidence in government," "county leadership," and "the way welfare is handled."

These data suggest that, with one special exception in the area of welfare services, more respondents viewed the program as helping to provide services—educational, health, job opportunity and income—than saw it as changing the area's institutional structure—county leadership, how things get decided. Observation of those items with special significance for changing the relationships between the poor and the leaders also supports this point. With regard to "opportunities the poor have for organized group action" "talk between poor people and local officials," "the say-so the poor have on important matters," "neighborhood leadership," and "the way important things get decided," a relatively small percentage of respondents perceived the program as having improved things.

Considerable similarity is observed with regard to the particular items viewed as helped the most and the ones seen as helped the least when responses from the six sets of interviewees are compared. However, there are certain significant variations. Considerably higher percentages of staff, board, leaders of the poor, and county leaders than LAG and non-LAG members felt the program had improved the opportunity the poor had to discuss their problems. A marked difference in view can also be observed among the groups regarding their assessment of the program's relative impact on the work skills of the poor. Board members and leaders of the poor ranked this low among the items in comparative effect, while others viewed it as relatively well served. Further, while other respondents saw the program's effect on job opportunities and level of income in a comparatively favorable light, staff members perceived these areas as relatively poorly served.

In another perspective these data reveal quite clearly the groups who saw the program as most helpful and those who saw it as least helpful. On 15 of the 17 items, a higher per cent of staff members than of any other group perceived the program as helpful. On ten of the 17 items the non-LAG members had the smallest per cent of all sets perceiving the program as helpful. County leaders were close seconds in lack of appreciation of the program. On six of the items, they had the smallest percentage favorable to the program's impact. Interestingly, the one item on which the most unfavorable stand was taken by neither non-LAG members nor county leaders was "confidence in government." Perhaps it is not surprising that the group required to serve as the final arbiter in the inevitable frictions arising from such an operation—the program's board of directors—should perceive the program as least effective on this item.

FINDINGS: THE PATTERN OF GENERAL AND DIRECTIONAL IMPACT PERCEPTIONS

The differential perceptions of the program's impact held by the six sets of respondents may be explored at a more generalized level by combining the responses to the 17 content items into one "general" impact measure and observing the pattern of relationship between this measure and that of "directional" impact derived from the second question put to the respondents. This latter directional measure reflects the percentage of the respondents who felt the program was helping the poor more than it was other segments of the population.

The one index of general impact was derived by summing, for each respondent, the coded answers to all 17 items. These sums ranged from 17 where a person answered all items *unfavorably* to 34 where a *favorable* response was given to every item. Inspection of the distribution of these scores revealed that the median fell within the score 28. All persons having a score of 17–28 were then classified as perceiving the effects of the program relatively unfavorably, while those with scores 29–34 were defined as having relatively favorable perceptions of the program impact.

The number and per cents of all respondents and of all in each set who had favorable perceptions of "general" and of "directional" impacts are shown in Table 2.[8] Interesting differences among the respondent sets are observable. On general impact, the staff held the most favorable view of the program. Next, in order, were members of local action groups, leaders of the poor, and board members. The groups least impressed by the program's general impact were non-LAG members of the sample rural population, and county leaders.

A somewhat different response pattern emerges with regard to percep-

[8] It should be kept in mind that the per cents favorable on general impact are partly functions of using the median as a base for dichotomizing favorable and unfavorable scores. A much higher per cent favorable to the program would have been manifest if the mid-point in range of possible scores had been made the basis of the dichotomy.

tions of directional impact. While the staff and LAG members were again the groups who perceived the program most favorably, the leaders of the poor saw the program least favorably, while non-LAG members, board members, and county leaders also held relatively unfavorable opinions.

Thus, while staff, local action group members, board, and non-LAG members keep their respective first, second, fourth and fifth positions on both measures, the rank order of the leaders of the poor and of the county leaders is reversed. County leaders with the smallest per cent perceiving the program to be generally helpful—only a little more than 40 per cent— had a much more favorable view (both absolutely and relative to others) of the program's directional effectiveness. On the other hand, the leaders of the poor, with a relatively high appreciation of the general impact of the program—almost 70 per cent favorable—manifest the smallest percentage of respondents who felt the program helped the poor more than the non-poor.

DISCUSSION

These varying perceptions of the different sets of respondents seem clearly related to their divergent group interests and concerns.[9] Staff, LAG members, and leaders of the poor, all of whom were directly involved in the activities of the program, emotionally committed to the interests of the poor, and less concerned than other groups with general county conditions, saw the program's directional impact less favorably than its general effectiveness. Board members, with some, but a less direct, association with day-to-day operations, with less commitment to the interests of the poor than the three above sets, and less concern than county leaders for general county conditions, perceived the two program impacts with about the same favorability.

County leaders, on the other hand, who had no direct association with the program, little commitment to the special interests of the poor, but great concern for general county conditions, perceived the program to help the poor considerably more than they felt it helped general conditions in the county.

Non-LAG members present a special case. They had no direct involvement with the program and no very specific concern for general county conditions. While a few more of them saw the CAP as helping the poor than perceived it as improving general county conditions, their difference on the two measures is relatively small. On neither dimension is this the respondent set perceiving the program least favorably; yet on both counts they viewed program operations as quite ineffective. Their responses seem

[9] In interpreting these data, the author draws upon a considerable period of direct observation of the community. As a part of the larger study of the Knox County Community Action Program, the author attended many meetings of the CAA Board, Association of Local Action Groups, and neighborhood LAG's, and executed numerous interviews in the 1966–1968 period. In addition, systematic observations were made during this time of the way in which different groups were involved in the initiation, development and resolution of a number of issues confronting the county.

TABLE 2

Extent of Favorable Perceptions of General and Directional Impacts by Different Respondent Sets
(Number and Per Cent of All Respondents, of All Respondents by Type Who Perceived the Community Action Program as Having Improved Conditions in the County—General Impact—and as Having Helped the Poor More than the Non-Poor—Directional Impact.)

	Total All Respondents (N-734)		CAP Staff (N-28)		Board Members (N-23)		Leaders of the Poor (N-36)		County Leaders (N-29)		LAG Members in Sample (N-79)		Non-LAG Members in Sample (N-539)	
	No.	Per Cent	No.	Per Cent	No.	Per Cent	No.	Per Cent	No.	Per Cent	No.	Per Cent	No.	Per Cent
General Impact	382	52.0	26	92.9	12	52.2	25	69.4	12	41.4	63	79.7	244	45.3
Directional Impact	399	54.8	23	82.1	11	52.4	16	44.4	16	55.2	56	70.9	277	51.8

more a manifestation of pervasive social apathy than of special concern for any differential interests.

It is, however, in the sharp contrast between county leaders and leaders of the poor where the effect of group interests, identifications, and aspirations are most clearly manifest. Identifying themselves more with the general interests of the county than with the poor, one would expect the county leaders to have higher aspirations for the improvement of county conditions than for helping the poor. Clearly, more of them (55 per cent on directional impact) saw the community action program as helpful to the poor than viewed it as improving county conditions (general impact—41 per cent). On the other hand, the leaders of the poor who had greater identification with the interests of the poor and less concern than county leaders for overall conditions, less often perceived the program as helpful to the poor (44 per cent on directional impact) and more often saw it improving the general conditions of the county (69 per cent on general impact).[10]

CONCLUSION

The major significance of this study lies in the answers it gives to two general questions—who holds the most and least favorable views of the effects of this rural community action program and what effects of it are perceived favorably by the largest and by the smallest number of people. Among the six categories of people chosen for study, the program is held in highest regard first by those who worked for pay on the CAP staff and secondly, by the poor people who became members, though not officers, of the neighborhood anti-poverty organizations. On the other hand, the groups holding the most unfavorable view of the program are the members of the program's board of directors and the poor citizens who did not participate at all in the services or operations of the program. Citizen leaders—both county influentials unrelated to the program, and leaders of the poor— exhibit a certain ambivalence in their perceptions of the CAP's effects. The leaders of the poor feel the program helped a great many aspects of community life, but they do not see it as strongly oriented to the special interests of the poor. By contrast, county leaders view the program's orientation to the poor favorably, but seriously question its contribution to various phases of community life.

Income and job, health, and educational services are the aspects of life perceived by most people to be helped by the program. On the other hand, the way welfare is handled, county leadership, the way important decisions are made, and confidence in government are the items the fewest people perceived to have been helped by the program.

One of the goals often attributed to community action programs is the

[10] On this point of relative favorability as between general impact and direction, it is perhaps noteworthy that of the six respondent sets the two least involved with the program were the only ones among whom a larger percentage perceived the program to be directed toward the poor than felt it was improving general conditions in the county.

development of procedures through which communities can more effectively deal with their poverty problems. Since most of the items closely related to elements of procedural change were among those the fewest people perceived to have been improved by the program, these data raise considerable questions about the achievement of this goal in Knox County.

32

PRIESTS, PROTESTS, AND POVERTY INTERVENTION[1]

PATRICK H. McNAMARA
The University of Texas at El Paso

THE CHURCHES' ROLE IN POVERTY INTERVENTION HAS NOT BEEN PARTICU-larly impressive if one judges by references in two of the more re-spected reviews of antipoverty and community action programs. Neither Moynihan nor Marris and Rein contains a single passage signalling the work of any church or churches as dynamic agents of change.[2] Is this simply another indication of the churches' alleged irrelevance in an era of rapid social change?

Lyle Schaller's small volume together with the study of Fish, Nelson, *et al.*, are reminders that churches have indeed been involved in anti-poverty efforts.[3] Schaller cites two national interfaith groups which emer-ged shortly after President Johnson's signing of the Economic Opportunity Act.[4] Such involvement, whether on the national or local level, enmeshes the churches in relationships with the political, economic, and welfare institutions characterizing a large American city. In fact, *The Edge of the Ghetto* singles out church leadership working "in coalition with other civic leaders" as the most important resource offered by the churches to the Chicago organization.[5] Yet it is precisely these alliances with political in-stitutions (particularly federal agencies) as well as other churches which Schaller terms "uneasy." "Can the church *freely* criticize the ally who is supplying ninety per cent of the resources for the war?"[6]

This question suggests that more specific analyses of church antipoverty involvement might well yield valuable sociological insights. *The Edge of the Ghetto* states four "conditioning dimensions which have shaped the

[1] Research reported in this study was undertaken during the author's research assistantship with the Mexican American Study Project, UCLA, 1966–1967. Assistance of the staff, and particularly the Project Director, Professor Leo Grebler, is gratefully acknowledged.

[2] Daniel P. Moynihan, *Maximum Feasible Misunderstanding: Community Action in the War on Poverty* (New York: The Free press, 1969); Peter Marris and Martin Rein, *Dilemmas of Social Reform: Poverty and Community Action in the United States* (New York: Atherton Press, 1967).

[3] Lyle E. Schaller, *The Churches' War on Poverty* (Nashville: The Abingdon Press, 1967); John Fish, Gordon Nelson, Walter Stuhr, and Lawrence Witmer, *The Edge of the Ghetto: A Study of Church Involvement in Community Organization* (Chicago: The University of Chicago Press, 1966).

[4] The Inter-Religious Committee Against Poverty was a coalition formed from the National Catholic Welfare Conference, the National Council of Churches, and the Synagogue Council of America; Women in Community Service (WICS) was formed from the National Council of Jewish Women, the National Council of Negro Women, the National Council of Catholic Women, and the United Church Women. Their main activity has been to recruit and screen girls for the Job Corps. (Schaller, *Churches' War on Poverty*, pp. 30–31).

[5] Fish, *et al.*, *Edge of the Ghetto*, p. 13.

[6] Schaller, *Churches' War on Poverty*, p. 84 (emphasis in the original).

✦ First published in Social Science Quarterly 50, No. 3 (December, 1969).

interaction of the churches and the community organization."[7] The first two dimensions—which for the authors "can help initiate Total Involvement"[8]—are pastoral leadership and denominational polity structure and sanction. The remaining two factors affecting "Total Involvement" of both church leadership and congregation[9] are situational (the historically-given traditions and sociocultural composition of the congregation) and the theological (broadly, is the denomination or congregation predominantly "comfort" or "challenge" oriented?).

The first three factors—pastoral leadership, denominational polity and sanction, and situational—are of special relevance to the present study. For Fish, Nelson, *et al.*, the pastor possesses an authority, varying from one denomination to another, "which gives him considerable latitude for independent action as well as power of persuasion."[10] A thoroughly convinced and firm pastor may well persuade the congregation to at least explore the possibilities of relating to a community or neighborhood organization. The denominational polity structure also influences action undertaken. The authors noted swifter responses to new ideas and activities in the Methodist and Roman Catholic Churches, whose pastors seemed more independent of their denominational "headquarters." Official pronouncements by a denomination also influence the response of local congregations.

The third or situational dimension (community context) forms a matrix in which the first two factors interrelate. The larger a denomination's membership, the more varied are its regional membership groups. Thus a variety of environmental constraints are to be expected—a theme familiar to students of formal organizations.[11] Within this situational dimension, the authors call attention to the "precipitating problem" (neighborhood racial change in their study) and existent community attitudes (toward race, change, the community itself). Both a local pastor and higher denominational leadership are usually aware of these "environmental climate" factors in initiating and pursuing any intervention or community action program.

This study explores the interfunctioning of these factors—pastoral leadership, denominational polity, and the the community situation—in a Roman Catholic setting. More specifically, it focuses on the largest low-income Catholic population in the United States: the almost five million Mexican Americans of Texas, New Mexico, Arizona, and California. It suggests, as

[7] Fish, *et al.*, *Edge of the Ghetto*, p. 146.

[8] *Ibid.*, p. 148. "Token Involvement describes a form of participation in which a congregation as a corporate unit is a member of the community organization, and a small group (perhaps a pastor and a few laymen) join in its activities." *Ibid.*, p. 144.

[9] "Total Involvement describes a form of participation in which the members of a congregation sense that their corporate membership in the community organization necessarily involves them as individuals." *Ibid.*, p. 145.

[10] *Ibid.*, p. 147.

[11] Cf., for example, W. Richard Scott, "Theory of Organizations," in R. E. L. Faris, ed., *Handbook of Modern Sociology* (Chicago: Rand McNally and Co., 1964), esp. p. 522.

a further specification of the interrelationships of pastoral leadership, polity structure, and situation, that the continued existence and visible success of priest-led poverty intervention programs is dependent upon two sets of factors. The first is a leadership context of support or at least no overt opposition from ecclesiastical superiors (bishops). The second varies according to an urban or small town setting. In the former, the key factor is alliance with other secular and religious institutions; in the latter, the priestly role of unique spokesman for the poor in a small community in which the prospect of federal aid is most attractive. Absence of one or more of these factors spells severe curtailment or even failure of the priests' efforts.

Data for this study consist of interviews with and newspaper accounts concerning 13 out of 75 priests interviewed in the course of a larger study.[12] The 13 are labeled "social action priests," i.e., they have devoted substantial time and interest to activities broadly aimed at improving the socio-economic status of Mexican Americans. "Substantial" time and interest were judged by two criteria: (1) publicity received from both secular and the Catholic press; (2) activity sustained over a comparatively long period (in contrast to a priest who may, for example, have demonstrated on some occasion or participated in a poverty program only through donation of parish facilities). The 13 priests are further divided into two subgroups: (1) eight directors of antipoverty programs: two large city directors and six small community directors; (2) five priests taking part in direct action (marching, picketing, etc.) on behalf of striking Mexican American agricultural field workers. To anticipate somewhat, these activity patterns constitute two different "situational dimensions" and markedly affect the viability of the intervention in question.

THE WAR ON POVERTY PRIESTS

Three characteristics of the region in which these priests were operating should be singled out: (1) a significant majority of Catholics in these southwestern dioceses are of Mexican background; (2) there are relatively few Catholics of affluent socioeconomic status; (3) in six out of the eight cases, the priests heading the programs operated in dioceses headed by bishops of progressive social policies, particularly in support of the right of union organization (a preliminary illustration of the denominational polity factor).

The Large City Directors. Father X, who had become a widely respected youth program director in a large southwestern city, was appointed director of one of the nation's largest antipoverty programs, funded for over three million dollars in a three-year period. His initial efforts included a broad gauge employment, tutorial, and recreational program receiving a wide spectrum of support from the city's civic organizations.

The programs had their opponents, of course. Political leaders grew

---

[12] Patrick H. McNamara, "The Roman Catholic Church in the Mexican American Community," in Leo Grebler, Joan Moore, and Ralph Guzman, et al., *The Mexican American People: The Nation's Second Largest Minority* (New York: The Free Press-Macmillan Co., forthcoming).

disturbed over charges that Neighborhood Youth Corps enrollees were registering non-citizens as voters. Ethnic militants claimed underrepresentation on the organization's staff and charged that enrollees were made to speak only English on the job. Protestant-sponsored community agencies maintained that the programs received a "disproportionate share" of the city's total antipoverty funding.

These crises were successfully weathered, however, in the contexts of two important factors. The first was strong denominational support. The priest's archbishop enjoyed a long-standing reputation as a champion of labor unions and supporter of minimum wage and medical care reforms in a region not noted for its union sympathies and social legislation. In other words, Father X operated in a diocesan climate of "social progressivism." He could rely on his ecclesiastical superior to oppose conservative political and economic interests.[13] This factor encouraged him to speak out strongly in rebuttal of the charges and to keep opponents successfully at bay. Second, the priest received wide institutional support from churches, schools, and important allies in the political sector. Apropos of the original committee which drafted the proposal for the Department of Labor, Father X remarked,

> There were 73 people . . . parents . . . youth themselves, and the 14 others were members of the community that were interested in juvenile delinquency: the director of boys' clubs, the juvenile judge, police chief, etc. Many of our members of the [present] Board of Directors are Protestants . . . we have the use of Protestant facilities.[14]

In fact, Father X particularly singled out Protestant church support ("including Mexican Protestant churches") as a key strategic alliance in enabling the program to withstand opposition.

This type of support from community institutions may be even more important, of course, when diocesan support (denominational polity and sanction) is not present. Father Y directed a program within a diocese in which the bishop's record, although by no means conservative, was still less than decisive in the area of progressive social reform. With the tacit consent of his superior, Father Y flew directly to Washington to secure funding of over $600,000, bypassing the city's principal war on poverty agency. The latter, he charged in a press interview, was "doing nothing for the poor." Partially for political reasons, other interest groups began to back him, including one of the city's leading daily newspapers as well as the weekly of organized labor in the area.

> It appears that while Project B : . . . got the headlines, Father Y and his 'Community Action, Inc.' got the money . . . where this leaves Project B . . . we don't know. But we do know that it's a feather in the cap of Father Y and we salute him for a job well done.[15]

[13] The bishop in question was instrumental in effecting a rather decisive Catholic representation and influence on the final board of directors of the city's major poverty program.

[14] Interview material.

[15] Editorial, a major southwestern daily newspaper, Oct. 6, 1965.

Such powerful support was not without its impact on the bishop. Father Y reported that friends informed him of his superior's reluctance to "touch him" because of unfavorable publicity which might arise from attempts to moderate his activities or even to remove him on other pretexts from his social action undertakings.

The Small Community Directors. The six small community directors enjoyed, like Father X, the active support of their respective bishops. What they lacked, however, was precisely the broad institutional support characterizing their big city colleagues. Operating in communities displaying a strong and visible social cleavage between "Anglos" and Mexican Americans living "on the other side of the tracks," they confronted

> an economic power structure dominated by the Anglo community who are again not really very highly educated. Maybe they have a grammar school education, a few a high school education. And they control everything. Their opposition is purely emotional.[16]

Without the leverage of a representative advisory board or the support of a friendly press, these priests operated within a narrower "situational dimension." They felt forced to channel their efforts into programs calculated to be least threatening to the dominant community (at least over the short run), for example, Operation Head Start and remedial instruction programs. (The latter had at least the advantage of involving local school officials.) Furthermore, the priests relied heavily on the fact that these communities often faced the alternatives of no funding at all, or of funding proposals drawn up by the chief spokesman for an ethnic population of low educational attainment and leadership experience. The priests could muster few organizational allies in any direct power confrontation.[17]

In summary, the interrelationships of leadership, denominational or diocesan policy, and community situation were such as to ensure the relative success of the programs in question. Both large city and small town priest directors could rely on at least the tacit backing of their superiors. This assurance encouraged them to exert vigorous leadership where it was needed. Roman Catholic polity structure, which traditionally is not open to response from the laity, enabled the priest directors to proceed regardless of opposition from conservative lay Catholics (and the interviews revealed a substantial amount of such opposition). Finally, the priests were able to render the institutional environment ultimately supportive, or at least not actively hostile. They either allied themselves with established community institutions (the press and organized labor are examples), or in the smaller communities, developed programs non-threatening to the local power structures. An added factor (which may be subsumed under

---

[16] Interview material.

[17] In one case, when the local school board adamantly refused to hire a single Mexican American as a teacher or teacher aide, the priest, aided financially by diocesan officials, put together his own headstart program utilizing the services of teaching sisters from another diocese. This move resulted in effectively removing prospective pupils—the vast majority of whom were Mexican American Catholics from the priest's own parish—from the school board's program.

the fourth or "theological" dimension cited previously), was general Catholic acceptance of their activities as not incompatible with a traditional function of the Church, bettering the lot of the poor. Within this latter framework, the priests were less vulnerable to charges of "meddling in politics" or "agitating for radical causes."

THE FIELD WORKER PRIESTS

The two areas of Mexican American agricultural workers' strikes—Delano, California and Texas' lower Rio Grande Valley—are characterized by deep socioeconomic cleavages. The struggle of farm workers vs. growers, particularly since Cesar Chavez assumed leadership of the workers' unionization movement, is well publicized. Structurally, Catholics are well represented on both sides of the conflict. In Texas, many of the growers are of Mexican background, as well. In such a situation, any individual or group championing the cause of one side is branded as a foe by the other and forfeits its support.

Since both field workers and growers make up the membership in parish and diocese, the clergy on both levels are caught in a painful dilemma. A local priest may well feel he has to be "prudent," and "consider the interests of both sides." As one priest expressed it to the writer, "I was afraid to mention [the strike] from the pulpit because I knew that whatever I said would easily be misinterpreted." The striking field workers, on the other hand, not surprisingly felt that the Church had "abandoned" them. As Cesar Chavez put it,

> We suspect that the Church is really, to put it very bluntly, missing the boat . . . there are a lot of jokes going around among us about the Church and about the priests who get up and preach the social teachings of the Church and turn right around and do exactly the opposite.[18]

One result of this situation was a kind of "moral vacuum," attracting social-action type priests from *other dioceses* to picket, march, even organize demonstrations. As one of the three farm-worker priests in Texas stated,

> We lent our moral weight to their cause. The strikers needed encouragement. They need advocates. . . . Just the physical presence of a priest satisfied the people's hunger for the Church to identify with them. Having done it I knew it was right, and it was done without ever compromising the priesthood.[19]

The priests organized a pilgrimage-march of farm workers. In doing so, they enjoyed the support of their own bishop, a noted progressive, who felt especially justified in permitting their intervention since the newly consecrated bishop of the diocese embracing the strike area had not yet arrived. His views were at the time unknown.

This mode of intervention did not, to say the least, spare the priests the

[18] Interview material.
[19] Interview material.

wrath of the local clergy and laymen. A local monsignor contemptuously referred to them as "intruders who do not speak for the Church." Growers flatly accused them of using the Roman collar to act as labor organizers. Some time after returning to their home diocese, they were informed by the new bishop that he wanted no more "outside help." He would solve his own problems.

Two of the priests returned a few months later to the strike area in open disregard of their superior's wishes. The strikers were, they asserted, "trying to break up a . . . serfdom down there, and as priests, certainly as individuals, we have a right to go there and help them."[20]

The axe fell swiftly. The priests were arrested for trespassing on private property, then released and sent back to their home diocese. Upon their arrival, their superior ordered them to a neighboring state for a mandatory retreat. When his disciplinary action was protested by four assistant pastors in a full-page interview article in the city's leading daily, the four were immediately suspended from their priestly duties.

A similar drama was played out in the case of two priests from a northern California diocese. Their private intervention in Delano (consisting of picketing, and on a second occasion, of pleading with strikebreakers from a private airplane by means of an amplified loudspeaker) resulted in a letter from their bishop ordering them under pain of possible suspension from priestly duties to refrain from all contact with persons connected with the strike, and not to make any statements publicly regarding the strike issues.

The free-wheeling intervention of the field worker priests stands in stark contrast to the organizationally protected activities of their colleagues in urban antipoverty programs. The field worker priests, bereft of any institutional support, nakedly challenged both ecclesiastical and secular power structures. They involved themselves not in such community-approved enterprises as curbing juvenile delinquency and teaching young people needed job skills, but in union organization which gave promise of restructuring an entire regional economy. Drastic retribution was the predictable response. Furthermore, in engaging in picketing and demonstrations, they were enacting unconventional and disturbing roles. No amount of personal charisma or exercise of dynamic leadership could ensure lasting viability of their intended reforms. They had violated core norms of their denomination (disobedience to one's bishop being the most serious violation); no appeals to higher laws of charity could outweigh such challenges to a traditionally authoritarian structure.

Priests, then, operating within more conventional structures of poverty intervention, perhaps meet Fish, Nelson, *et al.*'s leadership quality of "considerable latitude for independent action." And the typical Roman Catholic bishop does indeed afford his pastors freedom of action, at least in the sense that the pastor need not worry seriously about "how much the traffic will bear" out there in the congregation at Sunday Mass. But given a "situ-

[20] Interview material.

ation dimension" involving a serious challenge to entrenched (in this case, economic) institutions, apparently assailable only by direct confrontation, this same authority structure exerts very strong constraints, particularly if its exercise of power is not restrained by the priests' alliance with counter- vailing forces (the press, organized labor, interfaith groups). If the priests' motivation is strong enough, of course, they may choose to disregard ec- clesiastical norms and legitimate their intervention on what they consider more fundamental doctrinal norms—concern for "Christ's poor," rectifying injustices, and so forth. And in the longer run, this strategy will affect Church authorities.[21] It is no accident that the bishop of the diocese in which Delano is located has recently assigned a "permanent chaplain" to the striking farm workers. But the short-run consequences, as illustrated above, are likely to be disastrous.

From one point of view, clergymen should be most appropriate leaders in the war on poverty. Aside from the churches' doctrinal commitment to serve the poor and dispossessed, there is a presumption of altruistic moti- vation on the part of the clergyman. Marris and Rein, commenting on the difficulty of recruiting genuine leaders for the poor, remark,

> If the poor are to attract the able organizers they need, the defence of their interests must offer a career which rewards the ambitious with growing prestige and power. Community organization falters because it cannot offer any future to the neighborhood leaders it promotes but a lifetime of pa- rochial effort.[22]

By his calling the clergyman is supposedly motivated to defend the poor without the allurements of prestige and power, and he presumably can bestow upon the poor that respect without which, as Marris and Rein ob- serve, "the poor connot respect themselves."[23] But how can he engage in this effort within the "sharp cleavage" contexts discussed above? If, "as Weber pointed out, emanicipation is a crucial condition for the emergence of religious prophecy,"[24] is the convinced social action priest to step com- pletely outside the institutional norms and play the role of maverick pro- testor? Perhaps a more viable response lies in the development of more modest forms of emancipation, for example, a farm workers' chaplaincy. This relatively insulated substructure, provided its incumbents are allowed to experiment rather freely with their ministry, might well accelerate forces of progressive social change in both secular and ecclesiastical institutions.

[21] A fuller discussion of the effects of both types of intervention upon Church policy is found in Patrick H. McNamara, "Social Action Priests in the Mexican American Community," *Sociological Analysis,* 29 (Winter, 1968), pp. 177–185.

[22] Marris and Rein, *Dilemmas of Social Reform,* p. 186.

[23] *Ibid.,* p. 189.

[24] N. J. Demerath, III, and Phillip E. Hammond, *Religion in Social Context: Tradi- tion and Transition* (New York: Random House, 1969), p. 222.

33

THE EFFECTS OF URBAN RENEWAL UPON A BLACK COMMUNITY: EVALUATION AND RECOMMENDATIONS

J. ALLEN WILLIAMS, JR.

The University of Texas at Austin

F EW FEDERAL PROGRAMS HAVE BEEN MORE CONTROVERSIAL THAN URBAN renewal and few, if any, have been attacked from as many ideological vantage points.[1] Although the dysfunctional consequences of renewal projects have been well documented, some proponents appear to believe that recent changes in policy and administration have solved the previous problems.[2] The purpose of this paper is to present findings from a study of a recently completed urban renewal project and to make several recommendations based upon those findings.[3] The study is "evaluative" in that an attempt was made to assess the effects of the project in terms of the goals of urban renewal.

OBJECTIVES OF URBAN RENEWAL

Although the specific objectives of urban renewal are voluminous, the following goals appear to be among those most often cited as crucial for successful urban redevelopment: (1) to supply decent houses for every American family; (2) to provide a suitable living environment for every family; (3) to revitalize the urban areas by attracting and keeping the middle class in the central areas, thus increasing tax revenue and commerce; (4) to assist in ethnic desegregation of residential areas; and (5) to assist in alleviating social and personal problems by bringing families into contact with service agencies.[4]

[1] For excellent reviews of the literature concerning the controversy over urban renewal, see Jewel Bellush and Murray Hausknecht, eds., *Urban Renewal: People, Politics and Planning* (New York: Doubleday, 1967); Scott Greer, *Urban Renewal and American Cities* (Kansas City: Bobbs-Merrill, 1965); and Peter Marris, "A Report on Urban Renewal in the United States," in Leonard J. Duhl, ed., *The Urban Condition: People and Policy in the Metropolis* (New York: Basic Books, Inc., 1963), pp. 113–123.

[2] For example, see George M. Raymond, "Urban Renewal: Controversy," *Commentary*, 40 (July, 1965), pp. 72–80 and Joseph Epstein, "The Row Over Urban Renewal," in Judson R. Landis, ed., *Current Perspectives on Social Problems* (Belmont, Calif.: Wadsworth; second ed., 1969), pp. 284–295.

[3] A brief summary of this study is included in J. Allen Williams, Jr., *Blackshear Diagnostic Survey: A Description and Problem Analysis* (Austin, Texas: Prepared for The Urban Renewal Agency of the City of Austin, June, 1968: mimeographed). The study was supported through a contract with the Department of Housing and Urban Development. For a detailed analysis of the effect of the Kealing project on a sense of community, see Janice Catherine Freeman, *The Effects of Relocation Upon the Sense of Community among Afro-Americans* (unpublished MS: The University of Texas at Austin, Austin, Texas, January, 1969).

[4] Discussion of the origins and reasons for these objectives may be found in material cited in footnote 1 above. The reader is referred also to Robert C. Weaver, *The Urban Complex* (New York: Doubleday, 1966); Herbert J. Gans, "The Failure of Urban Renewal: A Critique and Some Proposals," *Commentary*, 39 (April, 1965), pp. 29–37; and James Q. Wilson, "Planning and Politics: Citizen Participation in Urban Renewal," *Journal of the American Institute of Planners*, 29 (Nov., 1963), pp. 242–249.

♦ First published in Social Science Quarterly 50, No. 3 (December, 1969).   377

THE RESEARCH DESIGN AND SAMPLE CHARACTERISTICS

An area in Austin, Texas, containing approximately 267 households was designated for renewal in 1957. Public hearings were held in 1963 and the project, entitled Kealing, went into execution. Land was purchased during the period of 1964 to 1968. About 32.0 per cent of the households remained in homes which could be rehabilitated. Thus, 182 households or 68.0 per cent were displaced from the area. The findings presented in this report are based on a random sample of 95 households drawn from a list of all those reported to have been displaced from the area. All of these households are black and all were interviewed by blacks. A number of techniques were used to assure the validity of the findings.[5]

Table 1 provides a general description of the Kealing sample. As can be seen, the sample may be characterized as a low-income population with limited education. Occupational prestige is typically quite low and many of the homes are female-headed. Average family size is small and many families are elderly or in late middle-age. A significant portion of the population appears to have been fairly stable in that over half (50.5 per cent) were home owners or buyers when living in Kealing.

FINDINGS

1. *Did all of the displaced households obtain decent housing?*

Condition of Housing. Table 2 shows the condition of dwelling units based upon interviewer estimates.[6] As can be seen, almost one out of three households did not obtain a "decent" home.

Cost of Housing. A problem created by many renewal projects is that displaced families have had to pay a larger percentage of their income for housing after relocation.[7] Obviously, improved housing at the expense of an increased financial burden is a questionable gain.

About 49.5 per cent of the sample were tenants in Kealing. Among the 44 households who continued to rent, 67.4 per cent are now making higher payments. Renters paying less in Kealing were paying a mean of $39.00 per month and, at the time of the survey, were paying $52.00.

Among Kealing owner-occupants, 60.4 per cent had their former homes paid for. Five of these became tenants after relocation making an average payment of $44.00 per month. Seven were able to purchase and completely

[5] Attempts to assure validity included pretesting the schedule, intensive interviewer training, matching interviewer-respondent ethnicity, call-backs when information was not clear or consistent, duplicate interviews on selected households and comparing "respondent recall" with data from identical questions collected from respondents in an area adjacent to Kealing.

[6] The interviewers were not trained appraisers, but their judgments of structures in another urban renewal area compared favorably with those made by experts. For example, whereas the urban renewal agency classified 56.0 per cent of the houses substandard, interviewers classified 53.6 per cent substandard.

[7] For example, on the basis of information on 25 renewal projects cited by Hartman, all but one show an increase in the amount of rent after relocation. See Chester W. Hartman, "The Housing of Relocated Families," *Journal of the American Institute of Planners*, 30 (Nov., 1964), pp. 266–282.

TABLE 1

Selected Characteristics of the Kealing Sample

Characteristics	Per cent (N = 95)
Annual Household Income	
$0,000–1,999	24.5
2,000–2,999	15.8
3,000–3,999	13.3
4,000–4,999	9.9
5,000 and above	36.5
Occupational Status of Household Head	
In job training	1.1
Retired	22.6
Disabled, unable to work	5.3
Unskilled workers	39.8
Semiskilled workers	14.0
Skilled workers	4.3
Clerical and sales	4.3
Small business owners, minor professionals	7.5
Lesser professionals	1.1
Education of Household Head	
0– 6 years	25.9
7–11 years	31.2
High school graduate	26.9
Some college training	12.9
College graduate or above	1.1
Not ascertained	2.2
Marital Status of Household Head	
Single	1.1
Married	39.8
Separated or divorced	25.9
Widowed	33.3

pay for another home. The remainder, 58.6 per cent of the home owners, purchased other homes and are now making an average house payment of $77.00. Thus, among former owners, only 24.1 per cent did not take on an increased financial burden.

Among former home buyers, 68.4 per cent are now buying other homes at an average increase of $33.00. Among the remaining seven households, three have been able to pay for homes and four have become tenants.

Thus, 70.5 per cent of all households in the sample took on an increased financial burden after relocation and 18.7 per cent of former owners and buyers have become tenants.

2. *Did all of the displaced households obtain a suitable living environment?*

Physical Characteristics. Respondents were asked to compare their present neighborhoods with the Kealing area on several physical characteristics. As can be seen from Table 3, the majority stated that there had been no

TABLE 2

Condition of Relocation Housing for Former Kealing Residents

Condition of Dwelling Unit	Per cent (N = 95)
Above average	15.8
Sound, average, in good shape	52.6
Deteriorating	25.3
Dilapidated	5.3
Not ascertained	1.0
Total	100.0

change. Interestingly, a number of respondents believe that the Kealing area was better. Given that Kealing was considered an area needing urban renewal, these findings suggest that many did not obtain a suitable living environment, at least in terms of these selected characteristics.

Convenience to Facilities. Without question a suitable living environment must include convenience to the facilities that are necessary for everyday living. This is especially true when many persons in the low-income population do not have their own source of transportation. Respondents were asked to compare their present neighborhood with Kealing on convenience to several important facilities. As can be seen in Table 4, the majority indicate little or no change. However, almost twice as many state that their new neighborhoods are less conveniently located than state that they are now more conveniently located.

Social Characteristics. Table 5 shows the respondents' opinions about changes in certain aspects of the social environment. As can be seen, the majority see no change. Among those perceiving a change, more feel that

TABLE 3

Comparison of Present Physical Conditions of the Neighborhood
With Neighborhood Conditions in Kealing
(in percentages)[a]

Area Condition	New Neighborhood Better	Same	Old Neighborhood Better
Area cleanliness	24.2	55.8	16.8
Street and sidewalk conditions	23.2	56.8	18.9
Lighting	20.0	50.5	26.3
Recreation for children	13.7	58.9	20.0

[a] The figures do not always equal 100.0 per cent since all of the 95 respondents did not respond to every item. Percentages are based upon all 95 households.

TABLE 4

Comparison of Convenience to Facilities in Present Neighborhood
with Convenience in Kealing
(in percentages)[a]

Facility	New Neighborhood More Convenient	Same	Old Neighborhood More Convenient
School	12.6	56.8	21.1
Church	2.1	61.0	27.4
Transportation	10.5	63.2	24.2
Shopping	13.7	62.1	21.1

[a] The figures do not always equal 100.0 per cent since all of the 95 respondents did not respond to every item. Percentages are based upon all 95 households.

things have improved regarding the honesty of the people and as a place to bring up children, but more prefer Kealing regarding safety after dark and police protection. This may be related to the "strangeness" of a new neighborhood and living further away from the central city.

3. *Was Kealing revitalized to provide a greater tax revenue and commerce?*
Although it is too early to evaluate the long-term effects of redevelopment of the Kealing area, it does appear that at least the short-term has been successful. Streets have been paved and widened, street lighting is better, a park has been developed and lots have been enlarged to meet present city requirements. According to the Urban Renewal Agency, tax producing property yielded $12,000 before urban renewal and $36,000 after redevelopment.

4. *Did relocation contribute to the ethnic desegregation of residential areas?*

TABLE 5

Comparison of Aspects of the Present Social Environment with
the Social Environment in Kealing
(in percentages)[a]

Social Condition	New Neighborhood Better	Same	Old Neighborhood Better
Honesty of the people	18.9	68.4	6.3
As a place to bring up children	22.1	60.0	10.5
Safe to be out alone after dark	9.5	74.7	13.7
Police protection	12.6	64.2	18.9

[a] The figures do not always equal 100.0 per cent since all of the 95 respondents did not respond to every item. Percentages are based upon all 95 households.

Data were available on the relocation addresses of 169 households displaced from Kealing (98.2 per cent of all those relocating in Austin). None of these households relocated into an Anglo neighborhood. Approximately 66.3 per cent relocated within one mile of the center of the Kealing area and the great majority of the others moved east, away from the city and still within the black community. It must be concluded, therefore, that this project in no way contributed to ethnic desegregation through relocation. Further, no Anglos have moved into the redeveloped Kealing area.

5. *Did displaced families receive assistance in alleviating social and personal problems?*

Urban renewal has been criticized for uprooting communities and thus contributing to or causing personal and social problems among displaced families.[8] Supporters have countered by suggesting that persons will be brought into contact with service agencies and that most slum communities are not really supportive so that "uprooting" has little adverse effect. Thus, two aspects of this goal may be examined—whether families did lose important social supports through displacement and whether they have been brought into touch with helping agencies.

Loss of "Community." Respondents were asked how they felt about moving. Approximately 62.1 per cent stated that they did not want to move. Respondents were then asked why they felt that way. Among the households disliking having to move, 42.4 per cent stressed factors associated with the community, for example, "All my friends were there." Another 30.6 per cent focused on financial problems and the remaining 27.0 per cent were primarily concerned with locational convenience or simply said that they disliked moving. Among those stating that they were glad to move or did not mind, the most common response, which accounted for only 10.5 per cent, was that the old house was in poor shape and moving was necessary. Thus, on the basis of this direct questioning, it appears that "loss of community" was highly salient for some, 26.3 per cent, but was not uppermost in the minds of the majority.

Almost half, 47.3 per cent, of former Kealing households had relatives living in the Kealing area. Virtually all of the respondents indicated that they had visited with their relatives at least once a week. Since 66.3 per cent of the households relocated within one mile of the renewal area, moving would not be expected to increase the difficulty of visiting relatives for the majority. As expected, only 21.0 per cent of those having relatives in the city (85.2 per cent of the sample) report increased difficulty. However, 64.7 per cent of those having greater difficulty in visiting relatives stated that they liked their Kealing neighborhood better whereas only 23.4 per cent of the other households report feeling that way.

[8] In addition to the works cited above, further discussion of this issue may be found in Marc Fried and Peggy Gleicher, "Some Sources of Residential Satisfaction in an Urban Slum," *Journal of the American Institute of Planners,* 27 (Nov., 1961), pp. 305–315; William H. Key, *When People Are Forced to Move* (mimeographed, May, 1967); Harry W. Reynolds, Jr., "The Human Element in Urban Renewal," *Public Welfare,* 19 (April, 1961), pp. 71–82; and Jane Jacobs, *The Death and Life of Great American Cities* (New York: Random House, 1961).

In addition to social ties with friends and relatives, relocation may disrupt group associations which are important and meaningful to community residents. However, it was found that few persons belong to voluntary associations, with the exception of church. Church appears to be a major form of social activity and approximately 90.5 per cent of all households attend. Among attenders, 30.2 per cent stated that relocation made attending their church more difficult or impossible. As with extended family interaction, an examination was made of the association between increased difficulty in attending church and attitudes toward the neighborhood. Among those encountering increased difficulty, 65.4 per cent stated that they liked their old neighborhood better. Only 13.3 per cent of those not finding it more difficult to attend their church stated that they preferred their old neighborhood.

Contact with Service Agencies. Respondents were provided with a list of all the major service agencies in the city and were asked, "Have you or anyone in your household been in contact at all with any of these agencies?" Excluding Urban Renewal, 63.4 per cent had never had any contact with any of the agencies. Another 20.4 per cent had used the services of the Texas Employment Commission, but had no contact with any other agency. On the basis of these data, it appears that few households have received agency assistance.

If few households were in need of assistance, then one would not expect to find a high percentage having been in contact with service agencies. To check for this possibility a careful examination was made of each interview schedule. Selecting only households with *serious* problems needing immediate attention yielded 23.6 per cent of the total.[9] Among these, twelve had no contact with any agency and another five have had contact with the Texas Employment Commission only. All of these households are believed to be eligible for at least one kind of service and many appear eligible for several. Further, many respondents expressed a desire for assistance and sought information from the interviewers.

RECOMMENDATIONS

As mentioned at the outset of this note, it has been argued that the faults of the "old Urban Renewal" of the 1950's have been eliminated. The findings from this study suggest that this is not true. However, the Kealing project was completed prior to the Housing and Urban Development Act of 1968. Thus, the following comments will focus on the very recent changes which have been introduced and an attempt will be made to evaluate their probable effect.

Clearly the most immediate and pressing need is to discover a way to rebuild or renew poverty areas without adversely affecting those who are

[9] The selection of serious problems included such conditions as persons needing immediate medical attention, persons physically disabled and unemployed, persons whose incomes were so limited that both parents and children were suffering from malnutrition, persons whose dwelling units were in such disrepair that they were unsafe for habitation.

displaced. In a letter dated April 19, 1968, HUD informed all urban renewal agencies that:

> It is the obligation of the locality carrying out a HUD-assisted project to assure that families and individuals who are displaced as a result of project activities are offered housing available on a *nondiscriminatory basis*— within a broad choice of neighborhoods—which is *decent*, safe, and sanitary, is *within their financial means*, and is *conveniently located* with respect to transportation and other public facilities.[10]

This requirement, if carried out, would alleviate some of the problems created by urban renewal. However, given that most cities do not have standard housing conveniently located to public facilities and within the financial means of low-income families, it would appear that this directive would either prevent urban renewal projects from being carried out or would force agencies to find ways of "getting around" the requirement.[11]

Congress has provided more funds for displaced households.[12] An owner-occupant may be eligible for a replacement housing payment "in an amount not to exceed $5,000. . . ." A family or single individual 62 years of age or older, or handicapped, may be eligible for a relocation payment of up to $1,000 over a period of two years. These increases in payments, while useful, do not appear sufficient to eliminate financial problems. The additional $41.67 per month for two years, for eligible tenants, will help provide better housing on a temporary basis only. It appears highly unlikely that the poorer owner-occupants will be able to purchase a well-located standard home with the additional relocation housing payment without having to go into debt.

Even if households received adequate monetary compensation for having to relocate out of the project area, this would not solve the problem of moving poorer families away from the central city. It would not solve the problems of forcing small businesses to move away from their clientele, moving persons who rent out rooms in their homes to provide themselves with necessary income, moving ill or elderly persons away from family or neighbors who care for them, moving families away from their friends, relatives, churches, and necessary facilities.

Some stress has been placed on rehabilitation rather than redevelopment since 1954 and this is again evidenced in the 1968 Act which authorizes a rehabilitation grant of up to $3,000 for owner-occupants with in-

---

[10] Local Public Agency Letter No. 456 from the Department of Housing and Urban Development, p. 2 (emphasis mine).

[11] It would appear that if standard housing which is conveniently located and within the financial means of the low-income population was available, then there would be scant need for urban renewal in the first place. Few families live in substandard housing because they want to.

[12] Public Law 90–448. This is an expansion of Section 114(c) of Title I of the Housing Act of 1949, as amended. The information provided in this paper comes from circular 1370.3, "Relocation Payment Provisions Authorized by the Housing and Urban Development Act of 1968—Initial Policies and Requirements," Jan. 23, 1969.

comes of $3,000 or less and a 20-year loan for those with larger incomes.[13] However, many are not eligible for these loans in renewal areas. For example, absentee owners are not eligible, many structures will be classified as "nonrehabilitable," structures must often be demolished for the expansion of facilities, for street widening, and in some cases because they are on "substandard" lots.

Since, as Marris has suggested, the aims of urban renewal may be incompatible, priorities among the objectives should be assigned on the basis of need. It would seem to the investigator that the primary focus of urban renewal should be on the low-income families living in slum areas. Given this, the goals of increasing tax revenue and even desegregation should be given less importance than the rehabilitation and preservation of communities.[14] At present, HUD requires that a substantial number of low or moderate-income housing units (a minimum of 20 per cent) be provided on land disposed of for residential construction or residential rehabilitation.[15] However, if communities are to be in fact preserved, then it would seem more realistic to base the minimum required on the number of households who wish to remain in the area. Further, the specification of "low- or moderate-income housing" should be changed to require that sufficient low-cost housing be provided for low-income families and sufficient moderate-cost housing for moderate-income families.[16] Since urban renewal must rely on private enterprise to construct the dwellings, agencies need to be provided with the means to offer the necessary incentives to builders to assure successful execution of the plan.

To assure that displaced families will be able to obtain the new housing at a minimum of inconvenience, execution of the plan should be carefully staged so that housing becomes available prior to displacement. Land

---

[13] Based upon information supplied by the Urban Renewal Agency of the City of Austin, Feb. 28, 1969.

[14] This does not mean that these objectives must be abandoned. Allowing low-income families to remain in the redeveloped area means that their property, at least for the owner-occupants, will probably increase considerably in value. Further, if households are brought into contact with service agencies at this time, then job training, counseling, and other public services could aid these families in upward mobility, thus increasing city revenue. Further, if the area is redeveloped creatively, with social as well as physical needs in mind, the area could attract members of other ethnic groups, thus contributing to desegregation. Finally, a number of households will be willing to relocate and these can be relocated in a way contributing to desegregation of other areas.

[15] *Urban Renewal Handbook: Land Marketing and Redevelopment*—RHA 7214. Chap. 3, Sect. 1, "Low and Moderate-Income Housing." For HUD policies on National Goals and Urban Renewal Priorities see 7202.1, "Program Policies and Directions," Chap. 1, Sect. 1.

[16] It must be recognized that the problem must be approached from at least two directions. First, adequate inexpensive housing must be developed, e.g., mass produced modular construction. Second, the income of the families must be increased to enable them to afford the housing since it is highly improbable that even the use of modern construction methods and materials will reduce the cost of housing to the income range of many of the families living in slum areas. For an excellent discussion of the income problem in relation to housing see, Jack E. Dodson, "Minority Group Housing in Two Texas Cities," in Nathan Glazer and Davis McEntire, eds., *Studies in Housing and Minority Groups* (Berkeley: University of California Press, 1960), pp. 84–109.

which is vacant, containing condemned structures or vacated by families who wish to move should be redeveloped first. When this is insufficient, temporary housing such as mobile homes, should be provided at no increase in cost to displaced families.

Assuming that the above objectives can be accomplished, urban renewal must still be provided with sufficient resources to take care of those households who will be adversely affected by either moving (the ill, elderly, disabled) or by demolition of structures (small businesses, persons who rent out rooms for a living). In the first case this will probably require the assistance of social workers, public health nurses and others trained to deal with problems of this nature. Additional financial aid and taking needs into consideration in the planning stage may suffice in the second instance.

34

ATTITUDES TOWARD HEALTH AND HEALTH CARE FACILITIES AMONG LOW INCOME YOUTH

JOSEPH M. CONFORTI
Rutgers University—Newark

THE HEALTH SERVICES FOR DISADVANTAGED YOUTH PROJECT BEGAN WHEN the officials of a state level department of health reviewed the Economic Opportunity Act of 1964 and found no provision of health services for the Neighborhood Youth Corps program (NYC).[1] They viewed the absence of such services as potentially impeding the success of the program on the grounds that any physical disabilities not corrected would limit the extent to which adolescents enrolled in the program could pursue work training. They also recognized that the program's eligibility criteria were so stringent as to admit only the poorest adolescents, who would not be able to acquire medical services from private physicians. Aware of deficiencies in the public medical facilities to which the enrollees had likely been limited, the health officials proposed a service-oriented project that would remove physical impediments to training through comprehensive physical examinations and the provision of any necessary remedial medical services.

When funds were requested for the project from the Office of Economic Opportunity (OEO), the officials were informed that funds were only available to demonstration projects and they were requested to indicate what the project would seek to demonstrate. The provision of services was not sufficient. The health officials thereupon shifted their concern from the provision of health services *per se* to a consideration of the implications of such services. They then reasoned that the NYC, in encouraging school dropouts to return to school or become work oriented, was designed to overcome the dropouts' alienation from major societal institutions, among which, it could be assumed, were medical and health service facilities. Such alienation, they reasoned, would result from experience assumedly limited to inferior outpatient clinics and emergency rooms, if that much. It was further assumed that the enrollees maintained negative attitudes toward health in general, by which was meant a lack of the concern about their health that the health officials considered a positive attitude.

In shifting from a focus upon the provision of services to a focus upon the attitudes and orientations of the enrollees, the health officials changed their definition of the problem the project would address. They no longer defined the problem as one of *physical disabilities* that might impede work training, but rather, as one of negative *attitudes* and alienation among the enrollees that had to be changed. This reorientation was of little consequence at that point, for while goals were redefined, the content of the project remained as planned.

---

[1] Information on the establishment of the project was gathered through a combination of participant observation and interviews with the project's directors.

♦ First published in Social Science Quarterly 50, No. 3 (December, 1969).

Following from the assumption that the enrollees had been limited to inadequate medical facilities in the past, it was proposed that they be exposed to a comprehensive examination and provided remedial treatment in terms of the most attractive organization of services possible. The model for such services was to be that of the private patient-physician arrangement.[2] This model was emphasized as a contrast to the enrollees' past experience that should serve to modify their attitudes and orientations. Given such a model, the project directors would likely have considered financing visits to private physicians at the best means of achieving their goals.[3] ̇

This was precluded by the insistence of OEO that all services be provided within local health facilities—the same community hospitals and clinics assumed responsible for the enrollees' alienation in the first place. The justification for such a prescription by OEO was that in anticipation of broad based community health services, hospitals should be encouraged to organize for the health care of low income people.

Thus the task for the project directors involved locating within the facilities from which the enrollees were assumed to be aliented, an organization of services so devised as to overcome their assumed alientation. Selection of such facilities lent significance to the reorientation of the project, for it placed primacy upon the facilities' modifying the attitudes and orientations of the enrollees, rather than upon modification of the facilities available to them.

ENROLLEES' ATTITUDES AND ORIENTATIONS

The attitudes, orientations and experiences that the enrollees brought to the project, though not taken into account in planning the services to be made available to them,[4] were elicited as part of an overall evaluation of the project and may be considered in terms of the assumptions made by the project directors.

One measure of the enrollees' orientations toward medical and health service facilities prior to their participation in the project consisted of a Guttman-type scale of attitudes toward doctors. In terms of this scale the enrollees were rather evenly arrayed from expressions of alienation to expressions of embracement of doctors, with slightly greater tendency toward

---

[2] This included such dimensions as the service arrangements being devised to make the enrollee feel welcome, having a single physician assume responsibility for an enrollee, providing the services in terms of a predictable time schedule (emphasizing appointments) and presenting an atmosphere of professional individualized care, rather than reluctant charity.

[3] Though reluctant to formally acknowledge such plans, informal conversation with the project directors elicited such sentiment. It was also manifested in a decision to use physicians in private practice rather than hospital interns. Furthermore, the project commenced with the enrollees of a specific NYC program being sent to a private practice clinic for their examinations and remedial care.

[4] The project directors chose to rely upon their own predilections and the directives of OEO in planning the project, rather than an assessment of the enrollees' expressed attitudes.

embracing than rejecting doctors, as indicated in Table 1.[5] In answering questions about specific kinds of medical experiences, they were over-

TABLE 1

NYC Enrollees' Pre-examination Attitudes Toward Doctors

	Alienated					Embracing
Scale Types	1	2	3	4	5	6
Percentage (N=809)	13.8	13.1	21.0	25.5	10.4	16.2

whelmingly satisfied with their experiences, as indicated in Table 2, somewhat more so with experiences involving a delimited doctor-patient relationship than with those related to hospitals. In regard to their attitudes

TABLE 2

NYC Enrollees' Pre-examination Attitudes Toward Previous Medical Experience

Experience	Per cent Satisfied	Per cent Dissatisfied	Per cent Neither Satisfied nor Dissatisfied	N
Visit to Doctor's Office	82.5	5.0	12.4	679
Hospital Inpatient	68.5	13.9	17.6	518
Hospital Outpatient	70.8	13.7	15.4	582
Physical Examination	84.1	5.7	10.2	636

toward health in general, examination through scaling again indicated a rather even distribution from negative attitudes to positive attitudes with a slight tendency toward the positive, as indicated in Table 3.

TABLE 3

NYC Enrollees' Pre-Examination Attitudes Toward Health

	Negative					Positive
Scale Types	1	2	3	4	5	6
Percentage (N=804)	8.1	12.4	29.9	23.0	13.7	12.9

[5] The N's of the tables presented vary on two bases: first, by virtue of the pre-examination and post-examination samples differing and, second, by virtue of some enrollees not answering all the questions used in the construction of scales. Scale items are available from the author upon request.

These findings do not substantiate assumptions of alienation and nega-tivity. Nor were such assumptions supported by more general questions put to the enrollees prior to their participation in the project. For example, another scale was devised to ascertain their orientations to the future. In terms of this scale they were rather evenly distributed from negative orien-tations to positive orientations, as indicated in Table 4. In response to an-

TABLE 4

NYC Enrollees' Pre-Examination Attitudes Toward the Future

	Negative				Positive
Scale Types	1	2	3	4	5
Percentage (N=787)	15.8	22.0	28.2	17.7	16.4

other question, asking them to anticipate how well off they would be dur-ing the next year, 90 per cent responded that they expected to be better off in the next year, 62 per cent of them choosing the most optimistic alter-native offered.

ORGANIZATION OF PROJECT SERVICES

With the exception of one private practice clinic available to a single NYC program, the only facilities hospitals made available to the project were their outpatient clinics and attendant resources. These were made available in a context of substantial reluctance on the part of several hos-pitals to participate in the project. Their reluctance revolved about two fears. First, that they would be inadequately compensated for the costs of the services they provided and, second, that participation might obligate them to provide such services beyond the duration of the project. Their re-luctance was aggravated by similarly negative reactions from the medical personnel recruited for the project. The main issue in their case was whether they would be paid directly by the project or indirectly through the hospital, while a secondary issue was the scope of their obligation in relation to their compensation.

These developments had two related consequences. One was that the project directors deemphasized their goal of the facilities' modifying the enrollees' attitudes, manifestly reducing the scope of the hospitals' obliga-tions. This left the hospitals relatively free to offer services in whatever form and context they chose. They were constrained only to the extent that they had to include in the examination a detailed medical history of each enrollee and to the extent that they *chose* to make their service arrange-ments attractive to the enrollees to encourage positive attitudes toward health and health care facilities. The other consequence was that the con-tent and form of the examinations and remedial services varied between hospitals, reflecting the hospitals' regular configuration of outpatient serv-ices.

The organization and quality of services in some of the hospitals contrasted sharply with the description of services promised the enrollees. Many of the enrollees reacted to the project with skepticism, and many expressed reluctance to take the examination.

Given the failure to achieve uniformly the desired organization of services, together with the absence of a clear-cut need for resocialization it may be expected that the project would not only fail to significantly reduce alienation and negativity among the enrollees, but also might increase such orientations and attitudes.

IMPACT OF PROJECT ON ENROLLEES

In considering the impact of the project, some methodological limitations need to be mentioned. The initial methodological strategy for determining the impact, panel analysis, was precluded by an unanticipated high rate of turnover among the enrollees, making it necessary to depend upon before only-after only comparisons of different samples. Further, the instruments focussing on enrollees' attitudes toward health services necessarily differed, being directed to the specific project experiences in one instance and general past experience in the other.

Non-cooperative enrollees. The first indications of the impact of the project appeared with the initial scheduling of examinations, when some enrollees refused to take examinations. Non-cooperation continued through both the examination and treatment phases.

Non-participation proved an elusive indicator of the enrollees' dispositions. Of 2,765 enrollees eligible for examinations, 1,100 received them, 244 refused them and 1,421 neither took the examination nor refused to take it.[6] The latter number includes both those who dropped out of NYC and those who repeatedly failed to keep examination appointments. What distinguished the non-cooperative from the non-examined was that the former verbalized refusal at some point. The 244 non-cooperative enrollees then represent 18 per cent of those who manifestly made a decision of taking or not taking the examination. Additional enrollees refused the treatment recommended for them. An estimated 500 received such recommendations, of whom 25 per cent refused it.

While direct contact with hospitals was limited to enrollees who refused treatment, those who refused examinations may nevertheless be considered in terms of the hospitals in which they *would have* received their examinations, since they knew where they were to be given and had knowledge of the hospital both from their peers who received examinations and from general community knowledge.

The participating hospitals were arrayed in rank order of conformity to the project directors' model of attractively organized services,[7] generating

[6] This latter figure includes 54 enrollees in NYC programs that never consummated examination arrangements with hospitals.

[7] Three judges independently rated each participating hospital in terms of 15 dimensions culled from proposals, directives and prescriptions offered by the state health officials on how the examination services should be organized to constitute an attractive arrangement in the manner of private practice medicine. The data consisted of observation reports on each of the hospitals, together with interviews of personnel,

a continuum of hospital organization from private practice to public clinic as the ideal types. The private practice type was characterized by an organization of services typical of a private physician's office or a private group practice clinic, and the public clinic type by organization typical of a hospital's outpatient clinic or emergency room.

When considered in terms of hospitals, enrollees associated with hospitals manifesting a public clinic type of organization were proportionally more likely to be non-cooperative than those associated with hospitals manifesting a private practice type of organization, as indicated in Table 5.

TABLE 5

Non-cooperative Enrollees, By Hospital Organization

	Hospitals			
	Private Practice a and b	c and d	e and f	Public Clinic Practice g and h
Potential Number of Examinees	395	383	516	1417
Percentage Non-cooperative	4.8	6.0	9.3	18.9

Cooperative enrollees. Of those enrollees who took the examination, their reactions to it were evenly arrayed from expressions of embracement to expressions of alienation, as indicated in Table 6. In comparison to pre-

TABLE 6

Cooperative Enrollees' Attitudes Toward
the Project Examination

	Alienated				Embracing
Scale Types	1	2	3	4	5
Percentage (N=462)	15.6	20.6	26.4	24.2	13.2

examination attitudes toward doctors (see Table 1), their reactions to the project examination do not constitute contrastingly positive orientations toward health service facilities. In terms of pre-examination attitudes toward past medical experiences (see Table 2), reactions to the project examination suggest that the project experience was alienating. An interpretation of alienation is further enhanced by taking into account the non-cooperative enrollees.

---

covering such aspects as site arrangement, personnel dispositions, equipment, handling of enrollees, organization and content of the examination, privacy and the general atmosphere prevailing during the examinations.

As with non-cooperative enrollees, the reactions of the cooperative enrollees to the project examination were related to the kinds of hospitals in which they received their examinations, as indicated in Table 7.

TABLE 7

Cooperative Enrollees' Attitudes Toward the Project
Examination, by Hospital Organization
(in percentages)

Attitudes Toward the Project Examinations: Scale Types	Hospitals			
	Private Practice a and b	c and d	e and f	Public Clinic Practice g and h
Alienated 1–2	18.0	27.0	30.0	40.0
Embracing 3–5	82.0	73.0	70.0	60.0
	100.0	100.0	100.0	100.0

The majority of cooperative enrollees emerged from the examination with positive attitudes toward health, as indicated in Table 8. In comparison to pre-examination attitudes toward health (see Table 3), this outcome

TABLE 8

Cooperative Enrollees' Post-Examination
Attitudes Toward Health

Scale Types	Negative		Positive	
	1	2	3	4
Percentages (N=563)	9.1	13.9	27.4	49.7

suggests a positive sensitizing through the project examination, seemingly as a consequence of sheer exposure to health facilities.

DISCUSSION AND CONCLUSION

When, early in the planning of the project, the project's directors focussed upon the attitudes of the NYC enrollees as their target for change, they supported their position by reference to a study of pre-induction draftees which suggested that those rejected on medical grounds suffered from inadequate facilities, inadequate education and a heritage of poverty.[8] Further support was offered by National Health Survey reports[9] and the

[8] The President's Task Force on Manpower Conservation, *One Third of a Nation* (Washington, D.C.: U.S. Government Printing Office, 1964).
[9] Department of Health, Education, and Welfare, *Vital and Health Statistics, Health Status and Family Income* (Washington, D.C.: U.S. Government Printing Office, 1964).

medical and social science literature dealing with the relationship between poverty and health practices.[10]

This literature suggests that low income people do not use medical and health facilities to the same extent that other people do and, further, that they are both alienated from such facilities and are unconcerned about their own health. However, this pertains to an adult population and generally does not make reference to adolescents. The findings of this study, in such a perspective, suggest that among low income people, alienation and negativity may not crystalize until adulthood, perhaps because adolescents are less likely to suffer illnesses than are other age categories.[11] This suggests that limited experience with illness among low income adolescents may tend to postpone those attitudes toward health observed among their elders, in spite of the medical facilities available to them during adolescence.

The findings of this study also suggest that the organization of health services available to low income adolescents has a direct bearing on their attitudes toward and utilization of such facilities. Furthermore, it appears that positive attitudes toward health in general *can* be encouraged rather easily.

In terms of policy, it is imperative that greater attention be paid to the *situational* basis of attitudes among the poor *as well as* to the attitudes themselves.

[10] Pearl Bierman, "Meeting the Health Needs of Low Income Families," *Annals of the American Academy of Political and Social Sciences*, 337 (Sept., 1961), p. 105. See also Lola M. Irelan, "Health Practices of the Poor," *Welfare in Review*, 3 (Oct., 1965), p. 1ff.; Earl L. Koos, *The Health of Regionville* (New York: Columbia University Press, 1954), chaps. 2–6; W. E. Mennie, "Health and Poverty," *Medical Services Journal, Canada*, 21 (Dec., 1965), pp. 787–814; Lee Rainwater, "The Lower Class: Health, Illness and Medical Institutions," (Mimeographed, March, 1965); and Daniel Rosenblatt and Edward Suchman, "Blue Collar Attitudes and Information Toward Health and Illness," in Arthur Shostack and William Gomberg, eds., *Blue Collar World*, (Englewood Cliffs, N.J.: Prentice-Hall, 1964), pp. 324–332.

[11] Congress, Senate, *Problems of Youth* (Washington, D.C.: U.S. Government Printing Office, 1964), p. 17.

Part VI
METHODOLOGICAL ISSUES IN
INTERVENTION RESEARCH

It was suggested earlier by Rossi (contribution 6), Sheppard (contribution 8), and Evans (contribution 22) that social-science methodology, though admittedly limited at this time, nonetheless can produce findings valuable to planners. Previous selections in this volume have provided some indication of the many methodological adequacies and inadequacies currently associated with intervention research.

The articles in this section are directly concerned with the mitigation of methodological problems in intervention research. Among contributions 35 through 42 are reviews of the literature on evaluative research and discussions of design, sampling, experimental control, analytical techniques, mathematical models, predictability, and respondent cooperation. Several of the contributions (36–40) are reports of program evaluation. They differ from those presentations of program evaluation in the previous section, however, in that the contributions here emphasize discussions of methodology as well as or rather than evaluative findings.

In contribution 35, sociologist Francis G. Caro identifies the major themes in recent social-science literature which he feels have direct implications for evaluative research. He focuses on those evaluation situations in which action programs are conducted by formal organizations and evaluative researchers are directly linked to the program administrators. His article discusses some of the basic issues in evaluative research, including choice of methodology, administration of such research, and implementation of research findings. Caro defines evaluative research as attempting to provide a program administrator with accurate information on the consequences of his actions.

The social-scientist program evaluators whose work was represented in Part V all had more or less direct contact with program administrators; at the very least they were expected to provide program personnel with information concerning intervention impact. Evans' (contribution 22) position in OEO headquarters was illustrative of a close structural relationship between a social scientist and policy makers at the national level. Williams' (contribution 33) research was funded by a local urban-renewal agency, to which he provided relevant feedback. Others in Part V, such as Vanecko (contribution 23), Zurcher (contributions 25 and 26), Lyden and Thomas (contribution 27), Bonjean and Crow (contribution 28), and Sutton (contribution 31) were contracted to gather data on the impact of local or regional intervention programs and to report their findings directly to national OEO.

Caro indicates that evaluative research is only one of the ways social scientists can contribute to programs of directed change; that way is illustrated in Part V. Other roles include participation in training programs, engaging in consulting, conducting basic research that has applied potential, and providing ideas which encourage rationality in the planning process. By their reflections, historical accounts, and critiques, the authors in Parts II, III, and IV have exemplified social scientists in the latter role —encouraging rationality in the planning process.

It is difficult to assess which of the two motivations for involvement in evaluative research mentioned by Caro—action interest or scientific interest—is the more salient among our contributors as a whole. Perhaps it is not simply a case of one motivation or another, but rather a mixture of interests in both the importance of planned social intervention and the scientific treatment of intervention effects. Individually considered, some of the contributors to this anthology seem to present their intervention arguments more fervently than others, and some appear to take greater pains to tie their efforts to theory and previous research.

Caro suggests that evaluative research may be sought by program administrators for a variety of covert reasons associated with sustaining or enhancing the program. Huitt (contribution 7), Trattner (contribution 9), Jones (contribution 11), Krause (contribution 13), Lineberry (contribution 14), and Zald (contribution 16) have discussed in detail some of the political, economic, and structural functions to which evaluative research can selectively be put to use by interventionists. The reports of Katz (contribution 17), Evans (contribution 19), Ford and Tollison (contribution 20), Ahearn (contribution 29), Bee (contribution 30), and Williams (contribution 33) indicate that an intervention organization's current policies do not or may not lead to the efficient realization of announced objectives. As Caro points out, this is an unwelcome possibility from the administrator's point of view, particularly if the program is being submitted to evaluative research.

Caro outlines dimensions on which evaluators and administrators are likely to differ, with the result that obstacles to coupling action with evaluative research are created. The dimensions are (1) service versus research, (2) time perspective, (3) methods, (4) status quo versus change, (5) explanations for failure, and (6) academic versus practical experience. The processes (and even some of the contents) of the differences in these orientations are not unlike those specified by Zurcher (contribution 25) as being endemic to poverty-intervention organizations. Perhaps the evaluative researcher himself is faced with enacting a version of "functional marginality." Caro comments that the researcher may be tempted to affiliate with power groups; but if he does, he will lose the freedom to hear all sides.

Caro notes what he feels are some of the major methodological problems facing evaluative research. Identification of independent and dependent variables is often difficult in practice, especially when the program is new or innovative and goals and strategies are not yet clearly delimited. The authors in Part II, reviewing the development of the goals and strategies of community-action programs, testify to that difficulty and its consequences.

Problems of adequate experimental control in evaluative research are especially critical, Caro points out. Gottlieb (contribution 4) and Rossi (contribution 6) comment, and Conforti (contribution 34) demonstrates, that the service orientation of intervention programs often precludes the establishment of control groups. That orientation, and the fact that intervention programs typically have been implemented before the evaluative researcher can begin his study, also make it difficult to obtain adequate premeasure or baseline data. The empirical program evaluations in Part V employ comparison groups rather than classic no-treatment control groups, and for the most part they do not have premeasures taken with the same subjects prior to program implementation. For example, Vanecko (contribution 23) establishes comparison groups by organizational status and acquires baseline data from retrospective accounts of respondents. Gove and Costner (contribution 24) compare members with nonmembers of neighborhood clubs. Zurcher (contribution 26) compares representatives of the poor with representatives of the nonpoor on a poverty board and contrasts time 1 with time 2 questionnaire measures. Lyden and Thomas (contribution 27) compare poverty-board members according to board status, having taken frequent measures of the interaction process over time. Bonjean and Crow (contribution 28) compare leadership patterns by ethnic group and assess change in those patterns by having asked respondents whether or not they had met one another through war-on-poverty activities. Ahearn (contribution 29) compares high-status with low-status indigenous nonprofessionals, using the respondents' prior employment histories as baseline data. Sutton (contribution 31) compares perceptions of OEO by various neighborhood and organizational statuses. Williams (contribution 33) compares housing and neighborhood data of displaced residents with, among other variables, respondents' retrospective accounts of housing and neighborhood conditions preceding relocation.

Unlike most of the research reported in the previous section, several of the selections presented in Part VI incorporate the classic no-treatment group, were able to obtain premeasures, or offer a logical substitute or variation on these characteristics of more sophisticated research designs.

William C. Berleman and Thomas W. Steinburn (contribution 36) report that in their evaluative research on a delinquency program the establishment of control groups was possible because of delay in the implementation of the service facility. This article indicates that, at the onset, antidelinquency intervention was severely circumscribed in time and clientele; and though the program did not represent a test of intervention, it did provide the evaluators with the opportunity to implement what they felt were rigorous procedural and evaluative techniques not generally employed in intervention research. Those techniques specifically were concerned with the selection and pretesting of experimental and control subjects. By collecting offense data on the entire population from which control and experimental subjects were drawn, Berleman and Steinburn could begin to answer questions concerning the accuracy of selection, the rates of attrition, and the levels of delinquent behavior exhibited by respondents. They also developed a coded recording system which, when used by service agents, supplied baseline data *prior* to full program implementation and to measurement of program impact.

Berleman and Steinburn represent the kind of *structural* research design which may overcome some of the control and pretest problems noted by Caro as associated with evaluative research. In contribution 37, sociologist Bruce C. Straits suggests an *analytical* research design of an intervention program which may provide statistical controls and noncontaminated premeasures for intervention subject groups. His article argues that drawing causal inferences about the factors influencing and sustaining cigarette smoking from surveys which are based on retrospective self-reports by smokers and ex-smokers is a difficult and uncertain task. His warning seems applicable to social-intervention research in general. To avoid that problem in his own study of antismoking intervention, Straits measured the relevant independent variables *prior* to smoking-clinic inducements and before the prospective clinic participants were invited to participate in the treatment program. Straits then used multiple discriminant analysis to "predict" which pretreatment variables were significantly related to posttreatment smoking behavior. He suggests that discriminant analysis can provide a predictive model for the impact of planned social intervention and can yield more useful evidence of the substantive relation of certain variables, such as attitudes, to program effectiveness than can more conventional designs.

Continuing with his outline of the methodological problems in intervention research, Caro observes that the prevailing conservatism in academic research regarding the rejection of the null hypothesis may be inappropriate when formulating decision criteria for evaluative studies and that caution should be used in drawing negative conclusions about the impact of innovative programs. In contribution 38, sociologist John H. Noble, Jr., comments on the uncertainty of evaluative research as a guide to social policy. Using a pretest-posttest control-group design with covariance adjustment techniques to control for subject attrition, Noble reveals that a delinquency-intervention program had no measurable impact upon the value orientations, attitudes, or self-concepts of program subjects, but did seem to reduce the extent of delinquent offenses for that group. Noble concludes that questions of statistical inference, measurement, substantive theory and value intrude upon the evaluator's attempt to judge the success or failure of planned social intervention. He advises, somewhat more elaborately than did Caro, that there may be uncertainties associated with the results of even the most carefully designed and executed evaluation of an intervention program and that statistical findings do not render an automatic verdict about the impact of that program. In order to minimize misinterpretations, Noble suggests that large-scale intervention programs should include opportunities for "true experiments" which can be designed, implemented, and analyzed under relatively controlled conditions—concurring in this respect with Rossi (contribution 6) and Berleman and Steinburn (contribution 36).

Noble's comments again raise the issue of the social scientist's role in planned social intervention. Should the researcher actually pronounce decisions about the "success" or "failure" of an intervention program? If he does make such pronouncements, will his judgment have any impact on the decision-making process? The reader is referred again to the differing perspectives which exist with respect to the social scientist's role (Parts I and II), as well as to the existing evidence with regard to the reality of the possibility that the social scientist himself may affect the decision process (Parts III and IV).

Caro identifies some other factors that are difficult to control and that could influence the outcome of intervention programs, such as the characteristics of the intervention site, the temporal factors of duration and continuity of program, and the interaction effect of traditional and innovative programs in an intervention agency. He suggests that in some cases participant observation may be more useful than formal experimentation as a means of understanding relevant program conditions. In Part V, Zurcher (contribution 25), Lyden and Thomas (contribution 27), Bee (contribution 30), and McNamara (contribution 32) demonstrated the feasibility of participant observation for evaluative research, or at least for isolating hypotheses for further comparative program assessment. In contribution 39, sociologist William L. Yancey also illustrates the use of participant observation in intervention research. However, Yancey's participation was at the level of intervention itself and thus was truly *participant* observation (Zurcher, Lyden and Thomas, Bee, and McNamara were, more correctly considered, *nonparticipant* observers). Yancey's study of unemployed Negro men suggests that a research strategy based on planned intervention provides social scientists with a "context of discovery" although it lacks many elements of a "context of proof." Yancey and his colleagues intervened into the lives of seven unemployed Negro men by encouraging them to seek employment. The researchers observed intervention effects by accompanying the men through several 8-hour days of job hunting. Personal, systematic, familial, and situational barriers to employment were revealed, suggesting that in some cases the active intervention of the researcher can be an essential component of the evaluative research itself.

In contrast to the "soft" approaches such as participant observation, mathematical and systems models have frequently been used, especially in industry and community studies, to provide a framework for the analysis of planned and unplanned social or technical change. In contribution 40, economists J. Ronnie Davis and Neil A. Palomba indicate that a game-theory model, the "prisoner's dilemma," is useful in predicting the outcome of a case of attempted social intervention. This article reveals some of the structural and interactional dynamics which affect the potential impact of the National Farmers Organization boycott intervention strategy. At the same time, Davis and Palomba's suggested model has relevance to Caro's suggestion that evaluative research needs analytical schemes which are sensitive to the *processes*, as well as the substantive impacts, of planned social intervention.

As mentioned above, Noble (contribution 38) indicated that in his opinion the researcher's choice of supporting theory can influence not only the range of methodologies usable for the study, but also the kinds of interpretations that are made from the data. In contribution 41, sociologist Leon Mayhew argues that aspects of Parsonian "action theory" can have critical relevance for intervention research. After reviewing those components of the theory which are relevant, Mayhew offers *ascription* as an additional theoretical concept which, as he illustrates with case material, helps to explain barriers to effective planned social intervention. Ascription defines those interactions which are governed by personal and informal criteria rather than impersonal and formal criteria. Like Krause (contribution 13), Lineberry (contribution 14), Zald (contribution 16) and Evans (contribution 22), Mayhew observes that "irrational" phenomena, of which ascription is one, are part of the social reality of the interfaces among organizations involved in planned intervention.

Like intervention research, planned social intervention involves human beings as "beneficiaries," "clients," "target groups," "subjects," "respondents," and so on. This is not to state a truism, but to call attention to the fact that just as people react differently to the demands of social-intervention programs, so also do they react differently to the requests of intervention research. In contribution 42, community-organization scholars Hans B. C. Spiegel and Victor G. Alicea challenge the feasibility of what they feel to be the traditional impersonal research or perception of low-income respondents. Among other factors, the emerging sense of community in low-income neighborhoods and the growing sense of cohesion among ethnic minority groups will make it increasingly difficult for the researcher in those communities to acquire *unrewarded* respondent cooperation. Spiegel and Alicea argue that some sort of exchange of services must be established between intervention researcher and respondent. They suggest various types of "trade-offs" which might accommodate the exchange process and facilitate research access.

A discussion of the role of respondents in planned social intervention and intervention research is not an inappropriate topic with which to close this anthology. In a sense it brings the reader full circle—from the role of the social scientist (contributions 1 and 2) to the role of the respondent (contribution 42). In the last analysis it is the respondent who is most important among an intervention program's cast of characters. He is the one to be served, both by the intervention program and by the evaluation of that program. Sometimes the exigencies and "irrationalities" of everyday program and research life are unduly allowed to obfuscate that responsibility.

35

APPROACHES TO EVALUATIVE RESEARCH: A REVIEW*

FRANCIS G. CARO

University of Colorado

S OCIAL SCIENCE WRITINGS ON APPROACHES TO THE EVALUATION OF ACTION programs are numerous but highly scattered. The present paper is an attempt to identify the major themes in recent social science literature with direct implications for evaluation research. The treatment is focused on situations in which action programs are conducted by formal organizations, and evaluative researchers are directly linked to program administrators. The material can be organized according to four major categories: (1) basic issues in evaluative research; (2) methodology; (3) administration of evaluative research; and (4) implementation of research findings.

BASIC ISSUES

Attempts to define evaluative research have focused on the specialized purposes of this form of research and on the methodology which distinguishes scientific from nonscientific evaluation. Brooks, Clinard, and Suchman, for example, all address themselves explicitly to the information sought in evaluative research. Brooks indicates that evaluation objectives include determination of: (1) the extent to which the program achieves its goal; (2) the relative impact of key program variables; and (3) the role of program as contrasted to external variables.[1] Clinard adds that the objectives may also include a test of the theories on 'which programs are based and a check on the efficiency of methods used.[2] Finally, Suchman defines evaluation as "the determination . . . of the results . . . attained by some activity . . . designed to accomplish some valued goal or objective."[3] He identifies four categories for evaluation: (1) effort (the amount of action); (2) effect (results of effort); (3) process (how an effect was achieved); and (4) efficiency (effects in relation to cost).[4]

Scientific evaluation is emphasized by Hyman and Wright when they specify the use of "methods that yield evidence that is objective, sys-

* This paper is Publication No. 111 of the Institute of Behavioral Science. The author is particularly indebted to Herbert Bynder and Marion Pearsall for their helpful suggestions.

1 Michael Brooks, "The Community Action Program as a Setting for Applied Research," *Journal of Social Issues,* Vol. 21, 1965, p. 34.

2 Marshall Clinard, *Slums and Community Development,* Free Press, New York, 1966, p. 240.

3 Edward Suchman, *Evaluative Research,* Russell Sage Foundation, New York, 1967, pp. 31–32; Edward Suchman, "A Model for Research and Evaluation on Rehabilitation," *Sociology and Rehabilitation,* American Sociological Association, Washington, D.C., 1966, p. 70.

4 Suchman, "A Model for Research and Evaluation on Rehabilitation," *op. cit.,* p. 68.

♦ Reprinted by permission of the Society for Applied Anthropology and of the author from *Human Organization* 28 (Summer, 1969), pp. 87–99.

tematic, and comprehensive."[5] For evaluation to qualify as research it is essential that measurements be based on some set of verifiable (and preferably quantitative) observations. The model of the classical experimental design thus represents a starting point for causal inferences regarding program effects. In this, the social scientist's approach contrasts with the impressionistic evaluation procedures often used by administrators and journalists.

At least in an idealized sense, evaluative research may be seen as a phase of systematic program development. That is, programs in response to some problem concern are preceded by a planning process that includes: (1) analysis of the problem; (2) specification of objectives; (3) evaluation of relevant existing programs; and (4) an exploration of possible alternatives. Program implementation is then followed by another evaluation phase which, in turn, contributes to further planning and program refinement. This planning, implementation, evaluation cycle may be repeated indefinitely until objectives are realized—or perhaps are discarded or altered on the basis of evaluation.

Evaluative research is, then, only one aspect of a process of planned change. It is a form of research which attempts to provide a program administrator with accurate information on the consequences of his actions. The results of evaluative research are a resource that may be used for the modification of programs to increase the likelihood of realization of long-term goals. Evaluative research may yield suggestions for action, but unless its findings are implemented, it does not bring about change.[6]

For social scientists interested in contributing to programs of directed change, evaluative research is only one possible role. Alternately social scientists may contribute to training programs and engage in consulting activities. Brooks, for example, suggests that social scientists may provide ideas for experimentation and encourage the greatest possible rationality in the planning process. They may aid in the identification of objectives and action alternatives and prediction of consequences of possible courses of action.[7]

Evaluative research, itself, also represents only one form of applied or action research since research may contribute to social action without assessing the effect of specific interventions. Research on the causes of problem behavior, the incidence and concentration patterns of social problems, and on public knowledge of and attitudes toward existing services may all have important policy implications without being specifically evaluative.

[5] Herbert Hyman and Charles Wright, "Evaluating Social Action Programs," in Paul Lazarsfeld, William Sewell, Harold Wilensky (eds.), *Uses of Sociology*, Basic Books, New York, 1967, p. 742.
[6] See, for example, Ronald Lippitt, Jeanne Watson, Bruce Westley, *The Dynamics of Planned Change*, Harcourt, Brace and Company, New York, 1958, pp. 91–126.
[7] Brooks, *op. cit.*, pp. 31-33. See also Warren Bennis, "Theory and Method in Applying Behavioral Science to Planned Organizational Change," *Journal of Applied Behavioral Science*, Vol. 1, 1965, pp. 337–360; Rensis Likert and Ronald Lippitt, "Utilization of Social Science," in L. Festinger and D. Katz (eds.), *Research Methods in Social Relations*, Holt, Rinehart, and Winston, New York, 1953, pp. 581–646.

Where action programs are carried out by a formal organization, evaluative research is most commonly sponsored by external funding sources and/or top administrators. Whether evaluative research is conducted by an internal unit of the organization or by outside consultants, evaluative researchers commonly are directly linked to a high level in the administrative structure. Those who actually carry out programs to be evaluated tend to be subordinate to those to whom evaluative researchers report. Although this structural arrangement puts the evaluative researcher in the same organizational position as an inspector or policeman, evaluative researchers insist that their role is quite different. Thus Likert and Lippitt emphasize

> . . . that the objective of the research is to discover the relative effectiveness of different methods and principles and that the study is in no way an attempt to perform a policing function. The emphasis must be on discovering what principles work best and why, and not on finding and reporting which individuals are doing their jobs well or poorly . . .[8]

Since formal evaluation of action programs is something less than a standard procedure, the conditions facilitating and impeding the development of the necessary research/action relationships warrant attention. In discussing their involvement in applied research, social scientists have tended to emphasize two positive themes. First, the social action goals of some social scientists parallel those of their clients; and their belief in the potential contribution of scientific evaluation to the development of effective action programs leads to involvement. Such social researchers may be personally concerned about an agency's potential target population (the poor, infirm, or aged), an organization's staff (their morale, compensation, or working conditions), the organization's mission (its productivity or profit), or a community (its growth or prosperity). A variation on this theme is cooperation with community agencies on the basis of an institutional service orientation. Secondly, the researcher's participation in evaluation may be based on his scientific interest in understanding organizations, communities, and/or social change where the action to be evaluated represents a test of some theoretically important hypothesis. Social scientists have been less inclined to identify more personal motives that may also be operating—for example, proximity to power, community prestige, or improved income. On the negative side, factors which have deterred social scientists from engaging in evaluative research include the low prestige accorded to applied research in academic circles, the uncertain implications for career development, reluctance to make policy recommendations on the basis of inadequate evidence, the possibility that the findings may be "misused," the imperfect "fit" between action problems and disciplinary interests, and anticipation of a number of methodological and operational problems which may detract from the validity, reliability, and the utility of the effort.

Possible contributions of evaluative research to action are usually

[8] Likert and Lippitt, "Utilization of Social Science," op. cit., pp. 31–33.

phrased in terms of the potential of this type of research for introducing greater rationality into organizational decision-making. Stated objectives of evaluation may include: (1) providing accounting information for funding sources; (2) feedback to administrators to aid in refining and improving the program; and (3) dissemination of program information to the general public.[9] However, a number of covert motives of actionists for engaging social scientists to "evaluate" programs have also been identified. Professional advice may be sought (consciously or unconsciously): (1) for arbitration to settle an internal dispute; (2) to justify decisions already made; (3) to support a bid for power; or (4) to postpone action.[10] Dexter adds that applied research may be used to place responsibility for a decision on someone outside the agency,[11] while other commentators have suggested that such research lends an aura of prestige to the action enterprise.[12] Or an administrator may hope to get special nonevaluative services from researchers—for example, the organization of information to justify further grant requests.[13]

Evaluative research may also have important disadvantages from the agency's perspective since it invites administrators to consider the possibility that their current policies do not lead to the efficient realization of announced objectives. Administrators' claims for programs are often unreasonably optimistic, and research results are therefore almost inevitably disappointing.[14] Similarly, changes in policies and practices suggested by the research findings may be unwelcome.[15] Practitioners may also feel that social scientists are unwilling or unable to provide information that is sufficiently relevant for policy decisions. At the same time, they may anticipate that the proposed research will impose serious restrictions on the activities of the agency's operating staff.

Therefore, while rational considerations suggest the coupling of action with evaluation research, there are a number of basic obstacles to putting this into practice. The obstacles can be summarized in terms of six orientations in which researchers and actionists are likely to differ markedly:

[9] See, for example, Brooks, *op. cit.*, p. 33; Suchman, *Evaluative Research*, pp. 1–6.

[10] Anthony Downs, "Some Thoughts on Giving People Economic Advice," *American Behavioral Scientist*, Vol. 9, September, 1965, pp. 30-32.

[11] Lewis A. Dexter, "Impressions about Utility and Wastefulness in Applied Social Science Studies," *American Behavioral Scientist*, Vol. 9, February 1966, pp. 9–10.

[12] See, for example, Hyman Rodman and Ralph Kolodny, "Organizational Strains in the Researcher-Practitioner Relationship," *Human Organization*, Vol. 23, 1964, pp. 171–182, reprinted in A. Gouldner and S. M. Miller (eds.), *Applied Sociology*, Free Press, New York, 1965, pp. 93–113; Herbert Bynder, "Sociology in a Hospital: A Case Study in Frustration," in A. Shostak (ed.), *Sociology in Action*, Dorsey Press, Homewood, Illinois, 1966, pp. 61–70; Robert Rosenthal and Robert Weiss, "Problems of Organizational Feedback," in Raymond Bauer (ed.), *Social Indicators*, M.I.T. Press, Boston, Massachusetts, 1966, pp. 302–340.

[13] S. M. Miller, "Evaluating Action Programs," *Trans-action*, Vol. 4, June 1967, p. 51; Elmer Luchterhand, "Research and the Dilemmas in Developing Social Programs," in Paul Lazarsfeld *et al.*, *Uses of Sociology*, Basic Books, New York, 1967, pp. 506–521.

[14] See, for example, Peter Rossi, "Evaluating Social Action Programs," *Trans-action*, Vol. 4, June 1967, pp. 51–53.

[15] Rodman and Kolodny, *op. cit.*, p. 104.

(1) Service *vs.* research; (2) Time perspective; (3) Methods; (4) *Status quo vs.* change; (5) Explanations for failure; and (6) Academic *vs.* practical experience.

Service vs. research.[16] Social scientists naturally emphasize the acquisition of knowlege in contrast to the practitioner's concern with the utilization of knowledge. Even where service and research functions are performed by a single person, situations may arise in which the two objectives are incompatible. Or the requirements of a research design may dictate some treatment or experimental control which appears nonoptimal from a service perspective. In cases which pose such conflicts, ideological and priority questions must be resolved.

Time perspective. While actionists are likely to emphasize the solution of immediate problems, researchers are more apt to stress the long-term resolution of problems.[17] This is similar to other suggestions that actionists tend to emphasize the uniqueness of each agency or program while researchers prefer to generalize in both time and space to all similar systems. In this sense, what is of theoretical significance to the scientist may be trivial or inconsequential from a practical viewpoint.[18]

Methods. Although actionists and researchers may agree on the use of rational methods in program development, they often do not mean the same thing by "rational." Research requirements, for instance, demand explicit statements of objectives and strategies which actionists find difficult or even undesirable to commit themselves to.[19] It is also difficult to comply with requests for evidence of direct relationship between administrative activities and organizational goals since evaluation studies tend to focus on organizational outputs to the neglect of activities which function primarily to maintain the organization as a viable system.[20] At another

---

[16] See, for example, Chris Argyris, "Creating Effective Relationships in Organizations" in R. Adams and J. Preiss (eds.), *Human Organization Research*, Dorsey, Homewood, Illinois, 1960, pp. 109–123; Howard Freeman, "Strategy of Social Policy Research," *Social Welfare Forum*, 1963, pp. 143–156; S. E. Perry and Lyman Wynne, "Role Conflict, Role Definition, and Social Change in Clinical Research Organization," *Social Forces*, Vol. 38, 1959, pp. 62–65; Roland Warren, *Social Research Consultation*, Russell Sage, New York, 1963, pp. 21–22.

[17] See, for example, Likert and Lippitt, *op. cit.*, p. 271; Herbert Shepard, "Nine Dilemmas in Industrial Research," *Administrative Science Quarterly*, Vol. 4, 1956, pp. 295–309; Warren, *op. cit.*, p. 21.

[18] See, for example, Arthur K. Davis, "A Prairie 'Dust Devil': The Rise and Decline of a Research Institute," *Human Organization*, Vol. 27, 1968, pp. 56–64; Lippitt *et al.*, *op. cit.*, p. 271; Robert K. Merton, "Role of the Intellectual in Public Bureaucracy," in *Social Theory and Social Structure*, Free Press, New York, 1957, pp. 207–224; Rodman and Kolodny, *op. cit.*, pp. 93–94.

[19] See, for example, Howard Freeman and Clarence Sherwood, "Research in Large-Scale Intervention Programs," *Journal of Social Issues*, Vol. 21, 1965, pp. 11–28; Peter Marris and Martin Rein, *Dilemmas of Social Reform: Poverty and Community Action in the U. S.*, Atherton Press, New York, 1967, pp. 191–207.

[20] Amitai Etzioni, "Two Approaches to Organizational Analysis: A Critique and a Suggestion," *Administrative Science Quarterly*, Vol. 5, 1960, pp. 257–278. Etzioni argues that most evaluation studies assume that all of an organization's energy is devoted to its publicly stated goals. In fact, some of its human and material resources must be channeled into keeping the organization alive. Without some emphasis on system maintenance, the organization could not bring together and coordinate all the activities needed to reach the primary objective.

level, the researcher's commitment to scientific decision-making procedures may run counter to the practitioner's confidence in intuition and the "art" of practice. In effect, practitioners use less rigorously objective or quantitative methods of evaluation than do their scientific counterparts.[21]

Status quo vs. change.[22] Researchers often have a vested interest in discovering inefficiency and encouraging change while practitioners are likely to prefer to conceal inefficiency and resist disruptive change. In part, the social scientists justify their claim to superior knowledge of human affairs by dramatizing inadequacies in conventional wisdom and existing social programs. Those who are responsible for administering social service enterprises are similarly inclined to assert *their* competence by claims about the success of past and current programs. Evaluating scientists are thus predisposed to see the need for change while administrators are inclined to defend their efforts and maintain the *status quo.*

Explanations for failure.[23] The researcher and the actionist are likely to emphasize different explanations for the persistence of social problems. While actionists seem to accept the theoretical premises on which programs are based as axioms to be taken for granted without further question, research evaluators may wish to examine them. As a result, practitioners may think in terms of expanding and improving present efforts where research workers prefer to consider current failures in relation to alternative approaches based on different explanations of the basic problem. The administrator wants information that will justify additional funds to expand operations, but the social scientist may be interested in finding more effective new programs to meet the old need. In addition, where both acknowledge difficulties in the implementation of programs,

[21] See, for example, Rodman and Kolodny, *op. cit.*, pp. 93–113; Warren, *op. cit.*, p. 22 ff.; Marris and Rein, *op. cit.*, pp. 191–207.

[22] See, for example, Chris Argyris, *Understanding Organizational Behavior*, Dorsey, Homewood, Illinois, 1960; Lippitt, Watson and Westley, *op. cit.*; Rodman and Kolodny, *op. cit.*, p. 97.

[23] Differences between researchers and actionists in their explanations for failure stem, in part, from differences in their orientations to the status quo. Because of the need to assert his competence, the practitioner has reason to defend the essential validity of his approach. When he is confronted with the persistence of the problem to which his efforts are addressed, the practitioner is not likely to abandon immediately his theoretical premises. By attributing failure to an insufficient application of his approach, he can acknowledge persistence of the problem without admitting to any personal or professional inadequacy. To the extent that he is successful in arguing that what is needed is "more of the same" the practitioner may also serve his professional interest in expanding the demand for his services. The social scientist, with no such commitment to established practices, is free to consider not only the utility of expanded services but also the theoretical premises on which programs are based. The social scientist's predisposition to call for change is also likely to lead to an interest in new approaches to problems.

(In cases where a social problem persists despite a contribution by researchers in the search for solutions, social scientists are likely to argue the need for more research. In their plea for an expansion of this effort, the researchers' response to failure is similar to that of practitioners'.)

the administrator is likely to look for explanations which are individual (e.g., incompetence, emotional disturbance) and moral (e.g., dishonesty or laziness) where the social scientist emphasizes nonmoral and structural factors.[24]

Academic vs. practical experience. Insofar as the researcher approaches social action from the perspective of a single academic discipline, his knowledge of practical affairs is likely to be highly incomplete.[25] Unless he has had work experience in the same kind of organization, he is also not likely to have much comprehension of or to develop empathy for the administrator's or practitioner's position.[26] In the same sense, it is difficult for practitioners with limited academic experience in the social sciences to understand the importance of the researcher's emphasis on methodology.

METHODOLOGICAL CONSIDERATIONS

A number of social scientists have produced manuals or texts on the techniques of evaluation research for students and/or practitioners.[27] In addition, some general works on field experiments are particularly relevant for evaluative research.[28] Others have written about methodological problems encountered in their own evaluative research, or have reviewed

[24] Part of what is at issue here is the social scientist's sensitivity to organizational structure and its impact on whoever occupies a particular position. Insiders, on the other hand, tend to explain everything in terms of *who* occupies the position; they praise or blame him as a person without considering the bureaucratic restraints he is subject to. Also involved is the social scientist's more secularized explanation of human behavior. Social scientists are more likely than practitioners to explain behavior in terms of factors which are outside the realm of free choice.

[25] See, for example, Argyris, "Creating Effective Relationships in Organizations," *op. cit.*, pp. 110–112; Brooks, *op. cit.*, p. 38; George Fairweather, *Methods of Experimental Innovation*, Wiley, New York, 1967; Merton, *op. cit.*, pp. 207–224.

[26] Political constraints, budgetary problems and limitations of personnel and facilities are among the realities which a social scientist preoccupied with programs is likely to gloss over. To the administrator, however, they are matters of vital importance.

[27] Samuel Hayes, *Measuring the Results of Development Projects*, UNESCO Monographs in Applied Social Sciences, New York, 1959; Elizabeth Herzog, *Some Guidelines for Evaluation Research*, HEW Children's Bureau, Washington, U. S. Government Printing Office, 1959; Fairweather, *op. cit.*; C. Selltiz, M. Jahoda, M. Deutsch, and S. Cook, "The Application of Social Research," in *Research Methods in Social Relations*, Holt, Rinehart, and Winston, New York, 1965, pp. 455–478; Suchman, *Evaluative Research*; Suchman, "A Model for Research and Evaluation on Rehabilitation"; Edward Suchman, "Principles and Practice of Evaluative Research," in J. Doby (ed.), *An Introduction to Social Research*, second edition, Appleton, Century, Crofts, New York, 1967, pp. 327–351; Hyman and Wright, *op. cit.*, pp. 741–782.

[28] For example, John French, "Experiments in Field Settings," in L. Festinger and D. Katz (eds.), *Research Methods in the Behavioral Sciences*, Holt, New York, 1963; Donald Campbell, "Validity of Experiments in Social Settings," *Psychological Bulletin*, Vol. 54, 1957, pp. 297–312; Donald Campbell and Julian Stanley, *Experimental and Quasi-Experimental Designs for Research*, Rand McNally, Chicago, 1966; Louis Barnes, "Organizational Change and Field Experiment Methods," in Victor Vroom (ed.), *Methods of Organizational Research*, University of Pittsburgh, 1967, pp. 57–111.

the work of others from a methodological perspective.[29] There is general agreement that, in principle, evaluative research is no different from other forms of social science research in terms of methodology. Nevertheless, the evaluation of social action presents a predictable set of specialized problems in terms of conceptualization, measurement, and interpretation.

A basic step in the formulation of evaluation research is the identification and measurement of dependent variables. The action objectives must be identified, operationalized, and measured. Suchman suggests that the formulation of objectives of action programs has five aspects: (1) the content of the objective (i.e., that which is to be changed by the program); (2) the target of the program; (3) the time within which the change is to take place; (4) the number of objectives (if they are multiple); and (5) the extent of the expected effect.[30] Freeman and Sherwood identify three ways in which the researcher may go about identifying objectives: (1) he may accept the actionist's statement of objectives; (2) he may guess at program objectives; or (3) he may participate in the formulation of objectives.[31] They recommend the last course. Freeman previously suggested that research findings would be more useful to policy makers if dependent variables are formulated in behavioral rather than attitudinal terms, and also, that where objectives are not likely to be realized in the immediate future, a distinction between ultimate, intermediate, and immediate goals is indicated.[32] If nothing else, this protects the researcher who must report evidence on goal-attainment long before the achievement of ultimate goals can possibly be measured.[33] Another and different consideration is the researcher's responsibility for identifying and measuring the possible undesired consequences of the programs being evaluated.[34]

Yet another consideration in evaluation studies is the "contamination" of the research project itself. Interviews and observations may well raise employee and client morale for no other reason than that the employees or clients are now receiving special attention they have never before had.[35] Campbell suggests that this problem can be minimized by using only post-test measurements,[36] while Seashore encourages procedures

---

[29] See, for example, Herbert Hyman, C. Wright, and T. Hopkins, *Applications of Methods of Evaluation*, University of California Press, Berkeley, 1962; William F. Whyte and Edith Hamilton, *Action Research for Management*, Dorsey, Homewood, Illinois, 1964; Stanley Seashore, "Field Experiences with Formal Organizations," *Human Organization*, Vol. 23, 1964, pp. 164–170; Avedis Donabedian, "Evaluating Quality of Medical Care," *Milbank Memorial Fund Quarterly*, Vol. 44, 1966, pp. 106–206; John Mann, *Changing Human Behavior*, Scribner's, New York, 1965, pp. 165–214.

[30] Suchman, *Evaluative Research*, pp. 39–41, 60–71; Suchman, "A Model for Research and Evaluation on Rehabilitation," pp. 64–65.

[31] Freeman and Sherwood, *op. cit.*, p. 17.

[32] Freeman, *op. cit.*, pp. 150–153; Freeman and Sherwood, *op. cit.*, p. 15. See also Suchman, *Evaluative Research*, pp. 52–59.

[33] See, for example, Marris and Rein, *op. cit.*, pp. 191–207.

[34] See, for example, Herzog, *op. cit.*, pp. 74–78; Hyman and Wright, *op. cit.*, p. 757.

[35] Whyte and Hamilton, *op. cit.*, p. 181.

[36] Campbell, *op. cit.*, pp. 303–307.

that minimize subjects' awareness of the research.[37] Hyman *et al.*, on the other hand, review a series of studies which show that the sensitizing or practice effects of pretesting are negligible.[38] In some cases, then, the effect of research as an intervention in its own right may be so slight as to be unimportant.

To assure that changes in the dependent variable can be attributed exclusively to the program, the classical experimental design is the accepted basic model for evaluative research. Inferences regarding program effects are based on the relative differences between pre- and post-measures of experimental and control groups to which subjects have been assigned. A number of factors may arise, however, that dictate departures from this ideal. For instance, the measurement problems discussed above may call for elimination of pretest measures or use of the Solomon four-group design.[39]

Problems of adequate control are perhaps even more critical, and Suchman suggests two basic obstacles to the effective use of control groups in evaluative research; (1) service orientation—actionists are reluctant to withhold services from randomly selected applicants; and (2) self-selection—there is usually no way to control the flow of persons who want services.[40] Mann similarly observes that in an organizational setting, innovative approaches may "spread like a disease" to control groups.[41]

Borgatta mentions five common objections to the use of control groups in therapeutic programs: (1) some who might most benefit from the therapy are included in the control group; (2) it is not fair to withhold treatment from some patients; (3) experimental research cannot solve the problems of therapists; (4) experiments are not needed since clinicians are competent and dedicated; and (5) if a treatment were not effective, it would not be used. He refutes these with the following arguments: (1) it is essential to the logic of experimental research that both the experimental and control group include persons who are likely to be affected by the treatment; (2) in the case of noneffective therapies, the withholding of treatment from some may, in the long run, be beneficial to all since it may encourage the development of more effective treatments; (3) any question with an empirical reference asked by clinicians can be subjected to scientific scrutiny; (4) clinical impressions are subject to error—experimental research is important for verification; and (5) the popularity of a treatment is not necessarily associated with its effectiveness.[42]

While some evaluation researchers insist that control groups are essential, others suggest design adjustments such as matching exposed and nonexposed subjects and using statistical analysis of covariance.[43] Hyman

[37] Seashore, *op. cit.*, p. 169.

[38] Hyman, Wright, and Hopkins, *op. cit.*, pp. 33–37.

[39] See, for example, Campbell, *op. cit.*, p. 305; Suchman, *Evaluative Research*, pp. 91–114.

[40] Suchman, "Principles and Practices of Evaluative Research," pp. 348–349.

[41] J. Mann, *op. cit.*, pp. 186–188.

[42] Edgar Borgatta, "Research: Pure and Applied," *Group Psychotherapy*, Vol. 8, 1955, pp. 263–277.

[43] Suchman, *op. cit.*, "Principles and Practice of Evaluative Research," pp. 340–349.

et al., on the other hand, recommend using the treatment group as its own control by measuring its stability prior to treatment over a period comparable in duration to the treatment period.[44] Hyman and Wright also suggest the use of comparison groups instead of, or in addition to, a control group.[45] Unlike the strict control group which receives no treatment, the comparison group receives an alternate treatment. Where practitioners are committed to giving some form of treatment, a comparison group design may be even more meaningful than a nontreatment control since the comparison groups can be linked to the action interests of various potential consumers of evaluative research. By being sensitive to the action alternatives open to funding sources, agency administrators, and practitioners, the researcher may add greatly to the potential influence of his work.[46] Finally Rossi suggests a strategy of a reconnaissance phase followed by an experimental phase.[47] Correlational designs are used to identify promising programs. Powerful controlled experiments are then used to evaluate the relative effectiveness of those programs which have passed the initial screening.

Sample size is another major methodological problem in terms of the kind of conclusions that can eventually be drawn from evaluative research. It is often realistic to expect that the impact of action programs will not be dramatic. Therefore, if evaluation is to document subtle but quite possibly important changes, large samples are necessary. For example, where interactions between programs and subject characteristics are anticipated, upward revision of the sample size is appropriate.[48] For similar reasons, the prevailing conservatism in academic research regarding rejection of null hypotheses may be less appropriate when formulating decision criteria for evaluation studies.[49] Caution may be called for in drawing negative conclusions about the impact of innovative programs. In any case, the decision criteria chosen have implications for the size of the sample to be selected.

Even where evaluation designs satisfy the basic requirements of the experimental model, there may be important limitations on data interpretation.[50] Most importantly perhaps, designs which only measure

[44] Hyman, Wright, Hopkins, *op. cit.*, pp. 20–37.

[45] Hyman and Wright, *op. cit.*, pp. 763–768.

[46] Carol Weiss, "Utilization of Evaluation: Toward Comparative Study," in *The Use of Social Research in Federal Domestic Programs*, U. S. Government Printing Office, Washington, D. C. 1966, pp. 426–435.

[47] Rossi, *op. cit.*, p. 53.

[48] Freeman, *op. cit.*, pp. 155–156.

[49] S. M. Miller, *op. cit.*, p. 444.

[50] For discussions of the problems involved in interpreting evaluation data and proposed solutions see, among others, Whyte and Hamilton, *op. cit.*, pp. 203–208; Hyman and Wright, *op. cit.*, pp. 741–782; Freeman and Sherwood, *op. cit.*, pp. 11–28; Weiss, *op. cit.*, pp. 426–435; Suchman, "Principles and Practice of Evaluative Research," pp. 327–351; J. Mann, *op. cit.*, pp. 165–214; Barbara Benedict, *et al.*, "The Clinical Experimental Approach to Assessing Organizational Change Efforts," *Journal of Applied Behavioral Science*, Vol. 3, 1967, pp. 347–380; S. M. Miller, "Prospects: The Applied Sociology of the Center-City," in A. Gouldner and S. M. Miller, *Applied Sociology*, Free Press, New York, 1965, pp. 441–456; Marris and Rein, *op. cit.*, pp. 191–207; P. Lasarsfeld, W. Sewell, and H. Wilensky, "Introduction," *The Uses of Sociology*, Basic Books, New York, 1967, pp. ix–xxxiii.

change in the dependent variable cannot explain the change process. Yet process analysis is precisely what is needed, especially when a given program is not working. The problem is compounded if the researcher accepts unquestioningly the official descriptions of a program's operations which all too often are only paper descriptions that have never been fully translated into action by the field staff. Rather, attention should be directed to actual operational processes and to an attempt to identify the basic concepts to which program effects might be attributed.

A related problem is the difficulty of designing research that can separate analytically the effects of program content from the personal influence of practitioners on their clientele. It is particularly difficult to distinguish between concepts or methods and the person applying them when the number of practitioners is small. Personality, social skills, staff enthusiasm, and faith in new programs become unusually important variables under the circumstances. The target population, too, may contribute effects through feelings of self-importance as persons selected for special attention (the "Hawthorne effect"), or through faith in the treatment being evaluated (the "placebo effect"). Such effects may be particularly likely where subjects are volunteers for an experimental program.

Many other uncontrolled or difficult-to-control factors that might help to explain program outcomes could be cited—for instance, physical and other characteristics of the experimental site; the temporal factors of duration and continuity of the treatment; the interaction effect of traditional on innovative programs in a particular agency; and the like. Questions arise also concerning the differential impact of the various components of large-scale programs. And uncontrolled exposure of subjects to several programs in communities making concerted efforts toward social change greatly hampers analysis of any single program. It is often difficult to determine whether new programs are supplements to or substitutes for earlier programs.

Somewhat related to the last point is the question of differences between new and already established programs with respect to methodological problems of evaluation. While innovation experiments may generate their own "halo" effect as suggested earlier, as new activities they undoubtedly require a certain amount of time to reach maximum efficiency. For this and other reasons, research designs suited to the evaluation of fully institutionalized programs may be inappropriate for assessing new programs. Indeed, as Marris and Rein indicate, action innovators developing exploratory programs prefer flexibility and freedom to modify their procedures in response to changing events.[51] Such actionists can be expected to resist the lengthy commitment to a particular intervention required for rigorous experimental purposes. They may quite correctly see the need for program modifications long before enough cases have been collected to satisfy the requirements of an experimental design. If evaluative research is to contribute to program development at this stage, it must provide rapid feedback. For this, the less formal research strategies associated with exploratory research are perhaps most appropriate.

[51] Marris and Rein, op. cit., pp. 191–207.

In this context, Lazarsfeld *et al.* observe that the decision process is continuous in action programs, and evaluation must take place at many points ("concurrent evaluation").[52] This requires a record of all decisions including notes on discarded alternatives and expected outcomes. It also suggests that participant observation may be more useful than formal experimentation at some points. Perhaps what is most needed is a judicious combination of experimental designs with a "natural history" type running account of events and actors before, during, and after planned interventions.[53]

While the basic logic for designing evaluation studies is simple, the methodological problems are obviously enormous. Circumstances may make it difficult to introduce a tight design or to develop a satisfactory measure of the dependent variable. People with action interests are likely to demand richer information, more rapidly, and more economically than rigorously trained social scientists can or are willing to provide. The social scientist who genuinely wants to make meaningful contributions to action faces a dilemma between the controlled purity of laboratory experimentation and the informational needs of administrators and other practitioners charged with making real life programs work. The major methodological problem for such scientists today is to devise procedural compromises which will at the same time minimize errors and lead to greater predictability.

THE ADMINISTRATION OF EVALUATION RESEARCH

Problems of design are not the only barriers to successful evaluative research. There are other obstacles in the organizational or interorganizational context in which such research is conducted. The most common arrangements are: (1) the researchers are themselves staff members in the organization whose programs are evaluated; or (2) the evaluators are consultants from an organization other than the one whose program is being evaluated. In either case, the unit initiating or sponsoring the evaluation is likely to have some formal link with the action agency's top administration. The evaluator's day-to-day contacts, however, are apt to be with the agency's line staff or even with members of a subcontracting organization. The research thus depends on cooperation from both agency administrators and lower-level personnel charged with implementing agency programs, to say nothing of the client population.

Basic questions immediately arise as to the researcher's authority and responsibility. Social scientists have typically maintained that ultimate responsibility for research design and execution is theirs even while advocating extensive collaboration and communication with clients and potential consumers of their findings. Yet many have found it difficult to maintain this position in the face of persons with vested interests in positions that give them a voice in the formulation and execution of research in their agencies, not to mention their power to interfere at

[52] Lazarsfeld, *et al.*, *op. cit.*, p. xv.
[53] Barbara Benedict, *et al.*, pp. 347–380.

critical points.[54] Even after research has been initiated, the problem of maintaining effective contact with policy makers remains. Administrators may "forget" to inform the researchers of problems or policy changes that emerge, and research people must continually compete with others for attention from top-local policy makers. In all of this, the specialized vocabularies of both may provide real or symbolic barriers to communication.

Whether or not researchers are agency employees, they are readily drawn into staff/management conflicts. Administrative acceptance of the utility of research certainly does not guarantee a similar acceptance from subordinates.[55] In fact, knowledge of the researchers' lines of communication with policy level personnel invites a staff view of them as management spies. Not surprisingly, staff awareness of potential criticism leads to protective devices for avoiding any publicizing of real or imagined mistakes. The researcher walks a tightrope between an affiliation with power groups and the freedom to hear all sides without becoming involved in internal conflicts. Repeated and emphatic assurances of confidentiality and anonymity are often necessary when dealing with employees in subordinate positions. Assurances to staff members that they will be informed of research findings may help to allay anxieties, but these can only be given when the evaluator has no reason to doubt an administrator's willingness to share findings openly and nonjudgmentally with his staff.

Research neutrality sometimes poses another problem with actionists who typically consider strong value commitment to their programs important. Bynder, for example, reports that his research in a social work unit of a general hospital was hindered by clinical values associated with the program.[56] Argyris, on the other hand, argues that a researcher who is sincerely concerned about his subjects' problems is more effective than one who subordinates his own humanitarianism to research demands. He postulates a process whereby research neutrality leads to subject alienation which in turn produces anxietiés in the researcher that result in invalid observations.[57] There would seem to be no easy balance between research objectivity and value commitment.

Even where agencies are openly committed to evaluation, the purely

54 For discussions of the establishment and maintenance of a proper collaborative relationship between researchers and practitioners see, for example, Freeman, op. cit., pp. 143–156; Joel Smith, et al., "Client Structure and the Research Process," in R. N. Adams and J. Preiss (eds.), Human Organization Research, Dorsey, Homewood, Illinois, 1960, pp. 41–56; Bynder, op. cit., pp. 67–68; Merton, op. cit., pp. 207–224; W. L. Slocum, "Sociological Research for Action Agencies: Some Guides and Hazards," Rural Sociology, Vol. 21, 1956, pp. 196–199; Luchterhand, op. cit., pp. 513–514.

55 A number of observers have noted that acceptance of evaluative research at upper administrative levels is often accompanied by suspicion of research at lower levels. See for example, Rodman and Kolodny, op. cit., pp. 101–102; Lippitt, et al., op. cit., pp. 270–271; Argyris, "Creating Effective Relationships in Organizations," op. cit., pp. 118–122; Whyte and Hamilton, op. cit., pp. 209–221; and Likert and Lippitt, op. cit., pp. 581–646.

56 Bynder, op. cit., pp. 63–69.

57 Argyris, op. cit., pp. 113–115.

mechanical demands of data-gathering create a burden. Particularly in situations where relations between administrators and their subordinates are strained, staff members may not comply with research demands. Staff members typically, perhaps correctly, consider themselves over-burdened with record-keeping. Typically, also, even where record-keeping is stressed and accepted, the records are not sufficiently accurate or complete to satisfy research criteria. At other levels too, research designs may fail to elicit adequate data for some of the reasons outlined above in the section on "Basic Issues." For example, when a research design calls for action inconsistent with immediate service goals, practitioners may disregard research needs in favor of providing services. Moreover, it is at this point that perceived differences in research and service orientations are likely to generate opposing actions.[58]

Even different conceptions of time may lead to mutual annoyance. As a research scientist, the evaluator is not used to turning in daily time sheets, but his failure to do so can be interpreted as a sign of indolence by an administrator attuned to time and cost criteria. "Thinking is not a tangible use of time, and therefore, could not be accepted in an agency which measured work in terms of clients interviewed, physicians contacted, meetings attended, and pages written."[59] An insecure social scientist may well direct his energies to appearing "busy" at this stage, to the detriment of long-term research objectives. He may also suffer from status ambiguities that further strain relationships if he is younger and has less clinical experience than his administrative or practitioner counterpart while having more formal education. This may be combined with an academic disrespect for "practical" people. Nonacademic managers and practitioners, in turn, may be defensive about their educational inferiority and be unduly sensitive to the apparent snobbism of research scientists.

As a result of such differences, the researcher measures himself by academic standards, prestige, and prerequisites which are denied him in the action setting, where he becomes an exposed and defenseless member of a minority group. The actionist, however, typically enjoys bureaucratic security against accusations of incompetency which may be threatened by evaluative research. Such personnel resort at times to organizational means of thwarting scientific evaluation and also to claims that "impractical" scientists are themselves incompetent to comprehend the practical problems of an action agency. There is little basis for mutual understanding where researchers receive only a certain surface prestige based on their professional credentials and administrators receive inadequate information of research goals, methods, and the possible practical utility of evaluative findings.

[58] A number of social scientists have noted annoyances which have emerged in their day-to-day working relationship with practitioners. See, for example, Rodman and Kolodny, op. cit., pp. 97–106; Selltiz, et al., op. cit., pp. 461–464; Bynder, op. cit., pp. 64–67; Rolf Schulze, "Communication to the Editor," American Sociologist, Vol. 2, 1967, pp. 96–97; Argyris, "Creating Effective Relationships in Organizations," op. cit., pp. 111–112; Luchterhand, op. cit., pp. 515–517; Shepard, op. cit., pp. 300–304.

[59] Bynder, op. cit., p. 67.

Two other basic problems may be mentioned in connection with the publication of the results of evaluative research:[60] (1) agencies tend to impose controls on the publication of "sensitive" data; and (2) if data *are* accepted for publication, practitioners want a share of the credit. In the former case, a negative report may threaten not only the agency's public "image" but also its access to funds. With respect to the second point, the question is whether administrators (who may conceive the social innovation) and implementers of programs (who may also supply data and keep records) should share authorship with the social scientists (who formulate the research design and are responsible for the final analysis). The researcher, with his focus on general principles rather than specific program content, may regard the report as primarily or exclusively a scientific publication for which he is solely responsible. The practitioner, on the other hand, focusing more on content, may feel he deserves major recognition for developing and administering the program. Traditional practices are far from standardized, but co-authorship and the listing of major data gatherers may at times be an appropriate solution.

A major issue in the administration of evaluative research is the relative effect on findings and their ultimate use of "inside" versus "outside" evaluators.[61] In this connection, Likert and Lippitt testify to some advantages on both sides: (1) outside researchers are better able to resist pressures toward subjectivity; (2) inside researchers are less likely to be able to conduct studies that question the policies and operating principles of top management; (3) yet an inside research group probably has more detailed knowledge of the organization; (4) where there is extensive internal distrust, outside researchers can probably get more valid data from individual members of the organization; (5) an inside research staff is in a better position to conduct continuing research; but (6) outside researchers may be more effective for a single study.[62] Luchterhand argues that there may be no such clearcut distinction in that some outsiders may act like insiders in the way they slant their accounts while insiders experiencing career deprivations in the organization may take more of an outsider's view.[63]

The general consensus seems to favor evaluation by outside research teams. The reasons cited, in addition to those already noted, run the gamut from belief that outsiders are more protected from problems of marginality and status incongruity to the notion that insiders may encounter more credibility problems in communicating results to outsider publics. It is also suggested that outside researchers are better able than

[60] Rodman and Kolodny, *op. cit.*, p. 100.

[61] Arguments regarding the relative superiority of evaluations by internal or external research agents are singularly inconclusive. For often conflicting views, see Likert and Lippitt, *op. cit.*, pp. 604–607; Luchterhand, *op. cit.*, p. 514; Rodman and Kolodny, *op. cit.*, pp. 106–107; Clinard, *op. cit.*, p. 243; Shepard, *op. cit.*, p. 306; S. M. Miller, "Evaluating Action Programs," *op. cit.*, pp. 38–39; William McEwen, "Position Conflict and Professional Orientation in a Research Organization," *Administrative Science Quarterly*, Vol. 1, 1956, pp. 208–224.

[62] Likert and Lippitt, *op. cit.*, pp. 604–607.

[63] Luchterhand, *op. cit.*, p. 514.

insiders to resist agency requests to do menial or other nonresearch tasks. Yet many reports end on a note of ambiguity; lone inside researchers may relieve some of their strains and disadvantages through the use of outside consultants; and outside researchers risk imposing inappropriate research designs if they cannot enlist adequate inside assistance.

A final but not insignificant aspect of the execution of evaluative research is the availability of funds for the necessary personnel and equipment. Action organizations nearly always operate with tight budgets. Given the often intangible and nonimmediate contribution of research, requests for research funds may be among the first to suffer in times of budget curtailment.

IMPLEMENTATION OF FINDINGS

For the social scientist whose objective is to contribute to the effectiveness of action programs, the implementation of research results is a critical phase in the evaluation process. Yet numerous writers have warned and demonstrated that meaningful action does not automatically flow from even the most carefully designed and conducted evaluative research. The "human" factors referred to in earlier sections are again in evidence here. Administrators may select findings consistent with their own analyses while ignoring others. Or negative findings may be dismissed by attacks on the research methods, on the alleged personal hostility of the researcher, and so on through the whole range of psychological and organizational defenses against real or imagined attacks.[64]

Various strategies have been proposed for insuring more objective reception and effective utilization of evaluative research.[65] Many of these begin with admonitions for an early specification of the researcher/practitioner relationship and closer cooperation and collaboration at each stage of the evaluative process. In this, some writers have stressed the influence of prestige and power factors on potential implementation. They note the importance of the researcher himself having a prestigious position in the action agency or some other organization and also of being linked with someone of high status in the action organization—a relationship which Sussman calls the "Merlin role."[66]

In a related vein, Likert and Lippitt urge the researcher to create an

[64] For some examples of cases in which findings of evaluative research were ignored or rejected by action personnel, see Rossi, *op. cit.*, pp. 51–62; Richard Hall, "The Applied Sociologist and Organizational Sociology," in Arthur Shostak (ed.), *Sociology in Action*, Dorsey, Homewood, Illinois, 1966, pp. 33–38.

[65] Among the discussions with relevance for the utilization of findings of evaluative research are Argyris, "Creating Effective Relationships in Organizations," *op. cit.*, pp. 109–123; Bennis, *op. cit.*, pp. 337–360; Likert and Lippitt, *op. cit.*, pp. 582–646; Floyd Mann and Rensis Likert, "The Need for Research on the Communication of Research Results," in R. Adams and J. Preiss (eds.), *Human Organization Research*, Dorsey, Illinois, 1960, pp. 57–66; Miller, "Evaluating Action Programs," *op. cit.*, pp. 38–39; Rosenthal and Weiss, *op. cit.*, pp. 302–340; Slocum, *op. cit.*, pp. 196–199; Suchman, *Evaluative Research*, pp. 162–166; Warren, *op. cit.*, pp. 22–28; Weiss, *op. cit.*, pp. 426–435; Whyte and Hamilton, *op. cit.*, pp. 183–222.

[66] Marvin Sussman, "The Sociologist as a Tool of Social Action," in A. Shostak (ed.), *Sociology in Action*, Dorsey, Homewood, Illinois, 1966, pp. 3–12.

"image of potential,"[67] which seems to be similar to Warren's suggestion that practitioners need assurance of the evaluating scientist's technical competence, his understanding of the practitioner's situation, and his personal integrity and decency in dealings with practitioners.[68] This is also the time to forestall any false hopes that evaluative research can provide answers to value questions or immediately solve practitioners' problems of "getting people to behave as we think they should."[69] It is argued that early involvement of action personnel in research planning and in the whole research process will lead to more realistic awareness of the potential contribution of research to action and also to greater commitment to the actual use of the findings.

Some of the same commentators have also stressed the relevance of content to final acceptance and implementation of evaluative findings. Certainly one rationale for working closely with potential consumers of research is to aid the researcher in addressing himself to questions with action implications—even though he may have to sacrifice some of his own professional interests, at least temporarily. Apparently research directed to policy questions, where recommendations fall within a framework of acceptable alternatives, is likely to get a favorable hearing,[70] although criticisms of an organization's basic goals may be ignored.[71] The strength of the scientist's findings will of course affect his potential for influencing policy decisions; and narrow, ambiguous results may— as much as any practitioner resistance—account for the failure of social scientists to be heeded.[72] The methodological limitations already discussed clearly detract from the researcher's ability to draw, with any certainty, conclusions regarding program effects.

Another obviously important consideration is the need for results to be available early enough to contribute to the making of decisions. A number of students of evaluation problems urge the reporting of interim findings before the interests of decision makers have a chance to lag, although others point to the scientific problems created when early feedback alters the experimental situation. At issue here is the previously mentioned problem of educating practitioners (and their publics) to committing themselves to particular practices long enough to satisfy research requirements for evaluation. A companion issue is the problem of developing methodologies that will reduce the time required for evaluating programs.

Timing is important, but so also is the form in which results are reported. As already noted, many social scientists engaged in action research believe their clients should be involved in planning and data-gathering (which implies early access to possible findings) from the start. A few recommend increasing the level of personal involvement with practitioners

[67] Likert and Lippitt, op. cit., pp. 582–584.
[68] Warren, op. cit., p. 28.
[69] Ibid., p. 22.
[70] Weiss, op. cit., pp. 427–430.
[71] Rosenthal and Weiss, op. cit., p. 326.
[72] Merton, op. cit., p. 210.

at the implementation stage,[73] in contrast to what may be the more common procedure of presenting an impersonal written report. And various gimmicks are suggested for reducing possible resistance. Argyris, for example, asks administrators for their own diagnoses first, to reduce the possibility that they will reject the research report as too "obvious."[74] Other writers emphasize the need for clear, concise, and even dramatic presentations. Still others, notably Mann and Likert,[75] suggest the efficacy of successive small group feedback meetings from the top administrative level down through the ranks of subordinates to clarify interpretations and thus stimulate greater interest in using the research results. They have found that pressures generated in small groups also increase commitment to changes based on the interpretation of data.

SOME CONCLUDING THOUGHTS

In view of the difficulties involved in formulating, designing, and executing evaluative research which may influence social policy, why should social scientists continue to concern themselves with such problems? In fact, some have argued that they should not. J. Mann, for example, claims —on the basis of an analysis of 181 evaluative studies in psychotherapy, counseling, human relations training, and education—that the methodological limitations imposed by natural settings are so great as to preclude genuinely scientific evaluative research.[76] He believes social scientists should contribute to human improvement, but that they can realize this objective only insofar as they can identify basic components of change processes and test them rigorously in strictly experimental settings. His approach would permit the utilization of more powerful research designs than are usually feasible in an action setting. Fairweather, on the other hand, argues that by integrating research and action, social scientists can contribute to the solution of social problems before they reach crisis proportions.[77] He advocates multidisciplinary teams of social scientists to define and study social problems in their natural settings. Such field research would in turn lead to the formulation of innovative solutions which could be organized and implemented to permit thoroughly scientific evaluation under natural rather than laboratory conditions.

Most others writing in this area are less optimistic but perhaps more realistically hopeful. They recognize the tremendous importance of massive governmentally inspired and sponsored intervention programs designed to solve critical problems. They urge policy makers to recognize the need for continuing scientific evaluation and provide adequate funding and administrative support. Since action will certainly continue to take priority over research, conditions for evaluative studies will be less than ideal. Yet social scientists can take steps to contribute more effectively to

[73] See, for example, F. Mann and Likert, *op. cit.*, pp. 59–66.
[74] Argyris, "Creating Effective Relationships in Organizations," *op. cit.*, pp. 116–118.
[75] F. Mann and Likert, *op. cit.*, pp. 59–66.
[76] J. Mann, *op. cit.*, pp. 165–214.
[77] Fairweather, *op. cit.*

action projects. They can sensitize themselves to the problems they are likely to face; they can sharpen their methods and strategies; and they can educate their actionist counterparts to the minimal requirements and limitations of problem-oriented research. The evaluative research that emerges may be imperfect from a strictly methodological perspective, but it is likely to be superior for practical as well as scientific purposes to the impressionistic accounts that now guide most action programs.

·36·

THE EXECUTION AND EVALUATION OF A DELINQUENCY PREVENTION PROGRAM*

WILLIAM C. BERLEMAN

THOMAS W. STEINBURN

Seattle Atlantic Street Center
Seattle, Washington

W HILE INCREASING EMPHASIS IS BEING PUT UPON COMMUNITY YOUTH projects aimed at "delinquency prevention" it is nonetheless "extremely rare to find written into an experimental project in this field a provision for even the most elementary kind of evaluation."[1] This would certainly seem to be the case if by delinquency prevention is meant the provision of a social service to children who are not yet officially adjudged delinquent and who therefore partake of the service without coercion and if by evaluation is meant an exhaustive and rigorous assessment of the service and the experimental design underlying that service. The Cambridge-Somerville Youth Study[2] still stands, thirty years after its inception, as the most rigorous evaluative study of delinquency prevention techniques applied in the open community among voluntary subjects. Because few projects since that study have applied a similar kind of scientific examination in assessing their service, it is safe to say that there is only the beginnings of a tradition of astute evaluation in delinquency prevention projects.[3]

* This investigation was supported by Public Health Service Research Grant, No. R11-MH-0082, from the National Institute of Mental Health.

[1] United Nations Consultative Group on the Prevention of Crime and the Treatment of Offenders, "Methods Used for the Prevention of Juvenile Delinquency," Geneva: The United Nations, MSOA, 61/SD 4, December, 1961, p. 4. mimeo.

[2] Edwin Powers and Helen Witmer, An Experiment in the Prevention of Delinquency: The Cambridge-Somerville Youth Study, New York: Columbia University Press, 1951; William McCord, Joan McCord, and Irving Kenneth Zola, Origins of Crime: A New Evaluation of the Cambridge-Somerville Youth Study, New York: Columbia University Press, 1959.

[3] By astute evaluation is meant reliance upon some form of the experimental design —that is, the comparison of an experimental, or treated group, with a control, or untreated group—in assessing the effectiveness of the delinquency prevention service. Other than the Cambridge-Somerville Youth Study, completed delinquency prevention projects utilizing the experimental design and engaging subjects who voluntarily participated in preferred services have been: 1) the Midcity Project (see Walter B. Miller, "The Impact of a Community Group Work Program on Delinquency Corner Boys," Social Service Review, 31 [December, 1957], pp. 390–406, and Walter B. Miller, "The Impact of a 'Total-Community' Delinquency Control Project," Social Problems, 10 [Fall, 1962], pp. 181–191); 2) the Maximum Benefits Project (see C. Downing Tait, Jr., M.D. and Emory F. Hodges, Jr., M.D. Delinquents, Their Families and the Community, Springfield: Charles C Thomas, 1962); 3) the New York City Youth Board's validation study of the Glueck Prediction Scale (see Maude M. Craig

♦ Reprinted by permission of the Society for the Study of Social Problems and of the authors from Social Problems 14 (Spring, 1967), pp. 413–423.

In 1962, the Seattle Atlantic Street Center, a small settlement house situated in Seattle's central area, undertook to evaluate its social work services to acting-out boys. With the aid of a National Institute of Mental Health grant, the Center commenced a five-year study. The study's second year, 1963–64, was designated as a pretest phase in which selection procedures, social work service, recording instruments, and evaluative techniques would be put into operation and refined. The remaining time, 1964 through 1967, would be devoted to the test phase proper.

The pretest phase was governed by an experimental design parallel to that planned for the test phase. In each phase, carefully screened seventh-grade junior high school boys would comprise a high-risk population, i.e., boys considered likely to act out in an anti-social way in excess of their peers. Acting out was defined simply as the objective evidence of a boy's social misbehavior as reported in police and school disciplinary files. By random selection boys in the high-risk population would be assigned to experimental and control groups. Those in the experimental group would be offered the Center's services; those in the control group would not.

The Center has now completed its pretest phase and has done an analysis of the pretest data to assess the impact of service. Major emphasis will be given the Center's procedural and evaluative methods rather than service and service impact. While the analysis reveals a trend suggesting a positive service impact, the reader is cautioned against making inferences about service effectiveness. The data fail to meet conventional criteria for the rejection of the null hypothesis. In addition, the number of treated pretest subjects was too small to support generalizing service impact to larger, more representative populations.

The pretest's importance lies in the rigor of its design and execution. Prior community based, delinquency prevention experiments have not collected and assessed sufficient data to speculate about the accuracy of their selection procedures or to contrast the experimental and control subjects' levels of acting out with that established by the remainder of the peer group from which the study's subjects were initially selected. Rates of service attrition have not been elucidated nor have the levels of acting out for attrition subjects been reported. Indeed, forms of "treatment," while often given elaborate theoretical underpinnings, have not been adequately explained in terms of kinds and amounts of simple attention shown experimental subjects by service agents, presumably because no consistent efforts have been made to collect such baseline data. Such deficiencies the Center's procedures attempted to overcome. What follows is an elaboration of the Center's pretest procedures. Particular attention will be given to (1) the selection of the pretest high-risk population,

and Philip W. Furst, "What Happens after Treatment: A Study of Potentially Delinquent Boys," Social Service Review, 39 [June, 1965], pp. 165–171); and 4) the Youth Consultation Service (see Henry J. Meyer, Edgar F. Borgatta, and Wyatt C. Jones, Girls at Vocational High: An Experiment in Social Work Intervention, New York: Russell Sage Foundation, 1965).

(2) an outline of the service with attention given the amount of time experimental boys were exposed to the service, and (3) the evaluation of service impact.

SELECTION OF THE HIGH-RISK BOYS

High-risk boys chosen for the pretest phase were Negroes who in the 1962–63 school year passed from one of Seattle's six most racially segregated elementary schools into the seventh grades of Seattle's two central area junior high schools. The population from which the high-risk boys were drawn numbered 167. The problem was to order the population along a continuum ranging from low-risk, or boys least likely to act out, through high-risk, or boys most likely to act out.

Two assumptions guided the placing of a boy in a risk category. The first assumption was that past misbehavior is predictive of future misbehavior. A record search was done on each boy to see if there was evidence of delinquent behavior in his career through the sixth grade, i.e., behavior judged delinquent by law, or acting-out behavior, i.e., anti-social behavior which had not been legally designated as being delinquent but was sufficiently serious to be found in official records. The Center's research staff carefully noted whether or not a boy's name appeared in juvenile court, police, school guidance, and school disciplinary files. In this manner the population was arrayed from those boys having no records —low-risk boys—through those having both community and school records—extreme high-risk boys.

The second assumption was that there might be other factors, in addition to the actual evidence of acting out, which could be predictive of acting-out behavior. It was assumed that the seventh-grade boys most likely to act out during their junior high school years would be those with backgrounds most closely resembling the backgrounds of boys who were then in the ninth grade and who had acted out while in junior high school. This required a search for factors, identifiable prior to the end of the sixth grade, that were associated with acting-out behavior by the end of the ninth grade. Factors closely associated with acting out could then be utilized in categorizing current seventh-grade boys into risk groupings. An exhaustive record search of boys in both groups was then conducted. Data regarding school grades, citizenship patterns, school attendance, home composition, health records, were collected and analyzed. If factors were found in the career of a seventh-grade boy which closely resembled factors found in the careers of acting-out ninth-grade boys, then it was "predicted" that the seventh-grade boy would act out while in junior high school.[4]

[4] This is a simplified account of an extremely complex prediction procedure. Essentially this was an application of multiple regression prediction techniques, utilizing forty-three criterion measures made available from police, school and court records, and seventy-six predictor measures made available from the same sources. The data were analyzed by extensive computer processing utilizing IBM Fortran programs written especially for the prediction problem. This procedure proved excessively costly and cumbersome considering the results obtained. See Bruce Bloxom, "Use of Predictor Accretion Selection Techniques in the Prediction of Acting-Out Behavior,"

Once the actual and predicted acting-out data had been compiled, it was possible to construct a matrix which crossed a boy's actual evidence of acting out with the prediction of his acting out in the future so that the population arrayed itself from the non-acting-out boys (those who had not acted out in the past and were predicted not to act out in the future) to the highest acting-out boys (those who had acted out in the past and were predicted to continue doing so). Since predictions of anti-social behavior are rightfully held suspect,[5] the Center refused to consider for selection those boys placed in the high-risk category by prediction alone. Also eliminated from consideration for selection were those boys who had acted out in the past but who were predicted not to act out in the future. For selection, then, the high-risk boys were confined exclusively to those who in the past had exhibited anti-social behavior and who were predicted to continue doing so. Anti-social behavior tended to break down into two categories: misbehavior in both the community and school[6] and misbehavior in the school alone. Table 1 illustrates the distribution of the population into risk categories.

TABLE 1

Distribution of Population into Risk Categories and of High-Risk Boys into Experimental and Control Boys

Prediction of Acting-Out 7th-9th Grade	Actual Evidence of Acting-Out Prior to 7th Grade			
	Neither	School Only	Community and School and Community Only	Total
Neither	49	15	6	70
School Only	22	30	3	55
		11 Exp. 19 Con.	3 Exp. 0 Con.	
		(High Risk Type I)	(High Risk Type III)	
Community and School and Community Only	11	15	13	39
		6 Exp. 9 Con.	8 Exp. 5 Con.	
		(High Risk Type II)	(High Risk Type IV)	
Total	82	60	22	164[a]

[a] The original population numbered 167; three boys were dropped because they had moved away.

Seattle: Seattle Atlantic Street Center, June, 1964, mimeo; and Herbert Costner, "Commentary on the Prediction Device Developed for the Atlantic Street Center," Seattle: Seattle Atlantic Street Center, June, 1964, mimeo.

[5] Elizabeth Herzog, "Identifying Potential Delinquents," Juvenile Delinquency, Facts and Facets, No. 5 (Washington, D.C.: Children's Bureau, U.S. Department of Health, Education and Welfare, 1960).

[6] Since it was exceedingly rare for a boy to have exhibited acting-out behavior in the community while not also being a problem in school, there was not a distinct acting-out-in-community-only category.

It will be noted that the high-risk boys occupy four cells of the matrix and that these cells can roughly be equated to types of severity, i.e., Type I, evidence of acting out in school only and predicted to continue doing so, being least severe, and Type IV, evidence of acting out in the community and school and predicted to continue doing so, being the most severe. Selection was weighted against the Center's social workers by assigning a higher proportion of the most serious types to the experimental group than to the control while the reverse was true for the least serious types. Table 1 shows this distribution by types. Once the number from each type to be assigned to the experimental group had been determined, the required number of specific cases was selected randomly.

The more serious high-risk boys were deliberately assigned to the workers in order to hedge against attrition. It would have been unrealistic to suppose that all twenty-eight high-risk boys assigned to the experimental group would wish to partake of the Center's services. If the experimental and control groups had been apportioned equally and if the expected refusals had been concentrated in the experimental Type III and Type IV boys, then it would have been questionable if the experimental and control groups were sufficiently similar to make valid comparisons. By concentrating the Type III and Type IV boys in the experimental group there would be little question but that the experimental boys might reasonably be anticipated to be as "bad," assuming no effective preventive treatment, as the control boys. Table 2 illustrates that twenty-one of the twenty-eight experimental boys were engaged in service and that these boys could be considered acting-out equivalents for their control counterparts with only nineteen per cent of the control group as opposed to thirty-eight per cent of the experimental group coming from the two "worst" types.

TABLE 2

Disposition of High-Risk Boys During Pretest Phase

High-Risk In Service	Experimental Boys		Control Boys		Total
	Category	Attrition	Control	Attrition	
Type IV	6	2	5	0	13
Type III	2	1[a]	0	0	3
Type II	5[c]	1	6	3	15
Type I	8	3	15	4	30
Total	21	7	26	7[b]	61

[a] This boy moved out of the community; all other experimental attrition boys refused to participate.

[b] These boys were not in attendance at the two central area junior high schools.

[c] One of these boys did not participate in the service himself but his mother did receive 18 hours of service from the worker.

RECORDING SERVICE AND ATTENTION GIVEN SUBJECTS

The staff for the pretest phase consisted of three trained male social workers. Through random assignment from each of the four high-risk categories two workers received the names of nine boys; one worker received the names of ten boys.[7] Boys comprising the control group were not made known to the workers so long as service was being given.

The workers then sent personal letters, one to the boy and one to the boy's parents or parental surrogates, inviting the boy to join a "club." Next, the workers arranged home visits. Depending upon the degree of recognition of a problem by the boy and his parents, the worker's interpretations ranged from the general, e.g., expressing the need for more constructive youth services in the central area, to the specific, e.g., recognizing the particular social difficulty in which the boy was involved.

Eventually the workers formed three groups composed of seven boys each. Each group met once a week at the Center for approximately two-and-a-half hours. Once the groups were established, the workers deliberately broadened their activity. Increasingly boys and their parents were seen in the schools and homes, usually as a result of chronic or emerging problems, such as delinquent behavior, school problems, or parent-child disagreements.

In order to keep an accurate account of these many contacts, the Center's social work and research staff devised a unique recording system by means of which the workers noted their activities in numerical code form.[8] This coded system allowed for the orderly accumulation of (1) the dates of a worker's contacts with a person in the client system, (2) the exact persons contacted, (3) the mode of contacts, (4) the duration of the contacts, (5) the problems encountered and the theoretical context into which those problems fell, and (6) the worker's response to those problems.

While an analysis of the data accumulated by this method cannot be presented here, one aspect of the worker's service—time spent with or on behalf of experimental subjects—deserves elaboration. This fundamental dimension of service has generally been so poorly documented in past delinquency prevention experiments that it is difficult to assess to what extent experimental subjects were in fact exposed to service agents. The scanty evidence suggests that in most experiments the subjects enjoyed

[7] The assignment of ten boys to one worker was the result of an error. Rather than the planned for twenty-seven experimental boys, twenty-eight boys were actually so designated. As Table 2 shows, attrition reduced the experimental population to twenty-one boys.

[8] The Center's recording procedure avoids many of the difficulties posed by each worker keeping process records in his own discursive style. By having all workers use a Recording Manual in which types of problem situations encountered are listed, grouped under theoretical headings and given code numbers, the consistency among workers is enhanced while the codes permit rapid computer tabulation and analysis. See James R. Seaberg, "Case Recording by Code," *Social Work* 10 (October, 1965), pp. 92–98 and Roy P. Wakeman, "Using Data Processing to Analyze Worker Activity," in *Social Work Practice, 1965,* New York: Columbia University Press, 1965, pp. 54–64.

only minimal contact with project staff.[9] Consequently, it remains unclear whether treatment methods have been ineffective or whether they have never really been tried.

It might be argued that the Center's pretest phase was deficient in that the experimental boys and the significant others were exposed to the workers for only five months (February, 1964 through June, 1964). During that time, however, the workers sought to provide intensive service. Of the twenty-one experimental boys considered permanently engaged in the pretest phase, the least time any boy was in direct contact with his worker was forty-five and one-half hours; the most was one hundred hours. Table 3 gives the total amounts of direct and indirect contact time the three workers had with the twenty-one boys and their significant others.

The median amount of service time a boy and his significant others received during the pretest was slightly in excess of seventy-five hours. In short, although the span of the pretest phase was brief, the service within that time was intense.

EVALUATION OF IMPACT

Two sources of data were available which reflected acting-out behavior: (1) the two junior high schools' disciplinary files[10] and (2) police

TABLE 3

Hours of Direct and Indirect Contact Twenty-One Experimental
Boys and Significant Others Had With Three Workers
February 1, 1964 Through June, 1964

	Experimental Boys	Families	Others	Total
Direct Contact (face-to-face)[a]	1377.50	127.00	11.75	1516.25
Indirect Contact (telephone, letters)	16.25	55.50	.50	72.25
Hours of Contact	1393.75	182.50	12.25	1588.50

[a] Direct contact includes group meetings, individual interviews, interviews with sub-groups, and family interviews.

[9] A review of the literature pertaining to previous delinquency prevention experiments regarding the exposure of experimental subjects to service agents suggests that exposure was generally minimal, that is, probably less than two contacts per month over the span of service. See William C. Berleman and Thomas W. Steinburn, "The Value and Validity of Delinquency Prevention Experiments," *Crime and Delinquency* 15 (October, 1969), pp. 471–478.

[10] Because procedures for collecting disciplinary data from schools other than the two central area schools were not established during the early phases of the experiment, the data that follow are based only on the records of boys in attendance at these two schools. Seven boys who moved to other schools are excluded for this reason.

records.[11] Data from school disciplinary files and police records were first obtained shortly after the close of the pretest service in June, 1964. One year after the end of service, in June, 1965, data were again collected from the schools and police. What follows is the procedure used for evaluating these data. In the interest of brevity, only school data will be used for illustrative purposes. While the police data were analyzed in the same manner, the fewer police contacts make police data more unstable as measures of service impact.

The data were analyzed in four time periods:

1. The Pre-Service Period: Since service did not begin until February, 1964, junior high school disciplinary records which accumulated from September, 1963 through January, 1964 were available for evaluation of school performance in the period just prior to service. All police contacts earlier than February, 1964 were included in the pre-service police data.[12] Data for this period are included to provide a before-service base for comparison of the different groups.

2. The Service Period: February, 1964 through June, 1964.

3. First Post-Service Period: July, 1964 through December, 1964.

4. Second Post-Service Period: January, 1965 through June, 1965.

In order to summarize the offenses which had accumulated in the school disciplinary and police records, judgments concerning the relative seriousness of every recorded offense were obtained from the Center's professional staff. These judgments were averaged and converted into weights and the resulting weights were then used to score each boy's record. Because school and police data are products of two quite different institutional and referral systems, school and police data were weighted and processed separately.[13]

Four indices derived from the school and police data were used to evaluate the performance of the pretest boys:

School and police data were gathered on the population of 164 Negro

[11] Juvenile Court records were also available. However, court records revealed so few contacts with the pretest population that no reliable index of acting-out behavior could be constructed from court data. The court records tended to reflect, only to a lesser degree, what was in the more comprehensive police records.

[12] Police offense data for these boys, most of whom were twelve or under prior to the pretest, were practically nonexistent in the six month period preceding service. This necessitated the accumulation of all prior police offense data. Police data relating to dependency were not considered.

[13] The school disciplinary items were weighted from one for minor infractions, such as chewing gum or eating candy in class, through thirty for major infractions, such as breaking and damaging school property. Police contacts were weighted in a similar manner. It should be noted that this weighting procedure was not used in the initial selection of high-risk boys. At the time of selection, it was simply noted whether or not a boy had a community and/or school record. (See selection above.) The use of a record/no record procedure for selection purposes and a graduated weighting procedure for evaluation purposes created some discrepancies; notably, that certain types of police contacts and many school guidance contacts, which figured in the selection procedure, were not used for evaluative purposes. Nonetheless, it was still evident that the two methods of identifying acting-out boys produced essentially the same results.

seventh grade boys from which the high-risk boys were drawn. Scores were generated for each time period for each of the boys in the four groups into which this population was then divided: (1) the experimental group, (2) the control group, (3) the service-attrition group, i.e., those boys selected for service but refused to participate,[14] and (4) the low-risk group, i.e., those boys not designated as high-risk in the selection process. Data on the last two groups have been included to enlarge the scope of the analysis. For example, inclusion of the attrition boys, even though a small group, sheds light on the possible biases introduced by refusals to accept service. The low-risk group provides data on the success of the selection procedure in identifying acting-out boys. These two groups and especially the low-risk group, also provide second level control groups for assessing general trends in school disciplinary and police contact activity. In most instances these two groups and the control group change in parallel.

Four indices derived from the school and police data were used to evaluate the performance of the pretest boys:

1. The first index gives the average offense score per boy in each of the four groups. This was derived by summing all offense scores accumulated by boys in each group and then computing an average score per boy per group. This index indicates the total performance of the group, and consequently is the most important of the four indices. (Table 4)

TABLE 4

Average School Disciplinary Score Per Boy in Each Group[a]

	Pre-Service (5 months)	Service (5 months)	First Post-Service (4 months)	Second Post-Service (6 months)
Attrition	48	66	116	52
Experiment	24	18	22	31
Control	19	27	18	25
Low Risk	6	15	11	22

[a] The total number of boys in each group for each period was: Attrition—4, 3, 3, 4; Experiment—21, 21, 19, 19; Control—26, 26, 26, 26; Low Risk—88, 88, 85, 85.

2. The second index reveals what percentage of boys within each group actually generated the total offense score for each group. This index serves as a corrective to the first index in that it would show if a few highly acting-out boys in any particular group were responsible for the average score borne by each boy in each group. It

[14] A fifth group composed of boys who moved out of the community could also be designated. This "area attrition" group could not be evaluated since they did not accumulate records in the designated schools or local police files, and so had to be eliminated from consideration.

TABLE 5

Per Cent of Boys With School Disciplinary Records

	Pre-Service (5 months)	Service (5 months)	First Post-Service (4 months)	Second Post-Service (6 months)
Attrition	75.0	100.0	100.0	100.0
Experiment	47.6	47.6	57.9	84.2
Control	57.7	65.4	53.8	53.8
Low Risk	27.3	34.1	40.5	38.8

would be expected, for example, that a significantly higher percentage of boys would act out among the high-risk boys than among the low-risk boys. (Table 5)

3. The third index shows the average severity of offenses committed by boys in each group. This was derived by dividing the sum of offense scores accumulated by each group by the number of offenses recorded. This index shows whether the boys engaged in "petty" offenses or in more serious offenses. (Table 6)

TABLE 6

Average Seriousness Per Disciplinary Contact[a]

	Pre-Service (5 months)		Service (5 months)		First Post-Service (4 months)		Second Post-Service (6 months)	
Attrition	22	(9)	14	(14)	14	(24)	17	(12)
Experiment	18	(28)	14	(27)	14	(29)	15	(39)
Control	15	(33)	14	(49)	16	(29)	15	(44)
Low Risk	11	(46)	14	(98)	15	(64)	15	(71)

[a] Figure in parentheses is the number of contacts for that period.

4. Finally, the fourth index gives the average severity score for those boys in each group who compiled records. This was derived by dividing the sum of offense scores accumulated by the number of boys who actually committed the offenses. This index, coupled with the second, shows whether the overall performance of a group stems primarily from the extensiveness or the intensiveness of acting-out behavior of its members. (Table 7)

In terms of the average score per boy in the groups (Table 4), the service-attrition group in the pre-service period was double the average score of the next highest group, the experimentals. In one sense, the service-attrition group represented a failure of the service, that is, a failure to engage those boys whose acting out was the greatest. On the other

TABLE 7

Average Score Per Boy With a School Disciplinary Record

	Pre-Service (5 months)	Service (5 months)	First Post-Service (4 months)	Second Post-Service (6 months)
Attrition	65	66	116	52
Experiment	51	37	37	37
Control	33	42	34	46
Low Risk	21	45	29	31

hand, even though these boys were excluded from the experimental boys for this analysis, the experimental boys still had a score about one-third higher than the control boys in the pre-service period, indicating that in spite of the biasing effect of attrition, the experimental group was still at least as "bad" as the controls. The low-risk group had an average score of only a third that of the controls. The other indices (Tables 6 and 7), except for the percentage of boys with school disciplinary records (Table 5), show essentially the same pattern.

In the service period, while the average disciplinary score per boy increased for the attrition, the control and the low-risk groups, it decreased for the experimental boys. Although the percentage of boys with records did not decrease for experimental boys, it did remain constant in the face

FIGURE 1

School Disciplinary Contacts

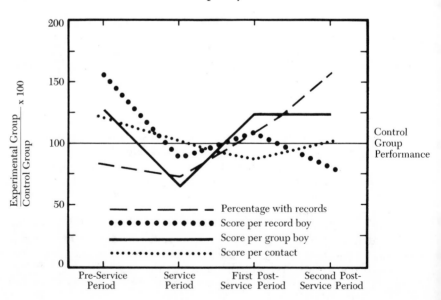

of increases for the other three groups. In general, the remaining two indices also show experimental group values decreasing while the other three groups register increases.

In the first post-service period, the direction of changes for the groups was somewhat more mixed. The experimental group went back up toward the level of performance of the pre-service period, while the other groups moved down toward their pre-service levels. To show this relative performance, the data on the experimental and control groups were converted to ratios.[15] These data appear in Figure 1.

In the pre-service period, on all but one index, the experimental group was performing at a poorer level than the control group. With the initiation of service, the experimental group improved its performance relative to the control group on every index, with the least improvement occurring in the percentage with records. It must also be noted that in the service period, the experimental group did as well as the control group or even better on all four indices. In the first post-service period, performance of the experimental group on three of the indices again became worse than that of the control group with a continued slight improvement in the score per contact index. In the last period, the average score per boy remained steady, the percentage with records and the score per contact both worsened and the average score per boy with a record improved relative to control group performance.

From these data, it can be seen that the experimental group initially was performing in school at a somewhat poorer level than the control group, that with service, the experimental group performed at a better level; and, with termination of service, the group reverted back toward the same relative level of performance it had prior to service.[16]

SUMMARY

The Seattle Atlantic Street Center's pretest phase involved the execution of a delinquency prevention experiment in the open community among voluntary subjects. Because the pretest study was severely circumscribed in time and population serviced, the pretest phase did not represent a test of service, but rather the opportunity for implementation of rigorous procedural and evaluative techniques not generally employed in this kind of experiment. By collecting offense data on the entire at-risk

---

[15] These data were standardized around the control group performance by the following formula:

$$\text{Ratio} = (100)\ (\text{EXPERIMENTAL})/(\text{CONTROL})$$

[16] Statistical tests of changes in performance for the experimental and control groups between the pre-service and service period, and the service and first post-service periods were made utilizing *Student's* t. The probability of the null hypothesis being true in the first comparison was between .10 and .05 ($t = 1.57$, $df = 45$). The probability of the null hypothesis being true in the second comparison was between .10 and .05 ($t = 1.64$, $df = 43$). Both tests are one-tailed tests. Although the data fail to meet conventional criteria for rejection of the null hypothesis, the joint probability of both null hypotheses being true lies between .01 and .0025. Because they were so few, data on police contacts were not tested for statistical significance; they tended to show, however, essentially the same patterns as the school data.

population from which control and experimental subjects were drawn, questions concerning the accuracy of selection, rates of attrition and levels of acting-out behavior exhibited by low- through high-risk groups could begin to be answered. In addition, a coded recorded system used by service agents supplied such baseline data as which subjects were actually receiving service in what amounts and forms.

While no in-depth analysis of the accumulated data is presented, the advantages of these or similar procedural methods and evaluative techniques are evident. Most generally, they suggest that a tidying of the experimental social laboratory is possible for more exact evaluations of intervening variables. With more complete data, inappropriate criticisms of prior delinquency prevention experiments, such as the tendency to castigate service or the theories undergirding service when it is not at all clear that service was actually given, can be avoided.

·37·
SOCIAL AND PSYCHO-PHYSIOLOGICAL CORRELATES OF SMOKING WITHDRAWAL[1]

BRUCE C. STRAITS
University of California, Santa Barbara

D RAWING CAUSAL INFERENCES ABOUT FACTORS INFLUENCING AND sustaining cigarette smoking from *surveys based on retrospective self-reports* by smokers and ex-smokers is a difficult and uncertain task. If, for example, a significantly higher proportion of ex-smokers than smokers report that their spouses are ex-smokers or nonsmokers, should this finding be attributed to mutual social influence (as a determinant of smoking behavior), to selective mate selection ("birds of a feather flock together"), or to both? If ex-smokers are more likely to express unfavorable attitudes toward smoking than are their cohorts who continue to smoke, should one conclude that relatively unfavorable attitudes toward smoking precipitate, support, or follow smoking cessation? Definite answers to such questions would seem to require a longitudinal study.

Longitudinal analysis of smoking behavioral change, however, is also beset with serious methodological problems. Unless one were willing to accept the unreasonable assumption that the social and psycho-physiological variables under investigation will not change significantly over time, it would be necessary to measure these variables just prior to any smoking behavioral change (or attempt). And this would involve very frequent monitoring of the study population, since the timing of cessation decisions under natural conditions cannot be predicted in advance. Frequent monitoring or interviewing of the same persons, however, is undesirable because the process of repeated interviewing may well, in and of itself, bring about changes in respondents' smoking habits— partly by sensitizing them to formerly unnoticed or avoided matters (possible health dangers and other costs of smoking, attitudes of spouse and close associates, and the like) and partly by heightening their awareness that they are under study (the guinea-pig effect). Further, sampling problems (particularly "panel mortality" or loss of some members of the study population over time), cost factors, and analysis problems (for

[1] The author served as a consultant for the Smoking Control Research Project, sponsored jointly by the Institute for Health Research and the Permanente Medical Group Kaiser Foundation Health Plan. The project was supported by Cancer Demonstration Grant No. 05-15-D67 from the Division of Chronic Diseases, United States Public Health Service.

For criticizing an earlier version of this article, I am indebted to Paul L. Wuebben and Thomas P. Wilson. I wish especially to thank Jerome L. Schwartz (Project Director) and Mildred Dubitzky (Project Research Psychologist) for their helpful suggestions and for special preparation of the data for this analysis.

♦ Published in this volume, by permission of the author, from duplicate manuscript prepared by the author for publication in the *Social Science Quarterly* 51 (June, 1970).

example, regression effects) would seem to virtually rule out longitudinal study of natural smoking cessation.

It appears, then, that research designs other than retrospective surveys or longitudinal (panel) studies must be developed to test causal explanations of smoking cessation. The present study employs a design which is essentially a mixture of experimental and longitudinal research procedures. In this hybrid design, the major drawback to longitudinal studies —the unpredictability of cessation decisions—is overcome by (experimentally) inducing the population under study to attempt smoking withdrawal during the *same* period of time. Measurement of the relevant independent (predictor) variables is obtained just prior to the cessation inducement and, most importantly, before the prospective participants are aware of their forthcoming withdrawal attempt.

METHOD

The Smoking Control Research Project was designed to evaluate the effectiveness of three smoking-withdrawal techniques (tranquilizers, individual counseling, group meetings) and to explore the social-psychological dynamics underlying smoking behavior.[2] Initially, a survey questionnaire was mailed in the fall of 1965 to 8,284 men, 25 to 44 years old, who belonged to the Kaiser Foundation Health Plan in Walnut Creek, California. Those respondents who smoked at least 10 cigarettes daily and indicated (on the questionnaire) that they were either *concerned* about their cigarette smoking or *might want to stop* were invited (mostly by telephone) to participate in an eight-week smoking-withdrawal clinic.

In order to isolate preexperimental and prehistory sources of variation, the technique of multiple discriminant analysis was used to analyze the questionnaire data obtained from the subjects *before* they were invited to participate in the treatment programs.[3] Essentially, this procedure involved a search for the questionnaire variables which, independently or in combination, were effective "predictors" of postclinic smoking behavioral change.

For purposes of analysis, the 252 treatment subjects were divided into five smoking-change categories based on their reported smoking behavior at the three follow-ups (end of treatment, four months, and one year): 50 *Successes* (subjects who maintained 85–100 per cent reduction in daily cigarette smoking at each checkpoint or for one year following the four-month or one-year follow-up); 42 *Recidivists* (former successes who resumed smoking at a less than 85 per cent reduction level); 45 *Continuing-Reducers* (persons who showed 15–84 per cent reduction at the

[2] For a more complete description of the study design (from which the summary above is adapted), see Jerome L. Schwartz and Mildred Dubitzky, "The Smoking Control Research Project: Purpose, Design, and Initial Results," *Psychological Reports*, 20 (1967), pp. 367–376.

[3] For a description of the maximum likelihood approach to discriminant analysis, see M. G. Kendall, *A Course in Multivariate Analysis* (London: Charles Griffin & Company, Ltd., 1957), Ch. 9; C. Radhakrishna Rao, *Advanced Statistical Methods in Biometric Research* (New York: Wiley, 1952), pp. 316–318; and William F. Massy, "On Methods: Discriminant Analysis of Audience Characteristics," *Journal of Advertising Research*, 5 (March, 1965), pp. 39–48.

end-of-treatment and/or four-month follow-up *and* at the one-year follow-up); 60 *Noncontinuing-Reducers* (former reducers who resumed smoking at a less than 15 per cent reduction level); and 46 *Failures* (persons who never reduced their smoking by at least 15 per cent from the preclinic level).

After a careful review of the relevant literature and an intial inspection of the distribution of questionnaire responses across the five clinic-outcome groups, 80 variables from the questionnaire were selected for the discriminant analysis.[4] Because some of the questionnaire items were of questionable theoretical relevance and many did not fully satisfy the statistical requirements of the discriminant model,[5] it was decided to group the variables into theoretically meaningful clusters and to interpret the findings, by and large, in terms of the predictor clusters rather than drawing inferences from single questionnaire items. Formation of indices of theoretical concepts from batteries of questionnaire items is a common practice, although it was unnecessary in the present study to follow the normal procedure of collapsing the items into a summary scale in advance of the analysis. Eight predictor clusters were formed from the available questionnaire items. The content and the underlying theoretical relevance of each cluster will be summarized below.

Interpersonal environments. Explicit in Festinger's theory of cognitive dissonance is the belief that "the human organism tries to establish internal harmony, consistency, or congruity among his opinions, attitudes, and values."[6] For cigarette smokers, there are two common ways that inconsistency may arise. First, they may acquire information which is dissonant with their present behavior, namely, the reports linking smoking with lung cancer and other diseases. Second, their opinions, attitudes, and values relating to smoking may not correspond with those of their friends and intimates. In the first instance, studies of personal influence have shown that a person faced with conflicting messages from the mass media (such as smoking-health questions) is likely to turn to his cohorts for their perception of the situation.[7] When a person's opinions, attitudes,

[4] Questionnaire items excluded from the analysis included those with low variability across the five clinic-outcome groups, those asked of only certain groups of respondents, and those with a high proportion of "no responses" or other suspicious peculiarities.

[5] Application of the regression model is valid in instances where the values of the independent variables are decided before the sample is drawn (as in categorical survey questions) and need not represent an underlying normal universe, provided that the dependent variable is normally distributed about the regression function. The converse applies in the discriminant model: the dependent variable may be predetermined (group membership), while the independent variables must be normally distributed with equal variance-covariance matrices for each group. Although one rarely encounters normal multivariate distributions in the behavioral sciences, the practice has been to employ a discriminant function if prediction is satisfactory.

[6] Leon Festinger, *A Theory of Cognitive Dissonance* (Stanford, Calif.: Stanford University Press, 1958).

[7] For example, Elihu Katz and Paul F. Lazarsfeld, *Personal Influence* (Glencoe, Ill.: Free Press, 1955); Herbert F. Lionberger, *Adoption of New Ideas and Practices* (Ames: Iowa State University Press, 1960); and Paul F. Lazarsfeld, Bernard Berelson, and Hazel Gaudet, *The People's Choice* (New York: Columbia University Press, 1948).

and values conflict with those of his friends, tension is usually produced which induces restoration of cognitive balance (consistency).[8] Because of the strains (imbalance) produced when only one member of a social group quits (for example, husband-wife) and the tendency to turn to others for their perception of an ambiguous situation such as smoking-health questions,[9] it was hypothesized that the cessation rate would be highest among the treatment subjects whose interpersonal environments were least supportive to smoking. Interpersonal environments were examined by asking the respondents to describe the smoking habits of their friends and intimates (including their wives), the reactions of their associates to their previous attempts (if any) to quit smoking, and the present attitudes of associates (friends, relatives, church groups) toward their smoking behavior. The respondents were also asked to indicate their parents' smoking habits and attitudes toward their smoking while they (the respondents) were growing up.

Attitudes toward smoking. To determine the extent to which preclinic attitudes[10] affected withdrawal in the present study, questionnaire responses relating to reasons for liking and disliking smoking, expressed reasons for wishing to give up smoking, general attitudes toward smoking, and acceptance of the smoking-health reports were included in the analysis. Also included were items regarding satisfaction with and concern about smoking, the certainty of the subject's desire to quit, and his expectation of how much he would be smoking in one year.

Personal health. Several studies have reported that a *present* physical ailment, especially one generally associated with smoking, is the most frequent reason given for quitting smoking, while health fears relating to the *future* (such as the possibility of getting lung cancer) are mentioned less often.[11] This does not exclude the possibility that lung cancer and other future health fears are important motivating factors in the dis-

---

[8] See especially F. Heider, *The Psychology of Interpersonal Relations* (New York: Wiley, 1958); Dorwin Cartwright and Frank Harary, "Structural Balance: A Generalization of Heider's Theory," in Dorwin Cartwright and Alvin Zander, eds., *Group Dynamics* (Evanston, Ill.: Row, Peterson, 1960), pp. 705–726; and Charles E. Osgood, "Cognitive Dynamics in the Conduct of Human Affairs," *Public Opinion Quarterly,* 24 (Summer, 1960), pp. 341–365.

[9] Because of the nature of the smoking habit, it is much harder for one individual to stop smoking if others in a small cohesive group continue to smoke. First, the ex-smoker reminds the rest of the group about a subject they wish to ignore—the possible dangers and disadvantages of smoking—and secondly, they remind him of the pleasure of smoking, which may be hard to ignore. A good illustration is a husband-wife dyad of smokers. If only one quits, the remaining member of the dyad may feel more uncomfortable about smoking, while the presence of cigarettes and cigarette smoke is a constant threat to the quitter.

[10] See Daniel Rosenblatt, Bernard Rosen, and Harvey Allen, "Attitudes, Information and Behavior of College Students Related to Smoking and Smoking Cessation," in Salvatore V. Zagona, ed., *Studies and Issues in Smoking Behavior* (Tucson: University of Arizona Press, 1967), pp. 67–72; and Bruce C. Straits, "Résumé of the Chicago Study of Smoking Behavior," *ibid.,* pp. 73–78.

[11] See, for example, E. Cuyler Hammond and Constance Percy, "Ex-Smokers," *New York State Journal of Medicine,* 58 (September 15, 1958), pp. 2965–2969; and Straits, *loc. cit.*

continuation of smoking, for individuals do not always give the real reasons for their actions—either because they are unaware of the real reasons or because they tend to conceal them. It seems plausible, however, that the difficulty experienced in smoking withdrawal is inversely related to the immediacy of the perceived harm of continued smoking (for example, having "smoker's cough" is more immediate than is the fear of incurring lung cancer). Some health problems, on the other hand, may support smoking continuation. A number of studies indicate that smokers are more anxious and involved in more stressful situations than nonsmokers and that smokers believe cigarettes to be an effective means of reducing tension in emotionally stressful situations.[12] To test these hypotheses, the personal-health cluster included questionnaire items relating to previous, present, and anticipated health problems. Both physical-health aspects (for example, heart disease, respiratory conditions) and emotional-health aspects (for example, anxiety, psychiatric consultation) were tapped.

Smoking history. The respondent's smoking history was compiled from responses relating to average daily cigarette, pipe, and cigar consumption; inhaling and other smoking patterns; attempts to quit (and difficulty of last attempt); duration of the habit; age at adoption of smoking; and changes in smoking over the past two years. It was hoped that pretreatment smoking patterns would help explain why some subjects succeeded in stopping while others did not. For example, if there is any truth in the addiction theory, the difficulty of quitting should increase with amount smoked. It was also hypothesized that smoking withdrawal would be inversely related to the number of serious pretreatment attempts to quit.

Personality: arousal seeking. Eysenck found English smokers more extroverted than nonsmokers, mean scores for extroversion increasing with number of cigarettes smoked.[13] As extroverts are characterized by orientation toward objects in the *outer* world (in contrast to introverts, who tend to be preoccupied with *internal* thought processes), this is consistent with the findings that smokers are heavy consumers of pleasure-giving objects in the external world, like coffee and alcohol.[14] In addition to oral indulgence, the factor of arousal seeking is supported by studies

[12] Social Research, Inc., *Cigarettes: Their Role and Function* (Chicago: Social Research, Inc., 1952); R. Davis, "Cigarette Smoking Motivation Study" (London: Research Services, Ltd., 1956); Joseph D. Matarazzo and George Saslow, "Psychological and Related Characteristics of Smokers and Nonsmokers," *Psychological Bulletin*, 7 (November, 1960), pp. 505–506; Caroline B. Thomas, "Characteristics of Smokers Compared with Non-Smokers in a Population of Healthy Young Adults, Including Observations on Family History, Blood Pressure, Heart Rate, Body Weight, Cholesterol and Certain Psychologic Traits," *Annals of Internal Medicine*, 53 (October, 1960), pp. 697–718; and M. Powell Lawton and Roswell W. Phillips, "The Relationship Between Excessive Cigarette Smoking and Psychological Tension," *American Journal of Medical Sciences* (October, 1956), pp. 397–402.

[13] H. J. Eysenck *et al.*, "Smoking and Personality," *British Medical Journal* (May 14, 1960), pp. 1456–1460.

[14] Matarazzo and Saslow, *op. cit.*; and Bruce C. Straits and Lee Sechrest, "Further Support of Some Findings About the Characteristics of Smokers and Nonsmokers," *Journal of Consulting Psychology*, 27 (June, 1963), p. 282.

relating the pharmacological action of the chemical constituents of cigarettes,[15] the sensuous aspects of handling cigarettes, and the interests of smokers in psychological arousal.[16] To test the hypothesis that the cessation rate would be lowest among the most active "arousal seekers," questionnaire items relating to consumption of coffee and alcoholic beverages, amount of television viewing, and self-imposed delay of gratification were included in the analysis.

Personality: risk aversion. Smokers have been found to believe things happen by chance more than do nonsmokers,[17] suggesting that nonsmokers have a higher degree of risk aversion. The finding in a study that smokers who have attempted withdrawal are less chance-oriented than those who have never attempted to quit prompted one explanation as to why heavy smoking is sustained in the face of strong evidence of its danger: "many current smokers have a chance-oriented, fatalistic outlook on life, which renders them less vulnerable to antismoking propaganda based on health threats."[18] Four questionnaire items concerned with safety and preventive health measures (for example, frequency of automobile-seatbelt use) were chosen as a measure of risk aversion.

Personality: personal security. A number of items were included in the questionnaire to measure *self-perceived* personal adjustment or contentment in such areas as work, achievement, and social situations. Most of the items were taken from Knutson's Personal Security Inventory.[19] Essentially, this is a measure of one's expressed confidence, security, or satisfaction with various aspects of his life. Presumably, the higher the level of personal adjustment at the beginning of treatment, the more

[15] Kissen discusses the possibility that cigarette smoking "stimulates a need for smoking by the pharmacological action of its chemical constituents"; see David M. Kissen, "Psycho-Social Factors in Cigarette Smoking Motivation," *Medical Officer,* 104 (December, 1960), pp. 365–372. This view has been supported by experiments where the cravings of chronic smokers were satisfied by injections of nicotine. During World War II, chewing tobacco and snuff became popular among workers in munitions factories, where smoking was prohibited, which Proosdy suggests was a means of reducing nicotine cravings; see C. Van Proosdy, *Smoking* (New York: Elsevier Publishing Company, 1960), p. 37.

[16] Levin hypothesized from his data that "some smokers may actually receive gratification from the cognition that they are flaunting danger"; see Martin Levin, "Perceived Risk in Smoking: An Exploratory Investigation," *Studies in Public Communication,* Committee on Communication, University of Chicago (Summer, 1959), pp. 54–60. Social Research, Inc., refers to the "perverse pleasure that many people derive from being self-defeating"; see Social Research, *op. cit.,* p. 8. McArthur echoes this theme: "The heavy smokers are often given to what the psychiatrist calls 'acting out.' Whether in war or marriage or the business jungle, these men frequently find a place where they can live dramatically" see Charles C. McArthur, "The Personal and Social Psychology of Smoking," in George James and Theodore Rosenthal, eds., *Tobacco and Health* (Springfield, Ill.: Charles C. Thomas), p. 294. See also Daniel S. P. Schubert, "Arousal Seeking as a Central Factor in Tobacco Smoking Among College Students," *International Journal of Social Psychiatry,* 11, No. 3 (1965), pp. 221–225.

[17] Straits and Sechrest, *op. cit.*

[18] Straits, *op. cit.,* p. 76.

[19] Andie Knutson, "Personal Security as Related to Station in Life," *Psychological Monographs,* 66 (1952), p. 376.

likely the subject will be successful in quitting. There are two different ways to deduce this hypothesis. First, individuals high in personal adjustment are more likely to have the necessary motivation and self-confidence to be able to stop smoking. Second, those low in adjustment may need cigarettes as a "crutch" to get through difficult situations or to promote pleasurable emotions.

Background factors. Finally, a number of common demographic and personal-background factors like education, occupation, family income, marital history, and religion were included as a residual predictor cluster. In essence, these background factors will be used as a synthetic (catchall) cluster to help explain smoking behavioral change not explained by the other clusters in the analysis.

RESULTS[20]

By the end of the eight-week program, 33 per cent of the treatment subjects had reduced their cigarette smoking by 85 per cent or more— the criterion for "success." (In fact, all but 9 of the 83 successful subjects had stopped smoking entirely.) All subjects were rechecked four months and one year after the end of the treatment program to find out how many cigarettes they were currently smoking. The initial success rate of 33 per cent for the treatment subjects fell to 21 per cent at the four-month follow-up and to 20 per cent one year after the treatment ended.[21]

Comparison of clinic-outcome groups. If it is assumed that the 80 independent variables approximately represent the social and psycho-physiological factors related to smoking withdrawal, the discontinuation process may be conceived as an 80-dimensional space in which each clinic-outcome group occupies a given position. If the members of a particular group were perfectly homogeneous with respect to the independent variables (that is, zero variance on all variables), the entire group may be represented as a single point in the 80-dimensional space. If, on the other hand, the values of the independent variables are not identical for every group member, the group may be visualized as a "swarm" of points (one for each unique set of variable values), the density of which decreases with increasing distance from the group center or centroid (a point defined by the group means on the 80 variables). The amount of dispersion about the group centroid is a function of the variances and covariances of the independent variables.

Numerous possibilities follow from the above conceptualization; for example: two or more groups may occupy similar positions within the

---

[20] This analysis is only one of many based on the Smoking Control Research Project. For a listing of the excellent publications of Jerome L. Schwartz and his project co-workers, see Jerome L. Schwartz and Mildred Dubitzky, "Psycho-Social Factors Involved in Cigarette Smoking and Cessation," final report of the Smoking Control Research Project (Berkeley, Calif.: The Institute for Health Research, September, 1968); pp. xiv–xv.

[21] For an evaluation of the treatment programs (none of which were very effective), see Jerome L. Schwartz and Mildred Dubitzky, "One-Year Follow-Up Results of a Smoking Cessation Program," *Canadian Journal of Public Health*, 59 (April, 1968), pp. 161–165.

80-dimensional space; they may occupy different but overlapping positions; they may occupy nonoverlapping but colinear positions; and they may be equally or unequally spaced apart.

Given the observed values of the independent variables for a particular individual (represented as a point in the 80-variable space), the person is classified as belonging to the group whose characteristics are most like his own. Essentially, the classification procedure assigns the individual to that group believed (on the basis of sample data) to have the highest probability density at the point determined by the individual's variable values.[22] The greater the overlap within the discriminant space among the members of a set of groups, the more difficult it is to discriminate between them to predict group membership.[23] For example, if the Recidivists closely resemble the Noncontinuing-Reducers, the two groups should be relatively close (within the space described by the 80 independent variables) compared to their distances from other groups. If this is true, the discriminant functions will not be very effective in "predicting" which of the two groups an individual belongs to, since a large proportion of the members of each group will be misclassified as belonging to the other. The distribution of classification errors will be used throughout this paper as a rough guide to judge the similarity of groups and the relative importance of the independent variables.

Although the typology of smoking-change categories appears to represent an ordinal-level measure of degree of success in smoking withdrawal, an exact ranking of the five groups is problematic. At stake is the ordering of the groups whose postclinic cessation patterns were intermediate between the polar groups of Success and Failure. Should Continuing-Reducers, for example, be classified as "more successful" than Recidivists, or vice versa? Implicit in this paper, as exemplified by the arrangement of column heads in Tables 1 and 2, is the following ordering:

Successes>Recidivists>Continuing-Reducers>Noncontinuing-Reducers>Failures

Some support for this ranking is provided by Table 1, which gives the proportion of correct and incorrect classifications for each of the five clinic-outcome groups based on the 80-variable discriminant functions. If the above ranking is correct, the degree of similarity (in terms of the independent variables) between any two groups in the ordered chain should become weaker (hence, fewer classification errors) with increasing distance (number of intervening groups) between the two. Such a pattern is moderately evident in Table 1. For instance, 80 per cent of the

[22] The computer program employed to compute discriminant functions (linear combinations of the independent variables) for each of the five groups is described in W. J. Dixon, ed., *Biomedical Computer Programs* (Los Angeles: Health Sciences Computing Facility, Department of Preventive Medicine and Public Health, School of Medicine, University of California, Los Angeles, 1965), pp. 587–598 (BMDO7M: Stepwise Discriminant Analysis). Computing assistance was obtained from the Health Sciences Computing Facility, UCLA, sponsored by NIH Grant FR-3.

[23] For a detailed description of classification procedures, see William W. Cooley and Paul R. Lohnes, *Multivariate Procedures for the Behavioral Sciences* (New York: Wiley, 1962), pp. 134–150.

Successes were correctly classified, while 8 per cent were misclassified as Recidivists, 6 per cent as Continuing-Reducers, 4 per cent as Noncontinuing-Reducers, and 2 per cent as Failures. In like fashion, the Failures were most likely to be misclassified as Noncontinuing-Reducers or as Continuing-Reducers, and least likely to be misassigned to the Success or to the Recidivist categories. It should be noted that although the proportion of correct predictions for each group is substantially larger than would be expected by chance, accuracy would be lower if the same discriminant functions (weighted linear combinations of the independent variables) were used to classify a *new* sample of individuals.[24]

TABLE 1

Comparison of Actual Smoking Behavior with Behavior Predicted by the Discriminant Functions[a]

Actual Behavior	Predicted Behavior						Number of Subjects
	Success	Recidivist	Continuing-Reducer	Noncontinuing-Reducer	Failure	Total	
Success	.80	.08	.06	.04	.02	1.00	(50)
Recidivist	.12	.64	.07	.07	.10	1.00	(42)
Continuing-Reducer	.04	.04	.74	.09	.09	1.00	(45)
Noncontinuing-Reducer	.06	.14	.10	.67	.03	1.00	(69)
Failure	.04	.04	.11	.09	.72	1.00	(46)

[a] The row entries show the proportion of correct and incorrect predictions for each treatment-outcome group. The first row, for example, discloses that 80 per cent of the Successes were correctly identified, while 8 per cent were misclassified as Recidivists, 6 per cent as Continuing-Reducers, 4 per cent as Noncontinuing-Reducers, and 2 per cent as Failures.

A pictorial representation of the major classification errors is shown in Figure 1. The degree of misclassification between a specific pair of groups is represented by a straight or a curved arrow, the length of which is (approximately) *inversely* proportional to the frequency of classification errors between the two groups. Consequently, groups which overlap to a considerable degree within the discriminant space (for example,

24 The discriminant coefficients (weights for the linear functions) that maximize discrimination in the given sample are not unbiased estimators of the "best" discriminant coefficients for new samples of data. For a discussion of this problem, see Ronald E. Frank, William F. Massy, and Donald G. Morrison, "Bias in Multiple Discriminant Analysis," *Journal of Marketing Research*, 2 (August, 1965), pp. 250–258. Since the purpose of using the classification procedure in the present application is to measure similarity among groups rather than to predict the behavior of unclassified individuals, this bias should not appreciably affect the findings.

FIGURE 1

Direction of major classification errors, drawn to approximate scale by separating groups by paths inversely proportional to the frequency of classification errors between them shown in Table 1.

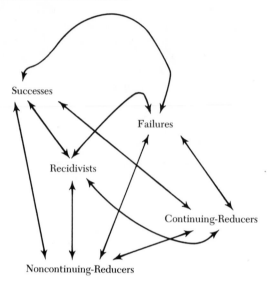

Recidivists and Noncontinuing-Reducers)[25] are connected by very short paths in Figure 1, whereas groups with less overlap are separated by longer paths. It was necessary to draw some curvilinear paths for the purpose of representing the relationships in two dimensions. If all except the four shortest paths (largest joint classification errors) were removed from Figure 1, the consequent chain (Successes⟷Recidivists⟷Noncontinuing-Reducers⟷Continuing-Reducers⟷Failures) would correspond to the ranking proposed above, with the exception of a reversal in the ordering of Continuing-Reducers and Noncontinuing-Reducers. The fact that the Recidivists were slightly closer to the Noncontinuing-Reducers than to the Continuing-Reducers within the discriminant space suggests that some of the predictor variables were associated with the inability to maintain a reduction in smoking behavior. More precisely, those clinic subjects who reported a relapse after initially achieving substantial or total reduction in smoking (Noncontinuing-Reducers and Recidivists) apparently have certain prominent characteristics in common. This possibility will be explored later.

It should be noted, however, that the degree of overlap between Recidivists and Noncontinuing-Reducers was not markedly greater than the overlap between several other pairs of groups within the discriminant

[25] Of the Noncontinuing-Reducers, 14 per cent were misclassified as Recidivists; of the Recidivists, 7 per cent were misclassified as Noncontinuing-Reducers.

space. In fact, the Noncontinuing-Reducers were almost as likely to be misclassified as Continuing-Reducers as they were to be misclassified as Recidivists. That the Successes were closer to the Recidivists than to the Continuing-Reducers in Figure 1 is highly suggestive of fundamental differences between clinic subjects who can stop smoking completely, at least for a brief period, and those who are only able to reduce their smoking.

Relative efficiency of predictor clusters. Table 2 presents the results of separate discriminant analyses for each predictor cluster. The Smoking History cluster played the most important role in discriminating among the clinic-outcome groups (40 per cent correctly classified by this cluster alone), closely followed by Interpersonal Environments (38 per cent correctly classified), Attitudes toward Smoking (34 per cent correctly classified), Risk Aversion (32 per cent correctly classified), Personal Health (31 per cent correctly classified), Background Factors (31 per cent correctly classified), Arousal Seeking (30 per cent correctly classified), and Personal Security (29 per cent correctly classified).

Table 2

Outcomes of Discriminant Analyses for Major Clusters of Predictor Variables

Predictor Cluster	Per Cent Correctly Identified					
	Successes	Recidivists	Continuing-Reducers	Noncontinuing-Reducers	Failures	Total
Smoking History	50	33	49	33	37	40
Personal Health	44	14	27	28	41	31
Interpersonal Environments	46	33	49	35	30	38
Attitudes toward Smoking	40	33	33	35	26	34
Personality: Personal Security	38	17	24	32	30	29
Personality: Arousal Seeking	18	26	40	26	43	30
Personality: Risk Aversion	42	24	40	30	22	32
Background Factors	44	31	29	23	30	31
All Clusters (80 variables)	80	64	73	67	72	71

The classification errors in Table 2 provide at least minimum support for the hypotheses underlying the eight predictor clusters. Each cluster independently predicted group membership somewhat better than chance expectancy, although the improvement over chance expectancy in some of the cases may not be statistically significant. The discriminatory power of the individual predictor clusters should not be interpreted as independent estimates of the relative importance of the various factors to smoking withdrawal, because the individual analyses shown in Table 2 do not take into account intercorrelations among the predictor clusters or interaction effects. The formation of attitudes toward smoking, for example, may partly be influenced by a person's interpersonal milieu, state of health, and smoking history.

Is it necessary to employ all eight predictor clusters to effectively predict group membership, or will a smaller number of clusters be nearly as efficient? Since it is not very practical to explore this question by computing discriminant functions for every possible combination of predictor clusters, an exploratory "stepwise" analysis was performed by combining clusters (adding one at each step) in decreasing order of their separate discriminatory power.[26] The cluster with the highest over-all discriminatory power (40 per cent), Smoking History, is particularly effective in correctly identifying the clinic subjects who achieved some degree of continued success (50 per cent of the Successes and 49 per cent of the Continuing-Reducers were correctly classified). Classification of all of the clinic-outcome groups was enhanced by the addition of Interpersonal Environments to Smoking History, which increased the total proportion of correct classifications slightly, to 50 per cent. Adding a third cluster, Attitudes toward Smoking, increases over-all discriminatory power to 56 per cent by mainly improving classification of Successes and Recidivists. The inclusion of a fourth cluster, Personal Health, substantially improves identification of the treatment Failures (an increase from 50 per cent to 70 per cent).

Adhering to the principle of maximizing prediction while minimizing the number of explanatory factors (predictors), the four predictor clusters mentioned above appear to yield the most parsimonious solution to the problem of finding the "best" set of predictor clusters.[27] Inclusion of the four remaining clusters (Arousal Seeking, Risk Aversion, Personal Security, and Background Factors) in the multiple discriminant analysis increases over-all discriminatory power slightly (an increase from 61 per cent to 71 per cent) by improving classification of Successes, Continuing-Reducers, and Noncontinuing-Reducers.[28]

Although the added improvement in discrimination contributed by the personality clusters is small, it is unwarranted to infer from these data that the three personality clusters are unrelated to smoking cessation. Rather, the discriminatory power of the personality clusters is greatly reduced in the presence of the previously entered predictor clusters, because some of the items contained in the previously entered clusters were correlated with items in the personality clusters.

[26] Limitations of space prohibit a detailed technical presentation of each discriminant analysis, a full explication of which may be obtained by writing the author.

[27] As in the case of regression analysis, a stepwise procedure may not always yield the most efficient set of predictors.

[28] This statement does not imply that the four remaining predictor clusters are useless from a theoretical standpoint. It should also be noted that the greater discriminatory power of the Attitudes toward Smoking, Personal Health, Interpersonal Environments, and Smoking History clusters may partly be attributed to the fact that they contain a larger number of variables than do any of the remaining predictor clusters—a consideration that would not be relevant if each of the variables in a given cluster were "perfect" measures of the underlying theoretical concept.

As an illustration of the problem of intercorrelations among the predictor clusters, consider the Failures, who, as a group, gave the most distinct set of responses to the questions included in the Arousal Seeking cluster.[29] Adding Arousal Seeking to a discriminant model incorporating Smoking History, Interpersonal Environments, and Attitudes toward Smoking, did not, however, appreciably improve classification of Failures (an increase from 50 per cent to 52 per cent). Apparently, the treatment Failures, who were most clearly distinguishable from the other treatment subjects on the basis of their responses to the questions included in the Arousal Seeking cluster, were also quite distinct in their responses to some of the questions on Smoking History, Interpersonal Environments, and Attitudes toward Smoking.

Discriminating variables. Previously the question was raised as to whether some characteristics distinguished between clinic subjects who achieved some degree of continued success (Successes and Continuing-Reducers) and those who relapsed after initially achieving substantial or total reduction in smoking (Recidivists and Noncontinuing-Reducers). Only a few of the 80 variables consistently differentiated between the two pairs of smoking-change groups. Most prominent were the questions relating to alcoholic beverages. The Recidivists and the Noncontinuing-Reducers reported slightly more frequent and heavier drinking than did the Successes and the Continuing-Reducers. This observation raises the interesting possibility that recidivism may occur during drinking occasions. In addition, the Recidivists and Noncontinuing-Reducers, as compared with the Successes and Continuing-Reducers, were less actively involved in voluntary organizations, were more likely to report that significant others were nonsmokers or wanted the respondent to quit, were more likely to have consulted a psychiatrist, and gave fewer reasons for liking smoking.

A search was also made for factors which discriminated between the clinic subjects who initially stopped completely (Successes and Recidivists) and those who only reduced their smoking (Continuing- and Noncontinuing-Reducers). Those who stopped completely, as compared with those who reduced their smoking, were found to be less favorable in their attitudes toward smoking, as well as lighter cigarette smokers and heavier pipe/cigar smokers. Subjects who initially stopped completely also were less likely to have smoking wives, more likely to have teen-age children, and less likely to have had recent contact with a physician for a specific health reason.

Contrary to the findings of retrospective studies of natural smoking cessation, the attitudinal variables were not major predictors of treatment success. Inspection of the distributions of attitudinal resposes for the five clinic-outcome groups *and* for the survey respondents who did not want to quit suggests that the presence of relatively unfavorable attitudes

---

[29] A larger proportion of treatment Failures (43 per cent) than any other outcome group were correctly identified solely on the basis of the Arousal Seeking cluster (see Table 2).

toward smoking may precipitate, but not strongly support, smoking withdrawal.

Some of the factors which seem to explain, in part, the observed patterns of complete or partial, continuing or noncontinuing, cessation have been discussed. The factors which emerged as the "best" predictors in the preceding analysis were generally variables with distributions that varied consistently across the five smoking-change groups. The impact of variables that "influenced" only one or two of the clinic-outcome groups, on the other hand, tended to be obscured in the omnibus five-group comparisons. Consequently, in order to explore the discriminating characteristics of Recidivists and Failures in greater detail, the two groups were compared *separately* with the Successes.

Successes as compared with Recidivists tended to have experienced greater difficulty in previous attempts to quit and to have had fewer smoking fathers while growing up. The discriminant analysis also disclosed that Successes were lighter consumers of alcoholic beverages, used automobile seatbelts more often, smoked pipes and/or cigars more frequently, watched television more often, drank more coffee, and were more likely to report a reduction in smoking during the two years prior to the time of the questionnaire.

The results of the discriminant comparison of Successes and Failures provided further insight into the complexity of the cessation process. First, as previously hypothesized, successful quitters are less fatalistic in their approach to life as evidenced by their greater concern with preventive safety measures such as fastening automobile seatbelts. The second most important predictor of cessation, the reported time interval between age when first tried smoking cigarettes and age when became a regular smoker, is more difficult to explain. Perhaps this is a measure of addiction or involvement in smoking, for the more "involved" smokers experienced greater difficulty in quitting. A small positive correlation between this presumed measure of involvement and the reported frequency of seatbelt usage partly explains why the discriminating ability of the former measure is enhanced after removal of the concomitant variation with the latter. That is, some of the subjects who seem unlikely candidates for success on the basis of their "involvement" in smoking do succeed because of their high degree of risk aversion.

Third, as also hypothesized, the presence of respiratory conditions or other ailments that are generally associated with or aggravated by smoking seems to help support nonsmoking. Subjects who only mentioned less immediate health concerns (for example, fear of incurring lung cancer) or weaker reasons for wanting to stop smoking (for example, the messiness of the habit) had greater difficulty in quitting. Individuals lacking immediate health reasons for quitting, however, often had other cessation "influences" going for them; for example, those who reported fewer respiratory conditions tended to be less fatalistic and less emotionally anxious. Finally, chances of treatment success are further increased if the individual has a history of relatively infrequent drinking and low anxiety.

SUMMARY AND CONCLUSIONS

In previous studies, complex patterns of smoking behavior have been most often summarized in terms of crude typologies, such as the trichotomy of smokers, ex-smokers, and nonsmokers. An attempt was made in the present study to develop more refined categories to characterize postclinic smoking patterns over a one-year period. Although the five formulated smoking-change categories (Successes, Recidivists, Continuing-Reducers, Noncontinuing-Reducers, and Failures) appear to represent an ordinal-level measure of success, it was unnecessary to postulate a unidimensional ordering of the five categories since discriminant analysis permits analysis of polytomous (categorical) dependent variables. By treating unidimensionality as a hypothesis to be investigated rather than as an untested assumption, some interesting findings that would have otherwise escaped notice were observed. In particular, it proved profitable to characterize cessation patterns along two dimensions of withdrawal: the *degree* (proportional reduction in amount smoked) and the *stability* (nonrecidivism to preclinic smoking habits). There is some evidence from the data that the two dimensions of cessation are influenced by different causal factors. Inability to maintain substantial or total reduction in smoking (recidivism), for example, may be associated with drinking behavioral patterns. Degree of reduction, on the other hand, was found to be related to prior smoking patterns, attitudes, and interpersonal environments.

The complexity of the cessation process defies simple description; factors influencing and sustaining withdrawal vary from smoker to smoker as do patterns of cessation (degree and stability). Nevertheless, certain general relationships were evident in the data. Considering all five smoking-change groups, a substantial portion of the reported postclinic changes in smoking could be "explained" by four *clusters* of predictor variables that were developed to characterize the subjects' smoking history, interpersonal environments, attitudes toward smoking, and personal health. Personality and background factors were less important predictors; their contribution was lessened through their interrelations with other variables.

Successful quitters (Successes) tended to be less chance-oriented, were more likely to have respiratory conditions, were less nervous or anxious, had demonstrated less dependence on cigarettes and alcohol, and were in interpersonal environments less supportive to smoking than those unable to quit (Failures). Clinic subjects who resumed smoking after stopping completely (Recidivists) tended to be more like Failures than Successes on the above-mentioned characteristics. In addition, Recidivists as compared with the long-term Successes reported less difficulty in previous withdrawal attempts, were more likely to have increased their rate of smoking in recent years, and reported less indulgence in cigarette substitutes (pipe/cigar smoking) and in related gratification activities (television viewing and coffee drinking).

The major deficiency of retrospective studies of smoking cessation is the possibility that some of the variables found to be correlated with cessation are *consequent* rather than antecedent or concomitant to the withdrawal attempt. For instance, the unsuccessful quitter may try to reduce his psychological discomfort by decreasing the importance of dissonant cognitions (for example, concern about health hazards of smoking) and/or by adding compensating positive cognitions (for example, smoking keeps weight down). Or, current smokers may report less concern for their health and greater fatalism than do ex-smokers because they believe this is what the researcher expects to find out.

Although most of the findings in the present study were in agreement with retrospective studies of natural cessation, some were not. Notable among the exceptions were the attitudinal data, including reasons for liking and disliking smoking, expressed reasons for wishing to give up smoking, general attitudes toward smoking, and acceptance of smoking-health reports. That the observed relationships between attitudes and cessation patterns were substantially weaker than previously reported may be attributed to the weaknesses of the retrospective approach discussed above. It is encouraging, on the other hand, to find support in these data for many other previously reported but causally suspect correlates of cessation, including risk aversion, respiratory conditions, anxiety, rate of smoking, drinking patterns, and interpersonal environments.

The conclusion should not be drawn that the research strategy described in this paper is methodologically superior to other approaches to the study of smoking behavioral change. Rather, the position is taken that, given the limitations and systematic biases (error) found in all research procedures, it is best to study smoking behavior by a wide variety of research techniques instead of placing unwavering emphasis on any single approach. For example, although the "experimental" aspects of the study reported here make it difficult to generalize about cessation under natural conditions, it is felt that this design provides "better" evidence of the substantive importance of certain variables, such as attitudes, to successful smoking discontinuation than that obtainable from conventional designs. Another design is necessary, however, to determine whether or not those variables affect cessation to the same degree under natural conditions.

38

THE UNCERTAINTY OF EVALUATIVE RESEARCH AS A GUIDE TO SOCIAL POLICY[1]

JOHN H. NOBLE, JR.

The Medical Foundation, Inc.

THIS PAPER FOCUSES UPON THE UNCERTAINTIES WHICH CONFRONT POLICY-makers and researchers as they come to grips with evaluative research and its products. It explores, through the vehicle of a case example, the uncertainties of results associated with even the most carefully designed and executed evaluation of an action demonstration program. The perspective afforded on what may be reasonably expected of evaluative research in action settings may prove helpful in the design and interpretation of an increasing number of programs being funded subject to evaluation.

Realistic appraisal of the uncertainties attached to evaluative efforts is important if public officials, administrators, and social scientists are to collaborate without disillusionment in obtaining "hard data" to support changes in social policy to improve standards of health, education, and welfare in the United States.

THE WEEKEND RANGERS PROGRAM

From 1963 to 1966 under Public Law 87–274 the President's Committee on Juvenile Delinquency and Youth Crime funded a variety of large-scale projects designed to demonstrate effectiveness in the prevention and control of juvenile delinquency. As part of the federally supported Boston Youth Opportunities Project, the Weekend Rangers Program sought to reduce the volume and seriousness of delinquent behavior among lower-class probationers under the supervision of Juvenile Courts in the Roxbury, North Dorchester, and Charlestown sections of Boston. On the theory that dysfunctional societal conditions cause affected youth to internalize values at variance with those of the dominant American culture, to feel alienated from the core society and its institutions, and, consequently, to engage more frequently in deviant behavior, the program attempted to reorient probationers randomly selected for treatment to what were considered the dominant American values and to reduce feelings of alienation. When less alienated and more oriented to middle-class mores, the probationers could be expected to refrain from law-violating behavior and to assume other behavioral and personality characteristics consistent with middle-class norms and values. Twelve weekends of work and recreation, guided group discussions, and self-government under supervision of interested adults in a camp setting were to accomplish the treatment goals.

Contemporary social structural and social psychological theories supported the major program assumption that probationers, if induced to

[1] Revision of a paper presented at the Joint Meeting of the American Society of Criminology and the American Association for the Advancement of Science, December 28, 1967.

embrace the values, attitudes, and self-concepts considered characteristic of dominant middle-class American society, would commit fewer and/or less serious offenses.[2] When synthesized, these theories link dysfunctional societal conditions or "objective anomie" to socially unacceptable behavior of such quality and magnitude that it comes to the attention of law enforcement agencies for adjudication and control. Dysfunctional societal conditions are thought to act upon affected individuals and groups by producing subjective anomie, alienation, variant value orientations, and an impoverished self-concept, all of which, in turn, incline the individual toward deviant behavior.

Since theorists generally agree that attitudes, value orientations or life style, antisocial behavior, good and bad self-concepts, and authoritarian personality have their origins in the socialization process,[3] some form of resocialization appeared to be the key to intervention. Attitude change theory suggested that change might occur if the Weekend Rangers Program fostered a nonthreatening, supportive environment where new information could be communicated, new needs, goals, and aspirations developed, where old attitudes could lose their appropriateness, and a degree of dissatisfaction with the old self occur.[4] Such an environment might accomplish a shifting of rewards and punishments if it provided a means of social control which freed staff from the usual authority role involving direct manipulation of rewards and punishment. Staff could then concentrate on developing relationships and teaching the role requirements and relevance of the middle-class value system.

[2] See Robert K. Merton, "Social Structure and Anomie: Continuities," *Social Theory and Social Structure* (Glencoe, Ill.: The Free Press, 1957), p. 162; Walter B. Miller, "Lower Class Culture as a Generating Milieu of Gang Delinquency," *Journal of Social Issues*, 14: 3 (1958), pp. 5–19; Florence R. Kluckhohn and Fred L. Strodtbeck, *Variations in Value Orientations* (Evanston, Ill.: Row, Peterson & Co., 1961), p. 4; Simon Dinitz, Frank R. Scarpitti, and Walter C. Reckless, "Delinquency Vulnerability: A Cross Group and Longitudinal Analysis," *American Sociological Review*, 27 (Aug., 1962), pp. 515–517; Albert K. Cohen and James F. Short, Jr., "Juvenile Delinquency," in Robert K. Merton and Robert A. Nisbet, eds., *Contemporary Social Problems* (New York: Harcourt, Brace & World, 1961), pp. 89–90; and Jerome Himelhoch, "Delinquency and Opportunity: An End and A Beginning of Theory," in Alvin W. Gouldner and S. Miller, eds., *Applied Sociology* (New York: The Free Press, 1965), pp. 189–206.

[3] S. Stansfeld Sargent and Robert C. Williamson, *Social Psychology*, 2nd ed. (New York: The Ronald Press, 1958), p. 224; Leonard Schneiderman, "Value Orientation Preferences of Chronic Relief Recipients," *Social Work*, 9 (July, 1964), pp. 13–18; Lee N. Robins, Harry Gyman, Patricia O'Neal, "The Interaction of Social Class and Deviant Behavior," *American Sociological Review*, 27 (Aug., 1962), pp. 480–492; Dinitz, Scarpitti, and Reckless, "Delinquency Vulnerability," p. 517; and Leo Srole, "Social Integration and Certain Corollaries," *American Sociological Review*, 21 (Dec., 1956), pp. 712–713.

[4] Daniel Katz, "The Functional Approach to the Study of Attitudes," *Public Opinion Quarterly*, 24 (Summer, 1960), pp. 163–204; Irving Sarnoff and Daniel Katz, "The Motivational Bases of Attitude Change," *Journal of Abnormal and Social Psychology*, 49 (Jan., 1954), pp. 115–124; Daniel Katz, Irving Sarnoff, and Charles McClintock, "Ego Defense and Attitude Change," *Human Relations*, 9 (Feb. 1956), pp. 27–46; and Herbert C. Kelman, "Processes of Opinion Change," *Public Opinion Quarterly*, 25 (Spring, 1961), pp. 57–78.

Accordingly, probationers were to have the opportunity both to examine and to experience alternatives between delinquent and nondelinquent values, attitudes, and behaviors. They were to confront the value system of the dominant middle class, to examine the system's instrumental value in achieving success, and to affirm or deny within the context of group discussion that they could benefit from a change in values, attitudes, and behavior. Group discussions were to be structured to allow airing of beliefs, attitudes, behaviors, satisfactions, and dissatisfactions without fear or jeopardy.

Since all human behavior is subject to regulation by family, peer, and public bodies, it was considered important that the probationers, under self-imposed circumstances, experience the utility and necessity of authority. Consequently, the program was to support the type of social structure which would permit the probationers to examine the role and legitimacy of authority in the camp setting for their own purposes. It was also to place major emphasis upon peer-group decision-making so that program participants might gain status and recognition not only for their own successful participation but for their willingness to involve others. Self-government appeared to be the type of social structure which both permitted examination of the role and legitimacy of authority and placed major responsibility upon the peer group for decision-making.[5]

Participation in work projects and group recreational activities was calculated to enhance the probationers' understanding of their responsibilities to themselves and to others by permitting staff to interpret the relevance of work and cooperation to success in the community. Finally, interaction with stable adults was to strengthen the probationers' sense of acceptable adolescent behavior and of appropriate (middle-class) adult values, attitudes, and behavior.

EVALUATIVE METHOD

The decision to conduct the evaluation of the Weekend Rangers Program according to experimental design reflected the conviction that such a procedure would maximize the yield of objective information and, therefore, best support inferences about the extent to which the program achieved valued goals.[6] A pretest-posttest control group design was adopted because previous experience in evaluating action demonstration programs forecast considerable attrition in the randomly designated experimental group due to refusal to participate and dropping out. This design made it

[5] The Provo Experiment in Delinquency Rehabilitation took a similar approach. It vested means control in the treatment group on the assumption that a treatment system would be most effective if the delinquent peer group was used as the means of perpetuating the norms and imposing the sanctions of the system. See LaMar T. Empey and Jerome Rabow, "The Provo Experiment in Delinquency Rehabilitation," *American Sociological Review*, 26 (Oct., 1961), p. 683.

[6] See Edward A. Suchman, *Evaluative Research* (New York: Russell Sage Foundation, 1967), p. 31, for a discussion of the distinction between *evaluation*, the general process of judging worthiness of activities, and *evaluative research*, the use of scientific method in making an evaluation.

possible to apply covariance adjustment techniques to pretest measures in order to equate statistically experimental and control groups after attrition had introduced possible bias. It also permitted control of the main effects of history, maturation, testing, instrument decay, regression, selection, and attrition, but not of possible interaction between testing and treatment.[7]

Eighty-four eligible males between the ages of 13½ and 16 under formal or informal supervision of the Juvenile Courts in Roxbury, North Dorchester, and Charlestown at the time of recruitment, stratified by race and probationary status, were randomly assigned to experimental and control groups.[8] Eligible probationers were pre- and posttested on questionnaires devised to measure anomie,[9] alienation,[10], authoritarianism,[11] dominant-variant value orientation,[12] and self-concept along the dimensions of assertiveness, likeableness, intelligence, nervousness, and responsibility.[13] Questionnaires were administered to probationers by researchers at district probation offices without prior notification of the impending program so that they would be less apt to "fake" responses as a way of either entering or avoiding the program.[14]

All extant Boston precinct police record data as of August 14, 1965, were collected on the probationer population. Only those reported incidents in which police either issued a warning or arrested the offending individual were defined as "offenses."[15] Reporting and monitoring systems, proceedings of staff orientation sessions, and testimonies of participants, camp personnel, and research staff yielded descriptive data on the program as actually implemented.

[7] See Donald T. Campbell, "Factors Relevant to the Validity of Experiments in Social Settings," *Psychological Bulletin*, 54 (July, 1957), pp. 297–312.

[8] Stratification served more to assure a racially balanced camp population than to control for differences of race and/or of probationary status, since covariance adjustment ultimately could be applied for control purposes.

[9] See Srole, "Social Integration," pp. 712–713, for the Anomia Scale.

[10] Gwynn Nettler, "A Measure of Alienation," *American Sociological Review*, 22 (Dec., 1957), pp. 670–677.

[11] The version of the F Scale appearing in Appendix A of Howard E. Freeman and Ozzie G. Simmons, *The Mental Patient Comes Home* (New York: Wiley & Sons, 1963), p. 236, was adopted.

[12] Variant value orientation was operationally defined as a departure from the following dominant orientation preference profile, as measured by a modification of R. P. R. Kluckhohn's urban form of the Kluckhohn-Strodtbeck Value Orientation Preference Schedule: a "doing" activity orientation, an "individualistic" relational orientation, a "future" time orientation, a "mastery-over-nature" man-nature orientation, and an orientation toward human nature which views it as a "mixture of good and evil." See Kluckhohn and Strodtbeck, *Variations in Value Orientations*, p. 12.

[13] Edgar F. Borgatta, "A Very Short Test of Personality: The Behavioral Self-Rating (BSR) Form," *Psychological Reports*, 14 (Feb., 1964), pp. 275–284.

[14] A small percentage of probationers had to be pretested at home or during the first weekend at camp because they resisted all efforts to get them to appear at the Probation Offices. Posttesting required similar follow-up.

[15] Sixty-five different offenses were identified, each written on a separate card, and the cards sorted by three judges into ten piles representing high to low seriousness. Average interjudge reliability in rating the seriousness of the offenses was .89 (Pearsonian r).

Comparison of 27 treated probationers with 26 probationers serving as controls via fixed-effect, two-way analysis of variance, using pretest scores as covariate adjustors, gave statistical evidence that the Weekend Rangers Program had no impact—positive or negative—on the value orientations, attitudes, or self-concept of the treated probationers. Neither race by itself nor race and treatment interacting showed any measurable effects.

Covariance analysis applied to data on the volume and seriousness of offenses occurring (1) three months during the program (November 13, 1964, to February 14, 1965), (2) six months after the program until police record data were collected (February 14, 1965, to August 14, 1965), and (3) nine months from program beginning until the date of data collection (November 13, 1964, to August 14, 1965), permitted evaluation over time of program impact on behavior. As shown by Tables 1 and 2, adjusted

TABLE 1

Adjusted Group Means on Six Criterion Variables

Variable	Experimental (N = 27)	Control (N = 26)
Number of offenses, 3 months during program	0.03	0.20
Seriousness of offenses, 3 months during program	0.22	0.76
Number of offenses, 6 months after program	0.28	0.44
Seriousness of offenses, 6 months after program	0.85	1.90
Number of offenses, 9 months during and after program	0.31	0.64
Seriousness of offenses, 9 months during and after program	1.08	2.24

TABLE 2

Significance of Adjusted Group Differences on Each of Six Criterion Variables

Variable	Wilks' Lambda	$F_{1,43}$	$F_{1,46}$	Probability
Number of offenses, 3 months during program	0.94	2.57		0.11
Seriousness of offenses, 3 months during program	0.98		1.19	0.28
Number of offenses, 6 months after program	0.98	0.84		—
Seriousness of offenses, 6 months after program	0.95		2.38	0.12
Number of offenses, 9 months during and after program	0.94	2.85		0.10
Seriousness of offenses, 9 months during and after program	0.95		2.69	0.10

group differences over the subdivided time span indicated a reduction in the volume and seriousness of offenses committed by treated probationers. These differences, however, were small and attained the 10 per cent level of significance only over the nine months between the beginning of the program and the date of data collection.

Adjusted group differences in volume of offenses committed three months during the program and in seriousness of offenses committed six months after the program came very close to the 10 per cent significance level—P = .11 and .12, respectively. On the other hand, group differences in volume of offenses committed six months after the program dropped to a chance level. These findings favor the supposition that the Weekend Rangers Program had greater initial impact on the volume of offenses committed by treated probationers but a more lasting effect on their seriousness.

DISCUSSION

Statistical findings do not render an automatic verdict about the success or failure of an action demonstration program, nor do they permit closure on earlier issues of program objectives, assumptions, and design. Uncertainty attends each step of the interpretative process as the analyst tries to juggle simultaneously questions of statistical inference, measurement, substantive theory, and values. These uncertainties are illustrated by consideration and discussion of several issues impinging upon judgment of success or failure of the Weekend Rangers Program.

Should differences between experimental and control groups which could have occurred by chance ten times in a hundred be accepted as statistically significant? The answer to this question depends upon (1) the decision-rule adopted and (2) reliability of measurement. While one and five percent levels of statistical significance are conventional in most social research, these levels are not immutable. The real issue is to establish a decision-rule which, under the circumstances, limits chances of reaching erroneous conclusions. Setting the alpha value of statistical significance at too stringent a level increases possibility of declaring true differences false (Type II error), whereas too lax a level increases chances of asserting true differences where none exist (Type I error).[16] When the social consequences of erroneously asserting true differences are not abhorrent, it seems reasonable to lessen the possibility of Type II error by establishing a larger than conventional alpha value of statistical significance. Thus, at the 10 percent level, acceptance as true of differences between experimental and control groups of the Weekend Rangers Program permits a one-in-ten chance of error. This does not seem too bad a wager, considering (1) the slight chance that acting upon the belief of program effectiveness would cause harm and (2) how little is known about the effectiveness of any of the delinquency control programs.

[16] William L. Hays, *Statistics for Psychologists* (New York: Holt, Rinehart and Winston, 1963), pp. 265–269.

On the other hand, when measurement is unreliable, one should be wary of accepting differences as true at larger than conventional alpha values. If, for example, the F-ratio in a fixed-effect analysis of variance falls below the value requisite to significance by virtue of the adopted decision-rule, the reason is not known without further information. One only knows that between-group variance did not exceed sufficiently within-group variance (error) to support assertion of true differences between gorups. A large amount of within-group variance may exist because the groups were essentially homogeneous or because measurement was so unreliable that it could not discriminate.[17] Within this context, reliability coefficients become important means of diagnosis.

With respect to the behavioral variables of the Weekend Rangers Program, reliability seemed adequate. Police record data, although probably somewhat biased by underreporting, provided a reasonably reliable measurement of the volume of offenses committed by the demonstration population. High average interjudge reliability (.89) was proof of the adequacy of the seriousness rating scale. Therefore, acceptance as true of differences between experimental and control groups in volume and seriousness of offenses appears warranted by the available evidence. Differences in attitudes, value orientations, and self-concept do not seem worthy of support as true differences because, in spite of fairly reliable underlying measures,[18] they did not attain the 10 per cent level of significance.

Should the Weekend Rangers Program by virtue of its known impact be considered substantively significant? Exposure to the program accounted for roughly 4 per cent of variance in the number and seriousness of offenses committed by probationers over a nine-month period. By "substantive significance" is meant, following Gold's definition,[19] statistical significance plus a sufficiently high degree of relationship between participation in the program and reduced volume and seriousness of delinquent behavior. But how is "suffiiciency" to be judged? Gold's advice in this admittedly subjective matter is to rely upon common sense and the nature of the problem.

Although attractive in theory, this criterion of substantive significance does not carry the analyst concerned with policy formulation far. No cumulative body of tested knowledge or general consensus exists against which results of a particular evaluation can be compared. Sociologists usually do

---

[17] As a matter of fact, when measurement is unreliable, one should be more disposed to interpret even an F-ratio attaining the critical alpha value for significance as a chance occurrence.

[18] Reliability coefficients for these measures varied from .13 to .76. Least reliable was the value orientation measure, the test-retest reliability of which was only .13. In terms of internal consistency, the rest of the measures ranged as follows: alienation (.25), authoritarianism (.49), anomie (.56), assertiveness (.22), likability (.68), intelligence (.64), nervousness (.68), and responsibility (.76). See Lee J. Cronbach, "Coefficient Alpha and the Internal Structure of Tests, *Psychometrika*, 16 (Sept., 1951), pp. 297–334, for a discussion of test reliability in terms of internal consistency as measured by the Kuder-Richardson formula 20 used in the present analysis.

[19] David Gold, "Statistical Tests and Substantive Significance," *American Sociologist*, 4 (Feb., 1969), pp. 44–45.

not report findings in terms of the degree of relationship involved—especially when the statistical significance of differences between means has been ascertained.[20] Thus, the will to believe or to disbelieve, as the case may be, may supplant more rational grounds for judgment.

Another approach to substantive significance appeals to theory which predicts the form and strength of relationships—requiring that a particular finding support specific expectations derived from theory.[21] Practically, this means isolating critical program components expected to account for the measured outcome of an action demonstration program. From the standpoint of the impact model underlying the Weekend Rangers Program,[22] the reduction in volume and seriousness of offenses without concomitant shifts in value orientations, attitudes, or self-concept was unexpected. As a matter of fact, it was surprising that any positive effects flowed from the program because social psychological conditions postulated as necessary for constructive change were not fostered. Staff threatened and, at times, abused probationers. They directly manipulated rewards and punishments to the point of physical coercion. With but few exceptions, the example provided by staff seemed better calculated to alienate than to draw acceptance of middle-class values.

Moral outrage at what happened, however, does not clarify or discriminate between contending hypotheses offering explanation of the results achieved by the program. First, the impact model which expected shifts in attitudes, values, and self-concept to lead to behavioral change may have been naive. Social scientists are still very unsure of the relationship between attitudes and behavior.[23] Inconsistency more than consistency appears to be the rule. Second, although need deprivation and coercion were rejected on ethical grounds as a suitable impact model to guide design of the Weekend Rangers Program, pragmatically this approach to attitude and behavior change may work.[24] Third, removing pro-

[20] Gold, "Statistical Tests." See also Thomas J. Duggan and Charles W. Dean, "Common Misinterpretations of Significance Levels in Sociology Journals," *American Sociologist*, 3 (Feb., 1968), pp. 45–46; and David Gold, "A Note on Statistical Analysis in the American Sociological Review," *American Sociological Review*, 22 (June, 1957), pp. 332–333.

[21] Denton E. Morrison and Ramon E. Henkel, "Significance Tests Reconsidered," *American Sociologist*, 4 (May, 1969), pp. 136–137.

[22] See Howard E. Freeman and Clarence C. Sherwood, "Research in Large-Scale Intervention Programs," *Journal of Social Issues*, 21 (Jan., 1965), p. 16, for a useful discussion of the meaning of "impact model" within the context of action demonstration evaluative research. "Impact model" is defined as "a set of theoretical concepts or ideas which trace the dynamics of how it is expected that the program will have the desired effects. . . ."

[23] See Howard J. Ehrlich, "Attitudes, Behavior, and the Intervening Variables," *American Sociologist*, 4 (Feb., 1969), pp. 29–34, for a review and critique of the positions taken.

[24] Parallels have been noted between Communist rectification programs, delinquency rehabilitation programs, and other traditional practices in religion, politics, medicine, and psychology. See Letter to Editor from Whitney H. Gordon and Reply by LaMar T. Empey and Jerome Rabow in *American Sociological Review*, 27 (April, 1962), pp. 256–258. Katz, "Functional Approach," p. 192, places need deprivation first in a list of conditions necessary for changing adjustment-based attitudes.

bationers from circulation on weekends over a three-month period may have produced the results achieved, by (1) reducing opportunity for delinquent behavior on weekends, (2) siphoning off energy which might have been expended on antisocial behavior on weekdays, or (3) interrupting habitual patterns of association enough to prevent more serious violations of the law—thus explaining the lag of seriousness in catching up with volume of offenses six months after the program had ended.

CONCLUDING REMARKS

Obviously, these and perhaps other alternative hypotheses explaining why such a program as the Weekend Rangers achieved the results that it did require additional controlled experimentation for an answer. Meanwhile, administrators and policymakers are pressed to reach decisions about the types of programs to launch in the effort to control delinquency among various segments of the juvenile population. They cannot wait for answers; nor is it likely that social scientists will provide answers for some time to come.

Under the circumstances, it seems advisable that planners under the guidance of policymakers proceed in such fashion that the knowledge-seeking enterprise is safeguarded. There should exist within large-scale intervention programs an insulated spot wherein true experiments can be designed, implemented, and analyzed. This entails establishing an organizational structure and staff capable of evaluating one or more innovative programs at a time. Massive subsidization may be necessary from time to time to gain the assent and cooperation of certain agencies whose traditional programs it seems advisable to evaluate. As for the rest, other innovative practices or momentarily feasible structural change strategies can be pursued without the need to evaluate outcomes.

Such a policy, if conscientiously followed by governmental officials and the large foundations, in time may yield considerably more knowledge about effective programs and practice than present sporadic and fragmented efforts afford.

39

INTERVENTION AS A STRATEGY OF SOCIAL INQUIRY: AN EXPLORATORY STUDY WITH UNEMPLOYED NEGRO MEN[1]

WILLIAM L. YANCEY

Vanderbilt University

THE NUMEROUS EVALUATIONS OF THE WAR ON POVERTY,[2] THE WORK IN "action-anthropology,"[3] of psychologists[4] and sociologists[5] in applied research, the studies of social change *per se,*[6] as well as traditional concerns of social scientists with the "unanticipated consequences of planned social change,"[7] rather clearly suggest that social change, planned or unplanned, makes possible the observation of structures and processes that might have been otherwise unrecognized. Examples are plentiful. It is clear from the recent work of Marris and Rein, Donovan, Brager and Purcell, and Moynihan, that evaluations of the War on Poverty have led to

[1] Revision of a paper presented at the annual meetings of the American Sociological Association, September, 1965. This paper is based in part on research aided by a grant from the National Institutes of Mental Health, Grant No.: MH-09189, "Social and Community Problems in Public Housing Areas." The author is indebted to Alvin W. Gouldner who has stimulated many of the ideas presented. Much of this is the result of our joint efforts.

[2] See Peter Marris and Martin Rein, *Dilemmas of Social Reform* (New York: Atherton Press, 1967); John C. Donovan, *The Politics of Poverty* (New York: Pegasus, 1967); George A. Brager and Francis P. Purcell, eds., *Community Action Against Poverty* (New Haven, Conn.: College and University Press, 1967); Daniel P. Moynihan, *Maximum Feasible Misunderstanding* (New York: The Free Press, 1969); and the special issue of the *Journal of Social Issues,* 21 (Jan., 1965) on poverty intervention.

[3] See Sol Tax, "The Fox Project," *Human Organization,* 17 (1958), pp. 17–19; Allan R. Holmberg, "The Research and Development Approach to the Study of Change," *Human Organization,* 17 (1958), pp. 6–12; James Spillius, "Natural Disaster and Political Crisis in a Polynesian Society," (Part II) *Human Relations,* 10 (1957), pp. 113–125; and Conrad M. Arensberg and Arthur H. Niehoff, *Introducing Social Change: A Manual for Americans Overseas* (Chicago, Ill.: Aldine Publishing Co., 1964.)

[4] See Kurt Lewin, "Frontiers in Group Dynamics: Concept, Method, and Reality in Social Science; Social Equilibria and Social Change," *Human Relations,* 1 (June, 1947), pp. 5–41; Ronald Lippitt, Jeanne Watson and Bruce Westley, *The Dynamics of Planned Change* (New York: Harcourt, Brace and World, Inc., 1958), and Warren G. Bennis, Kenneth D. Benne, and Robert Chin, eds., *The Planning of Change* (New York: Holt, Rinehart and Winston, 1962).

[5] Alvin W. Gouldner and S. M. Miller, eds., *Applied Sociology* (New York: The Free Press, 1965); Donald M. Valdes and Dwight G. Dean, eds., *Sociology in Use* (New York: MacMillan Co., 1965); Arthur B. Shostak, ed., *Sociology in Action* (Homewood, Ill.: The Dorsey Press, 1966); and Paul F. Lazarsfeld, William H. Sewell and Harold L. Wilensky, eds., *The Uses of Sociology* (New York: Basic Books, 1967).

[6] There are numerous examples. See Peter Marris, *Family and Social Change in an African City* (Chicago: Northwestern University Press, 1962); Mirra Komarovsky, *The Unemployed Man and His Family* (New York: Dryden Press, 1940); Robert K. Merton, "Manifest and Latent Functions," *Social Theory and Social Structure,* (Glencoe, Ill.: The Free Press, 1957), pp. 19–84; Alvin W. Gouldner, *Wildcat Strike* (New

✦ First published in Social Science Quarterly 50, No. 3 (December, 1969).

numerous insights into the institutional forces surrounding poverty in America.[8] This literature suggests that individual and institutional responses to change efforts are symptomatic of structural interests and relationships. As groups change, established relationships may either break down or become strained; emergent resistances to change provide information concerning latent interests, values, and interdependence.

INTERVENTION RESEARCH

In a word, there appears to be a latent function to the evaluation of planned social change. The research reported here attempted to take advantage of this function by purposefully intervening in subjects' everyday lives. These experiments did not focus on problems of proof (testing of previously stated hypotheses) nor did they focus on differences in observations taken before and after intervening. Rather, the continuous monitoring of the change effort by an observer closely involved in the research situation was emphasized.[9]

This paper reports the results of an exploratory study of seven lower class unemployed Negro men. We intervened in their lives by suggesting that they find a job, by offering a relatively large monetary reward if they were successful, and by remaining with them for several eight or more hour days as they sought work.

It was thought that by using such a research strategy we could not only obtain information concerning the process of job hunting in the lower class, but would also identify "latent structures" that either facilitate or impede the job hunting process.

We found that there are three periods during which the social scientist has an opportunity to make such observations. These are (1) at the outset of an intervention when the experimenter suggests the change to the subject, (2) during the actual process of change, and finally, (3) after change

York: Antioch Press, 1954); Amitai Etzioni, *Studies in Social Change* (New York: Holt, Rinehart and Winston, 1966); and John R. Seeley, "Crestwood Heights: Intellectual and Libidinal Dimensions of Research," in Arthur J. Vidich, Joseph Bensman and Maurice R. Stein, eds., *Reflections on Community Studies* (New York: John Wiley and Sons, 1964).

[7] See Robert K. Merton, "The Unanticipated Consequences of Purposive Social Action," *American Sociological Review*, 1 (1936), pp. 894–904; and Pitirim A. Sorokin, "Is Accurate Social Planning Possible?" *American Sociological Review*, 1 (1936), pp. 12–25.

[8] Marris and Rein, *Dilemmas*; Donovan, *Politics of Poverty*; Brager and Purcell, eds., *Community Action*; and Kenneth B. Clark, *Dark Ghetto* (New York: Harper and Row, 1965).

[9] Nathan Caplan has pointed out the limitations of traditional "before-after" experimental designs in his research on the effects of street-gang workers. He writes: "Whether this research method is adequate for identifying the variables that either contribute to or impair the efficacy of the specific method of treatment remains an open question. Thus far research has revealed little about the *processes* of behavior change and the causes of final effects." "Treatment Intervention and Reciprocal Interaction Effects," *Journal of Social Issues*, 24 (1968), p. 64.

has occurred and when the system receives feedback from secondary changes.

Even though the applied social scientist may view the change as worthwhile, this evaluation may be taken from his own frame of reference.[10] A "worthwhile" change, such as employment, may be objected to by unemployed men. This rejection appears to be derived, in part, from subjects' predictions concerning negative consequences of change. Whether accurate or not, the predicted disruption of rewards, or threats to values or interests serve as a major barrier to change.

For example, in one family, the husband, who had been previously diagnosed by state hospital doctors as schizophrenic and was therefore receiving disability compensation, was in the process of agreeing to participate in our experiment. His wife suddenly interrupted the conversation and objected to her husband's getting a job. She did not believe that he could hold a job, and as long as he remained unemployed and was classified as "disabled" his family could remain together and receive aid from the state. State law did not allow a medically able husband to live with his family if the family was receiving AFDC payments.

Here we can see that job-seeking by the male may be inhibited by his family's vested interest in maintaining government aid. This of course, is a familiar hypothesis; but our intervention efforts further enable us to see the actors in the situation *knowingly* and *deliberately* seeking to protect this secure source of income. Still, further, the wife interrupted the conversation when she saw her husband agreeing to look for a job. This suggests that it may be women in particular who act to protect an interest in maintaining governmental aid when this is possible, and who may actively inhibit male efforts to look for work. Males, on the other hand, may have an interest in getting a job in order to fulfill requirements of the male role. One can begin to see some of the functional relationships between the marginal economic status of men and the value of security on the part of women.

Barriers to social change can also be found in secondary meanings of the change goal. Unemployment has a stigma attached to it. One strategy that an unemployed man may use to remove this stigma is to "prove" to others that being unemployed is not his fault. It is not so much that he denies the stigma; he denies responsibility for it.[11] In one experiment, for example, the subject, who had been unemployed for three months, sought work in over one hundred different businesses and failed to get a job. A large proportion of these applications were in lumber yards even though he knew

[10] See Hyman Rodman, "Middle-Class Misconceptions about Lower-Class Families," in Arthur B. Shostak and William Gomberg, eds., *Blue-Collar World* (Englewood Cliffs, N. J.: Prentice-Hall, 1964), p. 59–69.

[11] See S. Zawadski and Paul Lazarsfeld, "The Psychological Consequences of Unemployment," *Journal of Social Psychology*, 6 (1935). The analysis here follows the work of Erving Goffman in *Stigma* (Englewood Cliffs, N. J.: Prentice-Hall, 1961) and Fred Davis, "Deviance Disavowal: The Management of Strained Interaction by the Visibly Handicapped," in Howard Becker, ed., *The Other Side* (New York: Free Press of Glencoe, 1964), pp. 119–137.

that construction and related industry were slow during the winter months. He never took back applications for jobs when they were given to him. He spent the early part of each day in a labor contracting organization where he could find only a part time job. He gave little commitment to the process of job hunting, and made few plans, as indicated by the fact that on one occasion he returned to one factory without realizing it. Many of his efforts were public performances, to which he apparently attached little private conviction. He presented a self that wanted a job, but at the same time in effect he sabotaged his own efforts and thereby "proved" to the researchers that there were no jobs available. Had he succeeded in getting a job this would have suggested that his previous months of unemployment were due to his laziness. By denying responsibility for being unemployed, he eliminated its stigma and, by this strategy, could maintain his image as a responsible male. In a word, successful change would have involved costs that are derived from the latent meaning of the change goal.

Costs derived from the latent meaning of the change *goal* are similar to those deriving from latent meaning of the *means* to that goal. An individual may reject an instrument of change because this involves additional costs derived from its meaning to him.

For example, one subject failed to use want ads as a means of getting a job, which it seemed to us would have been an obvious and rational way of job-hunting. On the last day of the experiment we intervened further by expressly suggesting that he buy a paper and use the want ads to find a job. Though there were several jobs advertised the respondent rejected all but one. In particular, he refused to ask for any job that required a specific characteristic or skill, no matter how low.

The use of want ads involves additional costs that are not present when one applies directly for a job at some factory. The man reading want ads knows that there are jobs available and if he is turned down for one of them, it implies some lack or deficiency on his part. This, of course, is more frustrating and demoralizing than being told that there are no jobs available. By avoiding want ads, then, the job hunter is better able to avoid placing himself in a situation that seemingly discredits him in some way.

One can also see from this that this job hunter seeks to reduce risks to his image of self as he searches for a job. Even though he may have wanted a job, he often does not allow himself to expect to get one, remains detached from job prospects, and thus does not run the risk of rejection. His behavior, then, is governed both by the desire to achieve the goal and also by pessimistic expectations and fear of rejection.

Although not normally seen as barriers to change, the sentiments that are expressed during the process of change point to tensions among an individual's perception of the social system, his interests, and his attempts to change his position. For example, one respondent spontaneously complained about caretakers, his union, the welfare agency, the employment service, and the food stamp agency. He did not, however, complain about the employer who had laid him off or the potential employers who did not hire him. His complaints about the caretakers indicated that he perceived *them* as owing him aid when he was unemployed, both in helping him find a job and in providing some form of welfare.

Under the pressure of the intervention, sentiments of a more general nature were elicited. For example, several times respondents expressed feelings of alienation by such statements as, "You can't really count on anything these days," and "The black man ain't got a chance these days." Such sentiments are not expressed in a vacuum but rather under a specific set of conditions. We can say from these data that these men seem alienated from the means of gaining employment, but we cannot make a statement about the generality of their alienation. We are able to spell out the precise conditions which elicit the sentiment and we are able to relate the abstract variable to specific actions.[12]

In addition to the barriers to change discussed above, intervention research provided knowledge of the direct costs of the change effort. In these experiments the researchers remained with the respondents for at least eight hours a day until they got a job. Thus, we developed a mobile observatory which enabled us to be with respondents as they drove into back alleys, across railroad tracks, down main thoroughfares or stopped abruptly in the middle of the street to look at a prospective employer.

From our mobile platform we were able to make detailed observations of the respondent's behavior. As a consequence we were able to see patterns that they probably would not have been able to verbalize. For example, we observed, in wonderment, during the first day of job hunting that subjects traveled long distances between job inquiries. Yet on the second or third day of the job hunt they went to an apparently fertile area —for example, an industrial park—and systematically went from one door to the next. After this happened with the first two men it became apparent that during the early part of their job hunting efforts they were following networks of friends and previous employers. It was only after they had exhausted these networks that they stopped "wasting time" traveling long distances and settled down to a more ecologically systematic pattern.[13]

Because we constrained ourselves to be with the subjects until they got a job, the costs of gaining employment were not only seen, but were also felt by us in a way that could not have been communicated to us through interviewing. We were sensitized to the frustrations of job hunting because we suffered much the same costs in terms of time, cold, number of refusals, and eventual hopelessness. The cessation of these costs to us were dependent on the applicant's getting a job and thus we had a real stake in his doing so as soon as possible. Field workers commonly felt that they could not have long endured the continued frustrations. These constraints made possible not only cognitive, but also affective reactions, on the part of the

[12] It is of interest to note that during initial interviews with these men most of them expressly denied having been subjected to racial discrimination.

[13] The importance of informal networks as sources of jobs for the working and lower class has been documented by several previous researchers. See Harold L. Sheppard and Herbert E. Striner, *Civil Rights, Employment and the Social Status of American Negroes* (Kalamazoo, Mich.: The W. E. Upjohn Institute for Employment Research, 1966).

researchers, to failures and frustrations. These, in turn, sensitized the researchers to the respondents' affective responses to failure, which in turn, led us to inquire how they coped with failure. We were led to the hypothesis that they did so by not becoming emotionally involved in job-searching.

There is one final barrier to social change. Aspects of the social system, when disturbed by successful change, may feed back on the actors in a negative manner. An example of the "negative feedback" can be seen in the case of the disruption of the unemployed man's leisure activities. The patterns of friendship that are developed during this period may be an important means to finding a job, but they must also be disrupted if the respondent finds a job. This breakdown or loss of previously rewarding relationships is also likely to act as a major barrier to job-hunting, or to job-keeping, if the search has been successful. This suggests that observation of social change, enables social scientists to make observations and inferences concerning the maintenance of specific patterns of behavior, norms and values that occur in social structure.

CONCLUSION

The underlying hypotheses of these experiments was something on the order of the following proposition: "Lower class men are unemployed because they lack motivation to seek work." From one perspective the experiments reviewed here were failures. Even with the considerable pressure placed on our subjects only one of the seven men obtained a part time job. Yet while we may be led to reject a hypothesis relating motivation to seek work to successful job hunting, we have generated little "hard" experimental evidence as to its incorrectness. The extraneous variables influencing the behavior of our subjects are both too numerous and too strong to allow serious consideration of this hypothesis.[14]

If we had followed the experimental mode of research, we might well have done a series of "pre-tests," designed to develop experimental control over the extraneous variables, thereby making possible the testing of the single hypothesis. Yet it is likely that this process would have narrowed the range of findings available to this research.[15] Indeed, it is the uncontrolled freedom for emergence of previously unrecognized variables that is the heart of the heuristic strategy suggested here.

Such an open-ended experiment as this, while enabling the social scientist to discover, places him in a poor position to prove. Without control over the extraneous variables we are unable to specify the relationships in-

[14] The ineffectiveness of current institutional efforts at motivating unemployed men to look for work was illustrated by one of our subjects, who after spending three days seeking work in some fifty factories and stores, suddenly remembered that he needed the names of five prospective employers to give the employment service in order to receive unemployment compensation. He suddenly walked down the block writing down the names of the first five companies that he passed. After this *diversion* he said, "Well now let's go over to where they have all those trucking companies, maybe they'll have something."

[15] See Robert K. Merton, "The Bearing of Empirical Research on Sociological Theory," in *Social Theory*, pp. 102–117.

volved, and are quite vulnerable to problems such as small sample and spurious relationships. The strategy used here is, to use Reichenbach's terms, one which provides a context of discovery and lacks the advantages of a context of proof.[16]

The strains that are produced under social change are obviously important to the applied social scientist. When he intervenes in a group he implicitly makes the promise that the social problems being dealt with will be remedied or improved. If attention is focused solely on the manifest structure of a group change may not be successful. Indeed, things may get worse, as with the case of local governments and community action programs,[17] immigrants and the political machines,[18] or slum dwellers and the economic and interpersonal investment they held in their neighborhoods.[19] Latent structure may be destroyed through the well-meaning efforts of the applied social scientist. Resources will be wasted; people will suffer; change efforts will fail. In contrast, purposeful intervention on a smaller scale may reveal some of these structures and functions, thereby facilitating later and more macroscopic change.

All of this has some implications concerning the relationship between pure and applied social science. Gouldner pointed out nearly a decade ago that most of the work in applied social science followed the assumption that applied social science is nothing but the application of knowledge obtained through pure research. He argued that applied social science was more than "nothing but" the application of pure knowledge, that indeed applied social science would result in the development of new concepts and information which could be added to and modify theoretical systems based on pure research.[20] Our results from these experiments in intervention research suggest that this is indeed the case.

[16] Hans Reichenbach, *The Rise of Scientific Philosophy* (California: The University of California Press, 1951).
[17] See especially Marris and Rein, *Dilemmas*; and Donovan, *Politics of Poverty*.
[18] Merton, "Manifest and Latent Functions."
[19] Marris, *Family and Social Change*; and Marc Fried, "Grieving for a Lost Home," in Leonard J. Duhl, ed., *The Urban Condition* (New York: The Free Press, 1963), pp. 151–171.
[20] Alvin W. Gouldner, "Explorations in Applied Social Science," *Social Problems*, 3 (Jan., 1956), pp. 169–181.

40

THE NATIONAL FARMERS ORGANIZATION AND THE PRISONER'S DILEMMA: A GAME THEORY PREDICTION OF FAILURE

J. RONNIE DAVIS
Iowa State University

NEIL A. PALOMBA
Iowa State University

IN RECENT YEARS THE NATIONAL FARMERS ORGANIZATION HAS ATTEMPTED to increase and stabilize its membership by efforts to augment farm prices and incomes. Through "holding" actions (dramatized by dumping milk, slaughtering and burying hogs, and burning grain), the NFO hoped to persuade a sufficiently large number of farmers to withhold certain farm products from markets and drive up farm prices and incomes. If a sufficiently large number of farmers collusively restrict output, the NFO argues, farm prices will be high and all farmers will fare better individually. However, only a few farmers have been persuaded by the argument, for reasons that are easily demonstrated through the use of game theory techniques.[1] In essence, as will be shown, the cooperative agricultural production withdrawals, i.e., "boycotts," of the NFO, have the attributes of a *public* good.[2] Moreover, until the NFO offers *private* goods to an augmented and stabilized membership, it is unlikely that its lobbying activities will be effective.

THE PRISONER'S DILEMMA

The now-famous Prisoner's Dilemma[3] is a two-person, non-zero-sum, noncooperative game which is credited to A. W. Tucker. In short, two suspects are arrested and separated. The prosecutor is certain that they are jointly guilty of a serious crime, but without their confession the evidence is insufficient to convict them at a trial. Accordingly, the prosecutor points out to each prisoner that he has the alternatives of confessing or not confessing to the crime for which they were arrested. If neither confesses, the

---

[1] Elementary price theory also clearly predicts the failure of such collusive arrangements, and economists are generally familiar with this technique of approaching cartels. In short, price theory emphasizes the enhanced marginal revenue possibilities associated with operating outside a cartel and the persistent threat of entry into the cartelized industry. These price theory reasons for the failure of such cooperative activities differ from the game theory reasons. Game theory (and a dash of the "new" public finance) emphasizes the lack of incentive to behave cooperatively *and* the public nature of the benefits in large-number cases.

[2] In contrast to purely private goods, a potential beneficiary of purely public goods cannot be excluded from consuming these goods even if he refuses to share the costs of providing them. See Paul A. Samuelson, "The Pure Theory of Public Expenditure," *Review of Economics and Statistics*, 36 (Nov., 1954), pp. 387–389.

[3] For an interesting argument that the Prisoner's Dilemma is not a genuine dilemma, or even a paradox, see R. L. Cunningham, "Ethics and Game Theory: The Prisoner's Dilemma," *Papers on Non-Market Decision Making*, 2 (1967), pp. 11–26.

♦ First published in Social Science Quarterly 50, No. 3 (December, 1969).

prosecutor states, he will try them on a much less serious crime, and they will receive minor punishment. If both confess, the prosecutor claims that he will recommend a reduced sentence for each prisoner. If one prisoner confesses and the other does not, however, the prosecutor states that he will recommend the maximum sentence for the prisoner who fails to confess and simple probation for the prisoner who does confess. Stated in terms of years, the strategic problem is

		Prisoner 2	
		Not Confess	Confess
Prisoner 1	Not Confess	1 year each	10 years for 1 0 years for 2
	Confess	0 years for 1 10 years for 2	5 years each

In a two-by-two matrix, therefore,

		Prisoner 2	
		Not Confess	Confess
Prisoner 1	Not Confess	$(1, 1)$ (x_1, x_1)	$(10, 0)$ (x_2, x_3)
	Confess	$(0, 10)$ (x_3, x_2)	$(5, 5)$ (x_4, x_4)

Without Collusion. If communication and collusion are not permitted, each prisoner has to behave under conditions of uncertainty regarding the other's strategy. With Prisoner 1 as a reference, it is seen that his best strategy is to confess, regardless of his assumption regarding Prisoner 2's behavior, since, on the one hand, the avoidance of 10 years dominates (is to be preferred to) the avoidance of one year, and on the other hand, the avoidance of one year dominates the avoidance of no imprisonment at all: $(x_3, x_2) > (x_1, x_1)$; $(x_4, x_4) > (x_2, x_3)$. The same is true for Prisoner 2 as a reference: $(x_2, x_3) > (x_1, x_1)$; $(x_4, x_4) > (x_3, x_2)$. Although the confess-confess set, (x_4, x_4), *dominates* all others, each prisoner would *prefer* the not confess-not confess set, (x_1, x_1).[4]

With Collusion. Even if communication and collusion were allowed, each prisoner would find a dual incentive to break an agreement and confess: (1) each has a chance of being freed if the other keeps the agreement and (2) each has a hedge against a heavier sentence if the other also breaks the agreement.[5] Accordingly, it appears that the prisoners cannot take ad-

[4] The x_1 and x_2 refer to the payoffs associated with not confessing, and the x_3 and x_4 refer to the payoffs associated with confessing.

[5] In experiments with *repetitive* play, individuals have tended to behave cooperatively (except when the terminal play was announced). See Anatole Rapoport and Albert M. Chammah, *Prisoners Dilemma* (Ann Arbor: University of Michigan Press, 1965), Ch. 5, who found that the proportion of cooperative responses approached 70 per cent with repeated play; Lester B. Lave, "An Experimental Approach to the Prisoner's Dilemma Game," *Quarterly Journal of Economics*, 76 (Aug., 1962), pp. 424–436, who reported similar results; and R. Duncan Luce and Howard Raiffa, *Games and Decisions* (New York: John Wiley and Sons, Inc., 1967), pp. 88–113.

vantage of the preferred not confess-not confess set unless assumptions favorable to such a movement are built into the model.[6]

A Generalization. The unusual characteristic of the Prisoner's Dilemma is the non-Pareto-optimality of the payoffs which are associated with the dominant choice set of the players. In generalized matrix notation, therefore, the Prisoner's Dilemma can be defined as

$$
\begin{array}{cc}
 & B_1 \qquad\qquad B_2 \\
\begin{array}{c} A_1 \\ A_2 \end{array} &
\begin{bmatrix} (x_1, x_1) & (x_2, x_3) \\ (x_3, x_2) & (x_4, x_4) \end{bmatrix}
\end{array}
$$

where

    i. $2x_1 > x_2 + x_3 > 2x_4,$

    ii. $x_3 > x_1,$

    iii. $x_3 > x_2,$ and

    iv. $x_4 > x_2.$[7]

THE NFO'S DILEMMA

None is a more classic example of the Prisoner's Dilemma than recent attempts by the NFO to persuade large numbers of farmers to withhold milk, hogs, grain, and even all farm production from the market in the effort to drive up the prices of these goods. For analytical purposes here, the details of such boycotts of farm output are unimportant. We can simply assume that there is a proposed collusion agreement among, say, milk producers to withhold production in order to drive up the price of milk. For each producer, the alternatives are (1) to cooperate or (2) not to cooperate. The payoff matrix for a single producer, therefore, is as follows:

$$
\begin{array}{c}
 & \text{All Other Producers } [B] \\
 & \text{Cooperate } [B_1] \qquad\qquad \text{Not Cooperate } [B_2]
\end{array}
$$

$$
\begin{array}{c}
\text{Cooperate } [A_1] \\[2em]
\text{Single Producer } [A] \\[1em]
\text{Not Cooperate } [A_2]
\end{array}
\begin{bmatrix}
\displaystyle\sum_{j=t+1}^{n} P_s Q_j - \sum_{j=1}^{t} P_o Q_j &
\displaystyle\sum_{j=t+1}^{n} P_o Q_j - \sum_{j=1}^{t} P_o Q_j \\[2em]
\displaystyle\sum_{j=1}^{t} P_o Q_j + \sum_{j=t+1}^{n} P_s Q_j &
\displaystyle\sum_{j=1}^{n} P_o Q_j
\end{bmatrix}
$$

[6] For example, Cunningham, "Ethics and Game Theory," p. 13, suggests that the prisoners can end up in the upper left-hand box if (a) they play cooperatively with an enforceable contract and each chooses rationally, (b) they choose irrationally, or (c) they choose rationally but each evaluates a year in prison for the other as equivalent to a year in prison for himself.

[7] This merely summarizes in notation the characteristics of the Prisoner's Dilemma, which have been noted above. Cf. A. Rapoport and C. Orwant, "Experimental Games: A Review," *Game Theory and Related Approaches to Social Behavior* (New York: John Wiley and Sons, Inc., 1964), p. 287.

where

P_o = original price,
P_s = price if the boycott is successful,
Q_j = quantity produced on j^{th} day,
t = number of days of boycott,
$n-t$ = number of days after the boycott, and

$$\sum_{j=t+1}^{n} P_sQ_j - \sum_{j=1}^{t} P_oQ_j > \sum_{j=1}^{n} P_oQ_j.\text{[8]}$$

Accordingly, if a single producer assumes that other producers will co-operate with the boycott, he has an incentive not to cooperate himself:

$$A_2B_1 \text{ dominates } A_1B_1, \text{ i.e., } \sum_{j=1}^{t} P_oQ_j + \sum_{j=t+1}^{n} P_sQ_j > \sum_{j=t+1}^{n} P_sQ_j - \sum_{j=1}^{t}$$

P_oQ_j. If the single producer assumes that other producers will not coop-erate with the boycott, he is again motivated not to cooperate himself:

$$A_2B_2 \text{ dominates } A_1B_2, \text{ i.e., } \sum_{j=1}^{n} P_oQ_j > \sum_{j=t+1}^{n} P_oQ_j - \sum_{j=1}^{t} P_oQ_j. \text{ To general-}$$

ize, since all individual producers are in this same position, none finds it rational to cooperate with the boycott. Although cooperative behavior implicit in choices A_1B_1 is associated with a greater payoff, the result is convergence to "antisocial" behavior implicit in choices A_2B_2.

If agricultural production boycotts involved a very small number of "players," a collusive movement from choices A_2B_2 to choices A_1B_1 might be forthcoming.[9] As a member of a large group, however, a producer can-not expect to influence the behavior of other individuals through his own actions. Each producer simply adjusts his behavior to the totality of others' behavior.[10] Moreover, insofar as the boycott is successful in increasing price, the boycott outcome is in the form of a *public* good. That is to say, if the price of milk is increased through the boycott, *any* farmer will be able to freely receive the advantage of the increase whether or not he par-ticipated in the boycott. Allowing an individual to volunteer his own con-tribution—cooperation with the boycott—to the cost of providing the commonly-shared benefits of the boycott leads simply to "free rider" be-havior (as demonstrated by the matrix). The "free riders" cannot really

[8] This assumption is based on evidence that price elasticities of demand for fluid milk are typically less than unity. The implication is that cooperatives operate generally on the inelastic portions of their demand curves for Class I milk and could increase net profits by selling smaller volumes of milk at higher prices. Cf. George W. Ladd and Milton Hallberg, "An Exploratory Econometric Study of Dairy Bargaining Coopera-tives," (Ames, Iowa: Research Bulletin 542; Iowa State University Agricultural and Home Economics Experimental Station, 1965).

[9] As Luce and Raiffa, *Games and Decisions*, p. 97, point out, farmers can and some-times do enter into forms of weak collusion, largely because of the repetitive nature of production decisions. Also, government has passed a great deal of legislation which interferes with such games.

[10] Cf. James M. Buchanan, *The Demand and Supply of Public Goods* (Chicago: Rand McNally Co., 1968), p. 85.

be bribed into the coalition by the cooperating beneficiaries (unless the number of beneficiaries from the boycott is very small). Collection of funds for any such cash transfer could not be accomplished voluntarily because the funds are earmarked for the "purchase" of a public good.

COERCION

An escape from the NFO's Dilemma would appear to be the outright coercion of uncooperative producers into cooperating with the boycott. The payoff matrix for a single producer would be transformed as follows:

$$
\begin{array}{c}
 & B_1 & B_2 \\
A_1 & \displaystyle\sum_{j=t+1}^{n} P_s Q_j - \sum_{j=1}^{t} P_o Q_j & \displaystyle\sum_{j=t+1}^{n} P_o Q_j - \sum_{j=1}^{t} P_o Q_j \\
A_2 & \displaystyle\sum_{j=1}^{t} P_o Q_j - C + \sum_{j=t+1}^{n} P_s Q_j & \displaystyle\sum_{j=1}^{n} P_o Q_j
\end{array}
$$

where
$C =$ the total costs associated with the threats (real or implied) of the boycotting organization against the uncooperative single producer.

If C were made sufficiently large by the boycotting organization (for example, by threatening to force the uncooperative single producer's trucks off the road), then the single producer would cooperate with the boycott: A_1B_1 dominates A_2B_1, i.e., $\displaystyle\sum_{j=t+1}^{n} P_s Q_j - \sum_{j=1}^{t} P_o Q_j > \sum_{j=1}^{t} P_o Q_j - C + \sum_{j=t+1}^{n} P_s Q_j$. Of course, if all other producers are not cooperating, there is no group to do the coercing, no C in A_2B_2, and A_2B_2 continues to dominate A_1B_2.

Most forms of coercion are illegal, so that the more a boycotting organization relied on it, the more pressure could be expected from society to prevent or eliminate it. Coercion is a means society is not likely to condone, and, if used, it cannot be expected to succeed.

BARGAINING

Is there any way that a boycotting organization can legally force the single producer to cooperate with a boycott? One possible method would appear to be an arrangement whereby the price increase would benefit only those belonging to the boycott organization. The payoff matrix for a single producer would then look as follows:

$$
\begin{array}{c}
 & B_1 & B_2 \\
A_1 & \displaystyle\sum_{j=t+1}^{n} P_s^b Q_j - \sum_{j=1}^{t} P_o Q_j & \displaystyle\sum_{j=t+1}^{n} P_o Q_j - \sum_{j=t}^{t} P_o Q_j \\
A_2 & \displaystyle\sum_{j=1}^{t} P_o Q_j + \sum_{j=t+1}^{n} P_o Q_j & \displaystyle\sum_{j=1}^{n} P_o Q_j
\end{array}
$$

where

P_s^b = price which the boycott organization contracts only for its members if the boycott is successful, and

$$\sum_{j=t+1}^{n} P_s^b Q_j \; - \; \sum_{j=1}^{t} P_o Q_j \; > \; \sum_{j=1}^{n} P_o Q_j.$$

In this situation, the single producer has an incentive to cooperate if the boycott group can successfully raise the price for its members' product until A_1B_1 dominates A_2B_1. In the real world, however, it is *unrealistic* to expect a group of producers to bargain with food processors for a higher product price exclusively for its members (especially when others are producing an identical product). As long as a significant number of producers believes that they can "ride free," they may stay out of a boycott organization, thereby dooming the boycott to failure.

This case roughly parallels the question of union security and "free riders" in the field of collective bargaining.[11] It might be argued, therefore, that the NFO's Dilemma could be solved by the formation of a bargaining union of farm producers with legal sanction (a Farmers' Wagner Act) and a "union shop" security clause.[12] If a farm organization could achieve majority recognition and establish a "union shop," in other words, it could bargain to raise P_o to P_s^b for all of its members. The "union shop" arrangement would imply that all producers belonged to the bargaining organization—at least as long as the bargaining organization had the support of a majority of producers.

Such a "union shop" arrangement would be unlikely to succeed, however. First of all, there is no satisfactory solution to the problem of what the nature of compulsion to affiliate (and pay dues) could be: compulsion could not really take the form of loss of employment (as in the traditional "union shop" arrangement). Also, whether the "union shop" would apply to farmers nationally, or only, say, to a particular state, is not easily decided. Moreover, a "union shop" might not serve to limit production: although a "union shop" presumably could impose sanctions against members who "overproduce," enforcement would be difficult.

SOME CONCLUDING REMARKS

Both price theory and game theory models predict the failure of collusive behavior which involves large numbers. In the game theory technique, it is clear that the success of NFO boycotts is dependent on a sufficiently large number of farmers' behaving irrationally. The single farmer's cooperation with such a boycott affects his enjoyment of its benefits by only $\frac{1}{m}$, where m is a very large number. On the cost side, each farmer (as

[11] Cf. Herbert R. Northrup and Gordon F. Bloom, *Government and Labor* (Homewood, Ill.: Richard D. Irwin, Inc., 1963), Ch. 8.

[12] The "union shop" arrangement would require all producers of a particular product to join the appropriate bargaining organization once that organization had secured the support of a majority of producers.

a member of a large group) can refuse to support voluntarily the NFO's activity without reducing his opportunity to enjoy whatever benefits are forthcoming. No large organization, including the NFO, can support itself by providing a public good.[13]

The Farm Bureau is one of the nation's largest lobbying organizations, but its *lobbying* activities do not provide an incentive for rational individuals to join the organization. The growth of this large pressure-group's membership is due instead to the Farm Bureau's provision of essentially *private* goods, primarily its myriad of business organizations, services which are for members only. The Farm Bureau's *lobbying* activities, which benefit members and outsiders alike, are a *by-product* of its provision of private services. The once-troubled Farmers Union has achieved strength and stability through its sponsorship of business organizations and its association with farm cooperatives.[14]

The NFO has been highly critical of the use of business institutions and government agencies to augment and stabilize membership. It has been particularly critical of the Farm Bureau's business activities. Nevertheless, the NFO cannot successfully base its membership appeal on the provision of a purely *public* good (higher farm prices and farm incomes). It appears that the NFO has only one alternative. It must build a large membership by providing *private* services to *members only*. Once it is very large and stable, it can lobby effectively.[15] It still would not be able, however, to affect farm prices or incomes by "holding" actions.

[13] As Mancur Olson, Jr., [*The Logic of Colective Action* (Cambridge, Mass.: Harvard University Press, 1965), pp. 15–16], has put it, "Just as a state cannot support itself by voluntary contributions, or by selling its basic services on the market, neither can other large organizations support themselves without providing some sanction, or some attraction distinct from the public good itself, that will lead individuals to help bear the burdens of maintaining the organization."

[14] Olson, *The Logic of Collective Action*, pp. 148–159.

[15] Cf. Richard E. Wagner, "Pressure Groups and Political Entrepreneurs: A Review Article," *Papers on Non-Market Decision Making*, 1 (1966), pp. 161–170.

41

ACTION THEORY AND ACTION RESEARCH*

LEON MAYHEW
University of Michigan

AT FIRST GLANCE THE USE OF THE WORD "ACTION" IN SOCIOLOGICAL DIS-
course to modify both "theory" and "research" might seem confusing.
Does the word have the same meaning in both instances? What is
common to both the abstract formulations of the so-called "grand" theory
of Talcott Parsons and his collaborators, and the more mundane and
practical research of those who design and evaluate programs of social
betterment?

A moment's reflection reminds us that, different as action research and
action theory might be in some respects, the term "action" does indeed
have a common meaning in both cases. When Parsons entitles a work
"The Structure of Social Action" and when a reform group christens its
organization "Action to Improve our Neighborhoods" the same meaning
is intended. In both cases the word "action" is intended to connote such
concepts as implementation, establishment, and realization. Parsons
would be as dissatisfied with the title "The Structure of Social Behavior"
as reformers would be unlikely to name their enterprise "Behavior to
Improve our Neighborhoods," for in both cases the names must connote
purposeful, goal directed, implementive conduct.

The fundamental premise of Parsonian action theory is that the elements of a social situation can be divided into two classes, the normative
and the conditional, and that social conduct is to be conceptualized as a
process whereby ideal norms are realized or implemented in the face of
realistic conditions. This is nowhere more clearly stated than in the conclusion to *The Structure of Social Action:*

> Action must always be thought of as involving a state of tension between
> two different orders of elements, the normative and the conditional. As
> process, action is, in fact, the process of alteration of the conditional
> elements in the direction of conformity with norms.[1]

This passage must not be regarded as evidence that Parsons is squarely
on the side of pure idealism. Parsons insists that both normative *and*
conditional elements always contribute to action; he rejects any methodological position that would attempt to reduce social reality to either
realistic conditions on the one hand or to values, norms, or intentions on
the other. The passage continues:

* Revised version of paper read at meeting of the Society for the Study of Social
Problems in August, 1965. Special appreciation is due to Albert J. Reiss, Jr. and
Albert Cohen who read and commented on an earlier draft.

[1] Talcott Parsons, *The Structure of Social Action,* Glencoe, Ill.: Free Press, 1949,
p. 732.

♦ Reprinted by permission of the Society for the Study of Social Problems and of
the author from *Social Problems* 15 (Spring, 1968), pp. 420–432.

Elimination of the normative aspect altogether eliminates the concept of action itself and leads to the radical positivistic position. Elimination of conditions, of the tension from that side, equally eliminates action and results in idealistic emanationism. Thus conditions may be conceived at one pole, ends and normative rules at the other, means and effort as the connecting links between them.[2]

Thus, according to Parsons, the only way to avoid the undesirable alternatives of positivism and idealism is to construct an *action* theory which, by taking human effort as its subject, relates ideal ends to realistic social conditions. Such a theory would presumably have critical relevance for action research for it should provide an account of how social reality opposes human intentions and shapes the consequences of social action.

The purpose of this paper is to explore the potentiality and the limitations of action theory as a guide to action research and, in so doing, to develop a critique of Parsonian theory that goes beyond the shibboleths of contemporary criticism. We are often told that Parsons can not deal with change or with conflict, or that his theory is only a set of categories, or that it is idealistic or conservative, without being given convincing and articulate accounts of the precise sense in which these charges are supposed to be true. This paper, while accepting the relevance and value of action theory to action research, will also attempt to specify one point at which action theory, as presently conceived, proves inadequate.

This inadequacy may be summarized in a few words: *Action theory is more successful in delineating the relations between goals and conditions than in relating conditions to each other.* Yet, successful social action (and successful action research) requires understanding of the interrelatedness of social conditions. In consequence, an investigator in any given situation is forced to graft on additional propositions which are imported from other sociological traditions in an *ad hoc* manner.

INSTITUTIONALIZATION

In order to specify the sense in which these rather cryptic statements are true it is necessary to establish in more substantive detail the relevant aspects of the theory of action. They may be summarized by providing a synopsis of what Parsons terms "the theory of institutionalization." Institutionalization is the process by which abstract ethical premises, such as values and norms, become transformed into concrete, established, and socially organized institutions. True to the initial premises of action theory such institutions must be regarded as joint products of the norms which they embody and of the social conditions which shaped their development. The first task is to establish a useful classification of the conditional elements.

During one phase of his career Parsons emphasized one type of condition above all others. In *The Social System* and *Towards a General Theory of Action* the predominant topic was the problem of adequate motivation. Institutionalization was conceived as a process whereby appropriate

[2] *Ibid.*

mechanisms of socialization and social control are instituted in order to insure that actors are adequately motivated to conform to normative obligations.[3]

In more recent papers, Parsons has developed a fuller, more inclusive description of the elements of institutionalization. They are said to be four in number.

1. *Specification.* If a social value is to be institutionalized there must be consensus in the population on the implications of the value for conduct. Consensus on an abstract value such as equality of opportunity is not enough; there must be agreement on the specific courses of action that the value requires. Is mere equal treatment of everyone required, or is it necessary to undertake positive programs to aid disadvantaged groups in the community? Who is responsible for implementing equality and what, exactly, are their responsibilities? Value traditions are susceptible to alternative versions and the shape of an established institution reflects the particular version that has become dominant in a population.[4]

2. *Ideology.* If a social value is to be institutionalized it must be supported by appropriate conceptions of the nature of the social world. Action is guided not only by conditions but by *perceptions* of conditions and thus, the patterns of belief within a population shape social institutions.[5] For example, equality of opportunity will have one meaning if some groups in the population are considered to be innately sub-human, and quite a different meaning if accepted social ideology alleges the essential equality of all groups.

3. *Interests.* Here we return to the concept of adequate motivation. Social values are institutionalized when patterns of interests are established which motivate actors to conform. However, Parsons' recent statements make it clear that the concept of adequate motivation is not to be confined to the problem of psychological motivation in the single actor. The patterns of the established interests of organized groups are an equally important factor in institutionalization. Furthermore, it must also be understood that institutionalization does not occur solely through socialization, that is, through transforming inner desires so that people want to do what they must do. Institutionalization may rest in large measure on the establishment of systems of rewards and sanctions, such as legal agencies or markets that create networks of interests upon which institutions may rest.[6] Thus, the emergence of real equality of opportunity may be supported by legislation, or by the economic costs of discrimination in an expanding economy, as well as by emotional commitments to equal treatment. The concept of "interests" will also lead us to examine

[3] Talcott Parsons, *The Social System,* Glencoe, Ill.: Free Press, 1951; and Talcott Parsons *et al., Towards a General Theory of Action,* Cambridge: Harvard U., 1951.

[4] Talcott Parsons, "An Outline of the Social System," in Talcott Parsons *et al.,* editors, *Theories of Society,* New York: Free Press, 1961, pp. 30–79. See p. 44.

[5] Talcott Parsons, "An Approach to the Sociology of Knowledge," *Transactions of the Fourth World Congress of Sociology,* International Sociological Association, Milan, 1959, pp. 25–29.

[6] For further elucidation of this point see Leon Mayhew, *Law and Equal Opportunity,* Cambridge: Harvard U., forthcoming.

the organization, capacities, and growth of groups that have an interest in pressing for or resisting change.

4. *Jurisdiction.* The fourth element of institutionalization concerns the access of systems of social control to actors. Jurisdiction presumes sovereignty in the classical sense, that is, institutionalization ultimately requires physical control over a territorial area.[7] However, jurisdiction must not be confused with sovereignty for it is a more inclusive term referring to access in a general sense. In order to successfully guarantee a normative order the agencies of social control must have not only physical access to non-conforming actors, they must also have access to information about non-conformity. Furthermore, in any social system in which legal protections are institutionalized, agencies of social control must have jurisdiction in the legal sense and access to sufficient information to provide legal proofs.[8] Jurisdiction, like the other components of institutionalization, is not only a condition of institutionalization; it is one of the factors shaping the form of established institutions. The structure of an institutional order is affected by the character of the relevant activity, its accessibility to the organs of control, and the channels of and barriers to communication in the population.

The importance of jurisdiction is illustrated by the jurisdictional difficulties involved in all attempts to enforce equality of opportunity. Real opportunity implies a set of well developed and readily available channels of individual growth and advancement in a complex array of social institutions and groups—schools, churches, business firms, neighborhoods, clubs, political groups, and many others. The implementation of equality of opportunity becomes quite difficult in the face of the many obstacles blocking access to these varied social arenas. The relative ease with which discriminatory acts can be disguised, and the definitions of some institutional spheres as private, tend to give attacks upon unequal opportunity a piecemeal and fragmentary character.

These four elements of institutionalization—specification, ideology, interests, and jurisdiction—are valuable concepts for the student of programs of social action. They sensitize the analyst to the barriers to success and to the dynamic forces that can be utilized to induce change. The categories help us to understand the form that action programs come to assume in practice.

In this bald statement the Parsonian theory may seem to present an excessively partial and one sided account of institutionalization. After all, in its broadest sense the term "institutionalization" refers to the transformation of fluid and undefined interaction into ordered social life, regulated by established norms and other controls. We must not overlook the interaction of concrete men, with concrete interests and problems, who confront each other and struggle to both secure their individual

---

[7] Talcott Parsons in James Rosenau, editor, *International Politics and Foreign Policy,* New York: Free Press, 1961, pp. 120–129.

[8] Parsons' own writings tend to emphasize the problem of physical control over a territorial area. The author has taken the liberty of extending this concept somewhat.

ends and order their collective life. From this perspective norms arise
naturally as a by-product (and to some extent a description) of patterns
of interaction.

Parsonian theory assumes just such a process. However, it also assumes
that this process occurs in the context of a larger social system. Hence, as
men face integrative problems they can draw upon common values. The
emergent normative order is not a mere utilitarian technique of coordination; it reflects and establishes the integrative values which order the
process of institutionalization. For this reason we can turn the process
around and view it from the point of view of the social system as a process of the establishment of values. The concrete viewpoints, interests,
and problems of the participants are not ignored; they appear as conditions of successful implementation. A stable institutional order presumes
support from participants and therefore emergent forms and specifications
of values will reflect their perspectives and interests. On the other hand,
unless we assume a prior natural order, no solution to an integrative
problem can adequately satisfy everyone. Accordingly, institutionalization
implies resistance, that is, it implies that some actors and groups must be
socialized to new normative definitions, ideologies, and goals if values are
to become institutionally established.

I have provided only the bare outline of the elements of a theory of
institutionalization. It is a theory which is still developing and it is capable
of producing more refined propositions about how values relate to social
conditions. The following propositions illustrate the types of hypotheses
that are suggested by the theory: (1) The versions of a value tradition
that are most likely to become institutionalized are those that are subject
to a visible test of compliance. (2) Values are more likely to become
established and embodied in institutions if important organized groups
have an interest in their implementation. (3) Values are more likely to
become established in sectors of the population which may obtain prestige
by seeking to implement them.

On the other hand, the theory as stated does not generate propositions
about important elements of these types of propositions. What are the
characteristics of a social structure that create visibility? Which groups
will organize to effectively secure their interests? How is the capacity to
gain prestige through normative activity distributed in society? The significance of this problem can be more clearly demonstrated by reference to
a particular piece of action research.

AN ILLUSTRATIVE EXAMPLE

During the early sixties the author was engaged in evaluative research
on the Massachusetts Commission Against Discrimination, a state agency
charged by law with an action program. Massachusetts law forbids discrimination by race, color, or religious creed in employment, housing,
education, and public accommodations; and the Commission Against
Discrimination has the task of implementing this law. Action theory provided an important initial insight, namely, that the factor of jurisdiction
would be of critical importance. Effective access to violators is an essen-

tial precondition of regulation. Therefore, it was important for any program of action research to evaluate the relative effectiveness of various strategies of access. This may sound extremely obvious; one might suppose that it would not be necessary to invoke the paraphernalia of action theory to arrive at such a conclusion. However, it was not obvious to the officials of the Massachusetts Commission Against Discrimination, who did not view access as problematical. From their point of view jurisdiction would come automatically as persons came to them to complain of discrimination. Their theory was that what may be called the "private law" strategy would be an effective means of obtaining access to violators.

The law provides that any person who feels that he has been a target of discrimination may bring a complaint to the commission. The commission has a responsibility for investigating such allegations and, if they find probable cause for believing them to be true, the commission must conciliate with the respondent and attempt to eliminate any discriminatory practice which the respondent may employ. The private complaint of the aggrieved individual is the key that unlocks the door to the company and legitimates commission investigation of the entire range of its policies and practices. The officials of the commission had no reason to doubt the effectiveness of this technique. What more effective means of discovering discrimination than to allow the targets of discrimination to activate the legal machinery? Those who are the most hurt will have the most reason to complain and this should lead to efficient use of the limited resources available for investigation.

The facts did not bear the commission out. Investigation unearthed the fact that the mean percent Negro employed at firms that had been targets of complaints was twice the percentage of Negroes in the labor force of the community. Further, most of the jobs in question were of a type that were already easily available to Negroes. There was a noticeable lack of pioneering, strategic complaints which would give the commission access to significant targets. On the other hand, certain structural forces helped to produce strategic complaints. Complaints of middle-class origin and complaints sponsored by organized groups were more strategic than complaints of lower-class origin brought by unaffiliated individuals. For this reason the private law approach achieved more effective jurisdiction in housing than in employment. Middle-class Negroes were effectively organized to use legal services in their quest for better housing.

At this point crucial questions must be asked. It is true that action theory led to recognition of the importance of jurisdiction and suggested some hypotheses relevant to problems of access, but did action theory provide any reason to doubt the assumptions of the commissioners? Did action theory provide any clues as to what structural phenomena would impede or facilitate access? In a very general sense these questions could be answered in the affirmative. Parsons has suggested that jurisdiction is closely associated with various "ascriptive bases" of social structure, particularly territorial location.[9] However, the findings can only be explained

---

[9] Talcott Parsons, *Theories of Society, op. cit.*, pp. 239–268.

by drawing upon sociological ideas of a type which find no place in action theory as it is presently constituted.

The findings are not inexplicable; in fact, they were not unexpected. We would not expect the private law approach to produce strategic complaints, for strategic complaints run counter to an established social structure. Private complaints reflect everyday life which in turn is *shaped by* social structure. The Negro citizen, as he looks for a type of work for which he is qualified, at a firm where he thinks employment is available (because his cousin who works there told him so), is likely to encounter treatment with the appearance of discrimination. He is likely to be wrong, for after all, his cousin *does* work there.

Recognition of the principle that aggregate behavior is shaped by social structure and some knowledge of how labor markets are structured help to explain the commission's experience. But action theory has no relevant hypotheses about the relation between the organization of recruitment in the labor market and the organization of legal access to the institution of employment.

RELATION BETWEEN INSTITUTIONAL SPHERES

It might be alleged at this point that this criticism of action theory is exceedingly cheap for we have merely noted the incompleteness of the theory. Many of the propositions and subpropositions of the theory are yet to be worked out, but that is true of any theory. However, the problems of action theory are more deeply rooted; it is not a matter of mere incompleteness. The problem is not that there are some propositions that action theory does not contain; there are whole categories of propositions that it cannot contain because its fundamental structure has no adequate place for them as it is presently constituted.

In action theory there are two basic types of conceptual apparatus for linking separate elements of a modern differentiated social structure. One is the concept of a *hierarchy of control* and the other is the concept of an *exchange*.

When two elements of social structure are said to be related in a "hierarchy of control" they are conceived to be at two different levels in a common system. The element at the higher level is said to "control" the element at the lower level and the lower level element is said to "set conditions" for the higher level element. This concept of two types of causation, control, and conditioning is peculiar to action theory and reflects its preoccupation with norms and conditions. Higher levels are generally seen to be more normative and to control the more realistic conditional levels below them. For example, values and norms are related as a hierarchy of control. Norms are specifications of values, but they also reflect the exigencies of the particular institutions which they regulate and have a more conditional character.[10] The concept of "equal opportunity" is only a value; it does not specify any particular obligations for any particular type of actor. If personnel directors in business firms come

[10] Talcott Parsons, "An Outline of the Social System," *loc. cit.*

to feel obligated to hire Negroes in all capacities for which they believe Negroes to be qualified, then a norm has developed. It is a specification or interpretation of the value of equal opportunity, but a relatively weak specification, that reflects such conditional elements as the structural position of personnel directors and their organizational roles and interests.

Two elements of social structure are related through exchange when they produce resources essential to each other's functioning. Often the exchange is facilitated through the institutionalization of a circulating media such as money. Parsons' paradigms for the analysis of exchange were first developed in *Economy and Society*[11] but exchanges are not limited to the economic sphere. Parsons has recently been treating power, influence, and commitment as circulating media analogous to money and this has permitted an expanded application of the exchange paradigm to exchanges between other institutional spheres.[12]

Now let us examine a particular social phenomenon that arises from a link between two areas of social life. Consider the problem of *de facto* school segregation which arises from links between housing as an institution and the institution of education. When school districts are drawn along neighborhood lines then the patterns of segregation that appear in housing will be reproduced in education. How should this be conceptualized within the framework of action theory? Certainly housing cannot be treated as higher in some control hierarchy than education in any simple sense. Nor is the opposite true. Residential patterns may become conditions for the implementation of educational goals if educators come to view racial balance as a desirable goal. But this is not an *explanation* of *de facto* segregation; it is only a statement that *de facto* segregation may become problematic in a social system. *De facto* segregation is not an "institutionalized norm" within the meanings of the lexicon of action theory for it is not a specification of a higher level value or intention. If segregation is truly *de facto* (and not disguised intentional discrimination), then it is by definition an unintended, accidental consequence or by-product of acts and decisions unrelated to racial questions.

It is also incorrect to treat *de facto* school segregation as an item of exchange between the two institutional spheres. It is neither a resource necessary for the effective functioning of educational institutions nor a resource essential to the neighborhood.

Neither of the linking paradigms of action theory are appropriate. *De facto* segregation is due to the facts that behavior is shaped by social structure, that sectors of social structure overlap, and that for this reason the structural patterns of one sector are reproduced in others. Social institutions are linked to each other by many deeply rooted ties; they share the same personnel and other resources, they are located in the same spatial context, and they have overlapping jurisdiction over the same activities. Social influences flow along all of these links.

[11] Talcott Parsons and Neil Smelser, *Economy and Society*, Glencoe, Ill.: Free Press, 1956.
[12] See for example Talcott Parsons, "On the Concept of Influence," *Public Opinion Quarterly*, 1962, pp. 37–62.

De facto segregation was not chosen as an example at random. It was chosen because of its connection with the example of action research given earlier. The social forces that operated to impede the jurisdiction of the Commission Against Discrimination were essentially the forces of *de facto* segregation. The social segregation and isolation of the Negro community is reproduced in all patterns of Negro activity, even in the pattern of complaints to the anti-discrimination agency. Complaints reflect the day-to-day problems and disappointments of the Negro citizen as he works, or seeks work or other opportunities. In turn, his day-to-day activity is shaped by an established social structure which has determined the range and character of his friendship circle, his neighborhood, his information, and his accessible opportunities. In consequence, the pattern of routine complaints reflects the established pattern and boundaries of community life; it does not extend to sectors of the community in which the potential complainant does not participate.

This complex embedding seems beyond the province of action theory as it is presently constituted because, in a certain sense, action theory lacks a theory of social structure. It has a theory of normative structure and a theory of organization but it provides an inadequate account of the patterning of structural conditions. To define social structure as *consisting in* institutionalized norms, as Parsons does,[13] is to open the way for a very sophisticated treatment of the normative dimensions of social structure and the impact of structural conditions on normatively patterned organization. On the other hand, such an approach says little about the non-normative factors that account for structural conditions.

THE PROBLEM OF ACTION PROGRAMS

To the student of social action programs this is a serious flaw. Action theory alerts him to the sources and consequences of resistance but it provides him with few clues as to what shape resistance will take. It insists that jurisdiction is important and it suggests (in the abstract) something about the consequences of the importance of jurisdiction. It tells us that visible, testable versions of value traditions are more likely to be institutionalized. But it does not permit us to predict patterns of jurisdiction effectively because it lacks conceptual apparatus for dealing with the structural mechanisms that determine patterns of access. Ideas about patterns of communication, spatial patterns, and patterns of allocation of resources can be introduced into the analysis and categorized as conditional elements. But this is an essentially *ad hoc* procedure, for the sources of these ideas must necessarily lie outside the province of action theory as it is presently stated.

This problem has extensive ramifications for it is met in variable guises in a wide variety of types of action research. Consider, for example, the distinction made in group dynamics between *resistance* to change and *interference* with change. The former occurs when the forces of opposition directly resist influence attempts, and the latter, when attempted changes

13 Talcott Parsons, "An Outline of the Social System," *op. cit.*, p. 61.

are hampered by "extraneous" forces with no direct involvement in the issue. For example, Lippitt *et al.* speak of interference when a proposal to build a new city hall is defeated, not because of direct opposition, but because of the greater urgency of a school building program.[14]

The forces of interference are said to be "extraneous" but they are none the less real or important. In any social system various institutional sectors share access routes to resources and, through this sharing, they are bound together. The "interests" component of institutionalization is inevitably affected by such sharing. In our example, both city administration and the school system are tied to the same system of bonding and taxation. In consequence, the use of resources by one affects the other's capacity to muster resources. Again, the problem is not one of exchanges between city administration and the schools, nor is it a case of a hierarchy of control. The capacity of the city administration to institutionalize new programs is affected by interests in other sectors of the community, and those interests derive, in part, from the patterns of organizational sharing that bind sectors together.

DIFFERENTIATION AND ASCRIPTION

To say that current action theory cannot deal with the structural problems outlined here is not to say that the theory cannot be reconstituted to allow for more recognition of the forces affecting structural conditions. One of the main purposes of this paper is to suggest one of the lines along which action theory might develop.

The solution to the problem lies in a reformulation of one of the problems to which Parsons has already devoted considerable attention, the problem of ascription. Ascription can be treated as a third concept for linking institutional spheres. Ascription is for Parsons the fusion of intrinsically separate functions in the same structural unit.[15] His theory of differentiation is essentially an attempt to uncover the forces that first break down ascription and then permit the stable establishment of structurally separate units for performing differentiated functions. Thus, when the family household becomes separate from economically productive units a variety of norms and processes of normatively regulated exchange emerge. These norms and processes serve to link the newly separated units and to relate them to the larger society.

Differentiation always presupposes that structures are initially fused. Parsons has suggested that in the first instance all structures are embedded in "ascriptive solidarities," that is, kinship, ethnic solidarities, primary groups, and the territorial community. The original embedding of social life in such ascriptive solidarities is taken for granted and what becomes problematic is how specialized functions become first emancipated and then stabilized as autonomous spheres of social life. The two major sources of stabilization are new normative controls and new processes of exchange,

[14] Ronald Lippitt, Jeanne Watson, and Bruce Westley, *The Dynamics of Planned Change*, New York: Harcourt, Brace, 1958, pp. 86–89.
[15] Talcott Parsons, "A Functional Theory of Change," in Amitai Etzioni and Eva Etzioni, *Social Change*, New York: Basic Books, 1964, pp. 83–97, esp. p. 90.

the two general mechanisms that serve to link separate institutions in action theory.[16]

The weakness in action theory is that it tends to assume that once functions become separated, only these two mechanisms link them whereas, in fact, they never become totally separated. Both are still residually located in ascriptive structures and linked to each other by virtue of this common location. The mutual influences that flow along these residual ascriptive links are very important. For example, even after the business firm and the household have been separated, the differentiated firm may recruit personnel by asking for recommendations from employees. These employees will tend to recommend friends, relatives, and neighbors thus perpetuating ascriptive patterns of employment within the firm.

It cannot be claimed that action theory refuses to admit the possibility of such residual links, but to admit the existence of a phenomenon is not theoretically equivalent to taking that phenomenon to be problematic. Theories may treat phenomena as problematic, as something whose attributes must be explained, or as something which is given. To cite one current theoretical issue, it is one thing to assume that there is great potential for conflict in human affairs and that since conflict is such a threatening force, social integration is problematic; it is quite another to take conflict as problematic and to seek to explain its origin and structure. Further, one may doubt the credentials of a theory of conflict resolution or integration that fails to account for the typical forms of conflict since the forms of resolution are presumably related to the structure of the conflict.

Similarly, sociological theory must not only admit ascriptive links, it must account for the patterns and the significance of those links. To do so is crucial to the theory of institutionalization for, as a norm becomes institutionalized in any given institutional sphere, it will encounter resistances transmitted to it from other institutional spheres along structural channels of an ascriptive type. For example, the author's investigation of the Massachusetts Commission Against Discrimination indicated that enforcement of the law against discrimination suffered because responsibility for initiating enforcement was embedded in the ethnic community most subject to unequal treatment. The ideal was supposed to be enforced within the sphere of employment but the structural links between employment, race, and law enforcement made many of the other patterns of Negro community life relevant obstacles to enforcement.

Finally, it should be emphasized again that there is no reason to suppose that what have here been called ascriptive links will be normatively defined. The fundamental structural commonalities that link differentiated institutions arise not only from normatively defined familial, communitarian, and ethnic solidarities but from the fact that both institutions are involved in a common ecological system, share a common constitutive order, and are staffed by the same population with all of its relevant population characteristics. Thus a viable action theory, if it is to account for the

[16] *Ibid.* See also *Theories of Society, op. cit.*, pp. 242–246.

crucial patterns of connection between institutional spheres, must confront, and systematically incorporate, such concepts as ecological dominance,[17] constitutive order,[18] and cohort structure.[19] It is not particularly difficult to merely assert that ascriptive links between institutions are conditions of institutionalization. The problem is to modify action theory so that its account of modern differentiated society systematically incorporates an adequate treatment of the functions and consequences of ascription.

THE SIGNIFICANCE FOR ACTION RESEARCH

The implications for action research are clear; investigators engaged in action research must be sensitive to the constraints that arise from the embedding of the targets of social action in networks of ascriptive ties. Ascriptive embedding can play a major part in establishing the jurisdictional problems, the counter-interests, and the ideological definitions that constitute barriers to effective social action.

The failure of many students of social action to appreciate the significance of this point is ironic, for most social action projects are themselves attacks upon ascription in one form or another. The problem of racial equality, to choose an example that has been prominent in this paper, is clearly a problem of ascription. And yet, for many years the attack on racial barriers proceeded upon the implicit assumption that overcoming the resistance of a few people in highly differentiated roles would solve the problem. If only personnel directors, real estate men, and school administrators could be made color blind, then equality of opportunity would follow. The "color-blind" theory has always underestimated the strength of ascriptive forces in the social system. A color-blind personnel director can often permit the established organization of personnel recruitment to do his discriminating for him, without engaging in any directly discriminatory conduct. Or an established seniority rule can automatically discriminate against members of minority groups who have been accepted for initial employment only in recent entering cohorts, thus effectively blocking upward mobility.

Nevertheless, for many years our conceptions of equal opportunity, our image of the nature of discrimination, our sense of the location of those interests that would resist equal opportunity, and our jurisdictional strategies have been founded on the assumption that unequal opportunity is a product of the intentional acts of discriminating officials. The prevalence of such acts obscures the more profound underlying capacity of ascriptive structures to reproduce themselves. The recent development of the concept of affirmative action to create equal participation is a product of our growing recognition that unequal opportunity is a case of ascription and must be treated as such.

[17] Amos Hawley, *Human Ecology*, New York: Ronald, 1950, p. 221.
[18] Albert Cohen, "The Study of Social Disorganization and Deviant Behavior," in Robert Merton *et al.*, *Sociology Today*, New York: Basic Books, pp. 461–484.
[19] Norman Ryder, "The Cohort in the Study of Social Change," *American Sociological Review*, 30 (December, 1965), pp. 843–861.

If the argument of this paper is sound, then it would seem likely that the strategy of affirmative action has analogues in other areas of social action. As we become more aware of the ascriptive barriers that interfere with social action, we will become more conscious of unanticipated and latent defects in our strategies for change; we will become more aware of the true extent of the requirements and costs of effective social reconstruction.

Although this paper has focused on the Parsonian version of action theory, its argument applies equally well to other action perspectives. It does not matter whether we treat institutionalization as the establishment and specification of the values of a social system or as the emergent establishment of patterns of interaction, for in either case we are interested in the relations between goals and obstacles. Whether we treat goals as ends for the system or as ends for particular actors within the system, ascription remains an important source for patterns of interference and resistance.

CONCLUSION

This paper should not be taken as one more contribution to the continuing series of attacks upon Parsonian theory as irrelevant to the conflicts and problems of the modern age. My fundamental premise is that action theory is inherently suited to the study of problems of social reconstruction. Moreover, Parsons has himself tried to bring the technical apparatus of the theory of the social system to bear on the problems of ascription. Recently, in "An Outline of the Social System," he suggested that institutions impinge upon one another because no concrete institution is ever completely unifunctional.[20] For example, top leadership in the business firm has an important set of political functions, and, in consequence, strictly economic criteria do not completely dominate the process of recruitment to high management positions. This line of argument suggests one mode of attack on the problem of residual ascription. At the same time, this limited strategy does not solve the problem adequately. Some continuing structural fusions may derive from continuing multiple functional problems in the same concrete social structures, but most of the ascriptive foci of modern society are more deeply rooted. They derive from the fact that the institutions of society must ultimately share the same personnel. They derive from the persistent staying power and functional capacity of ascription: in given economic contexts ascription is often very economical; in given political contexts ascription is very effective. Hence, new techniques for analyzing the functions and consequences of ascription deserve a high place on the agenda for the development of action theory.

[20] Talcott Parsons, "An Outline of the Social System," *op. cit.*, pp. 53–56.

42

THE TRADE-OFF STRATEGY IN COMMUNITY RESEARCH[1]

HANS B. C. SPIEGEL

Hunter College of the City University of New York

VICTOR G. ALICEA

Columbia University

T HE NEWLY-AWAKENED CONCERN OF GOVERNMENT WITH THE INVOLVEment of low-income residents in public decision-making, and the legislation to support this policy have reflected and helped to consolidate among target groups a feeling of kinship, identity, and a growing sense of power over their communities.[2] This emergent community or neighborhood "nationalism" has been accompanied by a closing of doors which in the past gave entry to the outside researcher and free access to data and information on the nature of slum life.

Most recently, some of the more sophisticated and highly organized low-income communities have developed a modus operandi with outside researchers. It is rooted in the very capitalistic system in which both the poor and the professional live: "If you want access to our pool of information and the experiences we can offer your technicians and professionals, then you must pay for it."

It would appear, then, that the era in which the low-income community served as a training ground or laboratory for people in human service professions and related disciplines may be a thing of the past. A more legitimate "gain-gain" relationship has evolved, in which both university and community can join hands on projects that each sees essential to its own welfare.

The human service professions have not been unresponsive to this emerging characteristic of low-income communities. Professional service programs involving low-income people as assistants to professionals and as links between the professional service and the recipients of these services are rapidly being developed.[3] Furthermore, professionals and low-income

[1] The research and comprehensive health planning projects referred to in this article were made possible by parallel grants No. 22012–01–69 and No. 22011–01–69 awarded by the U. S. Public Health Service, HEW, to the Planetarium Neighborhood Council, a resident group from the Mid-West Side of Manhattan and the Institute of Urban Environment, School of Architecture, Columbia University. The community health planning project is under the direction of Douglas Brian whose comments on the preliminary draft of this paper are greatly appreciated.

[2] See Hans B. C. Spiegel, ed., *Citizen Participation in Urban Development: Concepts and Issues* (Washington, D.C.: NTL Institute for Applied Behavioral Science, 1968); and Hans B. C. Spiegel and Stephen D. Mittenthal, *Neighborhood Power and Control: Implications for Urban Planning* (Springfield, Va.: Federal Clearinghouse for Scientific and Technological Information, 1969).

[3] See Arthur Pearl and Frank Riessman, *New Careers for the Poor; The Nonprofessional in Human Service* (New York: The Free Press, 1965). Further information on this topic is available from the New Careers Development Center, New York University.

♦ First published in *Social Science Quarterly* 50, No. 3 (December, 1969). 487

residents are collaborating not only on the type of services that should be brought into the neighborhood but also on how they are to be managed. A growing body of experience within the human service professions (social work, teaching, health services, and others) seems to indicate that such "gain-gain" trade-offs are practicable. However, for research and other data-gathering functions where the service or potential profit to the community is less tangible or of less immediate relevance, the problem of developing the gain-gain symbiotic relationship with the community becomes more difficult.

Traditionally, the researcher's approach to the community process has been objective, detached, silent—striving for invisibility: "Whenever possible investigators usually attempt to create an impression of the observer as a neutral psychologically non-visible person."[4] The researcher's model of work has been based on at least the following two values: maximizing the gathering of relevant data and minimizing the contamination of the processes being observed.

But how invisible is the researcher, particularly when he is operating in a community setting that is not his own? Experience in a number of communities has convinced us that the researcher is usually perceived as a highly visible outsider. Even if the researcher shares ethnic bonds with the subject group, the nature of his sponsorship may raise suspicions and hostility. "Who's paying you?" is a question the researcher is asked more than once. And even when the researcher honestly answers that it is a governmental agency seeking to formulate public policy, or an institution of higher education eager to enhance knowledge, or a service agency needing to document its work, he may still activate opposition from his subject. This is especially true when the subject is a community "gatekeeper" occupying a leadership position. At any rate, "researcher invisibility" is soon revealed to be a myth.

Another cogent question is posed by the target group: "How is your study going to help us—and help us now?" It will take some fancy explanations to convince the respondent that the research functions for the above type of sponsoring institutions are immediately relevant or directly beneficial to the neighborhood and its residents. Recently an incident of this type occurred in a meeting of one community's Policy Board of the Model Cities Program. Four researchers from a local university were present, silent, unobtrusive, and busy taking notes. They had been sanctioned by the local Model Cities Director. The meeting went on for about an hour with nothing of great importance taking place. Suddenly, the crucial issues caught fire. At this point, one of the local residents stood up and demanded to know the identity of the people taking notes. Each researcher was asked to describe what he was doing and the nature of its relevance to the community. None of the responses were acceptable. All were asked to leave on grounds that they "had nothing to offer the community."

These, then, are but a few of the vicissitudes involved in the delicate

---

[4] Claire Selltiz, Marie Jahoda, Morton Deutsch, and Stuart W. Cook, *Research Methods in Social Relations* (New York: Holt, Rinehart and Winston, 1963), p. 233.

process of gaining access to important data. One of the crucial questions is, therefore, "On what basis can research workers develop the necessary ties to low-income communities and thus legitimize their entry? One such mode of entry that is being used in a current project[5] might be characterized as a *quid pro quo* or "trade-off."

THE TRADE-OFF STRATEGY

The immediate objective of this strategy is to set up a symbiotic relationship between the two parties—researchers and the low-income community —which will result in mutual gain. The trade-off relationship results from negotiations between the researcher and the community, in which the researcher (contrary to the traditional role) provides certain specified goods and services in exchange for entry into, and relevant data from, the community. An explicit "contract" is drawn between the parties involved outlining the conditions of the trade-off.

Researchers have long operated on *implicit* trade-offs. For example, Ronald Lipitt, in reporting on the work of a group of researchers attempting to build a close relationship between the social scientist and consumers of research findings makes the point:

> Many organizations and groups are aware of the need to change their way of operating and are ready to collaborate in a scientific approach to their problem if they can see clearly that the research operation promises to yield a specific service.[6]

What are some of the goods and services that can be traded-off on the part of the researcher? One of the most elementary of trade-offs is, of course, the exchange of money for a specified service. Interviewers can be paid; community leaders can be compensated as consultants; indigenous research aides can be hired as data-gatherers.

Researchers are training low-income residents in some data-gathering skills and these residents are, in turn, being employed to perform functions previously carried out by professionals. Similarly, residents are being used as language interpreters as well as interpreters of the low-income neighborhood "cultures."

Employment in research enterprises, with the possibility of entering a career ladder as suggested above, can indeed mean significant employment to a number of low-income community members. However, the securing of jobs for selected individuals says little about how the community could profit directly from the findings of research. The example that follows highlights the use of the trade-off with particular emphasis on how a representative community group can obtain direct and immediate use of research findings.

---

[5] See footnote 1.

[6] Dorothy Mial and H. Curtis, eds., *Forces in Community Development* (Washington, D.C.: NTL Institute for Applied Behavioral Science, 1961), p. 73.

THE WEST SIDE PROJECT

A trade-off strategy was implemented in a collaboration between a neighborhood council and a university on New York's West Side. The goal of the neighborhood council (the Planetarium Neighborhood Council) was to provide for resident involvement in the planning of a comprehensive health center which is scheduled to rise within the next few years. The university group (the Institute of Urban Environment, School of Architecture, Columbia University) sought to gather data on the process of citizen participation in urban development. Stemming from a series of candid exchanges, both parties were made aware of mutual gains resulting from potential collaboration. The next step was to effectuate a trade-off.

The initial meeting that laid the groundwork for this collaboration dealt with an urgent matter for both groups: the requirement for simultaneous funding. The neighborhood council wished to secure a staff director/community organizer to give day-to-day leadership to the project. The university needed money to permit some of its staff members to engage in the research phase of the study. It was decided that parallel applications would be submitted to a potential funding source, thereby strengthening both cases. Before such parallel submissions, however, a memorandum of understanding was prepared between the two parties (and later included in both applications) setting forth the conditions of the trade-off.

A section of this memorandum (in which the Council states its expectations of the Institute) reads as follows:

> We encourage your staff to interview our staff, members of the program committees, the Planetarium Neighborhood Council—as well as cross check samplings of the community. As our staff pulls together masses of disparate information, we visualize calling on the Institute staff for informal guidance, as necessary. We expect the data your research team gathers (and interprets) to be available to us and our staff. We expect your research team to report regularly to our staff and appropriate program committees and to us, with as many written reports as practicable.

As the above indicates, the intended trade-off went considerably beyond the initial collaboration in federal grantsmanship; the main trade-off for the Neighborhood Council's willingness to be observed was the Institute's feedback of research findings and technical advice. It must be admitted that the Institute staff at first considered the price of this trade-off with mixed emotions. A myriad of methodological questions were raised: will the feedback of observed data hopelessly distort the very phenomenon we were trying to observe? Weren't we potentially observing and evaluating our own feedback performance? Could we, indeed, still be called "independent researchers" when we would discharge a potentially active role, far exceeding the norms of participant-observation?

We concluded that, while the purity of the research design would be somewhat affected, we would still be willing to pay the price demanded by the Neighborhood Council. Perhaps we rationalized, but we reasoned that *any* intervention into the research setting, no matter how delicately nondirective, would still constitute a form of contamination. More important, we felt that the data we were interested in gathering could only be obtained by searching interviews, anecdotal analysis, longitudinal observations—in short, through a researcher-subject relationship that demanded trust and mutual respect. And finally, we realized that our potential possession of significant data concerning participation and decision-making in the neighborhood group placed us, *ipso facto,* in a vulnerable political position. Therefore, we decided to take the risk of making this relationship explicit and as non-paternalistic as possible.

THE RESEARCHER-COMMUNITY ENCOUNTER

After the grants were secured, some initial questioning and even resistance to the role of the observer were still evident at neighborhood meetings. However, after clarifying the tasks of the researcher and explaining the nature and possible uses of the feedback that would be available to them, the members seemed to be satisfied. Toward the end of one meeting, the chairman pointed out that the researcher's "experience and familiarity with this type of project" would "make him a valuable asset, particularly in the initial stages."

Subsequent meetings suggest that the researcher was indeed called upon for a number of different services: (1) helping to draw up criteria for the selection of staff; (2) helping to evaluate interviews of prospective applicants; (3) suggesting ways in which other local citizens might be involved in planning; and (4) providing regular feedback to the neighborhood project director on questions of sub-committee development and organizational strategy.

These examples of services which the Institute has provided in keeping its end of the trade-off bargain can best be categorized under the rubric of "technical assistance." But technical assistance about what? One type of assistance is based on substantive advice concerning planning, community resources, and dealing with the city's human services hierarchy. The researcher, since he happens to be a person well versed in community action, sometimes appears to take on the stance of a consultant to the group. Just as the Neighborhood Council seems to respond easily and directly to the inquiries of the field investigator so he, in turn, is able to respond to technical inquiries quickly and competently.

The second type of technical assistance deals with the processes of organizational development and citizen involvement through which the Neighborhood Council is now moving. By way of periodic feedback of observations and individual consultations with Council members, the researcher can hold up a more or less "objective mirror" through which the Council can observe its own group development process. Once more, our field investigator has the kind of skills that enable him to perform this task even in such delicate situations as the previously cited interviewing for staff positions.

Does the trade-off strategy, then, depend on the technical assistance and consultative skills of the researcher? Undeniably, such skills are a great advantage in establishing the credibility of the trade-off for the community group which is thus able to see immediate results. It appears however, that a researcher less skilled in community action but equally motivated can share considerable data he has observed with the cooperating neighborhood organization. Further, he can share results of selected research instruments, summary statements, and help train research aides.

A crucial question remaining about the trade-off strategy of urban research is, of course, whether it produces more useful data than more conventional methods. We think it does, but qualifiedly so. It is our impression at this point that we have gained access to more significant data more quickly than with certain past studies dealing with comparable subject matter but where the interview schedule and/or observations were the main research tools. At any rate, the efficacy of the trade-off strategy is surely a matter for continuing evaluation.

We have no doubts that the trade-off strategy involves considerable risks to the research enterprise. All the perils of participant observation are present, for example;

> the participant observer faces especially severe difficulties in maintaining objectivity. . . . To get access to intimate data the observer allows himself to become absorbed in the local culture, but then this very absorption process makes him take for granted behavior that he should be trying to explain.[7]

But additional perils intrude themselves. One of the more obvious is the danger stemming from the researcher's multiplicity of roles—negotiator, technical advisor, and interpreter of research findings—and the ever present risk of role conflict. Such risks to which the researcher exposes his design are considerable. In the end, however, there may be few other options for the researcher who wishes to go beyond more conventional research methods. If the researcher wishes to intervene in an organized neighborhood, he should be willing to appear on the scene with something to offer—some visible goods or services. Otherwise the neighborhood may figuratively or literally close him out.

[7] Claire Selltiz, *et al., Research Methods,* p. 215.

INDEX

493